THE PRENTICE-HALL
ENCYCLOPEDIA OF
WORLD
PROVERBS

WOLFGANG MIEDER

MJF BOOKS

NEW YORK

Published by MJF Books
Fine Communications
Two Lincoln Square
60 West 66th Street
New York, NY 10023

Library of Congress Card Catalog # 96-77135
ISBN 1-56731-126-1

This edition published by arrangement with Prentice Hall/Career & Personal Development

Manufactured in the United States of America on acid-free paper

MJF Books and the MJF colophon are trademarks of Fine Creative Media, Inc.

10   9   8   7   6   5   4   3   2   1

Dr. Wolfgang Mieder, one of the world's most renowned folklorists, has written and edited more than 25 books and numerous articles in English or German on proverbs, fairy tales, legends, folksongs, nursery rhymes, and literary topics. Two of his English-language books are *International Proverb Scholarship: An Annotated Bibliography* (1982) and *The Wisdom of Many: Essays on the Proverb,* with Alan Dundes (1981). More recently he edited *Disenchantments: An Anthology of Modern Fairy Tale Poetry* (1985), and the fourth volume of his series on proverb research titled *Investigations of Proverbs, Proverbial Expressions, Quotations and Clichés* (1984) was published in Switzerland.

Dr. Mieder is a full professor of German language, literature, and folklore and also chairman of the Department of German and Russian at The University of Vermont. He studied at The University of Michigan, University of Heidelberg, and Michigan State University, and has achieved a distinguished teaching and scholarly record, including a guest professorship at The University of California at Berkeley.

In addition to lecturing widely on folklore, and in particular, on proverbs, in the United States and Europe, Dr. Mieder is a member of the American Dialect Society, serving on the Committee on Proverbial Sayings, and he was honored to become a Folklore Fellow of the American Folklore Society.

Among the more than 100 articles he has written are papers that deal with the function of proverbs in literature, proverb illustrations from medieval woodcuts to modern cartoons, proverbs used in psychological testing, and innovative proverb manipulations in advertisements. Dr. Mieder is also the editor of *Proverbium: Yearbook of International Proverb Scholarship.*

A proverb states, "Proverbs are the coins of the people."
It is to these people of all walks of life, of all races
and nationalities, that this collection of the world's proverbs
is dedicated in the hope that their wisdom, limited as it
might appear, be heeded throughout the world.

Acknowledgments

I would like to thank a number of friends and colleagues for their encouragement and support for the preparation of this large collection. I owe many thanks to Daniel Barnes, George Bryan, Heike Doane, Alan Dundes, Sandy Gavett, Betty Hoose, John Jewett, Dennis Mahoney, Kenneth Nalibow, Richard and Francine Page, Veronica Richel, Arthur Schwartz, David Scrase, Robert and Carol Stevens, as well as my relatives, Walter and Lucille Busker, William and Barbara Busker, Walter and Lee Busker, and John and Beverly Skinner. Of particular importance was the diligent and dedicated work that Elaine Scott did for the flawless preparation of the voluminous manuscript. Her commitment and interest in getting the collection completed certainly helped to bring this labor to a fruitful end. Finally, I would like to express to my wife Barbara Mieder my sincere appreciation for making it possible for me to spend hundreds of hours in my study amassing the materials for this international proverb collection. Her continuous interest in and steady support of my many research projects on proverbs have given me the strength to continue with them.

A Preview
of the Encyclopedia

This encyclopedia is for: Public speakers, speech writers, journalists, authors, educators, ministers, songwriters, lawyers, humorists, copywriters, artists, counselors, scientists—in short, everybody.

How proverbs can be used: In everyday conversation, journalistic writing, advertising, speeches of all types, in sermons, literature, debates, slogans, songs, legal argumentation, humorous quips, and other forms of human communications.

What proverbs provide: Wit, colorful language, imagery and authority. Proverbs strengthen an argument, help to disprove false statements, emotionalize a speech or article, educate the young pupil or student about people and human nature, and provide a humorous, ironical, or satirical mirror of the human condition everywhere.

Welcome to the Wonderful World of Proverbs

Behold the proverbs of a people.

CARL SANDBURG

The Prentice-Hall Encyclopedia of World Proverbs, the most ambitious work of its type, represents the largest collection available in a single volume. It is unique in that it contains proverbs only—not the sprinkling of quotations, maxims, aphorisms, and common phrases found in many such compilations.

Among the 18,520 entries are 5,000 English proverbs and 4,000 proverbs stemming from the major languages of the world (Anglo-American, Japanese, Chinese, Russian, Spanish, French, and German). The other half of the collection consists of proverbs from many languages from all continents: African (Swahili, Yoruba, and others); Indian (Hindi, Tamil, and others); Eastern Europe (dozens of languages including Bulgarian, Czech, Serbian, Croatian); Western Europe (Dutch, Basque, Swedish, among others); the Near East (including Egyptian, Lebanese, modern Hebrew); the Far East (Korean, Thai, Vietnamese); and also languages from the West Indies and Oceania. The result is a truly international proverb collection with texts in English translation. While most of the proverbs were located in collections that present them in English translations, a considerable number of them were translated for this collection from major collections in various languages.

Why have anthropologists, folklorists, and philologists and others bothered to collect thousands of proverbs throughout the world? The major reason is doubtlessly that proverbs are small pieces of human wisdom that have been handed down from generation to generation and that continue to be applicable and valid even in our modern technological age. Proverbs simply defined are concise statements of an apparent truth that have currency among the people because they contain a generally accepted insight, observation, and wisdom. The ancient proverb "One hand washes the other" is as true and applicable today as it was hundreds of years ago; its basic wisdom has been recognized by thousands of people in many parts of the world. This particular proverb mirrors the idea that our actions depend on reciprocity, and it expresses it in a short and easily remembered and recognizable sentence. What might take an entire paragraph to explain is expressed metaphorically in this short proverb, which contains in a nutshell the philosophy of the common people.

In nonliterate societies, anthropologists have found that studying the proverbs of a native tribe gives clues to the world view of its members regarding such matters as education, law, business, and marriage. There is no aspect of life that proverbs do not comment on, and in nonliterate societies they serve as rules of conduct and basic wisdom to be adhered to by subsequent generations.

Proverbs survive in more advanced societies where communication is based on various modes of writing and speaking. A cultural or literary historian, for example, can learn a great deal about the age of Shakespeare by studying the use of proverbs in his many plays. A careful reading of *Hamlet,* for example, will show that proverbs are useful as a ready-made linguistic tool in argumentation and persuasion, the effectiveness of which is further increased by creating linguistic puns in the actual proverb application. A few centuries later, one finds Charles Dickens using proverbs with a high frequency to depict the social ills of his time. And Carl Sandburg used proverbs in his poems concerning the American melting pot of various national and immigrant groups. For him the proverbs of the various immigrant groups helped blend the world view of this new society: "A code arrives; language; lingo; slang; behold the proverbs of a people, a nation."

A folklorist or sociologist with a particular interest in immigrants might well study the Hungarian steel workers and their proverbs in Gary, Indiana. Have some of the Hungarian proverbs been translated into English as subsequent generations have become more assimilated into the mainstream of American society? Do the proverbs of the old country still fit all aspects of modern American life? Does only the older generation use them, and how do the young people react today to this ethnic wisdom? These are questions that will help all of us understand members of ethnic groups better. With the increase in the Spanish speaking population in this country, it is important that we attempt to understand its traditional attitudes and social mores. Proverbs reflect such matters in a precise fashion, and an understanding of them will help to maximize meaningful communication.

Anyone interested in languages will, of course, recognize the value in knowing the proverbs of another language. Nobody really masters a foreign language without being able to understand its proverbs and communicate through them. The basic thoughts and opinions of another culture are expressed in them, and only by being able to use them can one hope to gain true fluency and be accepted by native speakers. In modern business and politics the understanding of proverbs plays a major role, often being the key to the success or breakdown of communications. It is a known fact that interpreters at the United Nations prepare themselves for their extremely sensitive job by learning proverbs of the foreign languages, since politicians often argue or attempt to convince their opponents by the use of a native proverb. No matter how sophisticated the debate, eventually every heated exchange can be reduced to an emotional war of proverbs.

For this reason, effective public speakers must have a good stock of proverbs at their immediate disposal. Convincing rhetoricians such as Cicero, Martin Luther, Winston Churchill, and Nikita Khrushchev, for example, are known to have been skillful artists in employing proverbs in their speeches.

Even advertising agents have learned to appreciate the traditional value of using proverbs as advertising headlines. Take for instance, a bank ad's "A penny saved is a penny earned," or a health food store's "An apple a day keeps the doctor away." Often the traditional proverb text is varied to catch the reader's attention and to create interest in reading the text of the ad. A proverb such as "Where there's a will, there's a way" can be reduced to the easily recognizable formula "Where there's X, there's Y," in which the X and Y can be replaced by anything the copywriter wishes to express. For example, "Where there's a car, there's a Ford."

Similarly, effective use of the proverb "Don't ask a man for a favor before he has had his lunch," was the basis of Time, Inc.'s Fortune Research Subscriber Census Card requesting information on readers' business interests and responsibilities.

In like manner, a high school principal's newsletter quoted the Chinese proverb "One kind word will warm three winter months" in reporting the outpouring of support and love for the school after a field-house break-in and loss of expensive equipment jeopardized the football team's schedule. Suffering and cruelty were mercifully replaced by hope and inspiration.

These are only a few examples of how proverbs continue to be of significance and practical use. In a world getting smaller through new technological advances almost every day, communication with new individuals and groups of people increases steadily. Each individual is, however, to a certain degree preprogrammed by the traditional proverb stock that continues to be handed down from generation to generation. At the same time, new proverbs are still being added to this repertoire, as can be seen by a relatively recent American coinage "Different strokes for different folks." An individual somewhere in this country used this sentence first; it was then picked up by others because of its basic underlying wisdom and its easily remembered structure and rhyme, and it slowly gained currency. This process was speeded along by the fact that the proverb became a title of a popular recording and a television show. By now this "wit of one" has become "the wisdom of many," and it is doubtlessly one of the most popular American proverbs. While such new proverbs are added to our basic stock, older ones may drop out since they no longer reflect newer attitudes. But a basic stock of proverbs remains in any ethnic or national group, and they continue to be effective expressions of the varied experiences of mankind everywhere.

Among the proverbs in this work are many of ancient origin, but which became current in the English language as well as many of the European languages. The Latin proverb *"In vino veritas"* exists, for example, as a direct translation in the English as "In wine there is truth," in French as *"La vérité est dans le vin,"* in German as *"Im Wein ist Wahrheit,"* in Italian as *"La verità è nel vino,"* in Spanish as *"En el vino está la verdad,"* and so on. Such universal proverbs are listed in the present collection as belonging to the English language without referring to the dozens of languages into which they have also been translated. For this reason, there are no specific references in this collection to ancient Greek, Latin, or Biblical proverbs.

Just as a proverb that is listed as belonging to the English language might also be found in several other European languages if it was translated from an ancient Latin proverb, for example, it is possible to find a proverb in this collection with a Spanish language designation, although it also exists in Portuguese or another Romance language. It is extremely difficult to ascertain in such cases in which language the proverb did in fact originate. This is particularly the case when two languages are linguistically and geographically very close, as is the case with Spanish and Portuguese, German and Dutch, Danish and Swedish. To ascertain the definite linguistic origin of each proverb in this collection would have meant hundreds of individual historical searches, literally one analysis for each proverb presented. This obviously could not be done, and for this reason each proverb received only one linguistic reference to that language in which it is particularly well known.

The organization of this collection follows that of the major scholarly compilations. The proverbs are arranged alphabetically according to key words and then are consecutively numbered. Under each key word (usually the noun-subject of the proverb), the texts are alphabetized as well, so that each proverb can be found easily and quickly. By looking under any key word, the user can discover what the Japanese, Russians, Spaniards, or whoever, say and think about adversity, behavior, dog, fidelity, honesty, law, love, merit, opportunity, payment, security, teacher, virtue, woe, youth, and countless other topics. This comparative aspect of the arrangement of proverbs makes this collection of the world's proverbs interesting and fascinating for everybody. There is a proverb for any and every situation, occasion, or condition!

Following the proverbs themselves is a sizable bibliography on proverb scholarship and other collections for further study or entertainment.

Proverbs are the true voice of all the people. *The Prentice-Hall Encyclopedia of World Proverbs* should have a universal appeal no matter what the cultural, societal, intellectual, professional or ethnic background the reader might have. It contains wisdom for everyone for every possible situation, for proverbs reflect the joys and sorrows, the fortune and misfortune, and the good and the bad of everyday life. The proverbs contain a basic philosophy of life or world view, which, though expressed in different metaphors, shows that common people around the world believe in mankind's desire to live a good and decent life. And despite the pessimistic attitudes in some of them, there appears to be present a certain pragmatic optimism in the majority of proverbs. They seem to say that "There is nothing new under the sun" and that "Hope springs eternal." By listening to and reading the proverbs of people of other nations, we might well come one step closer to understanding their frustrations, dreams, and wishes.

Wolfgang Mieder

Contents

Welcome to the Wonderful World of Proverbs   *ix*

A *(1–16)*

A Abbey Abbot Ability Above Absence Absent Abstinence Abundance Abuse Accident Accommodate Accomplice Accomplishment Accord Account Accountant Accuse Ache Acid Acknowledgment Acquaintance Acrobat Act (noun) Act (verb) Action Adam Add Admission Ado Adult Adulterer Adultery Advantage Adversity Advertisement Advertising Advice Advise Advisement Adviser Advising Affair Affection Affinity Affliction Afraid Afternoon Afterthought Age Aged (people) Agitation Agree Agreement Ague Aid Ailment Ale Alertness Alligator Almost Alms Alone Altar Ambassador Ambition Ambush Amendment American Amiss Anchor Angel Anger Angry Animal Ankle Answer (noun) Answer (verb) Ant Antagonist Antelope Anticipate Anvil Anxiety Anything Ape Apothecary Apparel Appear Appearance Appetite Apple Apple tree Apricot Archbishop Archer Architect Argument Arm Armpit Arms (weapons) Army Arrow Art Article Artisan Artist Ashamed Ashes Ask Asked Asking Ass Assertion Assistance Associate Assume Athlete Attain Attempt (noun) Attempt (verb) Attitude Auction Aunt Austerity Author Authority Avarice Avoidance Awl Ax(e) Axle

B *(17–53)*

Baby Bachelor Back Bacon Bad Bag Bagel Bagpipe Bait Bake Baker Baking Balance Bald Baldness Ball Bamboo Banana Bank (money) Bank (river) Banker Banquet Barbarian Barber Barefoot Bargain (noun) Bargain (verb) Bargainer Bargaining Bark (noun) Bark (verb) Barker Barley Barleycorn Barn Barrel Bashful Bashfulness Basket Bastard Bat Bath Battle Be Bead Bean Bear (noun)

CONTENTS

Bear (verb) Beard Bearskin Beast Beat Beating Beautiful
Beauty Because Bed Bedtime Bee Beef Been Beer Beetle Beg
Beggar Begging Begin Beginning Begun Behavior Behind Being
Belief Believe Believer Bell Belly Bellyful Beloved Bench Bend
Benefit Besom Best Betrayer Better Bill Bind Bird Bird-lime
Birth Bishop Bit (bridle) Bit (little) Bitch Bite Biter Bits Bitten
Bitter Bittern Bitterness Blab Black Blackberry Blacken Black-
smith Blade Blame (noun) Blame (verb) Blanket Blast Blessedness
Blessing Blind (adjective) Blind (people) Blister Block Blockhead
Blood Blossom (noun) Blossom (verb) Blot Blow (noun) Blow (verb)
Blue Blunder Blush Blushing Boast Boaster Boasting Boat
Boatman Body Bog Boil Bold Boldness Bolt Bond Bone Book
Boor Boot Booted Booty Born Borrow Borrowed Borrower
Borrowing Boss Bottle Bottom (behind) Bottom (ground, base)
Bough Boulder Bound Bounty Bow (archery) Bow (ship) Bow (verb)
Bowel Bowl (noun) Bowl (verb) Box Boy Bracelet Brag (noun)
Brag (verb) Braggart Bragger Bragging Brain Bramble Bran
Branch Brave (adjective) Brave (people) Bravery Braying Bread
Breadfruit Break Breakfast Breast Breath Breeches Breed
Breeding Breeze Brevity Brew Bribe (noun) Bribe (verb) Bribery
Bricklayer Bride Bridge Bridle Bright Brim Bring Brocade Brood
Brook Broom Broth Brother Bruise Bruit Brush Bubble Buck
Bucket Bud Budget Buffalo Bug Build Building (edifice) Building
(erecting) Bull Bull Ring Bullet Bullock Bun Burden Burdensome
Burial Burn Bush Bushel Business Businessman Busy Busybody
Butcher Butter Butterfly Button Buy Buyer Buying By Bygone

C (55–96)

Cabbage Cackle Caesar Cage Cake Calamity Caldron Calendar
Calf (cow) Calf (leg) Call Calligrapher Calling Calm Camel
Camp Can Candle Cane Cannonball Cannot Canoe Cantor Cap
Capon Captain Car Carabao Caravan Carcass Card Care (noun)
Care (verb) Career Carefulness Carelessly Carelessness Caress
Carpenter Carpentry Carriage Carrion Carrot Carry Cart
Cartwheel Carver Case Cash Cask Castle Cat Catch Catching
Cattle Cause Caution Cellar Cemetery Centipede Certainty Chafer
Chaff Chain Chair Chamber Chamois Chance Change (noun)
Change (verb) Chapel Chapter Character Charcoal Charitable
Charity Charm Chase (noun) Chase (verb) Chaste Chastity Chatter
Cheap Cheapest Cheapness Cheat (noun) Cheat (verb) Cheater
Cheating Cheek Cheer Cheerfulness Cheese Cheesecake Cherish
Cherry Chest (breast) Chest (trunk) Chick Chicken Chide Chief

CONTENTS

Child Childhood Children Chimney Chin Chip Choice Church
Cider Circumcision Circumstance Citizen Clam Claw Clay
Cleanliness Clemency Clergy Clerk Cleverness Climb (noun) Climb
(verb) Climber Cloak Clock Cloth Clothes Cloud Clout Clown
Coachman Coal Coat Coaxing Cobbler Cobra Cobweb Cock
Cockerel Cockroach Coconut Coffee Coffin Coin Coincidence Cold
Collection Color Colt Comb Come Comer Comfort Command
(noun) Command (verb) Commencement Commodity Community
Companion Company Comparison Competition Complain Complaint
Complimenting Compromise Comrade Concealer Conceit
Concentration Concern Concubine Condition Cone Confectioner
Conference Confession Confidence Conquer Conqueror Conscience
Consent Consequence Consideration Consistency Conspiracy
Consulting Contempt Content (adjective) Content (contentment)
Contentment Contest Contract Contrivance Control Conversation
Converse Cook (noun) Cook (verb) Cooking Coop Copper Cord
Cordial Cork Corn Corner Corporal Corpse Correction Corruption
Cost (noun) Cost (verb) Cottage Cotton Cotton tree Cough Council
Counsel (noun) Counsel (verb) Country Couple Courage Course
Court Courtesy Courtier Courtship Cousin Cover (noun) Cover
(verb) Covering Covetousness Cow Coward Cowardice Cowl Crab
Crabgrass Cradle Craft Craftsman Crane Craving Creak Cream
Crease Credit Creditor Credulous Creep Cricket Crime Cripple
Critic Criticism Crocodile Crooked Crop Cross Crotch Crow
Crowd Crown Cruelty Crumb Crust Cry Cuckold Cuckoo
Cunning Cup Cupidity Cur Cure (noun) Cure (verb) Curiosity
Currant Current Curry Curse Custom Customer Cut

D (97–130)

Dagger Damage Dance (noun) Dance (verb) Dancer Dancing
Danger Daring Darkness Darling Dart Daughter Daughter-in-law
Dawn Day Dead (adjective) Dead (noun) Deaf Deal Dealing Death
Debt Debtor Deceit Deceive Deceiver Deed Deem Deer Deer Hunter
Defeat Defect Defense Defer Delay Deliberate Deliberating
Delight Demand (noun) Demand (verb) Demon Demonstration
Denial Deny Depart Departure Depend Dependence Dependent
Depth Desert Deserve Desire (noun) Desire (verb) Despair
Desperate Despise Destiny Destitute Determination Determined
Devil Dew Diamond Dice Die Diet Difference Difficulty
Diffidence Dignity Dike Dilemma Diligence Dinner Dipper
Dipping Direct Direction Dirt Disagreement Disappoint Disaster
Disciple Discipline Discount Discourse Discredit Discreet Discretion

Discrimination Disease Disgrace Dish Dishonor Dislike Disobedience Disposition Dispute Disputing Distance Distinction Distress Distrust Diversity Dividend Divination Diviner Division Do Doctor Doer Dog Dogfight Doing Doll Dollar Done Donkey Door Doorstep Doorway Doubt (noun) Doubt (verb) Dough Dove Dowry Draff Dragon Dream (noun) Dream (verb) Dreaming Dress Drift Drink (noun) Drink (verb) Drinking Drive Driver Driving Drone Drop Dropping Droppings Drought Drown Drowning Drum Drunk (intoxicated) Drunk (noun) Drunkard Drunkenness Duck Dumpling Dung Dungeon Dunghill Dust Duty Dwarf Dwelling Dying

E *(131–146)*

Eagle Eagle-eyed Ear Early Earn Earth (soil) Earth (world) Ease Eat Eater Eating Echo Economy Edge Education Eel Effect Effort Egg Eggplant Elbow-grease Elder Elephant Elk Eloquence Embarrassed Ember Embrace Emerald Emperor Employment End Endeavor Endurance Endure Enemy Engagement Enmity Enough Entertainment Entrance Entrusted Envy (noun) Envy (verb) Equal Equality Err Errand Erring Error Escape Estate Estimate Eternity Eve Evening Event Everybody Everything Everywhere Evidence Evil Example Excellence Exception Excess Exchange Excuse (noun) Excuse (verb) Executioner Executor Exertion Expense Experience Expert Exterior Extreme Extremity Eye Eyelash Eyesight Eyewitness

F *(147–187)*

Face Fact Fagot Fail Failure Fair (beautiful) Fair (carnival) Fairy tale Faith Fall (noun) Fall (verb) Falling Falsehood Fame Familiarity Family Famine Fan Fancy Fare Farm Farmer Fashion Fasting Fat Fate Father Fatherland Fatigue Fault Fault-finder Favor Fear (noun) Fear (verb) Feast Feasting Feather Fed Fee Feed Feel Feeling Feet Fellow Fence Feud Fever Few Fewer Fiber Fiddle Fiddler Fidelity Field Fife Fifer Fig Fight (noun) Fight (verb) Figure (body) Figure (number) File Filth Find Fine Finery Finger Finish Fire Fireside Firewood Fish (noun) Fish (verb) Fisherman Fishing Fist Flame Flatter Flatterer Flattery Flavor Flea Flee Fleece Flesh Flight (fleeing) Flight (flying) Flint Flock Flogging Flood Floor Flounder Flour Flow Flower Fly (noun) Fly (verb) Flying Foal Fodder Foe Fog Folk Follower

CONTENTS

Folly Food Fool Foolish Foolishness Foot Football Footprint Footstep Forbearance Force Ford Forecast Foreigner Forenoon Foresight Forest Forethought Forewit Forget Forgetting Forgive Fortress Fortune Fortuneteller Foster Foundation Fountain Fowl Fox Fracture Fraud Fray Free Freedom Fretting Friar Friend Friendship Fright Frog Frost Froth Frugality Fruit Frying Frying Pan Fuel Fugitive Fun Fur Furniture Further Fury Future

G (189–209)

Gadfly Gain (noun) Gain (verb) Gaining Gait Gall Gallant Gallow Gambler Gambling Game Gap Gape Garden Gardener Garlic Garment Gate Gathering Gauntlet Gazelle Geese Gem General Generation Generosity Genius Gentility Gentle Gentleman Gentleness Get Ghost Giant Gift Gift Horse Ginger Girl Give Giver Giving Glacier Gladness Glass Glasses Glory Glutton Gluttony Go Goal Goat Go-between God Gods Gold Good Good-hearted Goodness Goods Goose Gossip Gossiping Gourd Govern Government Gown Grace Grain Grandchild Grant Grape Grasp Grass Grate Gratitude Grave Great Greatness Greed Greyhound Grief Grievance Grindstone Grocer Groom Ground Grove Grow Growth Grudge Guard Guarding Guess Guessing Guest Guide Guile Guilt Guilty Gun Gunpowder Gut Gutter Gypsy

H (211–246)

Habit Hack Hail Hair Half Halter Hammer Hammering Hand Handful Handicraft Handle Handsaw Handsome Hang Hanging Hap Happen Happiness Happy Hard Hardship Hare Harlot Harm Harpoon Harshness Harvest Haste Hasten Hastiness Hasty Hat Hatch Hatchet Hate Hatred Haughtiness Haughty Have Having Hawk Hay Hazard Head Headache Heady Heal Healing Health Healthy Heap Hear Hearer Hearing Hearsay Heart Hearth Heat Heaven Hedge Heed Heel Heir Hell Helm Help (noun) Help (verb) Helper Helping Hemlock Hemp Hen Herald Herb Herd Herder Here Hero Heroism Heron Herring Hesitate Hew Hide (skin) Hide (verb) High Highroad Highway Hill Hinge Hint Hippopotamus Hire Hiring Hit Hitch Hoe Hog Hold Hole Holiday Home Honest Honesty Honey Honeymoon Honor (noun) Honor (verb) Hood Hoof Hook Hope Hoping Horn (animal) Horn (instrument) Horse Horseshoe Hospitality Host Hostess Hostility Hot Hound Hour House Household Housekeeper Housewife

Human Humble Humility Humor Hunchback Hunger Hungry
Hunt Hunter Hunting Hunting-horn Hurry (noun) Hurry (verb)
Hurt (noun) Hurt (verb) Husband Husbandry Hut Hyena
Hypocrisy Hypocrite

I *(247–252)*

Ice Icon Idea Idiot Idle Idleness Idol Ignorance Ignorant Ill
Illness Ills Image Image-maker Imitation Imp Impatience Impossi-
bility Impression Improve Incense Inch Indecision Indolence
Indulgence Industry Inferior Influence Ingratitude Inheritance
Iniquity Injury Injustice Ink In-laws Inn Innkeeper Innocence
Innocent Inquire Inquiry Insect Instinct Instruction Instrument
Insult Intellect Intelligence Intention Interest Interpreter Intoxicated
Intoxication Intrigue Iron Itch (noun) Itch (verb) Ivory Ivy

J *(253–256)*

Jack Jackal Jade Jar (conflict) Jar (glass) Jealousy Jest (noun) Jest
(verb) Jester Jesting Jewel Jeweller Jill Job Join Joke Joking
Journey Joy Judge (noun) Judge (verb) Judgment Jug Jungle Junk
Just Justice

K *(257–263)*

Keep Keeper Kennel Kernel Kettle Key Kick Kid Kin Kind-
hearted Kindness King Kingdom Kinsfolk Kiss Kissing Kitchen
Kite Knapsack Knave Knavery Knee Knife Knock Knot Knout
Know Knowledge

L *(265–292)*

Label Labor (noun) Labor (verb) Laborer Lack Lad Ladder Ladle
Lady Lake Lamb Lambskin Lame Lamp Land Landlady Land-
lord Landmark Landowner Lane Language Lark Latch Late
Lather Laugh Laughter Lavishness Law Lawsuit Lawyer Laziness
Lazy Lead Leader Leading Leaf Leak (noun) Leak (verb) Leap
(noun) Leap (verb) Learn Learned (people) Learning Lease
Leather Leave Leaven Leaving Lechery Leg Legacy Leisure
Lemon Lend Lender Lending Lentil Leopard Lesson Letter Liar

Libel Liberty Lick Lid Lie (noun) Lie (verb) Life Lifeless Lifetime Light Lighthouse Lightning Like (equal) Like (verb) Likeness Lily Limb Linen Lining Link Lion Lion Skin Lip Liquor Listen Listener Literature Litter Little Live Livelihood Liver Living (noun) Living (people) Lizard Load Loaf Loafer Loan Lobster Lock Locust Log Loincloth Lonely Long Longing Look (noun) Look (verb) Looker-on Looking Looking-glass Lord (see God) Lord (men) Lose Loser Losing Loss Lot Louse Love (noun) Love (verb) Lover Loving Loyalty Luck Lucky Luggage Lure (noun) Lure (verb) Lust Luxury Lying

M *(293–341)*

Mad Madman Magistrate Maid Maiden Malice Man Manner Mantis Mantle Manure Marble Mare Mark Market Marketing Marksman Marriage Marry Marrying Mason Mass (crowd) Mass (holy) Master (noun) Master (verb) Mat Match Matchmaker Matter Maturity Maxim Mead Meadow Meal (food) Meal (grain) Meaning Means Measure (noun) Measure (verb) Meat Mecca Medal Meddle Meddling Medicine Meet Meeting Melancholy Melon Melon Seller Memory Men Mend Merchandise Merchant Merit Merry Message Messenger Metal Mice Midwife Might Mile Milk Mill Miller Millstone Mind Mine Minister Minnow Minute Miracle Mire Mirror Mirth Mischance Mischief Miser Miserly Misery Misfortune Misreckoning Miss Mistake Mistress Mistrust Misunderstanding Mix Mixture Mob Mocking Moderation Modesty Mole Moment Money Moneymaker Monk Monkey Moon Moonlight More Morning Morning Hour Morrow Morsel Moscow Mosque Mosquito Mote Moth Mother Mother-in-law Motherwit Motion Mountain Mourner Mouse Mouth Move Much Mud Mug Mule Multitude Murder Muse Mushroom Music Musician Musk Must Mustard Mutton Myrtle

N *(343–351)*

Nag Nail Naked Nakedness Name (noun) Name (verb) Native Nature Naught Nay Necessity Neck Nectar Need Needle Needy Negative Neglect Neighbor Neighborhood Nerve Nest Net Nettle Neutral Never New News Niceness Niggard Night Nightingale Nit Nobility Noble Nobody Nod Noise Nonsense Nose Nothing Nought Novice Number Nun Nurse Nurture Nut

O *(353–358)*

Oak Oar Oath Oatmeal Obedience Obligation Obstacle Occasion
Occupant Ocean Odds Offender Offense Offer Office Officer
Official Offspring Oil Ointment Old Older Omelet One Onion
Opinion Opium Opponent Opportunity Opposition Oppression
Oppressor Orange Orator Orchard Order Ornament Orphan
Ostrich Ounce Outbid Outergarment Oven Overeating Overseer
Overtake Owe Owl Owlet Own (property) Own (verb) Owner Ox

P *(359–395)*

Pace Pack (animals) Pack (bag) Padlock Pail Pain Painful Painter
Painting Palm Tree Pancake Paper Paradise Parasite Pardon
Parents Paris Parish Parrot Parson Part Partner Partridge Party
(entertainment) Party (people) Pass Passage Passion Past Pasturage
Pasture Patch Pate Path Patience Patient (adjective) Patient (noun)
Pattern Pauper Pause Pay (noun) Pay (verb) Paymaster Payment
Pea Peace Peacemaker Peach Peacock Pear Pearl Peasant Pebble
Peddler Pedestrian Pedigree Peg Pen Pence Penny Pension Peony
People Pepper Peppercorn Perfection Perhaps Perseverance
Persevere Person Persuasion Pestilence Peter Petticoat Pheasant
Philosopher Physician Piano Picture Piece Piety Pig Pigeon Pike
Pilgrim Pill Pilot Pin Pinch Pine Pint Pipe Piper Pit Pitch
Pitcher Pity (noun) Pity (verb) Place Plan Plank Planning Plant
(noun) Plant (verb) Plate Plating Platter Play (noun) Play (verb)
Playing Plaything Plea Pleasant Please Pleasure Pledge Plenty
Plough (noun) Plough (verb) Ploughman Plum Plummet Pocket
Poet Poetry Poison Pole Policy Politeness Politics Pond Pontoon
Pool Poor Poorer Pope Porcupine Porridge Portion Position
Possession Possessor Post Postpone Pot Pottage Potter Pottery
Pound Poverty Powder Power Practice (noun) Practice (verb) Praise
(noun) Praise (verb) Praising Prate (noun) Prate (verb) Prawn
Pray Prayer Preach Preacher Preaching Precaution Precept
Preference Presence Present Preserve Prettiness Pretty Prevention
Prey Price Pride Priest Prince Prison Prisoner Probability
Procession Procrastination Prodigal Profit Promise (noun) Promise
(verb) Promiser Promising Promptness Proof Proper Property
Prophet Propriety Prospect Prosperity Prostitute Prove Proverb
Provide Providence Providing Provision Prudence Psalm Public
Pudding Pull Pullet Pumpkin Punctuality Punish Punishment
Pup Pupil Puppy Purchase Purse Purse String Put

Q *(397–398)*

Quail Quality Quarrel (noun) Quarrel (verb) Question (noun) Question (verb) Questioning Quick Quietness Quill

R *(399–416)*

Rabbi Rabbit Rabble Race Rag Rage Raillery Rain (noun) Rain (verb) Rainbow Raindrop Raisin Rake Rancor Rank Rapier Rascal Rashness Rat Raven Razor Read Reap Reason Receive Receiver Receiving Reception Reckoning Reconcilement Reconciliation Recorder Rectify Red Redemption Reed Refusal Refuse (noun) Refuse (verb) Regret Regularity Reindeer Reinforcement Relation Relationship Relative Religion Remark Remedy Remember Remorse Removal Rent Repair Repeat Repentance Repetition Reply (noun) Reply (verb) Reprimand Reproach Reproof Reputation Repute Request Reserve Resignation Resolution Resolve Respect (noun) Respect (verb) Respite Response Rest Restraint Retreat Return (noun) Return (verb) Revenge (noun) Revenge (verb) Reverence Revolution Reward Rhinoceros Rhyme Rice Rice Field Rich (adjective) Rich (people) Riches Riddle Ride Rider Riding Right Righteousness Ring Ripe Rise (noun) Rise (verb) Riser Rising Risk River Rivulet Road Roadside Roast Rob Robber Robin Robin Hood Rock Rod Rogue Rome Roof Room Rooster Root Rope Rosary Rose Rowing Rub Rubbish Ruble Rudder Rule (noun) Rule (verb) Ruler Rum Rumor Run Runner Rush Rust

S *(417–465)*

Sabre Sack Sacrifice Saddle Sadness Safe Safety Sage Said Sail (noun) Sail (verb) Sailing Sailor Saint Salad Salary Sale Salmon Saloonkeeper Salt Salvation Salve Sand Sandal Sap Sapling Sardine Satisfaction Sauce Sausage Save Saver Saving Savor Say Saying Sayings Scald Scale Scandal Scar Scarcity Scarecrow Scepter Scheme Scheming Scholar Scholarship School Schoolboy Schoolmaster Scolding Score Scorn Scorning Scorpion Scrap Scratch Scratching Scribe Scythe Sea Seam Seaman Search (noun) Search (verb) Season Seat Seated Secrecy Secret (adjective) Secret (noun) Sect Secular Secure Security Seducer See Seed Seedling Seeing Seek Seeker Seem Seldom Self-interest Self-love Self-praise Self-preservation Self-respect Sell Seller Selvage Sense Sentence

CONTENTS

Separation Sermon Serpent Servant Serve Service Settle Seven
Shade Shadow Shaft Shake Shame Shameless Share Shark
Shaving Shearer Shed Sheep Shell Shelter Sheltering Shepherd
Shield Shilling Ship Shirt Shive Shoal Shoe Shoemaker Shoot
Shooting Shop Shore Short Shot Shoulder Shout Show (noun) Show
(verb) Shower Shrew Shrewdness Shrimp Shroud Shrub Sick
Sickle Sickness Side Sieve Sigh Sight Sign (noun) Sign (verb)
Silence Silent Silk Silver Silver mine Similarity Simpleton
Simplicity Sin Sing Singer Singing Single Sinner Sip Sit Sitting
Size Ski Skill Skilled Skin Skipper Skirt Skunk Sky Slander
(noun) Slander (verb) Slanderer Slap Slave Slavery Sleep (noun)
Sleep (verb) Sleeping Sleigh Slice Sling Slip Slipper Sloth Slothful
Slow Sluggard Slumber (noun) Slumber (verb) Slut Smart (verb)
Smartest Smell (noun) Smell (verb) Smile Smith Smoke Snail
Snake Snipe Snore Snow Soap Soft Soil Soldier Sole Something
Somewhat Son Song Son-in-law Soon Sorcerer Sore Sorrow Sort
Soul Sound Soup Sour Source Sovereignty Sow (noun) Sow (verb)
Sower Sowing Spade Spare Sparing Spark Sparrow Sparrow
Hawk Speak Speaker Speaking Spear Speck Spectacle Spectator
Speech Speed Spend Spender Spending Spice Spider Spinach
Spindle Spinning Spinster Spirit (ghost) Spirit (mind) Spit Spite
Splinter Spoil Spoke Sponge Spoon Spoor Sport Spot Spring
(season) Spring (water) Sprout Spur (noun) Spur (verb) Spy
Squinting Stab Stability Staff Stain Stair Stake Stand Standing
Star Starling Start (noun) Start (verb) State Statement Stay (noun)
Stay (verb) Steal Stealing Steed Steering Step Stew Stick Stile
Sting Stir Stitch Stocking Stomach Stone Stool Stop Store (noun)
Store (verb) Storm Story Stoup Strain Stranger Stratagem Straw
Stream Street Strength Stretch Stretching String Stripping Stroke
Struggle Stubbornness Student Studies Study Stumble (noun) Stumble
(verb) Stump Stupid Stupidity Subject Subtlety Succeed Success
Successor Suffer Sufferance Sufferer Suffering Suit Suitor Sultan
Sum Summer Sun Sun Dial Sunlight Sunshine Sup Superior
Supper Sure Surety Surf rider Surgeon Suspense Suspicion Swallow
(noun) Swallow (verb) Swan Swear Swearing Sweat Sweeping
Sweet Sweetheart Sweetness Swim Swimmer Swine Sword
Swordsman Sympathy

T (467–501)

Table Tace Tadpole Tael Tail Tailor Take Taker Tale Talent Talk
(noun) Talk (verb) Talker Talking Talmud Tapster Tar Tart Task
Taste (noun) Taste (verb) Tavern Tax Tea Teach Teacher Teaching

CONTENTS

Teapot Tear (cry) Tear (rip) Teasing Teeth Tell Telling Temper
Temple Temptation Tenant Tent Termite Testimony Thank Thanks
Thank you Thaw Thickness Thief Thieves Thing Think Thinking
Thirst Thistle Thong Thorn Thought Thread Threat Threaten
Threatener Three Three Things Threshold Thrift Thrifty Thrive
Throat Throw Thumb Thunder Thunderbolt Tickle Tidbit Tide
Tidings Tiger Tile Timber Time Timidity Tinker Tippler Tire
Titmouse Toad Tobacco Today Toe Together Toil Toll Tomato
Tomorrow Tone Tong Tongue Tool Tooth Toothache Top (lid) Top
(summit) Torah Torch Torment Tortoise Tower Town Toy Trace
Trade Tradition Train Traitor Tranquility Trap Trash Travel
(noun) Travel (verb) Traveler Tray Treachery Treason Treasure
Tree Tree-knot Trial Tribe Trick Trickery Trickster Trifle
Trooper Trot Trouble Trough Trousers Trout Troy True Trust
(noun) Trust (verb) Trusting Truth Try Trying Tsar Tub Tune
Turban Turn Twig Two Two Things Tyrant

U (503–504)

Ugliness Umbrella Unborn Uncertainty Underling Understand
Understanding Undertake Union Unity Unknown Unlooked
Unmannerliness Unmannerly Upbringing Use (noun) Use (verb)
Usurer Usury

V (505–510)

Valet Valiant Valley Valor Valuable Value Vanity Varnishing
Vegetable Veil Velvet Veneration Vengeance Venison Venture (noun)
Venture (verb) Vessel (container) Vessel (ship), Vice Victim Victor
Victory Vigilance Village Vinegar Vineyard Violence Violet
Violin Viper Virgin Virtue Visit Visiting Visitor Vodka Voice
Vow Vulture

W (511–555)

Wage Wager Wagon Wait Waiting Walk Walker Wall Wallet
Walnut Walnut Tree Wanderer Want (noun) Want (verb) Ware
Warm (adjective) Warm (verb) Warn Warning Warrior Wasp Waste
(noun) Waste (verb) Wastefulness Wasting Watch (noun) Watch
(verb) Watching Watchman Water Waterfall Watermelon Waterwheel Wave Wax Way Weak Weaker Weakest Weal Wealth

Weapon Wear Wearer Weary Weather Weatherwise Weaver Web
Wed Wedding Wedding Ring Wedge Wedlock Weed (noun) Weed
(verb) Weening Weigh Weight Welcome Well (adverb) Well
(adjective) Wench Whale Wheat Wheel Whelp Whet Whetstone
While Whim Whip Whisper (noun) Whisper (verb) Whistle (noun)
Whistle (verb) Wholeheartedness Whore Whoredom Whoring Why
Wicked (people) Wickedness Wide Widow Wife Wild Wile Will
(noun) Will (verb) Willow Win Wind Windmill Window Wine
Wing Winning Winter Winter Weather Wisdom Wise (adjective)
Wise (people) Wish Wisher Wishing Wit Within Witness
Witticism Wive (verb) Wives Wiving Woe Wolf Wolves Woman
Womankind Women Wonder Wood Woodcock Woodcutter Wooer
Wooing Wool Wool Seller Word Work (noun) Work (verb) Worker
Working Workman World Worm Worry Worship Worth Wound
Wrangler Wrath Wreck Wren Wretch Wretched Wrinkle Writing
Brush Wrong Wrong-doer

Y *(557–559)*

Yardstick Yarn Yawning Year Yeast Yesterday Yielding Yoke
Young Youth Youths

Z *(561)*

Zeal

Selected Bibliography *563*

A

1. He that says A, must also say B.
German

ABBEY

2. The abbey does not fail for want of one monk. *French*

ABBOT

3. As the abbot sings the sacristan responds. *Spanish*

ABILITY

4. Ability to swim is preservation of life. *African (Hausa)*

5. Suitable ability in the suitable place. *Japanese*

ABOVE

6. Those above are going down, those below are going up. *Hawaiian*

ABSENCE

7. A little absence does much good. *French*

8. Absence is a foe to love; out of sight out of mind. *Italian*

9. Absence is a shrew. *English*

10. Absence is foe to love; away from the eyes, away from the heart. *Spanish*

11. Absence sharpens love, presence strengthens it. *English*

12. Long absence changes friends. *French*

ABSENT

13. Long absent soon forgotten. *English*

14. The absent always bear the blame. *Dutch*

15. The absent are always in the wrong. *French*

16. The absent are always to blame. *Hebrew*

ABSTINENCE

17. Abstinence and fasting cure many a complaint. *Danish*

18. Abstinence is the best medicine. *Indian (Tamil)*

ABUNDANCE

19. Abundance does not spread, famine does. *African (Zulu)*

20. Abundance is from activity. *Turkish*

21. Abundance of money is a trial for a man. *Moroccan*

22. Abundance will make cotton pull a stone. *African (Hausa)*

1

23. The abundance of money ruins youth. *English*

ABUSE

24. Abuses are the result of seeing one another too often.
African (Swahili)

25. Abuse doesn't hang on the collar. *Russian*

26. Abuse is like a god that destroys his master. *Hawaiian*

27. Abuse of hospitality breaks the bridge. *African (Bemba)*

ACCIDENT

28. Accidents will happen. *English*

29. An accident is not like an expected result. *African (Yoruba)*

ACCOMMODATE

30. If you accommodate others, you will be accommodating yourself.
Chinese

ACCOMPLICE

31. The accomplice is as bad as the thief. *Portuguese*

ACCOMPLISHMENT

32. Accomplishment of purpose is better than making a profit.
African (Hausa)

33. Accomplishments will save a person. *Japanese*

34. An accomplishment sticks to a person. *Japanese*

35. He who boasts of his accomplishments will heap ridicule.
Philippine

36. Whatever accomplishment you boast of in the world, there is someone better than you. *African (Hausa)*

ACCORD

37. There is no good accord where every man would be a lord. *English*

ACCOUNT

38. Good accounts make good friends. *Greek*

39. The account of the donkey is different from the account of the donkey-man. *Turkish*

40. When accounts are examined, difficulties arise. *Indian (Tamil)*

ACCOUNTANT

41. The accountant is clever at numbers, but he is ignorant of his own accounts. *Indian (Tamil)*

ACCUSE

42. Accusing the times is but excusing ourselves. *English*

ACHE

43. The worst ache is the present ache. *Lebanese*

ACID

44. Sharp acids corrode their own containers. *Albanian*

ACKNOWLEDGMENT

45. Acknowledgment is half of correction. *Russian*

ACQUAINTANCE

46. One's acquaintances may fill the empire, but one's real friends can be but few. *Chinese*

47. Short acquaintance brings repentance. *English*

48. The more acquaintance the more danger. *English*

ACROBAT

49. Two acrobats cannot perform on one rope. *Lebanese*

ACT (noun)

50. A stupid act entails doing the work twice over. *Burmese*

ACT (verb)

51. Act honestly, and answer boldly.
Danish

ACTION

52. A good action always finds its recompense. *English*

53. A good action is better than a bad action. *African (Wolof)*

54. Action and reaction are equal.
American

55. Action is the proper fruit of knowledge. *English*

56. Brave actions never want a trumpet. *English*

57. Every one is responsible for his own actions. *Indian (Tamil)*

58. Good actions are not lost.
Turkish

59. Innocent actions carry their warrant with them. *English*

60. Never repent a good action.
Danish

61. Postpone not a good action.
Irish

ADAM

62. We are all Adam's children, but silk makes the difference. *English*

63. When Adam delved and Eve span, who was then the gentleman?
English

ADD

64. The more you add, the worse it gets. *Hebrew*

ADMISSION

65. Admission by the defendant is worth a hundred witnesses. *Hebrew*

ADO

66. Mickle ado and little help.
English

67. Much ado about nothing.
English

ADULT

68. The adult looks to deeds, the child to love. *Indian (Hindustani)*

ADULTERER

69. Were all adulterers to wear gray coats, the cloth would be expensive.
German

ADULTERY

70. Adultery is like dung; one goes far to do it. *African (Bemba)*

ADVANTAGE

71. A single advantage is worth a thousand sorceries. *Turkish*

72. Advantage is a better soldier than rashness. *English*

73. If you are modest, you are modest to your own advantage.
African (Yoruba)

ADVERSITY

74. Adversity and loss make a man wise. *Welsh*

75. Adversity brings knowledge, and knowledge wisdom. *Welsh*

76. Adversity flatters no man.
English

77. Adversity is easier borne than prosperity forgot. *English*

78. Adversity is the foundation of virtue. *Japanese*

79. Adversity makes a man wise.
French

80. Many can bear adversity, but few contempt. *English*

ADVERTISEMENT

81. An advertisement is the engine of commerce. *Russian*

ADVERTISING

82. Advertising is the mother of commerce. *Japanese*

ADVICE

83. A good advice is as good as an eye in the hand. *French*

84. A wife's advice is not worth much, but woe to the husband who refuses to take it. *Welsh*

85. A woman's advice is a poor thing, but he is a fool who does not take it. *English*

86. A woman's advice is but slender, yet he that refuses it is a madman. *English*

87. Advice after the mischief is like medicine after death. *Danish*

88. Advice comes too late when a thing is done. *English*

89. Advice is not compulsion. *German*

90. Advice once was worth a camel; now that it is free of charge, no one takes it. *Lebanese*

91. Advice should precede the act. *German*

92. Advice that ain't paid for ain't no good. *American*

93. Advice to a fool goes in at one ear and out at the other. *Danish*

94. Advice to all, security for none. *English*

95. Ask advice from everyone, but act with your own mind. *Yiddish*

96. Ask for advice, but do what you think is best. *Greek*

97. Crafty advice is often got from a fool. *Irish*

98. Do not ask advice of the ignorant. *Indian (Tamil)*

99. Give neither advice nor salt, until you are asked for it. *English*

100. Giving advice to a stupid man is like giving salt to a squirrel. *Indian (Kashmiri)*

101. Good advice is given, good esteem is not given. *Turkish*

102. He asks advice in vain who will not follow it. *French*

103. He who builds according to every man's advice will have a crooked house. *Danish*

104. He who seeks advice seldom errs. *Philippine*

105. He who will not accept an old man's advice will some day be a beggar. *Chinese*

106. He who will not take cheap advice, will have to buy dear repentance. *Danish*

107. If advice will not improve him, neither will the rod. *Greek*

108. In vain he craves advice who will not follow it. *English*

109. It is advantageous to follow advice, for you will succeed in life. *Philippine*

110. It is easy to give advice when all goes well. *Italian*

111. Let him who will not have advice have conflict. *Irish*

112. Never give advice unasked. *German*

113. Nothing is so liberally given as advice. *French*

114. One piece of good advice is better than a bag full. *Danish*

115. Take a woman's first advice and not her second. *French*

116. Take your wife's first advice. *English*

117. Take your wife's first advice, and not her second. *English*

118. The advice of the aged will not mislead you. *Welsh*

4

119. We may give advice, but we cannot give conduct. *American*

120. When a thing is done advice comes too late. *French*

121. Women's advice is cold advice. *English*

122. Write down the advice of him who loves you, though you like it not at present. *English*

ADVISE

123. No one is wise enough to advise himself. *German*

124. He who won't be advised, can't be helped. *German*

ADVISEMENT

125. There came never ill of good advisement. *Scottish*

ADVISER

126. A man is often a bad adviser to himself and a good adviser to another. *Irish*

127. Advisers are not givers. *Dutch*

128. Advisers are not the payers. *French*

129. He who works on the highway will have many advisers. *Spanish*

ADVISING

130. Advising is easier than helping. *German*

131. Advising is often better than fighting. *German*

AFFAIR

132. A great affair covers up a small matter. *African (Yoruba)*

133. He who could foresee affairs three days in advance would be rich for thousands of years. *Chinese*

134. Man's affairs are evaluated only after his coffin is closed. *Korean*

135. No one is wise in his own affairs. *Dutch*

136. The world's affairs are but a dream in spring. *Chinese*

137. Those who pry into other people's affairs will hear what they do not like. *Libyan*

138. We decide our affairs, then we rest them with God. *African (Jabo)*

AFFECTION

139. Strong affections give credit to weak arguments. *English*

AFFINITY

140. Affinity is a mysterious thing, but it is spicy! *Japanese*

AFFLICTION

141. After every affliction there is enjoyment. *Moroccan*

AFRAID

142. Be always a little afraid so that you never have need of being much afraid. *Finnish*

143. Be afraid and you'll be safe. *Irish*

AFTERNOON

144. The afternoon knows what the morning never suspected. *Swedish*

AFTERTHOUGHT

145. The afterthought is good, but forethought is better. *Norwegian*

146. The afterthought is good for nought, except it be to catch blind horses with. *English*

AGE

147. Age and wedlock bring a man to his nightcap. *English*

148. Age and wedlock tame man and beast. *English*

149. Age and wedlock we all desire and repent of. *English*

150. Age breeds aches. *English*

151. Age brings experience, and a good mind wisdom. *Greek*

152. Age does not give sense, it only makes one go slowly. *Finnish*

153. Age gives good advice when it is no longer able to give a bad example. *American*

154. Age is a sorry travelling companion. *Danish*

155. Age makes many a man whiter, but not better. *Danish*

156. Age must have allowance. *American*

157. For age and want save while you may, no morning sun lasts a whole day. *American*

158. If you want to avoid old age, hang yourself in youth. *Yiddish*

159. In old age one again becomes a child. *Japanese*

160. Old age and poverty are wounds that can't be healed. *Greek*

161. Old age does not announce itself. *African (Zulu)*

162. Old age is a hundred disorders. *Welsh*

163. Old age is not a blessing. *Russian*

164. Old age is ripeness. *American*

165. Old age is sickness enough of itself. *English*

166. Old age will not come alone. *Welsh*

167. The golden age never was the present age. *English*

168. Where old age is evil, youth can learn no good. *English*

169. With age comes wisdom. *American*

AGED (people)

170. The aged in council, the young in action. *Danish*

AGITATION

171. Popular agitation leads to justice. *Indian (Tamil)*

AGREE

172. Agree, for the law is costly. *English*

AGREEMENT

173. Agreement with two people, lamentation with three. *Indian (Kashmiri)*

174. An agreement is a kind of debt. *Moroccan*

175. An agreement is more valuable than money. *Russian*

176. An agreement will override custom. *Welsh*

177. An ill agreement is better than a good judgment. *English*

178. Better a lean agreement than a fat lawsuit. *German*

AGUE

179. Agues come on horseback, but go away on foot. *English*

AID

180. Without the aid of the divine, man cannot walk even an inch. *Chinese*

AILMENT

181. The ailment of the heart is known to one only. *African (Zulu)*

ALE

182. Ale in, wit out. *English*

183. Good ale needs no wisp. *Scottish*

184. Plenty know good ale but don't know much after that. *English*

ALERTNESS

185. Alertness and courage are life's shield.   *Philippine*

ALLIGATOR

186. The alligator lays eggs but it is not a fowl.   *Jamaican*

ALMOST

187. Almost is not eaten.
                              African (Zulu)

188. Almost kills no man.   *Danish*

ALMS

189. Alms given openly will be rewarded in secret.   *Chinese*

190. Alms never make poor. *English*

191. Alms quench sin.   *English*

192. Better give nothing than stolen alms.   *German*

193. Giving alms never lessens the purse.   *Spanish*

194. He who gives alms to the poor faces heaven.   *Philippine*

195. He who will not open the door to give alms will open it for the doctor.
                              Indian (Hindi)

196. No one ever became poor through giving alms.   *Italian*

197. The little alms are the good alms.   *French*

ALONE

198. Better alone than have a false friend for company.   *English*

199. Better be alone than in bad company.   *English*

ALTAR

200. He that serves at the altar ought to live by the altar.   *English*

AMBASSADOR

201. An ambassador bears no blame.   *Italian*

AMBITION

202. False ambition serves the neck.
                              Egyptian

AMBUSH

203. You cannot avoid what lies in ambush for you.   *African (Ovambo)*

AMENDMENT

204. Amendment is repentance.
                              English

AMERICAN

205. An American will go to hell for a bag of coffee.   *American*

AMISS

206. He that does amiss may do well.
                              English

ANCHOR

207. Better lose the anchor than the whole ship.   *Dutch*

ANGEL

208. A young angel, an old devil.
                              French

209. Nowadays you must go to heaven to meet an angel.   *Polish*

210. When the angels present themselves, the devils abscond.   *Egyptian*

ANGER

211. A lover's anger is short-lived.
                              Italian

212. Anger and haste hinder good counsel.   *English*

213. Anger dies quickly with a good man.   *English*

214. Anger edges valor.   *English*

215. Anger ends in cruelty.
                              Indian (Tamil)

216. Anger first, and pity afterwards.   *Indian (Tamil)*

217. Anger has no eyes.
Indian (Hindi)

218. Anger hears no counsel.
German

219. Anger increases love. *Italian*

220. Anger is a short madness.
English

221. Anger is a sworn enemy.
English

222. Anger is like a thorn in the heart.
Yiddish

223. Anger is the mother of treachery.
Welsh

224. Anger is the only thing to put off till tomorrow. *Slovakian*

225. Anger punishes itself. *English*

226. Anger with our friend, rather than constant friendship with our enemy.
Egyptian

227. Anger without power is a ready blow.
Egyptian

228. Anger without power is folly.
German

229. Don't drag for anger with a net, or push away your daily bread.
Malaysian

230. Dread the anger of the dove.
French

231. Great anger is more destructive than the sword. *Indian (Tamil)*

232. He who conquers his anger has conquered an enemy. *German*

233. If you are patient in one moment of anger, you will escape a hundred days of sorrow. *Chinese*

234. In proportion as anger comes, sense departs. *Turkish*

235. Kill your anger while it is small. *Slovakian*

236. Love's anger is fuel to love.
German

237. The anger of the prudent never shows. *Burmese*

238. When anger blinds the eyes, truth disappears. *Danish*

239. When anger ceases, revenge ceases. *Indian (Tamil)*

240. With anger you don't get too far.
Yiddish

ANGRY

241. He that is angry is not at ease.
English

242. He that is angry is seldom at ease. *Scottish*

243. He that is angry without a cause must be pleased without amends.
English

ANIMAL

244. A large animal is nice but difficult to feed. *African (Hausa)*

245. All animals sweat, but the hair on them causes us not to notice it.
African (Ashanti)

246. An animal has a long tongue, yet it can't recite a blessing. *Yiddish*

247. An animal that has just escaped from a trap fears a bent stick.
African (Annang)

248. Animals have long tongues but can't speak; men have short tongues and shouldn't speak. *Yiddish*

249. Every kind of animal can be tamed, but not the tongue of man.
Philippine

250. If a bush is surrounded, the animals in it are easily killed.
African (Yoruba)

251. When an animal is not going to bite you, it does not show its teeth at you. *African (Ashanti)*

8

ANKLE

252. Better be up to the ankles, than quite to over head and ears.   *English*

ANSWER (noun)

253. A soft answer turns away wrath.   *Dutch*

254. Give a civil answer to a civil question.   *American*

255. Half an answer also says something.   *Yiddish*

256. No answer is also an answer.   *Danish*

257. No is a good answer when given in time.   *Danish*

258. The shortest answer is doing.   *English*

259. To every answer you can find a new question.   *Yiddish*

ANSWER (verb)

260. If one has nothing to answer, it is best to shut up.   *Yiddish*

ANT

261. An ant hole may collapse an embankment.   *Japanese*

262. An ant is over six feet tall when measured by its own foot-rule.   *Slovenian*

263. Don't step even on an ant.   *Greek*

264. Even the ant has his bite.   *Turkish*

265. He who cannot raise an ant, and yet tries to raise an elephant, shall find out his folly.   *African (Yoruba)*

266. Many ants kill a camel.   *Turkish*

267. One who cannot pick up an ant and wants to pick up an elephant will some day see his folly.   *African (Jabo)*

268. The little ant at its hole is full of courage.   *African (Bemba)*

269. The tiny ant dares to enter the lion's ear.   *Armenian*

270. Where the sugar is, there the ants will be also.   *Philippine*

ANTAGONIST

271. Where there is no antagonist you cannot quarrel.   *Japanese*

ANTELOPE

272. A supposed antelope is not cooking in the pot.   *African (Ovambo)*

273. The antelope does not bear a child that cannot run.   *African (Hausa)*

ANTICIPATE

274. That which one most anticipates, soon comes to pass.   *English*

ANVIL

275. A good anvil does not fear the hammer.   *Italian*

276. A good anvil is not afraid of the hammer.   *Greek*

277. If the anvil is good, the work will be good.   *Indian (Tamil)*

278. If you are an anvil, be patient; if you are a hammer, strike hard.   *German*

279. If you are an anvil, bear the strokes, and if you become a hammer, strike.   *Lebanese*

280. If you are the anvil, suffer; if you are the hammer, strike.   *Rumanian*

281. One must be either anvil or hammer.   *French*

282. The anvil does not fear a good sledgehammer.   *Danish*

283. The anvil fears no blows.   *English*

284. The anvil is not afraid of the hammer. *German*

285. The anvil is used to noise. *German*

286. The anvil lasts longer than the hammer. *Italian*

287. When many strike on an anvil, they must strike by measure. *English*

288. When you are an anvil, bear; when you are a hammer, strike. *Spanish*

289. When you are an anvil, hold your still; when you are a hammer, strike your fill. *English*

ANXIETY

290. Anxiety breaks a man's backbone. *Hebrew*

291. To be prepared is to have no anxiety. *Korean*

ANYTHING

292. Anything for a quiet life. *English*

APE

293. An ape, a priest, and a louse, are three devils in one house. *Dutch*

294. An ape is an ape, though clad in purple. *English*

295. An ape is never so like an ape, as when he wears a doctor's cap. *English*

296. An old ape never made a pretty grimace. *French*

297. Apes are never more beasts than when they wear men's clothes. *English*

298. Apes remain apes, though you cloth them in velvet. *German*

299. No ape but swears he has the handsomest children. *German*

300. The ape kills her young with kindness. *English*

301. The higher the ape climbs the more he shows his rump. *French*

302. The higher the ape goes, the more he shows his tail. *English*

303. When apes climb high, they show their naked rumps. *Dutch*

APOTHECARY

304. Apothecaries would not give pills in sugar unless they were bitter. *English*

APPAREL

305. Apparel makes the man. *English*

APPEAR

306. Appear always what you are and a little less. *Greek*

APPEARANCE

307. Appearances are deceitful. *English*

308. Appearances aren't everything. *American*

309. The appearance of the wise differs from that of the fool. *African (Yoruba)*

APPETITE

310. A waiting appetite kindles many a spite. *English*

311. Appetite comes with eating. *French*

312. Appetite comes with the first mouthful and a quarrel starts with a word. *Lebanese*

313. He who restrains his appetite avoids debt. *Chinese*

314. It is difficult to satisfy one's appetite by painting pictures of cakes. *Chinese*

315. The less we eat, the greater is our appetite. *Vietnamese*

APPLE

316. An apple a day keeps the doctor away. *English*

317. An apple may happen to be better given than eaten. *English*

318. Beside the rotten apple the good one also spoils. *Russian*

319. Do not look for apples under a poplar tree. *Slovakian*

320. Don't pluck the apple while it is green; when it is ripe it will fall of itself. *Russian*

321. Eat an apple on going to bed, and you'll keep the doctor from earning his bread. *English*

322. Even a sour apple is gnawed by maggots. *Polish*

323. Everything round isn't an apple. *Armenian*

324. Handsome apples are sometimes sour. *Dutch*

325. In a good apple you sometimes find a worm. *Yiddish*

326. One rotten apple spoils the other. *Yiddish*

327. Rotten apples are the sweetest. *American*

328. Sour apples must also be eaten. *Estonian*

329. The apple does not fall far from the apple tree. *Russian*

330. The apple doesn't fall far from the tree. *Yiddish*

331. The apple doesn't roll far from the apple tree. *Russian*

332. The apple falls under the apple tree. *Rumanian*

333. The apple that ripens late keeps longer. *Serbo-Croatian*

334. The reddest apple has a worm in it. *Yiddish*

335. The ripe apple falls of itself. *Slovenian*

336. The rotten apple spoils its companion. *Spanish*

337. There's no making apples of plums. *German*

338. Whoever has bitten a sour apple will enjoy a sweet one all the more. *German*

APPLE TREE

339. No apple tree is immune from worms. *Russian*

APRICOT

340. The wild apricot may look ripe, but its taste is bitter. *Korean*

ARCHBISHOP

341. You cannot make a good archbishop of a rogue. *Danish*

ARCHER

342. A good archer is not known by his arrows, but his aim. *English*

343. The archer that shoots badly has a lie ready. *Spanish*

ARCHITECT

344. Everybody is the architect of his own fortune. *German*

ARGUMENT

345. Every argument has its answer. *Greek*

346. The arguments of the strongest have always the most weight. *French*

347. There's no argument like that of the stick. *Spanish*

ARM

348. Better something on the arm than all in the stomach. *Danish*

349. Don't stretch your arm farther than your sleeve will reach. *English*

350. Keep your broken arm inside your sleeve. *Chinese*

11

ARMPIT

351. One armpit cannot hold two watermelons.   *Turkish*

ARMS (weapons)

352. Arms and money require good hands.   *Spanish*

353. Arms, women, and books should be looked at daily.   *Dutch*

ARMY

354. A headless army fights badly.
                                   Danish

355. An army is driven back by courage and not by insults, however many.   *African (Ashanti)*

356. An army of a thousand is easy to find, but, ah, how difficult to find a general.   *Chinese*

357. An army stands until peace, and a lie does so till the truth is out.
                                  Russian

358. Every army that attacks not will be attacked.   *Irish*

359. If you wish to enjoy leisure, join the army.   *Polish*

360. It is an ill army where the devil carries the colors.   *English*

361. Two are an army against one.
                                Icelandic

362. When an army suffers defeat, a horn is not blown in its honor.
                         African (Ashanti)

363. Where the army passes there is no grass.   *Serbo-Croatian*

364. Without a general an army is lost.   *Greek*

ARROW

365. A single arrow is easily broken, but not ten in a bundle.   *Japanese*

366. If you have no arrows in your quiver, go not with archers.   *German*

367. If you sow arrows, you will reap sorrows.   *Philippine*

368. Never was good arrow made of a sow's tail.   *American*

369. The arrow often hits the shooter.   *English*

370. The arrow that has left the bow never returns.   *Iranian*

371. The arrow that is shot returns not back.   *Turkish*

372. The arrow you dropped will be collected by someone else.
                         African (Ovambo)

ART

373. Art and knowledge bring bread and honor.   *Danish*

374. Art has no enemy but ignorance.   *English*

375. Art improves nature.   *English*

376. Art is art, even though unsuccessful.   *Danish*

377. Art is long, life short.   *English*

378. Better is art than strength.
                                  English

379. In every art it is good to have a master.   *English*

380. It is a great art to laugh at your own misfortune.   *Danish*

381. Practice not your art, and it will soon depart.   *German*

382. The art is not in making money, but in keeping it.   *Dutch*

383. They who are skillful in art do not continue in slipper making.
                                  Turkish

ARTICLE

384. Good articles are not cheap.
                                Japanese

ARTISAN

385. A skilled artisan is not fussy about the material.   *Japanese*

ARTIST

386. An artist lives everywhere.
English

ASHAMED

387. He who is not ashamed does whatever he likes. *Egyptian*

ASHES

388. Ashes fly back in the face of him that throws them.
African (Yoruba)

389. Red-hot ashes are easily re-kindled. *Irish*

ASK

390. Ask too much to get enough.
Spanish

391. Better to ask than go astray.
Italian

392. He that asks faintly begs a de-nial. *English*

393. He that cannot ask cannot live.
English

394. He that is too proud to ask is too good to receive. *English*

395. If one asks, one does not err.
Yiddish

396. Never ask of him who has, but of him you know wishes you well.
Spanish

397. The less you ask, the healthier.
Yiddish

ASKED

398. Handsomely asked, hand-somely refused. *French*

ASKING

399. Asking costs little. *Italian*

400. By asking, one can find the way to Jerusalem. *Armenian*

401. By constantly asking, one can reach China. *Iranian*

402. Courteous asking breaks even city walls. *Russian*

403. He who is ashamed of asking is ashamed of learning. *Danish*

ASS

404. A contented ass enjoys a long life. *Portuguese*

405. A dull ass near home needs no spur. *English*

406. A dull ass near home trots without the stick. *Portuguese*

407. A goaded ass must trot. *French*

408. A hungry ass eats any straw.
Italian

409. An ass does not hit himself twice against the same stone. *Dutch*

410. An ass does not stumble twice over the same stone. *French*

411. An ass is but an ass, though laden with gold. *English*

412. An ass is most pleasing to an-other ass. *Slovakian*

413. An ass must be tied where the master will have him. *English*

414. An ass pricked must needs trot.
English

415. An ass was never cut out for a lap-dog. *English*

416. An ass with her colt goes not straight to the mill. *Spanish*

417. Asses carry the oats and horses eat them. *Dutch*

418. Asses die and wolves bury them. *English*

419. Asses must not be tied up with horses. *French*

420. Better an ass that carries me than a horse that throws me.
Portuguese

421. Better be carried by an ass than thrown by a horse. *Dutch*

422. Better have a bad ass than to be your own ass. *Spanish*

423. Better ride an ass that carries me than a horse that throws me. *English*

424. Better strive with an ill ass than carry the wood oneself. *English*

425. Do not load the ass with more than it can carry. *Maltese*

426. Every ass loves to hear himself bray. *English*

427. Every ass thinks himself worthy to stand with the king's horses. *English*

428. For a stubborn ass a stubborn driver. *French*

429. If you are born an ass, you will die one. *Hebrew*

430. It is a sorry ass that will not bear his own burden. *English*

431. It is better to strive with a stubborn ass than to carry the wood on one's back. *Spanish*

432. It is good to hold the ass by the bridle, and a scoffing fool by his wits' end. *English*

433. Jest with an ass, and he will flap you in the face with his tail. *English*

434. Make yourself an ass, and every one will lay his sack on you. *German*

435. No ass is lazy when tempted or teased by the manger. *Mexican*

436. Play with an ass and he will flirt his tail in your face. *Spanish*

437. Play with an ass, and he will slap your face with his tail. *Portuguese*

438. Rather an ass that carries than a horse that throws. *Italian*

439. The ass and his driver do not think alike. *German*

440. The ass and the driver never think alike. *Dutch*

441. The ass brays when he pleases. *English*

442. The ass carries corn to the mill, and gets thistles. *German*

443. The ass that brays most eats least. *English*

444. The ass that has not enough strength throws down his pack saddle. *Turkish*

445. The ass that is common property is always the worst saddled. *French*

446. The ass that is hungry eats thistles. *Portuguese*

447. The hungry ass runs more strongly than the horse. *Turkish*

448. The mountaineer's ass carries wine and drinks water. *French*

449. There's no making the ass drink when he is not thirsty. *Italian*

450. Though the ass may carry a sack of gold, it nevertheless feeds on thistles. *Danish*

451. To a rude ass a rude keeper. *English*

452. When an ass bears too light a load he wants to lie down. *Russian*

453. When an ass climbs a ladder, you may find wisdom in women. *English*

454. When the ass is too happy he begins dancing on the ice. *Dutch*

455. Wherever an ass falls, there will he never fall again. *English*

456. You cannot make an ass drink if he is not thirsty. *French*

ASSERTION

457. Assertion is no proof. *German*

ASSISTANCE

458. Assistance conquers a lion.
Moroccan

ASSOCIATE

459. Associate with the good and you will be one of them.   *Italian*

ASSUME

460. To assume is to be deceived.
Yiddish

ATHLETE

461. An athlete does not tell all his secrets.   *Turkish*

ATTAIN

462. It is best not to attain than to exceed.   *Japanese*

ATTEMPT (noun)

463. A bold attempt is half success.
Danish

ATTEMPT (verb)

464. Better not attempt anything that cannot be carried out.   *Philippine*

ATTITUDE

465. Attitudes don't prove anything.
American

AUCTION

466. At an auction keep your mouth shut.   *Spanish*

AUNT

467. Confide in an aunt and the world will know.   *Czech*

AUSTERITY

468. Austerity is an ornament, humility is honorable.   *Indian (Tamil)*

AUTHOR

469. Like author like book. *English*

AUTHORITY

470. Authority does not depend on age.   *African (Ovambo)*

471. He who has no authority will not have ceremonial drums.
African (Fulani)

AVARICE

472. Avarice bursts the bag. *French*

473. Avarice is the root of all evil.
African (Swahili)

474. The sea may be filled up, but man's avarice cannot be satisfied.
Korean

475. There are no limits to avarice.
Japanese

476. Whatever the avarice of a midwife, she doesn't come to the house of a bachelor.   *African (Hausa)*

AVOIDANCE

477. Avoidance is the only remedy.
English

AWL

478. Six awls make a shoemaker.
English

AX(E)

479. An axe for wax will not cut rock.   *African (Fulani)*

480. An axe is sharp on soft wood.
African (Ovambo)

481. An axe with a loose head is the bane of a man up a tree.
African (Hausa)

482. An axe without a handle does not cut firewood.   *African (Swahili)*

483. Evan a small axe is better than striking with a stick.
African (Ovambo)

484. He who continually uses an axe, must keep it sharp.

African (Hausa)

485. He who has the ax gives the whacks.   *Yiddish*

486. The axe attacks the forest from whence it got its own handle.

Indian (Hindi)

487. The ax forgets but the cut log does not.   *African (Shona)*

488. The axe strikes the chisel, and the chisel strikes the wood.   *Chinese*

489. The ax well familiar to oneself may be wielded on one's own foot.

Korean

490. There is no axe that cannot penetrate a tree.   *Turkish*

AXLE

491. If you don't grease the axle, you won't be able to travel.   *Russian*

~B~

BABY

492. A baby hires and enslaves you. *Maltese*

493. A baby is born with clenched fists and a man dies with his hands open. *Yiddish*

494. Folks that tend babies mustn't have pins about them. *American*

495. If the baby doesn't cry, they don't give it the breast. *Greek*

496. Kissing the baby touches the mother. *Thai*

497. Until the baby cries, the mother doesn't give him suck. *Rumanian*

498. When a baby grows, the crying changes. *African (Annang)*

499. When the baby cries, it is either hungry or in pain. *Greek*

500. You can't wean babies in a day. *American*

BACHELOR

501. A bachelor and a dog may do everything. *Polish*

502. A bachelor of arts discusses books; a pork butcher talks of pigs. *Chinese*

503. A lewd bachelor makes a jealous husband. *English*

504. Bachelors are but half of a pair of scissors. *American*

505. Old bachelors and old maids are either too good or too bad. *Basque*

506. We bachelors grin, but you married men laugh till your hearts ache. *English*

BACK

507. A child's back must be bent early. *Danish*

508. Back may trust but belly won't. *English*

509. He who offers his back should not complain if it is beaten. *Russian*

510. It is not all who turn their backs that flee. *Danish*

511. Not all who turn their backs are running away. *Swedish*

512. The ready back gets all the loads. *Latvian*

513. Though you may see another's back you cannot see your own. *Japanese*

514. Though you see the back of another you cannot see your own. *Japanese*

BACON

515. Bacon is not for dogs. *Polish*

516. He who can't get bacon must be content with cabbage. *Danish*

517. Where you think there is bacon there is no chimney. *English*

17

BAD

518. Bad is a bad servant, but worse is being without him.   *English*

519. Bad is never good until worse happens.   *Danish*

520. Better bad than without.   *English*

521. If you can't endure the bad, you'll not live to witness the good.   *Yiddish*

522. What is bad for one is good for another.   *French*

BAG

523. An old rice bag is ugly, but the thing inside is beautiful.   *African (Kpelle)*

524. Empty bags cannot stand upright.   *English*

525. He sins as much who holds the bag as he who puts into it.   *French*

526. The beggar's bag is bottomless.   *German*

527. The miser's bag is never full.   *Danish*

528. Too much breaks the bag.   *English*

BAGEL

529. If you eat your bagel, you'll have nothing in your pocket but the hole.   *Yiddish*

BAGPIPE

530. The bagpipe never utters a word till its belly is full.   *French*

BAIT

531. A little bait catches a large fish.   *Greek*

532. It is the bait that lures, not the fisherman or the rod.   *Spanish*

533. The bait hides the hook.   *English*

BAKE

534. As one bakes so one may brew.   *English*

BAKER

535. A hundred bakers, a hundred millers, and a hundred tailors are three hundred thieves.   *Dutch*

536. Be not a baker if your head be of butter.   *English*

BAKING

537. It is bad baking without flour and water.   *German*

BALANCE

538. The balance distinguishes not between gold and lead.   *English*

BALD

539. If the bald knew a remedy he would rub it on his own head.   *Turkish*

540. The bald need no comb.   *Polish*

541. You'll not believe he's bald till you see his brains.   *English*

BALDNESS

542. Baldness is a thing of dignity.   *African (Jabo)*

BALL

543. The more a ball is struck, the more it rebounds.   *Indian (Tamil)*

BAMBOO

544. A bamboo shoot never grows singly.   *Philippine*

545. A bamboo staff is the king of a vicious snake.   *Indian (Tamil)*

546. If a bamboo tube sounds loudly, it is empty.   *Philippine*

547. One bamboo does not make a row. *Chinese*

548. The bamboo stick makes a good child. *Chinese*

549. When eating bamboo sprouts, remember the man who planted them. *Chinese*

550. Young bamboo trees are easy to bend. *Vietnamese*

BANANA

551. A shriveled plantain banana is better than none at all. *Jamaican*

552. Not every long thing is a banana, nor is every round thing a walnut. *Lebanese*

553. One eats the banana and throws away the peel. *Vietnamese*

554. Only once does a banana bear. *Malaysian*

BANK (money)

555. Banks have no heart. *American*

BANK (river)

556. Who owns the bank owns the fish. *Russian*

BANKER

557. Ask the banker about gold, the jeweller about gems. *Turkish*

BANQUET

558. He that banquets every day never makes a good meal. *English*

559. There never was a banquet so sumptuous but someone dined ill at it. *French*

BARBARIAN

560. Control barbarians with barbarians. *Japanese*

BARBER

561. Barbers are correctors of capital crimes. *English*

562. Barbers learn to shave by shaving fools. *English*

563. He is a sorry barber who has but one comb. *Italian*

564. No barber shaves so close but another finds work. *English*

565. On a fool's beard the barber learns to shave. *French*

566. On poor people's beards the young barber learns his trade. *German*

567. One barber shaves another. *French*

568. The bad barber leaves neither hair nor skin. *Spanish*

BAREFOOT

569. He that goes barefoot must not plant thorns. *English*

BARGAIN

570. A bargain has charm for the customer. *Hebrew*

571. A bargain is a bargain. *English*

572. A cheap bargain wastes money. *Jamaican*

573. A doubtful bargain spoils the stomach. *Turkish*

574. At a good bargain pause and ponder. *Italian*

575. Bargains are dear. *Spanish*

576. Go to a man who is in a difficulty and you'll get a bargain. *Irish*

577. Good bargains are pickpockets. *English*

578. Good bargains are ruinous. *French*

579. Good bargains empty the purse. *Italian*

580. Good seems every bargain that is far away. *Irish*

581. It is a bad bargain where both are losers. *English*

582. It is an ill bargain where no man wins. *Scottish*

583. It is only good bargains that ruin. *French*

584. Let your bargain suit your purse. *Irish*

585. No one will get a bargain he does not ask for. *French*

586. On a good bargain, think twice. *English*

587. The bargain is ill made where neither party gains. *English*

BARGAIN (verb)

588. Bargain like a gypsy and pay like a gentleman. *Serbo-Croatian*

BARGAINER

589. The bargainer buys, not the praiser. *Slovenian*

BARGAINING

590. Bargaining teaches us how to buy. *Polish*

591. Through lack of bargaining one loses a cheap buy. *African (Hausa)*

BARK (noun)

592. His (or her) bark is worse than his (or her) bite. *English*

BARK (verb)

593. One cannot bark and run at the same time. *Irish*

BARKER

594. Great barkers are no biters. *English*

595. The greatest barkers bite not sorest. *English*

BARLEY

596. It is safe to lend barley to him who has oats. *Danish*

597. Too much barley makes the horse burst. *Turkish*

BARLEYCORN

598. A barleycorn is better than a diamond to a cock. *English*

BARN

599. Better a barn filled than a bed. *English*

600. Empty barns need no thatch. *English*

601. When the barn is full, you may thresh before the door. *English*

BARREL

602. A little barrel can give but a little meal. *English*

603. An empty barrel reverberates loudly. *Yiddish*

604. Empty barrels give the most sound. *Danish*

605. There is plenty of sound in an empty barrel. *Russian*

606. Two barrels of tears will not heal a bruise. *Chinese*

BASHFUL

607. It is only the bashful that lose. *French*

BASHFULNESS

608. At table bashfulness is out of place. *Italian*

609. Bashfulness is an enemy to poverty. *English*

610. Bashfulness is of no use to the needy. *Dutch*

BASKET

611. A basket cannot dam a stream for long. *Chinese*

612. A basket with its bottom burst is useless. *African (Yoruba)*

613. Don't fill your basket with useless shells of coconuts. *African (Swahili)*

614. He that makes one basket can make a hundred. *Spanish*

615. He who carries a basket of lime leaves footprints wherever he stops. *Chinese*

616. One basket of grapes does not make a vintage. *Italian*

617. What fills the small basket does not fill the large one. *African (Bemba)*

BASTARD

618. Even bastards can be cleansed with money. *Hebrew*

619. He who conceals his origin is a bastard. *Turkish*

BAT

620. A bat is not a bird. *African (Ovambo)*

BATH

621. At the baths all are equal. *Yiddish*

BATTLE

622. He who is well prepared has half won the battle. *Portuguese*

623. It is better to die in battle than to die of hunger. *Philippine*

624. To win the battle is easy; to secure the victory, difficult. *Korean*

625. What causes any battle to be lost is the needless fear of the enemy's strength. *Philippine*

626. Whatever has been taken in battle is sacred. *Russian*

BE (see BEEN)

627. One cannot be and have been. *French*

628. That which shall be, shall be. *English*

629. What will be cannot be escaped. *Russian*

630. What will be will surely happen. *Russian*

BEAD

631. Beads about the neck and the devil in the heart. *English*

BEAN

632. A bean in liberty is better than a comfit in prison. *English*

633. Beans are not equal to meat. *African (Ovambo)*

634. Beans grow where beans are planted, and limas where limas are planted. *Korean*

635. Every bean has its black. *English*

636. One bean spoiled the beans. *African (Fulani)*

637. One bean spoils the flour. *African (Hausa)*

638. One cannot get beans out of wild melons. *African (Ovambo)*

639. Sow beans in the mud and they'll grow like wood. *English*

640. Those soya beans that are mixed in the rice food of others would look bigger. *Korean*

641. Where soya beans were sowed, soya beans will sprout; where peas were sowed, peas will sprout. *Korean*

BEAR (noun)

642. A bear which is not tied up won't dance. *Russian*

643. A hungry bear does not perform. *Greek*

644. A hungry bear does not play. *Turkish*

645. Bear and bull catch no fox. *German*

646. Don't play with the bear if you don't want to be bit. *Italian*

647. Don't sell the bearskin before the bear is dead. *Dutch*

648. He who has taken the bear into the boat must cross over with him. *Swedish*

649. It is not easy to sting a bear with a straw. *Danish*

650. One thing thinks the bear, but another thinks his leader. *English*

651. The bear dances, but the gypsy takes the money. *Russian*

652. The bear doesn't dance for his own pleasure. *Rumanian*

653. The bear wants a tail and cannot be a lion. *English*

654. The she-bear thinks her cubs pretty. *Italian*

655. Two bears don't live together in one den. *Russian*

BEAR (verb)

656. What was hard to bear is sweet to remember. *Portuguese*

BEARD

657. A beard well lathered is half shaved. *Italian*

658. A long beard does not prevent a house going to bed hungry. *African (Fulani)*

659. A man without a beard is like a loaf that has no crust. *Latvian*

660. He who has a beard has a comb. *Greek*

661. If the beard were all, the goat might preach. *Danish*

662. It's good to learn to barber on someone else's beard. *Yiddish*

663. It is not the beard that makes the philosopher. *English*

664. The beard does not make the philosopher. *Italian*

665. The beard will (or will not) pay for the shaving. *English*

666. There is no beard so well shaven but another barber will find something more to shave from it. *Italian*

BEARSKIN

667. Never sell the bearskin till you have killed the bear. *French*

BEAST

668. A good beast heats with eating. *French*

669. Better a beast sold than bought. *English*

670. Every beast knows its time. *Polish*

671. He does not kill the beast who only looks at it. *African (Jabo)*

672. He who wants to travel far takes care of his beast. *French*

673. It is a strange beast that has neither head nor tail. *English*

674. The beasts plan ahead before entering the fields. *African (Jabo)*

675. The beast that goes always never wants blows.   *English*

676. The wild beast is not touched.   *African (Zulu)*

677. There is no beast so savage but sports with its mate.   *Spanish*

BEAT

678. One may as well be well beaten as badly beaten.   *French*

BEATING

679. You may as well give a good beating as a bad one.   *French*

BEAUTIFUL

680. Not that which is beautiful but that which pleases is beautiful. *Yiddish*

681. The beautiful is less what one sees than what one dreams.   *Flemish*

BEAUTY

682. A lazy beauty is fit only for the dunghill.   *Hawaiian*

683. A poor beauty finds more lovers than husbands.   *English*

684. An enemy to beauty is a foe to nature.   *English*

685. Beauty and folly are often companions.   *French*

686. Beauty and pride go to the grave.   *African (Swahili)*

687. Beauty and ugliness are in the face.   *Indian (Tamil)*

688. Beauty cannot be by force.   *Turkish*

689. Beauty carries its dower in its face.   *Danish*

690. Beauty displays perfection.   *Turkish*

691. Beauty does not ensnare men; they ensnare themselves.   *Chinese*

692. Beauty draws more than oxen.   *English*

693. Beauty is a good letter of introduction.   *German*

694. Beauty is a very fine thing, but you can't live on it.   *American*

695. Beauty is but a blossom.   *English*

696. Beauty is but dross if honesty be lost.   *Dutch*

697. Beauty is but skin deep.   *English*

698. Beauty is found only in one of a thousand.   *Indian (Tamil)*

699. Beauty is no inheritance.   *English*

700. Beauty is potent, but money is omnipotent.   *English*

701. Beauty is soon blasted. *English*

702. Beauty is the seasoning of virtue.   *Polish*

703. Beauty is the subject of a blemish.   *English*

704. Beauty may have fair leaves, yet bitter fruit.   *English*

705. Beauty of the chaste is a virtue, that of a whore a quality.   *Russian*

706. Beauty passes, but perfection remains with us.   *Turkish*

707. Beauty provokes thieves sooner than gold.   *English*

708. Beauty's sister is vanity, and its daughter lust.   *Russian*

709. Beauty suffers no pain.   *Irish*

710. Beauty will buy no beef.   *English*

711. Beauty will fade, but not goodness.   *Philippine*

712. Beauty will not make the pot boil.   *Irish*

713. Beauty will not season your soup.   *Polish*

714. Beauty will sit and weep, fortune will sit and eat.   *Indian (Tamil)*

715. Beauty without bounty avails nought.   *English*

716. Beauty without chastity, a flower without fragrance.
                                   Indian (Tamil)

717. Beauty without virtue is like a rose without scent.   *Danish*

718. Genuine beauty appears from the morning; no eye fluids will spoil it.
                                         Libyan

719. He who marries a beauty marries trouble.   *African (Yoruba)*

720. It's good to behold beauty and to live with wisdom.   *Yiddish*

721. It is not the greatest beauties that inspire the most profound passion.
                                         French

722. No one can live on beauty, but one can die for it.   *Swedish*

723. One can neither put beauty into the pot, nor loveliness into the kettle.
                                       Estonian

724. Personal beauty does not pay a debt.   *African (Ashanti)*

725. She that is born a beauty is half married.   *English*

726. She who is born a beauty is born betrothed.   *Italian*

727. Sweet beauty with sour beggary.   *English*

728. The beauty of a chaste woman makes bitter words.   *Irish*

729. The beauty of a loan is repayment.   *Russian*

730. The beauty of the corn cob is apparent in the inside only.
                              African (Swahili)

731. The beauty of the man is in his intelligence, and the intelligence of the woman is in her beauty.   *Moroccan*

732. There is no beauty but the beauty of action.   *Moroccan*

733. Though she may be a beauty, it is but one layer of skin.   *Japanese*

734. Woman's beauty, the forest echo, and rainbows soon pass away.
                                         German

BECAUSE

735. Because is woman's reason.
                                       Scottish

BED

736. A bed free from anxiety is the most agreeable of all things.
                                   Indian (Tamil)

737. A small bed will not hold two persons.   *African (Yoruba)*

738. As you make your bed, so will you lie on it.   *Russian*

739. As you make your bed, so will you sleep in it.   *Yiddish*

740. As you make your bed, so you lie down.   *Scottish*

741. As you make your bed, so you must lie on it.   *English*

742. Better a bed of wood than a bier of gold.   *Russian*

743. Better to go to bed supperless than to rise in debt.   *English*

744. Early to bed and early to rise, makes a man healthy and wealthy and wise.
                                        English

745. Even a golden bed does not help a sick person.   *Estonian*

746. Go to bed with the lamb, and rise with the lark.   *Scottish*

747. He who goes to bed hungry dreams of pancakes.   *Maltese*

748. If the bed would tell all it knows, it would put many to the blush. *English*

749. In bed, husband and wife; out of bed, guests. *Chinese*

750. Make your bed as well as you can. *Greek*

751. Not always does one sleep on a bed, sometimes one must sleep even on the ground. *African (Hausa)*

752. The warmest bed is mother's. *Yiddish*

753. Though they rest on the same bed, they dream of different things. *Korean*

754. Too much bed makes a dull head. *English*

755. When you have made your bed everybody wants to lie on it. *Russian*

756. Who goes to bed early and marries young will never repent. *Serbo-Croatian*

757. Who goes to bed supperless, all night tumbles and tosses. *English*

BEDTIME

758. Do not strip before bedtime. *French*

BEE

759. A bee is never caught in a shower. *English*

760. A dead bee will make no honey. *English*

761. Bees do not become hornets. *French*

762. Bees that have honey in their mouths have stings in their tails. *English*

763. Better have one bee than a host of flies. *Italian*

764. Every bee's honey is sweet. *English*

765. He's like the master bee that leads forth the swarm. *English*

766. One bee is as good as a handful of flies. *German*

767. One bee is better than a thousand flies. *Spanish*

768. The bees make honey but cannot eat it; the sea-swallows build nests but cannot live in them. *Vietnamese*

769. The bee stays not in a hive that has no honey. *Turkish*

770. The wise bee does not sip from a flower that has fallen. *Chinese*

771. When bees are old they yield no honey. *English*

772. Where bees are there is honey. *English*

773. Where the bee sucks honey, the spider sucks poison. *English*

BEEF

774. It is good beef that costs nothing. *English*

775. Such beef, such broth. *English*

BEEN (see BE)

776. What has been, may be. *English*

BEER

777. Better weak beer than an empty cask. *Danish*

778. The best beer is where the coachmen and the priests go for their drink. *Polish*

779. They who drink beer think beer. *American*

780. When the beer goes in the wits go out. *Danish*

BEETLE

781. However much the beetle is afraid it will not stop the lizard swallowing it. *African (Fulani)*

782. In the steppe even a beetle is meat. *Russian*

783. One beetle recognizes another. *Irish*

784. The beetle is a beauty in the eyes of its mother. *Egyptian*

BEG

785. Better beg than steal. *Dutch*

BEGGAR

786. A bashful beggar has an empty wallet. *Hungarian*

787. A beggar does not hate another beggar as much as one doctor hates another. *Polish*

788. A beggar never becomes a giver. *Greek*

789. A beggar pays a benefit with a louse. *English*

790. A beggar's purse is bottomless. *English*

791. A beggar who begs from another beggar will never get rich. *Jamaican*

792. A shameless beggar must have a shameful denial. *English*

793. Beg from beggars and you'll never be rich. *English*

794. Beggars are able to bear no wealth. *Scottish*

795. Beggars breed and rich men feed. *English*

796. Beggars cannot be choosers. *English*

797. Beggars make a free company. *English*

798. Better a live beggar than a dead king. *Chinese*

799. Better to die a beggar than live a beggar. *English*

800. Even a beggar will not cross a rotten wooden bridge. *Chinese*

801. He is a proud beggar that makes his own alms. *Scottish*

802. He will soon be a beggar that cannot say no. *Scottish*

803. If you associate with officials you will be a beggar, if with merchants you will be rich, if with Buddhist priests you will be asked for a contribution. *Chinese*

804. It is better to be a beggar than a fool. *English*

805. One beggar is enough at a door. *English*

806. One beggar is woe that another by the door should go. *English*

807. One beggar likes not that another has two wallets. *Danish*

808. Put a beggar into your barn and he will make himself your heir. *Spanish*

809. Set a beggar on horseback and he'll never alight. *English*

810. Set a beggar on horseback and he'll ride a-gallop. *English*

811. Set a beggar on horseback and he'll ride to the devil. *English*

812. Set a beggar on horseback and he'll ride to the gallows. *English*

813. Set a beggar on horseback and he'll run his horse out of breath. *English*

814. Set a beggar on horseback and he'll run his horse to death. *English*

815. Small invitation will serve a beggar. *English*

816. Sue a beggar and catch a louse. *English*

817. The beggar is never out of his way. *English*

818. The beggar may sing before the thief. *English*

819. When it rains porridge the beggar has no spoon. *Danish*

BEGGING

820. Better begging than theft. *African (Hausa)*

821. Constant begging only meets with constant refusal. *Irish*

BEGIN (see BEGUN)

822. As you begin the year, so you'll end it. *English*

823. Better never to begin than never to make an end. *English*

824. Good to begin well, better to end well. *English*

825. He begins to build too soon that has not money to finish it. *English*

826. He begins to die that quits his desires. *English*

827. He who begins badly, ends badly. *Spanish*

828. He who begins early helps himself a lot. *African (Bemba)*

829. He who begins ill finishes worse. *Italian*

830. He who begins much, finishes little. *German*

831. It is better not to begin than, having begun, to leave unfinished. *Czech*

832. To begin is to be half done. *Korean*

BEGINNING

833. A bad beginning may make a good ending. *German*

834. A good beginning is half the work. *Irish*

835. A good beginning is worth more than money. *Russian*

836. A good beginning makes a good ending. *English*

837. A hard beginning has a good ending. *English*

838. A hard beginning is a good beginning. *Scottish*

839. A light beginning, a heavy ending. *English*

840. Beginning and ending shake hands. *German*

841. Beginning and ending take each other by the hand. *Russian*

842. Every beginning is difficult. *English*

843. Everything must have a beginning. *French*

844. Evil beginning has evil end. *English*

845. From small beginnings come great things. *Dutch*

846. If there's a beginning there's an end. *Japanese*

847. If you know the beginning well, the end will not trouble you. *African (Wolof)*

848. Making the beginning is one third of the work. *Irish*

849. Such a beginning, such an ending. *English*

850. The beginning hot, the middle lukewarm, the end cold. *German*

851. The beginning is good if the end is good. *Philippine*

852. The beginning is most important. *Japanese*

BEGUN (see BEGIN)

853. Begun is half done. *German*

854. Better never begun as never ended. *Scottish*

855. Ill begun, ill done. *Dutch*

856. So begun, so done. *Dutch*

857. Soonest begun, soonest over.
English

858. Well begun is half done.
English

BEHAVIOR

859. Behavior denotes birth.
Malaysian

860. What reveals a man is his behavior in time of hunger.
African (Bemba)

BEHIND

861. Those who live together cannot hide their behinds from each other.
African (Ovambo)

BEING

862. Every living being likes a donation.
Russian

BELIEF

863. Belief is easier than investigation.
Serbo-Croatian

864. Belief is simpler than investigation.
Slovenian

BELIEVE

865. Believe not all you hear.
English

866. Believe not all you hear, tell not all you believe.   *Indian (Tamil)*

867. Believe well and have well.
English

868. Better believe it than go where it was done to prove it.   *English*

869. He that believes all, misses; he that believes nothing, hits not. *English*

870. Quick to believe is quickly deceived.   *Serbo-Croatian*

871. We soon believe what we desire.
English

872. Who is ready to believe, is easy to deceive.   *German*

BELIEVER

873. Quick believers need broad shoulders.   *English*

874. The believer asks no questions, while no answer can satisfy the unbeliever.   *Hebrew*

BELL

875. A cracked bell can never sound well.   *English*

876. A cracked bell will never be sounded.   *Spanish*

877. A fool's bell is soon rung.
English

878. A good bell is heard far, a bad one still farther.   *Finnish*

879. Bells call others to church but go not themselves.   *English*

880. Bells call to church but do not enter.   *French*

881. Everybody thinks that every bell echoes his own thoughts. *Slovenian*

882. Everyone thinks that all the bells echo his own thoughts. *German*

883. He is like a bell that will go for every one that pulls it.   *English*

884. He who cannot bear the clapper, should not pull the bell. *English*

885. He who hears but one bell hears but one sound.   *French*

886. One bell serves a parish.
Italian

887. One cannot ring the bells and walk in the procession.   *French*

888. One does not ring a bell for the deaf.   *Welsh*

889. The bell does not go to mass, and yet calls every one to it. *Italian*

890. The bell is loud because it is empty.   *Polish*

891. The higher the bell is hung, the shriller it sounds.   *German*

892. There is no need to fasten a bell to a fool, he is sure to tell his own tale.   *Danish*

893. When big bells ring, little ones are not heard.   *Serbo-Croatian*

894. When the bell begins to toll, Lord have mercy on the soul.   *English*

895. While the great bells are ringing no one hears the little ones.   *Danish*

BELLY

896. A belly full of gluttony will never study willingly.   *English*

897. A belly is nearer than a brother.   *Turkish*

898. A fasting belly may never be merry.   *English*

899. A fat belly did not invent gun powder.   *Greek*

900. A full belly counsels well.   *French*

901. A full belly is deaf to learning.   *Russian*

902. A full belly is neither good for flight nor for fighting.   *Spanish*

903. A full belly makes a heavy head.   *Indian (Bihar)*

904. A full belly makes a stiff back.   *Scottish*

905. A full belly neither fights nor flies well.   *English*

906. A full belly sets a man dancing.   *French*

907. A hungry belly has no ears.   *French*

908. A hungry belly hears nobody.   *Portuguese*

909. A hungry belly listens to no one.   *Spanish*

910. An empty belly hears nobody.   *English*

911. An empty belly is the best cook.   *Estonian*

912. An empty belly knows no songs.   *Greek*

913. An empty belly makes a lazy back.   *English*

914. Better belly burst than good drink lost.   *English*

915. Better belly burst than good victuals spoil.   *Dutch*

916. Better fill a glutton's belly than his eyes.   *English*

917. Full bellies make empty skulls.   *English*

918. He whose belly is full believes not him that is fasting.   *English*

919. If it were not for the belly, the back might wear gold.   *English*

920. It is easier to fill twenty bellies than one pair of eyes.   *Russian*

921. It is easy with a full belly to praise fasting.   *Serbo-Croatian*

922. It is hard to labor with an empty belly.   *Danish*

923. My belly cries cupboard.   *English*

924. My belly thinks my throat cut.   *English*

925. The belly carries the legs, and not the legs the belly.   *English*

926. The belly eight-tenths full needs no physician.   *Japanese*

927. The belly has no ears.   *English*

928. The belly hates a long sermon.   *English*

929. The belly is a bad adviser.   *German*

930. The belly is a scamp, it remembers not the good done to it.   *Russian*

931. The belly is not a mirror.   *Russian*

932. The belly is not a treasurer.
African (Hausa)

933. The belly is not filled with fair words. *English*

934. The belly overrules the head.
French

935. The belly robs the back.
English

936. The belly teaches all arts.
English

937. The full belly does not believe in hunger. *Italian*

938. The hungry belly and the full belly do not walk the same road.
Jamaican

939. When the belly is full, the bones like to stretch. *Irish*

940. When the belly is full, the bones would be at rest. *English*

941. When the belly is full the mind is among the maids. *English*

942. Your belly chimes it's time to go to dinner. *English*

943. Your belly will never let your back be warm. *English*

BELLYFUL

944. A bellyful is a bellyful. *English*

945. A bellyful is one of meat, drink, or sorrow. *English*

BELOVED

946. Your beloved is the object that you love, were it even a monkey.
Egyptian

BENCH

947. He who throws himself under the bench will be left to lie there.
Danish

948. One sits best on one's own bench. *Norwegian*

949. That bench is well adorned that is filled with virtuous women. *Danish*

BEND

950. Best to bend while it is a twig.
English

951. Better bend than break. *French*

BENEFIT

952. Benefits please like flowers, while they are fresh. *English*

953. He who feels the benefit should feel the burden. *American*

954. The last benefit is most remembered. *English*

BESOM

955. They have need of a besom that sweep the house with a turf. *English*

BEST

956. Better the best of the worst than the worst of the best. *Yiddish*

957. The best always goes first.
Italian

958. The best go first, the bad remain to mend. *English*

959. The best is best cheap. *English*

960. The best is best to speak to.
English

961. The best is the cheapest.
German

962. The best is what one has in his hand. *German*

963. You are always best when asleep. *English*

BETRAYER

964. Woe to him whose betrayer sits at his table. *Irish*

BETTER

965. If better were within, better would come out. *Scottish*

966. If it doesn't get better, depend on it, it will get worse. *Yiddish*

BILL

967. Better be the cock's bill than an ox's tail.   *Japanese*

BIND

968. Safe bind, safe find.   *English*

BIRD

969. A big bird cannot be trapped with chaff.   *African (Shona)*

970. A bird already caught is better than a beast that is still to be caught.
                                     Philippine

971. A bird has its weight, though a mere feather.   *African (Ovambo)*

972. A bird in the cage is worth a hundred at large.   *Italian*

973. A bird in the hand is worth two in the bush.   *English*

974. A bird in the nest is better than one hundred flying.   *Philippine*

975. A bird is not taken with the hand.   *Turkish*

976. A bird may be caught with a snare that will not be shot.   *English*

977. A bird may be ever so small, it always seeks a nest of its own. *Danish*

978. A bird never flew so high but it had to come to the ground for food.
                                        Dutch

979. A bird of the air shall carry it.
                                      English

980. A bird that agrees to be caught will find a way of escape.
                             African (Fulani)

981. A bird that has been hurt by an arrow will be frightened even by a crooked twig.   *Korean*

982. A caged bird longs for the clouds.   *Japanese*

983. A clever bird builds its nest with other birds' feathers.
                             African (Shona)

984. A flying bird knows its destination.   *Philippine*

985. A flying bird will sometimes fall.   *Japanese*

986. A good bird begins chirping while in the egg.   *Greek*

987. A little bird is content with a little nest.   *English*

988. A singing bird killed furnishes no flesh.   *Chinese*

989. A wise bird selects its tree.
                                      Chinese

990. An early bird hops far.   *Czech*

991. An ill bird lays an ill egg.
                                      English

992. As the bird is, such is the nest.
                                      English

993. As the old birds sing, the young ones twitter.   *German*

994. Bad bird, bad egg.   *German*

995. Better a bird in the hand than ten in the air.   *Dutch*

996. Better be a bird of the wood than a bird in the cage.   *Italian*

997. Better one bird tied up than a hundred flying.   *Hebrew*

998. Better to be a free bird than a captive king.   *Danish*

999. Birds are entangled by their feet, and men by their tongues. *English*

1000. Birds have nests, men have ancestors.   *Vietnamese*

1001. Birds of a color fly to the same place.   *Welsh*

1002. Birds of a feather flock together.
                                      English

1003. Birds of prey do not flock together.   *Portuguese*

1004. Birds of prey do not sing.
                                      German

1005. Birds perch with similar birds.
                                      Lebanese

31

1006. By going and coming a bird weaves its nest.   *African (Oji)*

1007. By little and little the bird makes his nest.   *English*

1008. By slow degrees the bird builds his nest.   *Dutch*

1009. Each bird loves to hear himself sing.   *English*

1010. Every bird admires its own nest.   *Turkish*

1011. Every bird has a hawk above it.   *Serbo-Croatian*

1012. Every bird is known by its feathers.   *English*

1013. Every bird likes its own nest.   *English*

1014. Every bird must hatch its own eggs.   *English*

1015. Every bird sings as it is beaked.   *Dutch*

1016. Every bird thinks its own nest beautiful.   *Italian*

1017. Every little bird has a long beak.   *African (Ovambo)*

1018. Far shooting never killed bird.   *English*

1019. Fine birds are commonly plucked.   *French*

1020. Full-fledged birds fly away.   *Chinese*

1021. He who buys a cage will want a bird.   *Polish*

1022. He who rents one garden will eat birds; who rents gardens, the birds will eat him.   *Hebrew*

1023. However high a bird may soar, it seeks its food on earth.   *Danish*

1024. If the bird drinks not at the stream, it knows its own watering place.   *African (Wolof)*

1025. If the bird had not sung, it wouldn't have been shot.   *Japanese*

1026. If you cannot get the bird, get one of its feathers.   *Danish*

1027. If you want a bird and a cage, buy the cage first.   *American*

1028. It is a brave bird that makes its nest in the cat's ear.   *Indian (Hindi)*

1029. It is a lazy bird that will not build its own nest.   *Danish*

1030. It is an ill bird that fouls its own nest.   *English*

1031. It is hard to catch birds with an empty hand.   *German*

1032. It is the beautiful bird that we put in the cage.   *Chinese*

1033. It is too late for the bird to scream when it is caught.   *French*

1034. Let each bird cry according to its kind.   *African (Hausa)*

1035. Let every bird hatch its own eggs.   *Manx*

1036. Let every bird sing its own note.   *Danish*

1037. Little birds do not plunge into arrows.   *African (Ovambo)*

1038. Little bird, little nest.   *Spanish*

1039. Little birds may pick a dead lion.   *English*

1040. Little by little the bird builds its nest.   *French*

1041. No bird flies and never rests.   *African (Zulu)*

1042. Old birds are hard to pluck.   *German*

1043. Old birds are not caught with cats.   *Dutch*

1044. Old birds are not caught with chaff.   *English*

1045. Old birds are not caught with new nets.   *Italian*

1046. One bird in the dish is better than a hundred in the air.   *German*

1047. One bird in the hand is better than ten on the tree. *Lebanese*

1048. One bird in the hand is better than two flying. *Dutch*

1049. One bird in the hand is better than two on the roof. *Danish*

1050. One bird in the hand is worth two flying. *Portuguese*

1051. One bird in your hand is better than ten birds in the sky.
African (Ashanti)

1052. Small birds must have meat.
English

1053. The bad bird fouls its own nest.
African (Ashanti)

1054. The bird builds his nest, then he flies up the hill. *African (Jabo)*

1055. The bird can drink much, but the elephant drinks more.
African (Wolof)

1056. The bird flies not without cause. *Turkish*

1057. The bird in full feathers flies.
Hawaiian

1058. The bird is known by his note, the man by his words. *English*

1059. The bird is not big until he spreads his wings. *African (Jabo)*

1060. The bird once out of hand is hard to recover. *Danish*

1061. The bird ought not to soil its own nest. *French*

1062. The bird seeks the tree, not the tree the bird. *Mexican*

1063. The bird that can sing and won't sing must be made to sing.
English

1064. The bird that walks straight into the snare is bound to be caught.
African (Hausa)

1065. The bird weaves its nest by going and coming. *African (Ashanti)*

1066. The bird which escapes from the cage never wants to come back.
Vietnamese

1067. The bird which has escaped from the snare it is vain to follow.
Australian (Maori)

1068. The early bird catches the worm. *English*

1069. The early bird gets the late one's breakfast. *English*

1070. The featherless bird lolls around. *Hawaiian*

1071. The first bird gets the first grain. *Danish*

1072. The late bird shakes its wings; the early one wipes its bill. *Estonian*

1073. The little bird starts with one straw. *African (Ovambo)*

1074. There are no birds of this year in last year's nests. *English*

1075. There is not a bird that does not know its eggs. *African (Ovambo)*

1076. Though a bird is hungry, it will not eat poisonous berries.
Indian (Tamil)

1077. Though the bird may fly over your head, let it not make its nest in your hair. *Danish*

1078. To scare a bird is not the way to catch it. *French*

1079. Too late the bird cries out when it is caught. *French*

1080. Two birds of prey do not keep each other company. *Spanish*

1081. When a big bird does not trouble to fly it goes to sleep hungry.
African (Ashanti)

1082. When a bird is in a snare, its cry is peculiar. *African (Oji)*

1083. When mature and on the wing, all birds will look after their own food.
Indian (Tamil)

1084. When the big bird dies the eggs rot. *African (Zulu)*

1085. Where there are birds there is cattle. *African (Ovambo)*

1086. Where there are birds there is water. *African (Ovambo)*

1087. Wise birds live in carefully chosen trees. *Japanese*

1088. With nets you catch birds and with presents, girls. *Yiddish*

1089. With one arrow two birds are not struck. *Turkish*

1090. You can tell a bird by its song and a man by his manner of speaking. *Greek*

1091. Young birds do not fly too far. *Jamaican*

BIRD-LIME

1092. Bird-lime is the death of a bird. *African (Yoruba)*

BIRTH

1093. At birth we bring nothing, at death we take away nothing. *Chinese*

1094. Birth is much but breeding more. *English*

1095. Birth is the remedy for death. *African (Hausa)*

1096. Birth is the remedy for sorrow. *African (Hausa)*

1097. One birth does not differ from another birth; as the slave was born, so was the free-born child. *African (Yoruba)*

BISHOP

1098. A living bishop is worth a hundred dead saints any time. *American*

BIT (bridle)

1099. A golden bit makes none the better horse. *Italian*

BIT (little)

1100. A bit in the morning is better than nothing all day. *English*

1101. Better a bit in the morning than fast all day. *Scottish*

BITCH

1102. If the bitch doesn't want it, the male dog won't be able to jump on. *Russian*

1103. If the bitch were not in such haste, she would not litter blind puppies. *German*

1104. The bitch will never bite its pups to the bone. *Haitian*

1105. The hasty bitch brings forth blind whelps. *English*

BITE

1106. A sheep's bite is never more than skin deep. *Italian*

1107. Better a friend's bite than an enemy's caress. *Danish*

1108. If you cannot bite, never show your teeth. *English*

1109. One bite brings another. *Danish*

1110. The bites of priests and wolves are hard to heal. *German*

BITER

1111. The biter is often bit. *French*

1112. The biter is sometimes bit. *English*

BITS

1113. Many bits make a pound. *Jamaican*

BITTEN

1114. Once bitten, twice shy. *English*

BITTER

1115. He who has not tasted bitter, knows not what sweet is. *German*

BITTERN

1116. A bittern makes no good hawk. *English*

BITTERNESS

1117. If there's bitterness in the heart, sugar in the mouth won't make life sweeter. *Yiddish*

1118. The bitterness of studying is preferable to the bitterness of ignorance. *Philippine*

1119. When bitterness preceeds sweetness, the sweetness becomes sweeter. *African (Annang)*

BLAB

1120. He that is a blab is a scab. *English*

BLACK

1121. Black will not become white, nor bitter sweet. *Indian (Tamil)*

1122. Black will take no other hue. *English*

1123. He that wears black must hang a brush at his back. *English*

1124. Two blacks will never make a white. *English*

1125. You can't wash the black off a black dog. *Russian*

BLACKBERRY

1126. Blackberries don't grow on every bush. *American*

BLACKEN

1127. By blackening another you do not whiten yourself. *Rumanian*

1128. Who blackens others, does not whiten himself. *German*

BLACKSMITH

1129. No one is a blacksmith at birth. *African (Ovambo)*

BLADE

1130. Better than a haftless blade is one which has a handle. *Malaysian*

1131. No blade is sharp enough when it strikes stone. *Philippine*

1132. The blade wears out the sheath. *French*

1133. There is no blade that can offer resistance to kindness. *Japanese*

1134. There is no dull blade to him who diligently sharpens it. *Philippine*

BLAME (noun)

1135. Absent, none without blame; present, none without excuse. *French*

1136. Blame is the lazy man's wages. *Danish*

BLAME (verb)

1137. Blame yourself as you would blame others; excuse others as you would excuse yourself. *Chinese*

1138. He that blames himself praises himself. *Polish*

1139. He that blames would buy. *English*

1140. To blame is easy, to do it better is difficult. *German*

BLANKET

1141. A big blanket makes a man sleep late. *Jamaican*

1142. Spread your blanket only as far as your feet. *Philippine*

BLAST

1143. The sharper the blast, the shorter it will last. *English*

BLESSEDNESS

1144. There is blessedness in adversity.   *Japanese*

BLESSING

1145. A blessing does not fill the stomach.   *Irish*

1146. Blessings are not valued till they are gone.   *English*

1147. Blessings never come in pairs; misfortunes never come singly. *Chinese*

1148. They have need of a blessing that kneel to a thistle.   *English*

BLIND (adjective)

1149. All are not blind that wink.
English

1150. Better be half blind than have both eyes out.   *English*

1151. Better to be blind than to see ill.
English

1152. He's so blind he can't see a hole through a ladder.   *English*

1153. None are so blind as those that will not see.   *English*

BLIND (people)

1154. It is only the blind who ask why they are loved who are fair.   *Danish*

1155. The blind are quick at hearing; the deaf are quick at sight.   *Chinese*

1156. The blind eat many a fly.
English

1157. The blind want only eyes.
Iranian

1158. When the blind leads the blind, indeed they will both fall into the water.   *Chinese*

1159. When the blind leads the blind, both fall into the ditch.   *English*

BLISTER

1160. He who gets blisters from the hoe handle will not die of hunger.
African (Swahili)

BLOCK

1161. As the block, so the chip.
Russian

BLOCKHEAD

1162. He who has to deal with a blockhead has need of much brain.
Spanish

BLOOD

1163. Blood boils without fire.
Spanish

1164. Blood cannot be turned into water.   *Albanian*

1165. Blood comes from much scratching.   *Indian (Kashmiri)*

1166. Blood doesn't turn into water.
Yiddish

1167. Blood is no water.   *Russian*

1168. Blood is not the remedy for thirst.   *African (Hausa)*

1169. Blood is not water.
Serbo-Croatian

1170. Blood is thicker than water.
English

1171. Blood will not wash away dirt.
African (Hausa)

1172. Human blood is all of a color.
English

1173. Let the blood be ever so thin, it is always thicker than water. *Danish*

1174. Like blood, like goods, and like age make the happiest marriage.
English

1175. The blood of the martyrs is the seed of the church.   *English*

1176. The nobler the blood the less the pride.   *Danish*

1177. There is no getting blood from a turnip.   *Italian*

1178. True blood may not lie. *English*

1179. When blood appears, it is apt to run.   *African (Annang)*

1180. You can't get blood out of a stone.   *English*

BLOSSOM (noun)

1181. Blossoms are not fruits. *Dutch*

1182. One blossom doesn't make a spring.   *Armenian*

1183. Timely blossom, timely fruit.
English

BLOSSOM (verb)

1184. What blossoms beautifully, withers fast.   *Estonian*

BLOT

1185. Clearing a blot with blotted fingers makes a greater blur.   *English*

BLOW (noun)

1186. A blow for a blow, and a wound for a wound.   *Irish*

1187. A blow from our lover is as sweet as the eating of raisins. *Egyptian*

1188. A blow passes on, a spoken word lingers on.   *Yiddish*

1189. A blow that is not struck is not actionable.   *Irish*

1190. A blow that is profitable does not hurt the neck.   *Egyptian*

1191. A blow with a reed makes a noise, but hurts not.   *English*

1192. A thousand blows on another man's back don't hurt.   *Greek*

1193. As the blow, so the pain.
Latvian

1194. Better a blow from a wise man than a kiss from a fool.   *Yiddish*

1195. It takes two blows to make a battle.   *English*

1196. Many blows fell great trees.
Norwegian

1197. One blow will not knock a strong man down.   *African (Hausa)*

1198. The first blow is as good as two.   *French*

1199. The first blow is half the battle.
English

1200. The second blow makes the fray.   *English*

BLOW (verb)

1201. Better blow hard than burn yourself.   *Danish*

1202. Blow first and sip afterwards.
English

1203. One cannot blow and swallow at the same time.   *Spanish*

1204. There is no need to blow what does not burn you.   *Danish*

BLUE

1205. True blue will never stain.
English

BLUNDER

1206. The blunders of physicians are covered by the earth.   *Portuguese*

BLUSH

1207. Better a blush in the face, than a spot in the heart.   *English*

BLUSHING

1208. Blushing is a sign of grace.
English

BOAST

1209. Don't boast when you depart, but when you arrive.   *Russian*

1210. Great boast, little roast. *Dutch*

1211. No one boasts of what belongs to another.   *African (Ashanti)*

BOASTER

1212. A boaster and a liar are all one.
English

1213. A boaster and a liar are near akin.   *Scottish*

1214. A great boaster was never a good rider. *Scottish*

1215. Believe a boaster as you would a liar. *Italian*

1216. Great boaster, little doer. *French*

1217. The boaster and the proud person are fools. *Japanese*

1218. The boaster dies before his days are fulfilled. *African (Hausa)*

1219. The boaster gets stuck in the mud. *Yiddish*

1220. The greater boasters are not the boldest men. *English*

BOASTING

1221. Boasting begins where wisdom stops. *Japanese*

BOAT

1222. A boat doesn't go forward if each one is rowing his own way. *African (Swahili)*

1223. A small boat must sail close to the shore, but a big one may go to the sea. *Philippine*

1224. Can't load a small boat with heavy cargo. *Chinese*

1225. Even if the boat has a sail, it won't go if there is no wind. *Philippine*

1226. He who owns the boat should give it a name. *Norwegian*

1227. If a boat has not a good bottom it cannot go to sea. *Jamaican*

1228. If you cannot pole a boat, don't meddle with the pole. *Chinese*

1229. Ill goes the boat without oars. *English*

1230. One boat does not load another. *African (Wolof)*

1231. The boat follows the helm, the woman follows her husband. *Vietnamese*

1232. The first in the boat has the choice of oars. *Dutch*

1233. The paper boat will sink some day. *Indian (Hindi)*

1234. The water is the same on both sides of the boat. *Finnish*

1235. When the boat reaches midstream, it is too late to stop the leak. *Chinese*

1236. When you travel by boat be prepared for a ducking. *Chinese*

BOATMAN

1237. The sleeping boatman does not know the streams he has passed. *Philippine*

1238. Too many boatmen will row the boat up the mountain. *Korean*

BODY

1239. A dead body has its coffin, and a live man his hut. *Russian*

1240. A little body does often harbor a great soul. *English*

1241. A living body is a dying body. *Japanese*

1242. A man's body buried in the snow will after a time come to light. *Chinese*

1243. Better a sick body than an ignorant mind. *Greek*

1244. Better that the body should suffer than that the soul be in torment. *Philippine*

1245. Do not refuse the body what it asks for. *Mexican*

1246. Great bodies move slowly. *English*

1247. One's body belongs to the Tsar, one's soul to God, and one's back to the squire. *Russian*

1248. One body cannot perform two services. *Chinese*

1249. The body is a sponge, the soul an abyss. *Yiddish*

1250. The body is felt by its owner. *African (Zulu)*

1251. The body is known by its owner. *African (Shona)*

1252. The body is more dressed than the soul. *English*

1253. The body is sooner dressed than the soul. *English*

1254. The body is the socket of the soul. *English*

1255. To bow the body is easy; to bow the will is hard. *Chinese*

1256. Where the body wants to rest, there the legs must carry it. *Polish*

BOG

1257. He who builds in a bog must not be sparing with the stakes. *Russian*

BOIL

1258. A boil is fine as long as it's under someone else's arm. *Yiddish*

BOLD

1259. Be not too bold with your betters. *English*

BOLDNESS

1260. Boldness in business is the first, second, and third thing. *English*

1261. Boldness is blind. *English*

1262. Boldness is royal power without a crown. *Hebrew*

1263. Boldness is the fruit of hope. *Philippine*

1264. Boldness takes cities. *Russian*

BOLT

1265. A bolt lost is not a bow broken. *English*

1266. A fool's bolt is soon shot. *English*

1267. A fool's bolt may sometimes hit the white. *English*

1268. A small bolt to the house is better than none at all. *Danish*

1269. This bolt never came out of your quiver. *English*

BOND

1270. Don't go on a man's bond in public, nor guarantee his debts in private. *Chinese*

BONE

1271. A bone in a mortar is no luck for the dog. *African (Hausa)*

1272. A bone is more valuable to a dog than a pearl. *Philippine*

1273. A dry bone is never licked. *Albanian*

1274. A meatless bone is the dog's. *African (Hausa)*

1275. Big bones are not cooked in the same pot. *African (Ovambo)*

1276. Bones bring meat to town. *English*

1277. Bones without meat are possible; meat without bones is not possible. *Yiddish*

1278. For the last-comer the bones. *French*

1279. He who will not give you a bone will not give you meat. *African (Ovambo)*

1280. No bones are broken by a mother's fist. *Russian*

1281. The bone given to you by the king is meat. *African (Ovambo)*

1282. The nearer the bone the sweeter the flesh. *English*

1283. There is no bone in a slanderous tongue. *Indian (Tamil)*

1284. There is no bone in the tongue, but it often broke a man's head. *Irish*

1285. Where the bone is softest there it will be gnawed.   *African (Fulani)*

1286. You can't get fat from a dry bone.   *Chinese*

1287. You may get something off a bone, but nothing off a stone.   *Danish*

BOOK

1288. A book gives knowledge, but it is life that gives understanding. *Hebrew*

1289. A book is a friend.   *American*

1290. A book that is shut is but a block.   *English*

1291. A book to a blind man signifies nothing.   *Irish*

1292. A book without a preface is like a body without a soul.   *Hebrew*

1293. A book without an index is like a house that is bolted and barred.   *Hebrew*

1294. A load of books does not equal one good teacher.   *Chinese*

1295. Books are preserved minds.   *Japanese*

1296. Books do not exhaust words; words do not exhaust thoughts.   *Chinese*

1297. If your books are unread, your descendants will be ignorant. *Chinese*

1298. It would be a very big book that contained all the maybes uttered in a day.   *French*

1299. Look at the book and sing as it directs.   *Chinese*

1300. One should not leap through a book from its end to its beginning.   *Hebrew*

1301. Take the book by its title; or, take the letter by its address. *Egyptian*

1302. There is no book that has not something bad in it, none that has not something good.   *Hebrew*

1303. To open a book brings profit.   *Chinese*

1304. Word by word the big books are made.   *French*

BOOR

1305. A boor can't be made into a gentleman.   *Russian*

BOOT

1306. A narrow boot will stretch, a broad one will shrink.   *Russian*

1307. An old boot and an old friend are the most dear.   *Polish*

1308. Two boots make a pair.   *Russian*

BOOTED

1309. They that are booted are not always ready.   *English*

BOOTY

1310. A fair booty makes many a thief.   *English*

BORN

1311. Better be born happy than pretty.   *Russian*

1312. Better to be born lucky than rich.   *English*

1313. Better unborn than untaught.   *English*

1314. First born, first fed.   *English*

1315. He that is born to be hanged will never be drowned.   *English*

1316. I was not born in a wood to be scared by an owl.   *English*

1317. We are born crying, live complaining, and die disappointed.   *English*

BORROW

1318. Borrow causes sorrow. *Yiddish*

1319. He may well be contented who needs neither borrow nor flatter.
English

1320. He that borrows must pay again with shame or loss.   *English*

1321. Neither borrow nor flatter.
English

1322. Not so good to borrow as be able to lend.   *English*

1323. Who readily borrows, readily lies.   *German*

1324. Who would borrow when he has not, let him borrow when he has.
English

BORROWED

1325. Long borrowed is not given.
German

BORROWER

1326. A habitual borrower quickly becomes impoverished.   *Philippine*

1327. Borrowers must not be choosers.   *French*

1328. The borrower runs in his own debt.   *American*

1329. The borrower who does not pay, gets no money lent to him.
African (Yoruba)

BORROWING

1330. Borrowing brings care. *Dutch*

1331. Borrowing is a wedding, paying back is mourning.
African (Swahili)

1332. He that goes a-borrowing goes a-sorrowing.   *English*

1333. He who is quick at borrowing, is slow in paying.   *German*

1334. They were bowing to you when borrowing, but you are bowing to them when collecting.   *Russian*

BOSS

1335. The boss is always right.
Russian

BOTTLE

1336. A full bottle won't shake; a half-empty one will.   *Chinese*

1337. It is only the first bottle that is dear.   *French*

1338. Let every man drink from his own bottle.   *American*

1339. With a bottle and a girl one does not count the hours.   *Polish*

BOTTOM (behind)

1340. If you haven't spanked a little bottom, don't threaten a big one. *Greek*

BOTTOM (ground, base)

1341. Do not wade where you see no bottom.   *Danish*

1342. It is best to begin at the bottom.
Hungarian

1343. It is too late to spare when the bottom is bare.   *Scottish*

1344. Maybe the bottom will turn out better than the top.   *Turkish*

1345. Start from the bottom to reach the top.   *African (Ovambo)*

BOUGH

1346. Short boughs, long vintage.
English

1347. The boughs that bear most, hang lowest.   *English*

BOULDER

1348. A boulder is the father of rocks.
African (Yoruba)

BOUND

1349. The bound must obey. *English*

BOUNTY

1350. Bounty being free itself, thinks all others so. *English*

BOW (archery)

1351. A bow long bent grows weak. *English*

1352. A bow overbent will weaken. *Scottish*

1353. A bow which is stretched to the limit breaks. *African (Bemba)*

1354. Draw not your bow before your arrow be fixed. *English*

1355. If the bow is drawn taut, the arrow will fly fast. *Chinese*

1356. If you are surety for the bow, you are surety for the arrow. *Chinese*

1357. Strain not your bow beyond its bent, lest it break. *Dutch*

1358. The bow must not be always bent. *Dutch*

1359. The bow that is always bent slackens or breaks. *Spanish*

1360. The bow will hit the target, depending on the bowman. *Japanese*

1361. The tightly strung bow will relax in time. *Japanese*

1362. Unbending the bow does not heal the wound. *Italian*

1363. Unstringing the bow does not cure the wound. *French*

BOW (ship)

1364. If the bow sinks, the stern follows. *Philippine*

BOW (verb)

1365. Better bow than break. *English*

BOWEL

1366. What is true of the buffalo's bowels is true of the cow's bowels. *Vietnamese*

BOWL (noun)

1367. Full bowls make empty brains. *English*

1368. One must exchange a bowl for a bowl of rice. *Vietnamese*

1369. You can't have more in the bowl than you have in the pot. *Yiddish*

BOWL (verb)

1370. It is easy to bowl downhill. *Yiddish*

BOX

1371. An open box tempts an honest man. *Portuguese*

BOY

1372. A boy knows not fire till it burns him. *African (Hausa)*

1373. A lazy boy and a warm bed are difficult to part. *Danish*

1374. A smiling boy seldom proves a good servant. *English*

1375. A spoiled boy won't be much good. *Maltese*

1376. An untoward boy may make a good man. *English*

1377. Boys will be boys. *English*

1378. Boys will be men. *English*

1379. Send a boy where he wants to go and you'll see his best pace. *African (Hausa)*

1380. Train a boy strictly, but a girl kindly. *Indian (Tamil)*

1381. While the boy is small, you can see the man. *Chinese*

BRACELET

1382. A single bracelet, even of silver, will not tinkle. *African (Fulani)*

1383. One bracelet will not jingle. *African (Hausa)*

BRAG (noun)

1384. Brag's a good dog but dares not bite.   *English*

1385. Brag is a good dog but Holdfast is a better.   *English*

1386. Brag's a good dog but that he has lost his tail.   *English*

BRAG (verb)

1387. They brag most that can do least.   *English*

BRAGGART

1388. A braggart is known by his headgear.   *African (Ovambo)*

BRAGGER

1389. Great braggers, little doers.
                                        English

BRAGGING

1390. Bragging never made a man.
                                        Maltese

1391. Bragging saves advertising.
                                        American

1392. Too much bragging drives away wisdom.   *Philippine*

BRAIN

1393. A brain is worth little without a tongue.   *French*

1394. All the brains are not in one head.   *Italian*

1395. Better brains in the head than riches and confusion.   *Greek*

1396. Borrowed brains have no value.
                                        Yiddish

1397. Brains of one person do not know what is going on in the back of your neck.   *African (Bemba)*

1398. Everyone thinks he has more than his share of brains.   *Italian*

1399. Half a brain is enough for him who says little.   *Italian*

1400. He carries his brains in his breeches-pocket.   *English*

1401. He who at thirty has no brains, will never purchase an estate. *Spanish*

1402. He who has not been given brains from above will not buy them at the apothecary.   *Czech*

1403. His brain is not big enough for his skull.   *English*

1404. Idle brains are the devil's workshop.   *English*

1405. If the brain sows not corn, it plants thistles.   *English*

1406. The brains are not in the beard.
                                   Indian (Hindi)

1407. The brains don't lie in the beard.   *English*

1408. There are many witty men whose brains can't fill their bellies.
                                       American

1409. When brains are needed, brawn won't help.   *Yiddish*

1410. Who has no brain needs brawn.   *Hebrew*

BRAMBLE

1411. He who sows brambles must not go barefoot.   *Spanish*

1412. He who sows brambles reaps thorns.   *Spanish*

BRAN

1413. He who mixes up with bran is eaten by pigs.   *Rumanian*

1414. If you get mixed with bran you'll soon be pecked by chickens.
                                        Libyan

1415. Much bran and little meal.
                                        English

BRANCH

1416. A crooked branch has a crooked shadow.   *Japanese*

1417. A young branch can be straightened, but a mature one breaks. *Philippine*

1418. Better is the branch that bends, than the branch that breaks. *Danish*

1419. Do not break the branch you climbed. *African (Ovambo)*

1420. He who pulls a fallen branch also drags away its leaves. *African (Shona)*

1421. Tall branches are apt to be broken. *Korean*

1422. The branch is seldom better than the stem. *Danish*

1423. The branch must be bent early that is to make a good crook. *Danish*

1424. The branch of one tree will not stick to another. *Indian (Tamil)*

1425. The highest branch is not the safest roost. *English*

1426. The old branch breaks when it is bent. *Danish*

1427. The topmost branch is not the safest perch. *English*

1428. The wet branch burns better than the dry stone. *Danish*

1429. There is often a withered branch on a green tree. *Norwegian*

BRAVE (adjective)

1430. Some have been thought brave, because they were afraid to run away. *English*

1431. Those who are brave get to eat. *Russian*

BRAVE (people)

1432. Seek the brave in prison and the stupid among the clergy. *Russian*

1433. The brave dies, his name remains. *Turkish*

BRAVERY

1434. Bravery is the fruit of a thousand hardships. *Philippine*

1435. Through bravery you win and through bravery you lose. *Polish*

1436. To run and stop is not bravery. *African (Fulani)*

BRAYING

1437. The braying of an ass does not reach heaven. *Italian*

BREAD

1438. A piece of bread in one's pocket is better than a feather in one's hat. *Swedish*

1439. Better bread with water than cake with trouble. *Russian*

1440. Better eat gray bread in your youth, than in your age. *Scottish*

1441. Better to eat bread in peace, then cake amidst turmoil. *Slovakian*

1442. Bread and cheese be two targets against death. *English*

1443. Bread and cheese is good to eat when men can get no other meat. *Scottish*

1444. Bread and salt never quarrel. *Russian*

1445. Bread by the color and wine by the taste. *English*

1446. Bread cries when eaten unearned. *Polish*

1447. Bread doesn't go looking for the belly. *Russian*

1448. Bread is better than the song of birds. *Danish*

1449. Bread is the staff of life, but beer's life itself. *English*

1450. Bread on a journey is no burden. *Russian*

1451. Bread, unless it be chewed, is not swallowed. *Turkish*

1452. Bread with eyes and cheese without eyes, and wine that leaps to the eyes. *English*

1453. Buttered bread always falls dry side up. *Hebrew*

1454. Crumb not your bread before you taste your porridge. *English*

1455. Cut bread cannot be put together again. *Latvian*

1456. Don't bite till you know whether it is bread or a stone. *Italian*

1457. Eat bread at pleasure, drink wine by measure. *French*

1458. Eaten bread is forgotten. *English*

1459. Every tomorrow brings its bread. *French*

1460. Everything revolves around bread and death. *Yiddish*

1461. He who doesn't want to make bread sifts the flour the whole day. *Greek*

1462. He who eats his bread alone saddles his horse alone. *Swedish*

1463. His bread is buttered on both sides. *English*

1464. However bad the bread it is better than cattle dung. *African (Hausa)*

1465. If one has eaten enough, bread becomes tasteless. *Estonian*

1466. If there's bread, there will be mice. *Russian*

1467. If you're hungry enough, you can eat dry bread. *Yiddish*

1468. If you have bread and butter, you have good luck. *Yiddish*

1469. If you have no bread, drink wine. *Russian*

1470. If you would eat bread don't remain sitting on the oven. *Russian*

1471. It's hard to eat a stranger's bread. *Yiddish*

1472. It is hard to pay for bread that has been eaten. *Danish*

1473. It is the bread that keeps one warm, not the fur. *Russian*

1474. Make bread while the oven is hot. *Iranian*

1475. No better bread than is made of wheat. *English*

1476. Oat bread today is better than cake tomorrow. *Serbo-Croatian*

1477. Stolen bread stirs the appetite. *French*

1478. The bread eaten, the company departed. *Spanish*

1479. The man who has bread to eat does not appreciate the severity of a famine. *African (Yoruba)*

1480. They that have no other meat, bread and butter are glad to eat. *English*

1481. To a starving man bread is sweeter than honey. *Lithuanian*

1482. When you can't get bread, oat cakes are not amiss. *Spanish*

1483. When you have bread, do not look for cake. *Polish*

1484. Who has no bread to spare should not keep a dog. *Spanish*

1485. Who has no more bread than need, must not keep a dog. *English*

1486. Whose bread I eat, his song I sing. *German*

1487. Without bread and wine even love will pine. *French*

1488. Without "Our Father" there is no bread. *Russian*

1489. Woe to him who remembers not the bread he eats.   *Irish*

1490. You can think as much as you like but you will invent nothing better than bread and salt.   *Russian*

1491. You will never get two breads of one cake.   *Scottish*

BREADFRUIT

1492. Look not at the breadfruit away out, it is not yours. Look at the breadfruit in front of you.   *Hawaiian*

BREAK

1493. Too much will soon break.   *German*

BREAKFAST

1494. A good breakfast cannot take the place of the evening meal.   *Chinese*

1495. The early breakfast is bought with gold.   *Moroccan*

BREAST

1496. A pair of women's breasts has more pulling power than a pair of oxen.   *Mexican*

1497. Breasts adorn a woman and uglify a man.   *Hebrew*

1498. Nobody will beat his own breast with a stone.   *Philippine*

BREATH

1499. A tyrant's breath is another's death.   *English*

1500. He who has bad breath cannot smell it.   *African (Ovambo)*

1501. It is hard to sup and blow with one breath.   *English*

1502. One man's breath, another's death.   *English*

1503. The first breath is the beginning of death.   *English*

1504. When you don't like someone you find his breath offensive.   *Greek*

BREECHES

1505. A new pair of breeches will soon draw down an old doublet.   *Scottish*

BREED

1506. Breed is stronger than pasture.   *English*

BREEDING

1507. A child's good breeding depends upon the parents.   *Philippine*

1508. Good breeding combined with wealth brings honor to a person.   *Philippine*

1509. One's breeding is shown by one's manners and speech.   *Philippine*

BREEZE

1510. Where there is no breeze the trees would not quiver.   *Malaysian*

BREVITY

1511. Brevity is the soul of wit.   *English*

BREW

1512. If you brew well, you will drink the better.   *Scottish*

BRIBE (noun)

1513. A bribe blinds the clever, and how much more so the fool!   *Hebrew*

1514. A bribe blinds the judge, for a bribe cannot give a true judgment.   *African (Yoruba)*

1515. A bribe will enter without knocking.   *English*

1516. Bribe is the enemy of justice.   *African (Swahili)*

BRIBE (verb)

1517. Neither bribe nor lose your right.   *English*

BRIBERY

1518. Bribery can split a stone. *Irish*

BRICKLAYER

1519. Too many bricklayers make a lopsided house.   *Chinese*

BRIDE

1520. A bride has no place at her in-laws' without the groom.   *Greek*

1521. A fair bride needs little finery.
Norwegian

1522. A foolish bride gets no presents.
Indian (Bihar)

1523. A sad bride makes a glad wife.
Dutch

1524. All brides are beautiful; all the dead are pious.   *Yiddish*

1525. At the wedding feast the least eater is the bride.   *Spanish*

1526. Brides and mothers-in-law are like dogs and monkeys.   *Japanese*

1527. Choose a bride and piece goods in the daytime.   *Japanese*

1528. First think of bread and then of the bride.   *Norwegian*

1529. If the bride can't dance, she finds fault with the musicians. *Yiddish*

1530. It is too late to pierce the ears of the bride when she is in her wedding chair.   *Chinese*

1531. No bride is ugly on her wedding day.   *Hebrew*

1532. The weeping bride makes a laughing wife.   *German*

1533. Train the bride when she first comes.   *Japanese*

1534. Weeping bride, laughing wife; laughing bride, weeping wife.
Russian

1535. When the bride is expecting, the wedding guests look away.
Yiddish

BRIDGE

1536. Build golden bridges for the flying foe.   *German*

1537. If you destroy a bridge, be sure you can swim.   *African (Swahili)*

1538. It is better to build bridges than walls.   *African (Swahili)*

1539. It is hard to turn tack upon a narrow bridge.   *English*

1540. Let every man praise the bridge he goes over.   *English*

1541. Make a bridge of silver for the fleeing enemy.   *Spanish*

1542. Never cross a bridge till you come to it.   *English*

1543. When the bridge is gone the narrowest plank becomes precious.
Hungarian

BRIDLE

1544. A bridle for the tongue is a necessary piece of furniture. *English*

1545. It is always well to keep hold of your horse's bridle.   *French*

BRIGHT

1546. He is only bright that shines by himself.   *English*

BRIM

1547. Better spare at brim than at bottom.   *English*

BRING

1548. He who brings is welcome.
German

BROCADE

1549. Silk brocade does not make a good mop.   *Japanese*

BROOD

1550. Bastard brood is always proud.
English

BROOK

1551. It is easier to stem the brook than the river.   *Danish*

1552. Little brooks make great rivers.
French

47

1553. Many shun the brook, and fall into the river. *German*

1554. The brook does not ascend the mountain. *African (Ga)*

BROOM

1555. A bad broom leaves a dirty room. *English*

1556. A new broom sweeps a new way. *Russian*

1557. A new broom sweeps clean. *Russian*

1558. A new broom sweeps well. *African (Ovambo)*

1559. An old broom is better than a new one. *African (Ga)*

1560. An old broom still sweeps the room. *Estonian*

1561. He who buys the broom can also buy the handle. *Italian*

1562. New brooms sweep clean. *English*

1563. The new broom sweeps the house best. *Irish*

1564. Those brooms can be sold cheapest which are stolen ready made. *German*

1565. You cannot be a broom and remain clean. *Hebrew*

BROTH

1566. Fat broth cannot be made of nothing. *French*

1567. Good broth may be made in an old pot. *English*

1568. Many esteem more of the broth than the meat boiled therein. *English*

1569. Much broth is sometimes made with little meat. *Danish*

BROTHER

1570. Brothers and sisters are like hands and feet. *Vietnamese*

1571. Brothers are like hands and feet. *Chinese*

1572. Even brothers keep careful accounts. *Chinese*

1573. If brothers disagree, the bystander takes advantage. *Chinese*

1574. The brother would rather see the sister rich than make her so. *English*

1575. The younger brother has the more wit. *English*

1576. The younger brother is the better gentleman. *English*

1577. With your brother eat and drink, but have no business. *Albanian*

BRUISE

1578. The bruises inflicted by a sweetheart are the brands of affection. *Hawaiian*

BRUIT

1579. Much bruit, little fruit. *English*

BRUSH

1580. He that wears black must carry a brush on his back. *Scottish*

BUBBLE

1581. Every bubble bursts. *Polish*

BUCK

1582. An old buck has still horns. *Latvian*

BUCKET

1583. Don't throw away the old bucket until you know whether the new one holds water. *Swedish*

1584. Every day the bucket goes to the well, but some day the bottom must drop out. *Jamaican*

1585. If the bucket has been long in the well, it ought to come out with water. *African (Hausa)*

1586. It is not necessary to fish up every bucket that falls into the well.
Italian

1587. The bucket goes so often to the well that it leaves its handle there.
Italian

1588. The bucket which frequents the well, in course of time, will get a spill.
Malaysian

BUD

1589. All the buds upon a bush do not blossom. *Indian (Kashmiri)*

1590. Buds will be roses, and kittens, cats. *American*

1591. If you don't crop it while it is a bud, it will grow into something that will require an ax. *Japanese*

1592. It's the bud that makes the gourd. *African (Hausa)*

1593. The bud becomes a rose and the rose a hip. *French*

BUDGET

1594. A tinker's budget is full of necessary tools. *English*

BUFFALO

1595. A buffalo does not feel the weight of his own horns.
Indian (Hindi)

1596. A single muddy buffalo will soon besmear the rest. *Malaysian*

1597. Buffaloes and bulls fight one another, but flies and mosquitoes die from the fight. *Vietnamese*

1598. No buffalo was ever beaten by its calf. *African (Zulu)*

1599. The buffalo which comes late will have to drink muddy water and eat dried grass. *Vietnamese*

1600. The fat buffalo will draw the lean buffalo. *Vietnamese*

1601. What is good for the buffalo is good for the cow. *Vietnamese*

1602. When one buys a buffalo one looks at his hoofs, when one marries a woman one looks into her ancestry.
Vietnamese

BUG

1603. The best way to put an end to the bugs is to set fire to the bed.
Mexican

BUILD

1604. He who builds and he who marries is never safe. *Swedish*

1605. What you build easily will fall quickly. *Slovenian*

BUILDING (edifice)

1606. A building of sand falls as you build. *African (Fulani)*

1607. A building without foundation is soon demolished. *Turkish*

1608. High buildings have a low foundation. *English*

BUILDING (erecting)

1609. Building and marrying of children are great wasters. *English*

1610. Building is a sweet impoverishing. *English*

1611. No good building without a good foundation. *English*

BULL

1612. A mad bull is not to be tied up with a packthread. *English*

1613. Don't help a bull out of a ditch, for when he's out he'll butt. *Malagasy*

1614. Faced by two goads no bull is brave. *Mexican*

1615. Feign death and the bull will leave you. *Portuguese*

1616. It is better to be a bull for a year than a cow for a hundred years. *Serbo-Croatian*

1617. It is easy to threaten a bull from a window. *Italian*

1618. Let him take the bull that stole the calf. *English*

1619. One cannot part two fighting bulls. *African (Wolof)*

1620. Take good care of the bull if you wish him to plough well for you. *Greek*

1621. Two bulls cannot live in one stable. *African (Swahili)*

1622. Two bulls can't rule in one pen. *Jamaican*

1623. Two bulls do not get on together in the same pen. *Moroccan*

1624. When the bull is old they turn him into the cow pasture. *Jamaican*

1625. You may play with a bull till you get his horn in your eye. *English*

BULL RING

1626. It isn't quite the same thing to comment on the bull ring and to be in the bull ring. *Mexican*

BULLET

1627. A wax bullet is not used to shoot an elephant. *African (Ashanti)*

1628. Bullets are shot by men and God deals them out. *Mexican*

1629. Every bullet has its billet. *English*

1630. Two bullets never go in one place. *American*

BULLOCK

1631. A good bullock requires but one blow, and a good woman only one word. *Indian (Tamil)*

1632. A vicious bullock will not be brought to market. *Indian (Tamil)*

1633. An unchastised bullock will not obey. *Indian (Tamil)*

BUN

1634. Half a bun in the hand is better than a whole bun in the shop. *African (Swahili)*

BURDEN

1635. A burden of one's own choice is not felt. *English*

1636. A voluntary burden is no burden. *Italian*

1637. Another man's burden is always light. *Danish*

1638. Every one feels his own burden heavy. *French*

1639. Everyone lays a burden on the willing horse. *Irish*

1640. Everyone thinks his burden heaviest. *English*

1641. He who carried one burden will soon carry a hundred. *French*

1642. It's a sad burden to carry a dead man's child. *English*

1643. Light burdens borne far become heavy. *French*

1644. None knows the weight of another's burden. *English*

1645. On an empty belly every burden is heavy. *Russian*

1646. Pray that you may not be a burden to your children. *Yiddish*

1647. The greatest burdens are not the gainfullest. *English*

1648. The heaviest burden is an empty pocket. *Yiddish*

BURDENSOME

1649. Nothing is so burdensome as a secret. *French*

BURIAL

1650. When the burial day is at your door, you do not pick and choose your grave diggers. *Jamaican*

BURN

1651. He that burns most shines most. *English*

1652. That which burns you not, cool not. *Dutch*

BUSH

1653. A bad bush is better than no shelter. *English*

1654. A little bush sometimes grows better than a big tree. *Jamaican*

1655. An ill bush is better than no shelter. *Scottish*

1656. Bushes have ears, walls have eyes. *Jamaican*

1657. He that fears every bush must never go a-birding. *English*

1658. He that peeps into every bush will hardly get into the woods. *German*

1659. One beats the bush, and another catches the bird. *German*

1660. One beats the bush and the other catches the bird. *Dutch*

1661. There is no bush so small but casts its shadow. *French*

BUSHEL

1662. A whole bushel of wheat is made up of single grains. *English*

1663. In a bushel of winning is not a handful of cunning. *English*

1664. It takes a bushel of corn to fatten a pig's tail. *American*

1665. Many take by the bushel and give with the spoon. *German*

BUSINESS

1666. Business is business. *English*

1667. Business is like the froth from an ox's mouth. *Japanese*

1668. Business is the salt of life. *English*

1669. Business makes a man as well as tries him. *English*

1670. Business opens business. *Turkish*

1671. Do not leave to morning the business of evening. *Turkish*

1672. Drive your business, let not that drive you. *American*

1673. Everybody's business is nobody's business. *English*

1674. He that does his own business hurts not his hand. *English*

1675. He that thinks his business below him will always be above his business. *English*

1676. If you would have your business done, go; if not, send. *American*

1677. In every business be steadfast. *Turkish*

1678. Let every one mind his own business, and the cows will be well tended. *French*

1679. Much business, much pardon. *English*

1680. Much business must have much pardon. *American*

1681. Never do business with a relative. *Turkish*

1682. One business begets another. *English*

1683. To establish a business is easy; to maintain it, difficult. *Korean*

1684. Who likes not his business, his business likes not him. *English*

BUSINESSMAN

1685. He who does not accept cash when offered is no businessman.
Chinese

BUSY

1686. Busy will have bands. *English*

1687. Some are very busy and yet do nothing. *English*

BUSYBODY

1688. Busybodies never want a bad day. *English*

BUTCHER

1689. Better pay the butcher than the doctor. *English*

1690. The butcher has no regard for the breed of the beast.
African (Yoruba)

1691. The butcher is not startled at the multiplicity of sheep. *Egyptian*

BUTTER

1692. All is not butter that comes from the cow. *Italian*

1693. Butter is gold in the morning, silver at noon, and lead at night.
English

1694. Butter is good for anything but to stop an oven. *English*

1695. Butter spoils no meat, and moderation injures no cause. *Danish*

1696. He must have plenty of butter who would stop everybody's mouth.
Danish

1697. It is not all butter that comes from the cow. *English*

1698. That which will not be butter must be made into cheese. *English*

1699. They that have good store of butter may lay it thick on their bread.
English

1700. They that have much butter, may lay it thick on their bread.
Scottish

1701. When you lack butter for the bread, it is not yet poverty. *Yiddish*

1702. Where there is butter there are flies. *Polish*

BUTTERFLY

1703. The butterfly often forgets it was a caterpiller. *Swedish*

1704. The butterfly that flies among the thorns will tear its wings.
African (Jabo)

BUTTON

1705. For a big button, a big buttonhole. *Philippine*

1706. You cannot sew buttons on your neighbor's mouth. *Russian*

BUY

1707. Better buy than borrow.
English

1708. Buy what you do not need, soon you will sell what you need. *Czech*

1709. It is better to buy than to receive. *Japanese*

1710. He that buys and lies shall feel it in his purse. *English*

1711. He that buys dearly must sell dearly. *English*

1712. He that buys land buys many stones; he that buys flesh buys many bones; he that buys eggs buys many shells; but he that buys good ale buys nothing else. *English*

1713. He who buys what he doesn't need steals from himself. *Swedish*

1714. It is better to buy dearly than to hunger direly. *Danish*

1715. It is good to buy when another wants to sell. *Italian*

1716. Tell me what you are eager to buy and I will tell you what you are.
Mexican

1717. Whether you buy or not, you can always barter a little. *Russian*

1718. Who buys cheap pays twice.
Slovakian

1719. Who buys dear and takes up on credit, shall ever sell to his loss.
English

BUYER

1720. Beware the buyer. *English*

1721. Buyers want a hundred eyes, sellers only one. *German*

1722. Good buyers but poor payers.
American

1723. The buyer needs a hundred eyes, the seller but one. *English*

1724. The buyer repents, the seller also repents. *Turkish*

1725. There are more foolish buyers than foolish sellers. *French*

BUYING

1726. Buying and selling is but winning and losing. *English*

1727. For overbuying there's no help but selling again. *French*

1728. It isn't the buying that teaches, it is the selling. *Russian*

BY

1729. By and by is easily said.
English

BYGONE

1730. Let bygones be bygones.
English

C

CABBAGE

1731. Better cabbage and peace than dainties and fretting.　*Greek*

1732. Cabbage is best after it is reheated seven times.　*Slovakian*

1733. He who would have good cabbage, must pay its price.　*Danish*

1734. If you are willing to eat cabbage stalks, you can accomplish a hundred affairs.　*Chinese*

1735. In the far off field the cabbages are fine.　*Greek*

1736. It is not enough to have cabbage, one must have something to grease it.　*French*

1737. Like seeks like and cabbages fertilizer.　*Greek*

1738. Together with the shrub the cabbage is beaten.　*Hebrew*

CACKLE

1739. You cackle often but never lay an egg.　*English*

CAESAR

1740. Render unto Caesar the things that are Caesar's.　*English*

CAGE

1741. A fine cage won't feed the bird.　*French*

1742. In the estimation of the nightingale, a cage of gold is a prison.　*Turkish*

1743. When the cage is ready the bird is flown.　*French*

CAKE

1744. A cake and a bad custom ought to be broken.　*French*

1745. All's not cake that's round.　*Libyan*

1746. Better is dry cake than having nothing to eat.　*Norwegian*

1747. Cakes are baked in a chatty, steeped rice is flattened in a mortar.　*Indian (Tamil)*

1748. I had rather my cake burn than you should turn it.　*English*

1749. One can get sick of cake, but never of bread.　*Russian*

1750. There is no cake but there is the like of the same make.　*English*

1751. Who owns the cake may wield the knife.　*Serbo-Croatian*

1752. You can't eat the rice cake in a picture.　*Japanese*

CALAMITY

1753. Calamity has no voice; suffering cannot speak to tell who is really in distress.　*African (Yoruba)*

1754. Calamity will teach. *Estonian*

1755. One calamity is better than a thousand counsels. *Turkish*

1756. One must not despise even a calamity. *Russian*

1757. Someone else's calamity doesn't add to your own wisdom. *Russian*

CALDRON

1758. Small and great, we all boil in the same caldron. *Rumanian*

CALENDAR

1759. No calendar is needed for dying. *Yiddish*

1760. The calendar is made by man; the weather by God. *Swedish*

CALF (cow)

1761. A calf's head will feed a huntsman and his hounds. *English*

1762. A calf is not found under an ox. *Armenian*

1763. A calf of little worth is better than an ox in which you have only a share. *Turkish*

1764. A calf takes after its mother, and a foal after its father. *Indian (Bihar)*

1765. A calf that goes with a pig will eat excrement. *Indian (Tamil)*

1766. A calf will not follow horses. *African (Hausa)*

1767. An affectionate calf gets to suck two cows. *Russian*

1768. As soon dies the calf as the cow. *French*

1769. Better my own ordinary calf than golden calves of others. *Korean*

1770. Every calf will find its slaughterer. *Polish*

1771. He who will steal a calf will steal a cow. *English*

1772. The calf belongs to the owner of the cow. *Irish*

1773. The calf of the carabao is tamed by gentle caresses. *Philippine*

1774. The calf takes after the mother. *African (Zulu)*

1775. The gentle calf sucks all the cows. *Portuguese*

1776. The largest calves are not the sweetest veal. *English*

1777. There is always a calf behind a cow, sometimes her own and sometimes another's. *Pashto*

1778. When the calf is drowned they cover the well. *Dutch*

1779. When the calf is stolen, the peasant mends the stall. *German*

1780. Who steals a calf, steals a cow. *German*

CALF (leg)

1781. If you give him your calf, he wants your thigh. *Malaysian*

CALL

1782. As you call, so will you be answered. *Albanian*

CALLIGRAPHER

1783. The good calligrapher is not choosy about his writing brush. *Japanese*

1784. The terrible calligrapher is choosy about his brushes. *Korean*

CALLING

1785. Every one to his own calling, and the ox to the plough. *Italian*

CALM

1786. Always a calm before a storm.
English

CAMEL

1787. A camel's dung points to the camel. *Lebanese*

1788. A camel that wants fodder stretches out its neck. *Iranian*

1789. A camel with bells is not lost.
Turkish

1790. As the camel, so the load.
Hebrew

1791. Many old camels carry the hides of young ones. *Hebrew*

1792. The camel carries the burden, the dog does the panting. *Turkish*

1793. The camel does not see his own hump. *Armenian*

1794. The camel does not see his own hump, he sees only the hump of his brother. *Moroccan*

1795. The camel has his projects, and the camel driver has his projects.
Egyptian

1796. The camel that leads the file pays no attention to the rear. *Turkish*

1797. The camel wants one thing and the camel driver wants another.
Lebanese

1798. The camel went to seek horns, and the ears which it possessed were cut off. *Hebrew*

1799. Though the camel go to Mecca forty years he does not become a pilgrim. *Turkish*

1800. You don't water a camel with a spoon. *Armenian*

CAMP

1801. Talk of camps, but stay at home.
English

CAN

1802. A noisy can is empty.
Philippine

CANDLE

1803. A candle lights others and consumes itself. *English*

1804. Burn a candle at both ends, and it will not last long. *Scottish*

1805. He needs a long candle who awaits the death of another. *Finnish*

1806. If you wall up a candle with boards, it will not shine. *Philippine*

1807. No candle is wanted to look for a fool. *Serbo-Croatian*

1808. The candle does not burn top and bottom. *Jamaican*

CANE

1809. Think not because the cane is bent the sugar's crooked too.
Malaysian

CANNONBALL

1810. Not all cannonballs hit.
German

CANNOT

1811. Cannot has no craft. *Scottish*

1812. What one cannot, another can.
English

CANOE

1813. A canoe is paddled on both sides. *African (Oji)*

1814. He who paddles two canoes, sinks. *African (Bemba)*

1815. Paddle your own canoe.
American

CANTOR

1816. All cantors are fools, but not all fools are cantors. *Hebrew*

1817. The cantor does not sing without a fee. *Hebrew*

CAP

1818. A cap sewn with pearls is not for a sore head. *Greek*

1819. Let him whom the cap suits wear it. *Irish*

1820. The cap burns on a thief. *Russian*

1821. To every fool his cap. *Dutch*

CAPON

1822. Capons were at first but chickens. *English*

1823. If you have not a capon, feed on an onion. *English*

1824. Who gives you a capon, give him the leg and the wing. *English*

CAPTAIN

1825. A wise captain carries more ballast than sail. *Jamaican*

1826. He who saves the ship is the captain. *Turkish*

1827. Many captains sink the ship. *Greek*

1828. Once a captain always a captain. *English*

1829. The captain of the ship means one way, the sailor another. *Egyptian*

1830. Too many captains and the ship rolls. *African (Swahili)*

1831. Too many captains run the ship aground. *Greek*

1832. Too many captains will sink the ship. *Libyan*

1833. Two captains cause one ship to sink. *Turkish*

1834. Two captains sink a ship. *Turkish*

CAR

1835. The front car upset is a warning to the next car following. *Korean*

CARABAO

1836. If a carabao with its four feet makes a wrong step, how much more man. *Philippine*

1837. Though you dress a carabao in silk, he will always return to the mud. *Philippine*

CARAVAN

1838. A caravan does not turn back at the howling of a dog. *Turkish*

1839. Life's caravan never turns back. *African (Swahili)*

1840. They don't unload the caravan for one lame donkey. *Iranian*

CARCASS

1841. Where the carcass is, the ravens will gather. *English*

CARD

1842. A pack of cards is the devil's prayer book. *German*

1843. Better play a card too much than too little. *English*

1844. Cards are the devil's books. *English*

1845. Many can shuffle the cards that cannot play well. *English*

CARE (noun)

1846. A pound of care will not pay an ounce of debt. *English*

1847. Care and diligence bring luck. *English*

1848. Care, and not fine stables, make a good horse. *Danish*

1849. Care brings on grey hairs and age without years. *German*

1850. Care is no cure.   *English*

1851. Care killed a cat.   *English*

1852. Care never paid a pound of debt.   *English*

1853. Care not would have it.
          English

1854. It is the farmer's care that makes the field bear.   *English*

1855. No matter how much care is taken, someone will always be misled.
          Philippine

1856. Take care of the pence.
          English

1857. Take care that you walk with your eyes open.   *Indian (Tamil)*

1858. When everyone takes care of himself, care is taken of all.   *English*

CARE (verb)

1859. Those who say they care least care most.   *American*

CAREER

1860. The career of falsehood is short.
          Pashto

CAREFULNESS

1861. Carefulness can go everywhere.
          Chinese

CARELESSLY

1862. If you are going to do something carelessly, it would be better to give it up entirely.   *Russian*

CARELESSNESS

1863. Carelessness is a great enemy.
          Japanese

1864. Every day the harm arising from carelessness is endured. *Turkish*

CARESS

1865. One gets a caress for a pinch and the other for a caress gets a slap!
          Yiddish

CARPENTER

1866. A carpenter is known by his chips.   *English*

1867. A carpenter is not a blacksmith.
          African (Ovambo)

1868. Such carpenter, such chips.
          English

1869. The worse the carpenter, the more the chips.   *Dutch*

CARPENTRY

1870. Carpentry is no trade for a monkey.   *Iranian*

CARRIAGE

1871. Better in an old carriage than in a new ship.   *Danish*

1872. If the carriage be not greased, it does not move on.   *Turkish*

1873. When the carriage has been smashed, they who show the road are many.   *Turkish*

CARRION

1874. A carrion kite will never make a good hawk.   *English*

1875. No carrion will kill a crow.
          English

CARROT

1876. Only in dreams are the carrots as big as bears.   *Yiddish*

CARRY

1877. He who carries nothing loses nothing.   *French*

1878. You can't carry what you can't lift.   *Latvian*

CART

1879. A creaking cart goes long.
          English

1880. An old cart well used may last out a new one abused.   *English*

1881. Creaking carts last the longest.
Dutch

1882. If you are sitting on his cart you must sing his song. *Russian*

1883. The best cart may overthrow.
English

1884. The overturning of the preceding cart is a warning to the cart following. *Japanese*

1885. To make the cart go you must grease the wheels. *Italian*

1886. What is fallen off the cart is gone. *Russian*

1887. When the cart breaks down, advisers are plentiful. *Armenian*

1888. Where there is a cart ahead there is a track hehind. *Chinese*

CARTWHEEL

1889. A cartwheel is a cartwheel.
American

CARVER

1890. Like carver like cook. *English*

CASE

1891. A good case is not difficult to state. *African (Ashanti)*

1892. A rotten case abides no handling. *English*

CASH

1893. Do not bargain when you are out of cash. *Hebrew*

1894. Who has the cash in his hand has the upper hand. *Hebrew*

1895. With a little cash in hand you have the upper hand. *Hebrew*

CASK

1896. A cask and an ill custom must be broken. *English*

1897. Empty casks make the most noise. *French*

1898. Every cask smells of the wine it contains. *Spanish*

1899. The cask always smells of the herring. *French*

1900. The cask can give no other wine than that it contains. *Italian*

1901. The full cask makes no noise.
Italian

1902. The fuller the cask, the duller its sound. *German*

CASTLE

1903. It is easy to keep a castle that was never assaulted. *English*

1904. The castle is not overthrown by precaution. *Japanese*

1905. The higher the castle the nearer to the lightning. *Russian*

CAT

1906. A bashful cat makes a proud mouse. *Scottish*

1907. A burnt cat shuns the fireplace.
Indian (Tamil)

1908. A cat and a rat cannot be kept at the same place. *African (Shona)*

1909. A cat is a lion in a jungle of small bushes. *Indian (Hindi)*

1910. A cat is a lion to a mouse.
Albanian

1911. A cat is called a domestic tiger, and the king of rats. *Indian (Tamil)*

1912. A cat is heavy if carried constantly. *Irish*

1913. A cat is not sold in a bag, but openly produced. *African (Ga)*

1914. A cat may look at a king.
English

1915. A cat may look at an emperor.
Dutch

1916. A cat pent up becomes a lion.
Italian

1917. A cat will not play after she is a year old. *Welsh*

1918. A cat with gloves will catch no mice. *Armenian*

1919. A halfpenny cat may look at a king. *Scottish*

1920. A meowing cat can't catch mice. *Yiddish*

1921. A mewing cat is never a good mouser. *Spanish*

1922. A muffled cat never caught a mouse. *French*

1923. A muzzled cat was never a good mouser. *English*

1924. A scalded cat dreads cold water.
French

1925. A scalded cat is afraid even of cold water. *Philippine*

1926. All cats are alike grey in the night. *Scottish*

1927. All cats are grey in the dark.
English

1928. All cats are not to be set down for witches. *French*

1929. An old cat laps as much milk as a young. *English*

1930. An old cat likes young mice.
Greek

1931. An old cat sports not with her prey. *English*

1932. An old cat will not learn dancing. *Moroccan*

1933. At night all cats are gray.
Russian

1934. Better have cats' good will than their ill will. *American*

1935. By night all cats are black.
Italian

1936. By night all cats are grey.
Dutch

1937. Cats and monks like fish; married women, kisses; and young girls, caresses. *Greek*

1938. Cat and mouse cannot be neighbors long. *African (Ovambo)*

1939. Cats hide their claws. *English*

1940. Cat will after kind. *English*

1941. Cat will not eat cat. *American*

1942. Don't buy a cat in a bag.
German

1943. Don't buy a cat in a sack.
Dutch

1944. Do not depend on the cat to guard the bacon, or the wolf the sheep.
Slovakian

1945. Don't send away your cat for being a thief. *Spanish*

1946. He has a good pledge of the cat who has her skin. *French*

1947. He's sure of a cat that has her skin. *English*

1948. He that denies the cat skimmed milk must give the mouse cream.
Russian

1949. He that will play with cats must expect to be scratched. *English*

1950. He who begrudges the cat's food finds his clothes eaten by the mice.
Greek

1951. He who hunts with cats will catch mice. *Danish*

1952. He who wants to play with a cat should be able to bear its scratches.
Lebanese

1953. He who will not feed his cat, let him feed his mice. *Welsh*

1954. If stretching were wealth, the cat would be rich. *African (Ga)*

1955. In the place where the cat is not found, there are plenty of rats. *Turkish*

1956. It is better to feed one cat than many mice. *Norwegian*

1957. It is too much to expect of a cat that she should sit by the milk and not lap it.   *German*

1958. Never has a begloved cat caught a mouse.   *Mexican*

1959. Never was cat or dog drowned that could see the shore.   *English*

1960. No one likes to bell the cat.
German

1961. No playing with a straw before an old cat.   *English*

1962. Old cats show great fondness for little, tender mice.   *Mexican*

1963. One plays with the cat until one feels the claws.   *Norwegian*

1964. Send not a cat for lard. *English*

1965. Small cats catch small mice.
Vietnamese

1966. The cat and dog may kiss, yet are none the better friends.   *English*

1967. The cat cannot catch the hare.
Turkish

1968. The cat does not cease to cry "miau."   *African (Ga)*

1969. The cat hates the dog that bites her.   *Welsh*

1970. The cat in gloves catches no mice.   *English*

1971. The cat invites the mouse to a feast.   *English*

1972. The cat is a good friend, only she scratches.   *Portuguese*

1973. The cat is friendly, but it scratches.   *Spanish*

1974. The cat is hungry when a crust contents her.   *English*

1975. The cat knows whose lips she licks.   *English*

1976. The cat knows whose meat she ate!   *Yiddish*

1977. The cat likes fish but she doesn't want to wet her paws.   *Yiddish*

1978. The cat that does not mew catches rats.   *Japanese*

1979. The cats that drive away mice are as good as those that catch them.
German

1980. The cat that is always crying catches nothing.   *Egyptian*

1981. The cat would eat fish but would not wet her feet.
English

1982. The cat would fain fish eat, but she has no will to wet her feet.
Scottish

1983. The more you rub a cat on the rump, the higher she sets up her tail.
English

1984. The scalded cat fears cold water.   *English*

1985. Though the cat winks she is not blind.   *English*

1986. To a good cat a good rat.
French

1987. Two cats and one mouse, two women in one house, two dogs to one bone will not agree long.   *German*

1988. Wake not a sleeping cat.
French

1989. What is born of a cat eats mice.
Rumanian

1990. What is born of a cat will catch mice.   *Czech*

1991. When cat and mouse agree, the farmer has no chance.   *Danish*

1992. When cats are mousing they don't mew.   *Dutch*

1993. When the cat and mouse agree, the grocer is ruined.   *Iranian*

1994. When the cat dies, the mice rejoice.   *African (Oji)*

1995. When the cat goes away, mice reign.   *African (Swahili)*

1996. When the cat has gone, the rats come out to stretch themselves.
Chinese

1997. When the cat is asleep, the mice dance around. *Yiddish*

1998. When the cat's away, it is jubilee with the mice. *Dutch*

1999. When the cat's away the mice will play. *English*

2000. When the cat is away the rats dance. *Italian*

2001. When the cat's away the rats will play. *Spanish*

2002. When the cat sleeps, the mice play. *Dutch*

2003. When the wild cat becomes a leopard, it will devour large beasts. *African (Yoruba)*

2004. Who does not keep a cat keeps mice. *Serbo-Croatian*

2005. Who hunts with cats will catch nothing but rats. *Dutch*

2006. Who is born of a cat will run after mice. *French*

2007. Who will not feed the cats must feed the mice and rats. *German*

2008. You can have no more of a cat than her skin. *English*

2009. Young cats will mouse, young apes will louse. *Dutch*

CATCH

2010. Do not catch everything that swims. *Russian*

2011. When we think to catch we are sometimes caught. *Spanish*

CATCHING

2012. Catching before spanking is the rule. *American*

2013. Catching is before hanging. *American*

CATTLE

2014. Do not mix your cattle with those of a chief. *African (Shona)*

2015. If the cattle are scattered the tiger seizes them. *Burmese*

2016. Little cattle, little care. *English*

2017. Old cattle breed not. *English*

CAUSE

2018. A good cause makes a stout heart and a strong arm. *English*

2019. A good cause needs help. *French*

2020. He that is angry without a cause must settle without amends. *Scottish*

2021. He who has an ill cause, let him sell it cheap. *English*

2022. If you grease a cause well it will stretch. *English*

2023. It is a bad cause that none dare speak in. *English*

2024. Make the best of a bad cause. *Scottish*

2025. Nobody hates anybody without cause. *African (Ga)*

2026. Plenty of words when the cause is lost. *Italian*

2027. Take away the cause and the effect must cease. *English*

2028. The best cause requires a good pleader. *Dutch*

2029. There is a cause for all things. *Italian*

2030. Who complains without cause, let a cause be made for him. *Welsh*

CAUTION

2031. Better caution at first than tears afterwards. *Yiddish*

2032. Caution brings speed in the end. *Hebrew*

2033. Caution is born of unpleasant experience. *Philippine*

2034. Caution is no cowardice; even fleas are armed. *Russian*

2035. Caution is the parent of delicate beer glasses.   *Dutch*

2036. Caution minimizes loss.
Philippine

2037. In prosperity caution, in adversity patience.   *Dutch*

2038. Much caution does no harm.
Portuguese

CELLAR

2039. An empty cellar makes an angry butler.   *Danish*

CEMETERY

2040. A cemetery never refuses a dead man.   *Lebanese*

2041. One passes by the cemetery so often that in the end one falls into it.
Russian

CENTIPEDE

2042. A centipede though dead will not fall.   *Japanese*

2043. Though the centipede has one of its legs broken, this does not affect its movement.   *Burmese*

CERTAINTY

2044. Better the certainty of a straddle.   *Irish*

2045. He that leaves certainty and sticks to chance, when fools pipe he may dance.   *English*

2046. Never quit certainty for hope.
English

2047. There is certainty as to the mother, uncertainty as to the father.
Hawaiian

CHAFER

2048. One chafer knows another.
Irish

CHAFF

2049. The king's chaff is better than other people's corn.   *English*

CHAIN

2050. All are not free who mock their chains.   *German*

2051. Chains of gold are stronger than chains of iron.   *English*

2052. He is not escaped who drags his chain.   *French*

2053. He is not free who drags his chain after him.   *Italian*

2054. One link snaps and the whole chain falls apart.   *Yiddish*

CHAIR

2055. A rickety chair will not long serve as a seat.   *Danish*

CHAMBER

2056. Empty chambers make foolish maids.   *English*

2057. The chamber of sickness is the chapel of devotion.   *English*

CHAMOIS

2058. The chamois climbs high and yet is caught.   *German*

CHANCE

2059. Chance is a dicer.   *English*

2060. Chance is better than meeting by agreement.   *Moroccan*

2061. Chance is no robbery.   *English*

2062. Have an eye to the main chance.   *English*

2063. He who does not take chances cannot expect to be rich.   *Philippine*

2064. He who trusts all things to chance makes a lottery of his life.
English

2065. He who waits for chance may wait a year. *African (Yoruba)*

2066. It is too late to grieve when the chance is past. *English*

CHANGE (noun)

2067. A change needed in a grandchild has to begin with the grandfather. *African (Swahili)*

2068. A change of rulers is the joy of fools. *Rumanian*

2069. A change of work is as good as a rest. *Irish*

2070. Changes never answer the end. *English*

2071. Change of fortune is the lot of life. *English*

2072. Change of masters, change of manners. *Scottish*

2073. Change of pasture makes fat calves. *English*

2074. Change of weather is the discourse of fools. *English*

2075. Change of women makes bald knaves. *English*

2076. Let it be worse, as long as it's a change. *Yiddish*

2077. Many a sudden change takes place on a spring day. *Irish*

CHANGE (verb)

2078. Who often changes, damages. *French*

CHAPEL

2079. There is no chapel so small but has its saint. *French*

CHAPTER

2080. The first chapter of fools is to esteem themselves wise. *English*

CHARACTER

2081. A good character is more valuable than gold. *Philippine*

2082. A good character is the real beauty that never fades. *Philippine*

2083. A man's character is revealed by his words. *Philippine*

2084. A man's character reaches town before his person. *Danish*

2085. Character comes before the teacher. *African (Hausa)*

2086. Character does not change. *Japanese*

2087. Character is a line on stone, none can rub it out. *African (Hausa)*

2088. Character is always corrupted by prosperity. *Icelandic*

2089. Every man's character is good in his own eyes. *African (Yoruba)*

2090. Everyone admires his own character. *Turkish*

2091. Look not at the shape, look at the character. *Turkish*

2092. Only by waiting is character known. *African (Hausa)*

CHARCOAL

2093. Not all that is black is charcoal. *Philippine*

CHARITABLE

2094. The charitable gives out at the door, and God puts in at the window. *English*

2095. He is not charitable that will not be so privately. *English*

CHARITY

2096. Charity and pride do both feed the poor. *English*

2097. Charity begins at home. *English*

2098. Charity does not come out of a prison. *Moroccan*

2099. Charity has no merit till the houseowner's hunger is satisfied. *Libyan*

2100. Charity is also a habit. *Yiddish*

2101. Charity protects you. *Indian (Hindustani)*

2102. Charity well regulated begins at home. *Spanish*

2103. If one could do charity without money and favors without aggravation, the world would be full of saints. *Yiddish*

2104. May your charity increase as much as your wealth. *Turkish*

2105. Well-regulated charity begins with one's self. *French*

CHARM

2106. A little charm and you are not ordinary. *Yiddish*

2107. Charm is better than beauty. *Yiddish*

CHASE (noun)

2108. A stern chase is a long chase. *English*

2109. He who goes out to the chase without a greyhound comes home without a hare. *Turkish*

CHASE (verb)

2110. He that chases another does not sit still himself. *Dutch*

CHASTE

2111. She is chaste who was never asked the question. *English*

CHASTITY

2112. A woman's jewel is her chastity. *Philippine*

2113. Chastity is a feminine grace. *Indian (Tamil)*

2114. You cannot set a watch upon chastity. *Hebrew*

CHATTER

2115. Much chatter, little wit. *Portuguese*

CHEAP

2116. It is as cheap sitting as standing. *English*

2117. What is cheap may also be bad. *Japanese*

CHEAPEST

2118. Cheapest is dearest. *Yiddish*

CHEAPNESS

2119. Cheapness costs dearly. *Mexican*

CHEAT (noun)

2120. Two cheats make an even bargain. *American*

CHEAT (verb)

2121. He is most cheated who cheats himself. *Danish*

2122. He that cheats in small things is a fool; but in great things is a rogue. *English*

2123. He that will cheat at play, will cheat you any way. *English*

2124. He who intends to cheat often cheats himself. *Philippine*

CHEATER

2125. It is fair and just to cheat the cheater. *Spanish*

CHEATING

2126. Cheating is more honorable than stealing. *German*

CHEEK

2127. A beautiful girl's cheeks are the foes of her chastity. *Greek*

CHEER

2128. Small cheer and great welcome makes a merry feast.   *English*

2129. Today a good cheer, tomorrow on the bier.   *English*

CHEERFULNESS

2130. Cheerfulness and goodwill make labor light.   *Danish*

2131. Cheerfulness gives sweetness to life.   *Philippine*

2132. Cheerfulness is the very flower of health.   *Japanese*

CHEESE

2133. After cheese comes nothing.   *English*

2134. Cheese and bread make the cheeks red.   *German*

2135. Cheese and money should always sleep together one night. *English*

2136. Cheese is gold in the morning, silver at noon, and lead at night.   *German*

2137. He who eats cheese finds water.   *Turkish*

2138. It is better to scrape the cheese than to peel it.   *Danish*

2139. You can't hang soft cheese on a hook.   *English*

CHEESECAKE

2140. You can't make cheesecakes out of snow.   *Yiddish*

CHERISH

2141. Cherish what you have and struggle for better.   *Greek*

CHERRY

2142. Eat not cherries with the great.   *English*

2143. It is dangerous to eat cherries with the great; they throw the stones at your head.   *Danish*

2144. It's not good to eat cherries with great men; they throw the stones and stalks into one's face.   *German*

2145. The cherry blossom among flowers, the warrior among men.   *Japanese*

2146. The cherry tree is known among others by its flowers. *Japanese*

CHEST (breast)

2147. Either your chest will be arrayed in medals or your head will be in the bushes.   *Russian*

CHEST (trunk)

2148. Open chests tempt even the righteous.   *Indian (Hindi)*

CHICK

2149. Out of a white egg often comes a black chick.   *Italian*

2150. The chick loved by God will grow up, though motherless.   *African (Hausa)*

CHICKEN

2151. A baby chicken sleeps under a hawk's tree without knowing it.   *African (Kpelle)*

2152. A chicken crows not in the presence of a rooster.   *African (Swahili)*

2153. A chicken has no bad luck in the morning.   *African (Annang)*

2154. A chicken that gets a sprained ankle is abandoned by its own mother.   *African (Annang)*

2155. Chickens feed capons.   *English*

2156. Do not eat your chicken and throw its feathers in the front yard.   *African (Kpelle)*

2157. My chicken is good, but my neighbor's looks better.   *Rumanian*

2158. Not even a chicken digs for nothing.   *Czech*

2159. The chickens are the country's, but the city eats them. *English*

2160. The chicken is no match for the knife. *African (Swahili)*

2161. While a bush fowl is being roasted, a chicken considers its own fate. *African (Annang)*

CHIDE

2162. He that sharply chides is ready to pardon. *English*

CHIEF

2163. A chief is known by his subjects. *Hawaiian*

2164. Where the chief walks, there questions are decided.
African (Ovambo)

CHILD (see CHILDREN)

2165. A burnt child dreads the fire.
English

2166. A burnt child fears the fire, and bitten child fears a dog. *Danish*

2167. A child, a drunkard, and a fool tell the truth. *Hungarian*

2168. A child does not break a land tortoise, but a child knows how to break a snail. *African (Ga)*

2169. A child does not know his father's poverty. *African (Kpelle)*

2170. A child does not look into the soup pot for nothing.
African (Ashanti)

2171. A child does not speak while a grown-up is talking. *African (Jabo)*

2172. A child is a blessing for any man's roof. *Rumanian*

2173. A child is a certain worry and an uncertain joy. *Swedish*

2174. A child is a child though he may be the ruler of a town. *Lebanese*

2175. A child is caressed by its mother, but an orphan is caressed by God. *Polish*

2176. A child is like a precious stone, but also a heavy burden.
African (Swahili)

2177. A child is like an axe; even if it hurts you, you still carry it on your shoulder. *African (Bemba)*

2178. A child is not scolded while he eats. *African (Ovambo)*

2179. A child learns quicker to talk than to be silent. *Norwegian*

2180. A child may crush a snail, but it will not crush a tortoise. *African (Oji)*

2181. A child may have too much of his mother's blessing. *English*

2182. A child much spoken of does not get very far. *African (Ovambo)*

2183. A child must creep until it learns to walk. *Danish*

2184. A child places reliance on its mother. *African (Zulu)*

2185. A child that does not cry dies in the cloth it is carried in.
African (Shona)

2186. A child that eats well thrives.
Indian (Tamil)

2187. A child who does not fear his father and mother will not live long.
African (Ovambo)

2188. A child who refuses the mother's advice does not live long.
African (Annang)

2189. A child with seven nannies often has an eye missing. *Russian*

2190. A cranky child has not been spanked. *African (Ovambo)*

2191. A crying child obtains milk.
Indian (Tamil)

2192. A crying child thrives.
Japanese

2193. A deformed child is the dearer to his parents.

Japanese

2194. A fatherless child is half an orphan; a motherless child is a whole one. *Estonian*

2195. A good child is a crown of honor for his parents.

African (Swahili)

2196. A good child soon learns.

English

2197. A lovely child has many names.

Hungarian

2198. A naughty child must be roughly rocked. *Danish*

2199. A pet child has many names.

Danish

2200. A respectful child is the wealth of his parents. *Philippine*

2201. A rich child often sits in a poor mother's lap. *Danish*

2202. A spoiled child is his parents' grief. *Philippine*

2203. A talkative child reveals his mother's secrets. *African (Kpelle)*

2204. A wandering child cannot eat his mother's food when it is hot.

African (Annang)

2205. A wise child is father's bliss.

English

2206. An old child sucks hard.

English

2207. As we teach a child, so he learns. *African (Jabo)*

2208. Ask the mother if the child be like his father. *English*

2209. Baptise your own child first.

Irish

2210. Better the child cry, than the mother sigh. *Danish*

2211. Better the child cry than the old man. *Danish*

2212. Better the child should cry than the father. *Yiddish*

2213. Boil not the pap before the child be born. *English*

2214. Bring up your beloved child with a stick. *Japanese*

2215. By crawling a child begins to walk. *African (Fulani)*

2216. Chastise a good child, that it may not grow bad, and a bad one, that it may not grow worse. *Danish*

2217. Even a child may beat a man who's bound. *English*

2218. Even without parents a child will grow up. *Japanese*

2219. Every mother's child is handsome. *German*

2220. Having an only child is like having one eye. *Yiddish*

2221. He that loves his child chastises it. *Dutch*

2222. He who does not whip the child does not mend the youth. *Spanish*

2223. He who takes the child by the hand takes the mother by the heart.

Danish

2224. If a child does not resemble its father, it resembles its mother.

African (Ovambo)

2225. If the child cries, let the mother hush it, and if it will not be hushed, let it cry. *Spanish*

2226. If the child doesn't cry, the mother doesn't find out. *Russian*

2227. If the child robs when he begins to walk, he will plunder a sheepfold when he grows older.

African (Wolof)

2228. If you're a child at twenty, you're an ass at twenty-one. *Yiddish*

2229. If you give a child your back it will ask to be carried in your arms.

Japanese

2230. Is it only when a child cries that he is given the breast.

African (Ashanti)

2231. It is a wise child that knows its own father. *English*

2232. It is better the child should cry than the father. *German*

2233. It is easier to bear a child once a year than to shave every day. *Russian*

2234. It is too late to cover the well when the child is drowned. *Danish*

2235. Let a child have its will and it will not cry. *Danish*

2236. Man is a child twice.

Estonian

2237. Many kiss the child for the nurse's sake. *English*

2238. Neither the child that is unchastised, nor the mustache that is untwirled will be right. *Indian (Tamil)*

2239. No child was ever born without having been conceived. *Philippine*

2240. No one sends a child on an errand and looks to see if he is pleased or not. *African (Ashanti)*

2241. Praise the child and you make love to the mother. *English*

2242. Quick child is soon taught.

English

2243. Send away your child and your foot rests, but your heart does not rest.

Jamaican

2244. Spare the rod and spoil the child. *English*

2245. The child looks everywhere and often sees nothing. *African (Wolof)*

2246. The child of a beggar eats when his mother has begged successfully.

African (Bemba)

2247. The child of a generous person does not die of hunger.

African (Bemba)

2248. The child of a snake is also a snake. *African (Bemba)*

2249. The child says nothing but what it heard by the fire. *English*

2250. The child that's born must be kept. *English*

2251. The child that is given all that he asks for will rarely succeed in life.

Philippine

2252. The child who gets a stepmother also gets a stepfather. *Danish*

2253. The child who has never had indigestion eats and eats.

African (Bemba)

2254. The dearer the child, the sharper must be the rod. *Danish*

2255. The motherless child is in the way when the stepmother bakes.

Finnish

2256. The weeping child will gain strength. *Indian (Tamil)*

2257. There's only one pretty child in the world, and every mother has it.

English

2258. Though a still-born child is brought forth, there is no escape from the midwife's fee. *Indian (Tamil)*

2259. To spoil a child is to kill it.

Chinese

2260. What the child hears at the fireside is soon known at the parish church. *French*

2261. What the child says, he has heard at home. *African (Wolof)*

2262. What the child sees is what the child does. *Irish*

2263. What you are as a child, you will be as a man. *Philippine*

2264. Whatever a child babbles, its mother will understand. *Yiddish*

2265. When the child is christened you may have godfathers enough.

English

2266. When you show the moon to a child, it sees only your finger.
African (Bemba)

2267. Who chastises his child will be honored by him; who chastises it not will be shamed. *Dutch*

2268. With a child in the house, all corners are full. *Yiddish*

2269. With seven nurses the child loses its eye. *Russian*

CHILDHOOD

2270. Childhood is a crown of roses, old age a crown of thorns. *Hebrew*

2271. Childhood is freedom.
Indian (Kashmiri)

2272. Childhood is without care.
Indian (Kashmiri)

CHILDREN (see CHILD)

2273. Better children weep than old men. *English*

2274. Better have many children than many riches. *Vietnamese*

2275. Children and chicken must be always picking. *English*

2276. Children and drunken men speak the truth. *Danish*

2277. Children and fools are prophets. *French*

2278. Children and fools have merry lives. *English*

2279. Children and fools speak the truth. *English*

2280. Children and money make a nice world. *Yiddish*

2281. Children are certain cares, uncertain comforts. *English*

2282. Children are certain sorrow, but uncertain joy. *Danish*

2283. Children are poor men's riches.
English

2284. Children are the riches of the poor. *Danish*

2285. Children are what they are made. *French*

2286. Children bring good fortune, children bring misfortune. *Yiddish*

2287. Children do not have as much affection for parents as parents have for them. *Japanese*

2288. Children do not understand the hearts of parents. *Japanese*

2289. Children have a hair of their father. *Flemish*

2290. Children have wide ears and long tongues. *English*

2291. Children learn from their parents. *Japanese*

2292. Children pick up words as pigeons peas, and utter them again as God shall please. *English*

2293. Children should be seen and not heard. *English*

2294. Children suck the mother when they are young, and the father when they are old. *English*

2295. Children take after their parents. *Maltese*

2296. Children when they are little make parents fools, when great, mad.
English

2297. Children who do their duty unprompted are as a life-preserving remedy. *Indian (Tamil)*

2298. Children will be children.
American

2299. Do not pray for gold and jade and precious things, but pray that your children and grandchildren may all be good. *Chinese*

2300. From bad matches good children are also born. *Yiddish*

2301. From children you must expect childish acts. *Danish*

2302. He that has children, all his morsels are not his own.   *English*

2303. He that has no children knows not what is love.   *English*

2304. He who chastises not his children is himself at last chastised.   *Turkish*

2305. If you love the children of others, you will love your own even better.   *African (Wolof)*

2306. Ignorant children are not better than calves.   *Indian (Tamil)*

2307. In whatever they do, children should consult their elders.   *Philippine*

2308. It is better not to live than to be dependent on children.   *Yiddish*

2309. Little children and headaches, great children and heartaches.   *Italian*

2310. Little children, little joys; bigger children, bigger sorrows.   *Yiddish*

2311. Little children, little sorrows; big children, great sorrows.   *Danish*

2312. Love your children with your heart, but train them with your hands.   *Russian*

2313. Of listening children have your fears, for little pitchers have great ears.   *Dutch*

2314. One cannot see the evil deeds of one's own children.   *Japanese*

2315. One cannot send other people's children without giving them anything.   *African (Ovambo)*

2316. Our neighbor's children are always the worst.   *German*

2317. Poor men's treasures are their children.   *Japanese*

2318. Pretty children sing pretty songs.   *Danish*

2319. Small children don't let you sleep; big children don't let you rest.   *Yiddish*

2320. Small children eat porridge, big ones eat their parents' hearts.   *Czech*

2321. Small children give you headache; big children, heartache. *Russian*

2322. Small children, small worries; older children, greater worries.   *Greek*

2323. The blessing of having many children has never broken a man's roof.   *Rumanian*

2324. The children of the same mother do not always agree.   *African (Wolof)*

2325. The daughter's children are dearer than one's own.   *Russian*

2326. The more children, the more debts; the more wives, the more misfortunes.   *Vietnamese*

2327. There are no filial children at the bedside of long-sick people.   *Chinese*

2328. What children hear at home soon flies abroad.   *English*

2329. What children hear their parents say by the fireside they repeat on the highway.   *Spanish*

2330. What small children wear out and pigs eat no one sees.   *Russian*

2331. When advanced in age we become children again.   *Japanese*

2332. When children stand still, they have done some ill.   *English*

2333. When it comes to one's own children, then everybody is blind.   *Yiddish*

2334. When you have your own children you will understand your obligation to your parents.   *Japanese*

2335. Who has no children does not know what love is.   *Italian*

2336. Widows' children turn out well.   *English*

CHIMNEY

2337. A smoking chimney in a great house is a good sign.   *English*

2338. It is easier to build two chimneys, than to maintain one.   *English*

2339. There is not always good cheer where the chimney smokes. *English*

CHIN

2340. He may swim boldly who is held up by the chin. *French*

CHIP

2341. Chips don't fall without being hacked from the tree. *Swedish*

2342. Chips never fly too far from the block. *Jamaican*

2343. He that hews above his head, may have the chip fall in his eye. *Scottish*

2344. Little chips kindle the fire, and big logs sustain it. *Portuguese*

2345. The shape of your chips is determined by your chopping. *Philippine*

CHOICE

2346. Don't be scared when you have no other choice. *Yiddish*

2347. He that has a choice has trouble. *Dutch*

2348. No choice is also a choice. *Yiddish*

2349. There is a choice of but two things, loss or gain. *Indian (Hindustani)*

2350. There's but bad choice where the whole stock is bad. *English*

2351. There is small choice in rotten apples. *English*

CHURCH

2352. A great church and little devotion. *Italian*

2353. Better come late to church than never. *Danish*

2354. Big churches, little saints. *German*

2355. New churches and new taverns are seldom empty. *German*

2356. The nearer the church the farther from God. *English*

2357. There can be no church without incense or candle. *Armenian*

2358. Where there's a church there's an inn not far away. *Latvian*

2359. Who is forced to go to church will not pray. *Slovenian*

CIDER

2360. He that drinks his cider alone, let him catch his horse alone. *American*

CIRCUMCISION

2361. Circumscision, confirmation, wedding, burial fee—all too soon to be paid! *Yiddish*

CIRCUMSTANCE

2362. Circumstances alter cases. *English*

2363. Small circumstances produce great events. *American*

CITIZEN

2364. The citizen is at his business before he rises. *English*

CLAM

2365. Clams cannot be taken in a field. *Japanese*

CLAW

2366. When one claw is caught, the whole bird perishes. *Russian*

CLAY

2367. Get the clay while it is still wet. *African (Swahili)*

2368. Unbeaten clay cannot be made into bricks. *Greek*

CLEANLINESS

2369. Cleanliness is next to godliness. *English*

2370. Cleanliness is part of glory.
Irish

2371. Cleanliness is the luxury of the poor. *Mexican*

2372. Cleanliness is the sister of holiness. *Maltese*

CLEMENCY

2373. Clemency is the support of justice. *Russian*

CLERGY

2374. Be neither intimate nor distant with the clergy. *Irish*

CLERK

2375. No one knows the parson better than the clerk. *Danish*

2376. The greatest clerks are not the wisest men. *English*

CLEVERNESS

2377. Cleverness and stupidity go together. *African (Ovambo)*

2378. What cleverness hides, cleverness will reveal. *African (Fulani)*

CLIMB (noun)

2379. Reckon the climb before reckoning the descent. *Lebanese*

CLIMB (verb)

2380. Don't climb too high and you won't have to fall. *Yiddish*

2381. He cannot climb up who cannot climb down. *Norwegian*

2382. He who climbs too high is near a fall. *Italian*

2383. He that climbs high, falls heavily. *German*

2384. Those who climb high, often have a fall. *Danish*

2385. Uphill one climbs slowly; downhill one rolls fast. *Yiddish*

2386. Who climbs high his fall is great. *English*

2387. He that never climbed never fell. *English*

CLIMBER

2388. Hasty climbers have sudden falls. *English*

CLOAK

2389. A borrowed cloak does not keep one warm. *Egyptian*

2390. A cloak is not made for a single shower of rain. *Italian*

2391. Another's cloak does not keep you warm. *Yiddish*

2392. Arrange your cloak as the wind blows. *French*

2393. Cut your cloak according to your cloth. *Scottish*

2394. Don't have your cloak to make when it begins to rain. *English*

2395. However bright the sun may shine, leave not your cloak at home. *Spanish*

2396. The cloak is precious to its wearer. *Hebrew*

2397. There's no making a good cloak of bad cloth. *Spanish*

2398. Truth's cloak is often lined with lies. *Danish*

2399. Where you lost your cloak, seek it. *Spanish*

CLOCK

2400. If it were not for the hands the clock would be useless. *Polish*

2401. The clock goes as it pleases the clerk. *English*

CLOTH

2402. A piece of cloth is not new for long; it is old for long. *African (Bemba)*

2403. A white cloth and a stain never agree.   *African (Yoruba)*

2404. Better coarse cloth than naked thighs.   *Danish*

2405. Better lose cloth than bread.   *English*

2406. Cloth and a wife, choose them not at night.   *Rumanian*

2407. Durable cloth is not easily torn.   *Philippine*

2408. Fine cloth is never out of fashion.   *English*

2409. It is a bad cloth that will take no color.   *English*

2410. Measure your cloth seven times, you can cut it but once.   *Russian*

2411. Of little cloth but a short cloak.   *French*

2412. The best cloth may have a moth in it.   *English*

2413. The best cloth has uneven threads.   *Spanish*

2414. When white cloth has been dipped in the dyeing vat, it is difficult to tell it from black.   *Chinese*

2415. Whenever white cloth is dipped in mud, it gets dirty.   *Philippine*

2416. You cannot take white cloth out of a tub full of indigo.   *Chinese*

CLOTHES

2417. Abroad we look at a man's clothes; at home we look at the man.   *Chinese*

2418. Borrowed clothes are either too tight or too loose.   *Philippine*

2419. Borrowed clothes do not keep one warm.   *Rumanian*

2420. Clothes conceal the blemish.   *Yiddish*

2421. Clothes make the man.   *Dutch*

2422. Even a packhorse driver looks well in fine clothes.   *Japanese*

2423. Ever since we wear clothes, we know not one another.   *English*

2424. Good clothes open all doors.   *English*

2425. He who wears too fine clothes, shall go about in rags. *African (Wolof)*

2426. If clothes remain long in the bag they rot.   *African (Yoruba)*

2427. If there is no one at home, don't leave clothes to dry before the fire.   *Chinese*

2428. It is good to hold the clothes of one who is swimming.   *Italian*

2429. Mend your clothes and you may hold out this year.   *English*

2430. New clothes have no lice.   *African (Ovambo)*

2431. With clothes the new are best; with friends the old are best. *Chinese*

2432. You may change the clothes, you cannot change the man.   *Chinese*

CLOUD

2433. A small cloud may hide both sun and moon.   *Danish*

2434. After the clouds are swept aside, brightness will appear.   *Philippine*

2435. All clouds do not rain.   *Dutch*

2436. Clouds are the sign of rain.   *African (Fulani)*

2437. Clouds may thunder and still not bring rain.   *Armenian*

2438. Every cloud has a silver lining.   *English*

2439. He that regards the clouds shall not reap.   *American*

2440. Not every storm cloud falls in rain.   *African (Fulani)*

2441. One cloud is enough to eclipse all the sun.   *English*

2442. The passing clouds can be seen, but passing thoughts cannot be seen.   *Australian (Maori)*

2443. The smallest of clouds can hide the sun.   *Armenian*

CLOUT

2444. Better a clout than a hole out.
English

CLOWN

2445. A clown enriched knows neither relation nor friend.   *French*

2446. Clowns are best in their own company, but gentlemen are best everywhere.   *English*

2447. Give a clown your finger, and he will take your hand.   *English*

2448. Give a clown your foot, and he'll take your hand.   *Spanish*

2449. Offer a clown your finger, and he'll take your fist.   *Dutch*

COACHMAN

2450. An old coachman loves the crack of the whip.   *Dutch*

COAL

2451. Glowing coals will be sparkling.   *English*

2452. If you touch a hot coal you burn yourself; a cold one, you blacken yourself.   *Greek*

2453. Let him that is cold blow at the coal.   *Scottish*

2454. Under white ashes there is glowing coal.   *Italian*

COAT

2455. A fine coat hides an empty belly.   *Serbo-Croatian*

2456. A ragged coat finds little credit.
Italian

2457. A smart coat is a good letter of introduction.   *Dutch*

2458. As the coat, so the lining.
Latvian

2459. Coats change with countries.
English

2460. He that has one coat cannot lend it.   *English*

2461. It is not the fine coat that makes the gentleman.   *English*

2462. Link by link the coat of mail is made.   *French*

2463. One cannot make a fur coat from a "Thank you".   *Russian*

2464. One does not tear one's coat because of the cleverness of sewing.
African (Hausa)

2465. One is received according to one's coat; one is dismissed according to one's brain.   *Russian*

2466. The silken coat also has fleas.
Estonian

2467. The white coat does not make the miller.   *Italian*

2468. Though your coat is dirty, you do not burn it.   *African (Oji)*

2469. You can't sew a coat out of thanks.   *Russian*

COAXING

2470. Coaxing is better than driving.
American

COBBLER

2471. If the cobbler sticks to his last, his pot is full.   *Yiddish*

2472. Let not the cobbler go beyond his last.   *English*

2473. The cobbler is always without boots.   *Russian*

2474. The richer the cobbler the blacker his thumb.   *English*

COBRA

2475. The cobra knows its length.
African (Ovambo)

COBWEB

2476. Where cobwebs are plenty, kisses are scarce. *English*

COCK

2477. A cock can't ride horseback although he has a spur. *Jamaican*

2478. A cock is valiant on his own dunghill. *Dutch*

2479. A good cock was never fat. *Portuguese*

2480. All cocks must have a comb. *Dutch*

2481. As the cock crows, the young cock learns. *Scottish*

2482. Better a cock for a day than a hen for a year. *English*

2483. Cocks make free with the horse's corn. *American*

2484. Cock, the village clock. *Polish*

2485. Even the cock is jealous concerning his hen. *Turkish*

2486. Even where there is no cock day dawns. *African (Zulu)*

2487. Every cock is brave on his own dunghill. *English*

2488. In the place where there are many cocks, the morning is early. *Turkish*

2489. It is a sorry house in which the cock is silent and the hen crows. *French*

2490. It is a very ill cock that will not crow before he be old. *English*

2491. It is an unhappy house where the cock is silent and the hen crows. *Czech*

2492. The cock crows, but daybreak is from God. *Lebanese*

2493. The cock crows but the hen goes. *English*

2494. The cock is a lord on his own dunghill. *German*

2495. The cock is bold on his own dunghill. *Italian*

2496. The cock is king on his own dunghill. *German*

2497. The cock often crows without a victory. *Danish*

2498. The young cock crows as he heard the old one. *English*

2499. Two cocks do not crow from the same roof. *African (Annang)*

2500. Two cocks in one house, a cat and a mouse, an old man and a young wife, are always in strife. *Dutch*

2501. Two cocks in one yard do not agree. *Italian*

2502. We do not know the cock in the egg. *African (Bemba)*

2503. Where the cock is the hen does not crow. *Portuguese*

2504. Young cocks love no coops. *English*

COCKEREL

2505. A fighting cockerel does not get fat. *Russian*

COCKROACH

2506. If the cockroach refuses to stay in its hole, the chicken refuses to stay hungry. *African (Annang)*

2507. The cockroach never wins its cause when the chicken is judge. *Haitian*

COCONUT

2508. A bad coconut spoils the good ones. *African (Swahili)*

2509. A coconut cannot compete with a stone. *African (Swahili)*

2510. A coconut shell full of water is an ocean to an ant. *Indian (Tamil)*

2511. He who cracks the coconut must eat the cream. *African (Swahili)*

2512. In a cluster of coconuts there is always a rotten one. *Philippine*

COFFEE

2513. Coffee has two virtues, it is wet and warm. *Dutch*

2514. Good coffee should be black like the devil, hot like hell, and sweet like a kiss. *Hungarian*

COFFIN

2515. Coffin carriers desire the year of the plaque. *Japanese*

2516. Even a coffin is made to measure. *Russian*

COIN

2517. Better five coins in hand than ten in prospect. *Greek*

2518. Golden coins make our crooked windows look straight. *Greek*

2519. Much coin much care. *English*

2520. One false coin spoils ten good ones. *Slovenian*

2521. The coin that is most current among us is flattery. *English*

2522. When coins rattle philosophers are silent. *Serbo-Croatian*

COINCIDENCE

2523. Coincidence defeats a well-laid plan. *Philippine*

COLD

2524. Every one feels the cold according as he is clad. *Spanish*

2525. The cold teaches one to steal charcoal. *Moroccan*

COLLECTION

2526. Partial collection of a debt is better than total loss. *Lebanese*

COLOR

2527. No color is deeper than black. *Iranian*

2528. The color does not come off a zebra. *African (Ovambo)*

COLT

2529. A colt you may break, but an old horse you never can. *English*

2530. A ragged colt may make a good horse. *English*

2531. A ragged colt may prove a good horse. *Scottish*

2532. Often has a tattered colt grown to be a splendid horse. *Irish*

2533. Ragged colts make the handsomest stallions. *German*

2534. What the colt learns in youth he continues in old age. *French*

2535. When you ride a young colt, see your saddle be well girt. *English*

2536. Wildest colts make the best horses. *English*

COMB

2537. What good is a gold comb to a bald man. *Armenian*

COME

2538. Come uncalled, sit unserved. *Scottish*

2539. First come, first served. *English*

2540. He that comes last makes all fast. *English*

2541. He who comes last is usually more fortunate than he who comes first. *Philippine*

2542. He who comes last sees least. *Norwegian*

2543. He who comes uncalled sits unserved. *English*

2544. Late come, late served.
American

2545. Lightly come lightly go.
English

2546. Quickly come, quickly go.
English

2547. They who come from afar have leave to lie. *Dutch*

2548. Who comes first, grinds first.
German

2549. Who comes last shuts the door.
Italian

2550. Who comes late lodges ill.
English

2551. Who comes seldom is welcome.
Italian

2552. Who comes unbidden departs unthanked. *German*

COMER

2553. The first comer grinds first.
French

2554. The last comers are often the masters. *French*

2555. The later comer gets the bones.
Greek

COMFORT

2556. It is poor comfort for one who has broken his leg that another has broken his neck. *Danish*

2557. The comfort of the bed is not experienced by the mattress.
Indian (Tamil)

2558. Who suffers much is likely to find comfort in very little. *Mexican*

COMMAND (noun)

2559. The command of custom is great. *English*

COMMAND (verb)

2560. He that commands well shall be obeyed well. *English*

2561. Little is done where many command. *Dutch*

COMMENCEMENT

2562. The commencement is easy but the maintenance is difficult.

COMMODITY

2563. Every commodity has its discommodity. *English*

2564. Rate your commodities at home, but sell them abroad. *English*

COMMUNITY

2565. Blame the community, it will stand everything. *Russian*

2566. Communities begin by building their kitchen. *French*

2567. Community is as strong as water, and as stupid as a pig. *Russian*

2568. Every community has its own customs and traditions. *Philippine*

2569. Nobody dare differ from the community. *Russian*

COMPANION

2570. A pleasant companion on a journey is as good as a post chaise.
French

2571. Everybody's companion is nobody's friend. *German*

2572. He is an ill companion that has a good memory. *English*

2573. He who has a companion has a master. *French*

2574. It is better to be alone than to have a bad companion. *Philippine*

2575. It is good to have companions in misery. *English*

2576. There are no companions in taste or color. *Russian*

COMPANY

2577. Better be alone than in bad company. *Spanish*

2578. Better to be beaten than be in bad company. *English*

2579. Cheerful company shortens the miles. *German*

2580. Choose your company before you drink. *English*

2581. Choose your company before you sit down. *Irish*

2582. Company in distress makes trouble less. *French*

2583. Company's good if you are going to be hanged. *English*

2584. For want of company welcome trumpery. *English*

2585. Good company makes short miles. *Dutch*

2586. If they do not want you in their company, go aside. *African (Yoruba)*

2587. In love, company is a nuisance. *Japanese*

2588. Keep bad men company and you'll soon be of their number. *English*

2589. Keep good men company and you shall be of their number. *English*

2590. One must look at a man's company. *Turkish*

2591. Plenty to eat and company is the feast. *African (Hausa)*

2592. Seven is company, and nine confusion. *Spanish*

2593. Shun evil company. *Irish*

2594. Tell me the company you keep, and I'll tell you what you are. *Dutch*

2595. Tell me your company, and I'll tell you who you are. *Irish*

2596. Tell me your company, and I'll tell you your manners. *English*

2597. The company makes the feast. *English*

2598. The smaller the company the greater the share. *Manx*

2599. Two is company and three is none. *English*

COMPARISON

2600. Comparisons are odious. *English*

2601. Comparison is not proof. *French*

COMPETITION

2602. Competition and reward induce a child to work. *African (Yoruba)*

COMPLAIN

2603. He that always complains is never pitied. *English*

2604. He who complains much does little. *African (Swahili)*

COMPLAINT

2605. Don't make complaints against a gift. *Japanese*

COMPLIMENTING

2606. Complimenting is lying. *English*

COMPROMISE

2607. A bad compromise is better than a good lawsuit. *French*

2608. A bad compromise is better than a successful suit. *Spanish*

2609. A lean compromise is better than a fat lawsuit. *Dutch*

COMRADE

2610. He who walks is not a comrade to him who rides. *Russian*

CONCEALER

2611. The concealer is as bad as the thief. *German*

CONCEIT

2612. Conceit and an empty purse are no companions.   *Yiddish*

CONCENTRATION

2613. Concentration brings near the distant camp.   *African (Fulani)*

2614. Too much concentration of thought does not produce a plan.
Japanese

CONCERN

2615. Of what does not concern you say nothing good or bad.   *Italian*

CONCUBINE

2616. Nobody can betray you so completely as your favorite concubine.
Russian

CONDITION

2617. Condition makes, condition breaks.   *Scottish*

2618. The first condition of friendship is to agree with each other.
Egyptian

2619. Who changes his condition changes fortune.   *Italian*

CONE

2620. A fir cone does not fall far from the tree.   *Estonian*

CONFECTIONER

2621. The confectioner likes bread best.   *Russian*

CONFERENCE

2622. Best is a conference from which comes peace.   *Irish*

CONFESSION

2623. A generous confession disarms slander.   *English*

2624. Any time of the day is good for confession.   *Hebrew*

2625. Confession by the defendant is as good as a hundred witnesses.
Hebrew

2626. Confession is the first step to repentance.   *English*

2627. Confession of a fault is half amends.   *Scottish*

2628. Open confession is good for the soul.   *Scottish*

2629. The confession of a fault removes half its guilt.   *Indian (Tamil)*

CONFIDENCE

2630. Confidence begets confidence.
German

2631. Confidence is half the victory.
Hebrew

2632. Mutual confidence is the pillar of friendship.   *Chinese*

2633. Too much confidence is destructive.   *Philippine*

2634. Woe to him who gives his confidence to a woman.   *Irish*

CONQUER

2635. He that would conquer must fight.   *English*

2636. Would you be strong, conquer yourself.   *German*

CONQUEROR

2637. The conquerors are kings; the defeated are bandits.   *Chinese*

CONSCIENCE

2638. A clear conscience can bear any trouble.   *English*

2639. A clear conscience is a good pillow.   *French*

2640. A clear conscience is a sure card.   *English*

2641. A clear conscience is more valuable than wealth. *Philippine*

2642. A clear conscience laughs at false accusations. *English*

2643. A clear conscience sleeps during thunder. *Jamaican*

2644. A good conscience is a continual feast. *English*

2645. A good conscience is a soft pillow. *German*

2646. A good conscience is the best divinity. *English*

2647. A guilty conscience is a self-accuser. *English*

2648. A guilty conscience needs no accuser. *Philippine*

2649. A guilty conscience runs and hides; it is ever fearful though. *Philippine*

2650. A guilty conscience self-accuses. *Scottish*

2651. A quiet conscience causes a quiet sleep. *English*

2652. A safe conscience makes a sound sleep. *Scottish*

2653. An evil conscience breaks many a man's neck. *English*

2654. Conscience is as good as a thousand witnesses. *Italian*

2655. Conscience is the nest where all good is hatched. *Welsh*

2656. Conscience is the sentry of virtue and righteousness. *Japanese*

2657. Conscience serves for a thousand witnesses. *English*

2658. If all your life you have had a clear conscience, you need not fear a knock at the door at midnight. *Chinese*

CONSENT

2659. An ignorant consent is no consent. *American*

CONSEQUENCE

2660. Suffer the consequences of your deeds. *Philippine*

CONSIDERATION

2661. Consideration is half conversion. *English*

2662. Consideration is the first born, calculation the next, wisdom the third. *African (Yoruba)*

2663. Consideration is the parent of wisdom. *English*

CONSISTENCY

2664. Consistency of action is the measure of greatness. *Indian (Tamil)*

CONSPIRACY

2665. Conspiracy is stronger than witchcraft. *Haitian*

CONSULTING

2666. Too much consulting confounds. *English*

CONTEMPT

2667. Contempt will sooner kill an injury than revenge. *English*

CONTENT (adjective)

2668. He has enough who is content. *French*

CONTENT (contentment)

2669. Content is all. *English*

2670. Content is happiness. *English*

2671. Content is more than kingdom. *English*

2672. Content is the philosopher's stone, that turns all it touches into gold. *English*

2673. Content is worth a crown. *English*

2674. Content lodges oftener in cottages than palaces. *English*

2675. He who wants content, can't find an easy chair. *English*

CONTENTMENT

2676. Contentment is an inexhaustible treasure. *Turkish*

2677. Contentment is happiness. *Korean*

2678. Contentment is the greatest wealth. *English*

CONTEST

2679. From trivial things great contests oft arise. *Dutch*

CONTRACT

2680. No one makes contracts with God. *Russian*

CONTRIVANCE

2681. Contrivance is better than force. *French*

CONTROL

2682. Self control excels control of a beast. *African (Hausa)*

CONVERSATION

2683. One evening's conversation with a superior man is better than ten years of study. *Chinese*

2684. The conversation between husband and wife no one knows about. *African (Ashanti)*

CONVERSE

2685. He that converses not, knows nothing. *English*

COOK (noun)

2686. A cook does not upset his own stomach. *Yiddish*

2687. A cook is known by his knife. *English*

2688. A lovelorn cook oversalts the porridge. *German*

2689. All are not cooks who wear long knives. *Dutch*

2690. An ill cook should have a good cleaver. *Scottish*

2691. Even if a cook were to cook a fly, he would still keep a wing for himself. *Polish*

2692. Every cook praises his own broth. *English*

2693. Cooks are not to be taught in their own kitchen. *English*

2694. He's an ill cook that can't lick his own fingers. *English*

2695. The more cooks, the worse broth. *Danish*

2696. Too many cooks burn the food. *Lebanese*

2697. Too many cooks oversalt the porridge. *Dutch*

2698. Too many cooks overspice the food. *Slovakian*

2699. Too many cooks spoil the broth. *English*

2700. When the cook and the steward fall out we hear who stole the butter. *Dutch*

2701. Where there are too many cooks the soup will be too salty. *Italian*

COOK (verb)

2702. He who cooks a bad thing, eats of it. *Egyptian*

COOKING

2703. Before cooking, one must have provisions. *African (Wolof)*

COOP

2704. When the coop is secure, the geese will grow fatter. *Yiddish*

COPPER

2705. Do not throw away your copper for the sake of gold's glitter.
African (Swahili)

2706. Everybody thinks of his copper as gold. *German*

CORD

2707. When the cord is tightest it is nearest snapping. *Danish*

CORDIAL

2708. Too much cordial will destroy.
English

CORK

2709. The cork is always bigger than the mouth of the bottle. *Estonian*

CORN

2710. A poor man's corn always grows thin. *Danish*

2711. Corn can grow on manure.
Yiddish

2712. Corn is not to be gathered in the blade but the ear. *English*

2713. Corn rustles less than straw.
Russian

2714. Do not spread your corn to dry at an enemy's door. *Spanish*

2715. Good corn is not reaped from a bad field. *Danish*

2716. He who farms is spared the trouble of buying corn.
African (Hausa)

2717. Much corn lies under the straw that is not seen. *English*

2718. No corn without chaff. *Dutch*

2719. Nobody carries corn to a worn out mill to be milled. *Mexican*

2720. One does not beat the corn on account of the chaff. *Russian*

2721. One reaps the same corn one sows. *Finnish*

2722. Sown corn is not lost. *English*

2723. The corn falls out of a shaken sheaf. *French*

2724. The corn passes from hand to hand, but comes at last to the mill.
Egyptian

2725. The corn that is taken to a bad mill, will be badly ground. *Danish*

2726. When there is nothing to eat but corn, rice is a luxury.
African (Hausa)

2727. There is no corn without weeds. *Polish*

2728. Very good corn grows in little fields. *French*

2729. When there is corn the measure will be found. *Russian*

2730. You can't grow corn on the ceiling. *Yiddish*

CORNER

2731. The corner of the house may be explored and seen, but not the corner of the heart. *Australian (Maori)*

2732. Three corners of the house rest upon the wife; the fourth upon the husband. *Slovakian*

CORPORAL

2733. Whoever takes the stick is the corporal. *Russian*

CORPSE

2734. A corpse and an uninvited guest stink after a couple of days.
Mexican

2735. As the corpse rots away grief grows less. *Maltese*

CORRECTION

2736. Correction brings fruit. *Dutch*

2737. Correction gives understanding. *English*

2738. Correction is good when administered in time. *Danish*

CORRUPTION

2739. The corruption of best is worst. *English*

2740. The corruption of one is the generation of another. *English*

COST (noun)

2741. Better is cost upon something worth than expense on nothing worth. *English*

2742. More cost more worship. *English*

2743. There's a daily cost, and all of it lost. *English*

2744. What you learn to your cost you remember long. *Danish*

2745. What you lose on the cost you will gain in the wear. *Malaysian*

COST (verb)

2746. It costs nothing to look. *Yiddish*

2747. It doesn't cost anything to ask. *Russian*

2748. It doesn't cost anything to look. *Russian*

2749. It doesn't cost anything to promise and to love. *Yiddish*

2750. What costs little is little esteemed. *English*

2751. What costs nothing is worth nothing. *Dutch*

COTTAGE

2752. A cottage in which you have not slept yet you should not praise. *African (Shona)*

2753. A thatched cottage with love is still better than a tile-roofed castle without it. *Vietnamese*

2754. Better a cottage for a home than a palace to visit as a stranger. *Welsh*

2755. Better inside a cottage than outside a castle. *Welsh*

2756. I'll not change a cottage in possession for a kingdom in hope. *English*

2757. It is better to live in a small cottage of one's own than in a palace with other people. *Maltese*

COTTON

2758. Cotton cannot play with fire. *Turkish*

COTTON TREE

2759. A cotton tree may be ever so big, but a little axe can fell it. *Jamaican*

COUGH

2760. A dry cough is the trumpeter of death. *English*

COUNCIL

2761. Do not bring weariness to a council by having all the talk to yourself. *Turkish*

2762. Every council brings forth war. *American*

2763. He who does not listen does not sit at the council. *African (Bemba)*

COUNSEL (noun)

2764. A woman's counsel is sometimes good. *English*

2765. A woman's first counsel is the best. *Danish*

2766. Alone in counsel, alone in sorrow. *Danish*

2767. Come not to counsel uncalled.
Scottish

2768. Counsel after action is like rain after harvest.   *Danish*

2769. Counsel before action.   *Dutch*

2770. Counsel breaks not the head.
English

2771. Counsel is no command.
English

2772. Counsel is nothing against love.
Italian

2773. Counsel is to be given by the wise, the remedy by the rich. *English*

2774. Counsel must be followed, not praised.   *English*

2775. Everybody knows good counsel except him that has need of it.
German

2776. Evil counsel is the root of misfortune.   *African (Hausa)*

2777. Good counsel comes overnight.
German

2778. Good counsel does no harm.
English

2779. Good counsel is lacking when most needed.   *English*

2780. Good counsel is no better than bad counsel if it be not taken in time.
Danish

2781. Good counsel never comes amiss.   *English*

2782. Good counsel never comes too late.   *German*

2783. He that refuses to buy counsel cheap, shall buy repentance dear.
English

2784. If the counsel be good, no matter who gave it.   *English*

2785. Ill counsel hurts the counsellor.
English

2786. Of hasty counsel take good heed, for haste is very rarely speed.
Dutch

2787. Receive an old man's counsel and a learned man's knowledge. *Greek*

2788. Short counsel is good counsel.
English

2789. Take counsel before it goes ill, lest it go worse.   *Dutch*

2790. Take not counsel in the combat.
English

2791. Taking counsel is a noble precept.   *Turkish*

2792. To give counsel to a fool is like throwing water on a goose.   *Danish*

2793. We have better counsel to give than to take.   *English*

2794. Where there's counsel, there's also love.   *Russian*

2795. Who follows his wife's counsel tumbles into hell.   *Hebrew*

2796. Woe to him who does not heed a good wife's counsel.   *Irish*

2797. Women's counsels are often fatal.   *Icelandic*

COUNSEL (verb)

2798. He that will not be counselled cannot be helped.   *English*

2799. Many want to counsel others without themselves knowing right from left.   *German*

COUNTRY

2800. A country may go to ruin but its mountains and streams remain.
Japanese

2801. A country without a king, a family without a head. *Indian (Tamil)*

2802. A country without freedom is like a prisoner with hands tied.
Philippine

2803. A fool's country is where his family is.   *Russian*

2804. A man's country is where he does well.   *English*

2805. As countries differ, their languages differ also. *Indian (Tamil)*

2806. Every country has its beauty. *Moroccan*

2807. Every country has its custom. *Spanish*

2808. If you want to have a country ruined, pray that it may have many heads. *Lebanese*

2809. So many countries, so many customs. *English*

2810. The country pays for all. *American*

2811. There are many people but there is only one native country. *Philippine*

2812. When a country is in disorder loyal men appear. *Japanese*

2813. When you enter a country, inquire as to what is forbidden; when you cross a boundary, ask about the customs. *Chinese*

COUPLE

2814. Every couple is not a pair. *English*

COURAGE

2815. Before the time great courage; when at the point, great fear. *Spanish*

2816. Courage beats the enemy. *Philippine*

2817. Courage ought to have eyes as well as arms. *English*

2818. Courage vanquishes some sufferings and patience the others. *Finnish*

2819. Courage without discretion is useless. *Philippine*

2820. Evading the enemy is true courage. *Philippine*

2821. It is courage that vanquishes in war, and not good weapons. *Spanish*

2822. Who has no courage must have legs. *Italian*

COURSE

2823. He who pursues a vicious course will try to lead others into the same. *Indian (Tamil)*

COURT

2824. At court, every one for himself. *English*

2825. Courts keep no almanacs. *English*

2826. One of the court, but none of the counsel. *English*

2827. Set foot into court and your hand goes into your pocket. *Russian*

2828. The court is straight but the judge is crooked. *Russian*

COURTESY

2829. A courtesy much entreated is half recompensed. *English*

2830. Courtesy is compatible with bravery. *Mexican*

2831. Courtesy on one side only lasts not long. *English*

2832. Courtesy that is all on one side cannot last long. *French*

2833. Even among intimate friends there should be courtesy. *Japanese*

2834. Excessive courtesy can harm no one. *Philippine*

2835. Full of courtesy and full of craft. *English*

2836. He may freely receive courtesies, that knows how to require them. *English*

2837. He that asks a courtesy promises a kindness. *English*

2838. It's a rank courtesy when a man is forced to give thanks for his own. *English*

2839. Lip courtesy avails much and costs little.   *Spanish*

2840. Proper courtesy should be observed even between close friends.
                                          Japanese

COURTIER

2841. A courtier should be without feeling and without honor.   *French*

COURTSHIP

2842. A short courtship is the best courtship.   *Manx*

COUSIN

2843. Too many cousins ruin the shopkeeper.   *Jamaican*

COVER (noun)

2844. According to your cover stretch your legs.   *Libyan*

COVER (verb)

2845. He that covers you, discovers you.   *English*

COVERING

2846. He whose covering belongs to others is uncovered.   *Libyan*

COVETOUSNESS

2847. Covetousness breaks the sack.
                                          English

2848. Covetousness brings nothing home.   *English*

2849. Covetousness is always filling a bottomless vessel.   *English*

2850. Covetousness is never satisfied till its mouth is filled with earth.
                                          Dutch

2851. Covetousness is the father of disease.   *African (Yoruba)*

2852. Covetousness is the father of unsatisfied desires.   *African (Yoruba)*

2853. Covetousness is the mother of ruin and mischief.   *English*

2854. Covetousness often starves other vices.   *English*

2855. When all sins grow old, covetousness is young.   *English*

COW

2856. A big cow is known by its hooves.   *African (Ovambo)*

2857. A cow among calves does not grow old.   *African (Ovambo)*

2858. A cow does not know the value of its tail until it is cut off.
                                  African (Swahili)

2859. A cow does not know what her tail is worth until she has lost it. *French*

2860. A cow eats moving, a horse eats standing.   *Indian (Tamil)*

2861. A cow from afar gives plenty of milk.   *French*

2862. A cow is milked by gentle handling.   *African (Hausa)*

2863. A cow is tied by its horns, a man by his tongue.   *Slovakian*

2864. A cow may be black, but her milk is white.   *Serbo-Croatian*

2865. A cow never goes so far that her tail does not follow.   *Norwegian*

2866. A cow that has been scorched by the sun will pant even on seeing the moon.   *Korean*

2867. A cow will not hear that the hay is dwindling away.   *Norwegian*

2868. A cow with a mouth has no milk.   *African (Zulu)*

2869. A lowing cow soon forgets her calf.   *English*

2870. A restless cow must be milked by force, and a gentle cow must be milked with kindness. *Indian (Tamil)*

2871. After dark every cow is black.
                                        Slovakian

2872. An ill cow may have a good calf. *Scottish*

2873. An ill-natured cow should have short horns. *Scottish*

2874. An old cow does not remember having been a calf. *Finnish*

2875. At night all cows are black. *Yiddish*

2876. Be the cow ever so poor it is not like a wild animal. *African (Fulani)*

2877. Better one cow in peace than seven in trouble. *Danish*

2878. Better one cow in the stable than ten in the field. *Yiddish*

2879. Black cows give white milk. *German*

2880. However much milk the cow has it will not milk butter. *African (Fulani)*

2881. If you buy the cow, take the tail into the bargain. *English*

2882. If you love the cow you will love the calf. *Jamaican*

2883. It is not for the good of the cow when she is driven in a carriage. *Danish*

2884. It is the old cow's notion that she never was a calf. *French*

2885. It is well that wicked cows have short horns. *Dutch*

2886. Like cow like calf. *English*

2887. Many a good cow has an evil calf. *English*

2888. Many a good cow has but a bad calf. *Manx*

2889. Milk the cow, but don't pull off the udder. *Dutch*

2890. Milk the cow that stands still. *English*

2891. Often a cow does not take after its breed. *Irish*

2892. The cow does not know the value of her tail till she has lost it. *Dutch*

2893. The cow does not sell straw. *Maltese*

2894. The cow finds it difficult to deliver its calf. *African (Zulu)*

2895. The cow gives good milk, but kicks over the pail. *English*

2896. The cow is milked by one who knows it. *African (Zulu)*

2897. The cow knows not what her tail is worth till she has lost it. *English*

2898. The cow licks no strange calf. *German*

2899. The cow that does not eat with the oxen either eats before or after them. *Spanish*

2900. The cow that's first up gets the first of the dew. *Scottish*

2901. The cows that low most give the least milk. *German*

2902. The cow withholds its milk when prodded, but it yields much when coaxed. *African (Zulu)*

2903. The laggard cow gets the sour grass. *Danish*

2904. Though a cow wanders here and there it does not trample its young. *African (Ovambo)*

2905. Though a cow yields three measures of milk, it is not desirable if it pulls down the roof. *Indian (Tamil)*

2906. Though it may yield a large pot of milk, a cow that destroys the roof is not desirable. *Indian (Tamil)*

2907. Though the cow gives a large pot of milk, it is not equal to the horse in speed. *Indian (Tamil)*

2908. When one cow has started to move it raises the others from their rest. *African (Ovambo)*

2909. Where the cow is, there is her calf. *Indian (Hindi)*

2910. You cannot sell the cow and sup the milk. *Scottish*

2911. You cannot take a cow from a man who has none. *Danish*

2912. You catch a cow by her horns, but a man by his words. *Jamaican*

2913. You may kill even a cow that aims to kill you. *Indian (Tamil)*

COWARD

2914. A coward's fear can make a coward valiant. *English*

2915. A coward has no scar. *African (Shona)*

2916. A coward often deals a mortal blow to the brave. *French*

2917. Better be a coward than foolhardy. *French*

2918. Between two cowards, he has the advantage who first detects the other. *Italian*

2919. Cowards are cruel. *English*

2920. Cowards die often. *English*

2921. Cowards don't play at cards. *Russian*

2922. Cowards have no luck. *German*

2923. Even a coward pursues him who runs away. *Czech*

2924. Make a coward fight and he will kill the devil. *English*

2925. Many would be cowards, if they had courage enough. *English*

2926. Nobody is a coward when his rights are trampled upon. *Philippine*

2927. The coward follows his mother. *African (Ovambo)*

2928. The real coward runs even if he is not wounded. *Philippine*

COWARDICE

2929. To evade danger is not cowardice. *Philippine*

COWL

2930. It is the cowl that makes the friar. *Dutch*

CRAB

2931. A crab does not beget a bird. *African (Ga)*

2932. A crab does not give birth to a bird. *African (Ashanti)*

2933. As the parent crab crawls, so does its young. *Philippine*

2934. Confused crabs miss their holes. *Japanese*

2935. The coral crab when cornered will fight for its life. *Philippine*

2936. The crab digs a hole according to its shell. *Japanese*

2937. The crab that lies always in its hole is never fat. *Manx*

2938. The greatest crabs are not always the best meat. *English*

2939. The sand crab is small, but digs a deep hole. *Hawaiian*

CRABGRASS

2940. Crabgrass grows overnight. *Yiddish*

CRADLE

2941. Cast not your cradle over your head. *English*

2942. What is learned in the cradle lasts till the grave. *French*

CRAFT

2943. A craft is a kingdom! *Yiddish*

2944. All the craft is in the catching. *English*

2945. Be not ashamed of your craft.
German

2946. Craft against craft makes no living. *English*

2947. Craft brings nothing home.
English

2948. Craft must have clothes, but truth loves to go naked. *English*

2949. He that has not craft, let him shut up shop. *English*

2950. Of all crafts, to be an honest man is the master craft. *English*

CRAFTSMAN

2951. If you are a craftsman, your wallet is full. *Yiddish*

2952. The bad craftsman quarrels with his tools. *African (Swahili)*

2953. The craftsman should be recognized by the tools of his craft.
African (Hausa)

CRANE

2954. A thousand cranes in the air are not worth one sparrow in the fist.
Egyptian

2955. The cranes are caught because they are lured by the bait. *Vietnamese*

2956. When the crane attempts to dance with the horse it gets broken bones. *Danish*

CRAVING

2957. Oft craving makes soon forgetting. *English*

2958. Shameless craving must have a shameless nay. *English*

CREAK

2959. That which creaks must be oiled. *Latvian*

CREAM

2960. Cream is thicker than water.
American

CREASE

2961. Better a crease in the shoe than a blister on the toe. *Estonian*

CREDIT

2962. Better sell cheap than for credit.
African (Hausa)

2963. Credit is better than ready money. *German*

2964. Credit is invisible fortune.
Japanese

2965. He that has lost his credit is dead to the world. *English*

2966. He who drinks on credit gets doubly drunk. *Rumanian*

2967. Nothing seems expensive on credit. *Czech*

CREDITOR

2968. Creditors have better memories than debtors. *English*

CREDULOUS

2969. Better be too credulous than too skeptical. *Chinese*

CREEP

2970. He that creeps falls not. *Dutch*

2971. One has to creep before one can go. *Finnish*

CRICKET

2972. Until the crickets sing it is not summer. *Greek*

CRIME

2973. A crime is always denied.
African (Zulu)

2974. Crime cries out for punishment.
Philippine

2975. It is easier for a cow to pass through the eye of a needle than to hide a crime. *Philippine*

2976. It's no crime to steal from a thief. *Yiddish*

2977. Many are cursed for the crime of one. *African (Ovambo)*

2978. What greater crime than loss of time? *English*

CRIPPLE

2979. A cripple in the right road beats a racer in the wrong road. *American*

CRITIC

2980. Critics are like brushers of noblemen's clothes. *English*

2981. Critics say more than the poet. *Indian (Bihar)*

2982. To be a critic is easier than to be an author. *Hebrew*

CRITICISM

2983. He who is critical is the one most deserving of criticism. *Philippine*

CROCODILE

2984. A crocodile cares not whether the water is deep or shallow. *Indian (Tamil)*

2985. A young crocodile does not die in the river. *African (Ga)*

2986. Don't think there are no crocodiles because the water's calm. *Malaysian*

2987. No crocodile shoves away carcass. *Philippine*

2988. Rather be swallowed whole by a crocodile, than nibbled by tiny fishes all the while. *Malaysian*

2989. There's a crocodile in every big river. *Philippine*

2990. Two crocodiles cannot agree. *African (Swahili)*

2991. Two crocodiles do not live in one hole. *African (Ga)*

CROOKED

2992. Unless you are crooked you can't get along in the world. *Japanese*

CROP

2993. A good crop, sell early; a bad crop, sell late. *Russian*

2994. A very good crop is worse than a very bad one. *Russian*

2995. Let your prayers for a good crop be short and your hoeing long. *Albanian*

2996. The future crop is known in the germ. *Indian (Tamil)*

CROSS

2997. Both the cross and the gallows are made of wood. *Polish*

2998. Crosses are ladders to heaven. *English*

2999. Every cross has its inscription. *English*

3000. Every one bears his cross. *French*

3001. Every one thinks his own cross the heaviest. *Italian*

3002. He that bears the cross blesses himself first. *Danish*

3003. The cross on the breast, and the devil in the heart. *English*

3004. There are many crosses upon a cemetery, but no cares. *Lithuanian*

3005. There is no cross that is not heavy. *Philippine*

3006. You are sure to find another cross if you flee the one you bear. *Mexican*

CROTCH

3007. One cannot run on two crotches. *Japanese*

CROW

3008. A crow does not lay dove's eggs. *Greek*

3009. A crow is never the whiter for often washing. *Danish*

3010. A flying crow always catches something. *Dutch*

3011. A once frightened crow is even afraid of a bush. *Russian*

3012. A sitting crow starves. *Icelandic*

3013. A whitewashed crow will not remain white long. *Chinese*

3014. As the crow is, so is its egg. *Philippine*

3015. Crows are black the whole world over. *Chinese*

3016. Crows are never the whiter for washing themselves. *English*

3017. Crows gather where the carrion lies. *Rumanian*

3018. Crows do not pick out crows' eyes. *English*

3019. Every crow thinks its own young one prettiest. *Scottish*

3020. From a crow's beak comes a crow's voice. *Greek*

3021. If the crows knew that they are black, they would not go about close to the storks. *Vietnamese*

3022. In its own nest even the crow will pick the vulture's eyes. *Russian*

3023. Like crow like egg. *English*

3024. Old crows are hard to catch. *German*

3025. One crow does not make a winter. *Dutch*

3026. One crow does not peck out another's eyes. *Dutch*

3027. The crow bewails the sheep, and then eats it. *English*

3028. The crow does not roost with the phoenix. *Chinese*

3029. The crow flies high but settles on a hog. *Yiddish*

3030. The crow thinks her own birds fairest. *English*

3031. The crow will find its mate. *Danish*

3032. When the crows sing the nightingales fly away. *Greek*

CROWD

3033. A crowd of people in a marketplace is like a puppet show. *Indian (Tamil)*

3034. He who does not mix with the crowd knows nothing. *Spanish*

3035. He who follows the crowd has many companions. *German*

3036. In a crowd one neither gets well fed nor starves. *African (Ovambo)*

CROWN

3037. A crown is no cure for the headache. *Dutch*

3038. The crown of a good disposition is humility. *Egyptian*

CRUELTY

3039. Cruelty is a tyrant that's always attended with fear. *English*

CRUMB

3040. Even crumbs are bread. *Danish*

3041. Where there are crumbs there will be mice. *Russian*

CRUST

3042. Even a crust is bread. *Finnish*

CRY

3043. Much cry and little wool.
English

CUCKOLD

3044. A discontented cuckold has not wit. *English*

3045. Cuckolds are kind. *English*

3046. It is better to be a cuckold and not know it, than be none, and everybody say so. *English*

3047. Let every cuckold wear his own horns. *English*

3048. The cuckold is the last that knows of it. *English*

3049. To be a cuckold and know it not is no more than to drink with a fly in the cup and see it not. *English*

3050. Who is a cuckold and conceals it carries coals in his bosom. *English*

CUCKOO

3051. Everybody thinks his own cuckoo sings better than another's nightingale. *German*

3052. One cuckoo doesn't make the spring. *Greek*

3053. The cuckoo doesn't sing until he sees the buds of spring. *Rumanian*

3054. The cuckoo sings while the lazy man sits and counts. *Rumanian*

CUNNING

3055. Cunning has little honor.
Danish

3056. Cunning is better than strength. *Irish*

3057. Cunning is followed by foolishness. *African (Ovambo)*

3058. Cunning is no burden.
English

3059. Cunning surpasses strength.
German

3060. The cunning of women is strong, and the cunning of the devil is weak. *Moroccan*

3061. The greatest cunning is to have none at all. *French*

3062. The most cunning are the first caught. *French*

3063. Too much cunning undoes.
English

CUP

3064. A full cup must be carried steadily. *English*

3065. It is hard to carry a full cup without spilling. *English*

3066. Such a cup, such a cruse.
English

3067. Such cup, such cover. *English*

3068. The cup finds not out its master's death. *African (Wolof)*

3069. When the cup is full carry it even. *Scottish*

3070. When the cup is fullest, then carry it most carefully. *English*

CUPIDITY

3071. Cupidity has no peak.
Japanese

CUR

3072. Brawling curs never want sore ears. *English*

CURE (noun)

3073. For the disease of stubborness there is no cure. *Yiddish*

3074. He that bewails himself has the cure in his hands. *English*

3075. Past cure, past care. *English*

3076. The cure for old age is the grave. *Russian*

3077. The only cure for sorrow is to kill it with patience. *Irish*

3078. There is no cure against a slanderer's bite.   *Danish*

CURE (verb)

3079. What can't be cured must be endured.   *English*

CURIOSITY

3080. Curiosity caused the roebuck to be shot in the eye.   *African (Ovambo)*

3081. Curiosity is endless, restless, and useless.   *English*

3082. Curiosity is ill manners in another's house.   *English*

3083. Curiosity often leads men into bitterness.   *African (Wolof)*

CURRANT

3084. One can't get currants without stalks.   *Pashto*

CURRENT

3085. You can't swim long against the current without cutting your throat as a pig does.   *American*

CURRY

3086. When the curry is tasty, the rice will be raw.   *Malaysian*

CURSE

3087. A curse is not a telegram: it doesn't arrive so fast.   *Yiddish*

3088. A curse spoken is like a donkey; it always follows its master.   *Greek*

3089. A curse will not strike out an eye, unless the fist go with it.   *Danish*

3090. A curse without causes does not pass through the door.   *Moroccan*

3091. Better to hear curses than to be pitied.   *Yiddish*

3092. Curses come back to yourself.   *Japanese*

3093. Curses come home to roost.   *English*

3094. Curses like chickens come home to roost.   *Jamaican*

3095. Neither with curses nor with laughter can you change the world.   *Yiddish*

3096. There is a curse on stolen goods.   *Serbo-Croatian*

3097. There is no worse curse than to desire a man's death.   *African (Efik)*

CUSTOM

3098. A bad custom is like a good cake, better broken than kept. *English*

3099. An old custom will prevail.   *Welsh*

3100. Custom and law are sisters.   *Slovakian*

3101. Custom becomes law.   *Spanish*

3102. Custom is a fifth nature.   *Egyptian*

3103. Custom is nature to a man.   *Turkish*

3104. Custom is rust that mocks at every file.   *Czech*

3105. Custom is second nature.   *English*

3106. Custom is stronger than law.   *Russian*

3107. Custom is the twin of the innate character.   *Egyptian*

3108. Custom makes all things easy.   *English*

3109. Custom without reason is but ancient error.   *English*

3110. Follow and adjust to current customs in order to get along with others.   *Philippine*

3111. National customs are national honors.   *Danish*

3112. Once is no custom.   *Dutch*

3113. To change customs is a difficult thing.   *Lebanese*

3114. When you enter a village, observe its customs.   *Korean*

CUSTOMER

3115. Cheated customers and satisfied customers balance each other.
                                        Malagasy

3116. Customers are the precious things; goods are only grass.   *Chinese*

3117. The customer is known to the shopkeeper.   *Indian (Kashmiri)*

CUT

3118. Cutting out well is better than sewing.   *English*

3119. Don't cut without measuring.
                                        Iranian

∽D∽

DAGGER

3120. In a narrow lane watch out for a dagger. *Chinese*

3121. No one murders with a golden dagger. *Indian (Hindi)*

DAMAGE

3122. Damage suffered makes you knowing, but seldom rich. *Danish*

DANCE (noun)

3123. As the dance so the music. *Polish*

3124. As you began the dance you may pay the piper. *Dutch*

3125. The dance is good when the music is good. *Philippine*

DANCE (verb)

3126. Dance alone and you can jump all you wish. *Greek*

3127. He who cannot dance declares that the ground is wet with rain. *Malaysian*

3128. If you dance you must pay the fiddler. *English*

3129. Not every one that dances is glad. *French*

3130. They who dance are thought mad by those who hear not the music. *English*

3131. When you go to dance, take heed whom you take by the hand. *English*

DANCER

3132. In the fiddler's house every one is a dancer. *French*

3133. The willing dancer is easily played to. *Hungarian*

3134. To a bad dancer even the hem of her skirt will be in the way. *Polish*

DANCING

3135. It's good dancing on another man's floor. *Dutch*

3136. More belongs to dancing than a pair of fine shoes. *Icelandic*

3137. They love dancing well that dance among the thorns. *English*

DANGER

3138. A common danger produces unity. *Slovakian*

3139. A danger foreseen is half avoided. *English*

3140. All is not lost that is in danger. *Spanish*

3141. Better pass a danger once than be always in fear. *English*

3142. Danger and delight grow on one stock. *English*

97

3143. Danger is next neighbor to security. *English*

3144. Danger makes men bold. *American*

3145. Danger past and God forgotten. *Scottish*

3146. Great dangers lead to great honors. *Greek*

3147. He is out of danger who rings the alarm bell. *Spanish*

3148. He that always fears danger always feels it. *English*

3149. He that fears danger in time seldom feels it. *English*

3150. He who turns aside avoids danger. *French*

3151. Shun danger and it will shun you. *Irish*

3152. The danger past, God is forgotten. *English*

3153. The danger past, our vows are soon forgotten. *English*

3154. The more danger, the more honor. *English*

3155. There's danger in delay. *American*

3156. Without danger we cannot get beyond danger. *English*

DARING

3157. Daring is noble business. *Russian*

DARKNESS

3158. Darkness and night are mothers of thought. *Dutch*

3159. The darkness of night is surer than the light of day. *Russian*

3160. The darkness of night will not prevent morn. *African (Fulani)*

DARLING

3161. Better be an old man's darling than become a young man's slave. *English*

DART

3162. A golden dart kills where it pleases. *English*

DAUGHTER

3163. A brilliant daughter makes a brittle wife. *Dutch*

3164. A daughter is a bad asset when the mother is to be wed. *Russian*

3165. A good daughter makes a good daughter-in-law. *Yiddish*

3166. After the daughter is married, then come sons-in-law in plenty. *French*

3167. Daughters and dead fish are no keeping wares. *English*

3168. Daughters and rotten fish should not be kept long. *Philippine*

3169. Daughters are easy to rear, but hard to marry. *German*

3170. Daughters are fragile ware. *Japanese*

3171. Daughters may be seen but not heard. *Dutch*

3172. Every only daughter has her charms. *Yiddish*

3173. He that would the daughter win must with the mother first begin. *English*

3174. One daughter helps to marry the other. *Italian*

3175. She spins a good thread that brings up her daughter well. *English*

3176. The crab's daughter does not bear a bird. *African (Oji)*

3177. The Rabbi's daughter is forbidden what the bathhouse keeper's daughter is allowed. *Yiddish*

3178. Two daughters and a back door are three arrant thieves. *English*

3179. When our daughter is married, sons-in-law are plenty. *Spanish*

3180. When you marry off a daughter, a hump is off your back. *Yiddish*

3181. Who the daughter would win, with the mother must begin. *German*

DAUGHTER-IN-LAW

3182. Daughter-in-law hates mother-in-law. *German*

3183. Even a clever daughter-in-law finds it hard to cook without rice. *Chinese*

DAWN

3184. However long the night, dawn will break. *African (Hausa)*

3185. With or without the crowing of the cock, dawn breaks. *Lebanese*

DAY

3186. A bad day has a good night. *English*

3187. A cold day or two or a little ice does not make winter. *American*

3188. A day in prison is longer than a thousand years at large. *Vietnamese*

3189. A day is long, but a lifetime is short. *Russian*

3190. A day to come shows longer than a year that's gone. *English*

3191. A day with your friend is better than a year with one who hates you. *African (Hausa)*

3192. A fine day is not a weather-breeder, but a fine day. *American*

3193. A spring day feeds the whole year. *Russian*

3194. Because of deceit day does not refuse to break. *African (Hausa)*

3195. Better reap two days too soon than one too late. *Dutch*

3196. Better the day, better the deed. *English*

3197. By day they're ready to divorce, by night they're ready for bed. *Yiddish*

3198. Day has its eyes, night has its ears. *Japanese*

3199. Don't think of the shortness of the day, but of the length of the year. *Malagasy*

3200. Every day brings a new light. *English*

3201. Every day brings forth its own sorrows. *Yiddish*

3202. Every day brings its bread with it. *English*

3203. Every day has its evening. *Danish*

3204. Every day has its fare. *Moroccan*

3205. Every day has its night. *Italian*

3206. Every day has its own fate. *Slovenian*

3207. Every day has its yoke; every hour its work. *Estonian*

3208. Every day is a messenger of God. *Russian*

3209. Every day is holiday with sluggards. *English*

3210. Every day is not holiday. *Dutch*

3211. Every day is not Sunday. *English*

3212. Every day is not yesterday. *English*

3213. Every day learns from the one that went before, but no day teaches the one that follows. *Russian*

3214. Everything may be bought except day and night. *French*

3215. Few days pass without some clouds. *English*

3216. It is a long day a day without bread. *French*

3217. It is day still while the sun shines. *English*

3218. It is never a bad day that has a good night. *English*

3219. No day so clear but has dark clouds. *English*

3220. No day so long but has its evening. *French*

3221. One day before you is better than ten years behind you. *Russian*

3222. One day blame, another day praise. *Indian (Tamil)*

3223. One day in perfect health is much. *Egyptian*

3224. One day is as good as two for him who does everything in its place. *French*

3225. One day is sometimes better than a whole year. *English*

3226. One day of pleasure is worth two of sorrow. *English*

3227. One day of prosperity is better than a year of poverty. *African (Hausa)*

3228. One day teaches the other. *Lithuanian*

3229. One day with the prosperous man is better than a year with the poor man. *African (Hausa)*

3230. One fair day assures not a good summer. *English*

3231. One fair day in winter makes not birds merry. *English*

3232. One good day often costs a hundred bad nights. *Swedish*

3233. One of these days is none of these days. *English*

3234. Pity the man who waits till the last day. *Irish*

3235. Praise a fair day in the evening. *Danish*

3236. Praise a fine day at night. *German*

3237. Praise not the day before night. *English*

3238. Praise the day in the evening. *Russian*

3239. That often happens in a day which does not happen in a hundred years. *French*

3240. The better day the better deed. *French*

3241. The days follow each other and are not alike. *French*

3242. The day has eyes and the night has ears. *Lebanese*

3243. The day is short and the work is long. *English*

3244. The day is sure to come when the cow will want her tail. *Danish*

3245. The day may come when the hawk and the eel may meet. *Philippine*

3246. The day obliterates the promise of the night. *Egyptian*

3247. The day of birth leads to death. *Indian (Tamil)*

3248. The days of poverty are more than the days of superfluity. *African (Ga)*

3249. The day we fear hastens toward us, the day we long for creeps. *Swedish*

3250. The day will dawn even without the rooster. *Armenian*

3251. The day you are unlucky, even the cold food burns. *African (Bemba)*

3252. The longest day must have an end. *English*

3253. There are many days in the year, and still more meals. *Danish*

3254. There is a day to be born and a day to die. *Chinese*

3255. There is a day to cast your nets and a day to dry your nets. *Chinese*

3256. There is no day without its night. *Portuguese*

3257. They take a long day that never pay. *English*

3258. To be for one day entirely at leisure is to be for one day an immortal. *Chinese*

3259. To learn what is good, a thousand days are not sufficient; to learn what is evil, an hour is too long. *Chinese*

3260. Treat the days well and they will treat you well. *African (Bemba)*

3261. What a day may bring, a day may take away. *English*

3262. When the day comes its counsel will come with it. *Manx*

3263. Who is tired of happy days, let him take a wife. *Dutch*

3264. Woe to him who waits until the last day. *Irish*

DEAD (adjective)

3265. When one is dead, it is for a long while. *French*

DEAD (noun)

3266. Don't bear a grudge against the dead. *Japanese*

3267. Let the dead rest. *German*

3268. One mourns for the dead seven days, but for a fool a whole lifetime. *Yiddish*

3269. The dead, and only they, should do nothing. *English*

3270. The dead and the absent have no friends. *Spanish*

3271. The dead are soon forgotten. *French*

3272. The dead have few friends. *English*

3273. The dead open the eyes of the living. *Portuguese*

DEAF

3274. None so deaf as those that won't hear. *English*

DEAL

3275. He who wants a good deal must not ask for a little. *Italian*

DEALING

3276. Plain dealing is a jewel. *English*

3277. Plain dealing is dead. *English*

3278. Plain dealing is praised more than practiced. *English*

DEATH

3279. After death one becomes important. *Yiddish*

3280. Any death is easier than death by the sword. *Irish*

3281. At your mother's death another one will not come. *African (Bemba)*

3282. Being thin is not death. *African (Hausa)*

3283. Better death than long sickness. *Welsh*

3284. Death alone measures equally. *Czech*

3285. Death answers before it is asked. *Russian*

3286. Death carries a fat Tsar on his shoulders as easily as a lean beggar. *Russian*

3287. Death combs us all with the same comb.   *Swedish*

3288. Death comes to us whether we are standing or sitting.   *Philippine*

3289. Death deals doubtfully.
                                    English

3290. Death defies the doctor.
                                    Scottish

3291. Death devours lambs as well as sheep.   *English*

3292. Death does not blow a trumpet.
                                    Danish

3293. Death does not come without a cause.   *Irish*

3294. Death for a common cause is beautiful.   *Russian*

3295. Death has no almanack.
                                    Russian

3296. Death has no mercy upon anyone.   *Lebanese*

3297. Death has no modesty.
                              African (Zulu)

3298. Death has the key to open the miser's chest.   *African (Ashanti)*

3299. Death in time of youth, poverty in time of age, are hard.   *Turkish*

3300. Death is a black camel that kneels at every door.   *Turkish*

3301. Death is a brother to the Russian soldier.   *Russian*

3302. Death is a camel that lies down at every door.   *Iranian*

3303. Death is blind.
                          African (Swahili)

3304. Death is concise like a good proverb.   *Russian*

3305. Death is not a sleeping room that can be entered and come out of again.   *African (Ashanti)*

3306. Death is the grand leveller.
                                    English

3307. Death is the last doctor.
                                    Swedish

3308. Death is the pursuer, disease the constant companion of man.
                                    Malagasy

3309. Death is the revealer of secrets.
                              African (Hausa)

3310. Death keeps no calendar.
                                    English

3311. Death may occur at six, or at a hundred years of age.   *Indian (Tamil)*

3312. Death never comes too late.
                                    Irish

3313. Death regards spring as winter.
                                    Russian

3314. Death rights everything.
                                    Maltese

3315. Death squares all accounts.
                                    English

3316. Death takes the poor man's cow and the rich man's child.   *French*

3317. Death when it comes will have no denial.   *English*

3318. Death will come uninvited.
                                    Lithuanian

3319. He pulls at a long rope who desires another's death.   *French*

3320. He that fears death lives not.
                                    English

3321. He waits long that waits for another man's death.   *Dutch*

3322. He who sees death, consents to sickness.   *Turkish*

3323. If one could know where death resided, one would never stop there.
                              African (Ashanti)

3324. If you start thinking of death, you are no longer sure of life.   *Yiddish*

3325. In death everyone is equal.
                                    Philippine

3326. Look upon death as a going home.   *Chinese*

3327. Men fear death as children do to go in the dark.   *English*

3328. No death without a cause.
Maltese

3329. No matter how long one may live, the day of death will come.
Indian (Tamil)

3330. On death all accounts are cancelled.   *Japanese*

3331. One cannot die before one's death.   *Russian*

3332. One is certain only of death.
Yiddish

3333. One man's death is another man's life.   *Maltese*

3334. Sometimes a quick death is better than a long life.   *Hungarian*

3335. Staying and staring is the death of the buck.   *African (Ovambo)*

3336. The death of a young wolf never comes too soon.   *English*

3337. The death of many is not wailed.   *African (Ovambo)*

3338. The death of one dog is the life of another dog.   *Manx*

3339. The death of the wolf is the health of the sheep.   *English*

3340. The death of wives and the life of sheep make men rich.   *English*

3341. The husband's death is the widow's sorrow.   *African (Yoruba)*

3342. There are not as many deaths as there are sorrows.   *Russian*

3343. Though you are starving to death, do not steal.   *Chinese*

3344. To the joyless man death is a blessing.   *African (Hausa)*

3345. Until death there is no knowing what may happen.   *Italian*

3346. We are living with death trailing us.   *Philippine*

3347. We do not even get death free of charge, for it costs us our life.
Russian

3348. What death takes it will not restore.   *Welsh*

3349. When death comes, the dog presses up to the wall of the mosque.
Turkish

3350. When death comes, the rich man has no money, the poor man no debt.   *Estonian*

3351. When death is on the tongue, repentance is not difficult.   *Polish*

3352. When death is there, dying is over.   *Russian*

DEBT

3353. A debt is extinguished by force of paying, a journey by force of walking.
Turkish

3354. A debt is not paid with words.
Turkish

3355. A debt of gold we can repay, kindness indebts till our dying day.
Malaysian

3356. A debt, of which there is no written acknowledgment, is not demanded.   *Turkish*

3357. A little debt makes a debtor, but a great one an enemy.   *English*

3358. A poor man's debt makes a great noise.   *English*

3359. An ounce of debt will not pay a pound of care.   *English*

3360. Better be in debt than in shame.   *Serbo-Croatian*

3361. Better go to bed without supper than to live with debts.   *Czech*

3362. Better old debts than old grudges.   *Irish*

3363. Better to go to bed supperless than run in debt.   *German*

3364. Debt is a bad companion.
Serbo-Croatian

3365. Debt is an evil conscience.
English

3366. Debt is better than death.
English

3367. Debt is the worst poverty.
English

3368. Debt is worse than poverty.
Slovakian

3369. Don't forget to pay your debts whether they have been forgotten or not. *Philippine*

3370. Everyone must pay his debt to nature. *German*

3371. Forgetting a debt does not pay it. *Irish*

3372. He that gets out of debt grows rich. *English*

3373. He who is without debt is without credit. *Italian*

3374. He who pays his debt adds to his capital. *Hebrew*

3375. He who pays his debts, betters his condition. *German*

3376. He who promises incurs a debt.
Spanish

3377. It is better to go to bed hungry than to wake up in debt. *Philippine*

3378. Of hunger and debt, debt is preferable. *African (Ashanti)*

3379. Old debts are better than old sores. *Scottish*

3380. Out of debt, out of danger.
English

3381. Out of debt, out of deadly sin.
English

3382. Reducing debt is better than swelling it. *African (Hausa)*

3383. The king's debts must be first paid. *American*

3384. Who pays a debt creates capital.
Italian

3385. With no debt there is no danger. *Japanese*

3386. Without debt without care.
Italian

3387. You cannot pay a debt with a noble pedigree. *Yiddish*

3388. You cannot pay a debt with a sigh. *Yiddish*

DEBTOR

3389. A debtor does not get angry.
African (Ga)

3390. Debtors are liars. *English*

DECEIT

3391. Deceit and treachery make no man rich. *Danish*

3392. In truth there is no deceit.
African (Ashanti)

3393. One deceit brings on another.
French

3394. The deceits of women are 99. The one which completes the 100, the devil knows it not. *African (Hausa)*

DECEIVE

3395. He that once deceives is ever suspected. *English*

3396. If a man deceive me once, shame on him; but if he deceive me twice, shame on me. *English*

3397. If you don't deceive, you won't sell it. *Russian*

DECEIVER

3398. A deceiver deceives himself.
Indian (Kashmiri)

DEED

3399. A deed well done pleases the heart. *English*

3400. A good deed bears interest.
Estonian

3401. A good deed is never lost.
English

3402. A good deed is the best prayer.
Mexican

3403. A good deed is written on snow.
Estonian

3404. All evil deeds are repaid on earth. *Greek*

3405. An evil deed has a witness in the bosom. *Danish*

3406. An evil deed, like smoke, cannot be hidden. *Philippine*

3407. Better a bad deed of a good person than a good deed of a bad one.
Yiddish

3408. By his deeds we know a man.
African (Jabo)

3409. Deeds are fruits, words are but leaves. *English*

3410. Deeds are love, and not fine phrases. *Spanish*

3411. Deeds are males, words are females. *English*

3412. Deeds are more fruitful than words. *Philippine*

3413. Deeds, not words. *English*

3414. Deeds, not words, are the true language of love. *Mexican*

3415. Each shameful deed carries with it its excuse. *Greek*

3416. Everybody should be rewarded for his own good deeds and punished for his own crimes. *Vietnamese*

3417. Evil deeds are like perfume; difficult to hide. *African (Jabo)*

3418. Evil deeds done in secret are seen by the spirits as a flash of fire.
Chinese

3419. For seven ill deeds, one needs to answer only once. *Russian*

3420. Good deeds are done by good people. *Hebrew*

3421. Good deeds are written on sand; bad deeds are graven upon rock.
Polish

3422. Good deeds never spoil.
African (Swahili)

3423. Good deeds return to the house of their author. *Iranian*

3424. Good deeds travel far; bad ones farther. *Russian*

3425. One deed is worth a thousand speeches. *American*

3426. One's own deed returns to oneself. *Korean*

3427. The bad deed turns on its doer.
Irish

3428. The best of the sport is to do the deed and say nothing. *English*

3429. The good deeds you do now are the treasure of the future. *Philippine*

3430. To see a man do a good deed is to forget all his faults. *Chinese*

DEEM

3431. Deem the best till the truth be tried out. *English*

DEER

3432. He who chases after a deer will take no notice of hares. *Korean*

3433. The deer that goes too often to the lick meets the hunter at last.
American

3434. Where the deer is slain, there will some of his blood lie. *English*

DEER HUNTER

3435. The deer hunter does not look at the hare. *Chinese*

DEFEAT

3436. One never reveals his defeats and the beating he has received from his wife. *Indian (Bihar)*

DEFECT

3437. Disclose not your defects even to a friend. *Indian (Tamil)*

3438. The defects in the eyelashes are not apparent to the eye.
Indian (Tamil)

3439. Though we see the seven defects of others, we do not see our own ten defects. *Japanese*

DEFENSE

3440. The best defense is offense.
American

DEFER

3441. Deferred is not annulled.
German

DELAY

3442. After a delay comes a let.
English

3443. After a delay comes a stay.
English

3444. All delay is to the good.
Hebrew

3445. Delays are dangerous. *English*

3446. Delays in love are dangerous.
Scottish

3447. Delay will lead to ruin.
Indian (Tamil)

3448. That is a wise delay which makes the road safe. *English*

DELIBERATE

3449. He who deliberates too much ruins his cause. *Burmese*

DELIBERATING

3450. Deliberating is not delaying.
English

DELIGHT

3451. Delights dwell as well in the cottage as the palace. *American*

DEMAND (noun)

3452. When the demand is a jest, the answer is a scoff. *English*

DEMAND (verb)

3453. He who demands does not command. *Italian*

DEMON

3454. Better be a demon in a large temple than a god in a small one.
Chinese

3455. Demons strike the timid.
Indian (Tamil)

DEMONSTRATION

3456. Mathematical demonstrations can no man gainsay. *American*

DENIAL

3457. A civil denial is better than a rude grant. *English*

3458. Better a friendly denial than an unwilling compliance. *German*

DENY

3459. Better to deny at once than to promise long. *Danish*

3460. He who denies everything confesses everything. *Spanish*

DEPART

3461. He who departs is forgotten daily. *Japanese*

DEPARTURE

3462. Departure on a journey is not death. *African (Fulani)*

3463. Every departure has an arrival.
Turkish

DEPEND

3464. Don't depend upon others—do it yourself. *Yiddish*

3465. He who depends on another dines ill and sups worse. *English*

DEPENDENCE

3466. Dependence is a poor trade.
English

DEPENDENT

3467. A dependent knows no happiness. *Indian (Bihar)*

DEPTH

3468. Do not step down unless you know the depth. *Indian (Tamil)*

DESERT

3469. Desert and reward seldom keep company. *English*

DESERVE

3470. First deserve and then desire. *English*

DESIRE (noun)

3471. A person's desires grow day by day. *Hebrew*

3472. A woman's wholehearted desire will pierce even a rock. *Japanese*

3473. Desires are nourished by delays. *English*

3474. Desire beautifies what is ugly. *Spanish*

3475. Desire conquers fear. *Irish*

3476. Desire doesn't equal destiny. *Malagasy*

3477. Desire has no rest. *English*

3478. Desire is for the handsome and rich. *Turkish*

3479. Desire is stronger than bondage. *Russian*

3480. Desire will entice beyond the bounds of reason. *Welsh*

3481. Every desire has wings. *Welsh*

3482. Excessive desire entails great loss. *Indian (Tamil)*

3483. If you have the desire, distance doesn't matter. *Philippine*

3484. If you have the desire, you must also have patience. *Russian*

3485. The desire to laugh is stronger than the desire to weep. *Burmese*

3486. The greater the inordinate desire, the greater the loss. *Indian (Tamil)*

3487. When the treasure house is full desire ceases. *African (Hausa)*

DESIRE (verb)

3488. He that desires but little has no need of much. *English*

DESPAIR

3489. Despair and hope are sisters. *Slovenian*

3490. Despair gives courage to a coward. *English*

3491. Despair never pays any debts. *American*

DESPERATE

3492. He is desperate that thinks himself so. *English*

DESPISE

3493. He that despises the little is not worthy of the great. *Dutch*

3494. If you despise yourself people will afterwards despise you. *Japanese*

DESTINY

3495. All destinies are not alike. *African (Ashanti)*

3496. Destiny and exertion must go together. *Indian (Tamil)*

3497. Destiny spoils plans. *Turkish*

3498. Even the swinging together of sleeves is preordained by destiny. *Japanese*

3499. He must stand high that would see the end of his own destiny. *Danish*

DESTITUTE

3500. The destitute does not live, but dies by inches. *Russian*

DETERMINATION

3501. There is nothing that cannot be achieved by firm determination.

Japanese

DETERMINED

3502. To him who is determined it remains only to act. *Italian*

DEVIL

3503. Better keep the devil at the door than turn him out of the house.

English

3504. Call not the devil, he will come fast enough unbidden. *Danish*

3505. Devils must be driven out with devils. *German*

3506. Do not make two devils of one.

French

3507. Even the devil cannot escape a woman. *Rumanian*

3508. Even the devil is not as black as he is painted. *Slovakian*

3509. Even the devil knows what is right, but he will not do it.

Serbo-Croatian

3510. Even the devil rocks the children of the rich. *Russian*

3511. Even the devil sometimes breaks his horns. *Japanese*

3512. Every devil has not a cloven foot. *English*

3513. Everyone has his own devil, and some have two. *Swedish*

3514. He must needs run, whom the devil drives. *Scottish*

3515. He that has swallowed the devil may swallow his horns. *Italian*

3516. He that is afraid of the devil does not grow rich. *Italian*

3517. He that is embarked with the devil must sail with him. *Dutch*

3518. He that sups with the devil needs a long spoon. *English*

3519. He that takes the devil into his boat, make the best of him. *English*

3520. He that the devil drives, feels no lead at his heels. *English*

3521. He who has once invited the devil into his house, will never be rid of him. *German*

3522. He who has shipped the devil, must carry him over the water.

English

3523. He who lives with a devil, becomes a devil. *Yiddish*

3524. If the devil catch a man idle, he'll set him at work. *English*

3525. If you buy the devil you must sell the devil. *English*

3526. Ill does the devil preserve his servant. *English*

3527. In time of war the devil makes more room in hell. *German*

3528. It is easy to bid the devil be your guest, but difficult to get rid of him. *Danish*

3529. It is not for nothing that the devil lays himself down in the ditch.

Danish

3530. It was surely the devil that taught women to dance and asses to bray. *English*

3531. Let the devil get into the church and he will mount the altar. *German*

3532. Let the devil into a church and he will climb into the pulpit. *Latvian*

3533. One devil does not make hell.

Italian

3534. One devil does not scratch out another devil's eyes. *Serbo-Croatian*

3535. One devil is like another.

English

3536. One devil knows another.
Italian

3537. Pulling the devil by the tail does not lead far young or old. *French*

3538. She devils are hard to tame.
English

3539. Talk of the devil and he'll appear. *English*

3540. Talk of the devil and you hear his bones rattle. *Dutch*

3541. The bigger the devil, the better soldier. *American*

3542. The devil can quote Scripture.
English

3543. The devil cannot go as far as a woman can. *Polish*

3544. The devil dares not peep under a maid's coat. *English*

3545. The devil does not destroy his own house. *Egyptian*

3546. The devil dreads holy water.
Maltese

3547. The devil gets up to the belfry by the vicar's skirts. *English*

3548. The devil has a chapel wherever God has a church. *English*

3549. The devil has his martyrs among men. *Dutch*

3550. The devil has no power over a drunkard. *English*

3551. The devil himself doesn't know where women sharpen their knives.
Latvian

3552. The devil is a busy bishop in his own diocese. *English*

3553. The devil is a knave. *English*

3554. The devil is an ass. *English*

3555. The devil is civil when he is flattered. *German*

3556. The devil is dead. *English*

3557. The devil is fond of his own.
Spanish

3558. The devil is God's ape. *English*

3559. The devil is good to his own.
English

3560. The devil is good when he is pleased. *English*

3561. The devil is in the dice.
English

3562. The devil is never so black as he is painted. *German*

3563. The devil is no match for a woman. *Polish*

3564. The devil is not always at a poor man's door. *French*

3565. The devil is not always at one door. *English*

3566. The devil is not so black as he is painted. *English*

3567. The devil is not so ugly as he is painted. *Italian*

3568. The devil is poor, he has no God. *Russian*

3569. The devil is seldom outshot in his own bow. *English*

3570. The devil is the root of all evil.
American

3571. The devil knows his Lord, but still practices evil. *Egyptian*

3572. The devil laughs when one thief robs another. *English*

3573. The devil lies brooding in the miser's chest. *English*

3574. The devil loves all colliers.
English

3575. The devil lurks behind the cross. *English*

3576. The devil makes pots and not lids. *Maltese*

3577. The devil often lurks behind the cross. *French*

3578. The devil often sits at the foot of the cross.   *Polish*

3579. The devil rebukes sin. *English*

3580. The devil rides upon a fiddlestick.   *English*

3581. The devil sits behind the cross.   *Dutch*

3582. The devil sometimes speaks the truth.   *English*

3583. The devil take the hindmost.   *English*

3584. The devil tempts some, but an idle man tempts the devil.   *English*

3585. The devil turns away from a closed door.   *Spanish*

3586. The devil was handsome when he was young.   *French*

3587. The devil was sick, the devil a monk would be; the devil was well, the devil a monk was he.   *English*

3588. The devil will be no saint though he be baptised in ninety-nine churches.   *Slovakian*

3589. The devil will take his own.   *English*

3590. The devil wipes his tail with the poor man's pride.   *English*

3591. The poorer one is, the more devils he meets.   *Chinese*

3592. The worst devil is the one who prays.   *Polish*

3593. There is a devil in every berry of the grape.   *English*

3594. Though the devil is up early, God is up before him.   *American*

3595. What the devil brings he also takes away.   *Russian*

3596. What the devil does in a year an old woman does in an hour.
                                        Moroccan

3597. When the devil finds the door shut he goes away.   *French*

3598. When the devil gets into the church he seats himself on the altar.
                                          Dutch

3599. When the devil grew old he became a monk.   *Rumanian*

3600. When the devil grows old he becomes a monk.   *Greek*

3601. When the devil grows old he turns hermit.   *French*

3602. When the devil grows poor he becomes a tax collector.   *Greek*

3603. When the devil prays, he has a booty in his eye.   *English*

3604. When the devil preaches, the world's near an end.   *English*

3605. When the devil quotes Latin, the priests go to prayers.   *English*

3606. When the devil says his paternosters he means to cheat you. *French*

3607. When the devil says his prayers he wants to cheat you.   *Spanish*

3608. Where none else will, the devil must bear the cross.   *English*

3609. Where the devil cannot succeed he sends an old woman.   *Polish*

3610. Where the devil doesn't have time to go, he sends a woman.
                                        Russian

3611. You may beat the devil into your wife, but you'll never bang him out again.   *English*

DEW

3612. If you rise too early, the dew will wet you.   *African (Wolof)*

3613. In the ant's house the dew is a flood.   *Iranian*

3614. Man's life is like a drop of dew on a leaf.   *Slovenian*

3615. No dew ever competed with the sun. *African (Zulu)*

3616. When there is dew there is no rain, when fruit is ripe there is no blossom. *Indian (Tamil)*

DIAMOND

3617. A diamond is valuable, though it lie on a dunghill. *English*

3618. A diamond, though men throw it in the mud, is still a diamond. *Turkish*

3619. Diamond cut diamond. *English*

DICE

3620. The best cast at dice is not to play. *Spanish*

DIE (see DYING)

3621. Better to die upright than to live on your knees. *Yiddish*

3622. He dies like a beast who has done no good while he lived. *English*

3623. He that dies pays all debts. *English*

3624. It is hard to die but it is harder to live. *Philippine*

3625. It's never too late to die or get married. *Yiddish*

3626. One has only to die to be praised. *German*

3627. The soldier will die in the field and the sailor in the sea. *Russian*

3628. To die is easy, to live is hard. *Japanese*

3629. Where one dies, there another gets up. *African (Hausa)*

3630. He that died half a year ago is as dead as Adam. *English*

DIET

3631. Diet cures more than doctors. *English*

DIFFERENCE

3632. There is a big difference between what one hears and sees. *Japanese*

3633. There is difference between living long and suffering long. *English*

3634. There is difference between staring and stark blind. *English*

3635. There is difference between staring and stark mad. *English*

3636. There is difference in servants. *English*

3637. There is no difference between blackness and blindness. *Greek*

3638. There is some difference between Peter and Peter. *English*

DIFFICULTY

3639. Difficulty makes desire. *English*

3640. Difficulties teach a man. *Turkish*

3641. Settle one difficulty, and you keep a hundred others away. *Chinese*

DIFFIDENCE

3642. Diffidence is the mother of safety. *English*

3643. Diffidence is the right eye of prudence. *English*

DIGNITY

3644. Dignity gains approval, meanness entails loss. *Indian (Tamil)*

3645. He who hurries cannot walk with dignity. *Chinese*

DIKE

3646. He who would drive another over three dikes must climb over two himself. *Danish*

3647. Where the dike is lowest the water first runs out. *Dutch*

DILEMMA

3648. Anything that releases you from a dilemma is useful.

African (Fulani)

DILIGENCE

3649. Diligence is the mother of good luck. *English*

3650. Diligence is the mother of success. *English*

3651. Diligence is the parent of fortune. *German*

3652. Diligence usually prospers. *Welsh*

3653. There is no diligence without a crown on its head. *Welsh*

3654. Too much diligence is hurtful. *English*

DINNER

3655. After dinner sit awhile; after supper walk a mile. *English*

3656. After dinner stand a while, or walk a thousand steps. *German*

3657. Better a good dinner than a fine coat. *French*

3658. For a good dinner and a gentle wife you can afford to wait. *Danish*

3659. He sups ill who eats up all at dinner. *English*

3660. He that saves his dinner will have the more for supper. *English*

3661. If you want your dinner, don't offend the cook. *Chinese*

DIPPER

3662. A dipper can't be used for an earpick. *Japanese*

DIPPING

3663. Dipping isn't drinking. *Yiddish*

DIRECT

3664. Better direct well than work hard. *English*

DIRECTION

3665. You can't ride in all directions at one time. *Yiddish*

DIRT

3666. Cast no dirt into the well that has given you water. *English*

3667. Dirt isn't fat: wash and it'll come off. *Russian*

3668. Dirt parts good company. *Scottish*

3669. Dirt will remove dirt, reproach will overcome reproach.

Indian (Tamil)

3670. Dirt will rub off when it is dry. *American*

3671. He that falls in the dirt, the longer he lies the fouler he is. *Scottish*

3672. He that flings dirt at another dirties himself most. *English*

3673. If you touch dirt, it will stick to your fingers. *Scottish*

3674. Meddle with dirt and some of it will stick to you. *Danish*

3675. The dirt always goes before the broom. *American*

3676. Throw dirt enough and some will stick. *English*

DISAGREEMENT

3677. The disagreements of women give birth to the wars of men.

Japanese

DISAPPOINT

3678. He who disappoints another is unworthy to be trusted.

African (Yoruba)

DISASTER

3679. Serious disasters come from small causes. *Japanese*

DISCIPLE

3680. The disciple does not surpass his teacher. *Japanese*

DISCIPLINE

3681. He who lives without discipline dies without honor. *Icelandic*

3682. Where there is discipline there is virtue; where there is peace there is plenty. *Danish*

DISCOUNT

3683. Discount is good pay. *American*

DISCOURSE

3684. Sweet discourse makes short days and nights. *English*

DISCREDIT

3685. Whatever you have to your discredit, be the first to tell it. *Hebrew*

DISCREET

3686. While the discreet advise, the fool does his business. *English*

DISCRETION

3687. A dram of discretion is worth a pound of wisdom. *German*

3688. An ounce of discretion is better than a pound of knowledge. *Italian*

3689. An ounce of discretion is worth a pound of learning. *English*

3690. Discretion is the better part of valor. *English*

3691. Give with discretion, accept with memory. *Czech*

DISCRIMINATION

3692. There is no discrimination in the forest of the dead. *African (Annang)*

DISEASE

3693. A deadly disease neither physician nor physic can ease. *English*

3694. A disease known is half cured. *English*

3695. Another man's disease is not hard to endure. *Yiddish*

3696. Desperate diseases must have desperate cures. *English*

3697. Diseases are the price of ill pleasures. *English*

3698. Diseases come by mountains and leave by driblets. *Thai*

3699. Diseases come on courier's horses, but go away on tired oxen. *Estonian*

3700. Diseases enter by the mouth, misfortunes issue from it. *Chinese*

3701. Disease will have its course. *English*

3702. If you know the disease, recovery is near. *Japanese*

3703. When the disease is not known there is no remedy. *Burmese*

3704. Worse than four hundred and four illnesses is the disease of poverty. *Japanese*

DISGRACE

3705. Disgraces are like cherries, one draws another. *English*

3706. Disgrace will attach to a king who has not a competent person near him. *Indian (Tamil)*

DISH

3707. All dishes need salt, but not all need spices. *Hebrew*

3708. Every new dish creates a fresh appetite in a glutton. *American*

3709. Many dishes make many diseases. *English*

3710. The dish wears its own cover. *English*

3711. The first dish pleases all.
English

DISHONOR

3712. Dishonor is worse than death.
Russian

DISLIKE

3713. Better dislike than contempt.
African (Fulani)

DISOBEDIENCE

3714. Disobedience is the father of insolence. *African (Yoruba)*

DISPOSITION

3715. A good disposition is the best treasure. *Indian (Tamil)*

3716. A good disposition makes a man liked. *African (Hausa)*

DISPUTE

3717. No and yes cause long disputes.
Danish

3718. Out of yes and no comes all dispute. *French*

DISPUTING

3719. Disputing and borrowing cause grief and sorrowing. *German*

3720. Great disputing repels truth.
French

3721. There is more disputing about the shell than the kernel. *German*

DISTANCE

3722. At a distance enjoy the fragrance of flowers. *Japanese*

3723. Distance lends enchantment.
American

3724. Distance preserves friendship.
Iranian

3725. Distance promotes close friendship. *Indian (Tamil)*

DISTINCTION

3726. One who attains distinction is immediately changed. *Polish*

3727. The distinction of big and little does not apply to snakes.
Indian (Tamil)

DISTRESS

3728. The distress of famine is worse than that of fire. *Indian (Tamil)*

3729. Two in distress make trouble less. *English*

3730. When distress doesn't show on the face, it lies on the heart. *Yiddish*

DISTRUST

3731. Distrust is poison to friendship.
Danish

3732. When distrust enters in at the foregate, love goes out at the postern.
English

DIVERSITY

3733. Diversity of humors breeds tumors. *English*

DIVIDEND

3734. Dividends from children is more precious than from money.
Yiddish

DIVINATION

3735. No divination without charcoal. *Libyan*

DIVINER

3736. Make me a diviner and I will make you rich. *English*

DIVISION

3737. Something to every one is good division. *German*

DO (see DONE)

3738. Better do it than wish it done.
English

3739. Better to do nothing than to make something into nothing.
Yiddish

3740. Do as others do and few will mock you. *Danish*

3741. Do good, and care not to whom.
Italian

3742. Do it well that you may not do it twice. *English*

3743. Do not all you can; spend not all you have; believe not all you hear; and tell not all you know. *English*

3744. Do nothing hastily but catching of fleas. *English*

3745. Do today what you want to postpone till tomorrow. *Lebanese*

3746. Do the likeliest and hope the best. *English*

3747. Do well, and dread no shame.
Scottish

3748. Do well and have well. *English*

3749. Do what you ought, and come what can come. *English*

3750. Do what you ought, and come what will. *Scottish*

3751. Do what you should and let the people talk. *German*

3752. Everybody does what he has learned. *German*

3753. He does much that does a thing well. *English*

3754. He that does most at once does least. *English*

3755. He that does what he should not shall feel what he would not. *English*

3756. He that does what he will does not what he ought. *English*

3757. He that is suffered to do more than is fitting will do more than is lawful. *English*

3758. He who does nothing does ill.
French

3759. If you can't do as you wish, do as you can. *Yiddish*

3760. If you're going to do something wrong, enjoy it! *Yiddish*

3761. It is easier to know how to do a thing than to do it. *Chinese*

3762. No one can do nothing and no one can do everything. *German*

3763. Nobody does everything, nobody does nothing. *German*

3764. None so busy as those who do nothing. *French*

3765. Self do, self have. *English*

3766. They can do ill that cannot do good. *Scottish*

3767. Those who do little expect the most. *American*

3768. To do nothing teaches to do evil. *Dutch*

3769. To do, one must be doing.
French

3770. We must do as we may, if we can't do as we would. *English*

3771. What we do willingly is easy.
English

3772. What you are doing do thoroughly. *French*

3773. What you do when you're drunk you must pay for when you're dry.
Scottish

3774. What you do when you are young will be what you will do when you get old. *Philippine*

3775. What you do yourself is well done. *Danish*

3776. What you want to do, do soon.
German

3777. When it is proper, then do it.
Indian (Kashmiri)

3778. Wherever you may be, do as you see done. *Spanish*

3779. Who does all he may never does well.   *Italian*

DOCTOR

3780. A clever doctor never treats himself.   *Chinese*

3781. A doctor and farmer know more than a doctor alone.   *German*

3782. A doctor cannot cure his own illness.   *Korean*

3783. A great doctor is accompanied by a great angel.   *Yiddish*

3784. After death the doctor.   *French*

3785. Before a doctor can cure one he will kill ten.   *Polish*

3786. Better no doctor at all than three.   *Polish*

3787. Doctors and gravediggers are partners.   *Yiddish*

3788. Doctors differ.   *English*

3789. Don't let yourself be operated upon by a doctor with a shaking hand.
                                                          Mexican

3790. Everyone is his own doctor.
                                                             Greek

3791. From a doctor and from a bathhouse attendant there are no secrets.   *Yiddish*

3792. Go not with every ailment to the doctor, nor with every plaint to the lawyer.   *Portuguese*

3793. Go not with every ailment to the doctor, with every plea to the lawyer, or with every thirst to the can.   *Spanish*

3794. If the doctor cures, the sun sees it; but if he kills, the earth hides it.
                                                         Scottish

3795. New doctor, new churchyard.
                                                          German

3796. No one becomes a good doctor before he has filled a churchyard.
                                                         Swedish

3797. Only a doctor can kill you without punishment.   *Hungarian*

3798. The doctor cures when he can smell money.   *Polish*

3799. The doctor demands his fees whether he has killed the illness or the patient.   *Polish*

3800. The doctor has a remedy for everything but poverty.   *Yiddish*

3801. The doctor is often more to be feared than the disease.   *French*

3802. The doctor who rides in a chair will not visit the house of the poor.
                                                          Chinese

3803. There is no doctor on the day of death.   *African (Fulani)*

3804. When everybody is doing well, the doctor is miserable.   *Hungarian*

DOER

3805. Ill doers are ill deemers.
                                                           English

DOG

3806. A bad dog gets the mange but he doesn't die of it.   *Greek*

3807. A bad dog never sees the wolf.
                                                           English

3808. A barking dog bites little.
                                                           English

3809. A barking dog is weak.
                                                         Japanese

3810. A barking dog was never a good biter.   *Spanish*

3811. A bashful dog never fattens.
                                                           German

3812. A biting dog does not bark.
                                                          Finnish

3813. A blind dog won't bark at the moon.   *Irish*

3814. A dog away from its accustomed place barks not for seven years.
                                                           Hebrew

3815. A dog barking at a shadow will set a hundred dogs to bark in unison.
Korean

3816. A dog can only dream of bones.
Russian

3817. A dog does not bite its master.
African (Shona)

3818. A dog does not die at the hand of its owner. *African (Bemba)*

3819. A dog doesn't enter if the door is not open. *Rumanian*

3820. A dog does not flee from a bone. *Irish*

3821. A dog does not take it ill when he is hit with bread. *Finnish*

3822. A dog has four feet but he can't walk four different paths. *Jamaican*

3823. A dog has nothing to do, and no time to rest. *Indian (Tamil)*

3824. A dog is a dog whatever his color. *Danish*

3825. A dog is better than an oppressor of men. *Iranian*

3826. A dog is brave at his own door.
Indian (Bihar)

3827. A dog is made fat in two meals.
English

3828. A dog is never offended at being pelted with bones. *Italian*

3829. A dog is sometimes more faithful than a child. *Yiddish*

3830. A dog is wiser than a woman, he does not bark at his master.
Russian

3831. A dog lying down has surrendered. *African (Shona)*

3832. A dog may look at a bishop.
French

3833. A dog once burnt will leave ashcovered embers alone.
African (Fulani)

3834. A dog once struck with a fireband dreads even the sight of lightning.
Indian (Bihar)

3835. A dog soiled with excrement laughs at another soiled with bran.
Korean

3836. A dog that fears barks more than he bites. *Slovakian*

3837. A dog that has forced its head into a pitcher is greedy.
African (Shona)

3838. A dog that means to bite does not show his teeth. *Turkish*

3839. A dog that stands still will never run across a bone. *Mexican*

3840. A dog, though he grows old, continues to bite. *Maltese*

3841. A dog who barks too often leads the wolf to the sheep. *Armenian*

3842. A dog will eat cockroaches rather than go without his supper.
Jamaican

3843. A dog will not cry if you beat him with a bone. *English*

3844. A dog will not howl if you strike him with a bone. *Scottish*

3845. A dog with a bone knows no friend. *Dutch*

3846. A dog with a full mouth will not bark. *African (Fulani)*

3847. A dog without teeth also attacks a bone! *Yiddish*

3848. A dog without teeth is just not a dog. *Yiddish*

3849. A good dog deserves a good bone. *English*

3850. A good dog hunts by instinct.
French

3851. A good dog never barks at fault.
French

3852. A good dog never gets a good bone. *French*

3853. A heedless dog is not fit for hunting.   *African (Jabo)*

3854. A heedless dog will not do for the chase.   *African (Yoruba)*

3855. A hungry dog is not afraid of cudgelling.   *French*

3856. A kitchen dog never was good for the chase.   *Italian*

3857. A lazy dog will not find even a bone.   *Philippine*

3858. A lean dog shames his master.   *Chinese*

3859. A living dog is better than a dead lion.   *English*

3860. A mad dog bites anything but himself.   *Libyan*

3861. A mad dog cannot live long.   *French*

3862. A male dog does not get food for his companion.   *African (Bemba)*

3863. A man's best friend is his dog, better even than his wife.   *Icelandic*

3864. A mischievous dog must be tied short.   *Italian*

3865. A modest dog seldom grows fat.   *Danish*

3866. A noisy dog is not fit for hunting.   *Indian (Tamil)*

3867. A scalded dog fears even the rain.   *Slovakian*

3868. A scalded dog thinks cold water hot.   *Italian*

3869. A silent dog will bite the heels.   *Indian (Tamil)*

3870. A sleeping dog should not be roused for food.   *African (Shona)*

3871. A small dog is a puppy until old age.   *Russian*

3872. A still dog bites sore. *English*

3873. A stupid dog will not do for the chase.   *African (Yoruba)*

3874. A tailless dog cannot express his joy.   *Albanian*

3875. A toiling dog comes halting home.   *English*

3876. A vicious dog bites its own master.   *German*

3877. A vicious dog must be tied short.   *French*

3878. A white dog is like a black dog.   *Greek*

3879. A wicked dog must be tied short.   *French*

3880. After a time even a dog makes a compromise with the cat. *Hungarian*

3881. All are not thieves whom the dog barks at.   *German*

3882. An ill-tempered dog has a scarred nose.   *Danish*

3883. An old dog barks not in vain.   *English*

3884. An old dog bites sore. *English*

3885. An old dog cannot be taught to sit up.   *Burmese*

3886. An old dog does not bark for nothing.   *French*

3887. An old dog does not bark in vain.   *African (Shona)*

3888. An old dog does not fight with a whelp.   *African (Ovambo)*

3889. An old dog does not grow used to the collar.   *Italian*

3890. An old dog does not growl for nothing.   *African (Ovambo)*

3891. An old dog does not howl at the stump of a tree.   *Basque*

3892. An old dog will learn no new tricks.   *English*

3893. An old dog will learn nothing.   *Albanian*

3894. Anyone who sees a leopard knows it is not a dog. *African (Hausa)*

3895. As the old dog barks, so the young one.   *English*

3896. Barking dogs don't bite. *Dutch*

3897. Be a dog ever so quick to start it will not catch a monkey swarming up a tree.   *African (Fulani)*

3898. Be on the watch when an old dog barks.   *Serbo-Croatian*

3899. Better a dog in peacetime than a soldier in war.   *Yiddish*

3900. Better a dog in times of peace than a man in times of rebellion.
                    Chinese

3901. Better a living dog than a dead lion.   *German*

3902. Better for a man to have even a dog welcome him than bark at him.
                    Irish

3903. Better have a dog fawn upon you than bite you.   *English*

3904. Better have a dog for your friend than your enemy.   *Dutch*

3905. Beware of a silent dog and a still water.   *English*

3906. Beware of the dog that does not bark.   *Portuguese*

3907. Bite not the dog that bites.
                    Danish

3908. By gnawing skin a dog learns to eat leather.   *Danish*

3909. Caress your dog, and he'll spoil your clothes.   *Dutch*

3910. Cut off the dog's tail, he remains a dog.   *Italian*

3911. Dead dogs bark not.   *English*

3912. Dead dogs don't bite.   *Dutch*

3913. Don't be afraid of a dog that barks.   *Greek*

3914. Do not give the dog bread every time he wags his tail.   *Italian*

3915. Do not judge the dog by his hairs.   *Danish*

3916. Don't snap your fingers at the dogs before you are out of the village.
                    French

3917. Don't trust a strange dog.
                    Slovakian

3918. Dogs bark as they are bred.
                    English

3919. Dogs bark at those they don't know.   *Italian*

3920. Dogs bark before they bite.
                    English

3921. Dogs bark more from custom than fierceness.   *English*

3922. Dogs become mad only during one season of the year, but man is foolish all the year around.
                    Vietnamese

3923. Dogs begin in jest and end in earnest.   *English*

3924. Dogs do not bark at a dead wolf.
                    Rumanian

3925. Dog does not eat dog.   *English*

3926. Dogs fight among themselves, but at the time of the jackal's cry they are united.   *Indian (Kashmiri)*

3927. Dogs fight over a bone and mourners over an inheritance. *Yiddish*

3928. Dogs gnaw bones because they cannot swallow them.   *English*

3929. Dogs have teeth in all countries.
                    Dutch

3930. Dogs keep the house and roosters announce daybreak with their crows.   *Vietnamese*

3931. Dogs show no aversion to poor families.   *Chinese*

3932. Dogs show their teeth when they dare not bite.   *American*

3933. Dogs that bark after a wagon keep out of the way of the whip.
                    American

3934. Dogs that bark at a distance never bite.   *English*

3935. Dogs that bark much don't bite.
German

3936. Dogs wag their tails not so much in love to you as to your bread.
English

3937. Dread silent dogs.   *Russian*

3938. Even a dog is king in his own place.   *Indian (Tamil)*

3939. Even a dog will not eat a quarrel between husband and wife.
Japanese

3940. Even the meanest dog wags its tail.   *German*

3941. Every dog barks differently.
Slovakian

3942. Every dog considers himself a lion at home.   *English*

3943. Every dog has his day. *English*

3944. Every dog has his day, and a bitch two afternoons.   *Scottish*

3945. Every dog is valiant at his own door.   *Irish*

3946. Every dog is valiant in his own kennel.   *French*

3947. Every dog rests at his own door.
African (Hausa)

3948. Every dog thinks himself a lion in his master's yard.   *Jamaican*

3949. Every dog will be lord on his own dunghill.   *Welsh*

3950. Fiddlers' dogs and flies come to feasts uncalled.   *English*

3951. He that lies down with dogs will get up with fleas.   *Danish*

3952. He that pelts every barking dog must pick up a great many stones.
German

3953. He that wants to hang a dog says that it bites the sheep.   *Danish*

3954. He who associates with dogs learns to pant.   *Russian*

3955. He who goes to bed with dogs will get up with fleas.   *Dutch*

3956. He who has a dog need not bark himself.   *Norwegian*

3957. He who lies down with dogs will rise with fleas.   *English*

3958. He who pets dogs must be childless.   *African (Ovambo)*

3959. He who travels with a dog may lie, but not one who travels with people.
African (Bemba)

3960. He who wants to kill his dog has only to say he is mad.   *Spanish*

3961. He who would have a bone from a dog must give the meat instead.
Norwegian

3962. Hungry dogs will eat dirty puddings.   *English*

3963. If a dog barks at you, stop his muzzle with bread.   *Rumanian*

3964. If dogs had their way there would be no horses.   *Serbo-Croatian*

3965. If the dog goes when the cat comes, there will be no fight. *Chinese*

3966. If the dog is not at home, he barks not.   *African (Wolof)*

3967. If the dog is patted on the head, it wags its tail.   *Philippine*

3968. If the old dog bark, he gives counsel.   *English*

3969. If you caress a dog, he will lick your mouth.   *Indian (Tamil)*

3970. If you have stepped over the dog, step over its tail too.   *Estonian*

3971. If you lie down with the dogs, you get up with the fleas.   *Yiddish*

3972. If you play with a dog, do not complain when it tears your clothes.
African (Annang)

3973. If you play with the dog, he will lick your face.   *Vietnamese*

3974. If you would wish the dog to follow you, feed him.   *English*

3975. In beating a dog, first find out who his owner is.   *Chinese*

3976. In every country dogs bite.   *English*

3977. Into the mouth of a bad dog often falls a good bone.   *English*

3978. It is a poor dog that is not worth whistling for.   *English*

3979. It is all one whether you are bit by a dog or a bitch.   *French*

3980. It's an ill dog that deserves not a crust.   *English*

3981. It is an ill dog that is not worth the whistling.   *Irish*

3982. It is better to irritate a dog than an old woman.   *Italian*

3983. It is difficult to teach an old dog to sit down.   *Icelandic*

3984. It is easy robbing when the dog is quieted.   *Italian*

3985. It is hard to make an old dog stoop.   *English*

3986. It is hard to teach old dogs to bark.   *Dutch*

3987. It is ill to waken sleeping dogs.   *Scottish*

3988. Keep a dog for three days and he will not forget your kindness, but three years kindness shown to a cat is forgotten in three days.   *Japanese*

3989. Keep hold of the bone and the dog will follow you.   *Irish*

3990. Let every dog carry his own tail.   *English*

3991. Let sleeping dogs lie.   *English*

3992. Little dogs start the hare but great ones catch it.   *English*

3993. Mad dogs get their coats torn.   *Danish*

3994. Many a dog is hanged for his skin, and many a man is killed for his purse.   *English*

3995. Many dogs are the death of the hare.   *Danish*

3996. Many make themselves a dog for the sake of a bone.   *Swedish*

3997. Not every dog that barks, bites.   *Russian*

3998. Not everyone the dogs bark at is a thief.   *Yiddish*

3999. Not every time a dog barks should a bone be thrown to it.   *Lebanese*

4000. One dog barks an inanity, ten thousand dogs assert its truth.   *Japanese*

4001. One dog barks at something and a hundred bark at the sound.   *Chinese*

4002. One must talk soothingly to the dog until one has passed him.   *French*

4003. One tells a dog there's a feast at your home, it says let me see it on the ground.   *African (Hausa)*

4004. Quarrelsome dogs get dirty coats.   *Irish*

4005. Quiet dogs and still water are dangerous.   *German*

4006. Satisfy a dog with a bone and a woman with a lie.   *Basque*

4007. Show a dog a finger and he wants the whole hand.   *Hebrew*

4008. Strike a dog with a bone and he'll not growl.   *Irish*

4009. The dead dog will bite no more.   *Indian (Tamil)*

4010. The dog barks and the caravan passes on.   *Turkish*

4011. The dog barks at the moon all night long, but the moon never hears him.   *Rumanian*

4012. The dog barks at the moon in vain. *Slovakian*

4013. The dogs bite the last. *German*

4014. The dog bites not his master. *Turkish*

4015. The dog does not eat hay, but he doesn't let the donkey eat it either. *Greek*

4016. The dog does not get bread every time he wags his tail. *German*

4017. The dog does not know how to swim until the water reaches his ears. *Russian*

4018. The dog gets into the mill under cover of the ass. *French*

4019. The dog has four feet, but he does not walk with them in four roads. *Haitian*

4020. The dog in his hunger swallows dung. *Hebrew*

4021. The dog is a lion in his own home. *Russian*

4022. The dog is boldest at home. *Norwegian*

4023. The dog knows how to eat bones. *Haitian*

4024. The dog knows the hand that gives him bread. *Turkish*

4025. The dog knows you by his tail. *Hawaiian*

4026. The dog may bark but the ant-hill will not run away. *Burmese*

4027. The dog says he will never commit adultery, but when he does so, he commits it with his own father's wife. *African (Ashanti)*

4028. The dog survives the winter but only his skin knows how. *Greek*

4029. The dog that barks much bites little. *Portuguese*

4030. The dog that barks much is never good for hunting. *Portuguese*

4031. The dog that bites does not bark in vain. *Italian*

4032. The dog that fetches will carry. *English*

4033. The dog that has been beaten with a stick is afraid of its shadow. *Italian*

4034. The dog that has left the house has no master. *African (Wolof)*

4035. The dog that hates to obey his owner will sleep without his supper. *Jamaican*

4036. The dog that's always on the go, is better than the one that's always curled up. *Irish*

4037. The dog that is forced into the woods will not hunt many deer. *Danish*

4038. The dog that kills wolves is killed by wolves. *Spanish*

4039. The dog that knows not how to bark brings the wolf to the sheep. *Turkish*

4040. The dog that means to bite doesn't bark. *Italian*

4041. The dog that strays too much loses his share. *Jamaican*

4042. The dog that wags its tail cannot be beaten. *Japanese*

4043. The dog wags his tail, not for you but for your bread. *Spanish*

4044. The dog which is known to be very swift is set to catch the hare. *African (Yoruba)*

4045. The dog will not get free by biting his chain. *Danish*

4046. The dog with many homes dies of hunger. *Slovakian*

4047. The foremost dog catches the hare. *English*

4048. The gardener's dog does not eat lettuce and will not let others eat it. *Italian*

4049. The hungry dog does not push on in the chase. *Turkish*

4050. The mad dog bites his master. *English*

4051. The scalded dog fears cold water. *English*

4052. The silent dog is the first to bite. *German*

4053. The smith's dog sleeps at the noise of the hammer and wakes at the grinding of teeth. *Spanish*

4054. The starving dog fears not the stick. *Japanese*

4055. The worst dog that is will wag his tail. *English*

4056. The wretched dog feels satisfied with the beating he received. *Indian (Tamil)*

4057. There are good dogs of all sizes. *French*

4058. There are more ways to kill a dog than hanging. *English*

4059. There is no dog, be he ever so wicked, but wags his tail. *Italian*

4060. Though a dog becomes fat, its meat is not edible. *Lebanese*

4061. Timid dogs bark most. *German*

4062. Trust not a dog's limp or women's tears. *Mexican*

4063. Two dogs do not share one bone. *Turkish*

4064. Two dogs fight for a bone and a third runs away with it. *German*

4065. Two dogs over one bone seldom agree. *German*

4066. Two dogs seldom agree over one bone. *Dutch*

4067. Wake not a sleeping dog. *Dutch*

4068. Wash a dog, comb a dog, still a dog remains a dog. *French*

4069. When a dog is hungry it eats even dung. *Hebrew*

4070. When an old dog barks, look out. *German*

4071. Where the dog drinks there he barks. *Serbo-Croatian*

4072. When the dog is awake, the shepherd may sleep. *German*

4073. When the dog is down, every one is ready to bite him. *Dutch*

4074. When the dog is drowning every one brings him water. *French*

4075. When the old dog barks he gives counsel. *Spanish*

4076. When two dogs fight for a bone, the third runs away with it. *Dutch*

4077. When you want to beat a dog, be sure to find a stick. *Yiddish*

4078. Where there are no dogs the fox is a king. *Italian*

4079. Where there are no dogs the wolves howl. *Serbo-Croatian*

4080. While the dogs are growling at each other the wolf devours the sheep. *French*

4081. While the dog gnaws a bone, he loves no company. *English*

4082. While the dogs yelp, the hare flies to the wood. *Danish*

4083. Who wants to beat a dog, soon finds a stick. *Dutch*

4084. Who yaps like a dog will be beaten like a dog.   *Polish*

4085. With two dogs they killed the lion.   *Hebrew*

4086. Young dogs have sharp teeth.   *Danish*

DOGFIGHT

4087. Dogfights draw children, children's fights draw parents.   *Japanese*

DOING (see DO)

4088. Doing is better than saying.   *English*

4089. He who is afraid of doing too much always does too little.   *German*

4090. In doing we learn.   *English*

4091. Whatever is worth doing is worth doing well.   *English*

DOLL

4092. Outwardly, a doll; within, the plague.   *Greek*

DOLLAR

4093. A dollar saved is as good as a dollar earned.   *American*

DONE (see DO)

4094. Could everything be done twice, everything would be done better.   *German*

4095. It isn't done as easily as it's said.   *Yiddish*

4096. Nothing is done while something remains undone.   *French*

4097. Self done is soon done.   *German*

4098. That's quickly done which is long repented.   *Dutch*

4099. That which is easily done is soon believed.   *English*

4100. That which is well done is twice done.   *English*

4101. What's done can't be undone.   *English*

4102. What is once done is never to be undone.   *English*

4103. What is well done is done soon enough.   *English*

DONKEY

4104. A donkey is a donkey even if he wears a saddle; and an old woman, no matter how she adorns herself, does not become a young one.   *Greek*

4105. A donkey is a donkey though it may carry the Sultan's treasure.   *Lebanese*

4106. A donkey is asked to a wedding either to carry water or to bring wood.   *Greek*

4107. A donkey that travels abroad will not return a horse.   *Hebrew*

4108. A starving donkey does not count the blows.   *Greek*

4109. An uninvited donkey has no place at a wedding.   *Greek*

4110. Better a sound donkey than a consumptive philosopher.   *Rumanian*

4111. Bucking will not rid a donkey of a load.   *African (Hausa)*

4112. Donkey tied, master tranquil.   *Greek*

4113. Everybody beats the donkey that has no owner.   *Turkish*

4114. He who took the donkey up to the roof should bring it down.   *Lebanese*

4115. Many donkeys need much straw.   *Basque*

4116. Only a donkey is patient under a load.   *African (Hausa)*

4117. The donkey has been to Jerusalem forty times, but he is still a donkey.   *Armenian*

4118. The donkey knows seven ways to swim; when he falls into the water, he forgets them all. *Armenian*

4119. The small donkey is the one that everybody rides. *Libyan*

4120. There's no making a donkey drink against his will. *Dutch*

4121. Two donkeys together will act alike and smell alike. *Iranian*

4122. When a donkey is well off he goes dancing on ice. *Czech*

4123. When the donkey wants to spite his master, he dies. *Armenian*

4124. You can recognize a donkey by his long ears, a fool by his long tongue. *Yiddish*

DOOR

4125. A door must either be open or shut. *French*

4126. A door once shut will not easily open again. *Hebrew*

4127. All doors open to courtesy. *English*

4128. An open door may tempt a saint. *English*

4129. An open door tempts a saint. *Spanish*

4130. At open doors, dogs come in. *English*

4131. Beware of a door that has many keys. *Portuguese*

4132. Do not bar your door after the storm. *Philippine*

4133. Every door has its own key. *African (Swahili)*

4134. Every door may be shut but death's door. *English*

4135. For every door that shuts, ten will open. *Philippine*

4136. He must stoop that has a low door. *English*

4137. He who comes late shuts the door. *Turkish*

4138. He who listens at doors hears more than he desires. *French*

4139. He who wishes to make a golden door drives a nail into it every day. *French*

4140. If you are rich, always shut your door. *African (Oji)*

4141. In a quarrel, leave the door open for a reconciliation. *Yiddish*

4142. Let everyone sweep before his own door. *German*

4143. Lock your door rather than suspect your neighbor. *Lebanese*

4144. Make not the door wider than the house. *English*

4145. Many open a door to shut a window. *Dutch*

4146. One door is locked, but another is wide open. *Russian*

4147. One must pass through the door or the window. *French*

4148. Sweep before your own door. *English*

4149. Sweep before your own door before you look after your neighbor's. *Dutch*

4150. The back door robs the house. *English*

4151. The door of charity is hard to open and hard to shut. *Chinese*

4152. The door of success is marked "push" and "pull." *Yiddish*

4153. The door of virtues is hard to open. *Chinese*

4154. The door to evil-doing is wide, but the return gate is narrow. *Yiddish*

4155. The door which is not opened for charitable purposes will be opened to the physician. *Hebrew*

4156. The last shuts the door.
German

4157. The open door invites the thief.
Dutch

4158. The postern door makes thief and whore.   *English*

4159. When one door shuts, a hundred open.   *Spanish*

4160. When one door shuts, another opens.   *English*

4161. When the door is low one must stoop.   *French*

4162. When you open a door, do not forget to close it, and treat your mouth the same way.   *Hebrew*

4163. Whoever brings finds the door open for him.   *Italian*

4164. You may shut your doors against a thief, but not against a liar.
Danish

4165. You must go behind the door to mend old breeches.   *English*

DOORSTEP

4166. The doorstep of the palace is very slippery.   *Polish*

DOORWAY

4167. Even the doorway of the rich is ashamed of the poor.   *Russian*

4168. He who finds a doorway too low must stoop.   *Russian*

DOUBT (noun)

4169. Doubts mean losing half of one's case beforehand.   *Czech*

DOUBT (verb)

4170. He doubts nothing who knows nothing.   *Portuguese*

4171. He who doubts nothing knows nothing.   *Spanish*

4172. When in doubt, do nothing.
English

4173. Who doubts errs not.   *French*

DOUGH

4174. So much dough, so many buns.
Latvian

DOVE

4175. He who makes himself a dove is eaten by the hawk.   *Italian*

4176. The dove recognizes its own ridgepole.   *Chinese*

4177. The dove shows its filial piety by sitting three branches below its parents.   *Japanese*

DOWRY

4178. Who wives for a dowry resigns his own power.   *French*

DRAFF

4179. He who mixes himself with the draff will be eaten by the swine.
Dutch

DRAGON

4180. A dragon stranded in a shallow water furnishes amusement for the shrimps.   *Chinese*

4181. Dragons beget dragons; phoenixes hatch out phoenixes.   *Chinese*

4182. When you paint a dragon, you paint his skin; it is difficult to paint the bones. When you know a man, you know his face but not his heart.
Chinese

4183. With money you are a dragon, without it you are a worm.   *Chinese*

DREAM (noun)

4184. A dream which has not been interpreted is like a letter unread.
Hebrew

4185. Dreams are dreadful but God is merciful.   *Russian*

4186. Dreams are froth.   *German*

4187. Dreams are lies. *French*

4188. Dreams go by contraries.
English

4189. Dreams of bliss and premature wisdom are not lasting.
Indian (Tamil)

4190. Golden dreams make men awake hungry. *English*

4191. Morning dreams are true.
English

4192. The dream is a fool and sleep's the master. *Yiddish*

4193. The dream of the cat is all about the mice. *Egyptian*

DREAM (verb)

4194. No one dreams of going to where they will kill him.
African (Ashanti)

DREAMING

4195. Dreaming of eating will not satisfy the hungry. *African (Fulani)*

DRESS

4196. A dress that is not worn wears itself out. *Armenian*

4197. The dress does not make the friar. *Spanish*

DRIFT

4198. Drift is as bad as unthrift.
English

DRINK (noun)

4199. A drink is shorter than a story.
Irish

4200. Drink and drought come not always together. *English*

4201. Drink in, wit out. *English*

4202. Drink washes off the daub and discovers the man. *English*

4203. Good drink drives out bad thoughts. *Dutch*

4204. When drink is in wit is out.
Scottish

DRINK (verb)

4205. He that drinks well sleeps well, and he that sleeps well thinks no harm.
English

4206. He who has drunk will drink.
French

4207. If you drink you die, if you don't drink you die, so it is better to drink.
Russian

4208. The more one drinks the more one may. *English*

4209. You cannot drink and whistle at the same time. *Danish*

DRINKING

4210. Where there's drinking, there's spilling. *Russian*

DRIVE

4211. Drive slowly, you will get farther. *Estonian*

4212. If you drive slowly, you'll arrive more quickly. *Yiddish*

DRIVER

4213. A good driver turns in a small space. *French*

4214. It is not good to be the driver of white horses or the servant of women.
Rumanian

4215. He is not a bad driver who knows how to turn. *Danish*

4216. The best driver will sometimes upset. *French*

DRIVING

4217. The one driving is like the one riding. *Russian*

DRONE

4218. Better feed five drones than starve one bee. *English*

DROP

4219. A drop and a drop cut through the rock. *Lebanese*

4220. A drop of water breaks a stone. *Italian*

4221. A drop of water in the eyes of the Tsar costs the country many handkerchiefs. *Russian*

4222. Drop by drop fills the tub. *French*

4223. Drop by drop wears away the stone. *French*

4224. Drops of water eat up stones. *Greek*

4225. Falling drops pierce the stone. *Japanese*

4226. Fat drops fall from fat flesh. *English*

4227. Many drops make a great flood. *Indian (Tamil)*

4228. Many drops make a shower. *English*

4229. The last drop makes the cup run over. *English*

4230. Through just a drop of indigo a jug of milk is lost. *Malaysian*

4231. To a drunkard even a drop is dear. *Lithuanian*

DROPPING

4232. Constant dropping wears the stone. *German*

DROPPINGS

4233. Old droppings do not stink. *African (Swahili)*

DROUGHT

4234. After drought comes rain. *English*

4235. After great droughts come great rains. *Dutch*

DROWN

4236. Drown not yourself to save a drowning man. *English*

4237. If one is fated to drown, he will drown in a spoonful of water. *Yiddish*

DROWNING

4238. He that is drowning shouts though he be not heard. *Italian*

DRUM

4239. A drum beaten on a hill is heard far and wide. *Chinese*

4240. A good drum does not require hard beatings. *Chinese*

4241. A poor man's drum is his belly. *African (Hausa)*

4242. As the drum beats, so goes the dance. *Malaysian*

4243. Beat your drum inside the house and your neighbors will not hear it. *Chinese*

4244. It is difficult to beat a drum with a sickle. *African (Hausa)*

4245. One must touch a drum before it will speak. *African (Jabo)*

4246. The drum knows its owner's hands. *African (Ovambo)*

4247. The drums sound according to the way they are struck. *Japanese*

4248. The noisiest drum has nothing but air inside. *Philippine*

4249. Where a big drum is beaten a small one must not be. *African (Fulani)*

4250. You can't hide a drum under a blanket. *Iranian*

DRUNK (intoxicated)

4251. Better be drunk than drowned. *English*

4252. He that is drunk is as great as a king. *English*

4253. When two say you're drunk, it's best to go to sleep. *Yiddish*

DRUNK (noun)

4254. A drunk can sleep it off, but never a fool. *Russian*

DRUNKARD

4255. A drunkard and a mad man are alike. *Indian (Tamil)*

4256. A drunkard is not he who thinks much, but he who gets drunk. *Serbo-Croatian*

4257. A drunkard's purse is a bottle. *English*

4258. Drunkards have a fool's tongue and a knave's heart. *English*

4259. The drunkard and the bartender both smell of whisky. *Yiddish*

4260. There are more old drunkards than old doctors. *French*

DRUNKENNESS

4261. Drunkenness and anger speak truly. *Irish*

4262. Drunkenness departed and reflection came. *Egyptian*

4263. Drunkenness reveals one's true mind. *Korean*

4264. Drunkenness reveals what soberness conceals. *English*

4265. Drunkenness will not protect a secret. *Irish*

4266. Where there is drunkenness, there is trouble. *African (Swahili)*

DUCK

4267. A duck will not always dabble in the same gutter. *English*

4268. All ducks do not dabble in one hole. *Jamaican*

4269. The duck knows where the lake is. *Greek*

DUMPLING

4270. Dumplings are better than flowers. *Japanese*

DUNG

4271. Dung is no saint, but where it falls it works miracles. *Spanish*

DUNGEON

4272. No sure dungeon but the grave. *English*

DUNGHILL

4273. He that is first on the dunghill may sit where he will. *Scottish*

DUST

4274. Dust does not rise because a dog-flea hops. *Burmese*

4275. Dust is always dust however near to heaven it may be blown. *Swedish*

4276. Even dust, if amassed enough, will form a great mountain. *Korean*

4277. Even dust when accumulated makes a mountain. *Japanese*

4278. He that blows in the dust fills his eyes with it. *English*

DUTY

4279. Do your duty and be afraid of none. *American*

4280. Duty is to be before devotion. *Mexican*

4281. Duty to parents is higher than the mountains, deeper than the sea. *Japanese*

4282. The filial duty of feeding one's parents is known even to the crow.

Japanese

DWARF

4283. A dwarf on a giant's shoulder sees farther of the two.   *English*

4284. When with dwarfs do not talk about pygmies.   *Chinese*

DWELLING

4285. Even though your dwelling contains a thousand rooms, you can use but eight feet of space a night. *Chinese*

DYING (see DIE)

4286. Dying is as natural as living.

English

4287. Dying is not child's play.

German

E

EAGLE

4288. Better be an eagle for a day than a rook for a whole year.
Rumanian

4289. Eagles catch no fleas. *Dutch*

4290. Eagles don't breed doves.
Dutch

4291. Eagles fly alone. *English*

4292. The eagle does not catch flies.
English

4293. The eagle does not hunt flies.
French

4294. The eagle does not war against frogs. *Italian*

4295. The eagle is the father of birds of prey. *African (Yoruba)*

4296. The eagle is the prince of fowls: the eagle is the prince of birds of prey.
African (Yoruba)

4297. The eagle will not pursue flies.
Indian (Hindi)

4298. You cannot fly like an eagle with the wings of a wren. *English*

EAGLE-EYED

4299. He is eagle-eyed in other men's matters, but as blind as a buzzard in his own. *English*

EAR

4300. Better to play with the ears than with the tongue. *English*

4301. Deaf ears give the tale-monger trouble. *Jamaican*

4302. Ears do not grow higher than the head. *Russian*

4303. He who has no ears, hears not.
African (Wolof)

4304. If the ear hears news of evil, the neck escapes being severed.
African (Hausa)

4305. It is the ear that troubles the mouth. *African (Ga)*

4306. Listen with each ear, then do judgment. *Manx*

4307. One pair of ears draws dry a hundred tongues. *English*

4308. The ears don't hear what the mouth utters. *Yiddish*

4309. The ears do not lose their interest. *African (Ovambo)*

4310. To rude words deaf ears.
French

4311. What one whispers in the ear is heard throughout the town. *Swedish*

4312. When the ear does not listen, the heart escapes sorrow. *Chinese*

4313. When the wolf's ears appear, his body is not far off.   *Danish*

4314. Wide ears and a short tongue is best.   *English*

EARLY

4315. Better early than late. *English*

EARN

4316. After one that earns comes one that wastes.   *Danish*

4317. First earn, then eat.
Indian (Hindi)

EARTH (soil)

4318. Black earth gives white bread.
Swedish

4319. Earth in the mouth of the dead, and rice in the mouth of the living.
Indian (Tamil)

4320. Earth is the best shelter.
English

4321. Earth must to earth. *English*

4322. Everything above falls to earth at the end.   *African (Hausa)*

4323. Heaped up earth becomes a mountain; accumulated water becomes a river.   *Chinese*

4324. If the earth had a mouth it would defend many.
African (Ovambo)

4325. Six feet of earth make all men equal.   *English*

4326. The earth covers the errors of the physician.   *Italian*

4327. The earth has ears, it hears every word.   *Turkish*

4328. The earth has ears; rumor has wings.   *Philippine*

4329. The earth hides as it takes the physician's mistakes.   *Spanish*

4330. The earth is always frozen to lazy swine.   *Danish*

4331. The earth produces all things and receives all again.   *English*

EARTH (world)

4332. Earth and heaven do not come together.   *African (Ga)*

4333. The earth is full of rumor.
Russian

4334. Earth laughs at him who calls a place his own.   *Indian (Hindustani)*

EASE

4335. A pennyworth of ease is worth a penny.   *English*

4336. Ease and success are fellows.
English

4337. He is at ease who has enough.
English

EAT

4338. Eat at pleasure drink by measure.   *English*

4339. Eat enough and it will make you wise.   *English*

4340. Eat little, sleep sound. *Iranian*

4341. Eat to live, not live to eat.
English

4342. Eat until you are half satisfied, and drink until you are half drunk.
Russian

4343. Eat-well is drink-well's brother.
English

4344. Eat whatever you like, but dress as others do.   *Egyptian*

4345. Eat when you're hungry and drink when you're dry.   *English*

4346. He that eats least eats most.
English

4347. He that eats till he is sick must fast till he is well.   *English*

4348. He that eats well and drinks well should do his duty well. *English*

4349. He that is ashamed to eat is ashamed to live.   *French*

4350. He who eats alone, coughs alone. *Egyptian*

4351. He who eats quickly works quickly. *Russian*

4352. To eat and to scratch, one has but to begin. *Spanish*

4353. To eat one must chew, to speak one must think. *Vietnamese*

4354. You eat and eat but you do not drink to fill you. *English*

4355. You should eat what you're given. *Russian*

EATER

4356. The quick eater does quick work. *Japanese*

EATING

4357. Eating a mouthful is better than waiting for a helping.
African (Hausa)

4358. Eating and drinking takes away a man's stomach. *Scottish*

4359. Eating and drinking wants but a beginning. *Scottish*

4360. Eating is preferable to amorousness. *Japanese*

4361. Eating teaches drinking.
Italian

4362. Too much eating and drinking leads to poverty. *Yiddish*

ECHO

4363. The echo knows all languages.
Finnish

ECONOMY

4364. Economy is a great revenue.
Dutch

4365. Economy makes men independent. *Chinese*

4366. It is easy to go from economy to extravagance; it is hard to go from extravagance to economy. *Chinese*

EDGE

4367. A good edge is good for nothing, if it has nothing to cut.
English

4368. Too keen an edge does not cut, too fine a point does not pierce.
French

EDUCATION

4369. Better education than wealth.
Welsh

4370. Education begins a gentleman, conversation completes him. *English*

4371. Education is life, not books.
African (Swahili)

4372. Education is light, lack of it is darkness. *Russian*

4373. There is no education that can surpass privations. *Japanese*

4374. Youthful education will prove beneficial. *Indian (Tamil)*

EEL

4375. All that breed in the mud are not eels. *English*

4376. An eel escapes from a good fisherman. *French*

4377. Eels of shallow water show their color. *Hawaiian*

4378. Even the most slippery eel and the clumsiest ladle may meet.
Philippine

4379. He that will catch eels must disturb the flood. *English*

4380. Taking an eel by its tail and a woman at her word leaves little in the hand. *Swedish*

4381. To squeeze an eel too hard is the way to lose it. *French*

4382. Who takes an eel by the tail and a woman at her word may say he holds nothing. *Italian*

4383. You cannot hide an eel in a sack. *English*

EFFECT

4384. The effects of an evil act are long felt.   *Irish*

4385. The effect speaks, the tongue need not.   *English*

EFFORT

4386. The efforts of the poor are their tears.   *Egyptian*

EGG

4387. A peeled egg doesn't leap into the mouth by itself.   *Yiddish*

4388. An egg in the mouth is better than a fowl in the fowlhouse.

African (Hausa)

4389. An egg is most valuable at Easter.   *Russian*

4390. Bad egg, bad chick.   *Dutch*

4391. Better an egg in peace than an ox in war.   *English*

4392. Better an egg today than a hen tomorrow.   *Albanian*

4393. Better an egg today than an ox tomorrow.   *Rumanian*

4394. Better half an egg than an empty shell.   *Dutch*

4395. Better today's egg than tomorrow's chicken.   *Greek*

4396. Don't boil eggs until the hen has laid them.   *Estonian*

4397. Eggs and vows are easily broken.   *Japanese*

4398. Eggs are not fried with wind.

Lebanese

4399. Eggs are put to hatch on chance.   *French*

4400. Eggs cannot be unscrambled.

American

4401. Eggs don't teach the hen.

Russian

4402. Eggs must not quarrel with stones.   *Chinese*

4403. Eggs that roll far from the nest often perish.   *Estonian*

4404. Even a round egg can be made square in the way you cut it; words can be sharp in the way you speak them.

Japanese

4405. Half an egg is better than an empty shell.   *English*

4406. He that will have eggs, must bear with cackling.   *Dutch*

4407. He who steals an egg will steal a camel.   *Lebanese*

4408. He who steals the egg will steal the hen.   *Welsh*

4409. He who treads on eggs must tread lightly.   *German*

4410. He who will have eggs, must bear with the cackling.   *German*

4411. If one steals a lot of eggs, one can also become rich.   *Yiddish*

4412. If you want to eat eggs, bear the cackling of the hen.   *Philippine*

4413. If you will have the hen's egg, you must bear her cackling.   *Scottish*

4414. Let him who wishes to hatch sit on his own eggs.   *Haitian*

4415. One rotten egg spoils the whole pudding.   *German*

4416. Put not all your eggs into one basket.   *Dutch*

4417. Rather the egg today than the hen tomorrow.   *Danish*

4418. Strike an egg against a stone and the yolk runs out at once. *Chinese*

4419. The egg of a white hen is the same as that of a black one.

Rumanian

4420. The egg of today is better than the fowl of tomorrow.   *Turkish*

4421. The more the eggs, the thicker the soup.   *Serbo-Croatian*

4422. To eat an egg, you must break the shell.   *Jamaican*

4423. Unlaid eggs are uncertain chickens. *Dutch*

4424. You can't play with eggs on a rock slab! *African (Hausa)*

EGGPLANT

4425. Eggplants do not grow on melon vines. *Japanese*

ELBOW-GREASE

4426. Elbow-grease gives the best polish. *English*

ELDER

4427. Respect the elders: they are our fathers. *African (Yoruba)*

4428. Reverence your elder, for the man excelling in age excels in wisdom. *African (Efik)*

4429. When there are no elders, the town is ruined; when the master dies, the house is desolate. *African (Yoruba)*

ELEPHANT

4430. An elephant can do nothing to a tamarind tree, except it be to shake it. *African (Wolof)*

4431. An elephant does not eat small berries. *African (Ga)*

4432. An elephant, however lean, is valuable. *Indian (Hindustani)*

4433. An elephant is not affected by sunshine or rain. *Indian (Tamil)*

4434. An elephant is not burdened by its tusks. *African (Shona)*

4435. An elephant will reach to the roof of the house. *African (Efik)*

4436. An elephant without a keeper is like a man without a wife. *Vietnamese*

4437. Don't meddle in assisting the elephant in carrying his tusks. *Thai*

4438. Don't waste spears on stabbing rhinos when elephants may still show up. *African (Shona)*

4439. Even an elephant may slip. *Indian (Tamil)*

4440. Even elephants will stumble, though they have four feet. *Malaysian*

4441. Even if the forest is undone, the elephant is above running. *African (Hausa)*

4442. However poor the elephant, it will be worth more than ten frogs. *African (Hausa)*

4443. If an elephant enters the forest and breaks trees it will not stop the hare breaking grass. *African (Fulani)*

4444. If the elephant were not in the wilderness, buffalo would be the greatest. *African (Jabo)*

4445. If you're going to move, move like an elephant, not like a hyena. *African (Hausa)*

4446. It is easy to cut to pieces a dead elephant, but no one dares attack a live one. *African (Yoruba)*

4447. It is one man who kills an elephant, but many people who eat its flesh. *African (Ashanti)*

4448. No one who is following an elephant has to knock the dew off the grass. *African (Ashanti)*

4449. On the death of an elephant the tusk remains, on the death of a tiger the skin. *Indian (Tamil)*

4450. One elephant does not raise a cloud of dust. *African (Ovambo)*

4451. The elephant and tiger are afraid of fire. *Indian (Tamil)*

4452. The elephant does not bite, it is that trunk one fears. *African (Hausa)*

4453. The elephant does not feel a flea bite. *Italian*

4454. The elephant does not see the fruit seed. *African (Ovambo)*

4455. The elephant dreams one thing, the elephant driver another. *Iranian*

4456. The elephant is bigger than the camel.   *Turkish*

4457. The elephant is frightened of the gnat.   *Hebrew*

4458. The elephant is killed because he has tusks.   *Chinese*

4459. The elephant makes a dust, and the buffalo makes a dust, but the dusk of the buffalo is lost in that of the elephant.   *African (Yoruba)*

4460. The sound of the bell is heard before the elephant makes its appearance.   *Indian (Tamil)*

4461. The young elephant is born with a thick skin.   *African (Ovambo)*

4462. To threaten an elephant you must carry a spear.   *African (Bemba)*

4463. Were no elephant in the jungle, the buffalo would be a great animal.
                                African (Ga)

4464. When the elephants in conflict lean, the mouse-deer gets killed in between.   *Malaysian*

4465. When two elephants jostle, that which is hurt is the grass.
                          African (Swahili)

4466. Where an elephant is being killed, none notices the death of a monkey.   *African (Hausa)*

4467. Where the elephant died you can tell by the bones.
                          African (Ovambo)

ELK

4468. Kill the elk in your youth if you would lie on its skin in your old age.
                                Finnish

ELOQUENCE

4469. An idiot's eloquence is silence.
                               Japanese

EMBARRASSED

4470. It is better to be embarrassed than heartbroken.   *Yiddish*

EMBER

4471. Blow not on dead embers.
                                  Irish

4472. Burning embers are easily kindled.   *Irish*

4473. Under white ashes lie often glowing embers.   *Danish*

EMBRACE

4474. The embrace at meeting is better than that at parting.   *Egyptian*

EMERALD

4475. Emeralds are easily broken.
                               Japanese

4476. Emeralds as well as glass will shine when light is shed on them.
                               Japanese

EMPEROR

4477. Even the emperor cannot feast from an empty dish.   *Serbo-Croatian*

4478. Even the emperor has straw-sandaled relatives.   *Chinese*

4479. Every one is emperor on his own ground.   *German*

4480. Only one can be emperor.
                                German

4481. To attend the emperor is like sleeping with a tiger.   *Chinese*

4482. Though the emperor has wealth, he cannot buy ten thousand years of life.   *Chinese*

4483. Where there is nothing, the emperor loses his right.   *Dutch*

EMPLOYMENT

4484. Employment in time of famine is like the warmth of a fire in the month of January.   *Indian (Kashmiri)*

4485. Out of employment, out of health.   *Indian (Hindustani)*

END

4486. Better the end of a feast than the beginning of a fray.   *Scottish.*

4487. Call no one blessed before his end. *Greek*

4488. Each end of the fire has its smoke. *African (Hausa)*

4489. Everything has an end excepting God. *Dutch*

4490. If the end is good everything is good. *Japanese*

4491. In the end it will be known who ate the bacon. *French*

4492. In the end things will mend. *English*

4493. The end crowns all. *English*

4494. The end crowns the work. *French*

4495. The end makes all equal. *English*

4496. The end of all things is death. *Dutch*

4497. The end of drinking is more thirst. *Irish*

4498. The end of every disgraceful action is repentance. *Turkish*

4499. The end of mirth is the beginning of sorrow. *Dutch*

4500. The end of our good begins our evil. *English*

4501. The end of the journey is reached by moving ahead. *African (Ovambo)*

4502. The end of the ox is beef, and the end of a lie is exposure. *Malagasy*

4503. The end of wrath is the beginning of repentance. *German*

4504. The end praises the work. *Italian*

4505. The end to a job is a crown. *Russian*

4506. The end tries all. *English*

4507. There is an end to every song. *Slovakian*

4508. Think on the end before you begin. *English*

ENDEAVOR

4509. No endeavor is worse than that which is not attempted. *Mexican*

ENDURANCE

4510. Endurance pierces marble. *Moroccan*

ENDURE

4511. He that can quietly endure overcomes. *English*

4512. He that endures is not overcome. *English*

4513. That which was bitter to endure may be sweet to remember. *English*

ENEMY

4514. A wise enemy is better than an unwise friend. *Indian (Kashmiri)*

4515. An enemy does not sleep. *French*

4516. An enemy may chance to give good counsel. *English*

4517. An enemy will give in, but a friend will argue. *Russian*

4518. An old enemy never becomes a friend. *Greek*

4519. An open enemy is preferable to a hidden friend. *Turkish*

4520. Be mild towards the wretched, but stern towards an enemy. *Irish*

4521. Better a good enemy than a bad friend. *Yiddish*

4522. Better a wise enemy than a foolish friend. *Lebanese*

4523. Better an open enemy than a false friend. *Danish*

4524. Better that my enemy should see good in me than I should see evil in him. *Yiddish*

4525. Beware of a reconciled enemy. *French*

4526. Beware of an enemy, even though he be only an ant. *Turkish*

4527. Even though you become the enemy of a good man, don't become the friend of a bad man.   *Japanese*

4528. Gossiping about the enemy brings war.   *African (Jabo)*

4529. He is an enemy who slanders one's name.   *African (Yoruba)*

4530. He that has no enemies has no friends.   *English*

4531. He who has three enemies must agree with two.   *German*

4532. He who is truthful may be the enemy of many.   *Indian (Tamil)*

4533. He who loses his enemy, weeps not for him.   *African (Wolof)*

4534. He who makes light of his enemy dies by his hand.   *Spanish*

4535. If we are bound to forgive an enemy, we are not bound to trust him.   *English*

4536. If you wish to have no enemy, do not lend.   *Philippine*

4537. It's easy to acquire an enemy; hard to acquire a friend.   *Yiddish*

4538. Little enemies and little wounds are not to be despised.   *German*

4539. Make no one an enemy without cause.   *Turkish*

4540. Many are brave when the enemy flees.   *Italian*

4541. One enemy is too many, and a hundred friends are too few.   *Italian*

4542. One enemy is too much for a man in a great post, and a hundred friends are too few.   *English*

4543. Repay your enemy with a favor.   *Japanese*

4544. Take heed of reconciled enemies.   *English*

4545. The angry and the weak are their own enemies.   *Russian*

4546. The enemy of a chief is he who has grown up with him from childhood.   *African (Ashanti)*

4547. The poor man's enemies are few, the rich man's friends are even fewer.   *Yiddish*

4548. The surest way to make enemies is to have too many friends. *American*

4549. There is no such thing as an insignificant enemy.   *French*

4550. When two enemies blow one horn, the third will have to suffer for it.   *Danish*

4551. When your enemy falls, don't rejoice; but don't pick him up either.   *Yiddish*

4552. When your enemy retreats, make him a golden bridge.   *Dutch*

4553. Your enemy makes you wise.   *Italian*

4554. Your enemy will not praise you, even though you catch a leopard and give it to him.   *African (Hausa)*

ENGAGEMENT

4555. Better to break off an engagement than a marriage.   *Yiddish*

ENMITY

4556. The enmity of the wise, rather than the friendship of the fool.   *Egyptian*

ENOUGH

4557. Enough is as good as a feast.   *English*

4558. Enough is better than a sackful.   *German*

4559. Enough is better than too much.   *Dutch*

4560. Enough is enough.   *English*

4561. Enough is enough, and too much spoils.   *Italian*

4562. He has enough who is contented with a little.   *English*

4563. More than enough is too much.   *English*

4564. There's not enough if there's not too much.   *French*

4565. There was never enough where nothing was left.   *Scottish*

ENTERTAINMENT

4566. When entertainment is discontinued friendship ceases.
      Indian (Tamil)

ENTRANCE

4567. When the entrance is carefully shut a dog does not come in. *Japanese*

ENTRUSTED

4568. Few are fit to be entrusted with themselves.   *English*

ENVY (noun)

4569. An enemy's envy is his own punishment.   *Indian (Tamil)*

4570. Better envy than pity. *German*

4571. Envy breeds hate.   *Yiddish*

4572. Envy cries of spite where honor rides.   *Dutch*

4573. Envy does not enter an empty house.   *Danish*

4574. Envy envies itself.   *German*

4575. Envy goes beyond avarice.   *French*

4576. Envy has smarting eyes.
      Latvian

4577. Envy hatches swans from rotten duck eggs.   *Russian*

4578. Envy is prosperity's manure.
      African (Fulani)

4579. Envy never dies.   *English*

4580. Envy never enriched any man.
      English

4581. Envy sees the sea but not the rocks.   *Russian*

4582. Envy shoots at others and wounds herself.   *English*

4583. Envy was never a good spokesman.   *Danish*

4584. If envy were a fever, all the world would be ill.   *Danish*

4585. If envy were a rash the whole village would be ill.   *Greek*

4586. If envy were leprosy, how many lepers in the world would be.
      Mexican

4587. Nothing sharpens sight like envy.   *English*

4588. The envious will die, but envy never.   *French*

4589. Where there is envy, there is meanness.   *Greek*

ENVY (verb)

4590. Better be envied than pitied.
      English

4591. He who envies, suffers.
      German

EQUAL

4592. It is good that equals consort together.   *African (Efik)*

4593. Jest with your equals. *Danish*

EQUALITY

4594. Where there is not equality there never can be perfect love.
      Italian

ERR

4595. Better to err than wittingly to sin.   *Hebrew*

4596. He who errs should be taught and not ridiculed.   *Philippine*

4597. To err is human.   *Dutch*

4598. Who errs in the tens errs in the thousands.   *Italian*

ERRAND

4599. Errands are small on a spring day.   *Icelandic*

4600. He that performs his own errand saves the messenger's hire.
Danish

ERRING

4601. Erring is not cheating.
German

ERROR

4602. Error is always in haste.
English

4603. Every error has its excuse.
Polish

4604. One error always leads to another.   *American*

4605. The first error is overlooked.
Manx

ESCAPE

4606. He who runs away and escapes, is clever.   *African (Wolof)*

ESTATE

4607. A great estate is not gotten in a few hours.   *French*

4608. An estate inherited is the less valued.   *Portuguese*

ESTIMATE

4609. The estimate made at home does not hold good at the market.
Rumanian

ETERNITY

4610. Eternity gives no answer.
African (Jabo)

EVE

4611. Every eve forms its own beauty.
English

EVENING

4612. A joyful evening may follow a sorrowful morning.   *English*

4613. A joyous evening often leads to a sorrowful morning.   *Danish*

4614. Evening is speedier than morning.   *Irish*

4615. In the evening one may praise the day.   *German*

4616. Only the evening will show what the day has been.   *Russian*

4617. The evening crowns the day.
English

4618. The later the evening, the fairer the company.   *German*

EVENT

4619. Coming events cast their shadows before.   *English*

4620. Great events are brought about by small beginnings.   *American*

4621. It is afterwards events are understood.   *Irish*

EVERYBODY

4622. Everybody has his ways.
American

4623. Everybody loves his own likeness.   *English*

EVERYTHING

4624. Everything ends in weeping.
Yiddish

4625. Everything goes to him who does not want it.   *French*

4626. Everything has a wherefore.
Dutch

4627. Everything has its price.
American

4628. Everything is best when it is ended.   *American*

4629. Everything new is pleasing, everything familiar is distasteful. *Irish*

4630. For everything there is a time and a judgment. *American*

EVERYWHERE

4631. He that is everywhere is nowhere. *English*

4632. He who would be everywhere will be nowhere. *Danish*

EVIDENCE

4633. There is not better evidence than something written on paper. *Philippine*

EVIL

4634. All evils save death may be amended. *Greek*

4635. Bear with evil and expect good. *English*

4636. Better prevent an evil than attend it. *American*

4637. Better suffer a known evil than change for uncertain good. *Spanish*

4638. Depart from evil and create good. *Russian*

4639. Evil condoned is evil consented. *Mexican*

4640. Evil follows good, good follows evil. *Japanese*

4641. Evil gotten, evil kept. *English*

4642. Evil gotten, evil spent. *English*

4643. Evil is easily learned by everyone. *Maltese*

4644. Evil is of old date. *Egyptian*

4645. Evil is soon believed. *English*

4646. Evil is soon done, but slowly mended. *Danish*

4647. Evil may spring from the tiniest thing. *Irish*

4648. Evil must be driven out by evil. *Danish*

4649. Evil to him that evil seeks. *English*

4650. Evil to him that evil thinks. *English*

4651. Evil will not be concealed. *Welsh*

4652. For every evil under the sun, there is a remedy, or there is none; if there be one, try and find it, if there be none, never mind it. *English*

4653. For great evils strong remedies. *Dutch*

4654. He that helps the evil hurts the good. *English*

4655. He that will no evil do, must do nothing that belongs thereto. *English*

4656. He who approves evil is guilty of it. *Indian (Tamil)*

4657. He who sows evil will harvest repentance. *Moroccan*

4658. He who wishes evil to another man will suffer his own loss. *Indian (Kashmiri)*

4659. Hide the evil; show the good. *Chinese*

4660. In every evil there is something good. *Russian*

4661. It is bad to do evil, but worse to boast of it. *English*

4662. It is easy to find evil but difficult to find goodness. *Philippine*

4663. No evil without its advantages. *English*

4664. Of two evils choose the least. *English*

4665. Of two evils choose the lesser, of two women, the third. *Hebrew*

4666. Pity the man who does evil and who is poor notwithstanding. *Irish*

4667. The evil done in the gloom of night will appear disclosed in the light of day.   *Mexican*

4668. The evil is soon done; the sore is aching long.   *Finnish*

4669. The last evil smarts most.
          English

4670. There is no evil without good.
          Russian

4671. There is no evil without some good in it.   *Russian*

4672. Who does not punish evil, invites it.   *German*

EXAMPLE

4673. A good example is the best sermon.   *English*

4674. An example is no proof.
          Yiddish

4675. Example is better than precept.
          English

4676. One bad example destroys more than twenty good ones build up.
          Hungarian

EXCELLENCE

4677. Excellence is no distinction among the excellent.   *Serbo-Croatian*

4678. The excellence of a man is a benefit to the public.   *Turkish*

EXCEPTION

4679. Exceptions prove the rule.
          English

EXCESS

4680. Anything in excess is unhealthy.   *Yiddish*

4681. Excess in clothes leads to debt, in spending to slavery, in eating to harm, in sleep to stupidity.   *Burmese*

4682. Excess is unhealthy.   *Yiddish*

4683. Excess mars perfection.   *Greek*

EXCHANGE

4684. A fair exchange brings no quarrel.   *Danish*

4685. Exchange is no robbery.
          German

4686. Fair exchange is no robbery.
          English

4687. He who wants an exchange despises his own.   *African (Hausa)*

EXCUSE (noun)

4688. A bad excuse is better than none.   *English*

4689. An excuse is nearer to a woman than her apron.   *Irish*

4690. Excuses are of no avail before God.   *Indian (Tamil)*

4691. Since excuses were invented, no one is ever in the wrong.   *Mexican*

4692. That which is customary requires no excuse.   *Italian*

4693. Without an excuse there's no respect.   *Yiddish*

EXCUSE (verb)

4694. He who excuses himself accuses himself.   *French*

4695. Who excuses, accuses.   *Dutch*

EXECUTIONER

4696. The executioner is a keen shaver.   *German*

4697. The executioner never lets the sword be passed across his own neck.
          African (Yoruba)

EXECUTOR

4698. Two executors and an overseer make three thieves.   *English*

EXERTION

4699. Exertion is a manly quality.
          Indian (Tamil)

4700. Exertion will succeed.   *Welsh*

EXPENSE

4701. He is wise who learns at another's expense.   *Norwegian*

4702. It is the petty expenses that empty the purse.   *Italian*

4703. Set your expense according to your trade.   *Dutch*

EXPERIENCE

4704. Experience is a long road.
    Swedish

4705. Experience is better than knowledge.   *Philippine*

4706. Experience is good, but often dear bought.   *Scottish*

4707. Experience is good, if not bought too dear.   *English*

4708. Experience is knowledge that makes not ashamed.   *Indian (Tamil)*

4709. Experience is sometimes dangerous.   *English*

4710. Experience is the best of schools.   *Lebanese*

4711. Experience is the best rule to walk by.   *American*

4712. Experience is the best teacher.
    German

4713. Experience is the father of wisdom, and memory the mother.
    English

4714. Experience is the mistress of fools.   *English*

4715. Experience is the mother of knowledge.   *English*

4716. Experience keeps a dear school, but fools will learn in no other.
    English

4717. Experience makes men wise.
    American

4718. Experience teaches fools.
    English

4719. Experience without learning is better than learning without experience.   *English*

4720. To hear it told is not equal to experience.   *Chinese*

4721. Without experience one gains no wisdom.   *Chinese*

EXPERT

4722. One is an expert on scholarly discourse, another on bristles, but all are experts on cantors.   *Yiddish*

4723. Two experts are never on good terms.   *African (Shona)*

EXTERIOR

4724. The exterior is the mirror of the interior.   *Indian (Tamil)*

EXTREME

4725. Extremes meet.   *English*

4726. One extreme produces another.
    English

EXTREMITY

4727. Every extremity is a fault.
    English

EYE

4728. A friend's eye is a good mirror.
    Irish

4729. A greedy eye had never a full belly.   *Scottish*

4730. A guest's eye is sharp sighted.
    Icelandic

4731. A lax eye spells a broken head.
    Malaysian

4732. A neighbor's eye is full of jealousy.   *Danish*

4733. A stranger's eye sees clearest.
    English

4734. Abroad one has a hundred eyes, at home not one.   *German*

4735. An evil eye can see no good.
    Danish

4736. Bad eyes never see any good.
German

4737. Before you are married keep your two eyes open; after you are married shut one. *Jamaican*

4738. Better eye out than always ache.
English

4739. Better to lose your eye than your good name. *Armenian*

4740. Cover your eyes in the village where everyone else is blind.
Armenian

4741. Doubt even your eyes, still less trust other people's words. *Russian*

4742. Eyes are great wealth.
African (Ovambo)

4743. Eyes can see everything except themselves. *Serbo-Croatian*

4744. Eyes do not see all.
African (Zulu)

4745. Eyes have no screen.
African (Swahili)

4746. Far from the eye, cheap to the heart. *Libyan*

4747. For the buyer a hundred eyes are too few, for the seller one is enough.
Italian

4748. Four eyes see more than two.
English

4749. Gone from the eyes and out of the heart. *Russian*

4750. He must have keen eyes that would know a maid at sight. *German*

4751. He that has but one eye had need look well to that. *English*

4752. He that has but one eye sees the better for it. *English*

4753. He who does not open his eyes must open his purse. *German*

4754. His eye is bigger than his belly.
English

4755. Hostile and envious are the eyes of neighbors. *Greek*

4756. If the eyes don't see, the heart won't break. *Spanish*

4757. If the eyes of a bride are beautiful, no need to examine the rest.
Hebrew

4758. If the eyes wouldn't see, the hands wouldn't take. *Yiddish*

4759. If you can't use your eyes, follow your nose. *Latvian*

4760. It is hard for a greedy eye to have an honest heart. *Scottish*

4761. Many are the eyes of the person whose spouse commits adultery.
African (Bemba)

4762. Many see more with one eye than others with two. *German*

4763. Men are born with two eyes, but with one tongue, in order that they should see twice as much as they say.
English

4764. Not all are asleep who have their eyes shut. *Italian*

4765. Nowhere in the world do eyes look satisfied. *Russian*

4766. One bad eye spoils the other.
German

4767. One eye is sufficient for the merchant, but a hundred are scarcely enough for the purchaser. *Basque*

4768. One eye of the master sees more than four eyes of his servants. *Italian*

4769. One eye of the master's sees more than ten of the servants'. *English*

4770. One sees with nothing so well as with the eyes. *Finnish*

4771. One who stays not before the other's eyes is soon forgotten. *Greek*

4772. Our eyes are our enemies.
Russian

4773. Shut your eyes if you are among the blind. *Hungarian*

4774. Shut your eyes when you laugh, and you'll never see a merry day. *English*

4775. Some have fine eyes and can't see a jot. *French*

4776. Strange eyes see more than one's own. *Swedish*

4777. That which is far from the eye is far from the heart. *Turkish*

4778. The eye and religion can bear no jesting. *English*

4779. The eyes are bigger than the belly. *Dutch*

4780. The eyes are the mirror of the soul. *Philippine*

4781. The eyes believe their own evidence, the ears that of others. *Swedish*

4782. The eyes believe themselves, the ears other people. *German*

4783. The eyes deceive. *Maltese*

4784. The eyes eat not but they know what will satisfy. *African (Fulani)*

4785. The eyes have one language everywhere. *English*

4786. The eye is blind if the mind is absent. *Italian*

4787. The eye is never satiated with seeing. *German*

4788. The eye is the pearl of the face. *English*

4789. The eyes of a stranger may be very large, but he does not see the inner things of the town. *African (Ga)*

4790. The eyes of the hare are not the same as the eyes of the owl. *Greek*

4791. The eye of the master fattens the steed. *French*

4792. The eye of the master makes the horse fat, and that of the mistress the chambers neat. *Dutch*

4793. The eye of the master will do more work than both his hands. *English*

4794. The eye of the sun cannot be hidden. *Egyptian*

4795. The eye of the thief glances about. *Hawaiian*

4796. The eye sees; the hand performs. *Greek*

4797. The eye should be blind in the home of another. *Irish*

4798. The eyes speak as much as the mouth. *Japanese*

4799. The eye that sees all things else sees not itself. *English*

4800. The eye will have his part. *English*

4801. The hen's eyes are where her eggs are. *Spanish*

4802. The hen's eyes are with her chickens. *French*

4803. The hen's eyes turn to where she has her eggs. *Portuguese*

4804. The master's eye and foot are the best manure for the field. *Dutch*

4805. The master's eye does more than both his hands. *German*

4806. The master's eye does more than the hands of two servants. *Estonian*

4807. The master's eye fats the horse. *English*

4808. The master's eye has its own effect. *Iranian*

4809. The master's eye makes the cow fat. *Turkish*

4810. The mistress's eye feeds the capon. *English*

4811. The parson's eye and the wolf's jaw will eat what they see. *Russian*

4812. Two eyes can see more than one. *English*

4813. Two eyes see better than one.
African (Wolof)

4814. Use your eyes in the field and your ears in the forest.   *Latvian*

4815. What the eyes do not see the heart does not desire.   *Russian*

4816. What the eye doesn't see, the heart doesn't feel.   *Yiddish*

4817. What the eye does not see the heart does not grieve for.   *Chinese*

4818. What the eyes see, the heart believes.   *German*

4819. What the eye sees not, the heart rues not.   *English*

4820. When the eye does not see, the heart does not grieve.   *Egyptian*

4821. Who buys wants a hundred eyes, who sells need have but one.
Dutch

4822. Who has but one eye must take good care of it.   *Dutch*

4823. With eyes you will not win love.
Lithuanian

4824. You can see the eye of a needle but fail to see the eye of an axe.
Philippine

4825. You may force a man to shut his eyes, but not to sleep.   *Danish*

EYELASH

4826. Eyelashes, though near, are not seen.   *Japanese*

EYESIGHT

4827. Eyesight is more powerful than hearsay.   *Icelandic*

EYEWITNESS

4828. One eyewitness is better than ten earwitnesses.   *English*

4829. The eyewitness observes what the absent does not see.   *Egyptian*

F

FACE

4830. A clean face needs no water.
Czech

4831. A fair face cannot have a crabbed heart. *English*

4832. A fair face is half a portion.
English

4833. A fair face may be a foul bargain. *English*

4834. A fair face will get its praise, though the owner keep silent. *Danish*

4835. A good face is a letter of recommendation. *English*

4836. A good face needs no band.
English

4837. A good face needs no paint.
English

4838. A king's face should give grace.
English

4839. A lovely face does not need adornment. *African (Swahili)*

4840. A man's face shows what is in his heart. *African (Hausa)*

4841. A pretty face and fine clothes do not make character. *Jamaican*

4842. A pretty face costs money.
Yiddish

4843. A pretty face doesn't make for a good wife. *Yiddish*

4844. A pretty face is half a dowry.
Hebrew

4845. A shining face goes with a full belly. *African (Hausa)*

4846. A smiling face is even better than hospitality. *(Lebanese*

4847. A smiling face removes unhappiness. *African (Hausa)*

4848. Better a red face than a black heart. *Portuguese*

4849. Do not show on your face what you feel in your heart.
African (Swahili)

4850. If you stay too near the fire, your face will get burned. *Vietnamese*

4851. One's face is the mirror of one's soul. *Mexican*

4852. The envious man's face grows sharp and his eyes big. *Spanish*

4853. The face is index of the heart.
English

4854. The face is the mirror of the heart. *Japanese*

4855. The face of an official is cold.
Turkish

4856. The face of Christ is like all men's faces. *Russian*

4857. The face tells the secret.
Yiddish

4858. The fairest face, the falsest heart.   *Scottish*

4859. We know men's faces, not their minds.   *Chinese*

4860. We see faces, we do not see hearts.   *Mexican*

FACT

4861. Facts are facts.   *American*

4862. Facts are stranger than fiction.   *American*

4863. Facts are stubborn things.   *English*

4864. Facts speak for themselves.   *American*

4865. Facts speak louder than words.   *American*

FAGOT

4866. There are fagots and fagots.   *French*

FAIL

4867. He who never fails will never grow rich.   *English*

FAILURE

4868. Failure is the source of success.   *Japanese*

4869. Failure teaches you more than success.   *Russian*

FAIR (beautiful)

4870. All that's fair must fade.   *Italian*

4871. Fair and softly goes far. *French*

FAIR (carnival)

4872. Buy at a fair but sell at home.   *English*

4873. Every one speaks of the fair as he himself finds it.   *Spanish*

FAIRY TALE

4874. With a fairy tale and with a lie you can lull only children to sleep.   *Yiddish*

FAITH

4875. Faith can move mountains.   *Russian*

4876. Faith in medicine makes it effectual.   *Indian (Tamil)*

4877. Faith makes god of a stone.   *Indian (Bihar)*

4878. Faith sees by the ears. *English*

4879. Faith will move Heaven.   *Korean*

4880. Who dies for his faith gains a kingdom.   *Russian*

4881. Who doesn't keep faith with God won't keep it with man.   *Dutch*

FALL (noun)

4882. One man's fall is another's uprising.   *African (Fulani)*

4883. The fall is allowed; to get up is commanded.   *Russian*

4884. We need not regret a fall if it is for a worthy cause.   *Philippine*

FALL (verb)

4885. Everything does not fall that totters.   *French*

4886. He falls low that cannot rise again.   *English*

4887. He that falls today may be up again tomorrow.   *English*

4888. He that is fallen cannot help him that is down.   *English*

4889. It is easier to fall than rise.   *English*

4890. No one falls low unless he attempts to climb high.   *Danish*

4891. The bigger they are the harder they fall.   *American*

4892. The harder you fall the higher you bounce. *American*

4893. To fall is easy; to get up is difficult. *Swedish*

FALLING

4894. By falling we learn to go safely. *Dutch*

4895. Falling is easier than rising. *Irish*

FALSEHOOD

4896. Falsehood is common, truth uncommon. *Hebrew*

4897. Falsehood is the beginning of theft. *Estonian*

4898. Falsehood never tires of going round about. *Danish*

4899. Falsehood often goes farther than truth. *Irish*

4900. Falsehood travels and grows. *Danish*

4901. Many destroy themselves by falsehood. *African (Efik)*

4902. One falsehood spoils a thousand truths. *African (Ashanti)*

4903. There is falsehood in fellowship. *English*

4904. There is falsehood in packing. *English*

FAME

4905. A good fame is better than a good face. *English*

4906. All fame brings envy. *English*

4907. All fame is dangerous. *English*

4908. Better a good fame than a good face. *Scottish*

4909. Common fame is a common liar. *English*

4910. Common fame is seldom to blame. *English*

4911. Common fame seldom lies. *Dutch*

4912. Fame and repute follow a man to the door. *Danish*

4913. Fame endures longer than life. *Irish*

4914. Fame is a magnifying glass. *English*

4915. Fame is but the breath of the people. *English*

4916. Fame is like gourds, it breaks. *African (Shona)*

4917. Fame, like a river, is narrowed at its source and broadest afar off. *English*

4918. Fame will last longer than wealth. *Welsh*

4919. From fame to infamy is a beaten road. *English*

4920. The fame of a warrior is precarious, while that of a man strong to cultivate food is lasting. *Australian (Maori)*

4921. Without money fame is dead. *Irish*

FAMILIARITY

4922. Familiarity breeds contempt. *English*

4923. Familiarity little by little gets into the drawers of the cupboard. *Maltese*

4924. If familiarity were useful water would not cook fish. *African (Fulani)*

FAMILY

4925. A decaying family will not listen to advice. *Indian (Tamil)*

4926. A family divided against itself will perish together. *Indian (Tamil)*

4927. A family out of debt is out of danger. *Indian (Tamil)*

4928. A large family gives beauty to a house. *Indian (Tamil)*

4929. A small family is soon provided for. *English*

4930. A wealthy family is not exposed to danger. *Indian (Tamil)*

4931. As the family is, so is the off-spring. *Russian*

4932. Every family has its own ugly member. *Russian*

4933. Family quarrels sow the seeds of poverty. *Japanese*

4934. If a family has an old person in it, it possesses a jewel. *Chinese*

4935. If the family lives in harmony, all affairs will prosper. *Chinese*

4936. In time of test, family is best. *Burmese*

4937. It's a poor family which has neither a whore nor a thief in it. *English*

4938. Large families bring poverty. *Greek*

4939. One family always sings one song. *Estonian*

4940. One family builds a wall, two families enjoy it. *Chinese*

4941. When the whole family is together, the soul is in place. *Russian*

4942. Whoever is ashamed of his family will have no luck. *Yiddish*

FAMINE

4943. Famine compels one to eat the fruit of all kinds of trees. *African (Yoruba)*

4944. Yearly guard against famine; nightly guard against thieves. *Chinese*

FAN

4945. There are no fans in hell. *Egyptian*

FANCY

4946. Fancy flees before the wind. *Scottish*

4947. Fancy is a fool. *English*

4948. Fancy may kill or cure. *English*

4949. Fancy requires much, necessity but little. *German*

4950. Fancy surpasses beauty. *English*

FARE

4951. Hard fare makes hungry bellies. *English*

4952. Light fare begets light dreams. *English*

FARM

4953. He who neglects his farm won't see a bright eye in his house. *African (Hausa)*

FARMER

4954. A farmer is known when at his field. *Indian (Bihar)*

4955. If a farmer becomes a king, he will still carry a basket on his back. *Hebrew*

4956. If the farmer fails all will starve. *American*

4957. The farmer hopes for rain, the traveler for fine weather. *Chinese*

4958. The farmer is master on his land. *German*

FASHION

4959. Everyone after his fashion. *English*

4960. Fashion is ruin to some people. *Japanese*

4961. The plain fashion is best. *English*

4962. What's in fashion will be out of fashion. *Japanese*

FASTING

4963. Fasting is easy with a chicken leg and a half-bottle of wine. *Yiddish*

4964. Fasting is the best medicine. *Indian (Hindi)*

4965. It is easy to preach fasting with a full belly. *Italian*

4966. Long fasting is no bread sparing. *Dutch*

4967. Long fasting is no economy of food. *German*

4968. Who goes fasting to bed will sleep but lightly. *Dutch*

FAT

4969. He who becomes fat must become thin, and he who flies must come down. *Moroccan*

4970. One need not worry about the fat, but just try to keep alive. *Russian*

FATE

4971. Fate and self-help equally shape our destiny. *Indian (Bihar)*

4972. Fate assists the courageous. *Japanese*

4973. Fate is with heaven. *Japanese*

4974. Fate leads the willing but drives the stubborn. *English*

4975. Fate makes a man dismount quicker than counsel. *African (Hausa)*

4976. No fate is worse than a life without a love. *Mexican*

4977. On the tip of the tongue lies the fate of the entire world. *Yiddish*

4978. One man's fate is another man's lesson. *African (Swahili)*

4979. The fate of one's parents is returned to their children. *Japanese*

4980. The fate of the lamb is that of its dam. *Indian (Tamil)*

FATHER

4981. A father maintains ten children better than ten children one father. *German*

4982. A miserly father has a thriftless son. *English*

4983. A miserly father makes a prodigal son. *French*

4984. Clever father, clever daughter; clever mother, clever son. *Russian*

4985. Father and mother are the most precious jewels on earth. *Philippine*

4986. Father earns and son spends. *Japanese*

4987. Father hands down, son hands down. *Korean*

4988. He who has neither father nor mother has no wisdom. *African (Ovambo)*

4989. He who teaches me for one day is my father for life. *Chinese*

4990. If the father is a good man, the son will behave well. *Vietnamese*

4991. If you live without being a father you will die without having been a human being. *Russian*

4992. It is a wise father that knows his own child. *English*

4993. Like father, like offspring. *Welsh*

4994. Like father, like son. *English*

4995. One cannot please everybody and one's father. *French*

4996. One father can support ten children; but it is difficult for ten children to support one father. *Yiddish*

4997. One father is more than a hundred schoolmasters. *English*

4998. Tell me who your father is, and I'll tell you who you are.   *Philippine*

4999. The father a saint, the son a devil.   *Italian*

5000. The father a saint, the son a sinner.   *Spanish*

5001. The father acquires wealth, the son destroys it.   *Indian (Tamil)*

5002. There are many fathers, but only one mother.   *Russian*

5003. When the father gives to his son, both laugh; but when the son gives to his father, both cry.   *Yiddish*

FATHERLAND

5004. It is a fine thing to die for one's fatherland, but a still finer to live for it.   *Hungarian*

FATIGUE

5005. Fatigue is better than a bed of down.   *American*

5006. On the day of victory no fatigue is felt.   *Egyptian*

FAULT

5007. A fault confessed is half redressed.   *African (Swahili)*

5008. A fault is sooner found than mended.   *English*

5009. A fault once excused is twice committed.   *English*

5010. A friend's fault should be known but not abhorred.   *Portuguese*

5011. A friend's faults may be noticed, but not blamed.   *Danish*

5012. Bear patiently that which you suffer by your own fault.   *Dutch*

5013. By concealing one fault another may arise.   *Indian (Tamil)*

5014. Confessing a fault makes half amends.   *English*

5015. Denying a fault doubles it.   *English*

5016. Don't find fault with what you don't understand.   *French*

5017. Everyone finds fault with his own trade.   *Italian*

5018. Everyone's faults are not written in their foreheads.   *English*

5019. Everyone knows how to find fault.   *English*

5020. Everyone puts his fault on the times.   *English*

5021. Faults are thick where love is thin.   *English*

5022. Fault-searchers are those who have the most faults.   *Philippine*

5023. He that commits a fault thinks everyone speaks of it.   *English*

5024. He who finds fault wants to buy.   *Spanish*

5025. He who likes you sees not your faults.   *African (Hausa)*

5026. He who loses is always in fault.   *Italian*

5027. He who loves you won't see your faults.   *African (Hausa)*

5028. If recognized, be not afraid to mend your fault.   *Korean*

5029. In every fault there is folly.   *English*

5030. It is easier to find faults in others than virtues in oneself.   *Yiddish*

5031. It is easier to spy two faults than mend one.   *English*

5032. It is hard for any man all faults to mend.   *English*

5033. It is well that all our faults are not written in our face.   *Scottish*

5034. Like fault like punishment.   *English*

5035. No one sees his own faults.   *German*

5036. One fault does but one pardon need. *English*

5037. One man's fault is another man's lesson. *English*

5038. The faults of a mother are visited on her children. *Indian (Tamil)*

5039. The first faults are theirs that commit them, the second theirs that permit them. *English*

5040. The first part of the night, think of your own faults; the latter part, think of the faults of others. *Chinese*

5041. When you sit alone, meditate on your own faults; when you converse, do not discuss the faults of others. *Chinese*

5042. Where no fault is, there needs no pardon. *English*

5043. Who excuses himself without being accused makes his fault manifest. *Italian*

FAULT-FINDER

5044. A fault-finder complains even that the bride is too pretty. *Yiddish*

FAVOR

5045. A favor ages sooner than anything else. *Greek*

5046. A king's favor is no inheritance. *English*

5047. An ounce of favor goes further, or is worth more, than a pound of justice. *French*

5048. Divine favor is common to all, material wealth is not. *Indian (Tamil)*

5049. Everything goes by favor and cousinship. *French*

5050. Favor and gifts disturb justice. *Danish*

5051. Favor will as surely perish as life. *English*

5052. For the smallest favor you become a debtor. *Yiddish*

5053. Great men's favors are uncertain. *English*

5054. Have no recollection of favors given; do not forget benefits conferred. *Chinese*

5055. He who asks the fewest favors is the best received. *Spanish*

5056. One favor qualifies for another. *English*

5057. The first time it is a favor; the second, a rule. *Chinese*

5058. To accept a favor is to lose your liberty. *Polish*

FEAR (noun)

5059. All fear is bondage. *English*

5060. Fear and love do not walk together. *Lithuanian*

5061. Fear and shame much sin does tame. *English*

5062. Fear gives wings. *English*

5063. Fear guards the vineyard. *Spanish*

5064. Fear has a quick ear. *English*

5065. Fear has large eyes. *Russian*

5066. Fear in the forest is shame at home. *African (Hausa)*

5067. Fear is a great inventor. *French*

5068. Fear is greater than danger. *Swedish*

5069. Fear is one part of prudence. *English*

5070. Fear is stronger than love. *English*

5071. Fear keeps the garden better than the gardener. *English*

5072. Fear makes people loving. *American*

5073. Fear never uses a donkey to ride away. *Mexican*

5074. Fear of the grave comes with old age.   *African (Swahili)*

5075. Fear of the law gives safety.
Greek

5076. Foolish fear doubles danger.
English

5077. He who dies from fears is not worth a place in the churchyard.
Czech

5078. He who fears to suffer, suffers from fear.   *French*

5079. If not for the fear of punishment, it would be sweet to sin.
Yiddish

5080. In a true heart, there is no fear.
African (Annang)

5081. It needs a high wall to keep out fear.   *Danish*

5082. Love, thieves, and fear make ghosts.   *German*

5083. Many a one threatens, while he quakes for fear.   *German*

5084. Seeing the case of another is enough to cause fear. *African (Hausa)*

5085. The greater the fear, the nearer the danger.   *Danish*

5086. Too much fear creates slavery.
African (Swahili)

5087. Where there is fear, there is shame.   *Greek*

5088. Where there is no fear, there is no pity.   *Estonian*

5089. Wise fear begets care. *English*

FEAR (verb)

5090. He who is feared by many, fears many.   *German*

5091. It's better to fear than to be frightened.   *Hungarian*

5092. It is folly to fear what one cannot avoid.   *Danish*

5093. It is good to fear the worst, the best will be the welcomer.   *Scottish*

5094. Two are less to fear than one.
Russian

FEAST

5095. A feast is not made of mushrooms only.   *English*

5096. Better than a feast elsewhere is a meal at home of tea and rice.
Japanese

5097. Don't praise the feast until you are going home.   *Czech*

5098. Enough is as good as a feast.
Scottish

5099. He who would enjoy the feast should fast on the eve.   *Italian*

5100. It is better coming to the beginning of a feast than to the end of a fray.
English

5101. It is better coming to the end of a feast than to the beginning of a fray.
English

5102. No feast like a miser's. *French*

5103. The feast passes and the fool remains.   *Italian.*

5104. The wedding feast is not made with mushrooms only.   *Spanish*

5105. There are no feasts in the world which do not break up at last.
Chinese

FEASTING

5106. Feasting makes no friendship.
English

FEATHER

5107. Feather by feather the goose is plucked.   *Italian*

5108. Fine feathers make fine birds.
English

5109. It is the feathers on a fowl that make it big. *African (Ashanti)*

5110. Let not him that fears feathers come among wild fowl.   *English*

5111. The feather makes not the bird.
English

FED

5112. Better fed than taught.   *French*

5113. Better unfed than untaught.
English

5114. Well fed but ill taught.   *French*

FEE

5115. A lean fee is a fit reward for a lazy clerk.   *English*

5116. No fee, no law.   *English*

5117. The physician's fee is not paid till the sickness is over.
African (Ashanti)

FEED

5118. The best feed of a horse is his master's eye.   *Spanish*

FEEL

5119. Feel for others as you feel for yourself.   *Indian (Tamil)*

FEELING

5120. Hurt feelings never heal completely.   *Philippine*

5121. When you give vent to your feelings, your anger leaves you.
Yiddish

FEET (see FOOT)

5122. All feet tread not in one shoe.
English

5123. Better the feet slip than the tongue.   *English*

5124. Do not stretch your feet beyond your carpet.   *Lebanese*

5125. Feet which are always on the move are not the feet of a hard-working man.   *Lebanese*

5126. He lifts his feet high who puts on boots for the first time.   *Chinese*

5127. Stretch your feet only as far as your covering goes.   *Pashto*

5128. The feet rest but the heart is not at ease.   *African (Fulani)*

5129. The gardener's feet do no harm to the garden.   *Spanish*

5130. The horse's front feet don't know what the back feet say. *Jamaican*

5131. Two feet in one shoe will never do.   *English*

FELLOW

5132. A crafty fellow never has any peace.   *English*

5133. A fellow who has been frightened by a mud-turtle will be startled at the mere sight of a kettle's lid. *Korean*

5134. A good fellow is a costly name.
Scottish

5135. An artful fellow is a devil in a doublet.   *English*

5136. An unlucky fellow gets hurt on his nose even when he tumbles backward.   *Korean*

5137. Don't kick a fellow when he's down.   *American*

5138. Even a worthless fellow can obtain the consent of a fool.   *Japanese*

5139. The fellow who has ten faults sneers at others for having one.
Korean

FENCE

5140. A fence between makes love more keen.   *German*

5141. A fence lasts three years, a dog lasts three fences, a horse three dogs, and a man three horses.   *German*

5142. A fence with supports is not overthrown by high winds.
Rumanian

5143. Between neighbors' gardens a fence is good. *German*

5144. Build a fence even between intimate friends. *Japanese*

5145. Every one tries to cross the fence where it is lowest. *Danish*

5146. Fences have ears. *Irish*

5147. Fences last the longest when the logs are peeled. *American*

5148. Good fences make good neighbors. *American*

5149. If you cross over the fence, you acquire other ideas. *Yiddish*

5150. No fence against ill fortune. *English*

5151. No fence is built for the eyes. *African (Ovambo)*

5152. On the other side of the fence, you have a change of heart. *Yiddish*

5153. There's no fence against a flail. *English*

5154. There must be a fence between good neighbors. *Norwegian*

5155. Where the fence is down everyone can get over. *Latvian*

5156. Where the fence is lowest, the devil leaps over. *German*

5157. Where there's a high fence there's a snowdrift. *Latvian*

FEUD

5158. Bridal feud is soon forgotten. *Scottish*

5159. The family feud is not to be interfered with. *African (Zulu)*

FEVER

5160. He who is with fever is not shown to the fire. *African (Bemba)*

5161. If you invest in a fever, you will realize a disease. *Yiddish*

FEW

5162. A few are no match for the many. *Japanese*

FEWER

5163. Fewer the better cheer. *English*

FIBER

5164. A single fiber does not make a thread. *Chinese*

FIDDLE

5165. The fiddle sings one tune and the bow another. *Greek*

FIDDLER

5166. He that dances must pay the fiddler. *American*

FIDELITY

5167. From a base person comes no fidelity, from a harlot no shame. *Turkish*

FIELD

5168. As the field, so the crops; as the father, so the sons. *German*

5169. Even though you have ten thousand fields, you can eat but one measure of rice a day. *Chinese*

5170. Fields have eyes, and the wilderness has ears. *Indian (Hindi)*

5171. Fields have eyes and woods have ears. *English*

5172. If your fields are not ploughed, your store house will be empty. *Chinese*

5173. Never leave your field in spring or your house in winter. *Chinese*

5174. Out of old fields comes new corn. *English*

5175. Take care of your field, and your field will take care of you. *German*

5176. The fertile field becomes sterile without rest. *Spanish*

5177. The neighbor's field is easy to hoe. *African (Ovambo)*

FIFE

5178. What comes from the fife goes back to the drum. *French*

FIFER

5179. The fifer of his own camp does not rejoice. *Egyptian*

FIG

5180. A fine fig is full of worms.
African (Zulu)

5181. If you break open a fig, you will see cavities here and there.
Indian (Tamil)

5182. The figs on the other side of the hedge are sweeter. *Serbo-Croatian*

5183. The more a fig is opened, the greater will be the number of worms found. *Indian (Tamil)*

5184. When you have figs in your haversack everybody seeks your friendship. *Albanian*

FIGHT (noun)

5185. Don't join in a fight if you have no weapons. *African (Swahili)*

5186. Rarely is a fight continued when the chief has fallen. *Irish*

FIGHT (verb)

5187. He that fights and runs away may live to fight another day. *English*

5188. The more you fight the more you get hurt. *Vietnamese*

FIGURE (body)

5189. A well-formed figure needs no cloak. *Portuguese*

FIGURE (number)

5190. Figures can't lie. *American*

5191. Figures will not lie. *American*

FILE

5192. A file will cut a file, diamonds cut diamonds. *Indian (Tamil)*

5193. It is a good file that cuts iron without making a noise. *Italian*

FILTH

5194. The more you stir filth, the worse it stinks. *Danish*

FIND

5195. Take heed you find not what you do not seek. *English*

FINE

5196. The beaten pay the fine.
French

FINERY

5197. So much finery, so much poverty. *American*

5198. Today in finery, tomorrow in filth. *German*

FINGER

5199. A single finger cannot catch fleas. *Haitian*

5200. A single finger cannot snap.
Indian (Tamil)

5201. A dry finger cannot take up salt. *Chinese*

5202. Better a finger off than always aching. *English*

5203. Don't put your finger into too tight a ring. *French*

5204. Do not thrust your finger through your own paper lantern.
Chinese

5205. Even the ten fingers cannot be of equal length. *Chinese*

5206. Fingers were made before forks. *English*

5207. Fingers which catch dirty things can be washed.

African (Bemba)

5208. Five fingers hold more than two forks. *German*

5209. If you can plug a hole with a finger, don't use your palm. *Slovakian*

5210. If you cannot say it, point to it with your finger. *French*

5211. Never put your finger between the tree and the bark. *French*

5212. No finger put into the mouth will come out without saliva.

African (Shona)

5213. No one puts his finger in another man's mouth and then beats him over the head. *African (Ashanti)*

5214. The fingers of the same hand are not alike. *Portuguese*

FINISH

5215. Once one has finished ringing, one should get out of the bell tower.

Russian

FIRE

5216. A distant fire does not burn.

African (Swahili)

5217. A good fire makes a quick cook.

Dutch

5218. A large fire often comes from a small spark. *Danish*

5219. A little fire that warms is better than a big fire that burns. *Irish*

5220. As fire is kindled by bellows, so is anger by words. *English*

5221. Better a little fire to warm us than a great one to burn us. *English*

5222. By labor fire is got out of a stone. *Dutch*

5223. Fire and gunpowder do not sleep together. *African (Ashanti)*

5224. Fire and pride cannot be hid.

English

5225. Fire and straw do not go together. *Greek*

5226. Fire and straw soon make a flame. *Danish*

5227. Fire and water are good servants but bad masters. *English*

5228. Fire drives out fire. *English*

5229. Fire drives the wasp out of its nest. *Italian*

5230. Fire in the heart sends smoke into the head. *German*

5231. Fire is a good slave, but a bad master. *Albanian*

5232. Fire is as hurtful as healthful.

English

5233. Fire is love and water sorrow.

English

5234. Fire is not quenched with fire.

Italian

5235. Fire is the rose of winter.

Armenian

5236. Fire straightens a crooked bar.

Greek

5237. Fire, water, and governments don't understand mercy. *Albanian*

5238. He that can make a fire well can end a quarrel. *English*

5239. He that will have fire must bear with smoke. *Dutch*

5240. He who blows in the fire will get sparks in his eyes. *German*

5241. He who cannot kindle a fire cannot love. *Finnish*

5242. He who dreads fire, guards himself even from smoke. *Turkish*

5243. He who plays with fire gets burned. *Philippine*

5244. He who warms himself by the fire must first put up with the smoke. *Serbo-Croatian*

5245. He who would enjoy the fire must bear the smoke. *Danish*

5246. If you light your fire at both ends, the middle will shift for itself. *English*

5247. It is a low fire that warms the soup. *African (Shona)*

5248. It is bad to be between two fires. *Danish*

5249. It is easy to kindle fire on an old hearth. *Welsh*

5250. It is easy to poke another man's fire. *Danish*

5251. It's good to poke the fire with somebody else's hands. *Yiddish*

5252. It is good to warm oneself by another's fire. *Dutch*

5253. It won't do to trifle with fire. *French*

5254. Kindle not a fire that you cannot extinguish. *English*

5255. Let him who is cold blow the fire. *French*

5256. Make no fire, raise no smoke. *English*

5257. No fire can cook a mess of stones. *Lebanese*

5258. No fire in the hearth, no bran in the mouth. *Indian (Tamil)*

5259. Of ready-cut logs it is easy to make a fire. *Russian*

5260. One lights the fire, the other fans it. *Greek*

5261. Only he who treads on the fire feels it. *Libyan*

5262. Put out the fire while it is small. *African (Hausa)*

5263. Secret fire is discovered by its smoke. *Spanish*

5264. Skeer your own fire. *English*

5265. Soft fire makes sweet malt. *English*

5266. Soon fire, soon ashes. *Dutch*

5267. Stir a fire with the poker and not with your hands. *Greek*

5268. The closer the fire the hotter. *English*

5269. The fire burns brightest on one's own hearth. *Danish*

5270. The fire heeds little whose cloak it burns. *Danish*

5271. The fire in the flint shows not till it's struck. *English*

5272. The fire is welcome within, when icicles hang without. *Danish*

5273. The fire of lust is more fierce than a smoking fire. *Indian (Tamil)*

5274. The fire of reeds is of rapid extinction. *Egyptian*

5275. The fire which is screened by elders is not dangerous. *African (Bemba)*

5276. The fire which lights us at a distance, will burn us when near. *English*

5277. The fire that does not warm me shall never scorch me. *English*

5278. The most covered fire is always the most glowing. *French*

5279. There is no fire when there is no wood. *African (Ovambo)*

5280. There is no fire without smoke. *Danish*

5281. There is no use in blowing a fire that burns well. *Danish*

5282. There is nothing more so red as fire. *African (Oji)*

5283. Well may he smell fire whose gown burns. *English*

5284. What is lost in the fire must be sought in the ashes. *Dutch*

5285. When you flee from fire, you run into water. *Yiddish*

5286. Where there is fire a wind will soon be blowing. *Polish*

5287. Where there's no fire there's no smoke. *Portuguese*

5288. Whether you tread on fire wittingly or unawares, it will burn you. *Indian (Tamil)*

5289. While your fire is burning, go cut up your pumpkin and cook. *Hebrew*

5290. Who wants fire, let him look for it in the ashes. *Dutch*

FIRESIDE

5291. There is no fireside like your own fireside. *Irish*

FIREWOOD

5292. If you do not gather firewood you cannot keep warm. *African (Ovambo)*

FISH (noun)

5293. A fish and a guest go bad on the third day and must be thrown out. *Basque*

5294. A fish begins to stink at the head. *Russian*

5295. A fish bites best on a silver hook. *Norwegian*

5296. A fish is a king in the water. *African (Hausa)*

5297. A fish is caught by its mouth, a man by his words. *Philippine*

5298. A fish should swim thrice: in water, in sauce, and in wine. *German*

5299. A small fish is better than a large cockroach. *Russian*

5300. A small fish makes the entire river water muddy. *Korean*

5301. A small fish on the table is better than a big one that still has to be caught. *Philippine*

5302. After a fish has matured, it ventures into the deep. *African (Annang)*

5303. All fish are not caught with flies. *English*

5304. All is not fish that comes to net. *English*

5305. Better are small fish than an empty dish. *English*

5306. Big fish are caught in deep waters. *Serbo-Croatian*

5307. Big fish eat little fish. *English*

5308. Big fish spring out of the kettle. *Dutch*

5309. Don't bless the fish till it gets to the land. *Irish*

5310. Don't cry fried fish before they are caught. *Italian*

5311. Don't rub your belly when the little fish is still in the pond. *Yiddish*

5312. Don't strike at fish in front of the trap. *Thai*

5313. Don't teach fishes to swim. *French*

5314. Every little fish expects to become a whale. *Danish*

5315. Fish and company stink in three days. *English*

5316. Fish and guests smell at three days old. *Danish*

5317. Fish are not bought at the bottom of the sea. *Moroccan*

5318. Fish begin to stink at the head. *German*

5319. Fish bred up in dirty pools will taste of mud. *English*

5320. Fish eats fish and he who has no might dies. *Libyan*

5321. Fish is not caught without a bait.   *Greek*

5322. Fish look for deeper waters and men for where it's better.   *Russian*

5323. Fish make no broth.   *English*

5324. Fish should swim thrice.   *English*

5325. From great rivers come great fish.   *Portuguese*

5326. Fry the big fish first and the little ones afterward.   *Jamaican*

5327. Get your fish but do not let the spear be badly bent.   *Malaysian*

5328. Great fish are caught in great waters.   *German*

5329. Great fish break the net.   *Dutch*

5330. Gut no fish till you get them.   *Scottish*

5331. He who sleeps catches no fish.   *Italian*

5332. He who wants to catch fish must not mind a wetting.   *Spanish*

5333. If there are no fish in this place, then drop your hook in another.   *Chinese*

5334. If you cannot catch fish, catch shrimps.   *Chinese*

5335. It is a silly fish that is caught twice with the same bait.   *English*

5336. It is good fish if it were caught.   *English*

5337. It is ill catching of fish when the hook is bare.   *English*

5338. It is in vain to cast nets in a river where there are no fish. *Spanish*

5339. It is in vain to look for yesterday's fish in the house of the otter.   *Indian (Hindi)*

5340. Large fish do not live in a small pond.   *Japanese*

5341. Little fish are sweet.   *Dutch*

5342. Little fish are the prey of great fish.   *Indian (Tamil)*

5343. Little fishes make the pike big.   *German*

5344. Little fishes slip through nets, but great fishes are taken.   *English*

5345. No fish without bones; no woman without a temper.   *Polish*

5346. No one should ask the fish what happens in the plain; nor should the rat be asked what takes place in the water.   *African (Yoruba)*

5347. Of all the fish in the sea, herring is the king.   *English*

5348. Old fish and young flesh do feed men best.   *English*

5349. Old fish and young ones don't get along in double harness.   *American*

5350. Old fish, old oil, and an old friend are the best.   *English*

5351. One fish makes the basket stink.   *Moroccan*

5352. Small fish mingle with big fish.   *Japanese*

5353. Tasty is the fish from someone else's table.   *Yiddish*

5354. That fish will soon be caught that nibbles at every bait.   *English*

5355. The best fish swim near the bottom.   *English*

5356. The big fish eat the little fish, the little fish eat the water-insects, and the water-insects eat the weeds and the mud.   *Chinese*

5357. The fish adores the bait.   *English*

5358. The fish can't be cooked if you don't have a chopping board.   *Philippine*

5359. The fish comes to the rod of him who waits.   *Estonian*

5360. The fish does not go after the hook, but after the bait.   *Czech*

5361. The fish in the well experiences no pleasure.   *African (Hausa)*

5362. The fish is caught from the head.   *Turkish*

5363. The fish lead a pleasant life; they drink when they like.   *German*

5364. The fish may be caught in a net that will not come to a hook.   *English*

5365. The fish sees the bait, not the hook.   *Chinese*

5366. The fish stinks from his head.   *Turkish*

5367. The fish that escaped is the big one.   *Chinese*

5368. The fish when grown big returns to his rivulet.   *African (Efik)*

5369. The fish will not look at bad bait; you can only bring home crabs.   *Hawaiian*

5370. The great fish eats the little.   *English*

5371. The little fish cannot swallow the big fish.   *Hawaiian*

5372. There are as good fish in the sea as ever came out of it.   *English*

5373. There are more fish in the sea than can be caught.   *Philippine*

5374. To eat fish one has to go angling.   *Vietnamese*

5375. Venture a small fish to catch a great one.   *English*

5376. When there's no fish, even the crayfish is a fish.   *Russian*

5377. You catch fish in troubled waters.   *Russian*

FISH (verb)

5378. He fishes on who catches one.   *French*

FISHERMAN

5379. A fisherman can see a fisherman from afar.   *Russian*

5380. If you're afraid to get wet, you'll never make a good fisherman.   *Armenian*

5381. When numerous fishermen combine together, multitudes of fish may be caught.   *Indian (Tamil)*

FISHING

5382. If you yawn when out fishing, you will get no fish.   *Hawaiian*

5383. It is good fishing in troubled waters.   *Dutch*

5384. No fishing like fishing in the sea.   *English*

5385. The end of fishing is catching.   *English*

FIST

5386. A shut fist gets only a closed hand.   *Irish*

5387. Don't swing your fists after the fight.   *Russian*

FLAME

5388. Sometimes the largest flame is soonest extinguished.   *American*

5389. The flame is not far from the smoke.   *Danish*

FLATTER

5390. Who flatters you has either cheated you or hopes to do so.   *Rumanian*

5391. Who knows not how to flatter knows not how to talk.   *Italian*

FLATTERER

5392. A flatterer's throat is an open sepulchre.   *English*

5393. Flatterers are cats that lick before and scratch behind. *German*

5394. Flatterers haunt not cottages. *English*

5395. The flatterer walks the middle of the road. *African (Ovambo)*

5396. There is no such flatterer as a man's self. *English*

5397. When flatterers meet, the devil goes to dinner. *English*

FLATTERY

5398. Flattery is sweet food for those who can swallow it. *Danish*

5399. Flattery listens well, but remembers little. *Norwegian*

5400. Flattery sits in the parlor, when plain dealing is kicked out of doors. *English*

5401. He that rewards flattery begs it. *English*

5402. There is flattery in friendship. *English*

FLAVOR

5403. He who feeds on leaves knows not the flavor of fruit. *Indian (Tamil)*

5404. There is no flavor in a swallowed morsel. *French*

FLEA

5405. It is easier to guard a bushel of fleas than a woman. *German*

5406. Nothing should be done in a hurry except catching fleas. *German*

5407. Only fleas are to be caught quickly. *Russian*

5408. The fatter the flea, the leaner the dog. *German*

FLEE

5409. He who flees, proves himself guilty. *Danish*

5410. To flee and to run are not all one. *Spanish*

FLEECE

5411. Better to give the fleece than the sheep. *English*

FLESH

5412. All flesh is not venison. *English*

5413. He loves sheep's flesh well that eats the wool. *English*

5414. He that never eats flesh thinks a pudding a fine bit. *Scottish*

5415. Ill flesh was never good broth. *Scottish*

FLIGHT (fleeing)

5416. Flight is the beginning of collapse. *Hebrew*

FLIGHT (flying)

5417. The flight of the eagle will not stop that of the sandfly. *African (Fulani)*

5418. When the flight is not high the fall is not heavy. *Chinese*

FLINT

5419. Strike a flint and you get fire; don't strike it and not even smoke will come. *Chinese*

FLOCK

5420. No flock without dog and shepherd. *Turkish*

FLOGGING

5421. Every one takes his flogging in his own way. *French*

FLOOD

5422. A flood can be controlled but lust, never. *Philippine*

5423. A flood is more easily controlled than love. *Philippine*

5424. A flood may be stopped but not a wagging tongue. *Philippine*

5425. After high floods come low ebbs. *Dutch*

5426. Every flood has its ebb. *Dutch*

5427. The highest flood has the lowest ebb. *English*

5428. There's no flood that doesn't recede. *Irish*

FLOOR

5429. He who lies on the floor doesn't fall down. *Norwegian*

5430. Let everyone sweep his own floor. *African (Ovambo)*

FLOUNDER

5431. The flounder does not return to the place he left when disturbed. *Australian (Maori)*

FLOUR

5432. If there be flour, cakes may be baked. *Indian (Tamil)*

5433. Make good flour, and do not blow the trumpet. *Spanish*

5434. The flour tastes bitter to the mouse who has had enough. *Slovakian*

5435. You must contrive to bake with the flour you have. *Danish*

FLOW

5436. A flow will have an ebb. *English*

5437. The flow of water and the future of human beings are uncertain. *Japanese*

FLOWER

5438. A fair flower springs out of a dunghill. *American*

5439. A flower won't fall from the branch if it is not God's will. *Philippine*

5440. A wild flower on the mountaintop would not change places with a rose in the garden. *Armenian*

5441. A withered flower and a faith lost never bloom to live again. *Mexican*

5442. All the flowers of a tree do not produce fruit. *African (Wolof)*

5443. Even the most beautiful flower has its thorns. *Philippine*

5444. Every flower has its scent. *Iranian*

5445. Fair flowers do not remain long by the wayside. *German*

5446. Fallen flowers do not return to branches; a shattered mirror does not again reflect. *Japanese*

5447. Flowers are the pledges of fruit. *Danish*

5448. Garden flowers are not as fragrant as the flowers of the field, but the flowers of the field do not last as long. *Chinese*

5449. He that paints a flower does not give it perfume. *Italian*

5450. In the garden of time grows the flower of consolation. *Russian*

5451. It is not every flower that smells sweet. *Italian*

5452. Look at the flowers and then break off a branch. *Japanese*

5453. Not all flowers are fit for nosegays. *German*

5454. One flower makes no garland. *English*

5455. Painted flowers are scentless. *German*

5456. Ten flowers together will make a nosegay. *Russian*

5457. The finest flower will soonest fade. *English*

5458. The handsomest flower is not the sweetest. *English*

5459. Where the flower is, the honey is also. *Russian*

5460. Where there are many flowers, the fruits are few. *Japanese*

5461. Yesterday's lovely flower is but a dream today. *Japanese*

5462. You raise flowers for a year; you see them for but ten days. *Chinese*

FLY (noun)

5463. A fly can drive away horses. *Greek*

5464. A fly does not mind dying in coconut cream. *African (Swahili)*

5465. A fly has its spleen. *English*

5466. A fly is nothing; yet it creates loathsomeness. *Egyptian*

5467. Big flies break the spider's web. *Italian*

5468. Even a fly has its anger. *Italian*

5469. Every fly has its shadow. *Portuguese*

5470. Flies and priests can enter any house. *Russian*

5471. Flies are caught more readily with a single drop of honey than with a cask of vinegar. *Turkish*

5472. Flies are easier caught with honey than with vinegar. *French*

5473. Flies come to feasts unasked. *English*

5474. Flies flock to the lean horse. *Italian*

5475. Flies go to lean horses. *English*

5476. Flies swarm where there is honey. *Indian (Tamil)*

5477. Flies will not light on a boiling pot. *French*

5478. Flies will tickle lions being dead. *English*

5479. Hungry flies bite sore. *English*

5480. Into a closed mouth no fly will enter. *Moroccan*

5481. Let every one keep off the flies with his own tail. *Italian*

5482. More flies are caught with a drop of honey than with a barrel of vinegar. *Danish*

5483. More flies are caught with a spoonful of syrup than with a cask of vinegar. *Dutch*

5484. More flies are taken with a drop of honey than a tun of vinegar. *English*

5485. No flies land on a boiling pot. *Spanish*

5486. No fly dares to get near a boiling kettle. *Mexican*

5487. No fly gets into a shut mouth. *Spanish*

5488. The biting fly gets nothing by alighting on the back of the tortoise. *African (Ashanti)*

5489. The biting fly has no one to come to his aid in trouble. *African (Ashanti)*

5490. The busy fly is in every man's dish. *Spanish*

5491. The fly does not kill, but it does spoil. *Hebrew*

5492. The fly flutters about the candle till at last it gets burnt. *Dutch*

5493. The fly heeds not death: eating is all to him. *African (Yoruba)*

5494. The fly that bites the tortoise breaks its beak. *Italian*

5495. The fly that stands on the carabao's back thinks that it is taller than the carabao. *Philippine*

5496. To a boiling pot flies come not. *English*

5497. When a fly does not get up off a dead body, he is buried with it.
African (Ashanti)

5498. With honey you can catch more flies than with vinegar.   *Yiddish*

5499. You must lose a fly to catch a trout.   *English*

FLY (verb)

5500. Everything that flies is not good to eat.   *Rumanian*

5501. If you must fly, fly well.
English

FLYING

5502. No flying without wings.
English

FOAL

5503. A young foal and an old horse draw not well together.   *Danish*

FODDER

5504. The best fodder is the master's eye.   *Dutch*

FOE

5505. A courageous foe is better than a cowardly friend.   *English*

5506. A foe is better than a dissembling friend.   *English*

5507. A foe vanquished is a foe no more.   *American*

5508. A secret foe gives a sudden blow.   *English*

5509. An intelligent foe is better than a silly friend.   *Turkish*

5510. Never tell your foe that your foot aches.   *English*

5511. One foe is too many, and a hundred friends are too few.   *German*

5512. There is no foe to the flatterer.
English

FOG

5513. A fog cannot be dispelled with a fan.   *English*

FOLK

5514. Busy folks are always meddling.   *English*

5515. False folk should have many witnesses.   *Scottish*

5516. Greedy folk have long arms.
Scottish

5517. Idle folks have the least leisure.
English

5518. Idle folks lack no excuses.
English

5519. Idle folks take the most pains.
English

5520. Lazy folk take the most pains.
English

5521. Little folks are fond of talking about what great folks do.   *German*

5522. More folks are wed than keep good houses.   *English*

5523. Needy folks are pleased with buttermilk.   *Irish*

5524. Poor folks are glad of porridge.
English

5525. Poor folk fare the best. *English*

5526. Rich folk have many friends.
Scottish

5527. Some folks are born to be lucky.
American

5528. Strong folks have strong maladies.   *German*

5529. The littler folks be, the bigger they talk.   *American*

5530. Threatened folks live long.
English

5531. Tired folks are quarrelsome.
French

5532. Young folk, silly folk; old folk, cold folk.   *Dutch*

5533. Young folks will be young folks.
American

FOLLOWER

5534. A good follower makes a good leader. *Philippine*

5535. There's no bad follower to a good leader. *Philippine*

FOLLY

5536. Folly grows without watering. *English*

5537. Folly is never long pleased with itself. *English*

5538. Folly is often sick of itself. *English*

5539. Folly is the most incurable of maladies. *Spanish*

5540. Folly is wise in her own eyes. *English*

5541. Folly may hinder a man of many a good turn. *English*

5542. Folly without faults is as radish without salt. *English*

5543. He who does not commit follies in his youth commits them in his old age. *Swedish*

5544. He who is aware of his folly is wise. *Yiddish*

5545. He who recognizes his folly is on the road to wisdom. *Norwegian*

5546. If folly were a pain, there would be groaning in every house. *Spanish*

5547. If folly were grief, every house would weep. *English*

5548. It is folly to drown on dry land. *Danish*

5549. It is folly to take a thorn out of another's foot and put it into your own. *Danish*

5550. Nobody so wise but has a little folly to spare. *German*

5551. The biggest folly of the fool is that he thinks he is smart. *Yiddish*

5552. The folly of one man is the fortune of another. *English*

5553. The shortest follies are the best. *French*

5554. Trying to outsmart everybody is the greatest folly. *Yiddish*

FOOD

5555. All food is good to eat, but all words are not fit to speak. *Haitian*

5556. Food and clothing from one's parents, knowledge from one's teacher. *Vietnamese*

5557. Food and drink both go to the belly. *African (Hausa)*

5558. Food given by another person is only a throat tickler, but food gained by the labor of one's own hand is the food which satisfies. *Australian (Maori)*

5559. Food is no more important than wisdom. *Irish*

5560. Food, the produce of your own labor, you may eat without stint. *Australian (Maori)*

5561. Food, which you will not eat, you do not boil. *African (Oji)*

5562. Food without hospitality is medicine. *Indian (Tamil)*

5563. Give food to the hawk you do not love. *Japanese*

5564. He who swallows his food hot burns his lips. *Latvian*

5565. If there is food in the house, a guest is no worry. *Pashto*

5566. If there is food left over in the kitchen, there are poor people in the street. *Chinese*

5567. More die by food than famine. *English*

5568. Nobody cooks food and places it in the road to seek a guest.

African (Oji)

5569. Rich food is not long stared at; but a good looking person is attractive.

Australian (Maori)

5570. Sufficient food and clothing will produce good manners. *Japanese*

5571. The best food is that which fills the belly. *Egyptian*

5572. The food earned by the plough is sweeter than that obtained by serving others. *Indian (Tamil)*

5573. The food is according to the year. *Moroccan*

5574. The food is cooked in a pot and the plate gets the honor. *Yiddish*

5575. There is no bad food in time of starvation. *Philippine*

5576. Weak food best fits weak stomachs. *English*

5577. Whatever satisfies hunger is good food. *Chinese*

5578. When food fails, the five senses fail. *Indian (Tamil)*

5579. When food or grain is scarce, all is scarce. *Indian (Tamil)*

FOOL

5580. A fool always comes short of his reckoning. *English*

5581. A fool and his goods are soon parted; a wise man and his poverty always remain united. *Russian*

5582. A fool and his money are soon parted. *English*

5583. A fool asks much, but he is more fool that grants it. *English*

5584. A fool at forty is a fool indeed. *English*

5585. A fool believes everything. *English*

5586. A fool believes the thing he would have so. *English*

5587. A fool can ask more questions in an hour than a wise man can answer in a year. *Yiddish*

5588. A fool can ask more questions than seven wise men can answer. *Italian*

5589. A fool can dance without a fiddle. *English*

5590. A fool doesn't age and cold water doesn't spoil. *Yiddish*

5591. A fool falls on his back and bruises his nose. *Yiddish*

5592. A fool gives and the clever one takes. *Yiddish*

5593. A fool goes to the baths and forgets to wash his face. *Yiddish*

5594. A fool grows without rain. *Yiddish*

5595. A fool hopes to get honey, even from wasps. *Russian*

5596. A fool, if he holds his tongue, passes for wise. *Spanish*

5597. A fool is always beginning. *French*

5598. A fool is always in the rain. *Polish*

5599. A fool is busy in every one's business but his own. *English*

5600. A fool is incurable. *Hebrew*

5601. A fool is known by his speech. *English*

5602. A fool is like other men as long as he is silent. *Danish*

5603. A fool is pleased by beauty alone. *Russian*

5604. A fool knows his own business better than a wise man knows that of others. *Italian*

5605. A fool knows more in his own house than a wise man in another's. *English*

5606. A fool laughs at himself. *African (Ovambo)*

5607. A fool looks to the beginning, a wise man regards the end.   *English*

5608. A fool loses and a clever man finds.   *Yiddish*

5609. A fool loses his estate before he finds his folly.   *English*

5610. A fool makes his doctor his heir.   *Hungarian*

5611. A fool makes two trips where a wise man makes none.   *Yiddish*

5612. A fool may chance to say a wise thing.   *Dutch*

5613. A fool may give a wise man counsel by a time.   *Scottish*

5614. A fool may make money, but it needs a wise man to spend it. *English*

5615. A fool may sometimes give a wise man counsel.   *English*

5616. A fool may throw a stone into a well which a hundred wise men cannot pull out.   *English*

5617. A fool needs a lot of shoes.   *Yiddish*

5618. A fool needs good luck.   *Norwegian*

5619. A fool never makes a good husband.   *American*

5620. A fool only wins the first game.   *Danish*

5621. A fool remains a fool. *Yiddish*

5622. A fool sometimes gives good counsel.   *Spanish*

5623. A fool thinks himself wise.   *English*

5624. A fool thinks of his belly only.   *Indian (Bihar)*

5625. A fool throws a stone into a well, and it requires a hundred wise men to get it out again.   *Italian*

5626. A fool throws a stone into the well and a thousand wise men cannot take it out.   *Greek*

5627. A fool when he has spoken has done all.   *Scottish*

5628. A fool will ask more questions than the wisest can answer.   *English*

5629. A fool will laugh when he is drowning.   *English*

5630. A fool will not be foiled.   *English*

5631. A fool will receive praise, and a wise man will receive blame.   *Manx*

5632. A fool will soon use up his money.   *Japanese*

5633. A half fool is a very wise man.   *Yiddish*

5634. A quiet fool is half a sage.   *Yiddish*

5635. A strange fool is a laughing stock; your own—a shame.   *Yiddish*

5636. Advising a fool is like striking cold iron.   *Greek*

5637. An easy fool is a knave's tool.   *English*

5638. An obliging fool is more dangerous than an enemy.   *Russian*

5639. An old fool is worse than a young simpleton.   *Danish*

5640. Answer a fool according to his folly.   *English*

5641. As the fool thinks, so the bell clinks.   *English*

5642. Avoid and pass by a fool and a madman.   *Japanese*

5643. Be vain and you will be known as a fool.   *Russian*

5644. Better a complete fool than half wise.   *Yiddish*

5645. Better a witty fool than a foolish wit.   *English*

5646. Better be a fool than a knave.   *English*

5647. By the time the fool has learned to play the game, the players have dispersed.   *African (Ashanti)*

5648. By their words we know fools, and asses by their ears. *English*

5649. Even a fool has one accomplishment. *Japanese*

5650. Even a fool may sometimes have one accomplishment. *Korean*

5651. Every fool can find faults that a great many wise men can't remedy. *English*

5652. Every fool is wise when he holds his tongue. *Italian*

5653. Every fool likes his bauble. *French*

5654. Every fool thinks he is clever enough. *Danish*

5655. Every fool wants to give advice. *Italian*

5656. Everyone has a fool in his sleeve. *French*

5657. Everyone is free to make a fool of himself. *Polish*

5658. Fools and little dogs are ladies' playfellows. *English*

5659. Fools and madmen speak the truth. *English*

5660. Fools and scissors may be put to use. *Japanese*

5661. Fools and weeds grow without rain. *Yiddish*

5662. Fools are free all the world over. *Dutch*

5663. Fools are known by their babbling. *English*

5664. Fools are lucky. *Russian*

5665. Fools are not sown nor ploughed, they grow of themselves. *Finnish*

5666. Fools are of all sizes. *English*

5667. Fools are pleased with their own blunders. *English*

5668. Fools are wise men in the affairs of women. *English*

5669. Fools build houses and wise men buy them. *English*

5670. Fools do foolish things. *Australian (Maori)*

5671. Fools don't have to be sown; they grow up by themselves. *Yiddish*

5672. Fools go in throngs. *French*

5673. Fools grow without watering. *English*

5674. Fools have fortune. *English*

5675. Fools invent fashions and wise men follow them. *French*

5676. Fools laugh at their own sport. *English*

5677. Fools live poor to die rich. *English*

5678. Fools love all that is good. *English*

5679. Fools may invent fashions that wise men will wear. *English*

5680. Fools must not be set on eggs. *German*

5681. Fools never know when they are well. *English*

5682. Fools no Latin know. *English*

5683. Fools refuse favors. *English*

5684. Fools rejoice at promises. *Russian*

5685. Fools rush in where angels fear to tread. *English*

5686. Fools set stools for wise men to stumble at. *English*

5687. Fools should not see half-done work. *Scottish*

5688. Fools tie knots and wise men loosen them. *English*

5689. Fools will be fools. *English*

5690. Fools will be meddling. *English*

5691. Forbid a fool a thing, and that he will do. *Scottish*

5692. From a fool you have trouble.
Yiddish

5693. From fools and children you will learn the truth.   *Greek*

5694. Half a fool is worse than a whole one.   *Hebrew*

5695. He has great need of a fool that plays the fool himself.   *English*

5696. He is a fool that deals with fools.   *English*

5697. He is a fool that forgets himself.
English

5698. He's a fool that is wiser abroad than at home.   *English*

5699. He is a fool that makes a wedge of his fist.   *English*

5700. He is a fool that praises himself, and he is a madman that speaks ill of himself.   *Danish*

5701. He is a fool that thinks not that another thinks.   *English*

5702. He is a fool who boasts of four things: that he has good wine, a good horse, a handsome wife, and plenty of money.   *Italian*

5703. He is a fool who does not consider his own interests.   *Maltese*

5704. He is a fool who does not know from what quarter the wind blows.
Italian

5705. He is a fool who makes a mallet of his fist.   *French*

5706. He is a fool who makes his physician his heir.   *French*

5707. He is a fool who thinks that another does not think.   *Italian*

5708. He is a great fool who forgets himself.   *French*

5709. He is fool enough himself who will bray against another ass. *English*

5710. He is fool enough that is not melancholy once a day.   *English*

5711. He that is well sheltered is a fool if he stir out into the rain.   *English*

5712. He that repents is a fool.
English

5713. He that sends a fool means to follow him.   *English*

5714. He that teaches himself has a fool as his master.   *English*

5715. He who claps his hands for the fool to dance is no better than the fool.
African (Yoruba)

5716. He who is born a fool is never cured.   *English*

5717. He who keeps quiet is half a fool; he who talks is a complete fool.
Yiddish

5718. He who listens to the advice of women is a fool.   *Indian (Tamil)*

5719. He who would make a fool of himself will find many to help him.
Danish

5720. If a fool could keep silent he would not be a fool.   *Swedish*

5721. If a fool has a hump nobody notices it; if the wise man has a pimple everybody talks about it.   *Russian*

5722. If a fool holds the cow by the horns, a clever man can milk her.
Yiddish

5723. If fools ate no bread, corn would be cheap.   *Dutch*

5724. If the fool knew how to be silent he could sit among the wise.   *Czech*

5725. If you keep calling a man a fool, he will become one.   *Armenian*

5726. It is a cunning part to play the fool well.   *English*

5727. Learned fools are the greatest fools.   *German*

5728. Learned fools exceed all fools.
German

5729. Make a fool pray to God, and he'll smash his forehead.   *Russian*

5730. Much abides behind what a fool thinks. *English*

5731. Never challenge a fool to do wrong. *French*

5732. No one is a fool always, everyone sometimes. *English*

5733. Nobody is twice a fool. *African (Ga)*

5734. None but fools lay wagers. *English*

5735. None plays the fool well without wit. *English*

5736. Nothing looks more like a man of sense than a fool who holds his tongue. *German*

5737. One does not cross a river with a fool. *African (Ovambo)*

5738. One fool always finds a greater fool to admire him. *French*

5739. One fool can ask more than ten wise men can answer. *Yiddish*

5740. One fool can drop a stone into a well that a hundred men cannot take out. *Philippine*

5741. One fool in a play is more than enough. *English*

5742. One fool is an expert on the other. *Yiddish*

5743. One fool makes a hundred. *Spanish*

5744. One fool makes many. *English*

5745. One fool may ask more questions than ten wise men can answer. *Danish*

5746. One fool praises another. *German*

5747. Only a fool would prefer food to a woman. *Irish*

5748. Only fools and fiddlers sing at meals. *English*

5749. Only fools rely on miracles. *Yiddish*

5750. Play with a fool at home and he will play with you in the market. *English*

5751. Praise a fool and you may make him useful. *Danish*

5752. Send a fool to the market and a fool he'll return. *English*

5753. Set a fool to catch a fool. *English*

5754. Sometimes a fool can say something clever. *Yiddish*

5755. That which a fool does at last, a wise man does at first. *English*

5756. The fool and the clown grow old worrying over others. *Greek*

5757. The fool continues procrastinating, the wise man waits a fit occasion. *Turkish*

5758. The fool cuts himself with his own knife. *French*

5759. The fool has his answer on the edge of his tongue. *Egyptian*

5760. The fool hunts for misfortune. *French*

5761. The fool knows more in his own house than the sage in other men's. *Italian*

5762. The fool plucks at a wasp's nest. *Philippine*

5763. The fool rejoices over his memories. *Greek*

5764. The fool runs away while his house is burning down. *English*

5765. The fool tells his cares to another who lives in comfort. *Finnish*

5766. The fool wanders, the wise man travels. *English*

5767. The fool who is silent passes for wise. *French*

5768. The fool will laugh when drowning. *Welsh*

5769. The higher the fool, the greater the fall. *English*

5770. The more fools, the more laughter. *French*

5771. The more riches a fool has, the greater fool he is. *English*

5772. The older a fool is, the worse he is. *English*

5773. There is a fool at every feast. *Dutch*

5774. There is no fool like a learned fool. *Italian*

5775. There is no fool like the old fool. *English*

5776. Though fools are told a thousand times the thing is useless. *Indian (Tamil)*

5777. Though the fool waits, the day does not. *French*

5778. Two fools in a house are too many. *English*

5779. We all have a fool under our cloaks, but some can hide it better than others. *Swedish*

5780. Were fools silent they would pass for wise. *Dutch*

5781. Were there no fools, bad ware would not be sold. *English*

5782. Were there no fools, there would be no wise men. *German*

5783. What a fool can spoil, ten wise men cannot repair. *Yiddish*

5784. What the fool does at last, the wise man does at first. *Spanish*

5785. When a fool goes shopping, the storekeepers rejoice. *Yiddish*

5786. When a fool has too many roses he plants thorns amongst them. *Russian*

5787. When a fool keeps quiet, you can't tell whether he is foolish or smart. *Yiddish*

5788. When a luckless fool kills a rooster, it still hops; when he winds a clock, it stops! *Yiddish*

5789. When fools go to market, peddlers make money. *Dutch*

5790. When the fool drops his bread it falls into the honeypot. *Russian*

5791. When the fool has made up his mind the market is over. *Spanish*

5792. When the fool is told a proverb, the meaning of it has to be explained to him. *African (Ashanti)*

5793. When you send a fool to the market, the merchants rejoice. *Yiddish*

5794. Where two fools meet, the bargain goes off. *English*

5795. While the cautious one ponders, the fool will cross the bridge. *Armenian*

5796. Who is born a fool is never cured. *Italian*

5797. With a fool you have no right to do business. *Yiddish*

5798. You don't show a fool a job half done. *Yiddish*

5799. You must not take offense at anything a fool does. *Yiddish*

5800. You should not ask a fool a question nor give him an explanation. *Yiddish*

FOOLISH

5801. The least foolish is wise. *English*

FOOLISHNESS

5802. As long as you understand your foolishness, you are smart! *Yiddish*

5803. Foolishness grows by itself, no need to sow it. *Czech*

5804. When foolishness sometimes succeeds, it is still foolishness. *Yiddish*

5805. When one talks too much, one talks foolishness. *Yiddish*

FOOT (see FEET)

5806. A bare foot is better than none. *English*

5807. A foot that stirs not gets nothing. *Irish*

5808. Better a crooked foot than a crooked mind. *Yiddish*

5809. Better badly mounted than proud on foot. *German*

5810. Better slip with the foot than with the tongue. *Italian*

5811. Every foot feels its own pinching. *Jamaican*

5812. He who falls by his foot shall rise again; he who falls by his mouth shall not rise. *African (Efik)*

5813. It's the lame foot that has the tight shoe. *Iranian*

5814. Keep something for the sore foot. *Scottish*

5815. On an unknown path every foot is slow. *Irish*

5816. One foot is better than two crutches. *English*

5817. One foot is better than two stilts. *French*

5818. The foot does not stay where there is no ground. *African (Hausa)*

5819. The foot has no eyes; it is blind. *African (Zulu)*

5820. The foot that travels the road is the one that is pricked by the thorn. *African (Jabo)*

5821. When one foot stumbles, the other is near falling. *Danish*

FOOTBALL

5822. Two to one is odds at football. *English*

FOOTPRINT

5823. No one buys a cow's footprint. *African (Ashanti)*

5824. Nobody will buy the footprints of a bullock. *African (Oji)*

FOOTSTEP

5825. The gardener's footsteps do not spoil the garden. *Mexican*

5826. The master's footsteps fatten the soil. *English*

FORBEARANCE

5827. Forbearance is no acquittance. *English*

5828. The word forbearance is the treasure of the household. *Chinese*

FORCE

5829. Force breaks force. *Russian*

5830. Force surpasses law. *German*

5831. Force without forecast is of little avail. *English*

5832. One usually succeeds not by force, but by ability. *Russian*

5833. There is great force hidden in a sweet command. *English*

5834. What force cannot do, ingenuity may. *Spanish*

FORD

5835. At the ford, they call someone who knows about it. *African (Bemba)*

5836. Don't jump into the water where there is no ford. *Iranian*

5837. First find the ford, then cross the river. *Armenian*

5838. He who has crossed the ford knows how deep it is. *Italian*

5839. If you don't know the ford, don't step into the water. *Russian*

5840. It's better to return from the center of the ford than drown in the flood. *Irish*

5841. Never praise a ford till you get one. *English*

5842. Praise the ford when you have crossed it. *Irish*

FORECAST

5843. Good forecast makes work easy. *Scottish*

FOREIGNER

5844. A foreigner scratches you where you do not itch. *Rumanian*

5845. The foreigner attaches a handle to an egg. *Turkish*

5846. There is no bitterer fruit than foreigners in one's land. *Rumanian*

FORENOON

5847. The longer forenoon, the shorter afternoon. *English*

FORESIGHT

5848. He who has foresight will be rewarded. *Philippine*

FOREST

5849. A forest that has sheltered you, you will not call a shrubbery. *African (Oji)*

5850. As long as there is a forest an axe will be found. *Russian*

5851. No forest without a bear. *Turkish*

5852. The farther into the forest, the more firewood. *Russian*

5853. The forest has ears, and the field has eyes. *Danish*

5854. When forests are cut, chips fly. *Russian*

FORETHOUGHT

5855. Forethought is easy, but regret is difficult. *Chinese*

FOREWIT

5856. One good forewit is worth two afterwits. *English*

FORGET

5857. He is lucky who forgets what cannot be mended. *German*

FORGETTING

5858. Forgetting is the cure for suffering. *African (Swahili)*

FORGIVE

5859. Forgive others easily, but yourself never. *Polish*

5860. Forgiven is not forgotten. *German*

FORTRESS

5861. A fortress on its guard is not surprised. *Spanish*

FORTUNE

5862. A great fortune depends on luck, a small one on diligence. *Chinese*

5863. A great fortune, in the hands of a fool, is a great misfortune. *English*

5864. A great fortune is a great slavery. *English*

5865. A man's best fortune, or his worst, is his wife. *English*

5866. An ounce of fortune is worth a pound of forecast. *English*

5867. An ounce of good fortune is worth a pound of discretion. *English*

5868. Bad fortune follows the poor man. *Yiddish*

5869. Do not rely on your present good fortune; prepare for the year when it may leave you. *Chinese*

5870. Don't trust in fortune until you are in heaven. *Philippine*

5871. Everything may be borne except good fortune. *Italian*

5872. Fortune aids the bold. *Spanish*

5873. Fortune and glass break soon. *Dutch*

5874. Fortune and love don't always favor the most deserving. *English*

5875. Fortune and misfortune are like the twisted strands of a rope. *Japanese*

5876. Fortune and misfortune are two buckets in a well. *German*

5877. Fortune and women are partial to fools. *German*

5878. Fortune can take from us nothing but what she gave us. *English*

5879. Fortune can take from us only what she has given us. *French*

5880. Fortune comes to him who strives for it. *Italian*

5881. Fortune does not stand waiting at any one's door. *Dutch*

5882. Fortune favors fools. *English*

5883. Fortune favors the bold. *English*

5884. Fortune favors the person who has been jilted. *Japanese*

5885. Fortune follows him who flees from it, and flees from him who seeks it. *Swedish*

5886. Fortune helps fools. *Italian*

5887. Fortune helps him that is willing to help himself. *English*

5888. Fortune is a woman; if you neglect her today, expect not to regain her tomorrow. *French*

5889. Fortune is like a wall that falls on those who lean on it. *Mexican*

5890. Fortune is like women: loves youth and is fickle. *German*

5891. Fortune is round; it makes one a king, another a dunghill. *Dutch*

5892. Fortune is variant. *English*

5893. Fortune knocks once at least at every man's gate. *English*

5894. Fortune lost, nothing lost; courage lost, much lost; honor lost, more lost; soul lost, all lost. *Dutch*

5895. Fortune makes you smart, because fortune makes you rich. *Yiddish*

5896. Fortune may fail us, but a prudent conduct never will. *American*

5897. Fortune often knocks at the door, but the fool does not invite her in. *Danish*

5898. Fortune provides shelter. *Yiddish*

5899. Fortune rarely brings good or evil singly. *English*

5900. From fortune to misfortune is a short step; from misfortune to fortune is a long way. *Yiddish*

5901. Good fortune closes the eyes, misfortune opens them. *Slovakian*

5902. He dances well to whom fortune pipes. *English*

5903. He that has no ill fortune, is troubled with good. *English*

5904. He who has the fortune brings home the bride. *German*

5905. If fortune calls, offer him a seat. *Yiddish*

5906. If fortune turns against you, even jelly breaks your tooth. *Iranian*

5907. If fortune turns against you, even the horse in the stable becomes a donkey. *Iranian*

5908. It is easy to manage when fortune favors you.   *Danish*

5909. The most friendly fortune trips up your heels.   *French*

5910. There is no good fortune which is not shadowed by misfortune.
Slovenian

5911. To the bold man fortune gives her hand.   *Spanish*

5912. When fortune's chariot rolls easily, envy and shame cling to the wheels.   *Danish*

5913. When fortune comes, it comes suddenly and without warning.
Philippine

5914. When fortune comes, open your doors.   *Italian*

5915. When fortune has departed, even yellow gold tarnishes; when good fortune comes, even iron shines brightly.   *Chinese*

5916. When fortune is good, you rule over the devils; when fortune is bad, they rule over you.   *Chinese*

5917. When fortune knocks, open the door.   *German*

5918. When fortune smiles, embrace her.   *English*

5919. When fortune smiles one may reign as a king.   *Indian (Tamil)*

FORTUNETELLER

5920. The fortuneteller cannot tell his own fortune.   *Japanese*

5921. The fortuneteller does not know his own future.   *Japanese*

FOSTER

5922. No longer foster food, no longer friend.   *English*

FOUNDATION

5923. It is forbidden to tell anything that has no foundation.
African (Kanuri)

FOUNTAIN

5924. At a little fountain one drinks at one's ease.   *French*

5925. When it dries up, one knows the worth of the fountain.   *Rumanian*

FOWL

5926. A fowl selects a single grain.
African (Oji)

5927. He that eats his fowl alone may saddle his horse alone.   *Spanish*

5928. It is the fowl with chicks that flees from the hawk.   *African (Hausa)*

5929. No one makes a fowl taboo and then eats its chickens.
African (Ashanti)

5930. One neighbor's fowl seems a goose to another neighbor.   *Turkish*

5931. The fowl is not aware of its danger before it is caught.
Indian (Tamil)

5932. The hungry fowl wakens early.
Jamaican

5933. Today's fowl is better than tomorrow's goose.   *Turkish*

5934. When a fowl eats your neighbor's corn, drive it away; another time it will eat yours.   *African (Oji)*

FOX

5935. A fox should not be of the jury at a goose's trial.   *English*

5936. A good fox does not eat his neighbor's fowls.   *French*

5937. A tired fox finds his tail heavy.
Serbo-Croatian

5938. An old fox does not run twice into the snare.   *German*

5939. An old fox is not caught in a trap. *Greek*

5940. An old fox need learn no craft. *English*

5941. At last foxes all meet at the furrier's. *Italian*

5942. At length the fox is brought to the furrier. *English*

5943. At length the fox turns monk. *English*

5944. Even foxes are caught. *Italian*

5945. Every fox looks after his own skin. *Danish*

5946. Every fox must pay his own skin to the flayer. *English*

5947. Foxes are all tail and women all tongue. *English*

5948. Foxes are caught with foxes. *Finnish*

5949. Foxes come at last to the furrier's. *French*

5950. Foxes dig not their own holes. *English*

5951. Foxes when sleeping have nothing fall into their mouths. *English*

5952. Good following the way where the old fox goes. *English*

5953. He that will deceive the fox must rise betimes. *English*

5954. He who has to do with foxes must look after his henroost. *German*

5955. He who would cheat the fox must rise early. *Spanish*

5956. If you would catch a fox you must hunt with geese. *Danish*

5957. It is a poor fox that has but one hole. *German*

5958. It is an ill sign to see a fox lick a lamb. *English*

5959. It is difficult to trap an old fox. *Danish*

5960. Let every fox take care of his own tail. *Italian*

5961. Nothing falls into the mouth of a sleeping fox. *French*

5962. Old foxes are hard to catch. *Dutch*

5963. Old foxes want no tutors. *English*

5964. Set a fox to catch a fox. *Danish*

5965. Take care of your geese when the fox preaches. *Danish*

5966. The fox comes forth from a hole you would not have expected. *Turkish*

5967. The fox does not go twice into the same trap. *Danish*

5968. The fox is cunning, but more cunning is he who catches it. *Rumanian*

5969. The fox is knowing, but more knowing he who catches him. *Spanish*

5970. The fox is taken when he comes to take. *English*

5971. The fox knows much, but more he that catches him. *English*

5972. The fox knows well with whom he plays tricks. *Spanish*

5973. The fox may grow grey, but never good. *English*

5974. The fox may lose his hair, but not his cunning. *Dutch*

5975. The fox praises the meat out of the crow's mouth. *English*

5976. The fox preys furthest from his hole. *English*

5977. The fox produces his tail as a witness. *Iranian*

5978. The fox says of the mulberries when he cannot get at them they are not good at all. *French*

5979. The fox sits but once on a thorn.
Armenian

5980. The fox thinks everybody eats poultry like himself.   *French*

5981. The fox will eat even marked chicken.   *Albanian*

5982. The more the fox is cursed, the better he fares.   *English*

5983. The more the fox is cursed, the more prey he catches.   *Italian*

5984. The old fox does not fear the trap.   *Turkish*

5985. Though the fox runs, the pullets have wings.   *Italian*

5986. What the fox can't reach he leaves hanging.   *Greek*

5987. When a fox is in his hole, the smoke fetches him out.   *Spanish*

5988. When foxes meet there is destruction among the fowls.   *American*

5989. When the fox dies, the fowls never mourn; for the fox never rears a chicken.   *African (Yoruba)*

5990. When the fox grows old it becomes a nun.   *Greek-*

5991. When the fox is hungry he feigns sickness.   *Greek*

5992. When the fox is hungry he pretends to be asleep.   *Greek*

5993. When the fox licks his paw, let the farmer look after his geese.
Danish

5994. When the fox preaches, beware the geese.   *English*

5995. When the fox preaches, take care of yourselves, hens.   *Italian*

5996. When the fox preaches to the goose the neck is in danger.   *Danish*

5997. When the fox starts preaching, look to your hens.   *Basque*

5998. When the fox wants to catch geese, he wags his tail.   *German*

5999. With foxes we must play the fox.
English

6000. You can have no more of the fox than his skin.   *English*

FRACTURE

6001. Fractures well cured make us more strong.   *American*

6002. With gentleness the fracture is repaired.   *Egyptian*

FRAUD

6003. Fraud and deceit are always in haste.   *English*

6004. Frauds and tricks will destroy reputation.   *Indian (Tamil)*

6005. Fraud is often the mother of gain, but gain is not always the son of fraud.   *Russian*

FRAY

6006. There is not often a fray without a broken head.   *American*

FREE

6007. He is not free that draws his chain.   *English*

FREEDOM

6008. A country's freedom cannot be bought by any amount of gold.
Philippine

6009. Freedom for the freed, paradise for the saved.   *Russian*

6010. Freedom from sickness is true happiness, and competence is true riches.   *Indian (Tamil)*

6011. Freedom is a fair thing.
Scottish

6012. You surrender your freedom where you deposit your secret.
Spanish

FRETTING

6013. A hundred years of fretting will not pay a halfpenny of debt. *French*

FRIAR

6014. Do what the friar says, and not what he does. *Spanish*

6015. Friars observant spare their own and eat other men's. *English*

6016. The friar preached against stealing and had a goose in his sleeve. *English*

6017. When a friar begs in the name of God he does so for himself too. *Mexican*

6018. Where friars abound keep your eyes open. *Spanish*

FRIEND

6019. A bad friend is no better than no friend. *Japanese*

6020. A fair-weather friend changes with the wind. *Spanish*

6021. A friend at one's back is a safe bridge. *Dutch*

6022. A friend in court is better than a penny in purse. *English*

6023. A friend in court is worth a penny in the purse. *Scottish*

6024. A friend in need is a friend indeed. *English*

6025. A friend in the market is better than money in the chest. *English*

6026. A friend is better than a thousand silver pieces. *Greek*

6027. A friend is better than money in the purse. *Dutch*

6028. A friend is known at the time of distress. *Lebanese*

6029. A friend is known in time of need. *French*

6030. A friend is never known till a man have need. *English*

6031. A friend is not known till he is lost. *Italian*

6032. A friend is not so easy to find as to lose. *Jamaican*

6033. A friend is not so soon gotten as lost. *English*

6034. A friend is recognized only in misfortune. *Russian*

6035. A friend is to be taken with his faults. *Portuguese*

6036. A friend remains a friend up to his pocket. *Yiddish*

6037. A friend to all is a friend to none. *English*

6038. A friend who leads one astray is an enemy. *Greek*

6039. A friend you get for nothing; an enemy has to be bought. *Yiddish*

6040. A friend you have to buy; enemies you get for nothing. *Yiddish*

6041. A good friend is better than silver and gold. *Dutch*

6042. A good friend is my nearest relation. *English*

6043. A good friend is often better than a brother. *Yiddish*

6044. A good friend is shown in a black day. *Turkish*

6045. A good friend is worth more than a bad brother. *Serbo-Croatian*

6046. A good friend never offends. *English*

6047. A near friend is better than a far-dwelling kinsman. *English*

6048. A new friend makes the old forgotten. *English*

6049. A reconciled friend is a double enemy. *English*

6050. A table friend is changeable. *French*

6051. A true friend is known in a doubtful matter. *English*

6052. A true friend is better than relations.   *Turkish*

6053. A true friend is the nectar of life.   *Indian (Tamil)*

6054. A well-known friend is a treasure.   *Chinese*

6055. All are not friends that speak us fair.   *English*

6056. All are not friends who smile on you.   *Dutch*

6057. Always treat your friends as when you first met them; then in old age you will have no hatred in your heart.   *Chinese*

6058. Among friends all things are common.   *English*

6059. An old friend is a mount for a black day.   *Turkish*

6060. An old friend is like a saddled horse.   *Pashto*

6061. As you pour out for your friend so must you drink.   *Russian*

6062. Be a friend to yourself, and others will be so too.   *English*

6063. Be a friend to yourself and others will befriend you.   *Scottish*

6064. Before you make a friend, eat a peck of salt with him.   *Dutch*

6065. Being without friends and without connections is like being a doctor without ointment.   *Russian*

6066. Better a friend at court than gold on the finger.   *Welsh*

6067. Better a new friend than an old foe.   *English*

6068. Better my friend think me strange than troublesome.   *Scottish*

6069. Better one friend with a dish of food than a hundred with a sigh.
                                        Yiddish

6070. Better to have a friend on the road than gold or silver in your purse.
                                        French

6071. Beware of a reconciled friend as of the devil.   *Spanish*

6072. Beware of your friends, not your enemies.   *Yiddish*

6073. Choose your friends like your books, few but choice.   *English*

6074. Correct your friend secretly and praise him publicly.   *Czech*

6075. Do not make friends with a woman, else you will live on tears.
                                        Hawaiian

6076. Eat and drink with a friend, but have no business transaction with him.   *Turkish*

6077. Everybody's friend and nobody's friend is all one.   *Spanish*

6078. Everybody's friend, everybody's fool.   *German*

6079. Everybody's friend, nobody's friend.   *Italian*

6080. Everyman's friend is often everyman's fool.   *Swedish*

6081. Fall not out with a friend for a trifle.   *English*

6082. For a friend seven versts do not make a detour.   *Russian*

6083. Friends agree best at a distance.
                                        Scottish

6084. Friends and mules fail in hard trials.   *Spanish*

6085. Friends and mules fail in the time of need.   *Indian (Hindi)*

6086. Friends and wine, the older the better.   *Japanese*

6087. Friends are known in time of need.   *Dutch*

6088. Friends are like fiddlestrings, they must not be screwed too tight.
                                        English

6089. Friends in prosperous times are many but in adversity you won't find one.   *Libyan*

6090. Friends may meet but mountains never. *English*

6091. Friends must part. *English*

6092. Friends should have a high wall between them. *Chinese*

6093. Friend to everybody, true to nobody. *Czech*

6094. Friends through fortune become enemies through mishap. *English*

6095. Friends while wine and meat are there, husband and wife while there are fuel and rice. *Chinese*

6096. Go often to your friend and you'll be treated coolly. *Japanese*

6097. God's friend, the priest's foe. *German*

6098. Good friends are better than pocket money. *Jamaican*

6099. Good friends settle their accounts speedily. *Chinese*

6100. Have but few friends though much acquaintance. *English*

6101. He cannot be a friend to any one who is his own enemy. *French*

6102. He's a friend that speaks well behind our backs. *English*

6103. He is a friend to none who is a friend to all. *Swedish*

6104. He is a friend who aids in adversity. *Indian (Tamil)*

6105. He is a true friend that loves me for my love and not for my goods. *English*

6106. He is called clever who cheats and plunders his friend. *French*

6107. He is my friend that grinds at my mill. *English*

6108. He never was a friend who has ceased to be one. *French*

6109. He that seeks to have many friends never has any. *Italian*

6110. He who causes one's starvation is not one's friend. *African (Yoruba)*

6111. He who is a friend of the forest cannot be an enemy of the tree. *Russian*

6112. He who is everybody's friend is either very poor or very rich. *Spanish*

6113. He who is his own friend will have the friendship of others. *Welsh*

6114. He who judges between two friends loses one of them. *French*

6115. He who lends to a friend makes an enemy. *Polish*

6116. He who plants the most has plenty to harvest and has many friends. *Philippine*

6117. He who seeks a constant friend goes to the cemetery. *Russian*

6118. Hold a true friend with both your hands. *African (Kanuri)*

6119. If a friend is honey, do not try to eat all of him. *Rumanian*

6120. If friends have faith in each other, life and death are of no consequence. *Chinese*

6121. If you drink with a friend, a thousand cups are too few; if you argue with a man, half a sentence is too much. *Chinese*

6122. If you have had enough of your friend, grant him a loan. *Russian*

6123. If you have one true friend, you have more than your share. *English*

6124. If you make friends on the road, your knife will be lost. *African (Oji)*

6125. If you want to lose your friend, grant him a loan. *Estonian*

6126. In distress a friend is best. *Welsh*

6127. In good times a friend has no value. *Philippine*

6128. In hardship you know your friends. *Japanese*

6129. In time of prosperity friends will be plenty.   *English*

6130. It is a good friend who helps one in poverty.   *Vietnamese*

6131. It is difficult to win a friend in a year; it is easy to offend one in an hour.

Chinese

6132. It is easier to fathom the depths of the sea than to find a true and sincere friend.   *Philippine*

6133. It is easier to visit friends than to live with them.   *Chinese*

6134. It is good to have friends but bad to need them.   *English*

6135. It is good to have friends everywhere.   *Italian*

6136. It's merry when friends meet.

English

6137. It is no use hiding from a friend what is known to an enemy. *Danish*

6138. It is not lost what a friend gets.

English

6139. Love your friend with his faults.

Italian

6140. Many a friend was lost through a joke, but none has ever been gained so.   *Czech*

6141. Many a man is a good friend but a bad neighbor.   *Danish*

6142. Many friends, no friend.

English

6143. Mistrust your best friend as if he were your worst enemy.   *Mexican*

6144. Never trust much to a new friend or an old enemy.   *Scottish*

6145. Old friends and old ways ought not to be disdained.   *Danish*

6146. Old friends and old wine are best.   *English*

6147. One friend watches for another.

English

6148. One learns much more from one's friends than from one's teacher.

Vietnamese

6149. One old friend is better than two new ones.   *Russian*

6150. One should go invited to a friend in good fortune and uninvited in misfortune.   *Swedish*

6151. Only he is a friend who is a friend when we are in difficulties.

Libyan

6152. Point out your friend to me and I will tell you what you are.   *Greek*

6153. Rather have a little something for your friend than a great something for your enemy.   *Italian*

6154. Real friends will share even a strawberry.   *Slovakian*

6155. Save a man from his friends, and leave him to struggle with his enemies.   *English*

6156. Self first, then your next best friend.   *English*

6157. Speak well of your friend; of your enemy neither well nor ill.

Italian

6158. Speak well of your friend, of your enemy say nothing.   *English*

6159. Tell me who your friends are and I'll tell you who you are.

Philippine

6160. The falling out of friends is the renewal of love.   *English*

6161. The false friend is like the shadow of a sundial.   *French*

6162. The father's friend is no friend of the son.   *African (Fulani)*

6163. The friend is known in the time of difficulty.   *Moroccan*

6164. The friend of a quarrel picker is quarrelsome.   *African (Ovambo)*

6165. The friend that can be bought is not worth buying.   *Irish*

6166. The friend that faints is a foe.
English

6167. There are three faithful friends, an old wife, an old dog, and ready money. *American*

6168. There is no better mirror than an old friend. *Japanese*

6169. There is no friend to a man like his mother. *Turkish*

6170. There is nothing like a true friend, loyal and faithful. *Philippine*

6171. They are rich who have true friends. *English*

6172. To meet an old friend in a distant land is like refreshing rain after a long drought. *Chinese*

6173. Too many friends spoil the dinner. *American*

6174. Trust not a new friend nor an old enemy. *English*

6175. Try your friend before you have need of him. *English*

6176. We can live without our friends, but not without our neighbors. *English*

6177. What you give to a good friend is not lost. *Polish*

6178. When a friend asks there is no tomorrow. *English*

6179. When friends meet, heart is warm. *Scottish*

6180. When I lent I was a friend, when I asked I was unkind. *English*

6181. When it is a friend that asks, don't wait till tomorrow to grant it. *Philippine*

6182. When two friends have a common purse, one sings and the other weeps. *English*

6183. When you have tea and wine, you have many friends. *Chinese*

6184. Where friends, there riches. *German*

6185. You are better friends at a distance. *Yiddish*

6186. Your friend lends and your enemy asks payment. *Dutch*

FRIENDSHIP

6187. A broken friendship may be soldered, but will never be sound. *English*

6188. A little for you and a little for me—this is friendship. *Indian (Kashmiri)*

6189. Friendship broken may be soldered, but never made whole. *Spanish*

6190. Friendship is friendship, but money has to be counted. *Russian*

6191. Friendship is friendship, but work is work. *Russian*

6192. Friendship is friendship, except when it comes to tobacco. *Russian*

6193. Friendship is good, though absence from friends is painful. *Irish*

6194. Friendship is like wine, the older the better. *Polish*

6195. Friendship is not laughing. *African (Kpelle)*

6196. Friendship is not to be bought at a fair. *English*

6197. Friendship is stronger than close relationship. *Indian (Tamil)*

6198. Friendship is stronger than kinship. *Yiddish*

6199. Friendship is the marriage of the soul. *Japanese*

6200. Friendship lasts as long as the pot boils. *Greek*

6201. Friendship, like mud, breaks when it dries up. *Philippine*

6202. Friendship that flames goes out in a flash. *English*

6203. If apart, long friendship, if together, the least touch will provoke hatred. *Indian (Tamil)*

6204. In the division of inheritance, friendship stands still. *Dutch*

6205. Make friendships with men better than yourself; better none than those like yourself. *Chinese*

6206. Reconciled friendship is a wound ill salved. *Italian*

6207. Sudden friendship, sure repentance. *English*

6208. The friendship of a brother-in-law lasts while one's sister lives. *Indian (Tamil)*

6209. The friendship of foes is like fire concealed in smoke. *Indian (Tamil)*

6210. The friendship of great men is like the shadow of a bush—soon gone. *French*

6211. The friendship of officials is as thin as paper. *Chinese*

6212. The friendship of the base is dangerous. *Indian (Tamil)*

6213. The friendship of the great is fraternity with lions. *Italian*

6214. The friendship of two depends on the forbearance of one. *Indian (Tamil)*

6215. There is no friendship in trade. *American*

6216. To preserve friendship one must build walls. *Italian*

6217. True friendship is like a single soul split in two to fill two bodies. *Mexican*

6218. While the pot boils friendship blooms. *English*

6219. You can't patch up a torn friendship. *Yiddish*

FRIGHT

6220. Fright is worse than a blow. *Moroccan*

6221. The fright is greater than the wound. *Welsh*

FROG

6222. A frog in a well is best off in the well. *Chinese*

6223. A frog in the well knows not the ocean. *Japanese*

6224. A frog likes water but not hot water. *African (Swahili)*

6225. A frog may kill an elephant. *African (Swahili)*

6226. Even a frog would bite if it had teeth. *Italian*

6227. He who likes frogs does not like fish. *African (Hausa)*

6228. If there is a marsh there will be frogs. *Russian*

6229. Old frogs like croaking. *African (Ovambo)*

6230. The frog at the bottom of a well believes that the sky is as small as a lid of a cooking pot. *Vietnamese*

6231. The frog enjoys itself in water, but not in hot water. *African (Wolof)*

6232. The frog forgets he was a tadpole. *Korean*

6233. The frog perishes by its own mouth. *Indian (Tamil)*

6234. The frog will jump back into the pool although it sits on a golden stool. *Dutch*

6235. The frog would like to have wings. *African (Ovambo)*

6236. The young of frogs are frogs. *Japanese*

6237. There is no frog that does not peep out of its pool. *African (Zulu)*

6238. Though you seat the frog on a golden stool, he'll soon jump off again into the pool. *German*

6239. You can't catch two frogs with one hand. *Chinese*

FROST

6240. Let him who fears the frost plant no vineyards.   *Serbo-Croatian*

6241. The first and last frosts are the worst.   *English*

6242. The frost hurts not weeds.
English

6243. The frost will surely pass.
African (Ovambo)

FROTH

6244. Froth always swims on the surface.   *American*

6245. Froth is no beer.   *Dutch*

FRUGALITY

6246. Frugality is an income.
English

FRUIT

6247. A fruit that ripens on the tree is delicious.   *Philippine*

6248. Better green fruit than ripe fruit that is wormy.   *Philippine*

6249. Fine fruit will have flies about it.   *American*

6250. Forbidden fruit is sweet.
English

6251. Fruit out of season, sorrow out of reason.   *English*

6252. Good fruit never comes from a bad tree.   *Portuguese*

6253. Graft good fruit all, or graft not at all.   *English*

6254. He that would eat the fruit must climb the tree.   *Scottish*

6255. He that would have the fruit must climb the tree.   *English*

6256. Late fruit keeps well.   *German*

6257. Let him who shook the fruit down pick them too.
African (Ovambo)

6258. No fruit falls from withered trees.   *Yiddish*

6259. Nothing so good as forbidden fruit.   *French*

6260. Ripe fruit does not remain on the branch.   *Indian (Tamil)*

6261. Ripe fruit falls of itself.
Indian (Tamil)

6262. Shake not the tree when the fruit is falling by itself.
Serbo-Croatian

6263. Sweet fruit usually has a bitter rind.   *Philippine*

6264. The fruit at the tips of branches are good.   *African (Ovambo)*

6265. The fruit falls not far from the stem.   *Dutch*

6266. The fruit must have a stem before it grows.   *African (Jabo)*

6267. The fruit of a good tree is also good.   *Greek*

6268. The fruit of a tree will fall at its foot.   *Indian (Tamil)*

6269. There is no fruit from a dry tree.   *Turkish*

6270. There is no hope of fruit from a tree which has been robbed of its flowers by the frost.   *Tibetan*

6271. There is no worse fruit than that which never ripens.   *Italian*

6272. When you eat a fruit, think of the man who planted the tree.
Vietnamese

FRYING

6273. Where there is frying there's a smell.   *Latvian*

FRYING PAN

6274. He has enough to do who holds the handle of the frying pan.   *French*

6275. He that holds the handle of the frying pan runs the risk of burning himself.   *French*

FUEL

6276. Fuel alone will not light a fire.
Chinese

6277. Fuel is not sold in the forest, nor fish on the shore of a lake.   *Chinese*

6278. Take away fuel, take away flame.   *English*

FUGITIVE

6279. A fugitive never stops to pick the thorns from his foot. *African (Yoruba)*

FUN

6280. Whether the fun pays for the powder is a matter of debate.
American

FUR

6281. Those with the same fur enter the same hole.   *African (Fulani)*

FURNITURE

6282. Better a little furniture than an empty house.   *Danish*

FURTHER

6283. The further off the better looked upon.   *English*

FURY

6284. The first stage of fury is madness, the end of it is repentance.
Lebanese

FUTURE

6285. He who has no care for the far future will have sorrow in the near future.   *Korean*

6286. Learn the future by looking at things past.   *Indian (Tamil)*

G

GADFLY

6287. Only a gadfly can sit on an elephant's back. *African (Hausa)*

GAIN (noun)

6288. Do not rejoice over the first gain. *Russian*

6289. Everyone fastens where there is gain. *English*

6290. Gain does not give as much pleasure as loss gives grief. *Greek*

6291. Great gain make work easy. *American*

6292. Great gains cover many losses. *English*

6293. Ill-gotten gain is scattered by the devil. *Greek*

6294. Light gains make heavy purses. *English*

6295. No gains without pains. *English*

6296. One man's gain is another's loss. *African (Hausa)*

6297. Small gains bring great wealth. *Dutch*

6298. Sometimes the best gain is to lose. *English*

6299. Who heeds not gain must expect loss. *English*

GAIN (verb)

6300. He who does not gain loses. *French*

6301. He who gains little gains much. *American*

6302. Lightly gained quickly lost. *English*

6303. Soon gained soon squandered. *French*

6304. To gain teaches how to spend. *English*

GAINING

6305. Fair gainings make fair spendings. *English*

GAIT

6306. The slow gait of the tortoise takes him far. *African (Swahili)*

GALL

6307. A little gall embitters much honey. *Spanish*

6308. A little gall makes a great deal of honey bitter. *Italian*

6309. A little gall spoils a great deal of honey. *French*

GALLANT

6310. A living gallant is better than a dead husband. *American*

GALLOW

6311. Who is doomed to the gallows will never be drowned. *Russian*

GAMBLER

6312. Gamblers know neither fathers nor sons. *Chinese*

6313. If a gambler can reform, then there is a cure for leprosy. *Chinese*

6314. If you help a gambler, it is as if you throw a hair into the fire.
Moroccan

6315. Rich gamblers and old trumpeters are rare. *German*

6316. The gambler is always a loser.
Maltese

6317. The hope of winning proves the gambler's undoing. *Irish*

6318. Young gambler, old beggar.
German

GAMBLING

6319. Gambling and boasting end in sorrow. *Indian (Tamil)*

6320. If you believe in gambling, in the end you will sell your house.
Chinese

GAME

6321. At the end of the game we see who wins. *Italian*

6322. At the game's end we shall see who gains. *English*

6323. He who looks on knows more of the game than he who plays. *German*

6324. If one piece is moved wrongly, the whole game is lost. *Chinese*

6325. It is a bad game where nobody wins. *Italian*

6326. It is an ill game that has not one trump. *English*

6327. It is well to leave off playing when the game is at its best. *French*

6328. The best game of dice is the one not played at all. *Hebrew*

6329. The game is not worth the candle. *English*

6330. There is not one game without an end. *African (Ovambo)*

6331. When the game is most thriving it is time to leave off. *Danish*

6332. When two play a game there must be a winner and a loser. *Yiddish*

GAP

6333. Every gap has its bush.
English

GAPE

6334. He must gape wide who would gape against an oven. *Dutch*

GARDEN

6335. A garden is like a babe; it does not grow fast. *African (Bemba)*

6336. A garden without a fence is like a dog without a tail. *Moroccan*

6337. A good garden may have some weeds. *English*

6338. A lazy man's garden is full of weeds. *Philippine*

6339. As the garden, so the gardener.
Hebrew

6340. Everyone has enough to do in weeding his own garden. *Flemish*

6341. The finest garden is not free from weeds. *English*

GARDENER

6342. As is the gardener, so is the garden. *English*

6343. In the garden more grows than the gardener sows. *Spanish*

6344. The gardener, for the sake of one rose, becomes the servant of a thousand thorns. *Turkish*

GARLIC

6345. Garlic makes a man wink, drink, and stink.   *English*

6346. He who does not eat garlic does not smell of garlic.   *Lebanese*

6347. However good garlic is, it will not be as good as an onion.
African (Hausa)

6348. If you don't eat garlic, you won't smell bad.   *Yiddish*

GARMENT

6349. A garment not worn is a prey to moths.   *Indian (Tamil)*

6350. Borrowed garments do not fit well.   *Japanese*

6351. Borrowed garments never sit well.   *English*

6352. One cannot make garments from cobwebs.   *Rumanian*

6353. One sews the garment, the other wears it.   *Yiddish*

6354. Our last garment is made without pockets.   *Italian*

6355. Rich garments weep on unworthy shoulders.   *French*

GATE

6356. A creaking gate hangs long.
English

6357. A gate once widened stays wide.   *Hebrew*

6358. He who has been shut out at the main gate must knock at the side entrance.   *Polish*

6359. The gates of tears are never shut.   *Yiddish*

GATHERING

6360. It is ill gathering of stones where the sea is bottomless.   *English*

GAUNTLET

6361. Make not a gauntlet of a hedging glove.   *English*

GAZELLE

6362. You cannot chase two gazelles.
African (Zulu)

GEESE (see GOOSE)

6363. Geese are plucked as long as they have feathers.   *Dutch*

6364. Roast geese don't come flying into your mouth.   *Dutch*

6365. Where there are geese there's dirt, and where there are women there's talking.   *Manx*

GEM

6366. Even a gem has a flaw.
Korean

GENERAL

6367. A drunken general is a bad commander.   *English*

6368. A general of a defeated army should not talk of tactics.   *Japanese*

6369. For one general to succeed, the bones of ten thousand soldiers lie drying.   *Japanese*

6370. There cannot be a general without soldiers.   *Turkish*

6371. Under a brave general there are no cowardly soldiers.   *Japanese*

6372. Under the command of a great general, there is no feeble soldier.
Korean

GENERATION

6373. One generation opens the road upon which another generation travels.
Chinese

6374. One generation plants the trees under whose cool shade another generation takes its ease.   *Chinese*

GENEROSITY

6375. Generosity is wealth.
African (Annang)

6376. The best generosity is that which is quick. *Egyptian*

GENIUS

6377. Genius is as tender as a skinned cat. *American*

GENTILITY

6378. Gentility without ability is worse than plain beggery. *English*

GENTLE

6379. Gentle is that gentle does.
English

GENTLEMAN

6380. A gentleman should have more in his pocket than on his back.
English

6381. A gentleman will do like a gentleman. *English*

6382. A gentleman without an estate is a pudding without suet. *English*

GENTLENESS

6383. Gentleness does more than violence. *French*

6384. Gentleness in the manner, but substance in the thing. *American*

6385. Gentleness skillfully subdues wrath. *Japanese*

GET

6386. He that gets forgets, but he that gives thinks on. *Scottish*

6387. Ill gotten, ill spent. *English*

6388. So got, so gone. *Dutch*

6389. Soon gotten, soon spent.
English

GHOST

6390. Nobody wars with ghosts.
African (Ga)

6391. To be a thousand days a ghost is not equal to being one day a man.
Chinese

GIANT

6392. A giant will starve with what will surfeit a dwarf. *English*

6393. It is not only giants that do great things. *African (Jabo)*

6394. Some think they are giants when they sit on the hump of a camel.
Russian

6395. The giant loves the dwarf.
English

GIFT

6396. A gift is not despised.
African (Ovambo)

6397. A gift long waited for is sold not given. *English*

6398. A wicked man's gift has a touch of his master. *English*

6399. Bound is he that takes gifts.
English

6400. Gifts are according to the giver.
German

6401. Gifts are effective means of persuasion. *Philippine*

6402. Gifts break a rock. *English*

6403. Gifts can soften even stone.
Philippine

6404. Gifts cripple the law, and grease makes the wheels go round.
Finnish

6405. Gifts enter without knocking.
English

6406. Gifts from enemies are dangerous. *English*

6407. Gifts make beggars bold.
English

6408. Gifts make friendship lasting.
Danish

6409. Great gifts are for great men.
English

6410. It is not the gift which is precious, it is the love. *Russian*

6411. Nothing freer than a gift.
Scottish

6412. The best gifts are those which expect no return. *Norwegian*

6413. The gift is not as precious as the thought. *Yiddish*

6414. To get a gift means to return one. *Hebrew*

6415. What gift is there that equals the gift of food! *Indian (Tamil)*

6416. What is bought is cheaper than a gift. *Portuguese*

GIFT HORSE

6417. Don't count the teeth of a gift horse. *Iranian*

6418. Don't look a gift horse in the mouth. *English*

6419. Never heed the color of a gift horse. *Italian*

GINGER

6420. The older ginger and cinnamon become, the more pungent is their flavor. *Chinese*

GIRL

6421. A fine girl and a tattered gown always find something to hook them.
French

6422. A girl draws more than a rope.
Spanish

6423. A girl in her time is like honey in the comb. *Rumanian*

6424. A girl is like a shadow; follow her, she runs; flee from her, she follows you. *Russian*

6425. A girl laughs after she has finished housework. *African (Shona)*

6426. A girl may be allowed to sin, otherwise she would have nothing to repent. *Russian*

6427. A girl unemployed is thinking of mischief. *French*

6428. A girl with a golden cradle doesn't remain long in her father's house. *Armenian*

6429. A girl without a needle is like a cat without a claw. *Estonian*

6430. A homely girl hates the mirror.
Yiddish

6431. A lovely girl attracts attention by her good looks, an ugly girl by the help of a mirror. *Maltese*

6432. A newlywed girl takes pride in her pregnancy. *Greek*

6433. A pretty girl is the kind of goods that's always in demand. *Yiddish*

6434. A quarrelsome girl will not be married. *African (Ovambo)*

6435. An untoward girl may make a good woman. *English*

6436. Even the wisest girl will yield to the boy who perseveres in his wooing.
Vietnamese

6437. Girls are wont to say no with their lips, but with their eyes they say yes. *Mexican*

6438. Girls will be girls. *American*

6439. Homely girls let themselves be seduced. *Yiddish*

6440. If a girl has no other virtues, even a freckle can be considered one.
Yiddish

6441. If the girls won't run after the men, the men will run after them.
American

6442. In the house where there are two girls, the cats die of thirst.

Rumanian

6443. It is easier to watch over one hundred fleas than one young girl.

Polish

6444. Little girls have little wit.

American

6445. That which a girl does not know adorns her. *Russian*

6446. The temple girl who could not dance said that the hall was not large enough. *Indian (Tamil)*

6447. When a girl is born all four walls weep. *Russian*

6448. When the girl is refined, the wife is a little dove. *Yiddish*

GIVE

6449. Better give than take. *English*

6450. Better give than take by a time.

Scottish

6451. Did you give, forget it; did you accept, mention it. *Hungarian*

6452. Give a little and you gain a lot.

Pashto

6453. He gives twice that gives quickly. *English*

6454. He to whom you give much will want more. *Estonian*

6455. He who gives quickly gives doubly. *German*

6456. He who gives to another bestows on himself. *English*

6457. He who gives you a little will give you much. *African (Fulani)*

6458. If you're given something, take; if you're beaten, run. *Russian*

6459. If you continually give you will continually have. *Chinese*

6460. If you give, give easily; if you accept, accept cheerily. *Hungarian*

6461. Neither give to all nor contend with fools. *English*

6462. No one is so liberal as he who has nothing to give. *French*

6463. They that give are ever welcome. *English*

6464. To give tardily is to refuse.

French

6465. Who gives to all denies all.

English

6466. Who gives to me, teaches me to give. *Dutch*

GIVER

6467. Let the giver be silent and the receiver speak. *Portuguese*

GIVING

6468. Giving is for the purpose of taking. *Japanese*

GLACIER

6469. It is no use trying to tug the glacier backwards. *Tibetan*

GLADNESS

6470. Gladness follows victory.

Hawaiian

GLASS

6471. A broken glass can't be hurt.

English

6472. Nothing more smooth than glass, yet nothing more brittle; nothing more fine than wit, yet nothing more fickle. *English*

6473. Who drains his glass in a single gulp is deemed greedy. *Hebrew*

GLASSES

6474. Glasses and lasses are brittle ware. *English*

6475. He pays for the glasses who breaks them. *French*

6476. To the blind, glasses are of no use. *Korean*

GLORY

6477. Hasty glory goes out in a snuff. *English*

6478. Sudden glory soon goes out. *English*

6479. The glory of ancestors should not prevent a man winning glory for himself. *Serbo-Croatian*

6480. There's no glory without sacrifice. *Philippine*

6481. Too much glory is half disgrace. *Yiddish*

6482. When glory comes memory departs. *French*

GLUTTON

6483. A glutton is never generous. *English*

6484. A glutton is never satisfied. *African (Ovambo)*

6485. A glutton young, a beggar old. *English*

6486. Who hastens a glutton chokes him. *English*

GLUTTONY

6487. Gluttony kills more than the sword. *English*

GO

6488. Better go about than fall into the ditch. *English*

6489. He goes far that never turns. *English*

6490. He goes not out of his way that goes to a good inn. *English*

6491. He goes safely who has nothing. *French*

6492. He that goes and comes makes a good voyage. *English*

6493. He that goes softly, goes safely. *English*

6494. He who does not go forward, stays behind. *German*

6495. If you can't go over, go under. *Yiddish*

6496. It is better to turn back than go astray. *German*

6497. One may go a long way after one is tired. *French*

6498. One never goes so far as when one doesn't know where one is going. *French*

6499. Tell me with whom you go, and I'll tell you what you do. *English*

6500. To go yourself is better than to send others; to do it yourself is better than to call upon others. *Chinese*

6501. Who goes softly goes safely, and he that goes safely goes far. *Italian*

GOAL

6502. The goal will not be reached if the right distance not be travelled. *Tibetan*

GOAT

6503. A dead goat does not fear the knife. *African (Ga)*

6504. A goat cannot be cooked with the hyena. *African (Hausa)*

6505. A goat is not a dog; one's own child is not a slave. *African (Ovambo)*

6506. A goat is not easy to fence in. *Norwegian*

6507. An old goat is never the more reverend for his beard. *English*

6508. Any goat can jump over a low fence. *Polish*

6509. Counting absent goats means counting even dead ones. *African (Shona)*

6510. Even a goat has his habits.
African (Ovambo)

6511. Every one fears a goat from in front, a horse from the rear and a fool on every side. *Yiddish*

6512. No matter how well you clean a goat, it will still smell like a goat.
Philippine

6513. The goat dwells among men for fear of the leopard. *African (Jabo)*

6514. The goat eats where it is tied.
Finnish

6515. The goat gives a good milking, but she casts it all down with her foot.
Scottish

6516. The goat learns wisdom from a cropped ear. *African (Hausa)*

6517. The goat must browse where she is tied. *English*

6518. The goat prefers one goat to a herd of sheep. *Armenian*

6519. The little goat follows its kind.
African (Ovambo)

6520. Where the goat is tied she must browse. *French*

GO-BETWEEN

6521. A go-between needs a thousand pairs of sandals. *Japanese*

GOD (see LORD)

6522. All is good that God sends.
Scottish

6523. All that God does is done for the best. *Hebrew*

6524. Ask God for as much as you like, but keep your spade in your hand.
Armenian

6525. Be contented with what God has given you. *Philippine*

6526. Before you find God, you are eaten by the saints. *Rumanian*

6527. Don't go to the threshold without God. *Russian*

6528. Even God does not satisfy all people. *Slovakian*

6529. Even God forgives fools.
Russian

6530. Even God gets out of a drunkard's way. *Rumanian*

6531. Even God who is God cannot please all the world. *Rumanian*

6532. Everyone for himself, God for us all. *Dutch*

6533. Everyone sneezes as God pleases. *Spanish*

6534. Fear God, and next to God, him that has no fear of God. *Polish*

6535. Fear God, but be wary of men.
Yiddish

6536. For a web begun God sends thread. *French*

6537. God alone understands fools.
French

6538. God belongs to rich and poor alike. *African (Ovambo)*

6539. God bless him who pays visits, and short visits. *Egyptian*

6540. God can shave without soap.
Polish

6541. God comes at last when we think he is furthest off. *English*

6542. God comes to see without a bell.
English

6543. God comes with leaden feet, but strikes with iron hands. *Scottish*

6544. God complains not, but does what is fitting. *English*

6545. God created a world full of many little words. *Yiddish*

6546. God cures, and the doctor gets the money. *Dutch*

6547. God cures the sick, and the doctor gets the money. *German*

6548. God defend me from my friends; I'll keep myself from my enemies. *English*

6549. God defend me from the still water, and I'll keep myself from the rough. *English*

6550. God delays, but never forgets. *Greek*

6551. God deliver me from a man of one book. *English*

6552. God did not join brains with beauty. *Polish*

6553. God does not bargain and God does not change. *Yiddish*

6554. God does not desert the man who defends himself. *Slovakian*

6555. God doesn't give horns to a cow that butts. *Russian*

6556. God does not hide a liar. *African (Swahili)*

6557. God does not let his eggs spoil. *African (Ovambo)*

6558. God does not like the lying tongue. *Irish*

6559. God does not measure men by inches. *Scottish*

6560. God does not pay weekly, but pays at the end. *Dutch*

6561. God drives the vessel where he will, no matter how the captain rants. *Iranian*

6562. God favors the bold. *Russian*

6563. God gave us teeth to hold back our tongue. *Greek*

6564. God gives all things to industry. *American*

6565. God gives birds their food, but they must fly for it. *Dutch*

6566. God gives clothes according to the cold. *Portuguese*

6567. God gives every bird its food but does not cast it into the nest. *Swedish*

6568. God gives man a cross according to his strength. *Russian*

6569. God gives potatoes, but with the peel. *Russian*

6570. God gives the cold according to the cloth. *French*

6571. God gives the day and provides the food for it. *Russian*

6572. God gives the grain, but we must make the furrow. *Czech*

6573. God gives the will, necessity gives the law. *Danish*

6574. God goes to him who comes to Him. *Russian*

6575. God has few friends, the devil has many. *English*

6576. God has often a great share in a little house. *English*

6577. God heals and the doctor gets the money. *Flemish*

6578. God heals, and the physician has the thanks. *English*

6579. God help the poor, for the rich can help themselves. *Scottish*

6580. God help the rich, for the poor can beg. *Scottish*

6581. God help the sheep when the wolf is judge. *Danish*

6582. God helps and the people oppress. *Maltese*

6583. God helps the early riser. *Spanish*

6584. God helps the kind. *Russian*

6585. God helps the navigator, but on condition that he rows. *Czech*

6586. God helps the poor man: He protects him from expensive sins. *Yiddish*

6587. God helps the strongest. *Dutch*

6588. God helps them that help themselves. *English*

6589. God helps three sorts of people: fools, children, and drunkards.
French

6590. God is a father; luck is a stepfather. *Yiddish*

6591. God is a giver.
Indian (Kashmiri)

6592. God is a good worker, but He loves to be helped. *Basque*

6593. God is above all. *American*

6594. God is above law. *American*

6595. God is an old worker of miracles. *Russian*

6596. God is at the end when we think he is farthest off it. *English*

6597. God is everywhere, except where he has his delegate. *German*

6598. God is great, but the devil is clever too. *Rumanian*

6599. God is in heaven and grass is on the earth. *Icelandic*

6600. God is no man's debtor.
Serbo-Croatian

6601. God is not as severe as he is said to be. *Irish*

6602. God is not rich; all He does is take from one and give to the other.
Yiddish

6603. God is not yet going on crutches. *Finnish*

6604. God is pleased with good people. *Indian (Kashmiri)*

6605. God is present not in strength, but in truth. *Russian*

6606. God is the best of witnesses.
Lebanese

6607. God is the blacksmith who does not forge for only one.
African (Bemba)

6608. God is the real physician.
African (Swahili)

6609. God knows well which are the best pilgrims. *English*

6610. God knows who is a good pilgrim. *French*

6611. God knows whose oil burns in the lamp. *Serbo-Croatian*

6612. God loves not a lying tongue.
Irish

6613. God loves the poor and helps the rich. *Yiddish*

6614. God loves the Trinity. *Russian*

6615. God makes and apparel shapes, but it is money that finishes the man.
English

6616. God makes no wreck without cause. *Swedish*

6617. God moves slowly yet his grace comes. *Irish*

6618. God needs no help when he cuts wood. *African (Ovambo)*

6619. God never pays his debts with money. *English*

6620. God often pays debts without money. *Irish*

6621. God permits, but not forever.
Portuguese

6622. God protect you from a woman's judgment and a fool's thrashing.
Rumanian

6623. God protects drunks and little ones. *Russian*

6624. God punishes but man takes revenge. *Yiddish*

6625. God punishes with one hand and blesses with the other. *Yiddish*

6626. God pursues sinners. *Greek*

6627. God puts a good root in the little pig's way. *French*

6628. God save me from him who studies but one book. *Italian*

6629. God save me from one who does not drink. *Italian*

6630. God save you from a bad neighbor, and from a beginner on the fiddle.
Italian

6631. God save you from a man who has but one business. *French*

6632. God saves the moon from the wolves. *French*

6633. God seizes late, but seizes harshly. *Iranian*

6634. God sells knowledge for labor, honor for risk. *Dutch*

6635. God sells wisdom for labor and suffering. *Russian*

6636. God sends corn and the devil mars the sack. *English*

6637. God sends fortune to fools. *English*

6638. God sends good luck and God sends bad. *English*

6639. God sends the remedy for the disease. *Yiddish*

6640. God shares out good things. *Irish*

6641. God shuts one door to open a hundred. *Serbo-Croatian*

6642. God sits on high and makes matches below. *Yiddish*

6643. God speaks a foreign tongue. *African (Ovambo)*

6644. God speaks for the man who holds his peace. *Mexican*

6645. God stays long but strikes at last. *English*

6646. God strikes not with both hands. *English*

6647. God takes care of a blind cow. *Indian (Bihar)*

6648. God takes care of an oppressed man. *Philippine*

6649. God takes care of fools, and drunken men. *Scottish*

6650. God takes care of those who take care of themselves. *Russian*

6651. God takes with one hand, and gives with the other. *Yiddish*

6652. God tempers the wind to the shorn lamb. *English*

6653. God wanted to chastise mankind so He sent lawyers. *Russian*

6654. God watches over fools. *Yiddish*

6655. God will cook the soup for him who has water, herbs, and wood. *Russian*

6656. God will help a ploughing man. *Polish*

6657. God will not drive flies away from a tailless cow. *African (Fulani)*

6658. God will provide, but a good bundle of straw will not be amiss. *Spanish*

6659. God will remain, friends will not. *Pashto*

6660. He's poor whom God hates. *Scottish*

6661. He that serves God for money, will serve the devil for better wages. *English*

6662. He thrives well that God loves. *English*

6663. He who does not speak, God does not hear. *Spanish*

6664. He who serves God has a good master. *English*

6665. Help yourself and God will help you. *Dutch*

6666. If God does not give, one cannot take. *Yiddish*

6667. If God doesn't will it, not even a blister will break out. *Russian*

6668. If God drenches you with His rain, He will dry you with His sun. *Slovenian*

6669. If God grants the day, he will also grant the nourishment.   *Russian*

6670. If God lived on earth, all his windows would be broken.   *Yiddish*

6671. If God wills, even a cock will lay an egg.   *Polish*

6672. If God wills it, even a broom can shoot.   *Yiddish*

6673. If we thanked God for the good things, there wouldn't be time to weep over the bad.   *Yiddish*

6674. In time comes he whom God sends.   *English*

6675. It is better to have to do with God than with his saints.   *French*

6676. Not even God can undo a blow received.   *Mexican*

6677. On whom God bestows an office, he provides brains to fill it.   *German*

6678. One God, one wife, but many friends.   *Dutch*

6679. Only God is without sin.   *Russian*

6680. Only God knows what is still to come.   *Maltese*

6681. Only God knows what man may have in his heart.   *Maltese*

6682. Praise God and love men.   *Russian*

6683. Pray to God but continue to row to the shore.   *Russian*

6684. Pray to God for a good harvest, but continue to hoe!   *Slovenian*

6685. Rely on God, but don't get out of line yourself.   *Russian*

6686. They are poor whom God hates.   *English*

6687. They are well guided that God guides.   *Scottish*

6688. They that worship God merely for fear, would worship the devil too, if he appear.   *English*

6689. To a vicious cow God doesn't give horns.   *Russian*

6690. To get near to God one need not climb the mountain.   *Russian*

6691. Trust in God and put your shoulder to the wheel.   *Polish*

6692. Trust in God, but tie your camel.   *Iranian*

6693. Trust not to God but upon good security.   *French*

6694. We all walk under God.   *Russian*

6695. What God decrees, man cannot prevent.   *Yiddish*

6696. What God does is probably for the best.   *Yiddish*

6697. What God joins together, let no man put asunder.   *German*

6698. What God made, he never mars.   *English*

6699. What God wants is deeds, not words.   *Philippine.*

6700. What God will, no frost can kill.   *English*

6701. What God wills, what God desires, that will be.   *Moroccan*

6702. Whatever God gives throw gratefully into your bag.   *Russian*

6703. When God denies a field rain He increases its dew.   *Russian*

6704. When God made the woman, He put beside her the distaff to distinguish her from man.   *Rumanian*

6705. When God means to punish a nation, he deprives the rulers of wisdom.   *German*

6706. When God so wills, the broom loses its handle.   *Hungarian*

6707. When God wants to break a man's heart, he gives him a lot of sense. *Yiddish*

6708. When God wants to make a poor man happy, he makes him lose his donkey and then find it again. *Armenian*

6709. When God will, all winds bring rain. *English*

6710. When God will not help, all the saints cannot help. *Serbo-Croatian*

6711. When God will not, the saints cannot. *Italian*

6712. When God wishes, even water can burn. *Russian*

6713. When God wishes to succor, men cannot destroy. *Yiddish*

6714. Where God builds a church, the devil builds a chapel. *German*

6715. Where God cooks, no smoke rises. *African (Bemba)*

6716. Where God does not make the key the lock is not secure. *Russian*

6717. Where God helps, nothing harms. *English*

6718. Who is pleased with little is not forgotten by God. *Russian*

6719. Whom God loves, his bitch litters pigs. *Spanish*

6720. Whom God will help none can hinder. *Scottish*

6721. Whom God wishes to punish, He deprives of his reason. *Russian*

6722. With one hand God punishes and with the other he blesses. *Yiddish*

6723. Woe to him who is not content with having God as his sustenance. *Irish*

6724. You cannot deceive God even by getting up early. *Russian*

6725. You cannot serve God and the devil. *Maltese*

GODS

6726. All the thousands and tens of thousands of gods are all one god. *Chinese*

6727. At steady gambling even the gods and immortals lose. *Chinese*

6728. Even the gods and immortals sometimes make mistakes. *Chinese*

6729. Gods and immortals sometimes lose their swords. *Chinese*

6730. Gods, devils and men are alike in actions and thoughts. *Tibetan*

6731. The gods don't allow us to be in their debt. *American*

6732. The gods see through everything. *Japanese*

6733. The gods themselves may be taken with gifts. *American*

6734. Whom the gods love die young. *English*

GOLD

6735. A spot in gold and a fault in a wise man are soon visible. *Finnish*

6736. All is not gold that glitters. *English*

6737. Better whole than patched with gold. *Danish*

6738. Don't think that all that glitters is gold. *African (Swahili)*

6739. Even gold is a thing of nought to the generous. *Indian (Tamil)*

6740. Fine gold in the hands of the unthrifty is of no value. *Indian (Tamil)*

6741. Gold brings gold, lack of gold a headache. *Iranian*

6742. Gold buys silver, but silver does not purchase gold. *Hebrew*

6743. Gold can come in all doors but Heaven's. *Indian (Hindi)*

6744. Gold does not buy everything.
Italian

6745. Gold dust blinds all eyes.
English

6746. Gold glitters even in the mud.
Yiddish

6747. Gold goes in at any gate except heaven's. *English*

6748. Gold grows (not) on trees.
American

6749. Gold is an orator. *English*

6750. Gold is but muck. *English*

6751. Gold is gold, though it be in a rogue's purse. *Danish*

6752. Gold is good but it may be dear bought. *Scottish*

6753. Gold is proved in the fire, friendship in need. *Danish*

6754. Gold is tested with fire; a woman with gold. *Yiddish*

6755. Gold is the glue, sinews, and strength of war. *English*

6756. Gold lies deep in the mountain, dirt on the highway. *German*

6757. Gold makes an honest man an ill man. *English*

6758. Gold should be sold to him who knows the value of it. *African (Yoruba)*

6759. Gold takes no rust. *Turkish*

6760. Gold though mixed with sand will always be gold. *Philippine*

6761. Gold without wisdom is but clay. *Slovakian*

6762. Gold, women, and linen should be chosen by daylight. *Basque*

6763. He is worth gold that carries it.
English

6764. He that has gold may buy land.
English

6765. He that wins gold, let him wear gold. *English*

6766. If there is gold in the house, there are money scales waiting outside to weigh it. *Chinese*

6767. No gold without dross.
English

6768. One may buy gold too dear.
English

6769. Pure gold does not fear the furnace. *Chinese*

6770. That is gold that is worth gold.
English

6771. The gold being gone, let us look to the silver. *Turkish*

6772. Today gold, tomorrow dust.
English

6773. When gold comes near to you, it glistens. *African (Oji)*

6774. When gold speaks every tongue is silent. *Italian*

6775. When gold speaks you may even hold your tongue. *English*

6776. When we have gold we are in fear, when we have none we are in danger. *English*

6777. When your gold dust is becoming finished, then you become prudent.
African (Ashanti)

6778. Yellow gold has its price; learning is priceless. *Chinese*

6779. Yellow gold is plentiful in the world; white-haired old friends are few. *Chinese*

GOOD

6780. Be good within reason, but never do evil. *Malaysian*

6781. Better a distant good than a near evil. *Portuguese*

6782. Better good afar off than evil at hand. *English*

6783. Better good and a little rather than bad and a lot of it. *Yiddish*

6784. By following the good you learn to be good. *Chinese*

6785. Do good and then do it again. *English*

6786. Good and evil are chiefly in the imagination. *English*

6787. Good and quickly seldom meet. *English*

6788. Good at a distance is better than evil at hand. *English*

6789. Good comes to better, and better to bad. *French*

6790. Good finds good. *English*

6791. Good is good, but better beats it. *Italian*

6792. He knows best what good is that has endured evil. *English*

6793. He that hopes not for good fears not evil. *English*

6794. He who is no good to himself is no good to another. *Yiddish*

6795. It is good to be neither high nor low. *Chinese*

6796. No good comes out of hurrying. *Yiddish*

6797. No good is got by wasting, but a good name is got by almsgiving. *Irish*

6798. None so good that's good for all. *English*

6799. Out of a great evil often comes a great good. *Italian*

6800. Set good against evil. *English*

6801. The good ones pay, the bad ones demand. *Yiddish*

6802. To talk good is not to be good; to do good, that is being good. *Chinese*

6803. What is good is not necessarily beautiful. *Japanese*

6804. When you have something good, you ought not look for something better. *Russian*

6805. Where there's no good within, no good comes out. *Dutch*

6806. With the good we become good. *Dutch*

GOOD-HEARTED

6807. The good-hearted has a heavy load. *Burmese*

GOODNESS

6808. Goodness is not tied to greatness. *English*

GOODS

6809. Better to cry over your goods than after them. *English*

6810. Common goods, no goods. *Dutch*

6811. Forbidden goods find many buyers. *Russian*

6812. From peddling small goods on the streets you don't make big fortunes. *Yiddish*

6813. Goods can be acquired, not children. *African (Bemba)*

6814. If everyone thought alike, no goods would be sold. *Libyan*

6815. Ill-gotten goods seldom prosper. *German*

6816. Ill-gotten goods thrive not. *English*

6817. Ill-gotten goods thrive not to the third heir. *English*

6818. Little goods, little care. *English*

6819. The best goods are the cheapest. *Dutch*

6820. When you have once gone out the door, we do not recognize the goods. *Chinese*

6821. Worldly goods come from avarice or what is forbidden. *Moroccan*

6822. Working slowly produces fine goods.   *Chinese*

GOOSE (see GEESE)

6823. A goose and a girl are never satisfied.   *Turkish*

6824. A goose drinks as much as a gander.   *Danish*

6825. A goose isn't a pig's comrade.
Russian

6826. A wild goose never lays a tame egg.   *English*

6827. It is a blind goose that knows not a fox from a fern bush.   *English*

6828. It is a silly goose that comes to a fox's sermon.   *English*

6829. It is an old goose that will eat no oats.   *English*

6830. Let a goose loose in oats and she will starve to death.   *Yiddish*

6831. The goose hisses, but does not bite.   *Dutch*

6832. The goose that has a good gander cackles loudly.   *Danish*

6833. The goose that has lost its head no longer cackles.   *Danish*

6834. When one goose drinks, all drink.   *German*

6835. When the goose trusts the fox then woe to her neck.   *Danish*

GOSSIP

6836. Gossip is like coal: If it does not char at least it will blacken.
Slovakian

6837. Gossip is the scum of water, action is the drop of gold.   *Tibetan*

6838. Gossip needs no carriage.
Russian

6839. It is easier to close a river than to stop gossip.   *Philippine*

6840. It is merry when gossips meet.
English

6841. Wherever there is gossip, there will be quarreling.   *Philippine*

GOSSIPING

6842. Gossiping and lying go together.   *English*

6843. Gossiping is the worst habit and the biggest calumny.   *Yiddish*

GOURD

6844. A water gourd gurgles when not full.   *Hawaiian*

6845. One will distinguish between the bitter gourd and the sweet.
African (Hausa)

GOVERN

6846. He who governs must know how to be strong.   *Maltese*

GOVERNMENT

6847. A tyrannical government is fiercer than a tiger.   *Japanese*

6848. An unjust government is better than corrupt subjects.   *Moroccan*

6849. Government is best which governs least.   *American*

GOWN

6850. That is the best gown that goes up and down the house.   *English*

6851. The gown does not make the friar.   *Italian*

6852. The gown does not make the monk.   *French*

6853. The gown is his that wears it, and the world his that enjoys it.
English

GRACE

6854. Grace grows after governance.
English

6855. Grace will last, beauty will blast.   *English*

6856. There is no grace in giving that which sticks to the fingers. *American*

GRAIN

6857. A grain does not fill a sieve, but it helps its fellow. *Spanish*

6858. A grain of caution is worth a pound of medicine. *American*

6859. A grain of prevention is worth a ton of remedy. *American*

6860. A grain of prudence is worth a pound of craft. *English*

6861. A single grain makes the balance heavier. *Egyptian*

6862. Every grain has its bran. *English*

6863. Grain by grain, a loaf; stone upon stone, a palace. *Slovenian*

6864. Grain by grain the hen fills her crop. *Spanish*

6865. He who sows his grain in the field puts his trust in Heaven. *Chinese*

6866. In the field the good grain is the other fellow's; on the road the pretty woman is the other man's wife. *Chinese*

6867. Of evil grain no good seed can come. *English*

6868. One grain fills not a sack, but helps his fellows. *English*

6869. One grain suffices to test a whole pot of boiled rice. *Indian (Tamil)*

6870. When the grain is weedy, we must reap high. *American*

6871. Without manure the growing grain will not yield a good crop. *Indian (Tamil)*

GRANDCHILD

6872. The first grandchild is more beloved than one's own child. *Japanese*

GRANT

6873. He grants enough that says nothing. *English*

GRAPE

6874. If you can't get grapes get an apple. *Russian*

6875. The sweetest grapes hang highest. *German*

6876. There is no grape without a stalk. *Turkish*

6877. With patience the sour grape becomes sweet and the mulberry leaf, satin. *Turkish*

GRASP

6878. He that grasps at too much holds nothing fast. *English*

6879. He who grasps all loses all. *Spanish*

6880. He who grasps at all holds nothing at the end. *German*

6881. He who grasps too much holds not firmly. *French*

6882. He who grasps too much holds nothing fast. *Italian*

6883. He who grasps too much lets much fall. *German*

GRASS

6884. As the grass cannot grow in the sky, so the dead cannot look out of the grave into the road. *African (Yoruba)*

6885. Bad grass does not make good hay. *Italian*

6886. Do not look for a string bag in the grass when the grass has been burnt. *African (Shona)*

6887. Grass does not grow on stones. *Greek*

6888. Grass grows not upon the highway. *Dutch*

6889. Grass grows not upon the highway, nor in the marketplace. *English*

6890. He that's afraid of every grass should not piss in a meadow. *Scottish*

6891. In a storm grass fares better than trees. *Russian*

6892. No grass grows in the marketplace. *English*

6893. No grass grows on a beaten road. *French*

6894. No grass grows on every man's road. *Flemish*

6895. No grass grows on the battlefield. *Polish*

6896. No grass grows under the stone that is often moved. *Swedish*

6897. No grass grows where the Turk's horse has trod. *English*

6898. Soft grass follows the wind. *Chinese*

6899. Soon grass, soon hay. *Dutch*

6900. The grass suffers in the fight of the tiger and buffalo. *Indian (Bihar)*

6901. The wild grass fears the frost, and the frost fears the sun. *Chinese*

6902. There are no two spears of grass alike. *American*

6903. Where everyone goes, the grass never grows. *German*

6904. While the grass grows the steed starves. *English*

GRATE

6905. Dirty grate makes dinner late. *English*

GRATITUDE

6906. Gratitude has gone to heaven and has taken the ladder. *Polish*

6907. Gratitude is what shows whether a gift is appreciated. *African (Hausa)*

GRAVE

6908. A grave is not dug before a person dies. *African (Zulu)*

6909. Better the grave than a life of want. *Welsh*

6910. Better the grave than slavery. *Serbo-Croatian*

6911. Graves are of all sizes. *English*

6912. He who eats when he is full digs his grave with his teeth. *Turkish*

6913. He who lies in the grave is well lodged. *German*

6914. The grave is already dug and man still continues to hope. *Yiddish*

6915. The grave is good rest. *English*

6916. The grave is our permanent home. *Maltese*

6917. We shall lie all alike in our graves. *English*

GREAT

6918. Great and good are seldom the same man. *English*

6919. The great and the little have need of one another. *English*

6920. The great put the little on the hook. *English*

6921. The great would have none great, and the little all little. *English*

6922. There would be no great ones, if there were no little. *English*

GREATNESS

6923. Greatness alone is not enough, or the cow would outrun the hare. *German*

6924. Where there is greatness, it shows itself. *African (Bemba)*

GREED

6925. Greed never finishes. *African (Swahili)*

6926. Greed will take you where you would not be.   *African (Fulani)*

GREYHOUND

6927. A greyhound finds its food in its feet.   *Irish*

6928. A greyhound forced to hunt catches no hare.   *Serbo-Croatian*

6829. In the long run the greyhound kills the hare.   *Spanish*

6930. The greyhound that starts many hares kills none.   *Spanish*

GRIEF

6931. All griefs with bread are less.
English

6932. Great griefs are mute.   *Italian*

6933. Grief and joy are a revolving wheel.   *Indian (Tamil)*

6934. Grief destroys even a hero.
Hebrew

6935. Grief for a dead wife lasts to the door.   *Italian*

6936. He who thinks of his own grief forgets those of others.   *Maltese*

6937. It is a grief to one beggar that another stands at the door.   *Dutch*

6938. New grief awakens the old.
English

6939. One grief drives out another.
English

6940. The anteater's grief is not the monkey's.   *African (Fulani)*

6941. The grief of parting and the agony of separation is the way of the world.   *Japanese*

6942. The grief of the head is the grief of griefs.   *English*

6943. The most recent grief is the heaviest to bear.   *Irish*

6944. There is no grief greater than that of a mother.   *Maltese*

6945. There is no grief so great as that for a dead heart.   *Chinese*

GRIEVANCE

6946. One grievance borne, another follows.   *Spanish*

GRINDSTONE

6947. Grinding and grinding wears out the hardest of grindstones.
Mexican

6948. He does not live in this world that can skin a grindstone.   *Danish*

GROCER

6949. The grocer does not open his shop for the sake of one customer.
Turkish

GROOM

6950. When the groom is desired, the bride doesn't need words.   *Yiddish*

GROUND

6951. He that lies on the ground can fall no lower.   *English*

6952. He who lies on the ground must expect to be trodden on.   *German*

6953. If you lie on the ground, you cannot fall.   *Yiddish*

6954. One doesn't build on foreign ground.   *Yiddish*

6955. The best ground has weeds.
Jamaican

6956. The best ground is the dirtiest.
English

6957. When you hold the ground you cannot fall.   *African (Annang)*

GROVE

6958. The distant grove you see surrounds either a house or a grave.
Chinese

GROW

6959. One cannot grow higher than oneself.   *Russian*

6960. The older one grows, the more one learns.   *Dutch*

GROWTH

6961. Without bending, there is no growth.   *Japanese*

GRUDGE

6962. A grudge is not held against a dead person.   *African (Zulu)*

6963. Don't bear a grudge and don't record it.   *Japanese*

GUARD

6964. He does not guard himself well who is not always on his guard.
French

6965. He who guards himself will not perish.   *African (Ovambo)*

GUARDING

6966. There's no guarding against the privy thief.   *French*

GUESS

6967. He who guesses well prophesies well.   *Italian*

GUESSING

6968. Guessing is missing.   *Dutch*

GUEST

6969. A constant guest is never welcome.   *English*

6970. A daily guest is a great thief in the kitchen.   *Dutch*

6971. A frequent guest becomes a burden.   *Yiddish*

6972. A guest and a fish after three days are poison.   *French*

6973. A guest eats much when he sees his hosts doing likewise.
African (Shona)

6974. A guest is like rain: when he lingers on, he becomes a nuisance.
Yiddish

6975. A guest, like a fish, stinks the third day.   *Dutch*

6976. A guest unwanted comes at meal time.   *Greek*

6977. A guest will not know what fasting means.   *Serbo-Croatian*

6978. An unbidden guest knows not where to sit.   *English*

6979. An unpleasant guest is as welcome as salt to a sore eye.   *Danish*

6980. Don't ask a guest if you may kill a fowl for him.   *Chinese*

6981. Even a welcome guest becomes a parasite on the third day. *Japanese*

6982. Even if you don't like your guests, welcome them with a smile.
Philippine

6983. Give the best you have to your guests.   *Philippine*

6984. Guests and fish will get old on the third day.   *Estonian*

6985. Guests only come to a happy house.   *Burmese*

6986. Guests should not forget to go home.   *Swedish*

6987. It costs money to be obliged to receive guests constantly. *Norwegian*

6988. It's an ill guest that never drinks to his host.   *English*

6989. One guest loves not another guest; the master of the house dislikes both.   *Turkish*

6990. One refuses to embrace the guest who comes too often.
Serbo-Croatian

6991. Seven days is the length of a guest's life.   *Burmese*

6992. The first day indeed a guest; the second, a nuisance; the third, a pest.
                                                                      Hebrew

6993. The guest is a guest, even if he stays a winter or a summer. *Moroccan*

6994. The guest of the hospitable treats hospitably.   *Egyptian*

6995. The unbidden guest is a burden.   *German*

6996. Though many guests are absent, he only who enlivens the party is missed.   *African (Yoruba)*

6997. When the guests have gone the host is at peace.   *Chinese*

6998. When the guest is in most favor, he will do well to leave.   *German*

6999. With a good guest, you are happy when he arrives; with a bad one, when he leaves.   *Yiddish*

GUIDE

7000. Bad guides may soon mislead.
                                                                      English

7001. He who goes out on a journey without a guide loses his way.
                                                                      Turkish

7002. One has no need of a guide to the village one can see.   *Rumanian*

7003. Without a guide, even into Paradise there is no entering.   *Turkish*

GUILE

7004. Guile excels strength.
                                                              African (Hausa)

GUILT

7005. Guilt is always jealous.
                                                                      English

GUILTY

7006. He who is guilty is the one who has much to say.   *African (Ashanti)*

7007. Strike the innocent that the guilty may confess.   *Egyptian*

GUN

7008. A gun is not so hard to buy as powder: A gun is bought one day, powder must be bought again and again.   *African (Yoruba)*

7009. A gun is not to be held carelessly.   *African (Yoruba)*

7010. A gun that does not go off leaves its owner in peril.   *African (Ovambo)*

7011. If there were only snails and tortoise, no gun would ever be fired in the jungle.   *African (Oji)*

GUNPOWDER

7012. Gunpowder and fire do not agree.   *African (Ga)*

GUT

7013. A full gut supports moral precepts.   *Burmese*

7014. Let the guts be full, for it is they that carry the legs.   *Portuguese*

GUTTER

7015. Better repair the gutter than the whole house.   *Portuguese*

7016. He who does not repair his gutter has a whole house to repair.
                                                                      Spanish

7017. The gutter by dropping wears the stone.   *Spanish*

GYPSY

7018. Every gypsy praises his own horse.   *Serbo-Croatian*

H

HABIT

7019. A habit acquired in youth is carried on in old age. *Philippine*

7020. A habit that has started at three will continue till eighty. *Korean*

7021. Habit becomes one's nature. *Japanese*

7022. Habits contracted in the cradle cleave to one till he goes to the burning ground. *Indian (Tamil)*

7023. Habit is a shirt of iron. *Slovenian*

7024. Habit is a shirt that we wear till death. *Russian*

7025. Habit is second nature. *Russian*

7026. Habit is stronger than resolution. *Welsh*

7027. Habit makes all things agreeable. *American*

7028. Old habits have deep roots. *Norwegian*

7029. The habits of early life will never be forgotten. *Indian (Tamil)*

7030. What becomes a habit does not change easily. *Greek*

7031. Wherever one goes, his habits follow. *Philippine*

HACK

7032. Even the best hack stumbles once. *German*

HAIL

7033. In time of drought even hail is welcome. *Greek*

HAIR

7034. A hair from the head of a woman can tie a large elephant. *Japanese*

7035. A hair of the dog that bit you. *English*

7036. Curly hair, curly thoughts. *Russian*

7037. Even a hair casts its shadow. *German*

7038. Even a thread of hair has its shadow. *Rumanian*

7039. Even the tiniest hair will cast a shadow upon the ground. *Mexican*

7040. Every hair casts its shadow. *Spanish*

7041. Gray hairs are death's blossoms. *English*

7042. Gray hairs do not always mean old age. *Philippine*

7043. It's bad combing where there is no hair. *Dutch*

7044. Long on hair, short on brains.
Russian

7045. One finds many gray hairs but few wise men. *Swedish*

7046. One hair at a time, and the man is bald at last. *German*

7047. One hair of a woman draws more than a bell rope. *German*

7048. One hair of a woman draws more than a team of oxen. *English*

7049. One hair on a maiden's head pulls harder than ten yoke of oxen.
Danish

7050. Short hair is soon brushed.
German

7051. When gray hairs begin to appear, the lust for life begins to disappear. *Mexican*

HALF

7052. It is best to take half in hand and the rest by and by. *English*

7053. The half is better than the whole. *English*

HALTER

7054. A short halter for a greedy horse. *Spanish*

7055. It is ill talking of a halter in the house of a man that was hanged.
English

HAMMER

7056. A golden hammer breaks an iron gate. *German*

7057. A silver hammer breaks an iron door. *French*

7058. Before the big hammer strikes one, the little hammer strikes two.
Indian (Tamil)

7059. It is better to be the hammer than the anvil. *Russian*

HAMMERING

7060. Without hammering there is no fastening. *Turkish*

HAND

7061. A beggar's hand is a bottomless basket. *Dutch*

7062. A broken hand works, but not a broken heart. *Iranian*

7063. A child's hand is soon filled and a child's anger soon emptied.
Swedish

7064. A closed hand catches no hawk.
Irish

7065. A hand in the water feels no pity for a hand in the fire. *Maltese*

7066. A hand that takes never gets tired. *Russian*

7067. A light hand makes a heavy pocket. *American*

7068. A little hand can often give great help. *Norwegian*

7069. A single hand makes no sound of handclapping. *Korean*

7070. A wet hand will hold a dead herring. *English*

7071. All is not at hand that helps.
English

7072. An empty hand is no lure for a hawk. *Scottish*

7073. Be it ever so dark the hand will not miss the mouth. *African (Fulani)*

7074. Clean hands want no washball.
English

7075. Cold hand, a warm heart.
German

7076. Dirty hands make clean money.
English

7077. Empty hands don't go to the mouth. *Indian (Hindustani)*

7078. For washing his hands none sells his lands. *English*

7079. From the fingers of a skillful hand water may leak.   *Japanese*

7080. Good hand, good hire. *English*

7081. Hand knows hand.
     Indian (Hindi)

7082. Hand washes hand, and finger, finger.   *Greek*

7083. Hand washes hand and stone polishes stone.   *Icelandic*

7084. He who is fed by another's hand seldom gets enough.   *Danish*

7085. He who puts his hands on his lap will suffer hardships in life.
     Philippine

7086. If the hands are empty the mouth is empty.   *Japanese*

7087. If the hand would do what the tongue says there would be no poverty.
     Indian (Hindi)

7088. If you applaud with one hand it will not be heard.   *African (Ovambo)*

7089. It is a bad hand that refuses to guard the head.   *Danish*

7090. Kiss the hand you cannot bite.
     Rumanian

7091. Liberal hands make many friends.   *Danish*

7092. Many hands at the carding but few at the dining.   *Greek*

7093. Many hands make light work.
     English

7094. Many hand soon make an end.
     German

7095. Many hands will carry off much plunder.   *English*

7096. Many kiss hands they would fain see chopped off.   *Spanish*

7097. Many kiss the hand they wish cut off.   *English*

7098. No one dares to slap the hand that gives.   *Philippine*

7099. Nothing enters into a closed hand.   *Scottish*

7100. One hand alone cannot carry a baby.   *African (Swahili)*

7101. One hand cannot clap.
     Indian (Hindustani)

7102. One hand cannot hold two watermelons.   *Lebanese*

7103. One hand claws another.
     English

7104. One hand full of money is stronger than two full of truth.
     Swedish

7105. One hand must wash the other, or both will be dirty.   *Danish*

7106. One hand washes the other, and both the face.   *English*

7107. One hand will not clasp.
     English

7108. One hand will not wash the other for nothing.   *Scottish*

7109. One stroke by the master's hand is better than ten from an apprentice.
     Libyan

7110. Put not your hand in a dog's mouth.   *American*

7111. Scatter with one hand, gather with two.   *English*

7112. Skilled hands eat trouts.
     Spanish

7113. Strike, but conceal the hand.
     American

7114. The busy hand does not beg.
     Armenian

7115. The folded hands gain no bread.   *Latvian*

7116. The hand applauds, the mouth assents.   *Hawaiian*

7117. The hand goes only where the leg goes.   *Irish*

7118. The hand helps the legs and the legs help the hands.   *Indian (Tamil)*

7119. The hands soon forget what the mouth promises.   *Russian*

7120. The hand that gives gathers.   *English*

7121. The hand that gives is above that which receives.   *Turkish*

7122. The hand that is ready to steal bran will be ready to steal money also.   *Indian (Tamil)*

7123. The hasty hand bungles things.   *Japanese*

7124. The hasty hand will do things wrong.   *Japanese*

7125. The idle hand gets nothing.   *Manx*

7126. The quick hand belongs to the skilled.   *Welsh*

7127. The right hand helps the left and the left the right.   *Indian (Tamil)*

7128. The right hand is slave to the left.   *Italian*

7129. The right hand itches to get money, the left hand to spend it.   *Russian*

7130. The right hand washes the left, and the left hand washes the right.   *Indian (Kashmiri)*

7131. The rough hand is the way to wealth.   *Philippine*

7132. The wise hand does not all that the tongue says.   *Spanish*

7133. Though the left hand conquer the right, no advantage is gained.   *Chinese*

7134. Though you are hungry, you do not eat with both hands. *African (Oji)*

7135. Under a glove the ugliest hand is hidden.   *Rumanian*

7136. What man's hands make, man's hands can destroy.   *German*

7137. What the hand plucks, the shoulder bears.   *Malaysian*

7138. When the hands are many, they can break down the stoutest of walls.   *Hebrew*

7139. When the hand ceases to give, the tongue will cease to praise. *Manx*

7140. When we compete in working, our hands quicken.   *African (Yoruba)*

7141. When you go to dance, take heed whom you take by the hand.   *Danish*

7142. When your hand is in the dog's mouth withdraw it gently.   *Irish*

7143. Where every hand fleeces, the sheep goes naked.   *English*

7144. With bare hands one establishes a family fortune.   *Korean*

7145. Without fingers the hand would be a spoon.   *African (Wolof)*

7146. You can't clap with one hand.   *Chinese*

HANDFUL

7147. A handful of good life is better than a bushel of learning.   *English*

7148. An handful of trade is an handful of gold.   *English*

7149. Handfuls make up a load.   *Irish*

HANDICRAFT

7150. A good handicraft has a golden foundation.   *Danish*

HANDLE

7151. Everything has two handles.   *Dutch*

7152. He who holds the handle of the frying pan turns it as he pleases.   *French*

7153. There must be a handle to an axe.   *Turkish*

HANDSAW

7154. A handsaw is a good thing, but not to shave with.   *English*

HANDSOME

7155. Handsome is not what is handsome, but what pleases.   *Italian*

7156. Handsome is that handsome does.   *English*

7157. He that is not handsome at 20, nor strong at 30, nor rich at 40, nor wise at 50, will never be handsome, strong, rich, or wise.   *English*

HANG

7158. Better be half hanged than ill wed.   *English*

7159. Better be half hanged than lose estate.   *English*

7160. He who is destined to hang won't drown.   *Yiddish*

7161. He who was born to be hanged will not be drowned, unless the water go over the gallows.   *Danish*

7162. Who will hang will never drown.   *Russian*

HANGING

7163. There is no hanging a man for his thoughts.   *American*

HAP

7164. Some have hap, some stick in the gap.   *English*

HAPPEN

7165. Nothing happens for nothing.   *French*

7166. Nothing is so new but it has happened before.   *Danish*

7167. What happens once may happen again.   *American*

HAPPINESS

7168. All happiness is in the mind.   *English*

7169. For finding happiness one must walk till he be wearied.   *Turkish*

7170. Happiness begins where ambition ends.   *Hungarian*

7171. Happiness is desired by all.   *Indian (Tamil)*

7172. Happiness is guarded by bold warriors.   *Indian (Hindi)*

7173. Happiness is not a horse, you cannot harness it.   *Russian*

7174. He that talks much of his happiness, summons grief.   *English*

7175. If you have happiness, don't use it all up.   *Chinese*

7176. Nobody reaps happiness without first undergoing hardships.   *Philippine*

7177. That is happiness which springs from virtue.   *Indian (Tamil)*

7178. There is no happiness without jealousy.   *Russian*

7179. Too much happiness ends in sorrow.   *Philippine*

7180. True happiness consists in making happy.   *Indian (Hindi)*

HAPPY

7181. Better be happy than wise.   *English*

7182. Happy is he that chastens himself.   *English*

7183. Happy is he that is happy in his children.   *English*

7184. Happy is he who knows his follies in his youth.   *English*

7185. He is not happy that knows not himself happy.   *English*

HARD

7186. Do not become too hard, lest you get broken.   *Russian*

7187. Hard against hard never was good.   *German*

7188. The hard gives no more than he that has nothing.   *English*

HARDSHIP

7189. There is no hardship that cannot be surmounted.   *Philippine*

7190. There is no hardship that will not end, no trouble that will not retreat.
                    African (Ovambo)

7191. There is no hardship without an end, no game without a parting.
                    African (Ovambo)

7192. When the hardship is at its height, relief is near.   *Philippine*

7193. Where there is no hardship, there is no pleasure and happiness.
                    Philippine

HARE

7194. A hare is not caught by sitting down.   *African (Hausa)*

7195. Even hares pull a lion by the beard when he is dead.   *Dutch*

7196. Every hare may pluck the dead lion's mane.   *German*

7197. Hares are caught with hounds, fools with praise, and women with gold.   *German*

7198. Hares are not caught by the sound of the drum.   *French*

7199. Hares are not caught with drums.   *Dutch*

7200. He that hunts two hares loses both.   *English*

7201. He that hunts two hares will catch neither.   *French*

7202. He who chases two hares will not catch even one.   *Japanese*

7203. He who hunts two hares at once, catches neither.   *Dutch*

7204. He who hunts two hares does not catch the one and let the other escape.   *Italian*

7205. He who hunts two hares from one bush is not likely to catch either.
                    Danish

7206. If you chase two hares one will escape.   *African (Shona)*

7207. In small woods may be caught large hares.   *Dutch*

7208. It is hard to catch hares with unwilling hounds.   *Dutch*

7209. It is hard to drive a hare out of a bush in which he is not.   *Irish*

7210. It is ill catching hares with drums.   *Dutch*

7211. Lame hares are ill to help.
                    English

7212. Many hares are hunted who haven't eaten cabbages.   *Polish*

7213. One catches the hare, and another eats it.   *German*

7214. One hunts the hare, and another eats it.   *Danish*

7215. The hare does not eat the grass around his burrow.   *Chinese*

7216. The hare is not the elephant's slave, the forest brought them together.
                    African (Hausa)

7217. The hare starts from where it is least expected.   *Spanish*

7218. The hare starts when a man least expects it.   *English*

7219. Two hares are not taken at once.   *Turkish*

7220. When we least expect it, the hare darts out of the ditch.   *Dutch*

7221. Who hunts two hares together catches neither.   *German*

HARLOT

7222. A harlot does not repent; and water in a jar does not become sour milk.   *Egyptian*

7223. A harlot has no faithfulness.
                                    Japanese

HARM

7224. Better the harm I know than that I know not.   *English*

7225. No harm, no force   *English*

7226. One does harm, and another bears the blame.   *English*

7227. The harm we do others we easily forget.   *Russian*

HARPOON

7228. A small harpoon can kill a whale.   *Philippine*

HARSHNESS

7229. The harshness of the mouth does not govern a house.
                              African (Bemba)

HARVEST

7230. Better a bad harvest than a bad neighbor.   *Serbo-Croatian*

7231. Harvest comes not every day, though it comes every year.   *English*

7232. Other people's harvests are always the best harvests, but one's children are always the best children.
                                    Chinese

HASTE

7233. An ill haste is not good.
                                    English

7234. Fool's haste is no speed.
                                    English

7235. Haste and careful work never go together.   *Greek*

7236. Haste and wisdom are things far odd.   *English*

7237. Haste comes not alone.
                                    English

7238. Haste is not strength.
                              African (Hausa)

7239. Haste is the sister of repentance.
                                    Moroccan

7240. Haste makes waste.   *English*

7241. Haste often rues.   *English*

7242. Haste trips up its own heels.
                                    English

7243. He that is too much in haste may stumble on a good road.   *French*

7244. In haste there is error. *Chinese*

7245. Make haste and leave nothing to waste.   *English*

7246. Make haste slowly.   *Greek*

7247. Make no more haste when you come down than when you went up.
                                    English

7248. Marry in haste and repent at leisure.   *Dutch*

7249. Nothing in haste but catching fleas.   *Dutch*

7250. Nothing to be done in haste but gripping of fleas.   *Scottish*

7251. The greater the haste, the greater the hindrance.   *Welsh*

7252. The more haste, worse speed.
                                    English

7253. There is no haste to hang true men.   *English*

7254. We do in haste what we repent at leisure.   *German*

HASTEN

7255. Hasten at leisure.   *German*

7256. Hasten leisurely.   *French*

HASTINESS

7257. Hastiness is the beginning of wrath, and its end repentance. *Dutch*

HASTY

7258. Be not too hasty, and you'll speed the better. *English*

7259. The hasty leaps over his opportunities. *Albanian*

HAT

7260. A broad hat does not always cover a venerable head. *English*

7261. A hat is not made for one shower. *English*

7262. Hat in hand goes through the whole land. *German*

7263. In a fight no broad hat can be put on. *Japanese*

7264. You can't make a hat out of a pig's tail. *Yiddish*

HATCH

7265. It is good to have a hatch before the door. *English*

HATCHET

7266. A small hatchet fells a great oak. *Portuguese*

HATE

7267. Hate does not build a house, it dissolves. *African (Ovambo)*

7268. Hate has no medicine. *African (Ga)*

7269. He who is sweating with hate cannot rule the country. *African (Ovambo)*

7270. The greatest hate springs from the greatest love. *English*

HATRED

7271. Better is the hatred of the wise than the friendship of fools. *Indian (Tamil)*

7272. Hatred is blind as well as love. *English*

7273. Hatred renewed is worse than at first. *Italian*

7274. Hatred with friends is succor to foes. *English*

HAUGHTINESS

7275. Haughtiness can do harm but you can't die from loving pleasure. *Yiddish*

HAUGHTY

7276. The haughty in prosperity are meanest in adversity. *American*

HAVE

7277. Better have it than hear of it. *English*

7278. Better to have than wish. *English*

7279. He that much has, much behoves. *English*

7280. He that will have all, loses all. *English*

7281. If you have, hold on to it; if you know, be silent; if you can, do! *Yiddish*

7282. Many have too much, but none have enough. *Danish*

7283. What one has, one doesn't want; and what one wants, one cannot have. *Yiddish*

7284. Who has nothing is nothing. *Italian*

HAVING

7285. Having is better than wanting. *African (Hausa)*

7286. Having is having, come whence it may. *German*

HAWK

7287. A hawk doesn't swoop on a stone ball unless there's a piece of meat on it. *African (Hausa)*

7288. Better a hawk in the hand than two in flight.   *Icelandic*

7289. Hawks will not carry off the fowl destined to crow.
African (Fulani)

7290. It is easy to reclaim a hawk that has lost its prey.   *English*

7291. It's hard to catch hawks with empty hands.   *Dutch*

7292. The avaricious hawk loses its talons.   *Japanese*

7293. The hawk is not frightened by the cries of the crane.   *Egyptian*

7294. The wise hawk conceals his talons.   *Japanese*

7295. Unmanned hawks forsake the lure.   *English*

7296. When the hawk hovers the owner of the fowls feels uneasy.
African (Yoruba)

7297. With empty hands men may no hawks lure.   *English*

7298. You cannot make a hawk of a buzzard.   *French*

HAY

7299. Hanged hay never fattens cattle.
English

7300. Make your hay before the fine weather leaves you.   *Irish*

HAZARD

7301. Better hazard once than be always in fear.   *English*

HEAD

7302. A bald head is soon shaven.
English

7303. A camel's head does not pass through the eye of a needle. *Turkish*

7304. A cool head and warm feet are the cause of long life.   *Japanese*

7305. A forgetful head makes a weary pair of heels.   *English*

7306. A good head does not want for hats.   *French*

7307. A head is not to be cut off because it is scabby.   *Danish*

7308. A scald head is soon broken.
English

7309. A smart head does not last long.
Yiddish

7310. A wise head keeps a shut mouth.   *Irish*

7311. A wise head makes a closed mouth.   *Irish*

7312. A wise head makes a still tongue.   *English*

7313. All heads are heads, but all luck is not luck.   *Jamaican*

7314. All heads are not sense-boxes.
French

7315. All heads have hair, but not all have brains.   *Philippine*

7316. An idle head is a box for the wind.   *English*

7317. Better be a chicken's head than an ox's rump.   *Japanese*

7318. Better be the head of a lizard than the tail of a lion.   *English*

7319. Better be the head of a pike than the tail of a sturgeon.   *English*

7320. Better be the head of a rat than the tail of a lion.   *Spanish*

7321. Better be the head of an ass than the tail of a horse.   *English*

7322. Better to be an ant's head than a lion's tail.   *Armenian*

7323. Better two heads than one, better one head than a hundred.   *Welsh*

7324. Big head, little wit.   *French*

7325. Do not enter where your head cannot pass through comfortably.
Russian

7326. Don't lie down with a healthy head in a sick bed.   *Yiddish*

7327. Every head must do its own thinking.   *African (Jabo)*

7328. Great head and little wit.
English

7329. Hair by hair the head becomes bald.   *Welsh*

7330. Hard heads suffer much.
Albanian

7331. He that has a head of butter must not come near the oven.   *Dutch*

7332. He that has a head of wax must not approach the fire.   *French*

7333. He that has a head of wax must not walk in the sun.   *English*

7334. He that has no head needs no hat.   *English*

7335. He who keeps his head at home, loses not his hat in the crowd.
Turkish

7336. He whose head has been cut off does not walk.   *African (Ovambo)*

7337. Head and feet kept warm, the rest will take no harm.   *English*

7338. If one hasn't got it in his head, he has it in his legs.   *Yiddish*

7339. If the head be left empty, it is not well.   *Turkish*

7340. If your head is made of butter, don't be a baker.   *French*

7341. In every head is some wisdom.
Egyptian

7342. It is difficult to get many heads under one hat.   *Danish*

7343. It is hard to put many heads under one hat.   *Swedish*

7344. It is no time to bow when the head is off.   *Scottish*

7345. Let not the tongue utter what the head may have to pay for.
Portuguese

7346. Let not the tongue utter what the head must pay for.   *Spanish*

7347. Many heads are better than one.   *Scottish*

7348. Many heads, many minds.
Dutch

7349. One cannot jump higher than one's head.   *Finnish*

7350. One good head is better than a hundred strong hands.   *English*

7351. One who has lost his head doesn't cry about having lost his hair.
Russian

7352. Scabby heads love not the comb.
English

7353. So many heads, so many minds.
Danish

7354. So many heads, so many wits.
English

7355. The bigger a man's head, the worse his headache.   *Iranian*

7356. The comforter's head never aches.   *English*

7357. The head doesn't wait for the tail.   *Russian*

7358. The heads of the gods are hidden in the clouds.   *Hawaiian*

7359. The head suffers because of the tongue.   *Slovakian*

7360. The head that bends is not cut off.   *Turkish*

7361. The head that is cut off does not shoot again.   *Turkish*

7362. There is many a good head under an old hat.   *Norwegian*

7363. There is often a wise head under a tattered hat.   *Slovakian*

7364. To protest and knock one's head against the wall is what everybody can do. *Italian*

7365. To wash an ass's head is but loss of time and soap. *French*

7366. Two heads are better than one. *English*

7367. Two heads don't fit into the same cap. *Greek*

7368. What one does not have in the head, one must have in the legs. *German*

7369. When the head aches all the body is the worse. *English*

7370. When the head aches all the limbs ache. *Danish*

7371. When the head does not work, the legs suffer. *Rumanian*

7372. When the head is a fool, the whole body can go to hell. *Yiddish*

7373. When the head is sick the whole body is sick. *Dutch*

7374. Where the head goes, there goes the trunk. *Hebrew*

7375. Where there is no head, woe to the feet. *Rumanian*

7376. Wherever the head goes, the foot also goes. *Turkish*

7377. Wherever the head goes, the tail follows. *Philippine*

7378. Who has no head should have legs. *Italian*

7379. You cannot shave a man's head in his absence. *African (Yoruba)*

HEADACHE

7380. He who does as he likes has no headache. *Italian*

7381. Neither hat nor crown help against headache. *Swedish*

HEADY

7382. He that is heady is ruled by a fool. *English*

HEAL

7383. One is not so soon healed as hurt. *English*

HEALING

7384. It is ill healing of an old sore. *English*

HEALTH

7385. Good health is the sister of beauty. *Maltese*

7386. He is young enough who has health, and he is rich enough who has no debts. *Danish*

7387. He who has not health has nothing. *French*

7388. Health and cheerfulness make beauty; finery and cosmetics cost money and lie. *Spanish*

7389. Health and money go far. *English*

7390. Health and wealth create beauty. *English*

7391. Health comes before making a livelihood. *Yiddish*

7392. Health is a crown and no one knows it save a sick person. *African (Swahili)*

7393. Health is better than wealth. *English*

7394. Health is great riches. *English*

7395. Health is not valued till sickness comes. *English*

7396. Health of the body is prosperity. *African (Hausa)*

7397. Health without money is a half-malady. *Italian*

7398. Health without money is half an ague. *English*

7399. When in good health one can earn money; one should save for the day when one is sick.   *Vietnamese*

7400. Without health, no wealth.
                                                Serbo-Croatian

HEALTHY

7401. He who would be healthy, let him be cheerful.   *Welsh*

7402. One can always be healthy so long as one is not ill.   *Russian*

7403. Who is not healthy at twenty, wise at thirty, or rich at forty, will never be either.   *Russian*

HEAP

7404. The more you heap, the worse you cheap.   *English*

HEAR

7405. He that hears much and speaks not at all shall be welcome both in bower and hall.   *English*

7406. He who hears one side only, hears nothing.   *English*

7407. Hear all, see all.   *English*

7408. Hear before you blame.
                                                American

7409. Hear first and speak afterwards.   *Spanish*

7410. Hear, see, and say nothing if you would live in peace.   *French*

7411. Hear twice before you speak once.   *English*

7412. "I heard" is not as good as "I saw."   *Chinese*

7413. None so deaf as he that won't hear.   *French*

7414. What one hears is doubtful; what one sees with one's own eyes is certain.   *Chinese*

HEARER

7415. Were there no hearers, there would be no backbiters.   *English*

HEARING

7416. From hearing comes wisdom; from speaking, repentance.   *English*

7417. Hearing a hundred times is not worth seeing once.   *Vietnamese*

7418. Hearing is never as good as seeing.   *Iranian*

7419. Hearing is not seeing.
                                        African (Swahili)

HEARSAY

7420. Better than hearsay is actual observation.   *Japanese*

7421. He who believes in hearsay lacks judgment.   *Philippine*

7422. Hearsay is half lies.   *Dutch*

7423. Hearsay is not like ocular testimony.   *Egyptian*

HEART

7424. A cheerful heart spins much flax.   *Serbo-Croatian*

7425. A drunk heart lied never.
                                                Scottish

7426. A fool's heart is in his tongue.
                                                English

7427. A gentle heart is tied with an easy thread.   *English*

7428. A glad heart seldom sighs, but a sorrowful mouth often laughs. *Danish*

7429. A good heart breaks bad fortune.   *Spanish*

7430. A happy heart is better than a full purse.   *Italian*

7431. A heart is a lock, but a lock can be opened with a duplicated key.
                                                Yiddish

7432. A heart is a lock: you need the right key to it.   *Yiddish*

7433. A heart of sympathy is the beginning of benevolence.   *Japanese*

7434. A heavy heart talks a lot.
Yiddish

7435. A kind heart is better than a crafty head.   *Manx*

7436. A kind heart loses nought at last.   *English*

7437. A lord's heart and a beggar's purse agree not.   *English*

7438. A loving heart is more precious than gold.   *Philippine*

7439. A maiden's heart is a dark forest.   *Russian*

7440. A man's heart is as changeable as the skies in autumn.   *Japanese*

7441. A proud heart and a beggar's purse agree not well together.   *English*

7442. A proud heart and a poor purse are ill met.   *Scottish*

7443. A royal heart is often hid under a tattered cloak.   *Danish*

7444. A small heart has small desires.   *English*

7445. A stout heart breaks ill fortune.
Portuguese

7446. A stout heart tempers adversity.
Dutch

7447. A wicked heart is poverty; hate is hunger.   *African (Ovambo)*

7448. A woman's heart and her tongue are not relatives.   *English*

7449. A woman's heart is as changeable as the eyes of a cat.   *Japanese*

7450. A woman's heart is as changeable as the weather in spring.   *Japanese*

7451. A woman's heart sees more than ten men's eyes.   *Swedish*

7452. After a good cry, your heart is lighter.   *Yiddish*

7453. All that is in the heart is written in the face.   *African (Fulani)*

7454. An embittered heart talks a lot.
Yiddish

7455. An envious heart frets itself.
English

7456. An innocent heart suspects no guile.   *Portuguese*

7457. As your heart, so is your word.
Russian

7458. Better a good heart than a fair face.   *Japanese*

7459. Easily changed is a woman's heart.   *Japanese*

7460. Every heart has its own ache.
English

7461. Every heart has secrets.
Yiddish

7462. Faint heart misses the chance; bravery wins a throne.   *Burmese*

7463. Faint heart never won fair lady.
English

7464. Have a clean heart and you may walk near the altar.   *Greek*

7465. He that has no heart ought to have heels.   *English*

7466. He whom the heart loves is the handsome one.   *Turkish*

7467. Hearts communicate with each other.   *Russian*

7468. Heart finds a way to heart.
Iranian

7469. Hearts may agree though heads differ.   *English*

7470. Humble hearts have humble desires.   *English*

7471. If the heart be stout, a mouse can lift an elephant.   *Tibetan*

7472. If the heart is firm, the body is cool.   *Chinese*

7473. If the heart is right the deeds will be right.   *Japanese*

7474. In every man's heart there is a sleeping lion.   *Armenian*

7475. It's a poor heart that never re-joices. *English*

7476. It is the heart that carries one to hell or to heaven. *African (Kanuri)*

7477. Large heart never loved little cream pot. *American*

7478. Let your heart go and it will lead you into slavery. *Russian*

7479. Man's heart is deeper than the sea, more secret than a tightly closed room. *Vietnamese*

7480. Men's hearts are as different as their faces. *Japanese*

7481. Nearest the heart, nearest the mouth. *Scottish*

7482. No heart is sadder than a penniless pocket. *Mexican*

7483. Not a long day, but a good heart rids work. *English*

7484. Not every heart that laughs is really cheerful. *Yiddish*

7485. One heart feels another's affections. *Yiddish*

7486. Set hard heart against hard lap. *English*

7487. Sweet heart and honey bird keep no house. *English*

7488. That which is in his heart is at the tip of his tongue. *Lebanese*

7489. The female heart is as unstable as water rolling on a lotus leaf. *Thai*

7490. The heart and the eye are the two agents of sin. *Hebrew*

7491. The heart does not grieve over what the eyes have not seen. *Slovakian*

7492. The heart does not lie. *Dutch*

7493. The heart has no window. *Russian*

7494. The heart is all. *American*

7495. The heart is no traitor. *Spanish*

7496. The heart is not a stone. *Russian*

7497. The heart is small and embraces the whole wide world. *Yiddish*

7498. The heart is something of a prophet. *Yiddish*

7499. The heart of a fool is on his tongue; the tongue of a wise man is in his heart. *Armenian*

7500. The heart of a little child is like the heart of the Buddha. *Chinese*

7501. The heart of one void of compassion is harder than iron. *Indian (Tamil)*

7502. The stoutest heart must fail at last. *American*

7503. To know one's self is to know others, for heart can understand heart. *Chinese*

7504. Were it not for hope, heart would break. *Scottish*

7505. What comes from the heart, goes to the heart. *German*

7506. What is in the heart will lead to the mouth. *African (Fulani)*

7507. What is nearest the heart is usually nearest the lips. *Irish*

7508. What the heart thinks the tongue speaks. *English*

7509. Whatever comes from the heart goes to the heart. *English*

7510. When one pours out his heart, he feels lighter. *Yiddish*

7511. When the heart is afire, some sparks will fly out of the mouth. *English*

7512. When the heart is bitter, sugar won't help. *Yiddish*

7513. When the heart is full of lust, the mouth is full of lies. *Scottish*

7514. When the heart is full, the eyes overflow. *Yiddish*

7515. When the heart is full, the tongue will speak.   *Scottish*

7516. When the heart is in love, beauty is of no account.   *Pashto*

7517. Where hearts are true, few words will do.   *English*

7518. Where the heart is past hope, the face is past shame.   *English*

HEARTH

7519. A hearth of your own is worth gold.   *German*

7520. Another's hearth does not spread the same warmth as your own.   *Russian*

7521. One's own hearth is worth gold.   *Dutch*

HEAT

7522. Heat belongs to all; cold varies with the clothing.   *Chinese*

HEAVEN

7523. Almighty Heaven is not indifferent to those whose hearts are earnest.   *Chinese*

7524. Better once in heaven than ten times at the gate.   *Dutch*

7525. For each man to whom Heaven gives birth the earth provides a grave.   *Chinese*

7526. He who is in hell knows not what heaven is.   *Italian*

7527. Heaven and hell can both be had in this world.   *Yiddish*

7528. Heaven has many cracks through which God can see.   *Russian*

7529. Heaven has no mouth but causes man to speak.   *Japanese*

7530. Heaven is Heaven.   *American*

7531. Heaven is not reached in a single bound.   *Philippine*

7532. Heaven is the help of the helpless.   *Indian (Tamil)*

7533. Heaven protects the good man.   *Chinese*

7534. Heaven who creates the elephant also creates grass.   *Vietnamese*

7535. Help yourself and heaven will help you.   *French*

7536. If Heaven creates a man, there must be some use for him.   *Chinese*

7537. If heaven rained milk, only the rich would have pitchers to catch it in.   *Russian*

7538. There's no getting to heaven in a coach.   *Italian*

7539. There is no going to heaven in a sedan.   *English*

7540. To follow the will of Heaven is to prosper; to rebel against the will of Heaven is to be destroyed.   *Chinese*

7541. What Heaven has ordained man cannot oppose.   *Chinese*

7542. When the heaven weeps, the earth lives.   *Hawaiian*

HEDGE

7543. A low hedge is easily leapt over.   *English*

7544. He who plants a hedge around his garden invites it to be jumped.   *Russian*

7545. Hedges have ears.   *English*

7546. Hedges have ears, and bushes have eyes.   *Welsh*

7547. Hedges have eyes.   *English*

7548. Hedges have no eyes, but they have ears.   *Italian*

7549. Where the hedge is lowest every one goes over.   *Dutch*

7550. Where the hedge is lowest men jump over.   *French*

7551. Where the hedge is lowest men may soonest go over. *English*

HEED

7552. Much heed does no harm. *English*

7553. Take heed is a fair thing. *English*

7554. Take heed is a good reed. *English*

7555. Too much taking heed is loss. *English*

HEEL

7556. Trust not a horse's heel nor a dog's tooth. *English*

HEIR

7557. An heir also inherits quarrels. *African (Ovambo)*

7558. Many heirs make small portions. *German*

7559. The heir thanks nobody but the sudden death. *African (Wolof)*

HELL

7560. He who would not go to hell, must not go to court. *Danish*

7561. Hell and Chancery are always open. *English*

7562. Hell is full of good intentions. *Italian*

7563. Hell is not so bad as the way to it. *Yiddish*

7564. Hell is paved with good intentions. *English*

7565. Hell is wherever heaven is not. *English*

7566. If there be a hell, Rome is built over it. *German*

7567. In hell one should pay court to the devil. *American*

7568. There is no hell like a troubled conscience. *English*

7569. They that be in hell ween there is no other heaven. *English*

HELM

7570. It is easy to sit at the helm in fine weather. *Danish*

7571. When the helm is gone the ship will soon be wrecked. *Danish*

HELP (noun)

7572. A little help does a great deal. *French*

7573. God's help is nearer than the door. *Irish*

7574. He sits well who can rise without help. *Danish*

7575. Mutual help in farming does not always coincide. *Irish*

7576. Slow help is no help. *English*

7577. Take help of many, advice of few. *Danish*

7578. That is a poor help that helps you from the featherbed to the straw. *Danish*

7579. There's always plenty of help when it's not wanted. *American*

7580. There is help for everything, except death. *Danish*

HELP (verb)

7581. Either it doesn't help or it isn't needed. *Yiddish*

7582. He helps little that helps not himself. *English*

7583. He who helps everybody, helps nobody. *Spanish*

7584. It is easy to help him, who is willing to be helped. *German*

7585. Many can help one. *German*

7586. One can't help many, but many can help one. *English*

HELPER

7587. A willing helper does not wait until he is asked.   *Danish*

HELPING

7588. There is no helping him who will not be advised.   *Italian*

HEMLOCK

7589. Hemlock is hemlock.

American

HEMP

7590. He who sows hemp will reap hemp; he who sows beans will reap beans.   *Chinese*

HEN

7591. A black hen lays a white egg.
Scottish

7592. A black hen will lay a white egg.   *English*

7593. A hen carried far is heavy.
Irish

7594. A hen does not break her own egg.   *African (Swahili)*

7595. A hen does not play with a cat.
African (Fulani)

7596. A hen frightened from her nest is hard to get back.   *American*

7597. A hen pecks one grain at a time, and lives with a full stomach.
Russian

7598. A hen with chicks is on the lookout for crows.   *African (Ovambo)*

7599. Better a hen in the hand than an eagle in the sky.   *Yiddish*

7600. Better a laying hen, than a lying crown.   *Scottish*

7601. Better walk before a hen than behind an ox.   *French*

7602. Black hens lay white eggs.
Dutch

7603. Even clever hens sometimes lay their eggs among nettles.   *Danish*

7604. Fat hens lay few eggs. *German*

7605. Grain by grain the hen fills her belly.   *English*

7606. He who feeds the hen ought to have the egg.   *Danish*

7607. Hens like to lay where they see an egg.   *Dutch*

7608. Hens that cackle much lay few eggs.   *Estonian*

7609. If the hen does not prate she will not lay.   *English*

7610. If the hen had not cackled we should not know she had laid an egg.
Italian

7611. It goes ill in the house where the hen sings and the cock is silent.
Spanish

7612. It is a bad hen that eats at your house and lays at another's. *Spanish*

7613. It is a bad hen that lays her eggs away from the farm.   *Danish*

7614. It is a bad hen that lays in neighbors' houses.   *German*

7615. It is a sad house where the hen crows louder than the cock.   *English*

7616. It is a sorry house where the hens crow and the cock is silent.
Italian

7617. It is better to have a hen tomorrow than an egg today.   *English*

7618. It is contrary to the house where the hen announces the dawn.
Japanese

7619. It is no good hen that cackles in your house and lays in another's.
English

7620. It is not the hen that cackles most which lays most eggs.   *English*

7621. It never goes well when the hen crows.   *Russian*

7622. Knowing hens lay even in nettles. *German*

7623. No one sells his laying hen without a good reason.
African (Ashanti)

7624. The gaily colored hen is not always the best layer. *Serbo-Croatian*

7625. The hen discovers her nest by cackling. *English*

7626. The hen flies not far unless the cock flies with her. *Danish*

7627. The hen is bad off when the egg teaches her how to cackle. *Danish*

7628. The hen lays an egg, and the cock feels pain in his bottom.
Moroccan

7629. The hen lays as well upon one egg as many. *English*

7630. The hen listens to the rooster's sermon and goes to look for a grain of corn. *Yiddish*

7631. The hen lives by pickings as the lion by prey. *Danish*

7632. The hen ought not to cackle in presence of the cock. *French*

7633. The hen that stays at home picks up the crumbs. *Portuguese*

7634. The miller's hen and widower's maid of want need never be afraid.
German

7635. The old hen is worth forty chickens. *Greek*

7636. There is little peace in that house where the hen crows and the cock is mute. *Italian*

7637. When hens are shedding their feathers they don't lay eggs. *American*

7638. When you have caught the mother hen, you pick up the chickens without difficulty. *African (Ashanti)*

7639. Woe to the house where the hen crows and the cock keeps silent.
Rumanian

HERALD

7640. No heralds in the grave.
English

HERB

7641. For every illness there is a herb growing. *Russian*

7642. The herb that can't be got is the one that brings relief. *Irish*

7643. The herbs to apply to a snake bite are quickly plucked.
African (Ashanti)

HERD

7644. A herd of cattle should not be without a bull. *Moroccan*

7645. Ill herds make fat wolves.
Scottish

7646. When the herd reversed direction, the lame became the leaders.
Armenian

HERDER

7647. The herder of the elephant will not fear it. *African (Fulani)*

HERE

7648. Better say here it is, than here it was. *English*

HERO

7649. At home, a hero, abroad, a coward. *Indian (Tamil)*

7650. Heroes are great lovers of the fair sex. *Korean*

7651. Heroes cannot stand side by side. *Japanese*

7652. Heroes know each other.
Japanese

7653. No man is a hero to his valet.
English

7654. The hero appears only when the tiger is dead. *Burmese*

7655. The hero when wounded becomes even braver.   *Philippine*

7656. The real hero doesn't tell that he is one.   *Philippine*

7657. There is no hero in the eyes of his servant.   *Japanese*

HEROISM

7658. Heroism consists in hanging on one minute longer.   *Norwegian*

HERON

7659. Herons do not eat herons' flesh.   *Chinese*

HERRING

7660. Better a salt herring on your own table than a fresh pike on another man's.   *Danish*

7661. Don't cry herrings till they are in the net.   *Dutch*

7662. Every herring must hang by its own gills.   *English*

7663. Set a herring to catch a whale.   *English*

HESITATE

7664. Who hesitates, regrets.   *Albanian*

HEW

7665. He that hews too high may get a chip in his eye.   *English*

HIDE (skin)

7666. The hide that is stretched is a dead one.   *Indian (Hindi)*

7667. You can't get two hides from one ox.   *Russian*

HIDE (verb)

7668. He that hides can find. *French*

7669. Hide nothing from your minister, physician, and lawyer.   *English*

7670. It is difficult to hide what everybody knows.   *Danish*

7671. They that hide can find.   *English*

HIGH

7672. It is hard to be high and humble.   *English*

HIGHROAD

7673. There is no highroad to happiness or misfortune; every man brings them on himself.   *Chinese*

HIGHWAY

7674. Every highway leads to Peking.   *Chinese*

7675. He that leaves the highway to cut short commonly goes about.   *English*

7676. He that sows in the highway tires his oxen, and loses his corn.   *English*

7677. Highways can be worn out, but not love and attachment.   *Vietnamese*

7678. No highway is safer than the one just robbed.   *Mexican*

HILL

7679. Every hill has its valley.   *Italian*

7680. Hills are green afar off.   *English*

7681. If the hill will not come to Mahomet, Mahomet will go to the hill.   *English*

7682. It is easier to run down a hill than up one.   *Chinese*

7683. Praise a hill but keep on the plain.   *English*

7684. The higher the hill the lower the grass.   *English*

7685. The little hill of a low district becomes a mountain.   *Turkish*

HINGE

7686. The hinge of a door is never crowded with insects.   *Chinese*

HINT

7687. A hint hits harder than the truth.   *Yiddish*

7688. A hint is about as good as a kick to some people.   *American*

HIPPOPOTAMUS

7689. A hippopotamus exceeds an elephant by one basket of flesh, and an elephant exceeds a hippopotamus by one basket of bones.   *African (Kanuri)*

7690. It is the mother hippopotamus which shows the little one how to dive.   *African (Bemba)*

HIRE

7691. If the hire be diminished, the work will be spoiled.   *Indian (Tamil)*

HIRING

7692. He's not worth hiring, who talks of tiring.   *English*

HIT

7693. He who once hits will ever be shooting.   *English*

7694. One does not always hit what one aims at.   *French*

HITCH

7695. An uneven hitch pulls badly.   *Slovakian*

HOE

7696. A hoe tells no lies.   *African (Shona)*

7697. If the new hoe wishes to know how tough the ground is, let him ask the old hoe.   *Jamaican*

7698. What one could have filled enough with a hoe, one now tries to fill with a spade.   *Korean*

7699. When you take another man's hoe to work with, you must wash it and put it back in its place.   *African (Oji)*

HOG

7700. A hog swimming cuts his own throat.   *American*

7701. A hog that's bemired endeavors to bemire others.   *English*

7702. A hog upon trust grunts till he's paid for.   *English*

7703. A measly hog infects the whole sty.   *Spanish*

7704. Better my hog dirty at home than no hog at all.   *English*

7705. Dead hogs have no fear of hot water.   *Jamaican*

7706. If you saw what the hog ate, you would never eat hog meat.   *Jamaican*

7707. It is hard to break a hog of an ill custom.   *English*

7708. No hog can trespass on his master's ground.   *American*

7709. The hog never looks up to him that threshes down the acorns.   *English*

HOLD

7710. Hold fast when you have it.   *English*

HOLE

7711. A hole is more easily patched than a crack.   *Philippine*

7712. Big hole, big stopper. *Estonian*

7713. Don't dig a hole for someone else, you'll only fall into it yourself.   *Russian*

7714. He who peeps through a hole may see what will vex him.   *English*

7715. Mend the hole while it is small.
Serbo-Croatian

7716. One may see through a wall, if there's a hole in it.   *German*

7717. The hole invites the thief.
Spanish

7718. The hole of lying is easily filled up.   *African (Hausa)*

7719. The hole of lying is not deep.
African (Fulani)

HOLIDAY

7720. It will not do to keep holidays before they come.   *French*

HOME

7721. A home without many children will not know happiness.   *Philippine*

7722. A pleasant home, a pleasant wife and pleasant furnishings enlarge a man's mind.   *Hebrew*

7723. At home it is always pleasant; far away from home it is always unpleasant.   *Chinese*

7724. Better at home than a mile away from it.   *Chinese*

7725. East or west, home is best.
Dutch

7726. Go home when the table is set and to church when the service is almost over.   *Armenian*

7727. He that lives always at home, sees nothing but home.   *English*

7728. He who remains at home will neither hear nor see.   *Maltese*

7729. Home is a pleasant word.
Scottish

7730. Home is home though never so homely.   *English*

7731. Home is where the heart is.
American

7732. It is home in the dog's mind where it has been three nights.
Finnish

7733. One's home is both paradise and hell.   *Rumanian*

7734. Place value on defending your home.   *African (Ovambo)*

7735. Ride softly that you may get home the sooner.   *English*

7736. The home is the wife's world; the world is the man's home.
Estonian

7737. The home which reared me forgets me not.   *Lebanese*

7738. The old home stands, but its owners disappear. *Australian (Maori)*

7739. Your own home—your own jurisdiction.   *Russian*

HONEST

7740. We are bound to be honest, but not to be rich.   *Scottish*

HONESTY

7741. A girl's honesty is like snow: when it melts the whiteness is no longer seen.   *Rumanian*

7742. A little with honesty is better than a great deal with knavery.
English

7743. Honesty is a fine jewel, but much out of fashion.   *English*

7744. Honesty is ill to thrive by.
English

7745. Honesty is no pride.   *Scottish*

7746. Honesty is plain, but no good fellow.   *English*

7747. Honesty is the best policy.
English

7748. Honesty lasts longest. *German*

7749. Honesty may be dear bought, but can never be an ill pennyworth.
Scottish

7750. Honesty may be dear bought, but can never be a dear pennyworth.
English

7751. There is more honesty in a penny than in five pounds. *English*

HONEY

7752. Cover yourself with honey and the flies will eat you. *English*

7753. Eat too much honey and it will become tasteless. *Libyan*

7754. He buys honey dear who has to lick it off thorns. *Dutch*

7755. He is a very bad manager of honey who leaves nothing to lick off his fingers. *French*

7756. He pays dear for honey who licks it off thorns. *French*

7757. He that handles honey shall feel it cling to his fingers. *English*

7758. He that has no honey in his pot, let him have it in his mouth. *English*

7759. He that stirs honey will have some of it stick to him. *Spanish*

7760. He who loves honey should be patient of the stinging of the bees.
Moroccan

7761. He who wants to eat honey should bear the sting of bees.
Lebanese

7762. He who would gather honey must brave the sting of bees. *Dutch*

7763. He who would steal honey must not be afraid of bees. *Danish*

7764. Honey is dear bought if licked off thorns. *English*

7765. Honey is not for asses. *French*

7766. Honey is not for the ass's mouth.
Portuguese

7767. Honey is sweet, but the bee stings. *English*

7768. Honey is sweeter after one has tasted something bitter. *Philippine*

7769. Honey is too good for a bear.
English

7770. Honey on the tongue, gall in the heart. *Yiddish*

7771. Honey was not made for the mouth of the ass. *Spanish*

7772. In the spot where honey is, flies too are found. *Turkish*

7773. It is dear honey that must be licked off thorns. *German*

7774. It is difficult to spit honey out of a mouth full of gall. *Danish*

7775. No honey without gall.
English

7776. Nothing better than honey to catch flies. *Mexican*

7777. The honey is not forgotten but the axe is. *African (Bemba)*

7778. To a sick man even honey tastes bitter. *Russian*

7779. Where the honey is spread there will the flies gather.
Indian (Hindi)

7780. Where there is honey, there flies gather. *Yiddish*

7781. You cannot handle honey without licking your fingers. *Slovenian*

HONEYMOON

7782. It will not always be honeymoon. *English*

HONOR (noun)

7783. After honor and state follow envy and hate. *Dutch*

7784. Better deserve honor and not have it than have it and not deserve it.
Portuguese

7785. Better die in honor than live in disgrace. *Vietnamese*

7786. Better poor with honor than rich with shame. *Dutch*

7787. Better retire in honor than advance in disgrace. *Serbo-Croatian*

7788. Do not lose honor through fear. *Spanish*

7789. Great honors are great burdens. *English*

7790. He who has acquired honor early commits many follies. *Swedish*

7791. Honor and ease are seldom bedfellows. *English*

7792. Honor and profit are not found in the same dish. *Indian (Hindi)*

7793. Honor and profit will not keep in one sack. *Portuguese*

7794. Honor blossoms on the grave. *French*

7795. Honor bought, temporal simony. *English*

7796. Honor cannot be bought. *Philippine*

7797. Honors change manners. *English*

7798. Honor is better than honors. *Flemish*

7799. Honor is measured by him who gives it, not by him who receives it. *Yiddish*

7800. Honor is much dearer than money. *Yiddish*

7801. Honor is unseemly for a fool. *English*

7802. Honors nourish arts. *English*

7803. Honor once lost never returns. *Dutch*

7804. Honor trusts honor. *Russian*

7805. Honor will buy no beef. *English*

7806. Honor will come at the end. *Hebrew*

7807. Honors will come to you by themselves if you don't run after them. *Yiddish*

7808. Honor without profit is a ring on the finger. *English*

7809. It is better to die in honor than live in disgrace. *Vietnamese*

7810. It is no honor for an eagle to vanquish a dove. *Italian*

7811. Regal honors have regal cares. *English*

7812. There is honor among thieves. *English*

7813. We cannot come to honor under coverlet. *English*

7814. Where honor ceases, there knowledge decreases. *English*

7815. Where there is honor there is no grief. *English*

7816. Where there is no honor there is no dishonor. *Portuguese*

HONOR (verb)

7817. Who honors not age is unworthy of it. *German*

HOOD

7818. The hood does not make the monk. *English*

HOOF

7819. You need not look after the hoofs of dead horses. *Rumanian*

HOOK

7820. He who does not bait his hook catches nothing. *German*

7821. He who does not bait his hook fishes in vain. *French*

7822. It is not the hook or the rod, but the bait that lures. *Spanish*

7823. It is vain to fish if the hook is not baited. *Italian*

7824. It is vain to fish without a hook, or learn to read without a book.
Danish

7825. The hook won't be bitten at unless it has bait.   *Philippine*

HOPE

7826. A good hope is better than a bad possession.   *English*

7827. A long hope is sweeter than a short surprise.   *Hungarian*

7828. Don't dangle by one slim hope.
Greek

7829. Good hope is better than a bad intention.   *Irish*

7830. Great hopes make great men.
English

7831. He that lives in hope, dances without a fiddle.   *English*

7832. He that lives in hope dances without music.   *English*

7833. He that lives on hope has a slender diet.   *Scottish*

7834. He that lives on hope will die fasting.   *English*

7835. He that thinks to thrive by hope may happen to beg in misery. *English*

7836. He that wants hope is the poorest man alive.   *English*

7837. He who lives on hope dies of hunger.   *Turkish*

7838. He whose coach is drawn by hope has poverty for a coachman.
Polish

7839. Hope and expectation are a fool's income.   *Danish*

7840. Hope and expectation are the brothers of boredom.   *Philippine*

7841. Hope deferred makes the heart sick.   *English*

7842. Hope for miracles but don't rely on one.   *Yiddish*

7843. Hope for the best and prepare for the worst.   *English*

7844. Hope helps.   *English*

7845. Hope holds up the head.
Scottish

7846. Hope is a good breakfast but a bad supper.   *English*

7847. Hope is a great deceiver.
Slovakian

7848. Hope is a lover's staff. *English*

7849. Hope is a sovereign balsam.
American

7850. Hope is as cheap as despair.
English

7851. Hope is born of despair.
Iranian

7852. Hope is grief's best music.
English

7853. Hope is the dream of the waking.   *Danish*

7854. Hope is the last thing to die.
Mexican

7855. Hope is the mother of fools.
Polish

7856. Hope is the pillar of the world.
African (Kanuri)

7857. Hope is the poor man's bread.
English

7858. Hope is worth any money.
English

7859. Hope keeps alive the poor; fear kills the rich.   *Finnish*

7860. Hope nourishes the living.
African (Fulani)

7861. Hope of long life beguiles many a good wife.   *English*

7862. Hope often blinks at a fool.
English

7863. Hope without work is like a tree without fruit.   *Lebanese*

7864. If hope were not heart would break.   *English*

7865. Stuff yourself with hope and you can go crazy.   *Yiddish*

7866. There is more hope of a fool than of him that is wise in his own eyes.   *English*

7867. Too much hope deceives.
          English

HOPING

7868. Hoping and waiting makes fools out of clever people.   *Yiddish*

HORN (animal)

7869. What has horns will gore.
          Dutch

7870. When the horns are off, it is too late to butt.   *Norwegian*

HORN (instrument)

7871. The bigger the horn, the louder the sound.   *Slovakian*

HORSE

7872. A bad horse eats as much as a good one.   *Danish*

7873. A boisterous horse must have a rough bridle.   *English*

7874. A borrowed horse and your own spurs make short miles.   *Danish*

7875. A common horse is always lean.
          Lithuanian

7876. A fast horse does not want the spur.   *Portuguese*

7877. A fine horse runs on by observing the shadows of the whip.
          Japanese

7878. A flea-bitten horse never tires.
          English

7879. A four-horse team cannot overtake the tongue.   *Japanese*

7880. A free horse is soon tired.
          English

7881. A galled horse does not care to be curried.   *French*

7882. A good horse and a bad horse need the spur; a good woman and a bad woman need the stick.   *Italian*

7883. A good horse is worth his fodder.   *Dutch*

7884. A good horse never lacks a saddle.   *Italian*

7885. A good horse often needs a good spur.   *English*

7886. A good horse should be seldom spurred.   *English*

7887. A groaning horse and a groaning wife never fail their master.
          English

7888. A halterless horse is not mounted.   *Turkish*

7889. A hired horse and one's own spurs make short miles.   *German*

7890. A hired horse tires never.
          English

7891. A horse has four legs and even he stumbles.   *Russian*

7892. A horse is not caught with an empty sack.   *Turkish*

7893. A horse is once a foal; man is a child twice in his lifetime.   *Czech*

7894. A horse is petted just before it is bridled.   *Slovakian*

7895. A horse knows its rider.
          African (Hausa)

7896. A horse may stumble, though he has four feet.   *Dutch*

7897. A horse that will not carry a saddle must have no oats.   *English*

7898. A horse will not avoid oats.
          English

7899. A horse with four feet may stumble by a time.   *Scottish*

7900. A hungry horse makes a clean manger.   *English*

7901 A running horse is an open sepulchre.   *English*

7902. A scabbed horse abides no comb. *English*

7903. A scabbed horse is good enough for a scald squire. *English*

7904. A scald horse is good enough for a scabbed squire. *English*

7905. A short horse is soon curried. *English*

7906. A weary horse finds even his own tail a burden. *Czech*

7907. A wounded horse trembles when he sees the saddle. *Greek*

7908. After the horse has been stolen, the stable door is locked. *Yiddish*

7909. All lay the load on the willing horse. *English*

7910. An old horse does not forget his path. *Japanese*

7911. An old horse learns not to amble. *Rumanian*

7912. An old horse won't spoil the furrows. *Russian*

7913. Another man's horse and your own spurs outrun the wind. *German*

7914. Be a horse ever so well shod, he may slip. *French*

7915. Better a blind horse than an empty halter. *Dutch*

7916. Better a poor horse than an empty stall. *Danish*

7917. Better ride a good horse for a year than an ass all your life. *Dutch*

7918. Cavalry horses delight in battle. *Chinese*

7919. Don't drive the horse with a whip, but with oats. *Russian*

7920. Don't look a given horse in the teeth. *Russian*

7921. Don't look at the teeth of a horse that you borrow. *Philippine*

7922. Don't refuse to sell your horse for the sake of a crown. *Irish*

7923. Do not spur a free horse. *English*

7924. Even a good horse cannot keep running always. *Irish*

7925. Even a good horse cannot wear two saddles. *Chinese*

7926. Even horses die from work. *Russian*

7927. Even if a horse is fed with sweets and bread, it will still prefer its hay. *Philippine*

7928. Every horse thinks his own pack heaviest. *English*

7929. Good horses make short miles. *English*

7930. He is a gentle horse that never threw his rider. *Scottish*

7931. He's a good horse that never stumbled, and a better wife that never grumbled. *Scottish*

7932. He is a weak horse that is not able to bear the saddle. *Scottish*

7933. He that cannot beat his horse, beats the saddle. *English*

7934. He that has neither horse nor cart, cannot always load. *English*

7935. He who advises you to buy a horse with a big belly will not help you feed him. *Haitian*

7936. He who buys a horse buys care. *Spanish*

7937. He who buys a horse takes the bridle with it. *Polish*

7938. He who has a white horse and a fair wife is seldom without trouble. *Danish*

7939. He who is carried by horses must deal with rogues. *American*

7940. He who rides the horse of greed at a gallop will pull it up at the door of shame. *African (Fulani)*

7941. Hobby horses are dearer than Arabians. *German*

7942. Horse and cow face the wind differently. *Chinese*

7943. Horses obey to the rein; women submit to the spur. *Mexican*

7944. However old the horse it is better than new sandals. *African (Hausa)*

7945. If a horse knew how small a man is compared to it, it would trample him. *Yiddish*

7946. If the horse did not blow on its oats it would swallow a lot of dust. *Russian*

7947. If the horse is mad, he who sits upon it is not also mad. *African (Ga)*

7948. Ill-matched horses draw badly. *Dutch*

7949. It is a bad horse that does not earn his fodder. *German*

7950. It is a good horse that has no fault. *French*

7951. It is a good horse that never stumbles. *English*

7952. It is a poor horse that is not worth its oats. *Danish*

7953. It's a very proud horse that will not carry his oats. *Italian*

7954. It's an ill horse that can neither whinny nor wag his tail. *English*

7955. It is better to be a horse than a cart. *American*

7956. It is difficult to tie an unborn horse to the manger. *Danish*

7957. It is hard to water a horse which does not hold down his head. *Finnish*

7958. It's not right for a race horse to despise the pace of a pony. *African (Hausa)*

7959. It is not the horse but the oats that draw the cart. *Russian*

7960. It is the bridle and spur that make a good horse. *English*

7961. It's the willing horse they saddle the most. *Jamaican*

7962. Lend not horse, nor wife, nor sword. *English*

7963. Let a horse drink when he will, not what he will. *English*

7964. Let the best horse leap the hedge first. *English*

7965. Look not a gift horse in the mouth. *English*

7966. Never spur a willing horse. *Italian*

7967. On a borrowed horse you cannot travel far. *Russian*

7968. Once a horse is born, someone will be found to ride it. *Hebrew*

7969. Once mounted on the horse one must be able to withstand his eventual starts and bolts. *Mexican*

7970. One can't shoe a running horse. *Dutch*

7971. One horse in the racecourse runs the fastest. *African (Hausa)*

7972. One may steal a horse while another may not look over the hedge. *English*

7973. One must plough with the horses one has. *German*

7974. Praise a horse after a month and a woman after a year. *Czech*

7975. Put no more on an old horse than he can bear. *English*

7976. Spur not a willing horse. *German*

7977. Take a horse by his bridle and a man by his word. *Dutch*

7978. Test a horse by riding him and a person by accompanying him. *Japanese*

7979. The best horse is just a carcass when it dies. *Yiddish*

7980. The best horse needs a whip, the wisest man advice, and the chastest woman a man.   *Yiddish*

7981. The best horse needs breaking.
English

7982. The best horse stumbles sometimes.   *Dutch*

7983. The biggest horses are not the best travelers.   *English*

7984. The blind horse is fittest for the mill.   *English*

7985. The fast horse soon gets tired.
Slovakian

7986. The horse ambles according to his master.   *Turkish*

7987. The horse can stand the horse's kick.   *Pashto*

7988. The horse is not judged by the saddle.   *German*

7989. The horse knows his rider, and a wife her husband.   *Indian (Tamil)*

7990. The horse must go to the manger, and not the manger to the horse.
Danish

7991. The horse must graze where it is tethered.   *Flemish*

7992. The horse next the mill carries all the grist.   *English*

7993. The horses of hope gallop, but the asses of experience go slowly.
Russian

7994. The horse that draws his halter is not quite escaped.   *English*

7995. The horse that draws most is most whipped.   *French*

7996. The horse thinks one thing, and he that saddles him another.
English

7997. The horse will go according as it is held by the bridle.
Indian (Kashmiri)

7998. The master's horse and one's own whip make fast driving. *Latvian*

7999. The slow horse reaches the mill.   *Irish*

8000. The willing horse is always most ridden.   *English*

8001. To a blind horse a nod is as good as a wink.   *English*

8002. Two horses are not tied to one stake.   *Turkish*

8003. When old horses get warm, they are not easily held in. *German*

8004. When the horse comes to the edge of the cliff it is too late to draw rein.   *Chinese*

8005. When the horse is starved you bring him oats.   *English*

8006. When they offer you a horse don't look at its teeth.   *Greek*

8007. When two ride on one horse, one must sit behind.   *English*

8008. When your neighbor's horse falls into a pit, you should not rejoice at it, for your own child may fall into it too.   *African (Yoruba)*

8009. Where the horse is tied, there it feeds.   *Philippine*

8010. Where the horse lies down, there some hairs will be found.
English

8011. Where the horse wallows the hair remains behind.   *Finnish*

8012. Who does not venture gets neither horse nor mule, and who ventures too much loses horse and mule.
French

8013. You may force a horse to the water, but you cannot make him drink.
Danish

8014. You may know the horse by his harness.   *English*

8015. You may take a horse to the water but you can't make him drink.
English

8016. You ride as you like on your own horse. *Russian*

HORSESHOE

8017. The horseshoe that clatters wants a nail. *Spanish*

HOSPITALITY

8018. To pass the night in the cold is better than the hospitality of a monkey.
Moroccan

HOST

8019. A merry host makes merry guests. *Dutch*

8020. Don't reckon without your host.
German

8021. He must be a clever host that would take the devil into his hostelry.
Danish

8022. He that reckons without his host must reckon twice. *English*

8023. It is hard to steal where the host is a thief. *Dutch*

8024. Like host like guest. *English*

HOSTESS

8025. A handsome hostess is bad for the purse. *French*

8026. The fairer the hostess, the fouler the reckoning. *English*

8027. Where the hostess is handsome the wine is good. *French*

HOSTILITY

8028. Hostility does not give birth to a child. *African (Ovambo)*

HOT

8029. Soon hot soon cold. *English*

HOUND

8030. A gentle hound should never play the cur. *English*

8031. Every hound is a pup until he hunts. *Irish*

8032. Hungry hounds make good hunting. *Serbo-Croatian*

8033. Many hounds are the death of the hare. *Dutch*

8034. Often the hound that was made fun of killed the deer. *Irish*

8035. The foremost hound catches the hare. *Scottish*

8036. The hound is lame till he sees the fox. *Armenian*

8037. The hungry hound thinks not of her whelps. *Irish*

HOUR

8038. An hour brings what a year does not. *Greek*

8039. An hour in the morning before breakfast is worth two all the rest of the day. *English*

8040. An hour lost is often a year lost.
Swedish

8041. An hour may destroy what an age was a-building. *English*

8042. An hour of pain is as long as a day of pleasure. *English*

8043. An hour of play discovers more than a year of conversation.
Portuguese

8044. Five hours sleeps a traveler, seven a scholar, eight a merchant, and eleven every knave. *English*

8045. Half an hour is soon lost at dinner. *English*

8046. Happy hours are very short.
Vietnamese

8047. Hours were made for slaves.
American

8048. In the hour of distress, a vow; in the hour of release, forgetfulness.

Hebrew

8049. It may come in an hour that will not come in a year.   *Scottish*

8050. Lose an hour in the morning and you'll be all day hunting for it.

English

8051. One hour today is worth two tomorrow.   *English*

8052. Pleasant hours fly fast.

English

8053. That may be done in an hour which we may repent all our life after.

English

8054. The darkest hour is before the dawn.   *English*

8055. The hours of parting are the warmest.   *Finnish*

HOUSE

8056. A house consumes standing still, an elephant when moving.

Indian (Tamil)

8057. A house established by oppression cannot long enjoy its prosperity.

Chinese

8058. A house filled with guests is eaten up and ill spoken of.   *English*

8059. A house full of gold is not worth a small bag of learning.   *Vietnamese*

8060. A house isn't beautiful because of its corners, but because of its tarts.

Russian

8061. A house needs a wife and a cat.

Norwegian

8062. A house of procrastination is a bad house.   *African (Swahili)*

8063. A house where one lives against one's will is no house.   *Hebrew*

8064. A house with two mistresses will be deep in dust.   *Iranian*

8065. A house with two owners will soon be neglected.   *Philippine*

8066. A house without a housewife is not a house.   *African (Ovambo)*

8067. A house without woman and firelight is like a body without soul or sprite.   *American*

8068. A little house has a wide mouth.   *English*

8069. A poor man's house is no place for a war horse.   *African (Hausa)*

8070. A small house has a wide throat.   *English*

8071. A small house may hold a thousand friends.   *Lebanese*

8072. After a house is burnt, one becomes cautious of fire.   *Korean*

8073. After visiting another man's house one notices rotten beams in one's own.   *Russian*

8074. Avoid the house of a prostitute.

Indian (Tamil)

8075. Better an empty house than an ill tenant.   *English*

8076. Better one house filled than two spilled.   *English*

8077. Better one's house too little one day than too big all the year after.

English

8078. Better one house troubled than two.   *English*

8079. Better to fill your house with stones than to have a stranger in it.

Indian (Kashmiri)

8080. Build a small house, and live thriftily.   *Indian (Tamil)*

8081. Burn not your house to fright away the mice.   *English*

8082. Choose not a house near an inn or in a corner.   *English*

8083. Each house has its long and its short; each door has its high and its low. *Chinese*

8084. Enter houses through their doors. *Lebanese*

8085. Every house has its cross. *Dutch*

8086. Everyone can keep house better than her mother till she tries. *English*

8087. Everyone in his own house, and God in all men's. *Spanish*

8088. Everyone seeks his own house. *Maltese*

8089. Everything the house gets is by favor of the door. *African (Hausa)*

8090. From a spark the house is burnt. *Dutch*

8091. Go not every evening to your brother's house. *Spanish*

8092. Go to your rich friend's house when invited, to your poor friend's without invitation. *Portuguese*

8093. He that burns his house warms himself for once. *English*

8094. He that would keep his house clean must not let priest or pigeon into it. *French*

8095. He who buys a house gets many a plank and nail for nothing. *German*

8096. He who lives in another man's house must be very careful with his manners and movements. *Philippine*

8097. He whose house is tiled with glass should not throw stones at his neighbor's. *Spanish*

8098. He will burn his house to warm his hands. *English*

8099. If one is not able at once to build a house, a shed is first erected. *African (Yoruba)*

8100. If you are not inside a house, you do not know about its leaking. *African (Kpelle)*

8101. If you go into a house, you must know where the exit is. *Philippine*

8102. In a good house all things are quickly ready. *English*

8103. In a minstrel's house everyone dances. *Rumanian*

8104. In a rich man's house the cloth is soon laid. *English*

8105. In a wealthy man's house there is no lean dog. *Japanese*

8106. It is no time to play chess when the house is on fire. *Italian*

8107. It is too late to come with water when the house is burnt down. *Italian*

8108. It is too late to throw water on the cinders when the house is burnt down. *Danish*

8109. Keep your house and your house will keep you. *English*

8110. Lawyers' houses are built on the heads of fools. *English*

8111. Many will find fault with a house newly built. *Indian (Tamil)*

8112. No house is too full of good feeling; it is given and then taken away. *Hawaiian*

8113. No house without a mouse, no barn without corn, no rose without a thorn. *German*

8114. One builds the house and the other lives in it. *Yiddish*

8115. One's house, one's castle. *English*

8116. One's own house is both heaven and hell. *Czech*

8117. Stay no longer in your friend's house than you are sure that you are welcome. *Scottish*

8118. The empty house is the wasp's estate.   *Indian (Hindustani)*

8119. The higher the house, the worse the storm.   *Norwegian*

8120. The house does not make the master, but the master makes the house.   *Czech*

8121. The house goes mad when women gad.   *English*

8122. The house in which there are no children is dark.   *Lebanese*

8123. The house of one's intimates isn't a market.   *African (Hausa)*

8124. The house of one who does not help to put out his neighbor's fire will soon be in danger.   *Polish*

8125. The house of the happy is secure.   *Welsh*

8126. The house of the oppressor shall fall in ruins.   *Lebanese*

8127. The house of the talkative person lets in rain.   *African (Zulu)*

8128. The house of the unjust oppressor is destroyed, though it should happen in distant times.   *Egyptian*

8129. The house shows the owner.   *English*

8130. The house that is built after every man's advice seldom gets a roof.   *Swedish*

8131. There is no wrongdoing in an empty house.   *Hawaiian*

8132. Travel east or travel west, a man's own house is still the best.   *Dutch*

8133. We cannot dwell in a house together without speaking one to another.   *African (Yoruba)*

8134. Were every one to sweep before his own house, every street would be clean.   *Dutch*

8135. What is wanted in the house is not given to the church.   *Serbo-Croatian*

8136. When house and land are gone and spent, the learning is most excellent.   *English*

8137. When my house burns, it is not good playing at chess.   *English*

8138. When the house burns, its debts fly up the chimney.   *Slovenian*

8139. When the house is burned down you bring water.   *English*

8140. When you get into a house, follow the rules of that house.   *Vietnamese*

8141. When you sweep the house, you find everything.   *Yiddish*

8142. Whose house is of glass must not throw stones at another.   *English*

8143. Your house is your own house.   *African (Ashanti)*

HOUSEHOLD

8144. Large household, thin soup.   *Estonian*

HOUSEKEEPER

8145. A fat housekeeper makes lean executors.   *English*

8146. A noble housekeeper needs no doors.   *English*

HOUSEWIFE

8147. If the housewife is stout, the loaves she bakes are large.   *Yiddish*

8148. When the housewife is a slattern, the cat is a glutton.   *Yiddish*

HUMAN

8149. As long as a human being lives he will learn.   *Libyan*

HUMBLE

8150. The humble-hearted is sure-stepped.   *Hawaiian*

HUMILITY

8151. Humility is the pillar of piety.
Philippine

8152. Humility is worse than pride.
Russian

8153. Too much humility is pride.
German

HUMOR

8154. A man of humor can hardly be a heartless scamp.   *American*

8155. Humor is like a cosset lamb.
American

8156. The stillest humors are always the worst.   *English*

HUNCHBACK

8157. The hunchback does not see his own hump, but he sees his brother's.
French

HUNGER

8158. At the working man's house, hunger looks in but dares not enter.
American

8159. Better hunger than disgrace.
African (Hausa)

8160. Extreme hunger will induce a man to break through a stone wall and steal.   *Indian (Tamil)*

8161. Go not with every hunger to the cupboard, nor with every thirst to the pitcher.   *Portuguese*

8162. Hunger and cold deliver a man up to his enemy.   *English*

8163. Hunger and ease is a dog's life.
English

8164. Hunger breaks through stone walls.   *English*

8165. Hunger cannot be satisfied by eating froth.   *Indian (Tamil)*

8166. Hunger cannot be washed away like dirt.   *African (Shona)*

8167. Hunger does not allow saving of money: hunger makes the body lean.
African (Yoruba)

8168. Hunger drives the wolf out of the woods.   *English*

8169. Hunger drives the wolf to the village.   *Serbo-Croatian*

8170. Hunger eats through stone walls.   *Dutch*

8171. Hunger finds no fault with the cookery.   *English*

8172. Hunger increases the understanding.   *Lithuanian*

8173. Hunger is a good cook.
African (Ovambo)

8174. Hunger is a slave, and satiation is its mistress.   *Moroccan*

8175. Hunger is cured by food, ignorance by study.   *Chinese*

8176. Hunger is felt by a slave and hunger is felt by a king.
African (Ashanti)

8177. Hunger is sharper than thorn.
English

8178. Hunger is the best cook.
German

8179. Hunger is the best sauce.
English

8180. Hunger is the remedy for poor cooking.   *African (Hausa)*

8181. Hunger looks in at the industrious man's door but dares not enter.
French

8182. Hunger makes a youngster old, repletion makes an old man young.
African (Hausa)

8183. Hunger makes forts surrender.
Greek

8184. Hunger makes hard beans sweet.   *English*

8185. Hunger makes the wolf come out of the forest.   *Turkish*

8186. Hunger means cultivating not begging.   *African (Bemba)*

8187. Hunger teaches many things.
Greek

8188. Hunger teaches you how to chew melon seeds. *African (Ovambo)*

8189. Hunger transmutes beans into almonds.   *Italian*

8190. Hunger will break through hard stone walls.   *Scottish*

8191. Hunger will make a monkey eat pepper.   *Haitian*

8192. In the time of repletion remember hunger; in the time of riches remember poverty.   *Russian*

8193. One does not embrace hunger.
African (Jabo)

8194. The hunger of your friend does not hinder sleep.   *African (Bemba)*

8195. To die full is better than walking in hunger.   *Turkish*

8196. What hunger desires is repletion.   *African (Oji)*

8197. When hunger slips in through the door, love flies out through the window.   *Yiddish*

HUNGRY

8198. Anyone who goes hungry for three days will steal.   *Korean*

8199. When you're hungry nothing is tasteless.   *Japanese*

HUNT

8200. He that hunts others must run himself.   *German*

HUNTER

8201. A dogless hunter must crawl in the hole himself. *African (Ovambo)*

8202. A hunter does not get rich with his companion's game.
African (Ovambo)

8203. All are not hunters that blow the horn.   *English*

8204. Even a hunter is sometimes caught in a trap.   *Japanese*

8205. Good hunters track narrowly.
Dutch

8206. Hunters never grow rich.
American

8207. If a hunter kills a buffalo in the bush, he must bring back a tail.
African (Swahili)

8208. If the hunter can't shoot, even his hound is left without a bite.
Yiddish

8209. The hunter in the chase is like the traveler on a journey.   *Turkish*

8210. The hunter pursuing the deer sees not the mountain.   *Japanese*

8211. The hunter who pierces the tree has not shot well.   *African (Wolof)*

8212. When the hunter comes from the bush carrying mushrooms, he is not asked for news of his hunting.
African (Ashanti)

HUNTING

8213. There is no hunting but with old hounds.   *French*

HUNTING-HORN

8214. You cannot make a good hunting-horn of a pig's tail.   *Danish*

HURRY (noun)

8215. Dress slowly when you are in a hurry.   *French*

8216. Nothing is ever well done in a hurry, except fleeing from the plague or from quarrels, and catching fleas.
Italian

8217. When in a hurry make a detour.
Japanese

HURRY (verb)

8218. It is better to always hurry than to be late once.   *Hungarian*

8219. One who hurries stumbles.
Greek

HURT (noun)

8220. A small hurt in the eye is a great one.   *English*

HURT (verb)

8221. He that hurts another hurts himself.   *English*

8222. It is easier to hurt than to heal.
German

HUSBAND

8223. A deaf husband and a blind wife are always a happy couple.
French

8224. A good husband makes a good wife.   *English*

8225. A good husband may have a bad wife, and a bad husband may have a good wife.   *Indian (Tamil)*

8226. A husband often makes the best physician.   *English*

8227. He is an ill husband that is not missed.   *English*

8228. Husband and wife are like one flesh.   *Yiddish*

8229. Husbands are in heaven whose wives scold not.   *English*

8230. If the husband drinks, half the house is burning; if the wife drinks, the whole house is ablaze.   *Russian*

8231. It is better to have a husband without love than jealous.   *Italian*

8232. The calmest husbands make the stormiest wives.   *English*

8233. The husband doesn't know what all the village knows.
Rumanian

8234. The husband is master of the home if the wife is out-of-doors.
Hebrew

8235. The husband is the head, the wife is the neck; she can turn him whichever way she wants.   *Russian*

8236. The husband is the head, the wife the crown on it.   *Slovakian*

8237. The husband is the law to his wife.   *Russian*

8238. The husband of the harlot is a base wretch by his own testimony.
Egyptian

8239. There is no such thing as a good husband or a sweet onion.
Rumanian

8240. To make a happy couple, the husband must be deaf and the wife blind.   *French*

8241. When husband and wife agree with each other, they can dry up the ocean with buckets.   *Vietnamese*

8242. When the husband earns well the wife spins well.   *Dutch*

8243. When the husband is a coach-man, he is not afraid of his wife's curses.   *Yiddish*

8244. Without a husband you are naked, without a companion you are in need.   *African (Ovambo)*

HUSBANDRY

8245. Good husbandry is good divinity.   *English*

HUT

8246. A hut is a palace to a poor man.
Irish

8247. In a hut one does not get wet, among the bulls one does not starve to death.   *African (Ovambo)*

HYENA

8248. A hyena does not drive a cow.
African (Ga)

8249. Hyena and dog can't share an abode.   *African (Hausa)*

8250. If the hyena were peaceful, the dog would not acknowledge it.
African (Hausa)

8251. No one gives a pig to a hyena to keep.   *African (Ga)*

8252. One does not give a hyena meat to look after.   *African (Hausa)*

8253. One does not put a hyena among goats.   *African (Ovambo)*

8254. The hyena is the cure for the biting dog.   *African (Hausa)*

8255. Whatever the hyena does by night at dawn it goes home.
African (Fulani)

8256. With rotten meat is the hyena caught.   *African (Hausa)*

HYPOCRISY

8257. Hypocrisy can find out a cloak for every rain.   *English*

8258. Hypocrisy is a sort of homage that vice pays to virtue.   *English*

HYPOCRITE

8259. A hypocrite is worse than a demon.   *Indian (Tamil)*

I

ICE

8260. Ice three feet thick is not frozen in a day. *Chinese*

8261. It is not easy to walk upon the devil's ice. *Danish*

8262. Trust not in one night's ice. *English*

8263. You do not know who is your friend or who is your enemy until the ice breaks. *Icelandic*

ICON

8264. An icon and a spade are made from the same tree. *Russian*

8265. Icons are not bought but exchanged. *Russian*

IDEA

8266. A swollen idea can bring ruin. *Burmese*

IDIOT

8267. The greater idiot ever scolds the lesser. *American*

IDLE

8268. Be not idle and you shall not be longing. *English*

8269. Better to be idle than ill occupied. *English*

8270. He is idle that might be better employed. *English*

IDLENESS

8271. Don't waste days in idleness; the bright spring will not come this way again. *Chinese*

8272. Idleness breeds lust. *Chinese*

8273. Idleness is hunger's mother, and of theft it is full brother. *Dutch*

8274. Idleness is the devil's bolster. *Danish*

8275. Idleness is the devil's workshop. *German*

8276. Idleness is the greatest prodigality. *American*

8277. Idleness is the greatest prodigality in the world. *English*

8278. Idleness is the key of beggary. *English*

8279. Idleness is the mother of all evil. *Greek*

8280. Idleness is the mother of poverty. *English*

8281. Idleness is the parent of all vice. *English*

8282. Idleness is the root of all evil. *English*

8283. Idleness is the seed of all evil. *Welsh*

8284. Idleness leads to boredom.
Hebrew

8285. Idleness makes the wit rust.
English

8286. Of idleness comes no goodness.
English

8287. There is no idleness without a thousand troubles. *Welsh*

IDOL

8288. The maker of idols does not worship them. *Russian*

IGNORANCE

8289. Better ignorance than bad news: Where ignorance is bliss it is folly to be wise. *African (Fulani)*

8290. Ignorance does not commit sins. *Russian*

8291. Ignorance is a voluntary misfortune. *English*

8292. Ignorance is an illness for which there's no medicine.
African (Hausa)

8293. Ignorance is an ungrateful guest. *Czech*

8294. Ignorance is better than imperfect knowledge. *Indian (Tamil)*

8295. Ignorance is more troublesome than poverty. *Burmese*

8296. Ignorance is the mother of devotion. *English*

8297. Ignorance is the mother of impudence. *English*

8298. Ignorance is the peace of life.
Indian (Kashmiri)

8299. Ignorance of a thing is darker than darkness. *African (Fulani)*

8300. Ignorance that supports me is better than wisdom which I must support. *Egyptian*

8301. Men's ignorance makes the pot boil for priests. *French*

IGNORANT

8302. It is better to be ignorant than to be mistaken. *Japanese*

ILL

8303. He that does ill hates the light.
English

8304. He that has done ill once will do it again. *English*

8305. He that's ill to himself will be good to nobody. *English*

8306. He that would do no ill must do all good or sit still. *English*

8307. Ill comes in by ells and goes out by inches. *English*

8308. Suffer the ill and look for the good. *English*

ILLNESS

8309. An imaginary illness is worse than a real one. *Yiddish*

8310. Illness comes by many roads but always uninvited. *Czech*

8311. Illness comes in a coach and goes away through the eye of a needle.
Rumanian

8312. Illness gives you the taste of health. *Hungarian*

8313. Illness is followed by death, leaving home by staying away.
African (Ovambo)

8314. Illness starts with the mouth.
Japanese

8315. No one buys illness with money. *Latvian*

8316. The illness of the rich is known to all, but not even the death of the poor.
Finnish

8317. Those who suffer from the same illness pity each other. *Korean*

8318. When you are busy you have no illness. *Japanese*

8319. Without illness and diseases one can get rich very soon.
Vietnamese

ILLS

8320. Desperate ills require desperate remedies. *French*

8321. For extreme ills extreme remedies. *Italian*

IMAGE

8322. The image of friendship is truth. *Egyptian*

IMAGE-MAKER

8323. An image-maker never worships the Buddha. *Chinese*

IMITATION

8324. Imitation is the sincerest form of flattery. *English*

IMP

8325. Even little imps when numerous are strong. *Japanese*

IMPATIENCE

8326. A little impatience spoils great plans. *Chinese*

8327. He who restrains his impatience to eat will find his food the sweeter. *African (Hausa)*

IMPOSSIBILITY

8328. No one is bound to do impossibilities. *French*

IMPRESSION

8329. Slight impressions soon fade. *English*

IMPROVE

8330. He who does not improve today will grow worse tomorrow. *German*

INCENSE

8331. Don't burn false incense before a true god. *Chinese*

INCH

8332. A lost inch of gold may be found; a lost inch of time, never. *Chinese*

8333. An inch in a miss is as good as an ell. *English*

8334. An inch in an hour is a foot a day. *English*

8335. An inch of a miss is as good as a spaw. *Scottish*

8336. An inch of gold will not buy an inch of time. *Chinese*

8337. An inch of time on the sundial is worth more than a foot of jade. *Chinese*

8338. An inch too short is as bad as an ell. *Dutch*

8339. Give him an inch and he'll take an ell. *Dutch*

INDECISION

8340. Indecision is the house of hunger. *African (Swahili)*

INDOLENCE

8341. A little indolence will bring great sorrow. *Indian (Tamil)*

8342. Indolence changes nectar into poison. *Indian (Tamil)*

8343. Indolence in youth will bring poverty in old age. *Indian (Tamil)*

8344. Indolence leads to poverty, inaction to ignorance. *Indian (Tamil)*

INDULGENCE

8345. Indulgence in the parent is not good for the child. *Indian (Tamil)*

INDUSTRY

8346. Industry in youth will support one in old age. *Indian (Tamil)*

8347. Industry is fortune's right hand and frugality her left. *English*

8348. Industry is the mother of wealth and well-being. *Philippine*

8349. Industry is the twin brother of prosperity. *Philippine*

8350. Industry need not wish. *American*

8351. Industry pays debts, while despair increases them. *American*

8352. When industry goes out of the door, poverty comes in at the window. *Dutch*

INFERIOR

8353. Inferiors have others below them. *Japanese*

INFLUENCE

8354. The influence of a fountain makes the brook flow. *African (Yoruba)*

INGRATITUDE

8355. Ingratitude dries up wells, and the time bridges fells. *English*

8356. Ingratitude is the daughter of pride. *English*

8357. Ingratitude is the world's reward. *German*

8358. Ingratitude is worse than witchcraft. *English*

8359. Ingratitude sickens benevolence. *German*

INHERITANCE

8360. The richest inheritance might become a burden. *Yiddish*

8361. Trust not to an inheritance; the produce of one's hands is sufficient for one. *African (Yoruba)*

INIQUITY

8362. He that sows iniquity shall reap sorrow. *English*

8363. He who sows iniquity shall reap shame. *Danish*

INJURY

8364. He that courts injury will obtain it. *Danish*

INJUSTICE

8365. Better suffer injustice than commit it. *Serbo-Croatian*

8366. Injustice has no price. *Estonian*

INK

8367. A lawyer's ink writes nothing until you have thrown silver into it. *Estonian*

8368. Ink dries quickly; tears don't. *Yiddish*

8369. Ink, if not used, will dry up. *Polish*

IN-LAWS

8370. Don't provoke your in-laws before sleeping with your wife-to-be. *African (Bemba)*

INN

8371. Find your inn before nightfall. *Chinese*

8372. The inn cannot pollute the virtuous, nor the church improve the wicked. *Polish*

8373. The nearer the inn, the longer the road. *German*

INNKEEPER

8374. An innkeeper never worries if your appetite is big. *Chinese*

8375. No one would be an innkeeper but for money. *Spanish*

INNOCENCE

8376. Innocence is no protection.
English

8377. Innocence itself sometimes has need of a mask. *English*

INNOCENT

8378. The innocent fears no accusation. *Philippine*

INQUIRE

8379. He that inquires much, learns much. *Danish*

INQUIRY

8380. Inquiry saves a man from mistakes. *African (Yoruba)*

INSECT

8381. The summer insect cannot talk of ice; the frog in the well cannot talk of Heaven. *Chinese*

8382. The summer insect knows not ice. *Japanese*

INSTINCT

8383. Hereditary instinct is stronger than upbringing. *Irish*

8384. Woman's instinct is often truer than man's reasoning. *English*

INSTRUCTION

8385. Instruction in old age is like engraving in dung. *Moroccan*

8386. Instruction in youth is like engraving in stones. *Moroccan*

8387. Instruction is wealth, and learning is fame. *Indian (Tamil)*

INSTRUMENT

8388. Let him play the instrument who knows how. *Spanish*

INSULT

8389. Insults are more painful than lashes. *Philippine*

8390. Insults do not cause a sore.
African (Bemba)

8391. Insult gives birth to insult.
Greek

8392. Run away from an insult but don't chase after honor. *Yiddish*

INTELLECT

8393. Where you need intellect, strength will not do. *Yiddish*

INTELLIGENCE

8394. Intelligence consists in recognizing opportunity. *Chinese*

8395. Intelligence is a man's capital.
Turkish

8396. Intelligence is not sold for money. *Turkish*

8397. Where there is intelligence there is knowledge. *Greek*

8398. With happiness comes intelligence to the heart. *Chinese*

INTENTION

8399. Many have good intentions, but something bad comes across them.
German

8400. The camel's intention is one thing, the camel driver's is something else. *Lebanese*

INTEREST

8401. Interest rules the world.
American

8402. Interest will not lie. *English*

INTERPRETER

8403. Every man is the best interpreter of his own words. *German*

INTOXICATED

8404. Become not intoxicated and you will not sin. *Hebrew*

INTOXICATION

8405. The intoxication of youth surpasses that of wine. *Rumanian*

INTRIGUE

8406. Women's intrigues surpass those of men. *Lebanese*

IRON

8407. Crooked iron may be straightened with a hammer. *Danish*

8408. Do not strike when the iron is cold. *Lebanese*

8409. Forge the iron while it's hot. *Russian*

8410. He who has many irons in the fire will let some of them burn. *Danish*

8411. If you continually grind a bar of iron, you can make a needle of it. *Chinese*

8412. If you have too many irons in the fire, some will burn. *Jamaican*

8413. If you put two pieces of iron together in the fire, one will be burned. *African (Oji)*

8414. Iron in repose will rust, while tubers rest and grow in girth. *Malaysian*

8415. Iron is cut by iron. *Indian (Kashmiri)*

8416. Iron may be rubbed so long that it gets heated. *French*

8417. Iron takes iron from the furnace. *Iranian*

8418. Iron that is not used soon rusts. *Portuguese*

8419. One beats iron while still hot. *African (Hausa)*

8420. One does not put two irons in the fire. *African (Hausa)*

8421. One does not use good iron to make nails, nor good men to make soldiers. *Chinese*

8422. Strike while the iron is hot. *English*

8423. The iron is struck while it is hot. *Moroccan*

8424. When the iron is hot, then is the time to strike. *Spanish*

ITCH (noun)

8425. An itch is worse than a smart. *English*

8426. He that will not bear the itch must endure the smart. *English*

8427. Itch and ease can no man please. *English*

ITCH (verb)

8428. Let him that itches scratch himself. *German*

8429. Whoever itches will be the one to scratch. *Malaysian*

IVORY

8430. Ivory does not grow in the mouth of a dog. *Chinese*

8431. Real ivory will not be eaten by insects. *Burmese*

8432. The poor man's ivory is a hog's tooth. *African (Oji)*

IVY

8433. The ivy destroys the oak. *American*

～J～

JACK

8434. A bad Jack may have as bad a Jill. *English*

8435. A good Jack makes a good Jill. *English*

8436. Every Jack has his Jill. *English*

8437. Every Jack shall have Jill. *English*

8438. Never a Jack but there's a Jill. *English*

JACKAL

8439. A jackal will not gore a bull. *African (Ovambo)*

JADE

8440. A jade eats as much as a good horse. *English*

8441. Better a lean jade than an empty halter. *English*

JAR (conflict)

8442. Women's jars breed men's wars. *English*

JAR (glass)

8443. A small but sturdy jar is better than a big broken one. *Philippine*

8444. If you hear a jar rattling, it is not full. *African (Hausa)*

8445. When two jars are dashed together, one must be broken. *Turkish*

JEALOUSY

8446. Jealousy is a pain which eagerly seeks what causes pain. *German*

8447. Jealousy is the life of love. *Japanese*

8448. Jealousy shuts one door and opens two. *English*

8449. Jealousy starts from the eye. *African (Zulu)*

8450. No jealousy, no love. *German*

8451. The jealousy of a wife is the key to her divorce. *Egyptian*

8452. The jealousy of the harlot is evidenced by adultery, that of the virtuous woman by weeping. *Egyptian*

8453. Where there's no jealousy, there's no love. *German*

JEST (noun)

8454. A jest breaks no bones. *English*

8455. A true jest is no jest. *English*

8456. Better lose a jest than a friend. *English*

8457. He that would jest must take a jest, else to let it alone were best. *Dutch*

253

8458. Jests are never good till they're broken. *English*

8459. Leave a jest when it pleases you best. *English*

8460. Said in jest, meant in earnest. *German*

8461. The truest jests sound worst in guilty ears. *English*

8462. The worst jests are those that are true. *French*

8463. When the jest is at its best, it will be well to let it rest. *German*

JEST (verb)

8464. Jest not in earnest. *German*

8465. Jest so that it may not turn to earnest. *Spanish*

JESTER

8466. Jesters do often prove prophets. *English*

JESTING

8467. It is ill jesting with edged tools. *English*

8468. Leave jesting while it pleases, lest it turn to earnest. *English*

8469. Long jesting was never good. *English*

JEWEL

8470. A jewel unless polished will not sparkle. *Japanese*

8471. None can guess the jewel by the casket. *English*

JEWELLER

8472. The jeweller knows the value of jewels. *Turkish*

JILL

8473. A good Jill may mend the bad Jack. *English*

JOB

8474. As the job, so the clothes. *Latvian*

8475. Do your own job and eat your own fruits. *Irish*

8476. He is lost who has seven jobs. *Libyan*

8477. Nothing is too far and no job is too hard if you like it. *Philippine*

8478. The job fears the craftsman. *Russian*

8479. The job's afraid of a master. *Russian*

JOIN

8480. What is joined may be separated. *Japanese*

JOKE

8481. A joke never gains over an enemy, but often loses a friend. *English*

8482. If there are no jokes, there is no joy. *Philippine*

8483. Jokes are a bad coin to all but the jocular. *English*

8484. There is no worse joke than a true one. *Spanish*

8485. True jokes never please. *French*

JOKING

8486. Joking starts merrily; it ends with sorrow. *Lebanese*

JOURNEY

8487. Every journey gives you its own flavor. *Libyan*

8488. From long journeys long lies. *Spanish*

8489. He who stops at every stone never gets to his journey's end. *French*

8490. It is a great journey to the world's end. *English*

8491. Nothing is lost on a journey by stopping to pray or to feed your horse. *Spanish*

8492. The journey of the masters is like a wedding feast for the servants. *African (Swahili)*

8493. To bait and to grease does not retard a journey. *Danish*

8494. We go quickly where we are sent when we take interest in the journey. *African (Wolof)*

8495. Who goes and returns makes a good journey. *French*

JOY

8496. After joy comes sorrow. *English*

8497. It is better to live in joy than to die in sorrow. *Yiddish*

8498. Joy and grief must be regulated by moderation. *Indian (Tamil)*

8499. Joy and sorrow are next-door neighbors. *German*

8500. Joy and sorrow are sisters. *Greek*

8501. Joy is always guarded by sorrow. *Philippine*

8502. No earthly joy is acquired without tears. *Philippine*

8503. No joy emanates from a lonely person. *Russian*

8504. No joy without annoy. *English*

8505. One is not kept alive by joy, nor does sorrow alone cause death. *Yiddish*

8506. One joy scatters a hundred griefs. *Chinese*

8507. Sudden joy kills sooner than excessive grief. *English*

8508. The drunken man's joy is often the sober man's sorrow. *Danish*

8509. The joy of the heart makes the face merry. *English*

8510. There can be no joy without food and drink. *Hebrew*

8511. When joy is exhausted, sorrow follows, and vice versa. *Korean*

8512. When joy is in the parlor, sorrow is in the passage. *Danish*

JUDGE (noun)

8513. A foolish judge passes brief sentence. *French*

8514. A good judge conceives quickly, judges slowly. *English*

8515. A judge is like a carpenter, what he wants he carves. *Russian*

8516. He goes safely to trial whose father is a judge. *Spanish*

8517. He who is judge between two friends loses one of them. *German*

8518. He who will have no judge but himself, condemns himself. *English*

8519. He whose father is judge goes safe to his trial. *English*

8520. If you would be a good judge, hear what every one says. *Portuguese*

8521. Judges should have two ears, both alike. *German*

8522. No judge should sentence a person he likes or one he dislikes. *Hebrew*

8523. No one is a good judge in his own cause. *Portuguese*

8524. Of ten reasons which a judge may have for deciding a case, nine will be unknown to men. *Chinese*

8525. There has not been found, nor will there be found, a juster judge than the field of battle. *Irish*

JUDGE (verb)

8526. Sit as crookedly as you like, but judge justly. *Russian*

8527. Who judges others, condemns himself. *Italian*

8528. Who suddenly will judge, hastens himself to repentance. *English*

JUDGMENT

8529. For good judgment ask old persons. *Japanese*

8530. He has a good judgment that relies not wholly on his own. *English*

8531. He that passes a judgment as he runs, overtakes repentance. *English*

8532. There is judgment in all things. *American*

8533. There is no judgment nor reprisal of proverbs. *Russian*

8534. Wrong judgment is due to inadequate defense. *Philippine*

JUG

8535. A mended jug lasts two hundred years. *Russian*

8536. Drop by drop the jug is filled. *Greek*

8537. Like jug, like lid. *Estonian*

8538. The jug goes to the well until it gets broken; the wolf goes to the herd until he gets killed. *Estonian*

JUNGLE

8539. A jungle inhabited by fierce tigers is better than a country ruled by a cruel tyrant. *Indian (Tamil)*

8540. The jungle will not be without a tiger. *Pashto*

JUNK

8541. When a junk is broken up the sharks are full of food. *Malaysian*

JUST

8542. Be just before you are generous. *English*

8543. Be just to all, but trust not all. *English*

JUSTICE

8544. Everyone prizes justice but shuts the door when it comes. *Swedish*

8545. If it is thought that justice is with us it will give birth to courage. *Japanese*

8546. Justice is as the rulers make it. *Rumanian*

8547. Justice is better than worship. *Indian (Kashmiri)*

8548. Justice is power. *Slovakian*

8549. Justice is the aider of the upright. *Turkish*

8550. Justice knows no friendship. *Estonian*

8551. Justice, like oil, will come to the surface, however deeply you have sunk it. *Russian*

8552. Justice never sinks nor burns. *Russian*

8553. Justice often leans to the side where the purse pulls. *Danish*

8554. Justice pleases few in their own house. *English*

8555. Justice watches the eye like a bird. *Turkish*

8556. No one likes justice brought home to his own door. *Italian*

8557. No one will do strict justice in his own case. *Indian (Hindi)*

8558. Rigorous justice is often injustice. *Slovenian*

8559. There is justice in the world, but it is blind. *Lithuanian*

8560. When justice comes, that which is false goes. *Turkish*

8561. Who refuses to submit to justice, must not complain of oppression. *German*

8562. With justice you can make a tour around the world; with injustice you cannot cross the threshold. *Russian*

≈ K ≈

KEEP

8563. It is merry to keep one's own.
English

8564. Keep some till furthermore come. *English*

KEEPER

8565. Better a good keeper than a good winner. *English*

KENNEL

8566. The dog's kennel is not the place to keep a sausage. *Danish*

KERNEL

8567. He that wants the kernel must crack the nut. *German*

8568. He that will eat the kernel must crack the nut. *English*

8569. He that would eat the kernel must crack the nut. *Scottish*

8570. He that would have the kernel must crack the shell. *Dutch*

8571. He who would eat the kernel must crack the shell. *Danish*

8572. If you wish for the kernel you must break the shell. *Slovenian*

KETTLE

8573. Everybody collects coals under his own kettle. *Finnish*

8574. Little kettles soon boil over.
Estonian

8575. Shake the kettle, and it will sing. *English*

8576. When the kettle boils over, it overflows its own sides. *Hebrew*

KEY

8577. A gold key opens every door.
Italian

8578. A gold or silver key will open any lock. *Slovakian*

8579. A golden key fits every door.
Polish

8580. A golden key opens all gates.
Hebrew

8581. A golden key opens every door except that of heaven. *Danish*

8582. A silver key can open an iron lock. *English*

8583. All keys hang not at one man's girdle. *English*

8584. Not all keys hang from one girdle. *Norwegian*

8585. The key that is used grows bright. *German*

8586. The used key is always bright.
English

KICK

8587. A kick from a mare never hurt a horse. *French*

8588. Every kick is a boost. *American*

8589. The kick of a mare never hurt a colt. *Italian*

8590. The kick of the dam hurts not the colt. *English*

8591. The kick of the female carabao is caress to the male. *Philippine*

8592. The mare's kicks are caresses to the horse. *Spanish*

8593. The mare's kick does not harm the colt. *Spanish*

KID

8594. What a kid can jump over, a goat can. *Albanian*

KIN

8595. Everyone is kin to the rich man. *English*

KIND-HEARTED

8596. The kind-hearted becomes a slave. *Burmese*

KINDNESS

8597. A forced kindness deserves no thanks. *English*

8598. A word of kindness is better than a fat pie. *Russian*

8599. Drinking kindness is drunken friendship. *English*

8600. He who has done you a kindness should never be ill-used. *African (Yoruba)*

8601. Kindness and evil are not forgotten. *African (Hausa)*

8602. Kindness breaks no bones. *German*

8603. Kindness is better than piety. *Yiddish*

8604. Kindness is lost that's bestowed on children and old folks. *English*

8605. Kindness is not just for the sake of others. *Japanese*

8606. Kindness is remembered, meanness is felt. *Yiddish*

8607. Kindness, wealth and self-restraint are essentials. *Indian (Tamil)*

8608. Kindnesses, like grain, increase by sowing. *English*

8609. Nothing grows old sooner than kindness. *French*

8610. One kindness is the price of another. *English*

8611. Too much kindness is of no profit to a child or man. *Turkish*

8612. Too much kindness to a man is not profitable, for he becomes ungrateful. *Turkish*

KING

8613. A good king is better than an old law. *Danish*

8614. A king and a snake are alike. *Indian (Tamil)*

8615. A kind is a king because of people. *African (Zulu)*

8616. A king promises, but observes only what he pleases. *English*

8617. A king should honor a man of letters. *Irish*

8618. A king without a good counsellor is like a wayfaring man who is blind. *Indian (Tamil)*

8619. A king without learning is but a crowned ass. *English*

8620. A subjectless king is no king. *African (Wolof)*

8621. All flatter a king. *Hebrew*

8622. As is the king, so are his people.
Spanish

8623. Even a king will approve of wise men. *Indian (Tamil)*

8624. Even kings bow at the threshold. *Czech*

8625. Every one is a king in his own house. *Portuguese*

8626. He who installs a king never rules with him. *African (Zulu)*

8627. In my own house I am a king.
Spanish

8628. In the kingdom of the blind, the one-eyed is king. *English*

8629. Kings and bears often worry their keepers. *English*

8630. Kings have long arms. *English*

8631. Kings have long hands.
Scottish

8632. Like king, like law; like law, like people. *Portuguese*

8633. Many kings do not rule the same country at the same time.
African (Ovambo)

8634. New king, new laws.
Hungarian

8635. New king, new way of life.
Philippine

8636. No king was ever a traitor, or pope excommunicated. *Spanish*

8637. On the road to the other world no one is king. *Japanese*

8638. Pay a just king homage due; unjust kings we should subdue.
Malaysian

8639. The king cannot always rule as he wishes. *German*

8640. The king has many treasures but he will still take whatever you give him. *Greek*

8641. The king likes the treachery, but not the traitor. *Spanish*

8642. The king of birds is the eagle.
Hebrew

8643. The king regards rebels with an evil eye. *African (Yoruba)*

8644. Though a king, he is the son of his mother. *Indian (Tamil)*

8645. To love the king is not bad, but a king who loves you is better.
African (Wolof)

8646. Two kings in one kingdom do not agree well together. *English*

8647. When a king has good counselors, then his reign is peaceful.
African (Ashanti)

8648. When a king makes a mistake, all the people suffer. *Chinese*

8649. Where nothing is, the king loses his right. *Scottish*

8650. Where there is nothing the king loses his rights. *French*

8651. Who serves two kings deceives one of them. *Hebrew*

8652. Woe to the kingdom whose king is a child. *English*

KINGDOM

8653. It is easy to govern a kingdom but difficult to rule one's family.
Chinese

KINSFOLK

8654. Many kinsfolk and a few friends. *English*

KISS

8655. A cunning person's kiss is like that of a mosquito. *Rumanian*

8656. A kiss must last long to be enjoyed. *Greek*

8657. A kiss of the mouth often touches not the heart. *English*

8658. Do not make me kiss, and you will not make me sin. *English*

8659. Frequent kisses end in a baby. *Hungarian*

8660. Kisses are first, and cusses come later. *Mexican*

8661. Kisses are like almonds. *Maltese*

8662. Kisses are the messengers of love. *Danish*

KISSING

8663. After kissing comes more kindness. *English*

8664. Kissing goes by favor. *English*

KITCHEN

8665. A fat kitchen is next door to poverty. *Italian*

8666. A fat kitchen makes a lean will. *French*

8667. A little kitchen makes a large house. *English*

8668. All that is said in the kitchen should not be heard in the parlor. *Scottish*

8669. No kitchen is forsaken where there is cabbage cooking. *Slovakian*

8670. The warm kitchen never lacks flies. *Czech*

KITE

8671. The kite flies because of the tail. *Hawaiian*

KNAPSACK

8672. An empty knapsack is heavier to carry than a full one. *Serbo-Croatian*

8673. Hang your knapsack where you can reach it. *Haitian*

KNAVE

8674. A knave discovered is a great fool. *English*

8675. A knave for one is a good man for another. *African (Ashanti)*

8676. An old knave is no babe. *English*

8677. Better kiss a knave than be troubled with him. *English*

8678. Every knave has a fool in his sleeve. *English*

8679. I'd rather have a knave than a fool. *English*

8680. If there were no knaves and fools, all the world would be alike. *English*

8681. It is as hard to please a knave as a knight. *English*

8682. It is better to quarrel with a knave than with a fool. *English*

8683. It is merry when knaves meet. *English*

8684. Knaves and fools divide the world. *English*

8685. Knaves imagine nothing can be done without knavery. *English*

8686. Once a knave and ever a knave. *English*

8687. One false knave accuses another. *English*

8688. The more knave, the better luck. *English*

8689. The more knave, the worse company. *English*

8690. Two cunning knaves need no broker. *English*

KNAVERY

8691. Knavery may serve a turn, but honesty never fails. *English*

8692. There is knavery in all trades. *English*

KNEE

8693. Supple knees feed arrogance.
English

KNIFE

8694. A dull knife slaughters no chicken. *African (Swahili)*

8695. A sharpened knife will not butcher a dead cow. *African (Fulani)*

8696. Do not go between the knife and the sheath. *African (Ovambo)*

8697. Even in the sheath the knife must be sharp. *Finnish*

8698. If a knife is lacking, a strip of bark will cut. *African (Fulani)*

8699. One knife keeps another in its sheath. *Italian*

8700. One knife whets another.
Italian

8701. Sharpening a knife doesn't frighten a horse. *African (Hausa)*

8702. The knife cuts not its sheath.
Turkish

8703. The knife for flaying an elephant needs not size but sharpness.
African (Hausa)

8704. The same knife cuts bread and fingers. *English*

8705. There was never a good knife made of bad steel. *American*

8706. What a knife has not cut a strip of bark will not cut. *African (Fulani)*

8707. When the knife is over a man's head, he remembers God. *Pashto*

8708. Who has no knife, may not eat pineapples. *Jamaican*

KNOCK

8709. Soft knocks enter hard blocks.
American

KNOT

8710. A knot in the tree spoils the axe; famine spoils friendship.
African (Efik)

8711. A tight knot cannot be formed in a thick rope. *Indian (Tamil)*

8712. Where the knot is loose the string slips. *English*

KNOUT

8713. The first knout is for the denouncer. *Russian*

8714. The knout isn't God, but it will find the truth. *Russian*

8715. You cannot always use the knout, sometimes the whistle will do.
Russian

KNOW

8716. All that is known is not told.
Egyptian

8717. Better known than trusted.
English

8718. Do not know too much or you will grow old. *Russian*

8719. He knows enough who knows how to live and keep his own counsel.
French

8720. He that knows himself best, esteems himself least. *English*

8721. He that knows little often repeats it. *English*

8722. He that knows nothing doubts nothing. *English*

8723. He that knows when he has enough is no fool. *English*

8724. He that knows you will never buy you. *English*

8725. He who knows but little quickly tells it. *Italian*

8726. He who knows does not talk; he who talks does not know. *Korean*

8727. He who knows little forgets little. *Norwegian*

8728. He who knows little soon tells it. *Spanish*

8729. He who knows not when he has enough is poor. *Japanese*

8730 He who knows nothing knows enough, if he knows how to be silent. *Italian*

8731. He who knows nothing never doubts. *Italian*

8732. He who knows when he has enough is fortunate. *Japanese*

8733. If you don't want anyone to know it, don't do it. *Chinese*

8734. Know thyself. *Greek*

8735. Know yourself and your neighbors will not mistake you. *English*

8736. Know yourself better than he does who speaks of you.
African (Wolof)

8737. None knows the weight of another's burden. *English*

8738. Not to know is bad, not to wish to know is worse. *African (Wolof)*

8739. The more you know the less will you sleep. *Russian*

8740. They that know one another, salute afar off. *English*

8741. They that think they know everything, know nothing. *English*

8742. Three know it, all know it. *Italian*

8743. To know everything is to know nothing. *Italian*

8744. To know is easier than to do. *German*

8745. We know what we have, but not what we shall get. *German*

8746. What one knows no one knows; what two know everyone knows. *Swedish*

8747. What three know, everybody knows. *Spanish*

8748. Who knows most believes least. *Italian*

8749. Who knows most, forgives most. *Italian*

8750. Who knows most says least. *French*

8751. You are known when you have plenty. *Hawaiian*

8752. You never know what you can do till you try. *English*

KNOWLEDGE

8753. He that increases knowledge increases sorrow. *Indian (Tamil)*

8754. He who has knowledge has power. *Iranian*

8755. If you desire knowledge study while still young, for when you are old, learning comes with difficulty.
Philippine

8756. Knowledge acquired in childhood is not soon forgotten. *Hebrew*

8757. Knowledge and timber shouldn't be much used until they are seasoned. *American*

8758. Knowledge comes through practice. *Irish*

8759. Knowledge has no enemy but ignorance. *English*

8760. Knowledge is a treasure. *English*

8761. Knowledge is a treasure, but practice is the key to it. *English*

8762. Knowledge is better than riches. *African (Efik)*

8763. Knowledge is light; ignorance is a cloud. *Philippine*

8764. Knowledge is no burden. *English*

8765. Knowledge is not always a water that washes away vices. *Russian*

8766. Knowledge is not to be concealed like a candle under a bushel.
American

8767. Knowledge is power. *English*

8768. Knowledge makes one laugh, but wealth makes one dance. *English*

8769. Knowledge of the Scriptures is the best wares. *Yiddish*

8770. Knowledge of the Torah is no deterrent to sin. *Yiddish*

8771. Knowledge unused is like a torch in the hand of a blind man.
Indian (Kashmiri)

8772. Knowledge without practice makes but half an artist. *English*

8773. Lack of knowledge is darker than the night. *African (Hausa)*

8774. Small knowledge moves slowly.
Hawaiian

8775. Thoroughly acquired knowledge does not fail. *Indian (Tamil)*

8776. When knowledge is least the will is strongest. *Norwegian*

8777. Where there is knowledge of the Scriptures there is wisdom. *Yiddish*

8778. With all your knowledge know thyself. *English*

8779. With knowledge you are nowhere lost. *Yiddish*

8780. Without knowledge, without sin. *German*

≈ L ≈

LABEL

8781. Don't rely on the label of the bag. *French*

LABOR (noun)

8782. A little labor, much health. *English*

8783. As the labor, so the pay. *German*

8784. He that will not endure labor in this world, let him not be born. *English*

8785. He who begins and does not finish loses his labor. *French*

8786. Labor has a bitter root, but a sweet taste. *Danish*

8787. Labor is bitter, but sweet is the bread which it buys. *Indian (Hindi)*

8788. Labor is light where love does pay. *English*

8789. Labor is the key to rest. *Indian (Hindustani)*

8790. Labor is vain in loss of time. *English*

8791. Labor warms, sloth harms. *Dutch*

8792. Past labor is pleasant. *English*

8793. The labor of the field brings grain. *Indian (Tamil)*

8794. The poor man's labor is the rich man's wealth. *English*

8795. Watching women is labor in vain. *German*

8796. Where there is no labor, there is no profit. *Indian (Tamil)*

LABOR (verb)

8797. He that labors and thrives, spins gold. *English*

8798. Labor to be as you would be thought. *English*

LABORER

8799. Every laborer is worthy of his hire. *German*

8800. The laborer is always in the sun; the landowner is always in the shade. *African (Yoruba)*

LACK

8801. He who lacks today is he who finds tomorrow. *African (Hausa)*

LAD

8802. An unhappy lad may make a good man. *English*

8803. If the lad goes to the well against his will, either the can will break, or the water will spill. *Scottish*

8804. Lads will be men. *Scottish*

LADDER

8805. He who places his ladder too steeply will easily fall backwards.
Czech

8806. He who would climb the ladder must begin at the bottom. *German*

8807. Step after step the ladder is ascended. *English*

LADLE

8808. To the big-mouthed the ladle is a spoon. *Turkish*

LADY

8809. For sake of the knight the lady kisses the squire. *French*

8810. It is easier to make a lady of a peasant girl than a peasant girl of a lady. *Dutch*

8811. When an old lady wants to feel happy, she recalls her dowry. *Hebrew*

LAKE

8812. Let me get over the lake, and I have no fear of the brook. *Dutch*

8813. There is no lake without frogs. *Turkish*

LAMB

8814. A lamb in the house, a lion in the field. *English*

8815. A lamb is as dear to a poor man as an ox to the rich. *English*

8816. A lamb when carried far becomes as burdensome as a sheep. *Irish*

8817. A mild lamb sucks at two mothers. *Rumanian*

8818. Every lamb knows its dam. *English*

8819. Lambs don't run into the mouth of the sleeping wolf. *Danish*

8820. More lambs are slaughtered than sheep. *Albanian*

8821. Outwardly a lamb, inwardly a wolf. *Greek*

8822. The lamb goes as far as the staggerer. *English*

8823. The lamb is a sheep in the long run. *Irish*

8824. Though lamb may be good, it is difficult to cook it to suit everyone's taste. *Chinese*

8825. Where the lamb is sheared, there is the wool. *Estonian*

LAMBSKIN

8826. As soon goes the lambskin to the market as the old sheep. *Scottish*

LAME

8827. If you mock the lame you will go so yourself. *English*

8828. The lame returns sooner than his servant. *English*

LAMP

8829. Everybody's lamp lights his own house. *Vietnamese*

8830. If you would have the lamp burn, you must pour oil into it. *German*

8831. Light your lamp before night overtakes you. *Greek*

8832. No lamp burns till morning. *Iranian*

8833. One lamp in a dark place is better than lighting a seven-story pagoda. *Chinese*

8834. The lamp does not light its own base. *Iranian*

8835. The lamp of one house cannot light two houses. *Chinese*

LAND

8836. Beautiful or not, it is my native land. *Chinese*

8837. Better a ruined than a lost land.
Dutch

8838. Better free in a foreign land than a serf at home. *German*

8839. Better poor on land than rich at sea. *Dutch*

8840. Every land its own custom, every wheel its own spindle.
Portuguese

8841. Everyone praises his own land.
Irish

8842. He that has lands has quarrels.
English

8843. He that has some land must have some labor. *English*

8844. Land was never lost for want of an heir. *English*

8845. Land which will raise hemp will produce any other crop.
American

8846. Many a one for land takes a fool by the hand. *English*

8847. Never forget your native land.
Philippine

8848. No land without stones, or meat without bones. *English*

8849. Not every land has all at hand.
German

8850. Our native land is our mother; a foreign country is our stepmother.
Russian

8851. The pleasant land is never near.
African (Hausa)

8852. Who buys land buys war.
Italian

LANDLADY

8853. If the landlady is fair, the wine is fair. *German*

LANDLORD

8854. A quick landlord makes a careful tenant. *English*

8855. If the landlord lives the tenant starves. *American*

LANDMARK

8856. A landmark is very well placed between the fields of two brothers.
French

LANDOWNER

8857. A landowner today, nothing tomorrow. *Russian*

LANE

8858. It is a long lane that has no turning. *English*

LANGUAGE

8859. As long as the language lives the nation is not dead. *Czech*

8860. Smooth language grates not the tongue. *English*

8861. That's not good language that all understand not. *English*

8862. Wherever you go, speak the language of that place. *Chinese*

8863. Who knows the language is at home everywhere. *Dutch*

LARK

8864. A lark is better than a kite.
American

LATCH

8865. A broken latch lasts longer than a good one. *English*

LATE

8866. A little too late is much too late.
German

8867. Better late ripe and bear, than early blossom and blast. *English*

8868. Better late than never. *English*

8869. Even though late it is better to do it than not to do it. *Japanese*

8870. It is too late to call again yesterday. *English*

8871. Never too late to learn. *English*

8872. Never too late to mend. *English*

8873. Never too late to repent. *English*

LATHER

8874. A good lather is half the shave. *English*

LAUGH

8875. Don't laugh at him who is old; the same will assuredly happen to us. *Chinese*

8876. He is not laughed at that laughs at himself first. *English*

8877. He laughs ill that laughs himself to death. *English*

8878. He may laugh that wins. *Scottish*

8879. He who laughs last, laughs best. *Russian*

8880. He who laughs much, weeps much. *Turkish*

8881. He'll laugh well that laughs longest. *French*

8882. Laugh and the world laughs with you, weep and you weep alone. *American*

8883. Let them laugh that win. *English*

LAUGHTER

8884. Laughter is heard farther than weeping. *Yiddish*

8885. Laughter makes good blood. *Italian*

8886. Much laughter, little wit. *Portuguese*

8887. No one has ever suffered loss because of laughter. *Japanese*

8888. The laughter of a child is the light of a house. *African (Swahili)*

8889. There will be a day when laughter comes to the mourners. *Turkish*

LAVISHNESS

8890. Lavishness is not generosity. *English*

LAW

8891. As fast as laws are devised, their evasion is contrived. *German*

8892. Better no law than law not enforced. *Danish*

8893. Fear not the law, but the judge. *Russian*

8894. Good laws often proceed from bad manners. *English*

8895. Harsh law creates guilt. *Russian*

8896. He that goes to law holds a wolf by the ears. *English*

8897. He who makes a law should keep it. *Spanish*

8898. It is the law that judges, not the judge. *Norwegian*

8899. Law governs man, and reason the law. *English*

8900. Law helps the waking, luck may come to the sleeping. *Danish*

8901. Law is a flag, and gold is the wind that makes it wave. *Russian*

8902. Law is a spider's web; big flies break through, but the little ones are caught. *Hungarian*

8903. Law makers should not be law breakers. *Scottish*

8904. Laws are spiders' webs; hornets pass through them, but flies are caught. *Russian*

8905. Laws catch flies, but let the hornets go free. *English*

8906. Laws go the way kings direct. *Spanish*

8907. Laws go where crusadoes please. *Portuguese*

8908. Laws have wax noses. *French*

8909. Laws without penalties are bells without clappers. *Czech*

8910. Much law but little justice. *English*

8911. New laws, new roguery. *German*

8912. No sooner is the law made than its evasion is discovered. *Italian*

8913. One natural law follows another, and the wolf the sheep. *Albanian*

8914. The law catches the small fish. *Maltese*

8915. The law devised, its evasion contrived. *Portuguese*

8916. The law does not show respect to relatives. *Vietnamese*

8917. The law gives sentence on what is apparent. *Turkish*

8918. The law grows of sin and does punish it. *English*

8919. The law is like a cobweb; a beetle breaks through, but a fly is caught. *Czech*

8920. The law is like a telephone pole: you can't jump over it, but you can get around it. *Russian*

8921. The law is like the shaft of a carriage—you can turn it wherever you please. *Russian*

8922. The law is not the same at morning and at night. *English*

8923. The law of the city is the citizen's honor. *Greek*

8924. The law says what the king pleases. *French*

8925. The law turns on golden wheels. *Rumanian*

8926. The law was not made for the captain. *American*

8927. The more law, the less justice. *German*

8928. The more laws, the more offenders. *English*

8929. The worst of law is that one suit breeds twenty. *English*

8930. There is no law but has a hole in it for those who can find it out. *German*

8931. There is no law written for a fool. *Russian*

8932. They that make laws should not break them. *English*

8933. To circumstances and custom the law must yield. *Danish*

8934. To know the law and do the right are two things. *Danish*

LAWSUIT

8935. Everyone is wiser after the lawsuit is ended. *Slovakian*

8936. He who has a lawsuit should go to a judge. *Hebrew*

8937. If the lawsuit has been adjourned overnight, the case is at an end. *Hebrew*

8938. The first who speaks of lawsuit is not always right. *African (Wolof)*

8939. The worst of a lawsuit is that out of one there grow a hundred. *Spanish*

8940. Though annoyed to death, do not file a lawsuit. *Chinese*

8941. Win your lawsuit and lose your money. *Chinese*

LAWYER

8942. A cunning lawyer beats the devil. *American*

8943. A good lawyer, an evil neighbor. *English*

8944. A good lawyer must be a great liar. *English*

8945. A wise lawyer never goes to law himself. *English*

8946. He who is his own lawyer has a fool for his client. *English*

8947. Lawyers and painters can soon change white to black. *Danish*

8948. Lawyers are bad Christians. *German*

8949. Lawyers play thunder with lives and property trusted to them. *American*

8950. No good lawyer ever goes to law himself. *Italian*

8951. The better lawyer, the worse Christian. *Dutch*

8952. The lawyers eat the kernel and the contending parties the shell of the nut. *Rumanian*

8953. With a young lawyer you lose your inheritance; with a young doctor your health. *Swedish*

LAZINESS

8954. Laziness is a load. *Irish*

8955. Laziness is not worth a pin unless it is well followed. *English*

8956. Laziness is the mother of all vices. *Philippine*

8957. Laziness is the mother of poverty. *Philippine*

8958. Laziness keeps on and on, but it arrives at poverty. *Turkish*

8959. Laziness lends a helping hand to fatigue: one must persevere, because fatigue must be felt every day. *African (Yoruba)*

8960. Laziness travels so slowly that poverty soon overtakes him. *English*

8961. What makes the road long is laziness to go. *African (Bemba)*

LAZY

8962. The lazy are not fed on honey. *Egyptian*

LEAD

8963. Do not be easily led, lest you become a child. *Hawaiian*

LEADER

8964. A leader not virtuous is worthless. *Indian (Tamil)*

8965. If the leader is good, the followers will be good. *Philippine*

8966. If the leader of the hunting party gets tired, then all are tired. *African (Ovambo)*

LEADING

8967. Good leading makes good following. *Dutch*

LEAF

8968. He that's afraid of leaves should not come into a wood. *Scottish*

8969. Leaves alone don't make a salad. *German*

8970. Leaves have their time to fall. *American*

8971. The leaf of a tree does not speak, nor does the road tell the traveler what lies ahead. *African (Ovambo)*

8972. There is no leaf that will not fall from the tree. *Philippine*

8973. Who is in fear of every leaf must not go into the wood. *Italian*

8974. With patience and time the mulberry leaf becomes a silk gown. *German*

8975. With the fall of one leaf we know that autumn has come to the world. *Japanese*

LEAK (noun)

8976. A little leak will sink a great ship.   *English*

LEAK (verb)

8977. That which leaks cannot stay full.   *African (Ovambo)*

LEAP (noun)

8978. One must step back to make the better leap.   *French*

LEAP (verb)

8979. He who would leap high must take a long run.   *Danish*

LEARN

8980. First learn, then discern.
English

8981. First learn, then form opinions.
Hebrew

8982. He is worth much who has learned much.   *Norwegian*

8983. Learn not and know not.
English

8984. Learn to say before you sing.
English

8985. Learn weeping and you shall laugh gaining.   *English*

8986. Never too late to learn.
Scottish

8987. No one is too old to learn.
German

8988. Once you learn something it is hard to unlearn.   *Greek*

8989. One learns by failing.   *French*

8990. Soon learned, soon forgotten.
English

8991. To learn and to be able is better than to beg.   *African (Fulani)*

8992. To learn to be industrious takes three years; to learn to be lazy takes only three days.   *Chinese*

8993. We are to learn while we live.
Scottish

8994. We learn by teaching.   *Italian*

8995. What is learned young is hard to lose.   *English*

8996. Who learns not how to suffer, learns not how to rule.   *Slovakian*

8997. You learn from those you associate with.   *Russian*

LEARNED (people)

8998. The most learned are not the wisest.   *Dutch*

LEARNING

8999. Even if we study to old age we shall not finish learning.   *Chinese*

9000. For a sackful of learning a cartful of wisdom is needed.   *Rumanian*

9001. Learning acquired in youth is an inscription on stone.
Indian (Tamil)

9002. Learning can suffer no damage.   *Indian (Tamil)*

9003. Learning cannot be inherited.
Yiddish

9004. Learning comes through work.
Irish

9005. Learning has no enemy but ignorance.   *American*

9006. Learning in a prince is like a knife in the hand of a madman.
English

9007. Learning is a bitter root, but it bears sweet fruit.   *Czech*

9008. Learning is a treasure which follows its owner everywhere. *Chinese*

9009. Learning is better than goods.
Moroccan

9010. Learning is like rowing upstream; not to advance is to drop back.
Chinese

9011. Learning is more substantial than accumulated riches.
Indian (Tamil)

9012. Learning is the eye of the mind.
English

9013. Learning is wealth that can't be stolen. *Philippine*

9014. Learning makes a good man better and an ill man worse. *English*

9015. Learning which does not advance each day will daily decrease.
Chinese

9016. Much learning, much sorrow.
English

9017. No learning without pain.
Slovakian

9018. The learning of things is better than the ignorance of them. *Moroccan*

9019. There are no national frontiers to learning. *Japanese*

9020. There is no short cut to learning. *Japanese*

9021. Where there is much learning, there is much folly too. *Rumanian*

9022. Without learning there is no knowing. *Japanese*

LEASE

9023. He never has a bad lease that has a good landlord. *English*

LEATHER

9024. Raw leather will stretch.
English

LEAVE

9025. Better leave than lack. *English*

9026. Better to leave than to maintain folly. *English*

LEAVEN

9027. A little leaven leavens a great mass. *French*

LEAVING

9028. Shameful leaving is worse than shameful eating. *English*

LECHERY

9029. Lechery and covetousness go together. *English*

LEG

9030. A broken leg is not healed by a silk stocking. *English*

9031. A wooden leg is better than no leg. *English*

9032. Because of a stupid head the legs have no rest. *Russian*

9033. Better a leg broken than the neck. *Dutch*

9034. Better walk on wooden legs than be carried on a wooden pier.
Danish

9035. Break the legs of an evil custom.
English

9036. He that has good legs has often bad boots. *German*

9037. Lose a leg rather than life.
English

9038. One pair of legs is worth two pairs of hands. *English*

9039. Stretch your legs according to your coverlet. *English*

9040. The wolf's legs feed him.
Russian

LEGACY

9041. If you come for the legacy, you often have to pay for the funeral.
Yiddish

LEISURE

9042. Leisure is the mother of sins and the stepmother of virtues. *Czech*

LEMON

9043. The lemon, after being squeezed, is thrown away.   *Polish*

LEND

9044. He that lends, gives.   *English*

9045. Lend and lose, so play fools.
                              English

9046. Lend never that thing you need most.   *English*

LENDER

9047. A lender does not hate part payment.   *African (Annang)*

LENDING

9048. Lending is ruinous to lenders and borrowers.   *Egyptian*

9049. Lending nurses enmity.
                              Egyptian

9050. Lending should be done with witnesses; giving, without witnesses.
                              Yiddish

LENTIL

9051. Lentils boil against their will.
                              Greek

9052. Lentils without onions are like a dance without music.   *Greek*

9053. You don't soak lentils in your mouth.   *Armenian*

LEOPARD

9054. A leopard does not sleep with a goat.   *African (Zulu)*

9055. A leopard is never enclosed together with goats.   *African (Shona)*

9056. A leopard is not embraced.
                        African (Swahili)

9057. A leopard licks its spots, black and white.   *African (Zulu)*

9058. If you find a leopard in your house, make him your friend.
                        African (Swahili)

9059. In a leopard the spots are not observed.   *English*

9060. It is difficult to encompass a leopard.   *African (Yoruba)*

9061. One does not embrace the leopard.   *African (Jabo)*

9062. The leopard and the goat do not sleep in the same house.
                        African (Swahili)

9063. The leopard has no heart.
                        African (Jabo)

9064. There is no leopard without a black spot.   *African (Zulu)*

9065. What has escaped from the leopard, still remains for the leopard.
                        African (Annang)

9066. When a leopard limps, a hare dares to demand for payment of a debt.
                        African (Annang)

9067. When the leopard dies, he leaves his skin; a man, his reputation.
                              Chinese

LESSON

9068. An evil lesson is soon learned.
                              English

9069. Constant seeing is the lesson for an ignorant man.   *African (Fulani)*

LETTER

9070. A letter from the heart can be read on the face.   *African (Swahili)*

LIAR

9071. A liar can go round the world but cannot come back.   *Polish*

9072. A liar is brother to the thief.
                              Philippine

9073. A liar is not believed when he speaks truth.   *English*

9074. A liar is the beginning of a thief.   *Japanese*

9075. A liar must have a good memory.   *Dutch*

9076. A liar never believes anyone else.   *Yiddish*

9077. A liar ought to lie with memory.   *Czech*

9078. A liar tells his story so often that he gets to believe it himself.
Yiddish

9079. Every liar has another liar as a witness.   *Greek*

9080. He who swears is a liar.
Italian

9081. Liars should have good memories.   *English*

9082. No one believes a liar even when he tells the truth.   *Yiddish*

9083. Once a liar, always a liar.
American

9084. One liar knows another.   *Irish*

9085. Show me a liar, and I'll show you a thief.   *English*

9086. The liar and thief are brothers.
Welsh

9087. The liar is not believed even when he tells the truth.   *Yiddish*

9088. The liar is short-lived.
Egyptian

9089. The liar is sooner caught than the cripple.   *Spanish*

LIBEL

9090. A libel hurts worse than a spear thrust.   *African (Hausa)*

9091. The worst libel is the truth.
Yiddish

LIBERTY

9092. Lean liberty is better than fat slavery.   *English*

9093. Liberty without rule is not worth a straw.   *English*

9094. Too much liberty spoils all.
English

LICK

9095. He who can lick can bite.
French

LID

9096. Be the lid ever so small it will not go in the pot.   *African (Fulani)*

9097. Don't lift off the lid too soon.
Chinese

9098. If there is a lid that does not fit there is a lid that does.   *Japanese*

LIE (noun)

9099. A lie begets a lie.   *English*

9100. A lie comes back sooner or later.
African (Bemba)

9101. A lie even after a year is a lie, truth has its abiding place.
African (Hausa)

9102. A lie has no legs.   *English*

9103. A lie in time of need is as good as the truth.   *Swedish*

9104. A lie is plump in private but lean in public.   *Malagasy*

9105. A lie stands on one leg, and truth on two.   *English*

9106. A lie stands on slippery ground.
Serbo-Croatian

9107. A lie you must not tell; the truth you don't have to tell.   *Yiddish*

9108. A necessary lie is harmless.
German

9109. A well-turned lie pays better than the truth.   *Rumanian*

9110. Better a lie that heals than a truth that wounds.   *Czech*

9111. Everything is useful, except that lies and slander bring no profit.
Moroccan

9112. He that hears much, hears many lies.   *Dutch*

9113. If a lie saves, truth is a surer saviour.   *Lebanese*

9114. If every lie were to knock out a tooth, many would be toothless.
                                 Swedish

9115. If lies are to find credence, they must be patched with truth.   *Danish*

9116. If lies were as heavy as stones to carry many would prefer the truth.
                                 Swedish

9117. In the presence of an expert a lie is not uttered.   *Turkish*

9118. Jesting lies bring serious sorrows.   *English*

9119. Lies and gossip have a wretched offspring.   *Danish*

9120. Lies are the salt of truth.
                                    Greek

9121. Lies have short legs.   *German*

9122. Lies have short wings. *English*

9123. Lies, however numerous, will be caught by truth when it rises up.
                              African (Wolof)

9124. Lies melt like snow.   *German*

9125. One lie draws ten after it.
                                  Italian

9126. One lie is a lie, two are lies, but three is politics!   *Yiddish*

9127. One lie makes many.   *English*

9128. Tell a lie and find out the truth.
                                  English

9129. Tell a lie, and you'll hear the truth.   *German*

9130. Ten no's are better than one lie.
                                   Danish

9131. The lie sinks like a plumb and comes up like a leaf.   *Rumanian*

9132. Though a lie be swift, truth overtakes it.   *Italian*

9133. Though a lie be well dressed, it is ever overcome.   *English*

9134. When lies finish in a free man's mouth, he will become a slave and be sold.   *African (Hausa)*

9135. When one erects a throne to lies one erects a gallows to truth. *Russian*

9136. Who tells a lie to save his credit, wipes his nose on his sleeve to save his napkin.   *English*

9137. Who travels alone tells lies.
                             African (Oji)

9138. With lies you will go far, but not back again.   *Yiddish*

LIE (verb)

9139. He may lie boldly who comes from afar.   *French*

9140. He may lie safely who comes from afar.   *Italian*

9141. It is easy to lie if you have come from afar.   *Czech*

9142. Lie, but don't overdo it.
                                  Russian

9143. They who come from afar are prone to lie.   *German*

9144. Whoever does not lie does not stay alive.   *African (Ovambo)*

LIFE

9145. A good life defers wrinkles.
                                 Spanish

9146. A good life has a good death.
                                 English

9147. A good life will have a good end.   *English*

9148. A handful of good life is better than seven bushels of learning. *French*

9149. A life of leisure and a life of laziness are two things.   *English*

9150. A life without love, a year without summer.   *Swedish*

9151. A long life has many shames.
Japanese

9152. A merry life ends in a poor man's will. *Greek*

9153. A merry life forgets father and mother. *French*

9154. All of life is a struggle.
Yiddish

9155. An ill life makes an ill end.
Scottish

9156. Despise your own life, and you are master of the lives of others.
Tibetan

9157. Fear life but do not fear death.
Russian

9158. He cannot lead a good life who serves without wages. *Italian*

9159. He who leads a useless life will die a miserable death. *Indian (Tamil)*

9160. Human life is like a candle.
Albanian

9161. If there is life there will be a cure. *Russian*

9162. In life beware of the law court; in death beware of hell. *Chinese*

9163. In this long transitory world life is short. *Japanese*

9164. It is one life whether we spend it in laughing or weeping. *Japanese*

9165. Life at court is often a short cut to hell. *Danish*

9166. Life has its ups and downs.
American

9167. Life in the world is like washing—you knead him who kneads you.
African (Hausa)

9168. Life in this world consists in mutual helpfulness. *Japanese*

9169. Life is a shuttle. *English*

9170. Life is a temporary stop, death is the journey home. *Vietnamese*

9171. Life is easy when one has labored well. *Philippine*

9172. Life is for one generation; a good name is forever. *Japanese*

9173. Life is half spent before we know what it is. *English*

9174. Life is light when compared to honor. *Japanese*

9175. Life is like a bubble that may vanish at anytime. *Philippine*

9176. Life is like a child's undershirt—short and soiled. *Yiddish*

9177. Life is like donkeys rubbing against each other: scratch me and I will scratch you. *Lebanese*

9178. Life is like smoke that is fleeting. *Philippine*

9179. Life is like the flame of a lamp; it needs a little oil now and again.
Indian (Kashmiri)

9180. Life is like the moon; now dark, now full. *Polish*

9181. Life is more fragile than the morning dew. *Japanese*

9182. Life is no more than a dream, but don't wake me up! *Yiddish*

9183. Life is sweet. *English*

9184. Life is the biggest bargain—we get it for nothing. *Yiddish*

9185. Life lies not in living but in liking. *English*

9186. Life lies open like a book.
American

9187. Life pends from a thread.
Mexican

9188. Life without a friend is death without a witness. *English*

9189. Life would be too smooth if it had no rubs in it. *English*

9190. Living life is not like crossing a field. *Russian*

9191. Long life has long misery.
English

9192. Man's life is filed by his foe.
English

9193. Man's life is like a candle in the wind, or like the frost upon the tiles.
Chinese

9194. Man's life is like an egg in the hands of a child.   *Rumanian*

9195. Man's life is like morning dew.
Korean

9196. Of evil life comes evil end.
English

9197. Our life is like a dayfly's.
Korean

9198. Our life is like candlelight that is flickering in the wind.   *Korean*

9199. The less you sleep, the more you get out of life.   *Yiddish*

9200. The life of man is as spotted as a woodpecker's coat.   *Latvian*

9201. The longer the life, the more the shame.   *Korean*

9202. The span of man's life is uncertain to the old and to the young alike.
Korean

9203. The ugliest life is better than the nicest death.   *Yiddish*

9204. There is life and death in the quiver.   *African (Ovambo)*

9205. To obey is life; to disobey is death.   *Hawaiian*

9206. To save a single life is better than building a seven-story pagoda.
Chinese

9207. We must not look for a golden life in an iron age.   *English*

9208. What life gives death takes.
Swedish

9209. When life is exhausted, death comes.   *Vietnamese*

9210. While there's life there's hope.
English

LIFELESS

9211. He is lifeless that is faultless.
English

LIFETIME

9212. If one morning you make a false step, a hundred lifetimes cannot redeem it.   *Chinese*

LIGHT

9213. Day light will peep through a little hole.   *Scottish*

9214. Every light has its shadow.
English

9215. Every light is not the sun.
English

9216. If not for the light, there would be no shadow.   *Yiddish*

9217. In vain you show light to the blind.   *Rumanian*

9218. Light is bad for sore eyes.
French

9219. Light travels like an arrow, and time like a shuttle.   *Chinese*

9220. One must not trim the light so closely that it goes out.   *Norwegian*

9221. The light is naught for sore eyes.
English

9222. The light is painful to sore eyes.
Italian

9223. The light of a hundred stars does not equal the light of the moon.
Chinese

9224. There is always light behind the clouds.   *American*

9225. There is more light than can be seen through the window.   *Russian*

9226. When the lights go out, the mice begin to dance.   *Yiddish*

9227. When the light is crooked, the shadow is crooked.   *Yiddish*

LIGHTHOUSE

9228. The base of a lighthouse is dark.   *Japanese*

LIGHTNING

9229. He who is struck by the lightning doesn't hear the thunder.
      Hungarian

9230. It does not thunder until after the lightning has flashed.   *Turkish*

9231. Lightning doesn't strike the nettle.   *Hungarian*

9232. The lightning more often strikes the peasant's tree than the noble's forest.   *Russian*

9233. Where there is lightning, there is thunder.   *Greek*

LIKE (equal)

9234. Like plays best with like.
      Danish

9235. Like will to like.   *English*

9236. Like will to like, be they poor or rich.   *Dutch*

LIKE (verb)

9237. One must needs like what one cannot hinder.   *French*

9238. When one has not what one likes, one must like what one has.
      French

LIKENESS

9239. Likeness causes liking. *English*

LILY

9240. Even a white lily casts a black shadow.   *Hungarian*

LIMB

9241. As long as one limb stirs, one does not think of the grave.   *Yiddish*

LINEN

9242. Fine linen often conceals a scabby skin.   *Danish*

9243. Foul linen should be washed at home.   *French*

9244. It is not clean linen only that makes the feast.   *English*

LINING

9245. There is a silver lining to every cloud.   *English*

LINK

9246. One link broken, the whole chain is broken.   *German*

LION

9247. A dead lion is kicked even by an ass.   *Hungarian*

9248. A lion doesn't catch mice.
      Russian

9249. A lion growls not in a den full of straw but in a den full of meat.
      Hebrew

9250. A lion is not a safe companion for all persons.   *Irish*

9251. A lion knows no danger.
      Indian (Tamil)

9252. A lion may be beholden to a mouse.   *English*

9253. Better to be eaten by a lion than to be eaten by a hyena.   *Lebanese*

9254. Destroy the lion while he is yet but a whelp.   *English*

9255. Even a weak lion is not bitten by a dog.   *African (Ovambo)*

9256. Even the lion must defend itself against flies.   *English*

9257. However debased the lion it will not play with a pig.
      African (Hausa)

9258. If one plays with a lion, let him beware of its paw.   *American*

9259. If the lion knew that he was going to find meat while still in the thicket he wouldn't go outside.
African (Hausa)

9260. If you live with a lion, wear the skin of a crocodile.   *African (Swahili)*

9261. In the heart of every brave man a lion sleeps.   *Turkish*

9262. Let sleeping lions lie!   *Yiddish*

9263. Lions are never caught with cobwebs.   *American*

9264. Not all that have claws are lions.   *African (Swahili)*

9265. The lion can't catch flies.
Armenian

9266. The lion dreads the gnat.
Hebrew

9267. The lion is known by his claws.
Italian

9268. The lion is known by his den.
Turkish

9269. The lion is not so fierce as he is painted.   *English*

9270. The lion is the pet of the forest: let every beast take heed how he feeds, for the lion does not eat stale meat.
African (Yoruba)

9271. The lion is valiant, the leopard treacherous.   *Turkish*

9272. The lion is vanquished by a fly buzzing in his ear.   *Armenian*

9273. The lion which has come to the end of its means is forced to eat grass.
African (Bemba)

9274. The lion which is alone cannot see his own mistakes.
African (Bemba)

9275. The lion which moves silently is the one that eats the meat.
African (Swahili)

9276. Two lions do not kill each other.
African (Swahili)

9277. Two lions equal ten hyenas.
African (Ovambo)

9278. Wake not a sleeping lion.
Turkish

9279. What the lion cannot, the fox can.   *German*

9280. When a lion fails to find meat it eats grass.   *African (Shona)*

9281. When the lion is dead the hares jump upon his carcass.   *Italian*

9282. When the lion roars the hyena is quiet.   *African (Ovambo)*

9283. When you play with a lion, do not put your hand in its mouth.
African (Swahili)

9284. You can tell a lion by his claws.
Greek

LION SKIN

9285. Lion skins were never had cheap.   *French*

LIP

9286. Like lips, like lettuce.   *English*

9287. Lips however rosy must be fed.
English

9288. Scald not your lips in another man's pottage.   *English*

9289. Sweet-melon lips, bitter-melon heart.   *Chinese*

9290. The lips of a scolding woman are always quivering.   *Hawaiian*

LIQUOR

9291. Good liquor needs no signboard.   *Japanese*

9292. Good liquor will make a cat speak.   *English*

9293. Pour in liquor and draw out the secret.   *Indian (Tamil)*

LISTEN

9294. He that won't listen, must feel.
German

9295. Listen much and speak little.
Lithuanian

9296. The one who listens is the one who understands. *African (Jabo)*

9297. There's no one as deaf as he who will not listen. *Yiddish*

LISTENER

9298. A good listener makes a good teacher. *Polish*

9299. Listeners hear no good of themselves. *English*

9300. There's always a listener where there's a speaker. *Finnish*

LITERATURE

9301. Literature does not lead men astray. *Chinese*

LITTER

9302. Don't build the sty until the litter comes. *Irish*

LITTLE

9303. A little of everything is nothing in the main. *English*

9304. Better long little, than soon nothing. *Scottish*

9305. By the little is known the much.
English

9306. Every little helps. *English*

9307. He that has little is the less dirty. *English*

9308. Little and often makes a lot in time. *German*

9309. Many a little makes a mickle.
English

9310. Not too little, not too much.
German

9311. Of a little take a little, of a mickle, mickle. *English*

9312. To whom a little is not enough, nothing is enough. *Greek*

9313. Who possesses little has the first right to it. *Egyptian*

LIVE

9314. All wish to live long, but none to be called old. *Danish*

9315. As you have lived, so shall you die. *Philippine*

9316. Better to live in low degree than high disdain. *English*

9317. Better to live well than long.
English

9318. But the longer we live, the more we learn of commodores. *American*

9319. Either live or die with honor.
Scottish

9320. Good or bad we must all live.
Italian

9321. He lives long that lives till all are weary of him. *English*

9322. He lives long that lives well.
English

9323. He lives unsafely that looks too near on things. *English*

9324. He that lives always at home sees nothing but the same. *English*

9325. He that lives ill, fear follows him. *English*

9326. He that lives long suffers much.
English

9327. He that lives overcomes.
English

9328. He that lives well is learned enough. *English*

9329. He that lives well, lives long.
Scottish

9330. He that lives well, sees afar off.
English

9331. He that lives wickedly can hardly die honestly. *English*

9332. If you live long enough, you will live to see everything. *German*

9333. It is hard to live, but it is harder still to die. *Albanian*

9334. Live and let live. *English*

9335. Live as you can, but die as you wish. *Russian*

9336. One cannot live by selling ware for words. *English*

9337. One must live long to learn much. *English*

9338. Since one lives one must suffer, but by suffering one gets wiser and better. *Vietnamese*

9339. Some want to live well and cannot, while others can live well and will not. *Yiddish*

9340. They live but ill who always think to live. *English*

9341. They live not most at ease that have the world at will. *English*

9342. They that live longest must die at last. *English*

9343. They that live longest must go farthest for wood. *English*

9344. They who live longest will see most. *English*

9345. To live is either to beat or to be beaten. *Russian*

9346. To live is to fight. *Estonian*

9347. To live long is to suffer long. *Danish*

9348. We must live by the quick and not by the dead. *English*

9349. We shall live till we die. *English*

9350. Who hastens to live soon dies. *Russian*

9351. Who lives well dies well. *English*

9352. Who lives will see. *French*

LIVELIHOOD

9353. A good livelihood is a cure for all ills. *Yiddish*

LIVER

9354. Chopped liver is better than miserable troubles. *Yiddish*

LIVING (noun)

9355. Living by yourself is better than living with a bad woman. *African (Hausa)*

9356. Living in peace is better than living as a king. *African (Hausa)*

9357. Living well is the best revenge. *English*

9358. There's no living without friends. *Portuguese*

LIVING (people)

9359. Only the living can praise God. *Russian*

LIZARD

9360. A lizard suns itself within reach of its hiding place. *African (Shona)*

9361. If the lizard were good to eat, it would not be so common. *Haitian*

LOAD

9362. It is easier to throw the load off the cart than to put it on. *Czech*

9363. It is not the load but the overload that kills. *Spanish*

LOAF

9364. Better half a loaf than none at all. *Danish*

9365. Do not steal a loaf from him that kneads and bakes. *Spanish*

9366. Half a loaf is better than no bread. *English*

9367. Loaves put awry into the oven come out crooked. *French*

9368. Send not your loaf in till the oven is hot. *English*

9369. The loaf in another's hand is always bigger. *Slovenian*

LOAFER

9370. Any loafer can get shrimps when the shrimps are plentiful.
Hawaiian

LOAN

9371. A borrowed loan should come laughing home. *English*

9372. A long-continued loan usually confers ownership. *Irish*

9373. Give a loan and make an enemy.
Indian (Hindustani)

9374. If loans were of any use, even wives would be lent. *Slovenian*

9375. Seldom comes a loan laughing home. *English*

LOBSTER

9376. The young lobster learns his manner of walking from the old lobster.
Slovakian

9377. Two small lobsters make a big one. *Manx*

LOCK

9378. A lock is a security against animals; nothing holds against man.
Estonian

9379. A lock is good only for an honest man. *Yiddish*

9380. All locks can be opened with a golden key. *Yiddish*

9381. Locks and keys are not made for honest fingers. *German*

9382. No lock avails against a hatchet.
French

9383. No lock will hold against the power of gold. *English*

LOCUST

9384. The locust lives only a little while, but it does great damage.
Rumanian

LOG

9385. A crooked log makes a good fire. *French*

9386. A single log doesn't warm the fireplace. *Yiddish*

9387. A small log will overthrow a big cart. *Rumanian*

9388. Crooked logs make straight fires. *English*

9389. One log does not burn long by itself. *German*

9390. The green log is burned with the dry ones. *Greek*

LOINCLOTH

9391. Better the poorest loincloth than nakedness. *African (Hausa)*

9392. He who is used to loincloth feels ill at ease in trousers. *Philippine*

LONELY

9393. To be lonely is better than to suffer offense. *Libyan*

LONG

9394. Long is not forever. *German*

LONGING

9395. Better go away longing than loathing. *English*

LOOK (noun)

9396. A cheerful look makes a dish a feast. *English*

9397. A valiant man's look is more than a coward's sword. *English*

9398. An honest good look covers many faults. *English*

9399. Looks are nothing—behavior is all. *American*

9400. Looks are one thing, and facts are another. *American*

9401. Looks breed love. *English*

9402. Not everybody is content with his looks, but everyone is content with his brains. *Yiddish*

9403. One look before is better than two behind. *Irish*

9404. Proud looks lose hearts, but courteous words win them. *English*

9405. A good looks of a woman are her dowry. *Maltese*

LOOK (verb)

9406. Don't look above you, rather look below you. *Japanese*

9407. He that looks not before finds himself behind. *English*

9408. Long looked for comes at last. *English*

9409. Look before you leap. *English*

9410. Look high and fall low. *English*

9411. Look not too high lest a chip fall in your eye. *English*

9412. You must look where it is not, as well as where it is. *English*

LOOKER-ON

9413. Lookers-on see most of the game. *English*

LOOKING

9414. Looking carefully is understanding. *African (Ovambo)*

LOOKING-GLASS

9415. The looking-glass is the enemy of ugly women. *Rumanian*

9416. They who are often at the looking-glass seldom spin. *Dutch*

LORD (see GOD)

9417. In the name of the Lord begins all mischief. *English*

9418. The Lord created two desires, one for good and one for evil. *Hebrew*

9419. The Lord will not fail to come, though he may not come on horseback. *Danish*

LORD (men)

9420. A lord without land is like a cask without wine. *Danish*

9421. Great lords and dogs do not close the door behind them. *Serbo-Croatian*

9422. Great lords have long hands, but they do not reach to heaven. *Danish*

9423. Great lords will have much, and poor folk can give but little. *Danish*

9424. Like lord like chaplain. *English*

9425. Lords and fools speak freely. *Danish*

9426. Many lords, many laws. *English*

9427. New lords, new laws. *English*

9428. When the lords come out of the councilhouse, they are wiser than when they went in. *German*

LOSE

9429. All is not lost that is delayed. *French*

9430. Better lost than found. *English*

9431. He has not lost all who has one cast left. *English*

9432. He loses many a good bit that strives with his betters. *English*

9433. He loses nothing that loses not God. *English*

9434. He who loses sins. *French*

9435. It is lost that is unsought. *English*

9436. It is not lost that comes at last. *English*

9437. Lose nothing for want of asking. *English*

9438. One who has nothing to lose can be reckless to any extent. *Indian (Bihar)*

9439. Who loses his due gets no thanks. *English*

LOSER

9440. Give losers leave to speak. *English*

LOSING

9441. Without losing you cannot win. *Russian*

LOSS

9442. After one loss come many. *French*

9443. Better a loss at sea than a bad debt at land. *English*

9444. Better two losses than one sorrow. *English*

9445. Don't be afraid of a loss, then you will get profit. *Russian*

9446. Even loss can be a profit. *Iranian*

9447. Loss embraces shame. *English*

9448. Losses teach men wisdom. *Serbo-Croatian*

9449. No great loss without some small profit. *Scottish*

9450. Reckon loss before reckoning gain. *Lebanese*

9451. The loss of one is a gain for two and a chance for twenty more. *English*

9452. The miser's loss is sudden. *Indian (Bihar)*

LOT

9453. Let every man be content with his own lot. *Scottish*

LOUSE

9454. A hungry louse bites sore. *Scottish*

9455. A louse is better than no meat. *English*

9456. Don't love the louse more than the hair. *Thai*

9457. The lean lice bite most. *Polish*

LOVE (noun)

9458. A boy's love is water in a sieve. *Spanish*

9459. A mother's love is best of all. *Indian (Hindi)*

9460. A pennyweight of love is worth a pound of law. *English*

9461. A secret love is always a true love. *Slovakian*

9462. All is fair in love and war. *English*

9463. All love is love, but self love is strongest. *African (Hausa)*

9464. Always in love, never married. *French*

9465. An old love doesn't rust. *Russian*

9466. An old love is lasting. *Russian*

9467. Be off with the old love before you are on with the new. *English*

9468. By beating love decays. *French*

9469. Don't be so much in love that you can't tell when the rain is coming. *Malagasy*

9470. Follow love and it will flee; flee love and it will follow thee.   *English*

9471. Follow love and it will flee you.
                                          Scottish

9472. For a little love you pay all your life.   *Yiddish*

9473. Forced love does not last.
                                          Dutch

9474. He that has love in his breast has spurs in his sides.   *English*

9475. He who forces love where none is found remains a fool the whole year round.   *German*

9476. He who marries for love has good nights and bad days.   *French*

9477. Hot love, hasty vengeance.
                                          English

9478. Hot love is soon cold.   *English*

9479. If love is a sickness, patience is the remedy.   *African (Fulani)*

9480. In love and war no time should be lost.   *American*

9481. In love, as in war, each man must gain his own victories.
                                          American

9482. In love is no lack.   *English*

9483. In love there are no distinctions between high and low.   *Japanese*

9484. It is easy to reconcile when there is love.   *Welsh*

9485. It is loving too much to die of love.   *French*

9486. Light love will change.
                                          English

9487. Lingering love breeds mislike.
                                          English

9488. Little love, little trust.   *English*

9489. Love, a cough, and smoke will not remain secret.   *French*

9490. Love, a cough, smoke, and money cannot long be hid.   *French*

9491. Love and a cough cannot be hid.   *English*

9492. Love and a king accept no partnership.   *Turkish*

9493. Love and blindness are twin sisters.   *Russian*

9494. Love and brandy have soothing aftereffects both.   *Mexican*

9495. Love and business teach eloquence.   *English*

9496. Love and eggs should be fresh to be enjoyed.   *Russian*

9497. Love and fear cannot be hidden.
                                          Russian

9498. Love and foolishness differ from each other only in name.
                                          Hungarian

9499. Love and hunger are the foundation stones of all things.   *Russian*

9500. Love and hunger don't dwell together.   *Yiddish*

9501. Love and knowledge live not together.   *English*

9502. Love and light cannot be hid.
                                          Scottish

9503. Love and lordship like no fellowship.   *English*

9504. Love and poverty are hard to conceal.   *Danish*

9505. Love asks faith, and faith asks firmness.   *English*

9506. Love begins at home.   *German*

9507. Love beyond measure afterwards brings hatred.   *Rumanian*

9508. Love blinds.   *African (Swahili)*

9509. Love blinds itself to all shortcomings.   *Lebanese*

9510. Love can do much, money can do all.   *German*

9511. Love comes after marriage.
                                          Icelandic

9512. Love conceals ugliness, and hate sees a lot of faults. *Irish*

9513. Love defies law. *Indian (Bihar)*

9514. Love demands faith, and faith firmness. *Italian*

9515. Love does much but money does all. *English*

9516. Love does not choose the blade of grass on which it falls. *African (Zulu)*

9517. Love does wonders, but money makes marriage. *French*

9518. Love drives out fear. *Czech*

9519. Love ends when the can is empty. *Icelandic*

9520. Love enters man through his eyes; woman through her ears. *Polish*

9521. Love expels jealousy. *French*

9522. Love, fire, cough, the itch, and gout are not to be concealed. *German*

9523. Love, grief, and money cannot be kept secret. *Spanish*

9524. Love grows with obstacles. *German*

9525. Love has made heroes of many and fools of many more. *Swedish*

9526. Love has no law. *Portuguese*

9527. Love has wings on its shoulders; matrimony has crutches under its arms. *Russian*

9528. Love is a dark pit. *Hungarian*

9529. Love is a fair garden, and marriage a field of nettles. *Finnish*

9530. Love is a flower which turns into fruit at marriage. *Finnish*

9531. Love is a ring, and a ring has no end. *Russian*

9532. Love is a sweet torment. *English*

9533. Love is above King or Kaiser, lord or laws. *English*

9534. Love is all-important, and it is it's own reward. *Indian (Tamil)*

9535. Love is an empire—it admires no partnership. *Turkish*

9536. Love is an excuse for its own faults. *Italian*

9537. Love is beyond reflection. *Japanese*

9538. Love is blind. *English*

9539. Love is blind to blemishes and faults. *Irish*

9540. Love is called the daughter of the skies because it grows wings quickly. *Hebrew*

9541. Love is full of busy fear. *English*

9542. Love is full of honey and gall. *Slovenian*

9543. Love is liberal. *English*

9544. Love is like butter, it's good with bread. *Yiddish*

9545. Love is like color which fades away. *African (Shona)*

9546. Love is like dew that falls on both nettles and lilies. *Swedish*

9547. Love is like fog, there is no mountain on which it does not rest. *Hawaiian*

9548. Love is master of all arts. *Italian*

9549. Love is meat and drink, and a blanket to boot. *American*

9550. Love is never without jealousy. *Scottish*

9551. Love is never without some thorns. *Slovakian*

9552. Love is no impartial judge. *Irish*

9553. Love is not found in the market. *English*

9554. Love is shown by deeds, not by words. *Philippine*

9555. Love is stronger than a giant.
Welsh

9556. Love is sweet, but it's nice to have bread with it. *Yiddish*

9557. Love is the loadstone of love.
English

9558. Love is the salt of life.
Philippine

9559. Love is the true price of love.
English

9560. Love is without law. *English*

9561. Love knows hidden paths.
German

9562. Love knows not labor. *Italian*

9563. Love lasts as long as the money endures. *English*

9564. Love laughs at locksmiths.
English

9565. Love levels all inequalities.
Italian

9566. Love lives in cottages as well as in courts. *English*

9567. Love lives in palaces as well as in thatched cottages. *Japanese*

9568. Love locks no cupboards.
English

9569. Love looks for love again.
English

9570. Love makes a good eye squint.
English

9571. Love makes a wit of the fool.
English

9572. Love makes labor light. *Dutch*

9573. Love makes men orators.
English

9574. Love makes time pass away, and time makes love pass away.
French

9575. Love needs no laws. *Slovakian*

9576. Love of lads and fire of chips is soon in and soon out. *English*

9577. Love of one's country is religion. *Lebanese*

9578. Love or fire in your trousers is not easy to conceal. *Swedish*

9579. Love overlooks defects and hatred magnifies shortcomings.
Lebanese

9580. Love, poverty, and care cannot be hidden. *Mexican*

9581. Love pursues profit. *Irish*

9582. Love rules its kingdom without a sword. *English*

9583. Love sees no faults. *English*

9584. Love starts from the eyes.
Russian

9585. Love suffers many disappointments. *Maltese*

9586. Love teaches asses to dance.
French

9587. Love tells us things which are not. *Russian*

9588. Love unexpressed is useless.
Philippine

9589. Love will creep where it cannot go. *English*

9590. Love will find a way. *English*

9591. Love will overcome everything.
Welsh

9592. Love without return is like a question without an answer. *German*

9593. Mother's love is always renewed. *French*

9594. New loves drive out the old.
Spanish

9595. No love is foul nor prison fair.
English

9596. Old and true love never rusts.
Hebrew

9597. Old love and old brands kindle at all seasons. *French*

9598. Old love burns strong.
American

9599. Old love does not rust.
German

9600. One always returns to one's first love. *French*

9601. One grows used to love and to fire. *French*

9602. One love expels another.
English

9603. One sees love after living together. *Hawaiian*

9604. See for love, and buy for money.
Scottish

9605. Self-love is blind. *Dutch*

9606. Short love brings a long sigh.
Rumanian

9607. Sometimes love has been implanted by one glance alone.
Egyptian

9608. Sound love is not soon forgotten.
English

9609. Superficial love is like smoke that dissipates. *Philippine*

9610. The course of true love never did run smooth. *English*

9611. The extreme form of passionate love is secret love. *Japanese*

9612. The greatest love is motherlove; after that comes a dog's love; and after that the love of a sweetheart. *Polish*

9613. The love of a woman, and a bottle of wine, are sweet for a season, but last for a time. *English*

9614. The love of money and the love of learning rarely meet. *English*

9615. The love of one's country is greater than love for parents.
Philippine

9616. The love of unearned money is the root of all evil. *American*

9617. The more violent the love, the more violent the anger. *Burmese*

9618. The people's love is the king's lifeguard. *English*

9619. There's love in a budget.
English

9620. There is no love without jealousy. *French*

9621. There is no such fiery love that would not be cooled down by marriage.
Russian

9622. Though love is blind, yet it is not for want of eyes. *English*

9623. Three things cannot be hidden: love, coughing, and poverty. *Yiddish*

9624. To understand your parents' love you must raise children yourself.
Chinese

9625. Too much love causes heartbreak. *Philippine*

9626. True love is sweet until the end.
Philippine

9627. True love shows itself in time of need. *Scottish*

9628. True love suffers no concealment. *Spanish*

9629. Unlucky in love, lucky at play.
English

9630. When love puts in, friendship is gone. *English*

9631. When passionately in love, one becomes stupid. *Japanese*

9632. Where love is in the case, the doctor is an ass. *English*

9633. Where love is, there's no lack.
English

9634. Where love reigns the impossible may be attained. *Indian (Tamil)*

9635. Where there is great love there is great pain. *Italian*

9636. Where there is love, there is also a quarrel. *Rumanian*

9637. Where there is love, there is God.   *Russian*

9638. Where there's no love, all faults are seen.   *German*

9639. Who has love in his heart has spurs in his sides.   *Italian*

9640. Without bread and salt love cannot exist.   *Polish*

LOVE (verb)

9641. Better love me little, but love me long.   *Yiddish*

9642. He loves me for little that hates me for nought.   *Scottish*

9643. He who loves a thing often talks of it.   *Egyptian*

9644. He who loves many won't marry anyone.   *Philippine*

9645. He who loves well, obeys well.   *Spanish*

9646. He whom we love is white even when unwashed.   *Russian*

9647. Love me little, love me long.   *English*

9648. Love me, love my dog.   *English*

9649. Love to live and live to love.   *English*

9650. Love well, whip well.   *American*

9651. One cannot love and be wise.   *English*

9652. That which is loved is always beautiful.   *Norwegian*

9653. They love too much that die for love.   *English*

9654. To love and be wise is impossible.   *Spanish*

9655. To love and to be wise are two different things.   *French*

9656. To those we love best, we say the least.   *Philippine*

9657. Who loves, believes.   *Italian*

9658. Who loves, fears.   *Italian*

9659. Who loves well, chastises well.   *French*

9660. Who loves well is slow to forget.   *French*

9661. Whom we love best, to them we can say least.   *English*

LOVER

9662. A lover is unmindful of any charcoal on the body.
African (Annang)

9663. As is the lover so is the beloved.
Italian

9664. Do not marry your lover, and never take back the man you have divorced.   *Lebanese*

9665. Let him not be a lover who has not courage.   *Italian*

9666. Lovers live by love as larks live by leeks.   *English*

9667. Lovers seek willingly new roads; the married seek the old.
Russian

9668. Lovers think others are blind.
Italian

9669. Lovers think that others have no eyes.   *Spanish*

9670. One cannot be a lover by force.
Turkish

9671. The lover walks in the snow and does not make his tracks visible.
Turkish

9672. The lover who suffers not anguish knows not the worth of pleasure.
Turkish

9673. To the partial eyes of a lover, pockmarks seem like dimples.
Japanese

9674. True lovers are shy, when people are by.   *English*

9675. You can tell lovers from their faces.   *African (Ovambo)*

9676. Young lovers wish, and married men regret.   *Indian (Hindustani)*

LOVING

9677. Loving and singing are not to be forced.   *German*

9678. Loving comes by looking.
English

9679. Loving one who loves another is a bellyful of trouble.   *African (Hausa)*

LOYALTY

9680. Loyalty is more valuable than diamonds.   *Philippine*

LUCK

9681. A little bit of luck is better than a ton of gold.   *Yiddish*

9682. All is luck or ill luck in this world.   *French*

9683. An ounce of luck is worth a pound of wisdom.   *French*

9684. An ounce of luck is worth more than a pound of gold.   *Yiddish*

9685. Bad luck often brings good luck.   *English*

9686. Bad luck rots and in the end one rejoices.   *African (Bemba)*

9687. Better luck than knowledge.
Greek

9688. Even for bad luck one needs luck.   *Yiddish*

9689. Few have luck, all have death.
Danish

9690. For good luck sleep and wait.
Japanese

9691. Good luck comes in at a smiling gate.   *Japanese*

9692. Good luck in cards bad luck in marriage.   *English*

9693. Good luck invites many mishaps.   *Japanese*

9694. Good luck is better than brains.
Serbo-Croatian

9695. Good luck is better than early rising.   *Irish*

9696. Good luck lurks under a black deuce.   *English*

9697. Good luck makes its way in by elbowing.   *Spanish*

9698. Good luck never comes too late.
English

9699. He that has no ill luck grows weary of good luck.   *Spanish*

9700. He that has the luck leads the bride to church.   *Dutch*

9701. He who has luck will have the winds blow him his firewood. *Libyan*

9702. If good luck comes, who doesn't? If good luck does not come, who does?   *Chinese*

9703. If it is to be luck, the bull may as well calve as the cow.   *Danish*

9704. If luck plays along, cleverness succeeds.   *Yiddish*

9705. If you are afraid of bad luck you will never get good luck.   *Russian*

9706. Ill luck comes by pounds and goes away by ounces.   *Italian*

9707. Ill luck enters by fathoms and departs by inches.   *Spanish*

9708. Ill luck is good for something.
English

9709. Ill luck is worse than found money.   *English*

9710. Luck and bad luck are driving in the same sledge.   *Russian*

9711. Luck and charm cannot be purchased in a store.   *Yiddish*

9712. Luck and ill luck are neighbors.
Norwegian

9713. Luck comes to those who look after it.   *Spanish*

9714. Luck for the fools and chance for the ugly.   *English*

9715. Luck has but a slender anchorage.   *Danish*

9716. Luck has much for many, but enough for no one.   *Danish*

9717. Luck is a lord.   *English*

9718. Luck is better than a hundred marks.   *Danish*

9719. Luck is like women who like fools best.   *Norwegian*

9720. Luck seldom lasts.   *Irish*

9721. Luck will carry a man across the brook if he is not too lazy to leap.
                                  Danish

9722. Luck will turn.   *American*

9723. Luck without sense is a perforated sack.   *Yiddish*

9724. Luck without wisdom is like a knapsack with holes.   *Russian*

9725. Once bad luck has come, open your gates.   *Russian*

9726. One's good luck is another's misfortune.   *Yiddish*

9727. Secret luck is not bothered by jealousy.   *German*

9728. Sit not idle, for your luck sits with you.   *Rumanian*

9729. Sometimes a piece of ill luck comes in handy.   *Yiddish*

9730. Speak little of your ill luck, and boast not of your good luck.   *Danish*

9731. The worse luck now, the better another time.   *English*

9732. There is luck in leisure.
                                  English

9733. There is luck in odd numbers.
                                  English

9734. There is luck in sharing a thing.   *Irish*

9735. There is no luck where there is no authority.   *Irish*

9736. Too much luck is dangerous.
                                  Russian

9737. What is bad luck for one man is good luck for another.
                         African (Ashanti)

9738. When ill luck falls asleep, let nobody wake her.   *English*

9739. When luck offers a finger one must take the whole hand.   *Swedish*

9740. Where luck is wanting, diligence is useless.   *Spanish*

9741. Who ventures nothing has no luck.   *Spanish*

9742. With luck, everything is possible.   *Yiddish*

9743. Without luck nothing will succeed.   *Yiddish*

9744. You must have good luck to catch hares with a drum.   *Danish*

LUCKY

9745. It's better to be lucky than wise.
                                  Irish

LUGGAGE

9746. Poor man's luggage is always light.   *Norwegian*

LURE (noun)

9747. Any lure is good that brings the bird to the net.   *Indian (Hindi)*

LURE (verb)

9748. He is easy to lure who is ready to follow.   *Danish*

LUST

9749. Lust causes a man to break into a house and rob.   *Indian (Kashmiri)*

9750. Lust is bottomless.
                         Indian (Hindi)

9751. Lust leads to love.   *Hebrew*

9752. Lust only longs for things forbidden.   *Hebrew*

9753. Rule lust, temper tongue, and bridle the belly. *English*

LUXURY

9754. Give us the luxuries of life, and we will dispense with the necessaries. *American*

LYING

9755. Lying and gossiping go hand in hand. *Spanish*

9756. Lying is the first step to the gallows. *German*

9757. Lying pays no tax. *Portuguese*

M

MAD

9758. Better be mad with all the world than wise alone. *French*

MADMAN

9759. A madman and a fool are no witnesses. *English*

9760. A madman makes people run. *Japanese*

MAGISTRATE

9761. An honest magistrate cannot succeed. *Chinese*

9762. An honest magistrate has lean clerks; a powerful god has fat priests. *Chinese*

MAID

9763. A maid and a virgin is not all one. *English*

9764. A maid that gives yields. *English*

9765. A maid that laughs is half taken. *English*

9766. A young maid married to an old man is like a new house thatched with old straw. *English*

9767. All are good maids, but whence come the bad wives? *English*

9768. An old maid becomes a faithful wife. *Yiddish*

9769. Better an old maid than a young whore. *Scottish*

9770. Every maid is undone. *English*

9771. He that woos a maid must come seldom in her sight. *Scottish*

9772. He that woos a maid must come seldom in her sight, but he that woos a widow must woo her day and night. *English*

9773. Maids say nay and take. *English*

9774. Maids should be seen and not heard. *English*

9775. Maids want nothing but husbands. *English*

9776. While the tall maid is stooping, the little one has swept the house. *English*

MAIDEN

9777. A maiden marries to please her parents, a widow to please herself. *Chinese*

9778. A maiden should pretty herself for strange bachelors and a young wife for her own husband. *Yiddish*

9779. A maiden with many wooers often chooses the worst. *Scottish*

9780. A neat maiden makes a dirty wife. *Scottish*

9781. Fair maidens wear no purses.
Scottish

9782. He that marries a maiden, marries a pokeful of pleasure. *Scottish*

9783. If one will not, another will; so are all maidens married. *Scottish*

9784. Maidens must be mild and meek, swift to hear, and slow to speak.
English

9785. Maidens say no and do it all the same. *German*

9786. The most to be pitied is a poor maiden in childbirth. *Yiddish*

9787. You must judge a maiden at the kneading trough, and not in a dance.
Danish

MALICE

9788. Malice has a sharp sight and strong memory. *English*

9789. Malice hurts itself most.
English

9790. Malice is mindful. *English*

9791. Malice never spoke well.
English

9792. Malice seldom wants a mark to shoot at. *English*

MAN (see MEN)

9793. A bald-headed man does not care for a razor. *African (Yoruba)*

9794. A blind man cannot judge colors. *English*

9795. A blind man doesn't care if lamp oil is expensive. *Armenian*

9796. A blind man does not show the way to a blind man. *African (Ga)*

9797. A blind man does not worry over the loss of a looking glass.
African (Hausa)

9798. A blind man is no judge of colors. *Italian*

9799. A blind man needs not to buy a mirror. *African (Fulani)*

9800. A blind man will not thank you for a looking glass. *English*

9801. A blind man would be glad to see it. *English*

9802. A brave man will face a situation no matter how dreadful.
Philippine

9803. A covetous man does nothing well till he dies. *English*

9804. A covetous man is good to none but worst to himself. *English*

9805. A dead man does not make war.
Italian

9806. A dead man does not speak.
Portuguese

9807. A dead man has neither relations nor friends. *French*

9808. A dead man pays no debts.
Serbo-Croatian

9809. A drowning man clings to a blade of grass. *French*

9810. A drowning man clutches at his own hair. *Greek*

9811. A drowning man grasps at water. *African (Swahili)*

9812. A drowning man will even clutch at a straw. *Russian*

9813. A drowning man will grasp the foam. *Armenian*

9814. A drowning man would catch at razors. *Italian*

9815. A drunken man may soon be made to dance. *Danish*

9816. A fortunate man may be anywhere. *English*

9817. A generous man has never gone to hell. *Irish*

9818. A good man can't be corrupted by the tavern nor a bad one reformed by the synagogue. *Yiddish*

9819. A good man is a man of goods.
French

9820. A good man is no more to be feared than a sheep. *English*

9821. A good man never hurts a tree.
Hungarian

9822. A good man protects three villages; a good dog, three houses.
Chinese

9823. A great man does not seize small things. *Japanese*

9824. A great man has not a great son.
American

9825. A greedy man will not die till he feels shame. *African (Fulani)*

9826. A guilty man is always self-conscious. *Yiddish*

9827. A heady man and a fool may wear the same cap. *English*

9828. A healthy poor man is worth half a rich one. *Chinese*

9829. A hungry man discovers more than a hundred lawyers. *Spanish*

9830. A hungry man is an angry man. *English*

9831. A hungry man smells meat afar off. *English*

9832. A late man brings trouble on himself. *Irish*

9833. A lazy man does not know he is lazy till he drives a tortoise away and it escapes. *African (Hausa)*

9834. A lazy man lies flat on his back; a lazy woman stretches out her legs.
Burmese

9835. A lazy man seeks easy employment: he would never choose a laborious one. *African (Yoruba)*

9836. A lazy man will destroy his own house. *Philippine*

9837. A lazy man will not bring a hare to market. *African (Hausa)*

9838. A little man fells a great oak.
French

9839. A little man may cast a great shadow. *English*

9840. A little man often casts a long shadow. *Italian*

9841. A loving man, a jealous man.
Italian

9842. A luckless man is like incense without fire. *Rumanian*

9843. A lucky man fares better than a brave man. *Greek*

9844. A man, a horse, and a dog are never weary of each other's company.
English

9845. A man alive is worth more than a pile of gold. *Vietnamese*

9846. A man always breaking off from his work never finishes anything.
African (Efik)

9847. A man among children will be long a child; a child among men will be soon a man. *English*

9848. A man apt to promise is apt to forget. *English*

9849. A man assailed is half overcome. *French*

9850. A man assaulted is half taken.
English

9851. A man at five may be a fool at fifteen. *English*

9852. A man at sixteen will prove a child at sixty. *English*

9853. A man believes that he has been born, he does not believe that he will die. *Turkish*

9854. A man can disgrace only himself. *American*

9855. A man can do no more than he can. *English*

9856. A man can hang himself from his own tree as well as from his neighbor's. *Russian*

9857. A man cannot be hanged for thinking. *American*

9858. A man cannot be known by his looks, nor can the sea be measured with a bushel basket. *Chinese*

9859. A man cannot bear all his kin on his back. *Scottish*

9860. A man cannot change his face but he can change his habit. *Philippine*

9861. A man cannot live by the air. *English*

9862. A man can't serve two mistresses—his country and his wife. *American*

9863. A man can't smoke and whistle at one time. *Jamaican*

9864. A man cannot spin and reel at the same time. *English*

9865. A man cannot wive and thrive in a year. *Scottish*

9866. A man conducts himself abroad as he has been taught at home. *Danish*

9867. A man deceives a man once. *Turkish*

9868. A man does not always aim at what he means to hit. *Danish*

9869. A man does not become a savant by licking ink. *Turkish*

9870. A man does not live a hundred years, yet he worries enough for a thousand. *Chinese*

9871. A man does not look behind the door unless he has stood there himself. *Danish*

9872. A man does not use one finger to take out an arrow. *African (Efik)*

9873. A man first builds a house and afterwards brings in the furniture. *Hebrew*

9874. A man forewarned is as good as two. *Spanish*

9875. A man goes out of his house for business, a woman to be looked at. *Finnish*

9876. A man has choice to begin love, but not to end it. *English*

9877. A man has many enemies when his back is to the wall. *English*

9878. A man has no worse friends than those he brings with him. *Scottish*

9879. A man has often more trouble to digest meat than to get it. *English*

9880. A man has plenty of time to choose a wife. *Finnish*

9881. A man in a foreign country is like a mad dog. *Indian (Kashmiri)*

9882. A man in distress or despair does as much as ten. *English*

9883. A man in extreme need will clutch even at a sharp blade. *Philippine*

9884. A man in passion rides a horse that runs away with him. *English*

9885. A man is a lion in his own cause. *English*

9886. A man is a man, even a ruined one. *Finnish*

9887. A man is a man if he have but a nose on his face. *English*

9888. A man is as old as he feels. *English*

9889. A man is attractive when he is not your husband. *African (Shona)*

9890. A man is bound by his word, an ox with a hempen cord. *Danish*

9891. A man is good if he makes others better men. *Russian*

9892. A man is handsome if he is only better looking than the devil. *Yiddish*

9893. A man is known by his acts. *Philippine*

9894. A man is known by his company. *English*

9895. A man is known by his works.
Philippine

9896. A man is not a dog.
African (Ovambo)

9897. A man is not a lord because he feeds off fine dishes. *Danish*

9898. A man is not known till he comes to honor. *Dutch*

9899. A man is not lean without cause. *African (Ga)*

9900. A man is not so soon healed as hurt. *English*

9901. A man is not stabbed with one spear. *African (Zulu)*

9902. A man is not sure of his meat till it is in his mouth. *English*

9903. A man is often too young to marry, but a man is never too old to love. *Finnish*

9904. A man is to be feared from his speech, water from its floods. *Turkish*

9905. A man is valued according to his own estimate of himself. *French*

9906. A man knows his companion in a long journey and a little inn.
English

9907. A man knows not whether he will see tomorrow. *African (Efik)*

9908. A man knows the faults of his neighbor but not his own. *Philippine*

9909. A man lives long in his native place. *Irish*

9910. A man loses his time who comes early to a bad bargain. *English*

9911. A man loves his own fault.
Indian (Kashmiri)

9912. A man's manners show his birth. *Philippine*

9913. A man may be an artist though he have not his tools about him.
English

9914. A man may be as strong as the buffalo, yet he has no horns.
African (Yoruba)

9915. A man may be young in years, and yet old in hours. *English*

9916. A man may bear till his back break. *English*

9917. A man may bind a sack, before it be full. *Scottish*

9918. A man may come soon enough to an ill bargain. *English*

9919. A man may hold his tongue.
English

9920. A man may live upon little, but he cannot live upon nothing. *English*

9921. A man may lose. *English*

9922. A man may lose his goods for want of demanding them. *English*

9923. A man may provoke his own dog to bite him. *English*

9924. A man may threaten yet be a-fraid. *French*

9925. A man may woo where he will, but wed where his wife is. *Scottish*

9926. A man must keep his mouth open a long while before a roast pigeon flies into it. *Danish*

9927. A man must not throw a gift at the giver's head. *English*

9928. A man must take such as he finds, or such as he brings. *English*

9929. A man need not look in your mouth to know how old you are.
English

9930. A man never fails among his own people. *Irish*

9931. A man never surfeits of too much honesty. *English*

9932. A man of courage never wants weapons. *English*

9933. A man of cruelty is God's enemy. *English*

9934. A man of gladness seldom falls into madness. *English*

9935. A man of learning is not suited to wield political power, for experience has shown that scholars make poor rulers. *Japanese*

9936. A man of many trades begs his bread on Sundays. *English*

9937. A man of straw is better than a woman of gold. *Portuguese*

9938. A man of straw is worth a woman of gold. *English*

9939. A man of words and not of deeds is like a garden full of weeds. *English*

9940. A man often kisses the hand he would like to see cut off. *Danish*

9941. A man on his death bed tells no lies. *African (Swahili)*

9942. A man sauntering has no business. *African (Efik)*

9943. A man should stay alive if only out of curiosity. *Yiddish*

9944. A man surprised is half beaten. *English*

9945. A man that breaks his word bids others be false to him. *English*

9946. A man that does what no other man does is wondered at by all. *English*

9947. A man that keeps riches and enjoys them not is like an ass that carries gold and eats thistles. *English*

9948. A man that will fight may find a cudgel in every hedge. *English*

9949. A man that would thrive must ask his wife's leave. *Scottish*

9950. A man travels as far in a day as a snail in a hundred years. *French*

9951. A man under no restraint is a bear without a ring. *English*

9952. A man warned is half saved. *German*

9953. A man who does one bad action will stoop to another. *African (Fulani)*

9954. A man who gets involved in an accident gets involved in tales. *African (Swahili)*

9955. A man who gives alms to be seen would never give in the dark. *Manx*

9956. A man who has but one eye must take good care of it. *French*

9957. A man who has no house is like a bird in the tree when a storm has broken. *African (Jabo)*

9958. A man who is pure and gentle is to the people like gold in the pocket. *Moroccan*

9959. A man who knows too many crafts cannot feed his family. *Chinese*

9960. A man who lives in two homes cannot catch a thief. *African (Annang)*

9961. A man who picks up a big stone does not intend to throw it. *Armenian*

9962. A man who puts his hand into the bee's hive gets stung by the bees. *African (Annang)*

9963. A man who talks of others behind their backs, another will talk of him in like manner. *African (Efik)*

9964. A man who throws stones at himself is not to be pitied. *Greek*

9965. A man who wants bread is ready for anything. *French*

9966. A man who wants to drown his dog says he is mad. *French*

9967. A man whose heart is not content is like a snake which tries to swallow an elephant. *Chinese*

9968. A man will rather hurt his body than displease his palate. *English*

9969. A man with a changeable spirit is not successful.   *Japanese*

9970. A man with a cough cannot conceal himself.   *African (Yoruba)*

9971. A man without a smiling face should not open a shop.   *Chinese*

9972. A man without a trade, a tree without fruit.   *Turkish*

9973. A man without a wife is like a horse without a bridle.   *Vietnamese*

9974. A man without children is like a horse without a tether.   *Moroccan*

9975. A man without determination is but an untempered sword. *Chinese*

9976. A man without enemies is like a river without stones.   *Rumanian*

9977. A man without knowledge is like a man groping in the dark.
Vietnamese

9978. A man without money is a bow without an arrow.   *English*

9979. A man without money is like a bird without wings.   *Philippine*

9980. A man without money is like a ship without sails.   *Dutch*

9981. A man without money is no man at all.   *English*

9982. A man without patience is like a lamp without oil.   *Greek*

9983. A man without reason is a beast in season.   *English*

9984. A married man is a caged bird.
Italian

9985. A merciful man is merciful to his beast.   *American*

9986. A naked man has less care than a man of wealth or a man of position.
Indian (Kashmiri)

9987. A night spent by the side of a wise man is worth more than a year caressed by a stupid man. *Vietnamese*

9988. A poor man buys what he can afford; a rich man what he wants.
Greek

9989. A poor man cannot afford to have whims.   *African (Swahili)*

9990. A poor man has a large stomach, not a large mouth.
African (Bemba)

9991. A poor man has few acquaintances.   *Danish*

9992. A poor man has no friend.
African (Oji)

9993. A poor man is like a torn sack.
Yiddish

9994. A poor man is pleased with whatever he gets.   *Irish*

9995. A poor man is recognized by his sandals.   *African (Ovambo)*

9996. A poor man wants some things, a covetous man all things.   *English*

9997. A poor man with intelligence is wealthy.   *Greek*

9998. A proud man has many crosses.
English

9999. A proud man is unacceptable even to his own household.   *Hebrew*

10000. A quarrelsome man has no good neighbors.   *American*

10001. A quiet man makes not the noise of an elephant.   *African (Ga)*

10002. A red-nosed man may not be a drunkard, but he will always be called one.   *Chinese*

10003. A resolute man cares nothing about difficulties.   *Indian (Tamil)*

10004. A rich man is known by his house.   *African (Ovambo)*

10005. A rich man is never ugly in the eyes of a girl.   *French*

10006. A righteous man who knows he is righteous is not righteous.   *Yiddish*

10007. A satisfied man does not know what a hungry man feels.
African (Fulani)

10008. A shamefaced man seldom acquires wealth. *Irish*

10009. A sick man despises not medicine. *African (Hausa)*

10010. A sick man sleeps, but not a debtor. *Spanish*

10011. A small man with education is of use to the state; of what use is a tall man who knows nothing? *Chinese*

10012. A sober man, a soft answer.
English

10013. A solitary man is either a brute or an angel. *English*

10014. A solitary man makes not an army. *Irish*

10015. A stingy man is always poor.
French

10016. A stubborn man brings in a snake for a hairdo. *African (Ovambo)*

10017. A stupid man conceives an idea only after the event. *Burmese*

10018. A talking man is no better than a barking dog. *American*

10019. A thankless man never does a thankful deed. *Danish*

10020. A thoughtless man is known by his speech. *African (Ovambo)*

10021. A timid man has little chance.
Danish

10022. A timid man is far from danger.
Irish

10023. A traveled man has leave to lie.
Scottish

10024. A true man and a thief think differently. *English*

10025. A wavering man is like a skein of silk. *English*

10026. A weeping man and a smiling woman are not to be trusted.
Indian (Tamil)

10027. A well-fed man can't understand a hungry one. *Russian*

10028. A well-fed man does not believe the hungry one. *Greek*

10029. A well-fed man does not give thanks. *African (Ovambo)*

10030. A well-read man is like a nicely cut stone. *Indian (Kashmiri)*

10031. A wicked man is his own hell.
English

10032. A willful man had need be very wise. *English*

10033. A willful man must have his way. *English*

10034. A willful man never wants woe.
English

10035. A willful man should be very wise. *Scottish*

10036. A wise man, a strong man.
German

10037. A wise man and a fool together know more than a wise man alone.
Italian

10038. A wise man begins in the end; a fool ends in the beginning. *English*

10039. A wise man carries his cloak in fair weather, and a fool wants his in rain. *Scottish*

10040. A wise man changes his mind, a fool never will. *English*

10041. A wise man conceals his intelligence; the fool displays his foolishness. *Yiddish*

10042. A wise man goes slowly but arrives surely at his goal.
Serbo-Croatian

10043. A wise man has his tongue in his heart. *Swedish*

10044. A wise man hears one word and understands two. *Yiddish*

10045. A wise man knows his own.
English

10046. A wise man knows what he says, a fool says what he knows.
Yiddish

10047. A wise man makes his own decisions, an ignorant man follows public opinion. *Chinese*

10048. A wise man may learn of a fool.
French

10049. A wise man never wants a weapon. *English*

10050. A wise man ought not to be ashamed to change his purpose.
English

10051. A wise man stumbles once over a peg. *Pashto*

10052. A wise man turns chance into good fortune. *English*

10053. A wise man walks on foot and a fool rides in a coach. *Yiddish*

10054. A wise man who has seen everything is not the equal of one who has done one thing with his hands.
Chinese

10055. A wise man will make more opportunities than he finds. *English*

10056. A wise man will make tools of what comes to hand. *English*

10057. A wise man won't call a fool a fool, but a fool will always call a wise man a fool. *Russian*

10058. A wise man will not reprove a fool. *Chinese*

10059. A wise man wonders at nothing. *American*

10060. A wise man would rather die than close his ears to the voice of reason. *Greek*

10061. A young man negligent, an old man necessitous. *English*

10062. After a feast a man scratches his head. *French*

10063. An angry man is a brother of the madman. *Lebanese*

10064. An angry man knows no reason. *Philippine*

10065. An envious man is a squint-eyed fool. *English*

10066. An envious man waxes lean with the fatness of his neighbor.
English

10067. An honest man does not make himself a dog for the sake of a bone.
Danish

10068. An idle man is the devil's pillow. *Dutch*

10069. An ignorant man is despised even by women. *Indian (Tamil)*

10070. An old man in the home is a curse, an old woman a blessing.
Hebrew

10071. An old man in the house is a snare in the house; an old woman in the house is a treasure in the house.
Hebrew

10072. An old man is a bed full of bones. *English*

10073. An old man is a child for a long time. *Icelandic*

10074. An old man is not to be laughed at. *African (Ovambo)*

10075. An old man never wants a tale to tell. *English*

10076. An old man will not dance to make laughter. *African (Fulani)*

10077. An ugly man does not often look into the glass. *Serbo-Croatian*

10078. Another man's trade costs money. *Portuguese*

10079. Anything can happen—even the rich man can knock at the poor man's door. *Russian*

10080. As a man dresses so is he esteemed. *Danish*

10081. As a man eats, so he works.
German

10082. As a man lives, so shall he die; as a tree falls so shall it lie.   *English*

10083. As for man wisdom, as for woman affection.   *Japanese*

10084. As long as a man is not dead, his chance of becoming wealthy is not over yet.   *Lebanese*

10085. As many steps a man has paced, so many sins has he committed.   *Russian*

10086. As the man is, so is his speech.   *Danish*

10087. As the man is worth his land is worth.   *French*

10088. Better a man of straw than a woman of gold.   *Rumanian*

10089. Better be the happy man than the happy man's son.   *Scottish*

10090. Better to lose with a wise man than to win with a fool.   *Yiddish*

10091. Between promising and performing a man may marry his daughter.   *English*

10092. Beware of the man of two faces.   *Dutch*

10093. Blessed be the man who knows his power and abstains from doing evil to others.   *Egyptian*

10094. Blessed is the man who has friends, but woe to him who needs them.   *Czech*

10095. Connected with a great man, you will advance.   *African (Efik)*

10096. Could a man foresee events he would never be poor.   *French*

10097. Either a strong man or a fool tells the truth.   *Pashto*

10098. Even a poor man wants to live.   *Yiddish*

10099. Even a wise man makes one error in a thousand considerations.   *Japanese*

10100. Even the proud man has to die; even the defiant will turn to dust.   *African (Ovambo)*

10101. Every gracious man is also a grateful man.   *English*

10102. Every ill man has his ill day.   *English*

10103. Every man a knave till found honest.   *English*

10104. Every man a little beyond himself is a fool.   *English*

10105. Every man after the fashion.   *English*

10106. Every man as he loves. *English*

10107. Every man as his business lies.   *English*

10108. Every man at his trade.   *American*

10109. Every man at thirty is a fool or a physician.   *Scottish*

10110. Every man bastes the fat hog.   *English*

10111. Every man before he dies shall see the devil.   *English*

10112. Every man bows to the bush he gets shelter of.   *Scottish*

10113. Every man can guide an ill wife but he that has her.   *Scottish*

10114. Every man can rule a shrew.   *English*

10115. Every man can rule a shrew but he who has her.   *English*

10116. Every man cannot hit the nail on the head.   *English*

10117. Every man cannot speak with the king.   *English*

10118. Every man carries his worth in his basket.   *Hebrew*

10119. Every man for himself.   *English*

10120. Every man for himself and God for us all.   *English*

10121. Every man for himself and the devil for all. *English*

10122. Every man gnaw on his own bone. *English*

10123. Every man has a fool in his sleeve. *English*

10124. Every man has a madness of his own. *Yiddish*

10125. Every man has a name.
African (Ovambo)

10126. Every man has his burden.
Yiddish

10127. Every man has his faults.
English

10128. Every man has his humor.
English

10129. Every man has his value.
French

10130. Every man has one fault.
Japanese

10131. Every man in his way. *English*

10132. Every man is a fool sometimes, and none at all times. *Scottish*

10133. Every man is a king at home.
English

10134. Every man is best known to himself. *English*

10135. Every man is blind in his own cause. *Scottish*

10136. Every man is blind to his own faults. *Yiddish*

10137. Every man is bold until he is at a public assembly. *Irish*

10138. Every man is dearest to himself.
German

10139. Every man is king in his own house. *Iranian*

10140. Every man is master at home.
Icelandic

10141. Every man is not born to be a boatswain. *English*

10142. Every man is not born with a silver spoon in his mouth. *Scottish*

10143. Every man is the architect of his own fortune. *English*

10144. Every man knows he will die but no one wants to believe it. *Yiddish*

10145. Every man knows the lining of his own cloak. *Serbo-Croatian*

10146. Every man likes his own praise best. *Danish*

10147. Every man must bear his own burden. *English*

10148. Every man must carry his own sack to the mill. *Danish*

10149. Every man must learn once.
American

10150. Every man must row with such oars as he has. *English*

10151. Every man rides his own hobby.
German

10152. Every man thinks he may live another year. *English*

10153. Every man thinks his own copper gold. *German*

10154. Every man thinks well of his own abilities. *African (Hausa)*

10155. Every man to his business.
English

10156. Every man to his craft.
English

10157. Every man to his taste.
French

10158. Every man to his trade.
English

10159. Every man wears his belt in his own fashion. *Scottish*

10160. Every man will shoot at the enemy, but few will gather the shafts.
English

10161. Every man wishes water to his own mill. *English*

10162. Every poor man is a fool.
English

10163. Every wise man has a measure of simplicity. *Russian*

10164. Every wise man has been attributed with his share of simplicities.
Russian

10165. For an honest man half his wits are enough; the whole is too little for a knave. *Italian*

10166. Fortunate is the man who has a happy old age. *Yiddish*

10167. Get the coffin ready and the man won't die. *Chinese*

10168. Give a grateful man more than he asks. *Portuguese*

10169. Give the wise man a hint and leave him to act. *Italian*

10170. Happy is the man who has a handsome wife close to an abbey.
French

10171. Happy man, happy dole.
English

10172. He is a clever man who can drive away hunger by working his jaw.
Jamaican

10173. He's a good man whom fortune makes better. *English*

10174. He is a man who acts like a man. *Danish*

10175. He's a silly man that can neither do good nor ill. *Scottish*

10176. He is a wise man who can make a friend of a foe. *Scottish*

10177. He's no wise man who cannot play the fool by a time. *Scottish*

10178. He is not a man who cannot say no. *Italian*

10179. He is not a thorough wise man who cannot play the fool on occasion.
Italian

10180. He is not a wise man that cannot play the fool. *English*

10181. He is truly a superior man who can watch a chess game in silence.
Chinese

10182. He who is a man does not make a mistake twice. *Turkish*

10183. He who rides in the chair is a man; he who carries the chair is also a man. *Chinese*

10184. However swift a man, he will not outstrip his shadow.
African (Fulani)

10185. If a clever man is angry, his wisdom quits him. *Hebrew*

10186. If a man does not receive guests at home, he will meet very few hosts abroad. *Chinese*

10187. If a man has folly in his sleeve, it will be sure to peep out. *Danish*

10188. If a man is evil, men fear him but Heaven does not; if a man is virtuous, men oppress him but Heaven does not. *Chinese*

10189. If a man is generally charitable, he will be unkind toward his wife.
Yiddish

10190. If a man knew where he would fall he would spread straw first.
Russian

10191. If a man once falls, all will tread on him. *English*

10192. If a man tells his secrets to his wife, she will bring him into the way of Satan. *African (Kanuri)*

10193. If a man wants a good dinner, he must pay for it. *American*

10194. If a man wants a hare for his breakfast he must hunt overnight.
English

10195. If man cheats the earth, the earth will cheat man. *Chinese*

10196. If the man lets a woman know what he has got in his saving box, she will marry him for his money.
Maltese

10197. If the poor man associates with the rich, he will soon have no trousers to wear. *Chinese*

10198. If the young man would, and the old man could, there would be nothing undone. *English*

10199. If you can't overcome a man, you would best call him your friend. *Jamaican*

10200. If you suspect a man, don't employ him; if you employ a man, don't suspect him. *Chinese*

10201. In bowing in a dark place each man follows his own inclination. *Chinese*

10202. In sleep man doesn't sin, but his dreams do. *Yiddish*

10203. In the land of promise a man may die of hunger. *Dutch*

10204. It's better to be with a wise man in hell than with a fool in paradise. *Yiddish*

10205. It is good to beat a proud man when he is alone. *French*

10206. It is hard for a man who stands to talk to one who is seated. *Russian*

10207. It is little that a talkative man escapes. *African (Fulani)*

10208. Let every man care about his own honor as best he can. *German*

10209. Let every man carry his own sack to the mill. *Danish*

10210. Let every man skin his own skunks. *American*

10211. Man builds castles, time ruins them. *Russian*

10212. Man builds the house, but woman makes the home. *Jamaican*

10213. Man can cure disease, but not fate. *Chinese*

10214. Man cannot be always fortunate; flowers do not last forever. *Chinese*

10215. Man cannot be measured by an ell. *Polish*

10216. Man cannot count on certain victory. *Japanese*

10217. Man carries the powder and God the bullets. *Polish*

10218. Man consecrates the land. *Rumanian*

10219. Man does what he can and God what He will. *English*

10220. Man for his courage, woman for her attractiveness. *Japanese*

10221. Man has a thousand schemes; Heaven has but one. *Chinese*

10222. Man has both life and death. *Rumanian*

10223. Man has two eyes, two ears, but only one mouth. *Yiddish*

10224. Man is a God to man. *English*

10225. Man is a pine tree, woman a wisteria vine. *Japanese*

10226. Man is a walking corpse. *Russian*

10227. Man is a wingless bird. *Lebanese*

10228. Man is a wolf to man. *English*

10229. Man is born to die. *Yiddish*

10230. Man is fire, woman is tow, and the devil comes and blows. *French*

10231. Man is for one generation; his name is for all ages to come. *Japanese*

10232. Man is for wartime, woman for peacetime. *Vietnamese*

10233. Man is Heaven and earth in miniature. *Chinese*

10234. Man is like pepper: not till you chew him do you know his heat. *African (Hausa)*

10235. Man is like the sheep: one readily follows after another. *Rumanian*

10236. Man is, of all creation, the spiritual intelligence. *Chinese*

10237. Man is only man by his money.
Egyptian

10238. Man is sometimes stronger than iron and at other times weaker than a fly. *Yiddish*

10239. Man is the head but woman turns it. *English*

10240. Man is the only animal that is hungry with his belly full. *American*

10241. Man is the slave of beneficence.
Egyptian

10242. Man is what he is, but not what he used to be. *Yiddish*

10243. Man keeps hoping till he goes to his eternal slumber. *Yiddish*

10244. Man knows where he came from but not where he is going.
African (Ovambo)

10245. Man learns as long as he lives and then dies ignorant.
Serbo-Croatian

10246. Man learns till his death.
Estonian

10247. Man learns till seventy but still dies an ignoramus. *Yiddish*

10248. Man looks only on the outside of things; God looks into the very heart.
African (Efik)

10249. Man loves but once. *German*

10250. Man plans many things; God alters his plans. *Greek*

10251. Man proposes but God disposes. *English*

10252. Man rears animals and animals keep man alive. *Vietnamese*

10253. Man rides, but God holds the reins. *Yiddish*

10254. Man sees the gain, not the danger. *Chinese*

10255. Man shoots, but God guides the bullet. *Polish*

10256. Man should take as companion one older than himself.
African (Wolof)

10257. Man thinks and God laughs.
Yiddish

10258. Man without woman is head without body; woman without man is body without head. *German*

10259. Many a man labors for the day he will never live to see. *Danish*

10260. May the man be damned and never grow fat who wears two faces under one hat. *English*

10261. Never have anything to do with an unlucky man or place. *American*

10262. No living man all things can.
English

10263. No man can do two things at once. *English*

10264. No man can live longer in peace than his neighbor pleases.
Scottish

10265. No man can master his own mind. *English*

10266. No man can please all.
English

10267. No man can serve two masters.
English

10268. No man can stand always upon his guard. *English*

10269. No man comes to heaven with dry eyes. *English*

10270. No man dares to be rude to his creditor. *Hebrew*

10271. No man is a hero in the eyes of his valet. *French*

10272. No man is born wise. *English*

10273. No man is going to die till his time comes. *American*

10274. No man is his craft's master the first day. *English*

10275. No man is so tall that he need never stretch, and none so small that he need never stoop. *Danish*

10276. No man knows what is good except he who has endured evil. *English*

10277. No man learns but by pain or shame. *Dutch*

10278. No man limps because another is hurt. *Danish*

10279. No man lives so poor as he was born. *English*

10280. No man lives without a fault. *English*

10281. No man loves his fetters, though they be made of gold. *English*

10282. No man makes haste to the market where there's nothing to be bought but blows. *English*

10283. No man so good, but another may be as good as he. *English*

10284. No man tells lies at death's door. *Hebrew*

10285. No man understands knavery better than the abbot who has been a monk. *French*

10286. On the day of trouble, a free man chooses patience. *African (Hausa)*

10287. Once a man repents, stop reminding him of what he did. *Hebrew*

10288. Once a man, twice a child. *English*

10289. One cannot be a wealthy man from the first. *Japanese*

10290. One honest man is worth two rogues. *English*

10291. One honest man scares twenty thieves. *English*

10292. One man is not bad because another is good. *Danish*

10293. One man knocks in the nail, and another hangs his hat on it. *German*

10294. One man laughs at another, and the devil at all. *Rumanian*

10295. One man likes sour cream and the other prayer. *Yiddish*

10296. One man may lead a horse to the water, but four and twenty will not make him drink. *Scottish*

10297. One man tells a falsehood, a hundred repeat it as true. *Chinese*

10298. One wise man is worth more than a million fools. *Greek*

10299. Out of stubbornness many a man goes from heaven to hell. *Yiddish*

10300. Praise no man till he is dead. *English*

10301. Respect a man, he will do the more. *English*

10302. Self is the man. *German*

10303. Send a wise man on an errand and say nothing to him. *English*

10304. She who loves an ugly man thinks him handsome. *Spanish*

10305. Show me the man, and I will show you the law. *English*

10306. Take a man by his word, and a cow by her horn. *Scottish*

10307. The blind man is not afraid of ghosts. *Burmese*

10308. The contented man, though poor, is happy; the discontented man, though rich, is sad. *Chinese*

10309. The cowless man cannot get rid of his poverty. *African (Ovambo)*

10310. The dead man is abused. *African (Ovambo)*

10311. The drowning man is not troubled by rain. *Iranian*

10312. The dumb man gets no land. *English*

10313. The envious man shall never want woe. *English*

10314. The experienced man is a small prophet. *Slovenian*

10315. The fat man knows not what the lean thinks. *English*

10316. The fearless man is the first to be wounded. *Serbo-Croatian*

10317. The generous man grows rich in giving, the miser poor in taking. *Danish*

10318. The good looking man is king, if there is no rich man near. *African (Hausa)*

10319. The great man makes the great thing. *American*

10320. The happy man cannot be ruined. *Scottish*

10321. The hasty man never wants woe. *English*

10322. The healthful man can give counsel to the sick. *English*

10323. The honester man, the worse luck. *English*

10324. The hungry man is not satiated by looking in the face of the full man. *Turkish*

10325. The intelligent man is the one that knows how to put two and two together. *Hebrew*

10326. The just man laughs and the guilty hides himself. *Serbo-Croatian*

10327. The lazy man is not ashamed of begging. *African (Ovambo)*

10328. The loyal man lives no longer than the traitor pleases. *Spanish*

10329. The lucky man waits for prosperity. *Irish*

10330. The man destined to happiness need not be in a hurry. *Chinese*

10331. The man has neither sense nor reason who leaves a young wife at home. *French*

10332. The man in pain suffers while his neighbors sleep. *Greek*

10333. The man of your own trade is your enemy. *Portuguese*

10334. The man on horseback knows nothing of the toil of the traveler on foot. *Chinese*

10335. The man shall have his mare again. *English*

10336. The man thinks he knows, but the woman knows better. *Indian (Hindustani)*

10337. The man who controls his wrath conquers his foe. *Greek*

10338. The man who does not demand his rights is buried alive. *Greek*

10339. The man who eavesdrops hears himself discussed. *Greek*

10340. The man who ensnares birds is always on the watch. *Hawaiian*

10341. The man who goes to law often loses an ox to win a cat. *Rumanian*

10342. The man who knows not what is good is not counted a man. *Turkish*

10343. The man who lives in a glass house does not throw stones at his neighbors. *Greek*

10344. The man who offers you tobacco and lime unasked is sure to go to heaven. *Indian (Bihar)*

10345. The man whose stomach is well filled has little sympathy with the wants of the hungry. *Irish*

10346. The man without eyes is no judge of beauty. *Irish*

10347. The married man has many cares, the unmarried one many more. *Finnish*

10348. The more you drive a man, the less he will do. *American*

10349. The mounted man doesn't believe the man that goes afoot. *Rumanian*

10350. The old man shows what the young man was.   *Swedish*

10351. The patient man cooks a stone till he drinks broth from it.
African (Hausa)

10352. The polite man has learned from the unpolite.   *Turkish*

10353. The poor man and the rich man do not play together. *African (Ashanti)*

10354. The poor man does not go on a journey.   *African (Bemba)*

10355. The poor man has his crop destroyed by hail every year.   *Spanish*

10356. The poor man has no friend.
African (Ashanti)

10357. The poor man has only one sickness, the rich man a hundred.
Czech

10358. The poor man pays for all.
Scottish

10359. The poor man seeks for food, the rich man for appetite.   *Danish*

10360. The poor man turns his cake and another comes and eats it.
English

10361. The poor man wants much, the miser everything.   *Danish*

10362. The properer man the worse luck.   *English*

10363. The rich man displays his wealth and the poor one his children.
Greek

10364. The rich man eats when it seems good to him, and the poor when he can.   *Serbo-Croatian*

10365. The rich man gets calves, the poor man children.   *Russian*

10366. The rich man has his brains in his billfold.   *Yiddish*

10367. The rich man has more relations than he knows.   *French*

10368. The rich man has only two holes to his nose, the same as the poor man.   *Polish*

10369. The rich man is a poor man indeed.   *African (Swahili)*

10370. The rich man plans for the future, but the poor man for the present.
Chinese

10371. The rich man transgresses the law, and the poor man is punished.
Spanish

10372. The rich man wonders how the poor man lives, but God helps him.
Russian

10373. The richest man carries nothing away with him but a shroud.
French

10374. The richest man, whatever his lot, is he who's content with what he has got.   *Dutch*

10375. The righteous man has many hardships.   *Japanese*

10376. The rude man shall be rudely treated.   *Greek*

10377. The satisfied man knows nothing of hunger, and the laughing man nothing of tears.   *Finnish*

10378. The sick man is free to say all.
Italian

10379. The silent man is most trusted.
Danish

10380. The singing man keeps his shop in his throat.   *English*

10381. The slothful man is the beggar's brother.   *English*

10382. The timid man loses many good things.   *Greek*

10383. The useless man is like sand; though it be rolled together it will not stay rolled.   *African (Hausa)*

10384. The well-fed man does not believe in hunger.   *Italian*

10385. The wet man fears no rain.
Rumanian

10386. The wily man doesn't buy snuff till he has sampled it.
African (Hausa)

10387. The wise man cannot recover the stone which the fool threw into the well.   *Serbo-Croatian*

10388. The wise man does at first what the fool does at last.   *Indian (Hindi)*

10389. The wise man does not hang his knowledge on a hook.   *Spanish*

10390. The wise man, even when he holds his tongue, says more than the fool when he speaks.   *English*

10391. The wise man has long ears and a short tongue.   *German*

10392. The wise man is deceived but once, the fool twice.   *English*

10393. The wise man must carry the fool upon his shoulders.   *English*

10394. The wisest man is guilty of folly.   *Yiddish*

10395. There is many a good man to be found under a shabby hat.   *Chinese*

10396. To a healthy man everything is healthy.   *Russian*

10397. To a hungry man it is always noon.   *Russian*

10398. To the grateful man give more than he asks.   *Spanish*

10399. Those or that which a man knows best, he must use most. *English*

10400. Though you are a prudent old man do not despise counsel. *Spanish*

10401. Today a man, tomorrow a cuckold.   *English*

10402. Today a man, tomorrow a mouse.   *English*

10403. Today a man, tomorrow none.
English

10404. Under a good cloak may be a bad man.   *Spanish*

10405. Until a man dies his value is not known.   *Turkish*

10406. Until a man takes trouble he does not get treasure.
Indian (Kashmiri)

10407. What a deaf man doesn't hear, he imagines.   *Yiddish*

10408. What a man says in private, Heaven hears as the voice of thunder.
Chinese

10409. What a sober man thinks, a drunkard speaks.   *Yiddish*

10410. What a wise man bewails makes the fool happy.   *Yiddish*

10411. What's a man but his mind?
English

10412. What one man eats and is satisfied by, another eats and dies.
African (Fulani)

10413. What the sober man keeps in his heart is on the tongue of the drunkard.   *French*

10414. What the sober man thinks, the drunkard tells.   *Dutch*

10415. When a divorced man marries a divorced woman, there are four opinions in the marriage bed.   *Hebrew*

10416. When a man becomes an old bachelor, he makes his own fireplace.
African (Yoruba)

10417. When a man grows angry his reason rides out.   *English*

10418. When a man has no one to play with he plays with his enemy.
African (Annang)

10419. When a man is disliked he is blamed for all kinds of things.
African (Ashanti)

10420. When a man is down, everybody runs over him.   *German*

10421. When a man is going down, everybody lends him a kick.
American

10422. When a man is poor he remembers old debts due him. *Chinese*

10423. When a man just sits and eats, even a mountain becomes nothing. *Japanese*

10424. When a man sees sunshine he dries his tobacco. *African (Efik)*

10425. When a poor man cries for help, only God will aid him. *African (Ovambo)*

10426. When a wise man talks to a fool, two fools are talking. *Yiddish*

10427. When drunk a man reveals his true self. *Japanese*

10428. When every man gets his own, the thief will get the gallows. *Scottish*

10429. When it rains soup the poor man has no spoons. *Swedish*

10430. When man is absent, the home is empty; when the woman is absent, the kitchen is empty. *Vietnamese*

10431. When the blind man carries the banner, woe to those who follow. *French*

10432. When the man oversleeps the wife can only look on. *Hawaiian*

10433. Where a man feels pain he lays his hand. *Dutch*

10434. Where a man never goes, there his head will never be washed. *Danish*

10435. Where a tall man puts up a thing, a short one cannot get it down. *African (Bemba)*

10436. Wherever a man goes to dwell, his character goes with him. *African (Yoruba)*

10437. Without a true friend the intelligent man cannot know the mistakes that he makes. *Chinese*

10438. You may be a wise man though you can't make a watch. *English*

MANNER

10439. Better good manners than good looks. *Irish*

10440. Look at the manners of others and mend your manners. *Japanese*

10441. Manners and money make a gentleman. *English*

10442. Manners make often fortunes. *English*

10443. Manners make the man. *English*

MANTIS

10444. The mantis seizes the locust but does not see the yellow bird behind him. *Chinese*

MANTLE

10445. Spread your mantle only as you can draw it. *Irish*

MANURE

10446. Better manure than unfertile soil. *African (Fulani)*

10447. He who carries manure gets soiled with it. *Maltese*

10448. Manure is the farmer's gold. *Estonian*

MARBLE

10449. Those that have marbles may play, but those that have none must look on. *English*

MARE

10450. A white mare needs washing; a pretty wife, watching. *Latvian*

10451. Once you have sold the mare you may burn the saddle. *Russian*

10452. The mare is not to be valued according to its housing and its ornaments in front. *Egyptian*

MARK

10453. Great marks are soonest hit. *English*

10454. He must shoot well who always hits the mark. *Dutch*

10455. Often shooting hits the mark. *German*

MARKET

10456. A market is not held for the sake of one person. *African (Fulani)*

10457. As the market goes wares must sell. *Scottish*

10458. As the market goes wives must sell. *English*

10459. Buy when it is market time. *German*

10460. Foresake not the market for the toll. *English*

10461. He loses his market who has nothing to sell. *Spanish*

10462. He that cannot abide a bad market deserves not a good one. *English*

10463. If you send no one to the market, the market will send no one to you. *African (Yoruba)*

10464. Make the best of a bad market. *Scottish*

10465. Markets have customs and communes have traditions. *Vietnamese*

10466. Once you have gone to market you have told the whole world. *Russian*

10467. One doesn't go to market with his own price. *Russian*

10468. One here, two there, so the market is filled up. *African (Yoruba)*

10469. The market is the best garden. *English*

10470. The market of debauch is always open. *Egyptian*

10471. There is no market for empty purses. *Russian*

10472. You may know by the market folks how the market goes. *English*

10473. You must sell as markets go. *English*

MARKETING

10474. It is bad marketing with empty pockets. *Dutch*

MARKSMAN

10475. A good marksman may miss. *English*

MARRIAGE

10476. A compulsory marriage does not endure. *Japanese*

10477. A late marriage, orphaned children. *Greek*

10478. A marriage between a young man and an old woman is made by the devil. *Philippine*

10479. An ill marriage is a spring of ill fortune. *English*

10480. At marriages and funerals friends are discerned from kinsfolk. *English*

10481. Early marriage, long love. *German*

10482. Even a good marriage is a time of trial. *Russian*

10483. For marriage and time wait for the final moment. *Japanese*

10484. Happy the marriage where the husband is the head and the wife the heart. *Estonian*

10485. He has a great fancy to marriage that goes to the devil for a wife. *English*

10486. If marriages be made in heaven, some had few friends there. *Scottish*

10487. In marriage cheat who can. *French*

10488. Marriage and cooking call for forethought. *Greek*

10489. Marriage and hanging go by destiny. *English*

10490. Marriages are made in heaven. *English*

10491. Marriages are not as they are made, but as they turn out. *Italian*

10492. Marriages are written in heaven. *French*

10493. Marriage is a lottery. *English*

10494. Marriage is heaven and hell. *German*

10495. Marriage is honorable but housekeeping is a shrew. *English*

10496. Marriage is no joke; it is not like rice which can be spat out if it is too hot. *Philippine*

10497. Marriage is not a mere trial; it is forever. *Philippine*

10498. Marriage is not a race; you can always get there in time. *Russian*

10499. Marriage is not like a patch which you can take off whenever you like. *Maltese*

10500. Marriage is the tomb of love. *Russian*

10501. Marriage leaps up upon the saddle, and repentance upon the crupper. *English*

10502. Marriage with peace is this world's Paradise; with strife, this life's Purgatory. *English*

10503. Marriage with the first wife is made in Heaven; with the second it's arranged by people. *Yiddish*

10504. Marriage without good faith is like a teapot without a tray. *Moroccan*

10505. More belongs to marriage than four bare legs in a bed. *English*

10506. One marriage is never celebrated but another grows out of it. *German*

10507. The best part of marriage is from the day of engagement to the wedding. *Maltese*

10508. There is marriage but there is no "dismarriage." *Russian*

MARRY

10509. Always say no, and you will never be married. *French*

10510. Before you marry consider what you do. *Portuguese*

10511. Before you marry make sure of a house wherein to tarry. *English*

10512. Before you marry reflect, for it is a knot you cannot untie. *Portuguese*

10513. He that goes to mary likes to know whether he shall have a chimney to his house. *English*

10514. He that marries late marries ill. *English*

10515. He who is about to marry should consider how it is with his neighbors. *English*

10516. He who marries does well, but who remains single does better. *German*

10517. He who marries ill, is long in becoming widowed. *Spanish*

10518. He who marries might be sorry; he who does not will be sorry. *Czech*

10519. If you marry in Lent you will live to repent. *English*

10520. It is better to marry a quiet fool than a witty scold. *English*

10521. It's good to marry late or never. *English*

10522. Marry and grow tame. *Spanish*

10523. Marry first and love will follow. *English*

10524. Married in a hurry and stuck for good! *Yiddish*

10525. Marry in haste and be sorry at your leisure. *Irish*

10526. Marry in haste, repent at leisure. *English*

10527. Married today, marred tomorrow. *French*

10528. Marry your daughters betimes, lest they marry themselves. *English*

10529. Marry your son when you will; your daughter when you can. *English*

10530. To marry once is a duty; twice a folly; thrice is madness. *Dutch*

10531. Who marries between the sickle and the scythe will never thrive. *English*

10532. Who marries does well, who marries not does better. *English*

10533. Who marries for love without money has merry nights and sorry days. *English*

MARRYING

10534. Marrying and dying are two things for which one is never late. *Yiddish*

10535. Marrying is easy, but housekeeping is hard. *German*

MASON

10536. He is not a good mason who refuses any stone. *Italian*

MASS (crowd)

10537. The masses are asses. *Yiddish*

MASS (holy)

10538. Mass and meat never hindered work. *English*

MASTER (noun)

10539. A bad master quarrels even with his broom. *Greek*

10540. A falling master makes a standing servant. *Scottish*

10541. A master of straw eats a servant of steel. *English*

10542. A master speaks but few words. *Greek*

10543. A real master needs no flagstaff. *Burmese*

10544. A sleepy master makes his servant a lout. *English*

10545. A thousand masters, a thousand methods. *Chinese*

10546. An ill master makes an ill servant. *English*

10547. An ill master makes bad scholars. *English*

10548. As the master is, so are his men. *Danish*

10549. As is the master, so is his dog. *Spanish*

10550. As the master, so the work. *German*

10551. Before you utter a word you are the master; afterwards you're a fool. *Yiddish*

10552. Better speak to the master, than the man. *English*

10553. Early master, soon servant. *Scottish*

10554. Even the walls of a house weep when the master is away. *Russian*

10555. Everyone has his master. *German*

10556. Everyone is a master and servant. *English*

10557. Everyone is master in his own house. *English*

10558. Good masters make good servants. *English*

10559. He can ill be master that never was scholar. *English*

10560. He is master of another man's life who is indifferent to his own. *Italian*

10561. He must indeed be a good master who never errs. *Dutch*

10562. He that is master must serve another. *English*

10563. He that is master of himself will soon be master of others. *English*

10564. He that would be master of his own must not be bound for another. *Scottish*

10565. He who builds by the roadside has many masters. *German*

10566. He who has studied himself is his own master. *Indian (Tamil)*

10567. He who has two masters to serve must lie to one of them. *Spanish*

10568. He who pays well is master of other men's purses. *Italian*

10569. He who rides the horse is his master. *Danish*

10570. He who serves many masters must neglect some of them. *Spanish*

10571. He who serves two masters must lie to one of them. *Italian*

10572. He who will not serve one master must needs serve many. *Italian*

10573. If masters are masters, servants are servants. *Japanese*

10574. If the master says the crow is white, the servant must not say it is black. *English*

10575. Like master, like man. *English*

10576. Master easy, servant slack. *Chinese*

10577. Masters should be sometimes blind, and sometimes deaf. *English*

10578. No better masters than poverty and want. *Dutch*

10579. None is born master. *English*

10580. Nothing so bad but it finds its master. *Dutch*

10581. The master does not ask the donkey if he may load him. *Serbo-Croatian*

10582. The master is kind but his hands hold the cane. *Yiddish*

10583. The master of the house is the servant of his guest. *Turkish*

10584. When the master is away the mice play on the table. *Rumanian*

MASTER (verb)

10585. Better master one than engage with ten. *English*

10586. Better master one than fight with ten. *Scottish*

MAT

10587. Though you sleep in a thousand-mat room, you occupy only one mat. *Japanese*

MATCH

10588. An ill-assorted match is the source of discord. *Japanese*

10589. Marry above your match, and you get a master. *Scottish*

MATCHMAKER

10590. Nine out of ten matchmakers are liars. *Chinese*

10591. The matchmaker gets the first cup and the first stick. *Russian*

10592. The unwed matchmaker looks for himself. *Greek*

MATTER

10593. A great matter puts a smaller out of sight. *African (Yoruba)*

10594. It is not matter but the mind. *English*

MATURITY

10595. Early maturity, early senility.
Japanese

MAXIM

10596. A good maxim is never out of season. *English*

MEAD

10597. Little mead, little need.
English

MEADOW

10598. A thin meadow is soon mowed.
English

10599. Better walk unshackled in a green meadow than be bound to a thornbush. *Danish*

MEAL (food)

10600. A forbidden meal is quickly eaten. *Swedish*

10601. A meal for the priest, a mouthful for the deacon. *Greek*

10602. A meal without salt is no meal.
Hebrew

10603. Better are meals many than one too merry. *English*

10604. He fasts enough that has a bad meal. *English*

10605. Quick at meals, quick at work.
English

10606. Two hungry meals make the third a glutton. *English*

MEAL (grain)

10607. There's no getting white meal out of a coal sack. *English*

MEANING

10608. The meaning is best known to the speaker. *French*

MEANS

10609. Live according to your means.
Danish

10610. Use the means, and God will give the blessing. *English*

MEASURE (noun)

10611. Feed by measure and defy the physician. *English*

10612. He that loves measure and skill often has his will. *English*

10613. Measure for measure. *English*

10614. Measure is a merry mean.
English

10615. Measure is medicine. *English*

10616. Measure is treasure. *English*

10617. When the measure is full, it runs over. *German*

MEASURE (verb)

10618. Better twice measured than once wrong. *Danish*

10619. Don't measure others by yourself. *Philippine*

10620. He that measures not himself is measured. *English*

10621. Measure seven times, but cut only once. *Russian*

10622. Measure ten times before you cut once. *Slovakian*

10623. Measure three times and cut once. *Italian*

10624. Measure twice, cut but once.
Scottish

MEAT

10625. A hungry man's meat is long in making ready. *Scottish*

10626. A piece of meat isn't the dog's portion unless it falls on the ground.
African (Hausa)

10627. All meat is not the same in every man's mouth. *English*

10628. All meats to be eaten, all maids to be wed. *English*

10629. Fat meat is known when taken close to the fire. *African (Hausa)*

10630. He who buys meat has to take the bone with it. *Norwegian*

10631. However lean the meat may be, it goes well upon bread. *Turkish*

10632. If there is no meat, be content with broth. *Philippine*

10633. If you miss the meat, take the soup. *Lebanese*

10634. Locust meat is better than pumpkin relish. *African (Shona)*

10635. Meat and mass hinder no man's journey. *English*

10636. Meat and mass hinder no man's work. *English*

10637. Meat does not rot in a day. *African (Shona)*

10638. Meat is made for mouths. *English*

10639. Meat is much but manners is more. *English*

10640. Meat is sold with bones. *Greek*

10641. Meat twice cooked and a friend twice reconciled are hardly ever good. *Czech*

10642. Much meat, much malady. *English*

10643. New meat begets a new appetite. *English*

10644. One man's meat is another man's poison. *English*

10645. Sweet meat will have sour sauce. *English*

10646. The meat close to the fire is best cooked. *African (Hausa)*

10647. There is no such thing as boneless meat. *Hebrew*

10648. When meat is in anger is out. *English*

10649. Who has eaten the meat knows how it tastes. *German*

MECCA

10650. Mecca is not far for him who intends to make the pilgrimage. *Lebanese*

MEDAL

10651. Every medal has its reverse. *French*

MEDDLE

10652. Meddle not in what you don't understand. *Portuguese*

MEDDLING

10653. Of little meddling, comes great rest. *English*

10654. Of much meddling, comes no sound sleeping. *English*

MEDICINE

10655. Even medicine when exceeded becomes poison. *Japanese*

10656. For lovesickness there is no medicine. *Japanese*

10657. If favored by fortune medicine will take effect in due time. *Indian (Tamil)*

10658. If there is neither food nor drink, plain water is medicine. *African (Hausa)*

10659. Medicine does not depend on the incantations of the sorcerer. *African (Annang)*

10660. Medicine is not roast beef. *Maltese*

10661. Medicine will not revive him doomed to die. *African (Hausa)*

10662. Medicines be not meat to live by. *English*

10663. No medicine can cure a vulgar man. *Chinese*

10664. The best medicine against troubles is to keep quiet. *African (Bemba)*

10665. There is no medicine against old age. *African (Yoruba)*

10666. There is no medicine for sexual passion. *Japanese*

10667. There is no medicine to apply to a fool. *Japanese*

10668. There is no medicine to cure hatred. *African (Ashanti)*

10669. There is no such thing as tasty medicine. *Hebrew*

10670. We must bear the medicine on account of its usefulness. *Egyptian*

10671. Without measure medicine will become poison. *Polish*

MEET

10672. Merry meet, merry part. *English*

10673. Those who meet must part. *Korean*

MEETING

10674. A hasty meeting, a hasty parting. *English*

10675. There's no meeting of the minds. *Russian*

MELANCHOLY

10676. To a lover, melancholy is no shame. *Turkish*

MELON

10677. A melon and a woman are hard to know. *Spanish*

10678. All that one cuts falls to the ground, except the melon. *African (Wolof)*

10679. Even a melon seed may come between husband and wife. *Iranian*

10680. From the roof of a house a melon may roll either of two ways. *Chinese*

10681. When the melon is ripe, it will drop of itself. *Chinese*

10682. You cannot carry two watermelons under one arm. *Serbo-Croatian*

10683. You can't pick up two melons with one hand. *Iranian*

MELON SELLER

10684. A melon seller never cries "bitter melons" nor a wine seller "thin wine." *Chinese*

10685. The melon seller declares his melon sweet. *Philippine*

10686. The melon seller shouts that his melons are sweet. *Chinese*

MEMORY

10687. Memory does not forget the promised kiss, but the remembrance of the kiss received is soon lost. *Finnish*

10688. Memory is the treasure of the mind. *English*

10689. Memory will slip, a letter will keep. *Welsh*

10690. Much memory and little judgment. *French*

10691. The memory of happiness makes misery woeful. *English*

MEN (see MAN)

10692. A hundred men will have a hundred different characters. *Vietnamese*

10693. A thousand men may live together in harmony, whereas two women are unable to do so although they be sisters. *Indian (Tamil)*

10694. All men are equal when they are underground. *Hebrew*

10695. All men can't be first. *English*

10696. All men can't be masters. *English*

10697. All men have not wives, and all women are not married.
African (Wolof)

10698. All men think all men mortal but themselves. *English*

10699. Angry men make themselves beds of nettles. *English*

10700. Angry men seldom want woe. *English*

10701. Bad men hurt a good cause. *American*

10702. Better men, better times. *American*

10703. Blind men are not afraid of snakes. *Japanese*

10704. Blind men should not judge colors. *Scottish*

10705. Clever men are often the servants of fools. *Chinese*

10706. Dead men bite not. *English*

10707. Dead men tell no tales. *English*

10708. Deaf men are quick-eyed and distrustful. *English*

10709. Deaf men go away with the blame. *English*

10710. Do as most men do, and men will speak well of you. *English*

10711. Drowning men catch at straws. *English*

10712. Drunken men never take harm. *English*

10713. Evil men, evil times. *American*

10714. Few men and much meat make a feast. *English*

10715. Follow good men and you will learn to be good; follow beggars and you will sleep outside the temple gates. *Chinese*

10716. Good men are a public good. *English*

10717. Good men are scarce. *English*

10718. Great men have great faults. *English*

10719. Great men may jest with saints. *German*

10720. Great men must be obliged. *American*

10721. Honest men do marry but wise men not. *English*

10722. Hungry men think the cook lazy. *English*

10723. Hurried men lack wisdom. *Chinese*

10724. Idle men are dead all their life long. *English*

10725. If all men pulled in one direction, the world would topple over. *Yiddish*

10726. If it is dark, all men are black. *African (Ga)*

10727. If men become sheep, the wolf will devour them. *English*

10728. If one hundred men call a sage a fool, he becomes one. *Albanian*

10729. If the wise men play the fool, they do it with a vengeance. *English*

10730. If two men feed a horse, it will be thin; if two men mend a boat, it will leak. *Chinese*

10731. If you do not ask their help, all men are good natured. *Chinese*

10732. In church, in an inn, and in a coffin, all men are equal. *Polish*

10733. Little men do not hang a bell on a hyena's neck. *African (Ovambo)*

10734. Lucky men need no counsel. *English*

10735. Many men are wise but few are good friends. *Greek*

10736. Many men, many minds. *Chinese*

10737. Men all make mistakes; horses all stumble. *Chinese*

10738. Men always meet but mountains never. *Rumanian*

10739. Men are a bundle of groundnuts, only when one opens them does one know the spotted ones.
African (Hausa)

10740. Men are all made of the same paste. *Rumanian*

10741. Men are as old as they feel, and women as they look. *Italian*

10742. Men are best loved furthest off.
English

10743. Men are blind in their own cause. *English*

10744. Men are crushed to death under the tongue. *Chinese*

10745. Men are easily good and easily bad. *Malagasy*

10746. Men are everywhere the same.
American

10747. Men are mountains and women are levers which move them. *Pashto*

10748. Men are never wise but returning from law. *English*

10749. Men are not to be measured by inches. *English*

10750. Men are willing to believe that which they most desire. *American*

10751. Men can bear all things except good days. *Dutch*

10752. Men carry their superiority inside; animals outside. *Russian*

10753. Men don't all go one road.
Malagasy

10754. Men don't die of threats.
Dutch

10755. Men dream in courtship but in wedlock wake. *English*

10756. Men fear a slip of their writing brush; women, a slip of their virtue.
Chinese

10757. Men fear death. *English*

10758. Men fear the gallows more than God himself. *Yiddish*

10759. Men have their privileges.
American

10760. Men ignore a barking dog.
Burmese

10761. Men in a hurry from dawn until sunset do not live long. *Chinese*

10762. Men know not their own faults; oxen know not their own strength.
Chinese

10763. Men may meet but mountains never. *English*

10764. Men mourn for those who leave fortunes behind. *Chinese*

10765. Men muse as they use. *English*

10766. Men must be sharpened by men; the knife must be ground on the stone. *Chinese*

10767. Men must sail while the wind serves. *Dutch*

10768. Men, not walls, make a city.
Chinese

10769. Men of a certain height must wear clothes of a certain length.
Chinese

10770. Men of principle have courage.
Chinese

10771. Men ought not to be one day without employment. *Chinese*

10772. Men trip not on mountains, they stumble over stones.
Indian (Hindustani)

10773. Men who are too cautious will never gain wisdom. *Chinese*

10774. More men have drowned in Bacchus' waters than in Neptune's.
Mexican

10775. Old men and travelers may lie by authority. *English*

10776. Old men are children for the second time. *Greek*

10777. Old men are twice children.
English

10778. Old men for consultation, young men for quarrels. *Japanese*

10779. Old men go to death; death comes to young men. *English*

10780. Old men will die and children soon forget. *English*

10781. Poor men do penance for rich men's sins. *Italian*

10782. Poor men have no souls.
English

10783. Poor men seek meat for their stomachs; rich men stomachs for their meat. *English*

10784. Prudent men choose frugal wives. *German*

10785. Rich men are often lean and poor men fat. *Yiddish*

10786. Rich men have no faults.
English

10787. Rich men have short memories.
Chinese

10788. Rich men may have what they will. *English*

10789. So many men, so many minds.
English

10790. The best of men are but men at the best. *English*

10791. The men of principle may be the principal men. *English*

10792. There are more men threatened than struck. *English*

10793. There are only two good men; one is dead, and the other is not born.
English

10794. Two blind men cannot guide each other. *African (Shona)*

10795. Two great men cannot stand side by side. *Japanese*

10796. Two men may meet, but never two mountains. *French*

10797. Two old men won't kill each other. *African (Shona)*

10798. We are usually the best men when in the worst health. *English*

10799. Weak men had need be witty.
English

10800. When all men speak, no man hears. *Scottish*

10801. When men are really friends, then even water is sweet. *Chinese*

10802. Where men are well used, they'll frequent there. *English*

10803. Wise men are caught in wiles.
English

10804. Wise men are silent, fools talk.
English

10805. Wise men care not for what they cannot have. *English*

10806. Wise men do not quarrel with each other. *Egyptian*

10807. Wise men go on foot and fools ride. *Yiddish*

10808. Wise men have their mouths in their hearts; fools have their hearts in their mouths. *English*

10809. Wise men in the world are like timber trees in a hedge—here and there one. *English*

10810. Wise men learn by others' faults, fools by their own. *English*

10811. Wise men make proverbs and fools repeat them. *English*

10812. Wise men propose and fools determine. *English*

10813. Without ordinary men, there would be no great men. *Japanese*

10814. Young men may die, old men must. *English*

10815. Young men think old men fools, but old men know the young men are.
English

MEND

10816. Who does not mend the old will never wear the new.   *Serbo-Croatian*

MERCHANDISE

10817. Love's merchandise is jealousy and broken faith.   *Italian*

10818. No merchandise is too expensive to one who has money. *Philippine*

MERCHANT

10819. A merchant that gains not loses.   *English*

10820. Careless merchant, future beggar.   *Greek*

10821. Every merchant praises his own merchandise.   *Russian*

10822. He is not a merchant bare that has moneyworth or ware.   *English*

10823. He that could know what would be dear need be a merchant but one year.   *English*

10824. He that loses is a merchant as well as he that gains.   *English*

10825. Merchants regard each other as foes.   *Japanese*

10826. Merchant today, beggar tomorrow.   *German*

10827. The merchant that loses cannot laugh.   *French*

MERIT

10828. Merit and renown are but gulls floating on the water.   *Chinese*

10829. The merit belongs to the beginner, should even the successor do better.   *Egyptian*

MERRY

10830. All are not merry that dance.   *English*

10831. Better be merry with something, as sad with nothing.   *Scottish*

MESSAGE

10832. He knocks boldly at the door who brings a welcome message.   *Danish*

10833. We should fear him who sends us with a message, not him to whom we are sent.   *African (Yoruba)*

MESSENGER

10834. Stay till the lame messenger come, if you will know the truth of the thing.   *English*

10835. When the messenger of death comes, all affairs cease.   *Chinese*

METAL

10836. Metal is tested by fire, man by wine.   *Japanese*

MICE (see MOUSE)

10837. As there are mice in the house, so are there thieves in the country.   *Korean*

10838. Dead mice feel no cold.   *English*

10839. Even mice do not go to an empty house.   *Serbo-Croatian*

10840. In old houses many mice, in old furs many lice.   *German*

10841. It takes a good many mice to kill a cat.   *Danish*

10842. Mice care not to play with kittens.   *English*

10843. Mice cease to fear the cat when she is too old.   *Burmese*

10844. The mice eat the miser's goods.   *African (Oji)*

10845. Too many mice have no lining for their nest.   *African (Shona)*

MIDWIFE

10846. Do not abuse midwives while there is a delivery.   *African (Swahili)*

10847. Too many midwives kill the baby. *Hebrew*

10848. Two midwives will twist the baby's head. *Iranian*

10849. When the midwife is incompetent she blames the child for it. *Mexican*

10850. Where there are many midwives, the baby is left with the umbilical cord uncut. *Rumanian*

MIGHT

10851. A handful of might is better than a sack full of right. *German*

10852. Better to have a handful of might than a bag of justice. *Czech*

10853. Might and courage require wit in their suite. *Danish*

10854. Might is not right. *Dutch*

10855. Might is overcome. *English*

10856. Might is right. *English*

10857. Might is two-thirds of right. *Irish*

10858. Might knows no right. *French*

10859. Where might is master, justice is servant. *German*

10860. Where might is right, right is not might. *German*

10861. Where there's no might there's no right. *Portuguese*

10862. Who bows to might loses his right. *German*

MILE

10863. Every mile is two in winter. *English*

MILK

10864. After getting burnt on milk, you'll start to blow even on water. *Russian*

10865. That which is taken in with the mother's milk only goes out with the soul. *Russian*

10866. To get milk and eggs you must not frighten the cow and hen. *Tibetan*

MILL

10867. A greedy mill grinds all kinds of corn. *Danish*

10868. A mill and a wife are always in want of something. *Italian*

10869. By going gains the mill, and not by standing still. *Portuguese*

10870. Do not set the mill on fire in order to burn the mice. *Rumanian*

10871. God's mill goes slowly, but it grinds well. *German*

10872. God's mill grinds slow but sure. *English*

10873. He who comes first to the mill is first served. *Danish*

10874. He who comes to the mill consents to his turn. *Turkish*

10875. He who goes to the mill gets befloured. *Italian*

10876. He who remains in the mill grinds, not he who goes to and fro. *Spanish*

10877. In vain does the mill clack, if the miller his hearing lack. *English*

10878. It is one thing in the mill, but another in the sack. *American*

10879. Mills and wives ever want. *English*

10880. Mills will not grind if you give them not water. *English*

10881. No mill, no meal. *English*

10882. No mill will grind wet corn. *Estonian*

10883. One who goes into a mill comes out covered with flour. *Greek*

10884. The mill cannot grind with water that's passed.   *English*

10885. The mill does not grind without water.   *Greek*

10886. The mill gains by going, and not by standing still.   *Spanish*

10887. The mill gets by going.   *English*

10888. The mill goes with the current and woman against it.   *Finnish*

10889. The mill that will grind must have water.   *Welsh*

10890. When one is in the mill one gets dusty.   *Finnish*

10891. When the mill grinds, flour; when tongues grind, trouble. *Russian*

MILLER

10892. An honest miller has a golden thumb.   *English*

10893. Every miller draws water to his own mill.   *Scottish*

10894. Many a miller many a thief.   *English*

10895. Millers and bakers do not steal, people bring to them.   *German*

10896. Put a miller, a tailor, and a weaver into one bag and shake them; the first that comes out will be a thief.   *English*

10897. The miller grinds more men's corn than one.   *English*

10898. The miller is never so drunk that he forgets to take his dues.
Danish

10899. The miller sees not all the water that goes by his mill.   *English*

10900. When the miller fights with the chimneysweep, the miller becomes black and the chimneysweep white.
Yiddish

MILLSTONE

10901. A millstone gathers no moss.
German

10902. It takes both millstones to grind the flour.   *Greek*

10903. The lower millstone grinds as well as the upper.   *English*

10904. The millstone that lies undermost also helps to grind.   *Danish*

MIND

10905. A concentrated mind will pierce a rock.   *Japanese*

10906. A contented mind is a continual feast.   *English*

10907. A mind enlightened is like the halls of Heaven; a mind in darkness is like the realm of Hell.   *Chinese*

10908. A princely mind will undo a private family.   *English*

10909. A willing mind makes a light foot.   *English*

10910. A woman's mind is like the wind in a winter's night.   *English*

10911. An eagle's mind never fits a raven's feather.   *American*

10912. Bearing in mind yourself, weigh others.   *Japanese*

10913. Careless mind, double work.
Greek

10914. Good mind, good find.
English

10915. He who pays is fairly entitled to speak his mind.   *French*

10916. His bashful mind hinders his good intent.   *English*

10917. If you wish to know the mind of a man, listen to his words.   *Chinese*

10918. It is better to go hungry with a pure mind than to eat well with an evil one.   *Chinese*

10919. It is mind that ennobles, not the blood. *German*

10920. Little minds like weak liquors are soonest soured. *English*

10921. Man's mind changes morning through evening. *Korean*

10922. My mind to me a kingdom is. *English*

10923. Nothing is difficult to a willing mind. *Italian*

10924. Nothing is impossible to a willing mind. *French*

10925. The mind is the lord of man's body. *Chinese*

10926. The mind of a woman is like the wind and the water. *Latvian*

10927. The mind of a workman is in his stomach. *Moroccan*

10928. The mind of the bird is on the millet. *Greek*

10929. The resolved mind has no cares. *English*

10930. What's on his mind is on his tongue. *Yiddish*

MINE

10931. Mine is better than ours. *American*

MINISTER

10932. A loyal minister will not serve two masters; a virtuous woman will not marry twice. *Korean*

MINNOW

10933. One must lose a minnow to catch a salmon. *French*

MINSTER

10934. Leave the minster where it is. *French*

10935. The nearer the minster the later to mass. *French*

MINUTE

10936. Take care of the minutes, and the hours will take care of themselves. *American*

MIRACLE

10937. Don't depend on miracles. *Yiddish*

10938. Miracles don't happen every day. *Yiddish*

MIRE

10939. If you will stir up the mire, you must bear the smell. *Danish*

10940. The more you stir the mire, the more it stinks. *German*

MIRROR

10941. A mirror can be the biggest deceiver. *Yiddish*

10942. A mirror reflects whatever is before it. *Indian (Tamil)*

10943. Don't sell a mirror to blind a person. *Japanese*

10944. In the mirror everybody sees his best friend. *Yiddish*

10945. In the mirror we see our form, in wine the heart. *German*

10946. The best mirror is an old friend. *English*

10947. The mirror fools none but the ugly. *Yiddish*

10948. There never was a mirror that told a woman she was ugly. *French*

MIRTH

10949. A pennyworth of mirth is worth a pound of sorrow. *English*

10950. An ounce of mirth is worth a pound of sorrow. *English*

10951. Mirth and mischief are two things. *English*

10952. The mirth of the world dures but a while. *English*

MISCHANCE

10953. After mischance everyone is wise. *French*

MISCHIEF

10954. Better a mischief than an inconvenience. *English*

10955. Everyone is wise when the mischief is done. *Spanish*

10956. He that mischief hatches, mischief catches. *English*

10957. Many a one is good because he can do no mischief. *French*

10958. Mischief all comes from much opening of the mouth. *Chinese*

10959. Mischief comes by the pound and goes away by the ounce. *English*

10960. Mischief comes not from a friend. *Turkish*

10961. Mischief comes soon enough. *Danish*

10962. Mischief has swift wings. *English*

10963. Mischief is ever too bold. *English*

10964. Mischief will be silent. *Welsh*

10965. The more mischief, the better sport. *English*

10966. Wherever there is mischief, there is sure to be a priest and a woman in it. *German*

MISER

10967. A miser and a liar come to terms quickly. *Greek*

10968. A miser is like a sow, useful only when dead. *Czech*

10969. Even a miser does not refuse his cook part of what he roasts. *African (Efik)*

10970. Misers are idol worshippers. *Yiddish*

10971. The miser and the pig are of no use till dead. *French*

10972. The miser ends by giving more, and the lazy man by going further. *Serbo-Croatian*

10973. The miser is like a donkey, he carries gold and silver and wants straw. *Moroccan*

10974. The miser will not prosper. *Indian (Tamil)*

MISERLY

10975. To be miserly is worse than to steal. *Yiddish*

MISERY

10976. He bears misery best that hides it most. *English*

10977. It is misery enough to have once been happy. *English*

10978. Misery acquaints a man with strange bedfellows. *English*

10979. Misery may be the mother when one beggar begs of another. *English*

MISFORTUNE

10980. A misfortune and a friar seldom go alone. *Italian*

10981. A misfortune borne patiently is as though it had not been. *African (Hausa)*

10982. A misfortune is better than the fear of it. *Welsh*

10983. A misfortune is like a cake of soap; at first it is large, then it becomes small. *Lebanese*

10984. Another's misfortune does not cure my pain. *Portuguese*

10985. Another's misfortune is only a dream. *French*

10986. Blessed is the misfortune that comes alone. *Italian*

10987. Don't laugh at someone else's misfortune, yours is on the horizon. *Russian*

10988. Each misfortune will show its own way. *Indian (Kashmiri)*

10989. Every misfortune is a counsel. *Turkish*

10990. Few bewail a fool's misfortune. *African (Fulani)*

10991. He of whom misfortune has taken hold will sprain his thumb, even when wiping his nose. *Polish*

10992. He who helps another in his misfortune becomes his master. *Indian (Tamil)*

10993. He who suffers misfortune may well look out for another. *Flemish*

10994. It is a misfortune to come to a law court, and law courts lie in wait for unfortunate people. *Vietnamese*

10995. It is well that misfortunes come but from time to time, and not all together. *Irish*

10996. Misfortune binds together. *Yiddish*

10997. Misfortune comes on horseback and goes away on foot. *French*

10998. Misfortune does not come with a bell on its neck. *Estonian*

10999. Misfortune draws misfortune in its train. *Moroccan*

11000. Misfortune is the beginning of evil. *Russian*

11001. Misfortune may turn out to be blessing. *Korean*

11002. Misfortune rides into the villages, but leaves them on foot. *Swedish*

11003. Misfortune seldom comes alone to the house. *Danish*

11004. Misfortune teaches us to pray. *Slovakian*

11005. Misfortune upon misfortune is not wholesome. *French*

11006. Misfortune, wood, and hair grow every day. *German*

10007. Misfortunes come on wings and depart on foot. *English*

11008. Misfortunes find their way even on the darkest night. *Czech*

11009. Misfortunes never come singly. *English*

11010. Misfortunes tell us what fortune is. *English*

11011. Misfortunes, when asleep, are not to be awakened. *English*

11012. Never rejoice in the misfortune of other people. *Maltese*

11013. One has always strength enough to bear the misfortunes of one's friends. *French*

11014. One misfortune brings on another. *Dutch*

11015. One misfortune is no disaster. *Russian*

11016. One misfortune shakes hands with another. *Swedish*

11017. Sudden misfortune, double misfortune. *Slovenian*

11018. The bitterest misfortune can be covered up with a smile. *Yiddish*

11019. The misfortunes of some people are advantages to others. *Egyptian*

11020. There are many who fall into the misfortunes of their companions. *Turkish*

11021. Upon every misfortune another misfortune. *Egyptian*

11022. Walk fast and you catch misfortune; walk slowly and it catches you. *Russian*

11023. When misfortune appears, open wide the gates.   *Russian*

11024. When misfortune comes in at the door, love flies out of the window.
German

11025. When misfortune is asleep, do not wake her.   *Russian*

11026. When misfortune is greatest relief is nearest.   *Irish*

11027. When misfortune knocks at the door, friends are asleep.   *Polish*

11028. When misfortune sleeps, beware of awakening it.   *Rumanian*

11029. Where misfortune befalls injuries follow.   *French*

11030. Wherever there are men there is also misfortune.   *Russian*

11031. Wise from the misfortune but not rich.   *Finnish*

MISRECKONING

11032. Misreckoning is no payment.
English

MISS

11033. A miss is as good as a mile.
English

11034. An infinitesimal miss may result in a thousand-mile difference.
Korean

MISTAKE

11035. A mistake is no reckoning.
French

11036. Better a mistake at the beginning than at the end. *African (Fulani)*

11037. Don't hesitate to acknowledge a mistake and correct it.   *Japanese*

11038. He who marries early makes no mistake.   *Turkish*

11039. In a multitude of words there will certainly be a mistake.   *Chinese*

11040. It is a mistake to go to a Buddhist monastery to borrow a comb.
Chinese

11041. Mistakes will happen.
American

11042. One mistake does not warrant the divorce of one's wife.
African (Swahili)

11043. One mistake naturally leads to another.   *American*

11044. The first mistake is a lesson and a teacher for those that follow.   *Greek*

11045. The mistakes of others are good teachers.   *Estonian*

11046. The mistakes of the doctor are covered by earth.   *Polish*

MISTRESS

11047. All is well when the mistress smiles.   *English*

11048. As the mistress, so the maid.
German

11049. He that makes his mistress a goldfinch may perhaps find her a wagtail.   *English*

11050. If you can kiss the mistress, never kiss the maid.   *English*

11051. Like mistress like maid.
English

11052. The mistress makes the morning, but the Lord makes the afternoon.
American

11053. The mistress of the mill may say and do what she will.   *English*

MISTRUST

11054. Mistrust is an axe at the tree of love.   *Russian*

11055. Mistrust is the mother of safety.
American

11056. When mistrust enters, love departs.   *Danish*

MISUNDERSTANDING

11057. Misunderstanding brings lies to town. *English*

11058. Misunderstandings are best prevented by pen and ink. *English*

MIX

11059. If you mix around, you learn quite a bit. *Yiddish*

MIXTURE

11060. Right mixture makes good mortar. *English*

MOB

11061. The mob has many heads but no brains. *English*

MOCKING

11062. Mocking is catching. *English*

MODERATION

11063. Moderation is medicine, excess is peril. *Burmese*

MODESTY

11064. Modesty is the emblem of goodness. *Philippine*

11065. Modesty is the ornament of a woman. *Indian (Tamil)*

11066. Too much modesty is half conceit. *Yiddish*

11067. When modesty becomes rare, disaster prevails. *Lebanese*

11068. Where there is modesty, there is virtue. *German*

11069. Where there's no modesty, there's no honor. *German*

MOLE

11070. A mole wants no lanthorn. *English*

11071. If a small mole appears, catch him, even if you are hunting for its mother. *African (Swahili)*

MOMENT

11072. A moment is worth a thousand gold pieces. *Korean*

11073. To one who waits, a moment seems a year. *Chinese*

11074. What the moment broke may take years to mend. *Swedish*

MONEY

11075. A rich man's money hangs him oftentimes. *English*

11076. All complain of their lack of money, none of their want of brains. *Rumanian*

11077. All things are obedient to money. *English*

11078. Bad money always comes back. *German*

11079. Being without money is always a mistake. *Yiddish*

11080. Better lose a little money than a little friendship. *Malagasy*

11081. Copper money makes rusty love. *Russian*

11082. Dally not with money or women. *English*

11083. Don't boast of your money because you can easily lose it. *Yiddish*

11084. Do not lend your money to a great man. *French*

11085. Even between parents and children money matters make strangers. *Japanese*

11086. Fair money can cover much that's foul. *Dutch*

11087. He is well off who has no money to lend to friends; he doesn't create enemies. *Yiddish*

11088. He that does lend does lose his money and friend. *English*

11089. He that gets money before he gets wit will be but a short while master of it. *English*

11090. He that has no money in his purse should have fair words on his lips. *Danish*

11091. He that has no money needs no purse. *English*

11092. He that has not money in his purse should have honey in his mouth. *French*

11093. He that plays his money ought not to value it. *English*

11094. He that shows his money shows his judgment. *Italian*

11095. He that wants money wants all things. *English*

11096. He who gives the money makes the fife play. *Turkish*

11097. He who has money does what he pleases. *Greek*

11098. He who has money has capers. *French*

11099. He who has money has the whole world! *Yiddish*

11100. He who has not married nor built a house doesn't know where his money has gone. *Libyan*

11101. He who has the money has the authority. *Yiddish*

11102. He who knows how to beg may leave his money at home. *Danish*

11103. He who loves money must labor. *African (Wolof)*

11104. He who sows money will reap poverty. *Danish*

11105. If a little money does not go out, great money will not come in. *Chinese*

11106. If one has money, one can even buy fairies. *Vietnamese*

11107. If one has money one will have servants. *Vietnamese*

11108. If two men unite, their money will buy gold. *Chinese*

11109. If we have not money, let us have honor. *Turkish*

11110. If you have money, take a seat; if you have none, take to your feet. *German*

11111. If you have money, you are wise and good looking and can sing well too. *Yiddish*

11112. If you have money, you can make even a cat dance. *Philippine*

11113. If you have money, you can make spirits turn the mill. *Chinese*

11114. If you have the money, you have the "say". *Yiddish*

11115. If you have the money, your opinion is accepted. *Hebrew*

11116. If you want to get rid of your friend, lend him money. *Hungarian*

11117. In buying cheap articles money is lost. *Japanese*

11118. It costs money to sin. *Yiddish*

11119. It's easier to earn money than to keep it. *Yiddish*

11120. It is not so good with money as it is bad without it. *Yiddish*

11121. Lend money to a bad debtor and he will hate you. *Chinese*

11122. Little money, little law. *English*

11123. Make money honestly if you can, but make money. *American*

11124. Misers' money goes twice to market. *Spanish*

11125. Money and friendship break the arms of justice. *Italian*

11126. Money answers all things.
English

11127. Money begets money. *English*

11128. Money borrowed is soon sorrowed.
French

11129. Money burns many. *French*

11130. Money buys everything except brains.
Yiddish

11131. Money can do everything.
Yiddish

11132. Money can put even gods to work for you. *Korean*

11133. Money causes conceit and conceit leads to sin. *Yiddish*

11134. Money comes and goes as the tide ebbs and flows. *Vietnamese*

11135. Money comes first and then the law. *Vietnamese*

11136. Money comes like earth scooped up with a needle; it goes like sand washed away by water. *Chinese*

11137. Money commands people and all things in the world. *Japanese*

11138. Money covers blame. *Turkish*

11139. Money does not smell. *Russian*

11140. Money doesn't tear one's pockets. *Latvian*

11141. Money gets the bride.
Lebanese

11142. Money goes to money. *Yiddish*

11143. Money goes where money is.
Russian

11144. Money governs the world.
English

11145. Money grows on the tree of patience. *Japanese*

11146. Money grows (not) on trees.
American

11147. Money has no smell. *English*

11148. Money hides a thousand deformities. *Chinese*

11149. Money in purse will be always in fashion. *English*

11150. Money in the purse dispels melancholy. *German*

11151. Money is a good servant but a bad master. *English*

11152. Money is a great traveler in the world. *English*

11153. Money is a master everywhere.
Czech

11154. Money is a mattress of thorns.
Maltese

11155. Money is ace of trumps.
English

11156. Money is an enemy. *Japanese*

11157. Money is lost only for want of money. *French*

11158. Money is money's brother.
Italian

11159. Money is more eloquent than a dozen members of parliament. *Danish*

11160. Money is no fool, if a wise man have it in keeping. *English*

11161. Money is not gained by losing time. *Portuguese*

11162. Money is often lost for want of money. *English*

11163. Money is power. *American*

11164. Money is round. *English*

11165. Money is round and rolls easily.
Rumanian

11166. Money is round; it must roll.
French

11167. Money is round; it rolls away from you. *Yiddish*

11168. Money is sharper than a sword.
African (Ashanti)

11169. Money is sweet balm.
Egyptian

11170. Money is that which art has turned up trump. *English*

11171. Money is the best soap—it removes the biggest stain.   *Yiddish*

11172. Money is the devil's eye.
                                    Rumanian

11173. Money is the measure of all things.   *Portuguese*

11174. Money is the sinew of love as well as of war.   *English*

11175. Money is the sinew of war.
                                    English

11176. Money is the sinews of trade.
                                    American

11177. Money is waiting to be counted.
                                    Latvian

11178. Money is welcome in a dirten clout.   *Scottish*

11179. Money is welcome though it comes in a dirty clout.   *English*

11180. Money is wise; it knows its way.
                                    English

11181. Money knows no day on which it is not welcome.   *African (Shona)*

11182. Money, land, and women are the roots of quarrel.
                          Indian (Hindustani)

11183. Money, like dung, does no good till it's spread.   *English*

11184. Money lost, nothing lost; courage lost, everything lost.   *Yiddish*

11185. Money loves to be counted.
                                    Russian

11186. Money makes dogs dance.
                                    French

11187. Money makes even a bastard legal.   *Hebrew*

11188. Money makes friends enemies.
                                    English

11189. Money makes marriage.
                                    English

11190. Money makes mastery. *English*

11191. Money makes the man.
                                    English

11192. Money makes the mare to go.
                                    English

11193. Money makes the merchant.
                                    English

11194. Money makes the old wife trot.
                                    English

11195. Money matters make strangers.
                                    Japanese

11196. Money must be made, or we should soon have the wolf at the door.
                                    American

11197. Money once gone never returns.
                                    American

11198. Money refused loses its brightness.   *English*

11199. Money rules the world. *Dutch*

11200. Money saved is as good as money gained.   *Danish*

11201. Money should always be counted even when found in the roadway.   *Serbo-Croatian*

11202. Money soothes more than a gentleman's words.   *Spanish*

11203. Money soothes more than the words of a cavalier.   *Portuguese*

11204. Money speaks; dogs bark.
                                    Hungarian

11205. Money taken, freedom forsaken.
                                    German

11206. Money talks.   *English*

11207. Money turns bad into good.
                                    Spanish

11208. Money unjustly gotten is but snow on which hot water is poured.
                                    Chinese

11209. Money will do more than my lord's letter.   *English*

11210. Money will make the pot boil.
                                    English

11211. Money will open a blind man's eyes and will make a priest sell his prayer books.   *Chinese*

11212. Money, wine, and women bring about the destruction of man.
Philippine

11213. Money wins the battle, not the long arm. *Portuguese*

11214. Money without love is like salt without pilchers. *English*

11215. Much money, many friends.
German

11216. Much money moves the gods.
Chinese

11217. Never spend your money before you have it. *English*

11218. No money, no mistress.
English

11219. No money, no Swiss. *English*

11220. No one takes money for thinking. *Rumanian*

11221. Nobody throws away his money for no reason. *Hebrew*

11222. Of money, wit, and virtue, believe one-fourth of what you hear.
English

11223. One never gets more than one's money's worth of anything. *French*

11224. Public money is like holy water—every one helps himself to it.
Italian

11225. Ready money can buy whatever is in stock. *Chinese*

11226. Ready money is a ready medicine. *English*

11227. Ready money will away.
English

11228. Ready money works great cures. *French*

11229. Sow not money on the sea lest it sink. *Dutch*

11230. The money you refuse will never do you good. *English*

11231. To have money is a good thing; to have a say over the money is even better. *Yiddish*

11232. Today for money, tomorrow for nothing. *German*

11233. To much money blinds the eyes.
Lebanese

11234. Too much money makes men mad. *English*

11235. When money speaks the truth keeps silent. *Russian*

11236. When money speaks the world keeps silent. *Swedish*

11237. When money talks everyone is silent. *Polish*

11238. When you have money, think of the time when you had none.
Japanese

11239. When you sow money, you reap fools. *Yiddish*

11240. Where money and counsel are wanting, it is best not to make war.
Danish

11241. Where money talks, arguments are of no avail. *German*

11242. Where there's money, there is the devil; but where there's none, there he is twice. *German*

11243. Who has no money in his purse must have honey in his mouth.
Italian

11244. Who has no money must have no wishes. *Italian*

11245. Who ventures to lend, loses money and friend. *Dutch*

11246. With money a donkey was ordained a priest. *Greek*

11247. With money one buys cherries.
Flemish

11248. With money one can even buy rabbit cheese. *Rumanian*

11249. With money you can influence the spirits; without it you cannot summon a man. *Chinese*

11250. Without money, it is no world. *Yiddish*

11251. You give money with your hand, but you go after it with your feet. *Russian*

MONEYMAKER

11252. The moneymaker is never tired. *Irish*

MONK

11253. A monk can't shave his own head. *Korean*

11254. A monk has no concern with a comb. *Burmese*

11255. A monk in his cloister, a fish in the water, a thief on the gallows. *German*

11256. A runaway monk never speaks well of his convent. *Dutch*

11257. A vagabond monk never spoke well of his convent. *Italian*

11258. Monks, mice, rats, and vermin seldom leave without harming. *German*

11259. More than a hood and a sad face is necessary to make a monk. *Albanian*

11260. The monk responds as the abbot chants. *French*

11261. The monk that begs for God's sake begs for two. *French*

11262. What a monk thinks he dares to do. *French*

MONKEY

11263. A monkey remains a monkey, though dressed in silk. *Spanish*

11264. An old monkey does not learn dancing. *Moroccan*

11265. As the parent monkey chatters, so does its young. *Philippine*

11266. Even a monkey may sometimes fall from the tree. *Korean*

11267. Even a monkey will not stay in a village divided against itself. *Indian (Tamil)*

11268. However foolish the monkey it will not play with the thorn tree. *African (Hausa)*

11269. Monkeys laugh at the buttocks of other monkeys. *Japanese*

11270. No matter how well a monkey is dressed, it remains a monkey. *Philippine*

11271. One monkey does not like another to get a bellyful. *African (Efik)*

11272. The monkey is happy when the dog is not there. *African (Swahili)*

11273. The monkey who is alone does not amuse himself in front of many. *African (Bemba)*

11274. When you see a monkey on a tree it has already seen you. *African (Fulani)*

MOON

11275. Don't love the moon more than the sun. *Thai*

11276. Let anyone who despises the position of the moon get up and correct it. *African (Hausa)*

11277. The moon also shines, but does not warm. *Russian*

11278. The moon shines even in the house of the outcast. *Indian (Tamil)*

11279. You can't outrun the moon. *Yiddish*

MOONLIGHT

11280. Moonlight does not dry the malt. *African (Ovambo)*

MORE

11281. The more the merrier. *English*

11282. The more the merrier; the fewer the better fare. *English*

MORNING

11283. A foul morning may turn to a fair day. *English*

11284. A glaring sunny morning, a woman that talks Latin, and a child reared on wine never come to a good end. *French*

11285. A misty morning may prove a good day. *Scottish*

11286. The early morning is the time to find the people at home. *Hawaiian*

11287. The morning is wiser than the evening. *Russian*

11288. This morning knows not this evening's happenings. *Chinese*

11289. To get up early for three mornings is equal to one day of time. *Chinese*

11290. What is not good in the morning will hardly be good by night. *Jamaican*

MORNING HOUR

11291. The morning hour has gold in its mouth. *German*

MORROW

11292. No one knows what the morrow will bring. *Yiddish*

MORSEL

11293. A large morsel chokes a child. *African (Yoruba)*

11294. A morsel eaten gains no friend. *English*

11295. A restive morsel needs a spur of wine. *French*

MOSCOW

11296. In Moscow there is never a scarcity of bread. *Russian*

11297. Moscow wasn't built in an instant. *Russian*

11298. Moscow was set ablaze by a one-copeck candle. *Russian*

11299. To some people Moscow is a mother, and to others a step-mother. *Russian*

MOSQUE

11300. The mosque is no place to dance. *Iranian*

11301. The mosque is no place to tie one's donkey. *Iranian*

11302. When the mosque is open, the dog forgets its manners. *Iranian*

MOSQUITO

11303. The mosquito is without a soul, but its whizzing vexes the soul. *Turkish*

MOTE

11304. A mote may choke a man. *English*

11305. Every mote is a beam. *English*

MOTH

11306. He dreads a moth who has been stung by a wasp. *Albanian*

11307. The moth does most mischief to the finest garment. *Italian*

11308. When the moth flies around the flame, it burns itself to death. *Chinese*

MOTHER

11309. A busy mother makes a lazy daughter. *Irish*

11310. A mother becomes a liar and a thief for the love of her children.
Maltese

11311. A mother refuses to go far lest her baby cries. *African (Annang)*

11312. A mother that has lost many children by death, hates the idea of her child taking a nap. *African (Annang)*

11313. A nimble mother makes a lazy daughter. *Scottish*

11314. A tender-hearted mother makes a scabby daughter. *French*

11315. An indulgent mother makes a sluttish daughter. *Dutch*

11316. As is the mother such is the child, as is the yarn such is the cloth.
Indian (Tamil)

11317. As mother and father, so daughter and son. *Greek*

11318. As the mother goat leaps, so does its young. *Philippine*

11319. Even if your mother is not a good woman, she is your mother nevertheless. *African (Ashanti)*

11320. Every mother thinks her child is beautiful. *Yiddish*

11321. He who flatters the mother will hug the daughter. *Estonian*

11322. He who has no mother sucks his grandmother. *African (Wolof)*

11323. Inquire about the mother before you marry a girl. *Lebanese*

11324. It's the mother who can cure her child's tears. *African (Hausa)*

11325. Like mother like daughter.
English

11326. Look at the mother before you take her daughter in marriage.
Indian (Tamil)

11327. Look at the mother rather than her daughter. *Japanese*

11328. Mother and daughter-in-law never praise each other. *Vietnamese*

11329. One kisses the child for the mother's sake, and the mother for the child's sake. *German*

11330. See the mother, and then marry the daughter. *Rumanian*

11331. See the mother, comprehend the daughter. *Pashto*

11332. The husband's mother is the wife's devil. *German*

11333. The mother is to the child what the king is to the nation. *Vietnamese*

11334. The mother of a hero is the first to weep. *Serbo-Croatian*

11335. The mother of a second child is midwife to the mother of a first child.
Indian (Tamil)

11336. The mother of the coward does not grieve for him. *Egyptian*

11337. There is no mother like the mother that bore us. *Spanish*

11338. There is no such thing as a bad mother. *Yiddish*

11339. Though a mother give birth to nine sons, all nine will be different.
Chinese

11340. Though your mother be poor, she is still your mother.
African (Ovambo)

11341. When a mother shouts at her child "Bastard," you can believe her.
Yiddish

11342. With your mother you will not want, but alone you will.
African (Ovambo)

MOTHER-IN-LAW

11343. Mother-in-law and daughter-in-law are a tempest and hailstorm.
English

11344. The mother-in-law remembers not that she was a daughter-in-law.
English

11345. There is but one good mother-in-law and she is dead. *English*

MOTHERWIT

11346. A handful of motherwit is worth a bushel of learning.   *Spanish*

11347. An ounce of motherwit is worth a pound of clergy.   *English*

11348. An ounce of motherwit is worth a pound of schoolwit.   *German*

MOTION

11349. Motions are not marriages.
    English

MOUNTAIN

11350. A mountain and a river are good neighbors.   *English*

11351. A mountain cannot be moved with a splinter.   *Yiddish*

11352. A mountain does not meet another mountain, but man meets man.
    Rumanian

11353. Although a mountain is high there is still a way to reach its top; although the road is full of danger one can always find a way to get through it.
    Vietnamese

11354. Always taking out without giving back, even the mountains will be broken down.   *Libyan*

11355. Behind every mountain lies a vale.   *Dutch*

11356. Gradually from chippings a mountain is made.   *Indian (Kashmiri)*

11357. If the mountain will not come to Mahomet, Mahomet must go to the mountain.   *Russian*

11358. If you don't climb the high mountain, you can't view the plain.
    Chinese

11359. Mountains cannot meet, but men can.   *Yiddish*

11360. The higher the mountain the lower the vale, the taller the tree the harder the fall.   *Dutch*

11361. The mountain was in labor and produced a mouse.   *English*

11362. Though not stumbling over a mountain, we stumble over an anthill.
    Japanese

11363. When climbing a high mountain, take no step backward.   *Chinese*

11364. You can't climb a mountain by a level road.   *Norwegian*

MOURNER

11365. The chief mourner does not always attend the funeral.   *American*

MOUSE (see MICE)

11366. A mouse can build a home without timber.   *American*

11367. A mouse eats the food in the house.   *African (Ovambo)*

11368. A mouse in time may bite in two a cable.   *English*

11369. A mouse must not think to cast a shadow like an elephant.   *English*

11370. A mouse with but one hole easily meets its death.
    African (Ovambo)

11371. An old mouse does not eat cheese.   *Maltese*

11372. Better a mouse in the pot than no flesh at all.   *English*

11373. Don't make yourself a mouse, or the cat will eat you.   *English*

11374. Don't show the mouse the door of the house.   *Moroccan*

11375. Even if the mouse were the size of a cow, he would be the cat's slave nevertheless.   *African (Ashanti)*

11376. In his dreams a mouse can frighten a cat.   *Armenian*

11377. In time a mouse will gnaw through a cable.   *Dutch*

11378. It is a bold mouse that makes her nest in the cat's ear.   *Danish*

11379. It is a poor mouse that has but one hole. *Dutch*

11380. It must be a bold mouse that can breed in the cat's ear. *English*

11381. One mouse eats the clothes and all the mice get into trouble. *Greek*

11382. The escaped mouse ever feels the taste of the bait. *English*

11383. The mouse does not leave the cat's house with a bellyful. *Italian*

11384. The mouse goes abroad where the cat is not lord. *English*

11385. The mouse in its hole is a king. *Moroccan*

11386. The mouse is knowing, but the cat more knowing. *Danish*

11387. The mouse may find a hole, be the room ever so full of cats. *Danish*

11388. The mouse that has only one hole is easily taken. *English*

11389. The mouse that keeps going round the trap will at last get noosed by it. *Maltese*

11390. The mouse that knows but one hole is soon caught by the cat. *Spanish*

11391. To a mouse, there is no greater beast than a cat. *Armenian*

11392. Two cannot dine off one mouse. *Russian*

11393. When the mouse has had its fill, the meal turns bitter. *Dutch*

11394. When the mouse laughs at the cat, there is a hole. *African (Wolof)*

MOUTH

11395. A clean mouth and honest hand will take a man through any land. *German*

11396. A closed mouth and open eyes never did anyone harm. *German*

11397. A closed mouth catches no flies. *English*

11398. A closed mouth makes a wise head. *English*

11399. A cool mouth and warm feet live long. *English*

11400. A foul mouth must be provided with a strong back. *Danish*

11401. A wanderer with a mouth will not get lost. *African (Ovambo)*

11402. All mouths must be fed. *English*

11403. An enemy's mouth seldom says well. *English*

11404. An open mouth remains not hungry. *Turkish*

11405. Everything the mouth says, it does not do. *African (Kpelle)*

11406. Guard your mouth as though it were a vase, and guard your thoughts as you would a city wall. *Chinese*

11407. He who guards his mouth often guards his life. *Swedish*

11408. He who has bitter in his mouth, spits not all sweet. *English*

11409. He who has had his mouth burnt is prudent on another occasion. *Turkish*

11410. He who has once burnt his mouth, always blows his soup. *German*

11411. He who will stop every man's mouth must have a great deal of meal. *English*

11412. He who would close another man's mouth should first tie up his own. *Danish*

11413. If the mouth is fastened shut, no quarrel arises. *Japanese*

11414. If you speak with a cunning mouth, I listen with a cunning ear. *African (Annang)*

11415. In the morning the mouth smells, but there are good words in it.
African (Oji)

11416. Instead of opening your mouth, open your eyes. *Turkish*

11417. It is better to blow than burn your mouth. *Dutch*

11418. It is hard to blow with a full mouth. *Dutch*

11419. It is the mouth that cuts the throat. *African (Hausa)*

11420. Keep your mouth shut and your eyes open. *English*

11421. Mouth and heart are wide a-part. *German*

11422. Nothing falls into the mouth of a sleeping fox. *Spanish*

11423. One man's mouth destroys cit-ies. *Rumanian*

11424. One mouth does nothing with-out another. *English*

11425. Out of the abundance of the heart the mouth speaks. *Dutch*

11426. People's mouths can't be sewn up like sacks. *Greek*

11427. The drunken mouth reveals the heart's secrets. *German*

11428. The mouth does not know that its master is afraid. *African (Ga)*

11429. The mouth eats what it is given. *African (Shona)*

11430. The mouth is easy to open but difficult to close. *African (Shona)*

11431. The mouth is not worn away by dint of talking. *Turkish*

11432. The mouth is the gate of misfor-tune and evil. *Japanese*

11433. The mouth is the helper and can redeem. *African (Bemba)*

11434. The mouth is the interpreter of the heart. *Estonian*

11435. The mouth is the shield to pro-tect oneself. *African (Zulu)*

11436. The mouth knows what it will say, not what it will be answered.
African (Hausa)

11437. The mouth may talk, but keep your hands busy. *Hawaiian*

11438. The mouth of any who eats onion will smell. *African (Hausa)*

11439. The mouths of certain people are always clacking. *Hawaiian*

11440. The mouth of the slanderer is as fire exposed to the wind.
Indian (Tamil)

11441. The mouth of the young bird is big. *Turkish*

11442. The mouth often utters that which the head must answer for.
Danish

11443. The mouth that forbids is the mouth that allows. *Hebrew*

11444. The mouth that says yes, says no. *Spanish*

11445. The mouth that speaks not is sweet to hear. *Irish*

11446. Though a man may miss other things, he never misses his mouth.
African (Yoruba)

11447. What is sweet in the mouth is not always good in the stomach.
Danish

11448. When the mouth opens, lies come forth. *Indian (Tamil)*

11449. When the mouth stumbles it is worse than the foot. *African (Oji)*

11450. You can stop the mouth of a river but not the mouth of man.
Philippine

MOVE

11451. Who moves picks up, who stands still dries up. *Italian*

MUCH

11452. Much would have more.
English

MUD

11453. Cast no mud into the well from which you have drunk. *Hebrew*

11454. He who is in the mud likes to get another into it. *Spanish*

11455. Mud chokes no eels. *English*

11456. One who throws mud gets himself soiled as well. *African (Swahili)*

11457. The mud that you throw will fall on your own head. *Iranian*

MUG

11458. More are drowned in the mug than in the sea. *German*

MULE

11459. A mule and a woman do what is expected of them. *Spanish*

11460. A mule laden with gold is welcome at every castle. *Armenian*

11461. He who rides the mule shoes it. *French*

11462. He who wants a mule without fault must walk on foot. *Spanish*

11463. Mules make a great fuss about their ancestors having been horses. *German*

11464. One mule scrubs another. *English*

11465. The mule long keeps a kick in reserve for its master. *French*

MULTITUDE

11466. The multitude is like a flock of sheep. *Turkish*

MURDER

11467. After murder expect justice. *Maltese*

11468. Murder breeds murder. *American*

11469. Murder will out. *English*

MUSE

11470. The muses love the morning. *English*

MUSHROOM

11471. In the eyes of the jealous a mushroom grows into a palm tree. *Russian*

MUSIC

11472. As the music goes, so goes the dance. *Philippine*

11473. If the music changes so does the dance. *African (Hausa)*

11474. If we pay for the music we will take part in the dance. *German*

11475. Music befits a house where there is a wedding. *Turkish*

11476. Music has no charms for a buffalo. *Indian (Bihar)*

11477. Music helps not the toothache. *English*

11478. Talk of music only to a musician. *Chinese*

MUSICIAN

11479. All musicians are brothers. *Welsh*

11480. When a musician has forgotten his note, he makes as though a crumb stuck in his throat. *English*

MUSK

11481. Look not for musk in a dog's kennel. *English*

MUST

11482. Must is a hard nut. *German*

11483. Must is a king's word. *English*

11484. When one must, one can.

Yiddish

MUSTARD

11485. Mustard is very uncivil because it takes one by the nose. *English*

11486. Mustard makes a weak man wise. *American*

MUTTON

11487. Mutton is meat for a glutton.

English

MYRTLE

11488. The myrtle is always a myrtle, though it be among nettles. *Italian*

N

NAG

11489. Every nag imagines himself to be a fancy trotter. *Russian*

NAIL

11490. A nail secures the horseshoes, the shoe the horse, the horse the man, the man the castle, and the castle the whole land. *German*

11491. Do not hang all on one nail. *German*

11492. Drive not a second nail till the first be clinched. *English*

11493. Drive the nail that will go. *English*

11494. He who grudges the nail, loses the hoof. *Rumanian*

11495. He who heeds not the lost shoe-nail will soon lose the horse. *German*

11496. One nail drives in another. *Dutch*

11497. One nail drives out another. *English*

NAKED

11498. The naked don't fear robbery. *Russian*

NAKEDNESS

11499. Nakedness turns around; hunger goes straight. *Rumanian*

NAME (noun)

11500. A good name comes after a while, but a bad name is soon obtained. *Indian (Kashmiri)*

11501. A good name covers theft. *Spanish*

11502. A good name is a rich inheritance. *German*

11503. A good name is better than fine clothes. *Vietnamese*

11504. A good name is better than gold. *Philippine*

11505. A good name is more precious than gold. *Irish*

11506. A good name is the root of wealth. *Indian (Kashmiri)*

11507. A good name is worth gold. *English*

11508. A good name keeps its lustre in the dark. *English*

11509. A good name replaces a shirt that is missing. *Russian*

11510. A name doesn't harm a man if a man doesn't harm the name. *Estonian*

11511. Evil name is evil fame. *English*

11512. Get a name to rise early, and you may lie all day. *Scottish*

11513. Good name is better than riches.   *English*

11514. He's born in a good hour who gets a good name.   *English*

11515. He that has an ill name is half hanged.   *English*

11516. If you can't spread my fame, don't besmirch my good name! *African (Jabo)*

11517. One has the name and another the worth.   *Greek*

11518. That never ends ill which begins in God's name.   *English*

11519. The name given to a child becomes natural to it.   *African (Yoruba)*

11520. The name of an honest woman is worth much.   *Scottish*

NAME (verb)

11521. Sooner named, sooner come.
English

NATIVE

11522. If the natives eat rats, eat rats.
African (Swahili)

NATURE

11523. Good nature and talent are worth more than a large fortune.
Philippine

11524. Human nature is the same all the world over.   *American*

11525. Ill natures never want a tutor.
English

11526. Nature and love cannot be hid.
German

11527. Nature draws more than ten oxen.   *English*

11528. Nature draws stronger than seven oxen.   *German*

11529. Nature follows its course and a cat the mouse.   *Greek*

11530. Nature gives what no man can take away.   *English*

11531. Nature hates all sudden changes.   *Scottish*

11532. Nature is nature.   *American*

11533. Nature is the true law. *English*

11534. Nature passes nurture. *English*

11535. Nature requires little, fancy much.   *German*

11536. Nature, time, and patience are the three great physicians.   *English*

11537. Nature will have her course.
English

11538. There is nature in all things.
American

NAUGHT (see NOUGHT)

11539. Naught is never in danger.
English

11540. Naught is that muse that finds no excuse.   *English*

NAY

11541. A woman's nay is no denial.
English

NECESSITY

11542. Great necessities call out great virtues.   *American*

11543. Necessity alters the law.
Russian

11544. Necessity and opportunity may make a coward valiant.   *English*

11545. Necessity became a law.
American

11546. Necessity becomes will.
Italian

11547. Necessity breaks iron.   *Dutch*

11548. Necessity has compulsion in it.
American

11549. Necessity has no law. *English*

11550. Necessity is a hard dart.
English

11551. Necessity is stronger than choice.   *Welsh*

11552. Necessity is the mother of invention. *English*

11553. Necessity knows no law. *Dutch*

11554. Necessity makes sour sweet. *Norwegian*

11555. Necessity must speak. *American*

11556. Necessity seeks bread where it is to be found. *German*

11557. Necessity skips, necessity dances, necessity sings songs. *Russian*

11558. Necessity teaches arts. *German*

11559. Necessity teaches even the lame to dance. *German*

11560. Necessity teaches new arts. *Norwegian*

11561. Necessity teaches to eat white bread. *Russian*

11562. Necessity turns lion into fox. *Iranian*

11563. Necessity unites hearts. *German*

11564. Necessity will buy and sell. *Welsh*

11565. Necessity will teach one to eat white bread. *Russian*

11566. Where necessity speaks, it demands. *Russian*

NECK

11567. Where there is a neck there will be a yoke. *Russian*

NECTAR

11568. If in excess even nectar is poison. *Indian (Tamil)*

NEED

11569. He has great need of a wife that marries mamma's darling. *English*

11570. Need and night make the lame to trot. *English*

11571. Need makes greed. *Scottish*

11572. Need makes the naked man run. *English*

11573. Need makes the old wife trot. *English*

11574. Need makes virtue. *Scottish*

11575. Need will have its course. *English*

11576. Needs must go when the devil drives. *English*

11577. The need knows no price. *Russian*

11578. The needs of the monkey are not those of the anteater. *African (Fulani)*

11579. When need is greatest, help is nearest. *German*

11580. When the need is highest, the help is nighest. *English*

NEEDLE

11581. A hot needle burns the thread. *African (Ga)*

11582. A needle is small but its metal is strong. *African (Kpelle)*

11583. A needle with a piece of string will not be lost. *African (Hausa)*

11584. A needle with a small eye should be threaded slowly. *Thai*

11585. He who steals a needle will steal an ox. *Korean*

11586. If a needle can pierce it don't chop with an ax. *Burmese*

11587. If he steals a needle, he will steal a cow. *Moroccan*

11588. If you invest a needle, you'll realize a needle. *Yiddish*

11589. If you lose your needle in the grass, look for it in the grass. *Chinese*

11590. In the end a needle weighs heavy. *Flemish*

11591. It takes a needle to get a thorn from one's foot. *Iranian*

11592. Needle and thread do the work well. *Greek*

11593. No needle has two sharp points. *Chinese*

11594. The needle is small, but it sews costly garments. *Rumanian*

11595. The needle makes clothes, but the needle is naked herself. *Jamaican*

11596. Though small, a needle is not to be swallowed. *Japanese*

11597. Where goes the needle, there goes the thread. *Russian*

11598. Who steals a needle steals also a nail. *Finnish*

NEEDY

11599. He that is needy when he is married shall be rich when he is buried. *English*

NEGATIVE

11600. Two negatives make an affirmative. *English*

NEGLECT

11601. A little neglect may breed great mischief. *English*

NEIGHBOR

11602. A faithful neighbor is the best guardian. *Albanian*

11603. A good neighbor is better than a brother far off. *Danish*

11604. A near neighbor is better than a distant cousin. *Italian*

11605. A near neighbor is better than a distant relative. *Russian*

11606. A neighbor that is near is better than a relative of no benefit. *Turkish*

11607. Better a near neighbor than a distant cousin. *Italian*

11608. Better good neighbors that are near than relatives far away. *Chinese*

11609. Choose the neighbor before the house, and the companion before the road. *Moroccan*

11610. Choose your neighbor before you buy your house. *African (Hausa)*

11611. Close neighbors are better than cousins in the distance. *Korean*

11612. He has ill neighbors that is fain to praise himself. *English*

11613. He's an ill neighbor that is not missed. *English*

11614. He who can give has many a good neighbor. *French*

11615. He who has bad neighbors is fain to praise himself. *Danish*

11616. He who slanders his neighbor makes a rod for himself. *Dutch*

11617. Hold him not for a good neighbor that's at table and wine at every hour. *English*

11618. If your neighbor is an early riser, you will become one. *Albanian*

11619. In time of trouble a near neighbor is better than a distant brother. *Icelandic*

11620. Keep well with your neighbors, whether right or wrong. *German*

11621. Love your neighbor, but don't pull down the fence. *German*

11622. Love your neighbor, but do not throw down the dividing wall. *Indian (Hindi)*

11623. Love your neighbor, but put up a fence. *Russian*

11624. Love your neighbor yet pull not down your hedge. *English*

11625. Neighbor once over the hedge, neighbor over it again. *German*

11626. No one has peace longer than his neighbor wishes. *Swedish*

11627. No one is rich enough to do without his neighbor.   *Danish*

11628. One cannot keep peace longer than his neighbor will let him.   *German*

11629. Shut your door and you will make your neighbor good.   *Portuguese*

11630. The bad neighbor gives a needle without thread.   *Spanish*

11631. To have a good neighbor is to find something precious.   *Chinese*

11632. When neighbors quarrel, lookers-on are more apt to add fuel than water.   *Danish*

11633. When you go to your neighbors, you find out what is happening at home.   *Yiddish*

11634. You may live in peace when your neighbors permit.   *Indian (Hindi)*

11635. You must ask your neighbor if you shall live in peace.   *English*

11636. Your neighbor is your teacher.   *Egyptian*

NEIGHBORHOOD

11637. Examine the neighborhood before you choose your house.   *Chinese*

11638. It is better to live in a good neighborhood than to be known afar.   *Norwegian*

NERVE

11639. Nerve succeeds!   *Yiddish*

NEST

11640. As the nest, so the bird; as the father, so the child.   *Serbo-Croatian*

11641. Don't stir up a hornet's nest.   *Malaysian*

11642. Prepare a nest for the hen and she will lay eggs for you.   *Portuguese*

11643. To every bird its nest seems fair.   *French*

NET

11644. A new net won't catch an old bird.   *Italian*

11645. Better go home and make a net than dive into a pool after fish.   *Chinese*

11646. It is better to go home and make your net than to gaze longingly at the fish in the deep pool.   *Japanese*

11647. It is better to go home and weave a net than to stay on the shore and watch the fish.   *Philippine*

11648. The net fills though the fisherman sleeps.   *English*

11649. The old net catches animals, the new does not.   *African (Efik)*

11650. The rough net is not the best catcher of birds.   *English*

11651. When the net is worn out with age, the new net encircles the fish.   *Australian (Maori)*

11652. Without a net don't face the pool.   *Japanese*

NETTLE

11653. Better be stung by a nettle than pricked by a rose.   *English*

11654. He that handles a nettle tenderly is soonest stung.   *English*

11655. He who throws nettles over his neighbor's fence has them growing again in his own garden.   *Russian*

11656. Nettles are never frostbitten.   *Slovenian*

11657. Nip a nettle hard, and it will not sting you.   *English*

11658. That which is to become a good nettle must sting early.   *Swedish*

11659. Where nettles thrive roses cannot grow.   *Russian*

NEUTRAL

11660. Neutrals think to tread on eggs and break none.   *German*

NEVER

11661. Never is a long day.   *English*

NEW

11662. Always something new, seldom something good.   *German*

11663. The new is always liked, though the old is often better. *Danish*

11664. What is new is always fine.
French

11665. When the new is there, the old is forgotten.   *Vietnamese*

NEWS

11666. Bad news has wings.   *French*

11667. Bad news is always true.
Spanish

11668. Bad news is soon told.
American

11669. Bad news is speedily heard.
Turkish

11670. Bad news is the first to come.
Italian

11671. Believe no news until it is old.
Welsh

11672. Do not fret for news; it will grow old and you will know it.
Spanish

11673. Good news is not always to be interpreted as certain.   *Mexican*

11674. Good news is rumored and bad news flies.   *Spanish*

11675. Good news may be told at any time, but ill in the morning.   *English*

11676. He knocks boldly at the door who brings good news.   *French*

11677. He that brings good news, knocks boldly.   *English*

11678. He that tells his wife news, is but newly married.   *English*

11679. He was scarce of news who told that his father was hanged. *English*

11680. Ill news is commonly true.
English

11681. Ill news travels fast.   *Italian*

11682. In the world, there is no news that has not been heard.   *Turkish*

11683. News is interesting from the mouth of him who tells it first.
African (Yoruba)

11684. No news is good news.
English

11685. Stay a little and news will find you.   *English*

11686. The news of a good deed travels far, but that of a bad one farther.
Polish

NICENESS

11687. Overniceness may be underniceness.   *English*

NIGGARD

11688. The niggard spends as much as he who is liberal, and in the end more.
French

NIGHT

11689. A blustering night, a fair day.
English

11690. A dark night brings fear, but man still more.   *African (Fulani)*

11691. A dark night has no witnesses.
Serbo-Croatian

11692. A dark night is light to those who plot evil.   *Philippine*

11693. A sleepless night is the worst punishment.   *Yiddish*

11694. Many seek good nights and lose good days.   *Dutch*

11695. Merry nights make sorry days.
English

11696. Night brings the crows home.
English

11697. Night has no friend. *French*

11698. Night is followed by day, famine by abundance. *African (Ovambo)*

11699. Night is the mother of counsel.
English

11700. Night is the mother of plots.
Welsh

11701. Nights of pleasure are short.
Lebanese

11702. No night is so long that day will not follow it. *Finnish*

11703. One night does not suffice to make an elephant rot.
African (Bemba)

11704. The night and the day are as long as ever they were. *Irish*

11705. The night brings counsel.
French

11706. What is done by night appears by day. *English*

11707. When night comes, fear is at the door; when day comes, fear is on the hills. *Pashto*

11708. You must start by night to arrive by day. *Iranian*

NIGHTINGALE

11709. A nightingale cannot sing in a cage. *English*

11710. Even in a golden cage, the nightingale is homesick. *Armenian*

11711. It is better to hear the nightingale sing than the mouse gnaw.
Italian

11712. Nightingales can sing their own song best. *English*

11713. Nightingales don't feed on fairy tales. *Russian*

11714. The nightingale cannot live in a cage. *Greek*

11715. Two nightingales do not perch on one bough. *Turkish*

NIT

11716. Nits will be lice. *English*

NOBILITY

11717. It is a sign of nobility to patronise. *Irish*

11718. Nobility imposes obligations.
French

11719. Nobility of soul is more honorable than nobility of birth. *Dutch*

11720. Nobility, without ability, is like a pudding wanting fat. *Scottish*

11721. True nobility is invulnerable.
French

NOBLE

11722. He is more noble that deserves than he that confers benefits. *English*

11723. Noble is that noble does.
German

11724. The more noble, the more humble. *English*

NOBODY

11725. Nobody calls himself rogue.
English

11726. Nobody has too much prudence or virtue. *English*

11727. Nobody is fond of fading flowers. *English*

NOD

11728. A nod for a lord is a breakfast for a fool. *English*

11729. A nod for a wise man, and a rod for a fool. *English*

11730. A nod is as good as a wink to a blind horse. *Irish*

11731. A nod of an honest man is enough. *English*

NOISE

11732. He that loves noise must buy a pig. *English*

NONSENSE

11733. He who speaks much is sure to talk nonsense. *Greek*

NOSE

11734. A big nose never spoiled a handsome face. *French*

11735. A dog's nose and a maid's knees are always cold. *English*

11736. Don't poke your nose into someone else's monastery with your own regulations. *Russian*

11737. He that has a great nose thinks everybody is speaking of it. *English*

11738. It is better to leave the child's nose dirty than wring it off. *French*

11739. Let him who feels he has a dirty nose wipe it. *French*

11740. Put not your nose in the pot which doesn't boil for you. *Rumanian*

11741. The nose knows not the savor of salt. *African (Hausa)*

11742. Who blows his nose too hard makes it bleed. *French*

NOTHING

11743. By doing nothing we learn to do ill. *English*

11744. He that does nothing does ever amiss. *English*

11745. He that has nothing is frighted at nothing. *English*

11746. He that has nothing is not contented. *English*

11747. He who has nothing fears nothing. *French*

11748. It's more painful to do nothing than something. *English*

11749. Nothing comes unmixed. *American*

11750. Nothing has no savor. *English*

11751. Nothing have, nothing crave. *English*

11752. Nothing is easy to the unwilling. *English*

11753. Nothing is given for nothing. *English*

11754. Nothing is good or ill but by comparison. *English*

11755. Nothing is gotten without toil and labor. *English*

11756. Nothing is had for nothing. *French*

11757. Nothing is impossible. *English*

11758. Nothing is impossible to a willing heart. *English*

11759. Nothing is lost in a good market. *English*

11760. Nothing is more easily blotted out than a good turn. *English*

11761. Nothing is perfect. *Yiddish*

11762. Nothing is so new as what has long been forgotten. *German*

11763. Nothing is stolen without hands. *English*

11764. Nothing is to be bought in the market without a penny. *English*

11765. Nothing kindles sooner than fire. *English*

11766. Nothing should be bought that can be made or done without. *American*

11767. Nothing that is violent is permanent. *American*

11768. Nothing to be got without pains. *English*

11769. Nothing will come of nothing. *English*

11770. There's nothing but is good for something. *English*

11771. There's nothing like trying in this world. *American*

11772. Where nothing is, a little does ease. *English*

11773. Where nothing is, nothing can be had. *English*

11774. Where nothing is, the king must lose his right. *English*

NOUGHT (see NAUGHT)

11775. He that has nought shall have nought. *English*

11776. Nought can restrain consent of twain. *English*

11777. Nought is good for the eyes, but not for the stomach. *German*

11778. Nought needs no hiding place. *German*

NOVICE

11779. He who has been first a novice and then an abbot knows what the boys do behind the altar. *Spanish*

NUMBER

11780. The number drowned in alcohol is in excess of those drowned in water. *Indian (Tamil)*

NUN

11781. When the nuns dance the devil does not weep. *Rumanian*

NURSE

11782. A nurse spoils a good housewife. *English*

11783. Nurses put one bit in the child's mouth and two in their own. *English*

11784. Nurses should not have pins about them. *American*

11785. One kisses the nurse for the sake of the child. *German*

NURTURE

11786. Nurture passes nature. *English*

NUT

11787. Give someone nuts and he will throw the shells at you. *Hebrew*

11788. He that wishes to eat the nut does not mind cracking the shell. *Polish*

11789. One bad nut spoils all. *African (Ga)*

O

OAK

11790. An oak is not felled at one stroke. *English*

11791. Great oaks from little acorns grow. *English*

11792. Oaks may fall when reeds stand the storm. *English*

OAR

11793. Every one must row with the oars he has. *Dutch*

11794. Let him stay at the oar who has learned to row. *Danish*

11795. Without oars you cannot cross in a boat. *Japanese*

OATH

11796. An unlawful oath is better broken than kept. *English*

11797. It is ill to make an unlawful oath, but worse to keep it. *Scottish*

11798. The oaths of one who loves a woman are not to be believed. *Spanish*

OATMEAL

11799. Where there is store of oatmeal, you may put enough in the crock. *English*

OBEDIENCE

11800. Obedience to the tongue causes repentance. *Egyptian*

11801. Obedience to women makes one enter hell. *Moroccan*

11802. Willing obedience depends upon him who commands. *Philippine*

OBLIGATION

11803. Woe to him who fails in his obligations. *Irish*

OBSTACLE

11804. Every obstacle is for the best. *Greek*

OCCASION

11805. An occasion lost cannot be redeemed. *English*

11806. Great occasions make great men. *American*

11807. Occasion is bald behind. *English*

11808. One should not kiss the occasion that has a dirty mouth. *Russian*

OCCUPANT

11809. It is the occupant who knows where the house leaks. *African (Hausa)*

OCEAN

11810. To a fool the ocean is knee deep.
Russian

11811. The ocean cannot be emptied with a can. *Yiddish*

11812. The ocean is not choosy about a small stream. *Japanese*

ODDS

11813. Odds will beat anybody.
English

11814. There are odds in all things.
English

OFFENDER

11815. The offender never pardons.
English

OFFENSE

11816. Keep your offense in your bosom, and you may meet as before.
Chinese

OFFER

11817. Fair offer is no cause of emnity.
Scottish

11818. Never refuse a good offer.
Italian

OFFICE

11819. All offices are greasy.   *Dutch*

11820. An office that will not afford a man his victuals is not worth two beans. *English*

11821. No office so humble but it is better than nothing.   *Dutch*

11822. Offices may well be given, but not discretion. *English*

11823. Office without pay makes thieves. *German*

11824. Sometimes it is not the office that makes the man but the man that makes the office. *Hebrew*

11825. The office teaches the man.
German

11826. They that buy an office must sell something. *English*

OFFICER

11827. Good officers will make good soldiers. *American*

OFFICIAL

11828. An official never flogs a bearer of gifts. *Chinese*

11829. If you talk to an official you must talk roubles. *Russian*

11830. The official who can't lie may as well be out of the world. *Spanish*

OFFSPRING

11831. Unworthy offspring brag the most of their worthy descent. *Danish*

OIL

11832. He that measures oil shall anoint his fingers. *English*

11833. No one extracts the oil but the oil presser. *Egyptian*

11834. So long as there is oil in the lamp, don't give up hope.   *Maltese*

11835. To cast oil in the fire is not the way to quench it. *English*

11836. Too much oil extinguishes the light. *American*

11837. When the oil has burned dry, the lamp goes out. *Chinese*

11838. When the oil is exhausted, the flame goes out. *Japanese*

11839. You can't beat oil out of chaff.
Chinese

11840. You cannot get oil out of a wall.
French

OINTMENT

11841. Precious ointments are put in small boxes. *French*

OLD

11842. As the old ones sing, the young ones twitter.   *German*

11843. Honor the old, teach the young.
Danish

11844. None so old that he hopes not for a year of life.   *English*

11845. Old and tough, young and tender.   *English*

11846. Though old and wise, yet still advise.   *English*

11847. What the old chew, the young spit out.   *Yiddish*

11848. What the old ones sing, the young ones whistle.   *Dutch*

11849. When old, one finds it difficult to follow the world.   *Japanese*

OLDER

11850. The older the more covetous.
English

11851. The older the wiser.   *English*

11852. The older the worse.   *English*

OMELET

11853. Omelets are not made without breaking of eggs.   *English*

ONE

11854. One is no number.   *English*

11855. One's too few, three too many.
English

11856. Where one is wise, two are happy.   *English*

ONION

11857. A dealer in onions is a good judge of scallions.   *French*

11858. He who counts the onions and garlic shouldn't eat the stew.
Armenian

11859. He who introduces himself between the onion and the peel, does not go forth without its strong smell.
Egyptian

11860. Keep on peeling an onion and it will disappear.   *Armenian*

11861. Onion and garlic are born brothers.   *Russian*

11862. Onions, smoke, and a shrew make a good man's eyes water. *Danish*

OPINION

11863. A man's own opinion is never wrong.   *Italian*

11864. Not every opinion is truth.
Czech

11865. Opinion rules the world.
English

11866. Opinion slays and opinion keeps alive.   *Indian (Hindustani)*

11867. People's opinion has crucified Christ.   *Russian*

11868. Woe to him who deems his opinion a certainty.   *Irish*

OPIUM

11869. One must ask the delight of opium from one that smokes it.
Turkish

OPPONENT

11870. He who knows himself as well as his opponent will be invincible.
Korean

OPPORTUNITY

11871. Easily had opportunities are easily lost.   *Japanese*

11872. He who lets opportunities pass by achieves something only with difficulty.   *Philippine*

11873. Opportunities mean rubies.
Turkish

11874. Opportunity brings success.
Russian

11875. Opportunity is a precious companion. *American*

11876. Opportunity is the cream of time. *English*

11877. Opportunity kills a lion.
Moroccan

11878. Opportunity knocks only once.
English

11879. Opportunity makes desire.
Dutch

11880. Opportunity makes the thief.
English

11881. When an opportunity is in your hand do not allow it to pass. *Turkish*

OPPOSITION

11882. Opposition to everyone is a mistaken act. *Turkish*

OPPRESSION

11883. Oppression will make a wise man mad. *Scottish*

OPPRESSOR

11884. Oppressors sleep not day or night. *Indian (Tamil)*

11885. The oppressor will not be helped by God. *Moroccan*

ORANGE

11886. A divided orange tastes just as good. *Chinese*

11887. A rotten orange rots a whole boatload. *Maltese*

11888. A stolen orange is better tasting than your own. *African (Bemba)*

ORATOR

11889. He is a good orator who convinces himself. *English*

ORCHARD

11890. It is easy to rob an orchard when no man keeps it. *English*

ORDER

11891. Before giving orders learn to submit yourself. *Rumanian*

11892. Don't give an order after listening only to one side. *Japanese*

11893. Give orders and do no more, and nothing will come of it. *Spanish*

11894. Obey orders or break owners.
American

ORNAMENT

11895. Man's ornament is his mind.
Lebanese

ORPHAN

11896. An orphan eats too much, a bitter heart talks too much. *Yiddish*

11897. An orphan is not in the habit of weeping. *African (Ovambo)*

11898. When an orphan suffers, nobody notices; when he rejoices, the whole world sees it. *Yiddish*

OSTRICH

11899. An ostrich chick is too much for a hawk to pick up. *African (Hausa)*

11900. An ostrich is too great to alight on a branch. *African (Hausa)*

11901. Everything that has feathers flies, except the ostrich.
African (Wolof)

OUNCE

11902. The last ounce broke the camel's back. *American*

OUTBID

11903. Be not too hasty to outbid another. *English*

OUTERGARMENT

11904. The outergarment conceals the inner torment. *Yiddish*

OVEN

11905. An old oven is easier to heat than a new one. *French*

11906. It is folly to gape against an oven. *French*

11907. It is useless to gape against an oven. *Danish*

11908. One cannot be at the oven and the mill at the same time. *French*

OVEREATING

11909. From overeating one suffers more than from not eating enough. *Yiddish*

OVERSEER

11910. A good overseer is better than an ill worker. *Scottish*

OVERTAKE

11911. He overtakes at last who tires not. *English*

OWE

11912. He who owes is in all the wrong. *English*

OWL

11913. Although the owl has large eyes, he can't see as well as a mouse. *Japanese*

11914. An owl is the king of the night. *English*

11915. Every one thinks his owl a falcon. *German*

11916. The owl is not accounted the wiser for living retiredly. *English*

11917. The owl is small, its screech is loud. *Indian (Tamil)*

11918. The owl thinks all her young ones beauties. *English*

11919. The owl thinks her children the fairest. *Danish*

OWLET

11920. An owlet is a beauty in the eyes of its mother. *Russian*

OWN (property)

11921. Own is own. *English*

11922. To everyone his own is not too much. *German*

OWN (verb)

11923. He who owns something knows all about begging. *African (Hausa)*

OWNER

11924. An owner of a house knows about its leaking. *African (Kpelle)*

11925. It is the owner of the farm who drives off a leopard, not another man. *African (Hausa)*

11926. Let the owner of the garden remove his own thistles. *Hebrew*

11927. The dog's owner is the one who can take the bone from its mouth. *African (Jabo)*

11928. The owner has authority to work. *African (Fulani)*

11929. The owner of the bed knows his bed bug. *African (Fulani)*

OX

11930. A butting ox is better than a lonely bed. *Indian (Hindustani)*

11931. A long-horned ox, though it may not butt, will have that reputation. *Malaysian*

11932. After an ox is lost, one repairs its stable. *Korean*

11933. An old ox makes a straight furrow. *English*

11934. An old ox will find a shelter for himself. *English*

11935. An ox and an ass don't yoke well to the same plough. *Dutch*

11936. An ox is taken by the horns, and a man by the tongue. *English*

11937. An ox when weariest treads surest. *English*

11938. From one ox you can't skin two hides. *Yiddish*

11939. He who drives oxen speaks of oxen. *Finnish*

11940. He who ploughs with young oxen makes crooked furrows. *German*

11941. If an ox won't drink, you can't make him bow his head. *Chinese*

11942. It is in vain to lead the ox to the water if he is not thirsty. *French*

11943. It is not the big oxen that do the best day's work. *French*

11944. Old oxen have stiff horns. *Danish*

11945. Old oxen tread hard. *German*

11946. One blind ox will lead a thousand oxen astray. *Indian (Kashmiri)*

11947. One ox can't be sold to two butchers. *Latvian*

11948. Oxen go with oxen, horses with horses. *Japanese*

11949. Take an ox by his horn, a man by his word. *French*

11950. The black ox treads on one's foot. *English*

11951. The fierce ox becomes tame on strange ground. *Spanish*

11952. The ox comes to the yoke at the call of his feeder. *Spanish*

11953. The ox forgets it was once a calf. *Slovakian*

11954. The ox is caught by its horns, man by his tongue. *Czech*

11955. The ox is never weary of carrying his horns. *Haitian*

11956. The ox is not aware of its strength. *Yiddish*

11957. The ox lives safely as long as the knife is being sharpened. *Finnish*

11958. The ox ploughs the field, and the horse eats the grain. *Chinese*

11959. The ox that ploughs is not to be muzzled. *Egyptian*

11960. The ox will not flee the hare. *African (Ovambo)*

11961. The tired ox plants his foot firmly. *Spanish*

11962. When the ox falls, everyone sharpens their knives. *Yiddish*

11963. When the ox falls, its slayers are many. *Hebrew*

11964. Where the ox is slaughtered, there the blood is sprinkled. *Estonian*

11965. Whoever is an ox of his own choice finds pleasure in the licking of his yoke. *Mexican*

11966. With luck, even your ox will calve. *Yiddish*

11967. You may force an ox to the water, but you cannot make him drink. *Danish*

P

PACE

11968. A lasting, leisurely pace goes farther than a tiring trot. *Mexican*

11969. He that stumbles and falls not, mends his pace. *French*

11970. Soft pace goes far. *English*

11971. The pace of a donkey matches the oats it eats. *Hebrew*

PACK (animals)

11972. If you get into the pack you need not bark, but wag your tail you must. *Russian*

PACK (bag)

11973. A little pack serves a little peddler. *French*

PADLOCK

11974. A bad padlock invites a picklock. *English*

PAIL

11975. It is not known what milk pail will come back with a handle. *African (Zulu)*

PAIN

11976. Better a pain in your heart than shame before men. *Yiddish*

11977. Even pain has its joy. *Slovakian*

11978. Great pain and little gain make a man soon weary. *English*

11979. Great pains quickly find ease. *English*

11980. He who has suffered can sympathize with those in pain. *Indian (Bihar)*

11981. He who is in pain should go to the doctor. *Hebrew*

11982. He who lives long knows what pain is. *French*

11983. If pains be a pleasure to you, profit will follow. *English*

11984. If you give the pain freedom you will have to lie down and die. *Russian*

11985. No pains, no gains. *Scottish*

11986. Pains are the wages of ill pleasures. *English*

11987. Pain is forgotten where gain follows. *English*

11988. Pain is preferable to remedy in some cases. *Indian (Bihar)*

11989. Pain is the price that God puts upon all things. *English*

11990. Pain is the seed of pleasure. *Japanese*

11991. Pain past is pleasure. *English*

11992. The pain of the little finger is felt by the whole body. *Philippine*

11993. The stomach pain is a great pain. *Indian (Kashmiri)*

11994. There is no one in the world without pain. *Turkish*

11995. There is pain in getting, care in keeping, and grief in losing riches. *English*

11996. There is pain in prohibition. *Irish*

11997. When in pain it's best to be alone. *Japanese*

11998. When someone has a pain, that's what he talks about. *Russian*

PAINFUL

11999. It is more painful to do nothing than something. *English*

PAINTER

12000. A good painter can draw a devil as well as an angel. *English*

12001. A good painter need not give a name to his picture, a bad one must. *Polish*

12002. Painters and poets may lie by authority. *English*

PAINTING

12003. Let no woman's painting breed your heart's fainting. *English*

PALM TREE

12004. On the palm tree that yields nuts the birds will tarry. *African (Jabo)*

12005. When you see the palm tree, the palm tree has seen you. *African (Wolof)*

PANCAKE

12006. The first pancake is like a lump. *Russian*

12007. There is no making pancakes without breaking the eggs. *Italian*

12008. You can't make pancakes without breaking eggs. *Spanish*

PAPER

12009. Neither sign a paper without reading it, nor drink water without seeing it. *Spanish*

12010. Paper and brush may kill a man; you don't need a knife. *Chinese*

12011. Paper bears anything. *French*

12012. Paper can stand anything. *Russian*

12013. Paper does not blush. *Italian*

12014. Paper is patient. *German*

12015. The fairer the paper the fouler the blot. *English*

12016. You can't use paper to wrap up fire. *Chinese*

PARADISE

12017. Even in paradise it is not pleasant to be alone. *Rumanian*

12018. Even under a single fir tree with a crust of bread is paradise. *Russian*

12019. Fool's paradises are wise men's purgatories. *English*

12020. He that will enter into Paradise must have a good key. *English*

PARASITE

12021. A parasite cannot live alone. *African (Ovambo)*

12022. A parasite has no root; every tree is its kindred. *African (Yoruba)*

PARDON

12023. The pardon may be severer than the penalty. *Norwegian*

PARENTS

12024. Good parents, happy marriages; good children, fine funerals. *Chinese*

12025. He who respects his parents never dies. *Greek*

12026. If you do not support your parents while alive, it is of no use to sacrifice to them when dead. *Chinese*

12027. It is difficult for parents to guarantee the virtues of their sons and daughters. *Chinese*

12028. Let the parent punish the child. *African (Swahili)*

12029. Once parents used to teach their children to talk; today children teach their parents to keep quiet. *Yiddish*

12030. Parents are the first teachers of the children. *Burmese*

12031. Parents can give a dowry but not luck. *Yiddish*

12032. Parents can provide everything except good luck. *Yiddish*

12033. The parents can see best the character of the child. *Japanese*

12034. There is one thing one cannot buy, one's parents. *Hebrew*

12035. What the parents are, so will the children be. *Philippine*

12036. When one would be filial one's parents are gone. *Japanese*

12037. With such a parent there is such a child. *Japanese*

PARIS

12038. Paris was not built in a day. *French*

PARISH

12039. A mad parish, a mad priest. *Italian*

12040. A mad parish must have a mad priest. *English*

PARROT

12041. An old parrot never gets tame. *Indian (Bihar)*

12042. The parrot will utter what it is taught. *Indian (Tamil)*

PARSON

12043. For timber, even a parson is a thief. *Russian*

PART

12044. He that repairs not a part, builds all. *English*

PARTNER

12045. Do not be the partner of one more powerful than yourself. *Turkish*

PARTRIDGE

12046. The partridge loves peas, but not those which go into the pot with it. *African (Wolof)*

PARTY (entertainment)

12047. At other people's parties one eats heartily. *Yiddish*

PARTY (people)

12048. It is hard to please all parties. *Scottish*

12049. It takes two parties to make a quarrel. *English*

12050. The absent party is still faulty. *English*

12051. When one party is willing the match is half made. *American*

PASS

12052. Everything passes, everything breaks, everything wearies. *French*

PASSAGE

12053. At the narrow passage there is no brother and no friend. *Egyptian*

12054. The worse the passage, the more welcome the port. *English*

PASSION

12055. Destroy all passion when you light the lamp before the Buddha.
Chinese

12056. Hot passion cools easily.
Japanese

12057. Passion will master you if you do not master your passion. *English*

12058. The best passion is compassion.
Jamaican

12059. When passion enters at the fore-gate, wisdom goes out of the postern.
English

PAST

12060. Consider the past and you will know the future. *Chinese*

12061. He that praises the past blames the present. *Finnish*

12062. He who brings up something from the past should have his eye put out. *Russian*

12063. The past is as clear as a mirror, the future as dark as lacquer. *Chinese*

PASTURAGE

12064. Bad pasturage makes sheep shabby. *Jamaican*

PASTURE

12065. Fat pastures make fat venison.
French

PATCH

12066. Better a patch than a hole.
Welsh

12067. Better to have an ugly patch than a beautiful hole. *Yiddish*

12068. Patch by patch is good husban-dry, but patch upon patch is plain beggary. *English*

12069. The best patch is off the same cloth. *English*

12070. There is no better patch than one off the same cloth. *Spanish*

PATE

12071. A bald pate is quickly shaved.
Philippine

PATH

12072. A path has ears.
African (Ashanti)

12073. Every path has a puddle.
English

12074. It is the path you do not fear that the wild beast catches you on.
African (Ashanti)

12075. The just path is always the right one. *Yiddish*

12076. The middle path is the safe path. *German*

12077. Whoever strays from known paths may lose his way. *Philippine*

PATIENCE

12078. An ounce of patience is worth a pound of brains. *Dutch*

12079. Begin with patience, end with pleasure. *African (Swahili)*

12080. For what cannot be cured, pa-tience is the best remedy. *Irish*

12081. Have patience so that you will succeed. *Philippine*

12082. He preaches patience that never knew pain. *English*

12083. He that has no patience has nothing. *English*

12084. He that has patience has fat thrushes for a farthing. *English*

12085. He who has patience gets what he wants. *Greek*

12086. If you do not have patience you cannot make beer. *African (Ovambo)*

12087. In whatever you do unless you have patience you will not succeed.
Japanese

12088. Let patience grow in your garden. *English*

12089. Patience and hard work will overcome everything. *Russian*

12090. Patience carries with it half a release. *English*

12091. Patience conquers. *English*

12092. Patience conquers destiny.
Irish

12093. Patience cures many an old complaint. *Irish*

12094. Patience extracts sweetness from sourness. *Lebanese*

12095. Patience is a flower that grows not in every garden. *English*

12096. Patience is a good nag, but she'll bolt. *English*

12097. Patience is a plaster for all sores. *English*

12098. Patience is a plaster for every wound. *Irish*

12099. Patience is a virtue. *English*

12100. Patience is a virtue that causes no shame. *Irish*

12101. Patience is an ointment for every sore. *Welsh*

12102. Patience is as a dish of gold.
Indian (Kashmiri)

12103. Patience is bitter but its fruit is sweet. *Japanese*

12104. Patience is safety, haste is blame. *Turkish*

12105. Patience is the best of dispositions: he who possesses patience, possesses all things. *African (Yoruba)*

12106. Patience is the best remedy.
English

12107. Patience is the cure for an old illness. *Irish*

12108. Patience is the greatest prayer.
Indian (Hindi)

12109. Patience is the key of joy.
Turkish

12110. Patience is the key to all things.
Iranian

12111. Patience is the key to relief.
Lebanese

12112. Patience is the universal remedy. *African (Hausa)*

12113. Patience is the virtue of asses.
French

12114. Patience is wealth to its possessor. *African (Hausa)*

12115. Patience makes all hardships light. *Estonian*

12116. Patience, money, and time bring all things to pass. *English*

12117. Patience surpasses learning.
Dutch

12118. Patience will not spoil.
African (Fulani)

12119. Patience will pierce even a rock. *Japanese*

12120. Patience with poverty is all a poor man's remedy. *English*

12121. True patience consists in bearing what is unbearable. *Japanese*

12122. Where there is patience everything is possible. *Maltese*

12123. Who has patience sees his revenge. *Italian*

12124. With patience all is done.
Greek

12125. With patience you can drain a brook. *Yiddish*

12126. With patience you can even bore through granite. *Yiddish*

PATIENT (adjective)

12127. He who is patient obtains.
Libyan

PATIENT (noun)

12128. A patient that can swallow food makes the nurse doubtful.   *Malagasy*

12129. It is no time to go for the doctor when the patient is dead.   *Irish*

12130. Patients of the same disease sympathize with each other. *Japanese*

12131. That patient is not like to recover who makes the doctor his heir.
English

PATTERN

12132. The pattern of the reed lining of the house may be followed by the eye, but not the pattern or figuring of the heart.   *Australian (Maori)*

PAUPER

12133. A proud pauper and a rich miser are contemptible beings. *Italian*

12134. No one so hard upon the poor as the pauper who has got into power.
Danish

12135. Nobody will give a pauper bread, but everybody will give him advice.   *Armenian*

PAUSE

12136. Prudent pauses forward business.   *English*

PAY (noun)

12137. No pay smells bad.   *Hawaiian*

PAY (verb)

12138. He that cannot pay, let him pray.   *English*

12139. He that pays another remembers himself.   *English*

12140. He that pays beforehand shall have his work ill done.   *English*

12141. He that pays last never pays twice.   *English*

12142. He who pays well is well served.   *French*

12143. He who pays well may borrow again.   *German*

12144. It is hard to pay and pray too.
English

12145. It pays to advertise.   *American*

12146. Once paid never craved.
English

12147. Pay at once, delay is bad.
Indian (Tamil)

12148. Pay for work done is like jasmine.   *Indian (Kashmiri)*

12149. Pay what you owe, and be cured of your complaint.   *Spanish*

12150. Pay what you owe, and what you're worth you'll know.   *English*

12151. Pay with the same dish you borrow.   *English*

12152. Who pays soon borrows when he will.   *French*

PAYMASTER

12153. A good paymaster is keeper of others' purses.   *Spanish*

12154. A good paymaster needs no surety.   *English*

12155. An ill paymaster never wants excuse.   *English*

12156. From a bad paymaster get what you can.   *English*

12157. The good paymaster is lord of another man's purse.   *English*

12158. There are two bad paymasters: those who pay before, and those who never pay.   *English*

PAYMENT

12159. To work without payment is better than sitting idle.   *Turkish*

PEA

12160. Eat peas with the king and cherries with the beggar.   *English*

12161. He who sows peas on the highway does not get all the pods into his barn.   *Danish*

12162. Who has many peas may put the more in the pot.   *English*

PEACE

12163. A bad peace is better than a good war.   *Russian*

12164. A meager peace is better than a fat quarrel.   *Latvian*

12165. Better a lean peace than a fat victory.   *English*

12166. Better a little in peace and with right than much with anxiety and strife.   *Danish*

12167. Better an unjust peace than a just war.   *German*

12168. Better keep peace than make peace.   *Dutch*

12169. Eternal peace only lasts till the first fight.   *Russian*

12170. For the sake of peace one may even lie.   *Yiddish*

12171. He knows enough that can live and hold his peace.   *English*

12172. He that will live in peace and rest must hear and see and speak the best.   *English*

12173. He who holds a sword will maintain peace.   *Polish*

12174. Hear, see, and say nothing if you would live in peace.   *Italian*

12175. If you like peace don't contradict anybody.   *Hungarian*

12176. If you want to be at peace, you must learn to be passive.   *Philippine*

12177. In peace do not forget war.   *Japanese*

12178. It is safest making peace with sword in hand.   *English*

12179. Make peace with men, and quarrel with your sins.   *Russian*

12180. Of all wars peace is the end.   *Scottish*

12181. Peace and a well-built house cannot be bought too dearly.   *Danish*

12182. Peace at home takes war to other countries.   *African (Ovambo)*

12183. Peace feeds, war wastes; peace breeds, war consumes.   *Danish*

12184. Peace is better than easy warfare.   *Irish*

12185. Peace is more fattening than food.   *African (Ovambo)*

12186. Peace is not sold for evil.
African (Ovambo)

12187. Peace is the father of friendship.
African (Yoruba)

12188. Peace makes plenty.   *English*

12189. Peace must be bought even at a high price.   *Danish*

12190. Peace pays what war gains.
Serbo-Croatian

12191. Tell not all you know, nor judge of all you see, if you would live in peace.   *Spanish*

12192. There is no lasting peace without battle.   *Polish*

12193. There is no peace until after enmity.   *Egyptian*

12194. There must be peace in the district to have law and order in the country.   *African (Ovambo)*

12195. To a man equipped for war, peace is assured.   *Irish*

12196. When there is peace in the house, a bite suffices.   *Yiddish*

12197. Where there is peace, God is.
English

12198. Where there is peace, there is blessing.   *Yiddish*

12199. Without peace there can be no national prosperity.   *Philippine*

12200. You cannot have peace longer than your neighbor chooses.   *Danish*

PEACEMAKER

12201. A peacemaker often receives wounds.   *African (Yoruba)*

12202. No matter who comes off well, the peacemaker is sure to come off ill.   *Irish*

PEACH

12203. One peach rotting, one hundred are damaged.   *Japanese*

PEACOCK

12204. A peacock has too little in its head and too much in its tail.   *Swedish*

12205. Peacock, look at your legs.   *German*

12206. The peacock has fair feathers but foul feet.   *English*

12207. What the peacock has too little on his head, he has too much on his tail.   *German*

PEAR

12208. A single ripe pear is better than a whole basketful of unripe pears.   *Indian (Kashmiri)*

12209. Don't shake the tree when the pears fall off themselves.   *Slovakian*

12210. He who eats pears with his master should not choose the best.   *Italian*

12211. No pear falls into a shut mouth.   *Italian*

12212. Pears and peaches are not often found on the same tree.   *American*

12213. The best pears fall into the pigs' mouths.   *Italian*

12214. The pear falls from the pear tree.   *Greek*

12215. The pear falls not far from its tree.   *Turkish*

12216. The pear falls under the pear tree.   *Albanian*

12217. When the pear is ripe, it falls.   *German*

PEARL

12218. He who searches for pearls should not sleep.   *Libyan*

12219. The pearl lies at the bottom of the sea, while the corpse floats on the surface.   *Rumanian*

PEASANT

12220. A peasant between two lawyers is like a fish between two cats.   *Spanish*

12221. An ennobled peasant does not know his own father.   *Dutch*

12222. Every peasant is proud of the pond in his village because from it he measures the sea.   *Russian*

12223. For the sake of a proverb a peasant walked to Moscow.   *Russian*

12224. If a peasant has a lot, he hauls it on a cart.   *Russian*

12225. The most stupid peasants get the largest potatoes.   *Swedish*

12226. The peasant carries the sack, whatever you put in it.   *Russian*

12227. When a peasant gets rich, he knows neither relations nor friends.   *Spanish*

12228. Where the peasant is poor the whole country is poor.   *Polish*

PEBBLE

12229. A pebble and a diamond are alike to a blind man.   *English*

12230. Amongst men some are pebbles, but others are jewels.   *Indian (Hindustani)*

12231. One pebble doesn't make a floor.   *African (Hausa)*

PEDDLER

12232. Every peddler praises his own needles. *Spanish*

12233. Every peddler thinks well of his pack. *English*

12234. Let the peddler carry his own burden. *English*

12235. The little peddler a little pack does serve. *English*

PEDESTRIAN

12236. One hears pedestrians sing most of the riding songs. *Russian*

PEDIGREE

12237. Ask not after a good man's pedigree. *Spanish*

PEG

12238. A forked peg will not enter the ground. *Turkish*

12239. A peg for every hole. *French*

PEN

12240. A pen often reaches further than a sword. *Swedish*

12241. God's pen does not make any mistakes. *African (Swahili)*

12242. Not always the pen, often the weapon writes the law. *Hungarian*

12243. Pen and ink is wit's plough. *English*

12244. Pen and ink never blush. *English*

12245. Pens may blot but they cannot blush. *English*

12246. What's been written by pen can't be cut off by an axe. *Russian*

PENCE

12247. Take care of the pence and the pounds will take care of themselves. *English*

PENNY

12248. A hard-earned penny lives a lifetime. *Russian*

12249. A penny at a pinch is worth a pound. *English*

12250. A penny at hand is worth a dollar at a distance. *Yiddish*

12251. A penny earned is better than a shilling given. *English*

12252. A penny for your thought. *English*

12253. A penny in pocket is a good companion. *English*

12254. A penny in purse will bid me drink, when all the friends I have will not. *English*

12255. A penny in the purse is better than a friend at Court. *English*

12256. A penny in time is as good as a dollar. *Danish*

12257. A penny of your own is better than a peso of your neighbor's. *Philippine*

12258. A penny saved is a penny earned. *English*

12259. A penny saved is twice earned. *German*

12260. A penny spared is better than a florin gained. *Dutch*

12261. A single penny fairly got is worth a thousand that are not. *German*

12262. An ill won penny will cast down a pound. *Scottish*

12263. Better a frequent penny than a rare shilling. *Hungarian*

12264. Better a quick penny than a dallying shilling. *English*

12265. Every penny counts. *Hebrew*

12266. Every penny that is taken is not clear gain. *English*

12267. He that does not save pennies will never have pounds. *Danish*

12268. He who was born to pennies will never be master of dollars. *Danish*

12269. If you don't save the penny, you'll not have the dollar. *Yiddish*

12270. In for a penny in for a pound. *English*

12271. No penny, no pardon. *English*

12272. No penny, no Paternoster. *English*

12273. One penny in the pot makes more noise than when it is full. *Dutch*

12274. One penny is better on land than ten on the sea. *Danish*

12275. Penny and penny laid up will be many. *English*

12276. Penny is penny's brother. *German*

12277. Penny piled on penny will make a heap. *Libyan*

12278. Sometimes a penny well spent is better than a penny ill spared. *English*

12279. That which is stamped a penny will never be a pound. *Danish*

12280. The penny is ill saved that shames the master. *English*

12281. The penny is well spent that gets the pound. *English*

12282. The penny is well spent that saves a groat. *English*

12283. The penny is well spent that saves the spending of two. *Welsh*

12284. There's no companion like the penny. *English*

12285. Who will not lay up a penny shall never have many. *English*

PENSION

12286. Pension never enriched a young man. *English*

PEONY

12287. The peony is large, but useless to man; the jujube blossom, though small, ripens into precious fruit. *Chinese*

12288. Though the peony is beautiful it is supported by its green leaves. *Chinese*

PEOPLE

12289. A people without faith in themselves cannot survive. *Chinese*

12290. Advise people to do good deeds, never urge people to bring in lawsuits against one another. *Vietnamese*

12291. As you respect old people you will be yourself blessed with longevity. *Vietnamese*

12292. Avoid offending three classes of people—officials, customers, and widows. *Chinese*

12293. By their tongues people are caught, and by their horns, cattle. *Irish*

12294. Crafty people do not share the same bedroom. *African (Zulu)*

12295. Eat and drink with your own people, but do no business with them. *Serbo-Croatian*

12296. Every people has its prophet. *American*

12297. Go out and see how the people act. *Hebrew*

12298. Hasty people will never make good midwives. *English*

12299. He that builds on the people, builds on the dirt. *English*

12300. He who builds on the public way must let the people have their say. *German*

12301. He who serves the people has a bad master. *German*

12302. If it would help to pray to God, then people would be hiring others to pray for them. *Yiddish*

12303. If two people tell you you are drunk, go to sleep. *Russian*

12304. If you wish to succeed, consult three old people. *Chinese*

12305. It's more important to please people than to please God. *Yiddish*

12306. It is only at the tree loaded with fruit that people throw stones. *French*

12307. Learn your way from old people. *Estonian*

12308. Let people talk and dogs bark. *German*

12309. Many people see things but few understand them. *Yiddish*

12310. More people are drowned in the glass than in the sea. *Latvian*

12311. Not all people can be driven by the same stick. *Lebanese*

12312. Not all the people who weep over your corpse are your friends. *African (Jabo)*

12313. Old people have always new pains. *Swedish*

12314. Old people see best in the distance. *German*

12315. Old people tend to be critical of the young, forgetting their own past ignorance. *Philippine*

12316. One gets to know people during games and on journeys. *Russian*

12317. Only that is good which other people praise. *Russian*

12318. Ordinary people are as common as grass, but good people are dearer than an eye. *African (Yoruba)*

12319. People always sing the tune that pleases their host. *Yiddish*

12320. People are masters over people till arriving at the throne of God. *Turkish*

12321. People are not alike like guinea fowl, nor identical like quail. *African (Ovambo)*

12322. People become man and wife because they are predestined to each other by fate. *Vietnamese*

12323. People can say anything. *Russian*

12324. People count up the faults of those who keep them waiting. *French*

12325. People get drunk not from too much wine, but from not enough time. *Russian*

12326. People know people, and horses know their riders. *Moroccan*

12327. People lend only to the rich. *French*

12328. People may get tireder by standing still than by going on. *American*

12329. People of the same stock are friendly. *Irish*

12330. People often change and seldom for the better. *German*

12331. People take more pains to be damned than to be saved. *French*

12332. People that want a will seldom want an excuse! *American*

12333. People will not lie about anything that can be found out. *Hebrew*

12334. Poor people entertain with the heart. *Haitian*

12335. Rich people are everywhere at home. *German*

12336. Scratch people where they itch. *French*

12337. Small people often live in big houses. *Swedish*

12338. Some people are born lucky. *American*

12339. Some people are masters of money, and some are slaves. *Russian*

12340. The common people look at the steeple. *English*

12341. The little among certain people are great among other people.

Egyptian

12342. There are people who place a basket on your head to see what you carry. *African (Wolof)*

12343. Two people fit easier into one grave than under one roof. *Slovakian*

12344. Two people make two brains and one person only one.

African (Bemba)

12345. Wealthy people have many worries. *Japanese*

12346. When one goes to a town inhabited by squint-eyed people, one must squint one's eyes. *Thai*

12347. When people meet, they speak.

Hebrew

12348. When people say someone is crazy, believe it. *Yiddish*

12349. When people talk about something, it is probably true. *Yiddish*

12350. Where people love you, go rarely; where you are hated, go not at all. *Yiddish*

12351. Where there are many people, there are many words.

African (Swahili)

12352. Wise people keep their mouth closed, strong people keep their arms folded. *Vietnamese*

12353. Young people and dogs take many useless steps in an hour. *Czech*

12354. Young people must be taught, old ones be honored. *Danish*

12355. Young people will be young people the world over. *American*

PEPPER

12356. Pepper has a beautiful face with an ugly temper.

African (Annang)

12357. Put not pepper in other people's meals. *Rumanian*

12358. The red pepper, though small, is hot. *Korean*

PEPPERCORN

12359. Don't judge a peppercorn by its smallness, crack it and see how sharp it is. *Iranian*

PERFECTION

12360. Of every perfection there is a decline. *Turkish*

12361. Perfection can't be expected in this world. *American*

PERHAPS

12362. "Perhaps" and "never mind" are born brothers. *Russian*

PERSEVERANCE

12363. Perseverance brings success.

Dutch

12364. Perseverance is everything.

African (Yoruba)

12365. Perseverance kills the game.

English

12366. Sooner or later perseverance achieves. *American*

PERSEVERE

12367. He who perseveres will succeed. *Vietnamese*

PERSON

12368. A bad person is better than an empty house. *African (Ga)*

12369. A crafty person is consumed by other crafty people. *African (Zulu)*

12370. A dead person has no mouth.

Japanese

12371. A drenched person doesn't mind the rain. *Slovakian*

12372. A drowning person clings even to thorns. *Philippine*

12373. A fleeing person is not choosy about his road. *Japanese*

12374. A good person doesn't need a letter of recommendation; for a bad one, it would do no good. *Yiddish*

12375. A lazy person acquires no food. *Yiddish*

12376. A lazy person chews empty coconut shells. *African (Swahili)*

12377. A patient person has all the wealth that there is in this world. *African (Jabo)*

12378. A person bitten by a snake becomes frightened at the sight of a dragged rope. *Lebanese*

12379. A person dies before we appreciate him. *African (Jabo)*

12380. A person does not become clever by carrying books along. *African (Swahili)*

12381. A person does not lay on one side throughout the sleep. *African (Annang)*

12382. A person is not a palm nut which we cut open to see what it is inside. *African (Jabo)*

12383. A person is not always what he appears to be. *Japanese*

12384. A person is not corn that you peel and see the seeds. *African (Kpelle)*

12385. A person is not his words. *African (Kpelle)*

12386. A person is praised when dead. *African (Zulu)*

12387. A person without a spiritual director is as a body without a head. *Irish*

12388. A person without self-control is like a boat without a rudder. *Philippine*

12389. A restless person gets himself into a jam. *Philippine*

12390. A sick person does not hide his buttocks. *African (Bemba)*

12391. A sick person eats but little and spends much. *Serbo-Croatian*

12392. A stingy person dies in a sickly condition. *Lebanese*

12393. A stinking person does not know his own foul odor. *Japanese*

12394. A wealthy person is a selfish person. *African (Ovambo)*

12395. An armless person can not clean a fish dish. *Hawaiian*

12396. An idle person is the devil's cushion. *English*

12397. An industrious person soon succeeds. *Philippine*

12398. An ungrateful person loses his way. *Burmese*

12399. An unskillful person inspects his tools. *Japanese*

12400. Every person has his own idiosyncrasies. *Yiddish*

12401. For a deaf person, one doesn't celebrate two masses. *Russian*

12402. For a hungry person there is no coarse food. *Japanese*

12403. He who does not know a famous person surely will hear of him. *African (Hausa)*

12404. However good a person is, he has some weakness. *Philippine*

12405. Lazy persons will eventually lose even their trousers. *Philippine*

12406. Let each person drive away his own wasps. *Japanese*

12407. No one person possesses all the virtues. *Yiddish*

12408. Persons of imperfect learning have no reputation. *Indian (Tamil)*

12409. Persons of little learning are always talkative. *Indian (Tamil)*

12410. Seven persons don't wait for one. *Russian*

12411. Talented persons are short lived. *Japanese*

12412. The cunning person dies in cunning. *African (Zulu)*

12413. The famished person is not choosy about his food. *Japanese*

12414. The generous person gives and the miser is sorrowful.
Indian (Kashmiri)

12415. The guilty person flees from his own shadow. *Philippine*

12416. The ignorant person is like a cock out of season. *Turkish*

12417. The lazy person has no legs.
Egyptian

12418. The one-eyed person is a beauty in the country of the blind. *Egyptian*

12419. The person going home is not stopped by the dusk. *African (Bemba)*

12420. The person who beats the drum must also know the song.
African (Bemba)

12421. The person who goes ahead controls others. *Japanese*

12422. The person with least knowledge talks most. *Irish*

12423. The sick person knows the intensity of his suffering. *Indian (Tamil)*

12424. The third person makes good company. *Dutch*

12425. The unselfish person will draw a prize. *Japanese*

12426. There is no person without a fault. *Japanese*

12427. Three persons together, bitter world. *Japanese*

12428. Three persons together are the foundation of a quarrel. *Japanese*

12429. To know a person one must live in the same house with him. *Irish*

12430. Two persons never lit a fire without disagreeing. *Irish*

12431. Wealthy persons and spittoons become filthier as accumulation takes place. *Japanese*

12432. Whether a person is good or bad can be known by the friends with whom he associates. *Japanese*

PERSUASION

12433. The persuasion of the fortunate sways the doubtful. *English*

PESTILENCE

12434. There is no worse pestilence than a familiar enemy. *English*

PETER

12435. There's no harm in robbing Peter if you pay Paul with it. *American*

PETTICOAT

12436. A woman's petticoat is the devil's binder. *Rumanian*

12437. Near is my petticoat, but nearer is my smock. *English*

PHEASANT

12438. Had the pheasant not screamed it would not have been shot. *Japanese*

PHILOSOPHER

12439. Many talk like philosophers and live like fools. *English*

PHYSICIAN

12440. A good physician heals the illness of his country. *Japanese*

12441. A physician does not drink medicine for the sick. *African (Ga)*

12442. A physician has no business with one who is not sick. *Philippine*

12443. Deceive not your physician, confessor, or lawyer. *Spanish*

12444. Few physicians live well.
English

12445. He is a good physician who cures himself. *English*

12446. If you wish to die soon, make your physician your heir. *Rumanian*

12447. Only physicians may murder with impunity. *Slovenian*

12448. Physician, heal thyself. *English*

12449. Physicians and Buddhist priests are better if old. *Japanese*

12450. Physicians and judges murder with impunity. *Russian*

12451. Physicians' faults are covered with earth. *English*

12452. Physicians kill more than they cure. *English*

12453. The inexperienced physician makes a humpy churchyard. *Czech*

12454. The physician cannot prevent death. *African (Swahili)*

12455. The physician does not drink the medicine for the patient. *African (Ashanti)*

12456. The physician of anger is reason. *Greek*

12457. The physician who accepts no fee is worth no fee. *Hebrew*

12458. Until the physician has killed one or two he is not a physician. *Indian (Kashmiri)*

12459. Whatever a physician prescribes is a remedy. *Indian (Tamil)*

PIANO

12460. Everyone is eager to play the piano, but very few are willing to carry it on. *Mexican*

PICTURE

12461. A picture is worth a thousand words. *English*

12462. Painted pictures are dead speakers. *English*

12463. The picture of a rice cake does not satisfy hunger. *Japanese*

PIECE

12464. Someone else's piece is always sweeter. *Russian*

PIETY

12465. Filial piety is the source of many good deeds and the beginning of all virtue. *Japanese*

12466. Filial piety moves heaven and earth. *Chinese*

12467. Piety, prudence, wit, and civility, are the elements of true nobility. *German*

PIG

12468. A clean pig makes lean bacon. *Serbo-Croatian*

12469. A pig bought on credit grunts all the year. *Spanish*

12470. A pig may fly, but it isn't a likely bird. *English*

12471. A pig never becomes a sheep. *Greek*

12472. A pig won't spare even the most beautiful fruit. *Albanian*

12473. A pretty pig makes an ugly old sow. *English*

12474. As the pig, so the squeal; as the man, so the manner. *Slovakian*

12475. Everyone has a black pig in his house. *Chinese*

12476. Feed a pig and you'll have a hog. *English*

12477. Give a pig a chair, he'll want to get on the table. *Yiddish*

12478. Give a pig when it grunts and a child when it cries, and you will have a fine pig and a bad child. *Danish*

12479. Give the trough and the pigs will appear. *Russian*

12480. He that has but one pig easily fattens it. *Italian*

12481. He who lies in the sty will be eaten by the pigs. *Yiddish*

12482. If you pull one pig by the tail all the rest squeak. *Dutch*

12483. Let every pig dig for itself. *Manx*

12484. Old pigs have hard snouts. *German*

12485. One pig knows another. *Irish*

12486. The lazy pig does not eat ripe pears. *Italian*

12487. The pig dreams of its trough. *Finnish*

12488. The pig knows no meal hours. *Russian*

12489. The pig snatches the best apple. *Yiddish*

12490. The stillest pig sucks the most milk. *Jamaican*

12491. The worst pig gets the best acorn. *Spanish*

12492. The worst pig often gets the best pear. *English*

12493. The young pig grunts like the old sow. *English*

12494. There's no need to grease the fat pig's rump. *French*

12495. To lazy pigs the ground is always frozen. *Swedish*

12496. What satisfies the pig also fattens him. *Serbo-Croatian*

12497. When the pig has had a bellyful it upsets the trough. *Dutch*

12498. When the pig is proffered hold up the poke. *English*

12499. Where a pig burrows there are roots. *Latvian*

12500. Young pigs grunt as old swine grunted before them. *Danish*

PIGEON

12501. A blind pigeon may sometimes find a grain of wheat. *Danish*

12502. Do not abstain from sowing for fear of the pigeons. *French*

12503. Full pigeons find cherries bitter. *English*

12504. Pigeon flies with pigeon, hawk with hawk. *Iranian*

12505. Roast pigeons don't fly through the air. *Dutch*

PIKE

12506. The pike knows the bottom of the lake, and God the bottom of the sea. *Finnish*

PILGRIM

12507. Pilgrims seldom come home saints. *German*

PILL

12508. Bitter pills are gilded. *German*

12509. Bitter pills may have blessed effects. *Scottish*

12510. Bitter pills may have wholesome effects. *English*

12511. If the pills were pleasant, they would not want gilding. *English*

12512. Pills must be swallowed, not chewed. *German*

PILOT

12513. A good pilot is not known when the sea is calm and the weather fair. *Danish*

12514. The best pilots are ashore. *Dutch*

12515. Too many pilots wreck the ship. *Chinese*

PIN

12516. Even a pin is worth bending down for. *Polish*

12517. He that will not stoop for a pin will never be worth a pound. *English*

12518. He that will steal a pin will steal a better thing. *English*

PINCH

12519. Pinch yourself to find out how much it hurts others. *Pashto*

PINE

12520. As the pine and the cedar endure the frost and snow, so intelligence and wisdom overcome dangers and hardships. *Chinese*

12521. No one can cut down a pine and live to see the stump rotten. *American*

12522. The pine wishes herself a shrub when the ax is at her root. *English*

PINT

12523. A pint is a pound the world over. *American*

PIPE

12524. He'll dance to nothing but his own pipe. *English*

12525. No longer pipe, no longer dance. *English*

PIPER

12526. They that danced should pay the piper. *American*

PIT

12527. He falls into the pit who leads another into it. *Spanish*

12528. He who digs a pit for another should take his own measure. *Estonian*

12529. He who digs a pit for his brother will fall into it. *Moroccan*

12530. He who digs a pit for others falls into it himself. *German*

12531. If you dig a pit for someone else, you fall in it yourself. *Yiddish*

PITCH

12532. He that touches pitch shall be defiled. *English*

12533. He who handles pitch, besmears himself. *German*

12534. If you touch pitch you will be defiled. *Dutch*

PITCHER

12535. A pitcher is taken to the fountain many times, but one time it is not. *Greek*

12536. Little pitchers have wide ears. *English*

12537. The pitcher goes often to the well, but is broken at last. *English*

12538. The pitcher goes so often to the well that it leaves its handle or its mouth. *Spanish*

12539. The pitcher that goes often to the fountain leaves there either its handle or its spout. *Italian*

12540. There never was a pitcher that wouldn't spill. *American*

12541. Whether the pitcher strike the stone, or the stone the pitcher, woe be to the pitcher. *Spanish*

PITY (noun)

12542. A foreigner's pity is like a thorn's shadow. *Rumanian*

12543. He deserves no pity that chooses to do amiss twice. *English*

12544. Pity cures envy. *English*

12545. Pity has pure intentions. *Yiddish*

12546. Pity is a poor plaster. *English*

12547. Pity is but one remove from love.   *English*

12548. Pity without relief is like mustard without beef.   *English*

12549. Show pity to the lowly, obedience to the lofty.   *Turkish*

PITY (verb)

12550. He that pities another remembers himself.   *English*

PLACE

12551. A charred place smells a long time.   *Russian*

12552. A place for everything, and everything in its place.   *English*

12553. A sitting in one place makes a man sleep.   *African (Efik)*

12554. A woman's place is in her home.   *American*

12555. Any place in the yellow earth will do to bury a man.   *Chinese*

12556. Don't sleep in a troubled place, and you won't dream a troubled dream.
                                    Iranian

12557. East, West, there is no place that surpasses home.   *Japanese*

12558. He is in no place who is everywhere.   *Italian*

12559. He quits his place well that leaves his friend there.   *English*

12560. He who quits his place loses it.
                                     French

12561. High places have their precipices.   *English*

12562. It is not good to unpack in an open place.   *Indian (Tamil)*

12563. No one can be caught in places he does not visit.   *Danish*

12564. No place is as desirable as home.   *Japanese*

12565. One always knocks oneself in the sore place.   *French*

12566. That place seems good where we are not.   *Yiddish*

12567. The place to get top speed out of a horse is not the place where you can get top speed out of a canoe.
                          African (Hausa)

12568. The unlikeliest places are often likelier than those that are likeliest.
                                    English

12569. There are more places than the parish church.   *English*

12570. There is no place to be compared to my house.   *Japanese*

12571. There is no such place in the world from which a path would not lead to hell.   *Hungarian*

12572. Your place of abode directs your spirit.   *Japanese*

PLAN

12573. Form your plans before sunrise.
                          Indian (Tamil)

12574. If you want a plan by which to stop drinking, look at a drunken man when you are sober.   *Chinese*

12575. Make your whole year's plans in the spring, and your day's plans early in the morning.   *Chinese*

12576. One plans ahead but plans go awry.   *Maltese*

PLANK

12577. Tread not on a rotten plank.
                                   Turkish

PLANNING

12578. Planning is in the power of man; executing is in the hands of Heaven.   *Chinese*

PLANT (noun)

12579. A climbing plant does not stay alone.   *African (Ovambo)*

12580. A noble plant suits not with a stubborn ground. *English*

12581. From a bad seed will sprout a bad plant. *Philippine*

12582. Plants often removed never thrive. *German*

12583. The young plant grows from the parent stem. *African (Zulu)*

PLANT (verb)

12584. Some plant and harvest and others eat and give blessings. *Greek*

PLATE

12585. A damaged plate laughs at a broken plate. *African (Shona)*

12586. Every plate that is made breaks. *Pashto*

PLATING

12587. When the plating goes, the base will show. *Malaysian*

PLATTER

12588. He who comes too late finds the platter turned over. *Flemish*

PLAY (noun)

12589. A child's play does not last long. *African (Swahili)*

12590. A play may conceive a baby. *Korean*

12591. Every play must be played, and some must be the players. *Scottish*

12592. Fair play is a jewel. *English*

12593. Fair play is good play. *English*

12594. He that will cheat in play will not be honest in earnest. *Scottish*

12595. It is difficult for one man to act a play. *Chinese*

12596. It is no play to play with fire. *Welsh*

12597. Leave off while the play is good. *Scottish*

12598. No play without a fool in it. *English*

12599. Play, women, and wine undo men laughing. *English*

12600. Turn about is fair play. *English*

12601. What is play to one is death to another. *Indian (Bihar)*

12602. What is play to the cat is death to the mouse. *Danish*

12603. What is play to the strong is death to the weak. *Danish*

PLAY (verb)

12604. Better play for nothing than work for nothing. *Scottish*

12605. He plays best who wins. *German*

12606. He plays well that wins. *English*

12607. It is not clever to play but to stop playing. *Polish*

12608. Play, but don't try to retrieve your losses. *Russian*

PLAYING

12609. Playing and joking lead to quarrelling. *Maltese*

PLAYTHING

12610. Playthings for the cat, but tears for the mouse. *Russian*

PLEA

12611. A plea is always better than a threat. *Slovakian*

12612. An ill plea should be well pleaded. *English*

PLEASANT

12613. If pleasant it will be shortlived, if unpleasant longlived. *African (Fulani)*

PLEASE

12614. He had need rise betimes that would please everybody.   *English*

12615. He is not yet born who can please everybody.   *Danish*

12616. He that all men will please shall never find ease.   *English*

12617. He that would please all and himself too undertakes what he cannot do.   *English*

12618. If you want to please everybody, you'll die before your time.   *Yiddish*

12619. It is hard to please all. *English*

12620. It is hard to please everybody, yet it is harder to fool anyone.
Philippine

12621. Please the eye and plague the heart.   *English*

12622. Trying to please is always costly.   *Yiddish*

PLEASURE

12623. Consider not pleasures as they come, but as they go.   *English*

12624. Everyone takes his pleasure where he finds it.   *French*

12625. Every pleasure has a pain.
English

12626. Follow pleasure and pleasure will flee; flee pleasure and pleasure will follow thee.   *English*

12627. For one pleasure a thousand pains.   *French*

12628. From short pleasure long repentance.   *French*

12629. He who is in the midst of pleasure forgets everything else.
Philippine

12630. In hawks, hounds, arms, and love, for one pleasure a thousand pains.
French

12631. In war, hunting, and love, for one pleasure a hundred pains.
Portuguese

12632. Let pleasure overcome you and you learn to like it.   *English*

12633. Momentary pleasure is inferior pleasure.
Indian (Tamil)

12634. Never pleasure without repentance.   *English*

12635. No pleasure like misery when it does not last long.
Indian (Hindustani)

12636. Our pleasures are shallow; our sorrows are deep.   *Chinese*

12637. Pleasure first with pain to follow.   *Malaysian*

12638. Pleasure has a sting in its tail.
English

12639. Pleasure is the seed of pain; pain is the seed of pleasure. *Japanese*

12640. Pleasure is the seed of trouble.
Indian (Hindi)

12641. Pleasures steal away the mind.
Dutch

12642. Short pleasure, long lament.
English

12643. Short pleasure often brings long repentance.   *Danish*

12644. Stolen pleasures are sweetest.
English

12645. Sweetest pleasures are the shortest.   *American*

12646. The pleasures of the mighty are the tears of the poor.   *English*

12647. There is more pleasure in loving than in being beloved.   *English*

12648. Where there is pleasure there is pain.   *Japanese*

PLEDGE

12649. Pledge yourself and you've sold yourself.   *Yiddish*

PLENTY

12650. Plenty and envy lie down together. *African (Hausa)*

12651. Plenty breeds pride. *English*

12652. Plenty is strength. *American*

PLOUGH (noun)

12653. A much-used plough shines; stagnant waters stink. *Estonian*

12654. A plough that works, shines, but still water stinks. *Dutch*

12655. A used plough shines; standing water stinks. *German*

12656. Better have one plough going than two cradles. *English*

12657. Don't yoke the plough before the horses. *Dutch*

12658. He that by the plough would thrive, himself must either hold or drive. *English*

12659. He that trusts to borrowed ploughs will have his land lie fallow. *English*

12660. Never let the plough stand to catch a mouse. *English*

12661. The more a plough is used the brighter it becomes. *Slovenian*

12662. The plough goes not well if the ploughman hold it not. *English*

12663. Where the plough shall fail to go, there the weeds will surely grow. *English*

PLOUGH (verb)

12664. One ploughs, another sows, who will reap no one knows. *Danish*

12665. Plough deep while others sleep and you shall have corn to sell and keep. *English*

12666. Plough or plough not, you must pay your rent. *English*

12667. You must plough with such oxen as you have. *English*

PLOUGHMAN

12668. A bad ploughman beats the boy. *English*

12669. The ploughman has no time for mischief. *Russian*

PLUM

12670. A black plum is as sweet as a white. *English*

12671. If one receives a plum, one must return a peach. *Vietnamese*

PLUMMET

12672. Every plummet is not for every sound. *English*

POCKET

12673. A priest's pocket is not easily filled. *Danish*

12674. Empty pockets, empty promises. *Burmese*

12675. If your pocket gets empty, your faults will be many. *Libyan*

12676. It is too late to spare when the pocket is bare. *German*

12677. Put no more in the pocket than it will hold. *English*

POET

12678. A poet is a poor man. *African (Swahili)*

12679. Everyone is not born a poet. *English*

12680. It is not good to be the poet of a village. *German*

12681. Poets are born, but orators are made. *English*

POETRY

12682. In composing poetry you need no teacher. *Japanese*

POISON

12683. A poison embitters much sweetness. *English*

12684. Control poison with poison.
Japanese

12685. Even if we are surrounded by poison we will not die of it if we do not take it.   *Philippine*

12686. One poison drives out another.
English

12687. Poison is killed by boiling, and what will not poison you will fatten you.   *American*

12688. Poison is poison though it comes in a golden cup.   *English*

12689. Poison is the medicine of poison.   *Indian (Tamil)*

POLE

12690. The longest pole gets the persimmon.   *American*

POLICY

12691. Policy goes beyond strength.
English

POLITENESS

12692. Excessive politeness assuredly conceals conceit.   *Chinese*

12693. Great politeness usually means "I want something."   *Chinese*

12694. Politeness is not slavery.
African (Swahili)

12695. Politeness pleases even a cat.
Czech

12696. When politeness is overdone it becomes flattery.   *Japanese*

POLITICS

12697. Politics has no religion.
Lebanese

12698. Politics makes strange bedfellows.   *American*

POND

12699. Little ponds never hold big fish.
American

PONTOON

12700. An old pontoon often capsizes.
African (Bemba)

POOL

12701. Standing pools gather filth.
English

12702. What was a deep pool yesterday is but a shallows today.   *Japanese*

POOR

12703. He is not poor that has little, but he that desires much.   *English*

12704. He is poor indeed that can promise nothing.   *English*

12705. He that feeds the poor has treasure.   *English*

12706. He who laughs at the poor will become the butt of other's jokes.
Yiddish

12707. Poor and liberal, rich and covetous.   *English*

12708. The poor are cured by work, the rich by the doctor.   *Polish*

12709. The poor are not those who have little, but those who need much.
Swedish

12710. The poor have no leisure.
Japanese

12711. The poor have their own troubles and the rich their own.   *Maltese*

12712. The poor must dance as the rich pipe.   *German*

12713. The poor must pay for all.
English

12714. The poor think, the rich laugh.
Yiddish

12715. Twice a year the poor are badly off: summer and winter.   *Yiddish*

12716. When poor, liberal, when rich, stingy.   *Spanish*

POORER

12717. The poorer, the more generous.
Russian

POPE

12718. After one Pope another is made.
Italian

12719. Death spares neither Pope nor beggar. *Portuguese*

12720. He who has the Pope for his cousin may soon be a cardinal.
German

12721. He who never budges from Paris will never be Pope. *French*

12722. One living Pope is better than ten dead. *Italian*

12723. The Pope and a peasant know more than the Pope alone. *Italian*

12724. We cannot all be Pope in Rome.
German

12725. Where the Pope is there is Rome. *Italian*

PORCUPINE

12726. A porcupine will not mind needle grass. *African (Fulani)*

PORRIDGE

12727. Better porridge in peace than chocolate in alarm. *Mexican*

12728. He who has brewed the porridge must eat it himself. *Russian*

12729. Hot porridge will soak old crusts. *English*

12730. Old porridge is sooner heated than new made. *English*

12731. The porridge is cooled on the top. *African (Ovambo)*

12732. You can't cook porridge with a fool. *Russian*

12733. You won't spoil the porridge with butter. *Russian*

PORTION

12734. If you eat, eat a portion, but do not eat all. *African (Oji)*

POSITION

12735. It's not the position that makes the man, but the man the position.
Russian

12736. The higher the position, the greater the hardship. *Vietnamese*

POSSESSION

12737. Fast and loose is no possession.
English

12738. Possession is as good as a title.
French

12739. Possession is nine points of the law. *English*

12740. Possession satisfies. *Irish*

POSSESSOR

12741. The possessor came before the seeker. *African (Hausa)*

POST

12742. Little posts cannot support heavy weights. *Chinese*

12743. The post supports the roof and keeps it from falling in the hut.
African (Ovambo)

POSTPONE

12744. It is better to postpone than to forget. *Icelandic*

POT

12745. A cracked pot never fell off the hook. *Italian*

12746. A cracked pot will hold sugar.
Indian (Tamil)

12747. A little pot is soon hot. *English*

12748. A pot belonging to partners is neither hot nor cold. *Hebrew*

12749. A pot does not boil when not looked after. *African (Zulu)*

12750. A pot in the wind does not cook. *African (Ovambo)*

12751. A pot that belongs to many is ill stirred and worse boiled. *English*

12752. A small pot boils quickly. *African (Swahili)*

12753. A watched pot never boils. *English*

12754. Every family cooking pot has one black spot. *Chinese*

12755. Everyone knows what is boiling in his own pot. *Haitian*

12756. Every pot has its matching lid. *Philippine*

12757. Every pot has two handles. *English*

12758. For a lucky man the pot boils without fire. *Rumanian*

12759. If in the pot, it will come into the spoon. *Indian (Tamil)*

12760. If there's nothing in the pot, there's nothing on the plate. *Yiddish*

12761. Like pot, like lid. *Estonian*

12762. Place the pot on the stones after you've lit the fire. *African (Swahili)*

12763. Small pots soon run over. *Swedish*

12764. That which has been eaten out of the pot cannot be put into the dish. *Danish*

12765. That which will not make a pot may make a pot lid. *English*

12766. The earthen pot must keep clear of the brass kettle. *English*

12767. The flawed pot lasts longest. *French*

12768. The larger the pot, the more rice adheres. *Malaysian*

12769. The pot always calls the kettle an ugly name. *American*

12770. The pot boils best on your own hearth. *Danish*

12771. The pot calls the kettle black. *English*

12772. The pot cooks best on its own stove. *Indian (Hindi)*

12773. The pot that boils too much loses its flavor. *Portuguese*

12774. There is no pot so ugly but finds its cover. *Spanish*

12775. What is in the pot will come out in the ladle. *Iranian*

12776. When one pot hits another, both break. *Rumanian*

12777. When the pot boils over, it cools itself. *English*

12778. When the pot is full it will boil over. *Scottish*

12779. When you tap the pot, you see where the crack is. *African (Ashanti)*

12780. You can't boil the pot with green sticks. *Jamaican*

POTTAGE

12781. Blow your own pottage and not mine. *English*

POTTER

12782. Every potter praises his pot, especially if cracked. *Spanish*

12783. Every potter vaunts his own pot. *French*

12784. Potters never fail to praise their pots, the more so when they are cracked. *Mexican*

12785. The potter drinks water from a broken pot. *Iranian*

12786. The potter knows where to place the handle. *Greek*

POTTERY

12787. Pottery and fine porcelain must not quarrel. *Chinese*

POUND

12788. A thousand pounds and a bottle of hay is all one at Doomsday. *English*

12789. In a thousand pounds of law there's not an ounce of love.   *English*

POVERTY

12790. Do not look for poverty; it will find you.   *Polish*

12791. Do not wake poverty when it sleeps.   *Polish*

12792. Happy poverty overcomes everything.   *Yiddish*

12793. He bears poverty very ill, who is ashamed of it.   *English*

12794. He that is in poverty is still in suspicion.   *English*

12795. He who is content in his poverty is wonderfully rich.   *English*

12796. Honest poverty is thinly sown.   *French*

12797. If you don't want to resign yourself to poverty, resign yourself to work.   *African (Hausa)*

12798. It is poverty that causes the free man to become a slave.   *African (Ashanti)*

12799. Neither great poverty nor great riches will hear reason.   *English*

12800. One does not throw away the stick that drives off poverty.   *African (Hausa)*

12801. Poverty and anger do not agree.   *Egyptian*

12802. Poverty and hunger have many learned disciples.   *German*

12803. Poverty and love are hard to conceal.   *Norwegian*

12804. Poverty and wealth are twin sisters.   *Albanian*

12805. Poverty benumbs intelligence.   *Vietnamese*

12806. Poverty breeds strife.   *English*

12807. Poverty brings nagging.   *Greek*

12808. Poverty destroys a man's reputation.   *African (Yoruba)*

12809. Poverty does not destroy virtue, nor does wealth bestow it.   *Spanish*

12810. Poverty follows the poor.   *Hebrew*

12811. Poverty generates resourcefulness.   *Russian*

12812. Poverty has a thick head.   *Yiddish*

12813. Poverty has no kin.   *Italian*

12814. Poverty hides wisdom.   *Yiddish*

12815. Poverty is a sort of leprosy.   *French*

12816. Poverty is an enemy to good manners.   *English*

12817. Poverty is disgrace.   *African (Hausa)*

12818. Poverty is no crime.   *Russian*

12819. Poverty is no disgrace, but also no great honor.   *Yiddish*

12820. Poverty is no disgrace, just so it isn't filthy.   *Yiddish*

12821. Poverty is no sin.   *Spanish*

12822. Poverty is no sin, but it is a branch of roguery.   *Spanish*

12823. Poverty is no vice but an inconvenience.   *English*

12824. Poverty is no vice but something far worse.   *Russian*

12825. Poverty is not a shame, but the being ashamed of it is.   *English*

12826. Poverty is not a sin, it is something worse.   *Russian*

12827. Poverty is not a vice.   *French*

12828. Poverty is the common fate of scholars.   *Chinese*

12829. Poverty is the mother of all arts and trades.   *English*

12830. Poverty is the mother of health.
English

12831. Poverty is the mother of the arts. *Slovakian*

12832. Poverty is the reward of idleness. *Dutch*

12833. Poverty makes a free man become a slave. *African (Oji)*

12834. Poverty makes a man dull witted. *Japanese*

12835. Poverty makes strange bedfellows. *English*

12836. Poverty makes us acquainted with strange bedfellows sometimes.
American

12837. Poverty parts fellowship.
English

12838. Poverty passes by an industrious man's door. *Greek*

12839. Poverty pursues the poor.
Hebrew

12840. Poverty reveals itself first on the face. *Yiddish*

12841. Poverty will not drive away freedom. *African (Hausa)*

12842. Poverty without debts is perfect riches. *Lebanese*

12843. The poverty of the learned is better than the wealth of the unlearned.
Indian (Tamil)

12844. There is no poverty where there is virtue and no wealth or honor where virtue is not. *Chinese*

12845. There is no virtue that poverty destroys not. *English*

12846. When poverty comes in at the door, friendship flees out at the window. *Scottish*

12847. When poverty comes in at the door, love flies out of the window.
English

12848. When poverty crosses the threshold, love flies out of the window.
African (Swahili)

12849. When poverty enters from the window, love goes out of the door.
Maltese

12850. With a brush and a needle poverty can be covered up. *Yiddish*

POWDER

12851. Powder doesn't refuse fire, nor fire fuel. *Malagasy*

POWER

12852. Do not leave undone what is in your power to do. *Turkish*

12853. Every power is subject to another power. *African (Shona)*

12854. It is not in the pilot's power to prevent the wind from blowing.
Spanish

12855. Much power makes many enemies. *English*

12856. Power and violence shut the mouth. *Maltese*

12857. Power often goes before talent.
Danish

12858. Power seldom grows old at Court. *English*

12859. Power weakens the wicked.
English

12860. Where the power, there the law.
Russian

PRACTICE (noun)

12861. Let your practice keep step with your knowledge. *Chinese*

12862. Practice comes half way to meet every effort. *Welsh*

12863. Practice is better than a teacher. *Welsh*

12864. Practice is second nature.
Welsh

12865. Practice is the mother of perfection.
Welsh

12866. Practice makes perfect.
English

12867. Practice makes the master.
German

PRACTICE (verb)

12868. Practice what you preach.
English

12869. Who practices nothing shall have nothing.
English

PRAISE (noun)

12870. A man's praise in his own mouth does stink.
English

12871. Faint praise is akin to abuse.
Danish

12872. Faint praise is disparagement.
English

12873. Little praise is dispraise.
Indian (Hindi)

12874. Old praise dies unless you feed it.
English

12875. Praise has killed the antelope.
African (Annang)

12876. Praise is but the shadow of virtue.
English

12877. Praise makes good men better and bad men worse.
English

12878. Praise paves the way to friendship.
Danish

12879. Praise without profit puts little into the pot.
English

12880. Sing his praise who gives you food.
Indian (Bihar)

12881. The praise of fools is censure in disguise.
English

12882. Too much praise is a burden.
English

12883. True praise roots and spreads.
English

12884. Without praise you cannot sell; without disparagement you cannot buy.
Russian

PRAISE (verb)

12885. Avoid those who always praise you.
African (Swahili)

12886. He that praises himself, spatters himself.
English

12887. He that praises publicly, will slander privately.
English

12888. He who praises himself will be humiliated.
Yiddish

12889. It's better to praise yourself than to disparage others.
Yiddish

12890. Praise at parting.
English

12891. Praise little, dispraise less.
American

12892. Rather than be praised, try not to be slandered.
Japanese

12893. What you cannot praise do not disparage.
Russian

PRAISING

12894. Praising is not loving.
German

PRATE (noun)

12895. Prate is prate, but it is the duck that lays the eggs.
English

PRATE (verb)

12896. He who prates much, lies much.
German

PRAWN

12897. The prawn does not know of the hump on its back.
Malaysian

PRAY

12898. Better to pray for yourself than to curse another.　　　　*Yiddish*

12899. He that would learn to pray, let him go to sea.　　　　*English*

PRAYER

12900. A short prayer reaches heaven.　　　　*English*

12901. Before going to war say one prayer, before going to sea, two, before getting married, three.　　　　*Polish*

12902. Compulsory prayers never reach heaven.　　　　*Slovakian*

12903. If the dog's prayer were accepted, there would be a shower of bones from heaven.　　　　*Turkish*

12904. If you do nothing for your fellow man, then all your prayers to the Buddha are in vain.　　　　*Chinese*

12905. It is better to offer your prayers to the spirits than to man.　　　　*Chinese*

12906. Of prayer there must be acceptance.　　　　*Turkish*

12907. Prayer is heard best at night.　　　　*Yiddish*

12908. Prayer or no prayer, you can't eat out of an empty bowl.　　　　*Slovakian*

12909. Prayers and provender hinder no journey.　　　　*English*

12910. Prayers to God and service to the Tsar are not lost.　　　　*Russian*

12911. The prayer ascends and the blessing descends.　　　　*Yiddish*

PREACH

12912. He preaches well that lives well.　　　　*English*

PREACHER

12913. Cold preachers make bold sinners.　　　　*American*

12914. Everyone is a preacher under the gallows.　　　　*Dutch*

12915. He that will not be saved needs no preacher.　　　　*English*

12916. There are many preachers who don't hear themselves.　　　　*German*

PREACHING

12917. He is past preaching to who does not care to do well.　　　　*French*

12918. It is bad preaching to deaf ears.　　　　*German*

12919. There is no good in preaching to the hungry.　　　　*German*

PRECAUTION

12920. Precaution must be taken in advance.　　　　*Japanese*

PRECEPT

12921. Precepts may lead but examples draw.　　　　*English*

PREFERENCE

12922. Woe to him who gives a preference to one neighbor over another.　　　　*Irish*

PRESENCE

12923. A good presence is letters of recommendation.　　　　*English*

12924. Presence does more than the written word.　　　　*Greek*

PRESENT

12925. A present looks for a present.　　　　*Russian*

12926. Accept a present and you have sold your freedom.　　　　*Hungarian*

12927. Little presents maintain friendship.　　　　*French*

12928. Presents keep friendship warm.　　　　*German*

12929. Small presents keep friendship warm.　　　　*Slovenian*

PRESERVE

12930. Preserve the old, but know the new. *Chinese*

PRETTINESS

12931. Prettiness dies first. *English*

12932. Prettiness makes no pottage. *English*

PRETTY

12933. Pretty is as pretty does. *American*

12934. You don't have to be pretty if you are charming. *Yiddish*

PREVENTION

12935. Prevention is better than cure. *English*

12936. Prevention of desire equals theft of possessions. *African (Fulani)*

PREY

12937. When its time has arrived, the prey comes to the hunter. *Iranian*

PRICE

12938. If the prices are equal, choose the best. *Moroccan*

12939. Prices and lifetimes are in the hands of God. *Lebanese*

12940. When prices go down buy; when prices go up sell. *Maltese*

PRIDE

12941. A little pride is good even in a wild horse. *English*

12942. He who is weeping has no pride. *Indian (Tamil)*

12943. If pride were an art, how many doctors we should have. *Italian*

12944. If you sow pride, you will reap war. *Philippine*

12945. Overdone pride makes naked side. *English*

12946. Pride and grace dwell never in one place. *English*

12947. Pride and poverty are ill met, yet often seen together. *English*

12948. Pride breakfasted with Plenty, dined with Poverty, and supped with Infamy. *English*

12949. Pride brings curses. *African (Hausa)*

12950. Pride costs us more than hunger, thirst, and cold. *English*

12951. Pride feels no frost. *English*

12952. Pride feels no pain. *Irish*

12953. Pride goes before, shame follows after. *English*

12954. Pride had rather go out of the way than go behind. *English*

12955. Pride in children is more precious than money. *Yiddish*

12956. Pride in prosperity turns to misery in adversity. *English*

12957. Pride invites calamity; humility reaps its harvest. *Chinese*

12958. Pride is as loud a begger as want, and a great deal more saucy. *English*

12959. Pride is the author of every sin. *Irish*

12960. Pride is the sworn enemy to content. *English*

12961. Pride is unbecoming in women. *Hebrew*

12962. Pride lies on the dungheap. *Yiddish*

12963. Pride makes the crab go sideways. *Jamaican*

12964. Pride may lurk under a threadbare cloak. *English*

12965. Pride must abide. *English*

12966. Pride never left his master without a fall. *Scottish*

12967. Pride scorns the vulgar, yet lies at its mercy. *English*

12968. Pride soars as high as the sky. *Philippine*

12969. Pride swells with flattery. *Serbo-Croatian*

12970. Pride that dines on vanity sups on contempt. *American*

12971. Pride went out on horseback and returned on foot. *Italian*

12972. Pride will have a fall. *English*

12973. Pride will spit in pride's face. *English*

12974. The pride of the poor does not endure. *Danish*

12975. The pride of the rich makes the labors of the poor. *English*

12976. There is no pride like that of a beggar grown rich. *French*

12977. When pride is in the saddle, shame is on the crupper. *English*

12978. When pride rides, shame lacqueys. *English*

12979. Where pride leads shame follows. *Welsh*

PRIEST

12980. A dumb priest never got a parish. *Irish*

12981. A priest does not accept another priest nor a deacon another deacon. *Greek*

12982. A priest helps a priest. *Hebrew*

12983. A priest is not chosen by the length of his beard. *Serbo-Croatian*

12984. As is the priest, so is the parish. *Russian*

12985. As the priest, so the blessing. *Polish*

12986. Bad priests bring the devil into the church. *English*

12987. It is his own child the priest baptizes first. *Irish*

12988. Like priest like people. *English*

12989. No priest, no mass. *English*

12990. One loves the priest and another his wife. *Russian*

12991. Priest and peasant together know more than the priest alone. *Serbo-Croation*

12992. Priests also smile pleasantly on your women. *German*

12993. Priests and women never forget. *German*

12994. Priests bless themselves first. *German*

12995. Priests, friars, nuns, and chickens never have enough. *Italian*

12996. Priests love pretty wenches. *English*

12997. Priests should not prate out of the cónfessional. *German*

12998. Some like the priest and some like the priest's wife. *Greek*

12999. Some like the priest, some his wife, and some his daughter. *Russian*

13000. Such is the priest, such is the clerk. *English*

13001. The priest and the cock sing on an empty stomach. *Russian*

13002. The priest does not eat pilaff every day. *Turkish*

13003. The priest ever returns to his temple and the merchant to his shop. *Chinese*

13004. The priest forgets that he was clerk. *English*

13005. The priest loves his flock, but the lambs more than the wethers. *German*

13006. The priest to his book, the peasant to his plough. *Danish*

13007. Whatever the priest tells you to do, do it; what you see him do, do not.
Greek

PRINCE

13008. All are not princes who ride with the emperor.   *Dutch*

13009. As princes fiddle, subjects must dance.   *German*

13010. If the prince wants an apple, his servants take the tree.   *German*

13011. Never joke in the presence of a prince.   *Chinese*

13012. Princes have long hands and many ears.   *German*

13013. Princes use men as the husbandman uses bees.   *French*

13014. Princes will not be served on conditions.   *French*

13015. The prince that is feared of many must of necessity fear many.
English

13016. To censure princes is perilous, and to praise them is lying.   *Italian*

13017. When the prince wants a minister to die, he dies.   *Chinese*

PRISON

13018. A prison made of pearls and gold is still a prison.   *Philippine*

13019. He who was born in a prison remembers a prison.   *Greek*

13020. Never seemed a prison fair, or a bride ugly.   *German*

13021. Never seemed a prison fair or mistress foul.   *French*

13022. There is no prison like a guilty conscience.   *Welsh*

PRISONER

13023. A prisoner does not choose his task.   *African (Hausa)*

PROBABILITY

13024. A thousand probabilities do not make one truth.   *English*

PROCESSION

13025. It is an ill procession where the devil bears the cross.   *English*

13026. It is an ill procession where the devil holds the candle.   *English*

13027. No matter how long the procession is, it will surely wind up in church.   *Philippine*

PROCRASTINATION

13028. Procrastination is the thief of time.   *English*

PRODIGAL

13029. A young prodigal, an old beggar.   *English*

13030. The prodigal robs his heir, the miser himself.   *English*

13031. Young prodigal in a coach will be old beggar barefoot.   *English*

PROFIT

13032. Even in Mecca profit is all the same.   *African (Hausa)*

13033. Everyone is wise for his own profit.   *Portuguese*

13034. If the profits are great, the risks are great.   *Chinese*

13035. Little profit comes from constant drunkenness.   *Irish*

13036. No profit without pains.
Scottish

13037. Profit and loss are companions.
Hebrew

13038. Profit and loss are twin brothers.   *Estonian*

13039. Profits and losses walk in the same shoes.   *Russian*

13040. Profits don't live without losses.
Russian

13041. Profit is better than fame.
Danish

13042. Profit is the brother of loss.
Turkish

13043. Profit surpasses pride.
African (Swahili)

13044. Small profits and often are better than large profits and seldom.
German

13045. Small profits are sweet.
Danish

13046. Take a profit from your loss.
Japanese

13047. There is hardly any profit in reluctant work.   *Maltese*

13048. What is none of my profit shall be none of my peril.   *Scottish*

13049. Without trouble there is no profit.   *African (Hausa)*

13050. You would not know where to put all the profits if there were no losses.   *Russian*

PROMISE (noun)

13051. A fair promise binds a fool.
French

.3052. A promise breaker is in the wrong way.   *Indian (Tamil)*

13053. A promise is a charge to keep.
Indian (Kashmiri)

13054. A promise is a debt.   *Irish*

13055. A promise is a debt you should not forget.   *Philippine*

13056. A promise is a loan.
African (Ovambo)

13057. A promise made at an inn never leaves it.   *Latvian*

13058. A youth's promise is like froth.
Welsh

13059. All promises are either broken or kept.   *English*

13060. Every promise is a debt.
Italian

13061. Great promise, small performance.   *English*

13062. It is easier to make a promise than to fulfill it.   *Iranian*

13063. Nothing weighs lighter than a promise.   *German*

13064. Old promises are left behind.
Australian (Maori)

13065. Promise is debt.   *English*

13066. Promises and pie crusts are made to be broken.   *English*

13067. Promises don't fill the belly.
German

13068. Promises make debts. *German*

13069. Promises make debts, and debts make promises.   *Dutch*

13070. The little promise you promised is not forgotten.   *African (Bemba)*

13071. What appears full of promise often turns out a failure.   *Irish*

PROMISE (verb)

13072. Easily promised, quickly forgotten.   *Japanese*

13073. Easy to promise, hard to fulfill.
Yiddish

13074. He is poor that cannot promise.
Scottish

13075. He that promises too much means nothing.   *English*

13076. To promise and give nothing is a comfort for a fool.   *English*

13077. To promise is easy, to keep is troublesome.   *Danish*

13078. Who promises much is most likely to fulfill very little.   *Mexican*

PROMISER

13079. No greater promisers than they who have nothing to give.   *Dutch*

PROMISING

13080. Promising and performing are two things. *French*

13081. Promising is one thing, performing another. *German*

13082. Promising is the eve of giving. *English*

PROMPTNESS

13083. Promptness carries the day. *Australian (Maori)*

PROOF

13084. An ounce of proof is worth a ton of assertions. *American*

13085. The proof of the pudding is in the eating. *English*

13086. The soldering is proof of the goldsmith. *Burmese*

PROPER

13087. He is proper that has proper conditions. *English*

PROPERTY

13088. A fool's property is the prey of all. *Indian (Bihar)*

13089. A poor man's property does not increase. *African (Ovambo)*

13090. He who possesses no property is but half a man. *Indian (Tamil)*

13091. He who takes care of his property will not be robbed. *Indian (Tamil)*

13092. Lawful property is not lost. *Turkish*

13093. Property is the remedy for disgrace. *African (Hausa)*

13094. Property not looked after perishes. *Indian (Tamil)*

13095. The property of food is the support of life. *Indian (Tamil)*

13096. The sick man's property belongs to the doctor. *African (Hausa)*

13097. Touch my property touch my life. *American*

13098. Unguarded property teaches people to steal. *Lebanese*

PROPHET

13099. A prophet is with honor save in his own country. *Indian (Bihar)*

PROPRIETY

13100. Better die than turn your back on propriety. *Chinese*

13101. Propriety governs the superior man; law, the inferior man. *Chinese*

PROSPECT

13102. One cannot live upon prospects. *American*

13103. Prospect is often better than possession. *English*

PROSPERITY

13104. He who swells in prosperity, will shrink in adversity. *English*

13105. In prosperity think of adversity. *Dutch*

13106. Prosperity and beautiful women are the most treacherous things in the world. *Slovenian*

13107. Prosperity discovers vice, adversity virtue. *American*

13108. Prosperity forgets father and mother. *Spanish*

13109. Prosperity gets followers, but adversity distinguishes them. *English*

13110. Prosperity glitters and adversity shrivels. *Libyan*

13111. Prosperity is the fruit of industry, while idleness begets poverty. *Australian (Maori)*

13112. Prosperity lets go the bridle. *English*

13113. The prosperity of the ship owner is at the mercy of the wind.
Indian (Tamil)

13114. When prosperity smiles, beware of its guiles. *Dutch*

PROSTITUTE

13115. A prostitute knows how to deprive one of his money. *Indian (Tamil)*

13116. The prostitute who has no customer reproaches her own mouth to have no charm. *Vietnamese*

PROVE

13117. That which proves too much proves nothing. *English*

13118. Who proves too much proves nothing. *French*

PROVERB

13119. A good proverb does not strike one in the brow, but full in the eye.
Russian

13120. A proverb can't be judged.
Russian

13121. A proverb does not tell a lie; an empty pipe does not burn. *Estonian*

13122. A proverb is always wise.
Russian

13123. A proverb is the horse of conversation. *African (Yoruba)*

13124. A proverb never tells a lie.
Lebanese

13125. A proverb says what man thinks. *Swedish*

13126. A wise man who knows proverbs reconciles difficulties.
African (Yoruba)

13127. Old proverbs are the children of truth. *Welsh*

13128. One who applies proverbs gets what he wants. *African (Shona)*

13129. Proverbs are butterflies, some are caught, others escape. *Russian*

13130. Proverbs are not vain words.
Polish

13131. Proverbs are the coins of the people. *Russian*

13132. Proverbs are the daughters of daily experience. *Dutch*

13133. Proverbs beautify speech.
Russian

13134. Proverbs cannot be contradicted. *Irish*

13135. The proverb cannot be bettered.
Irish

13136. The proverb comes from the intellect, and the intellect from the proverb. *Russian*

13137. There is no proverb without a grain of truth. *Russian*

13138. Though the proverb is abandoned, it is not falsified. *Irish*

13139. When the occasion comes, the proverb comes. *African (Oji)*

13140. You can't argue against a proverb, a fool, or the truth. *Russian*

13141. You can't get around a proverb.
Russian

PROVIDE

13142. Provide for the worst, the best will save itself. *English*

PROVIDENCE

13143. Providence is better than rent.
English

PROVIDING

13144. Providing is preventing.
English

PROVISION

13145. Although you have many provisions, you will see the end of them.
African (Wolof)

13146. Provision in season makes a rich house. *Scottish*

13147. Without provisions, one does not start upon a journey.   *Turkish*

PRUDENCE

13148. An ounce of prudence is worth a pound of gold.   *English*

13149. Prudence does no harm.
    German

13150. Prudence looks before as well as behind.   *American*

PSALM

13151. He that can't sing psalms, let him pray.   *American*

PUBLIC

13152. He that does anything for the public is accounted to do it for nobody.   *English*

13153. He who serves the public has a sorry master.   *Italian*

13154. It's bitter and bad when the public is wrong.   *Yiddish*

13155. Who serves the public serves a fickle master.   *Dutch*

13156. Who serves the public, serves no one.   *Italian*

PUDDING

13157. Better some of a pudding than none of a pie.   *English*

13158. Cold pudding settles love.
    English

13159. Handle the pudding while it is hot.   *Scottish*

13160. Pudding before praise. *English*

13161. Those that eat black pudding will dream of the devil.   *English*

13162. Too much pudding will choke a dog.   *English*

PULL

13163. It is easier to pull down than to build up.   *English*

PULLET

13164. A pullet in the pen is worth a hundred in the fen.   *English*

PUMPKIN

13165. A young pumpkin now is better than a full grown one later on.
    Hebrew

13166. Every pumpkin is known by its stem.   *Hebrew*

13167. The pumpkin has no unripe parts.   *African (Jabo)*

PUNCTUALITY

13168. Punctuality is the soul of business.   *English*

PUNISH

13169. Who punishes one threatens a hundred.   *French*

PUNISHMENT

13170. Many without punishment, but none without fault.   *English*

13171. Punishment is lame, but it comes.   *English*

13172. Punishment is not putting to death, it is improving character.
    African (Hausa)

13173. The best way to avoid punishment is to fear it.   *Chinese*

13174. The punishment of one's conscience is heavier than that of the law.
    Philippine

13175. Undeserved punishment is better than deserved punishment.
    Indian (Tamil)

PUP

13176. He who has a pup as good as has a dog.   *African (Hausa)*

PUPIL

13177. Every pupil as he is taught.
    Irish

PUPPY

13178. A puppy does not hunt rabbits with a big dog.   *African (Ovambo)*

13179. A three-day-old puppy does not fear a tiger.   *Korean*

13180. It is bad for puppies to play with bear cubs.   *Danish*

PURCHASE

13181. No purchase like a gift.
French

PURSE

13182. A full purse makes the mouth run over.   *English*

13183. A full purse never wanted a friend.   *Scottish*

13184. A heavy purse makes a light heart.   *English*

13185. A heavy purse makes a light-hearted spirit.   *Yiddish*

13186. A light purse is a heavy curse.
English

13187. A light purse makes a heavy heart.   *English*

13188. A purse cries before leaving the pocket.   *Russian*

13189. An empty purse and a new house make a man wise, but too late.
English

13190. An empty purse causes a full heart.   *English*

13191. An empty purse fills the face with wrinkles.   *English*

13192. An empty purse frights away friends.   *English*

13193. An empty purse is the devil.
English

13194. Ask your purse what you should buy.   *English*

13195. Be it better, be it worse, be ruled by him that has the purse.   *Scottish*

13196. Be it better, be it worse, do after him that bears the purse.   *English*

13197. Better a lean purse than an empty stomach.   *English*

13198. Empty is the purse that holds other folk's money.   *Swedish*

13199. He that has a full purse, never wanted a friend.   *Scottish*

13200. He that shows his purse longs to be rid of it.   *English*

13201. He who cannot pay with his purse must pay with his hide.
German

13202. He who has his purse full preaches to the poor man.   *French*

13203. Heavy purses and light hearts can sustain much.   *Dutch*

13204. If you put nothing into your purse, you can take nothing out.
English

13205. If you sell your purse to your wife, give your breeches into the bargain.   *Scottish*

13206. It is easy to be generous out of another man's purse.   *Danish*

13207. It is ill to make a silk purse of a sow's ear.   *Scottish*

13208. Keep your purse and your mouth closed.   *English*

13209. Let your purse be your master.
English

13210. Little and often fills the purse.
English

13211. Near is my purse, but nearer is my soul.   *English*

13212. One may steal nothing save a lawyer's purse.   *French*

13213. So it goes in this world: one has the purse, the other has the money.
Yiddish

13214. That is but an empty purse that is full of other men's money.   *English*

13215. The longest purse will prevail.
American

13216. The purse of the dead man is turned inside out. *Greek*

13217. There's no making a silk purse of a sow's ear. *Dutch*

13218. Usurers' purses and women's plackets are never satisfied. *English*

13219. When the purse is light there is no vitality. *Japanese*

13220. Wrinkled purses make wrinkled faces. *English*

13221. You can't make a silk purse out of a sow's ear. *English*

PURSE STRING

13222. The purse strings are the most common ties of friendship. *English*

PUT

13223. If you put something in, you can take something out. *Yiddish*

Q

QUAIL

13224. The quail is very small but can tire both horse and rider.
Serbo-Croatian

QUALITY

13225. Quality without quantity is little thought of. *Scottish*

13226. When quality opens the door there is poverty behind. *English*

QUARREL (noun)

13227. An old quarrel is easily renewed. *Italian*

13228. Avoiding a quarrel is better than asking forgiveness.
African (Hausa)

13229. Female quarrels breed court cases. *African (Shona)*

13230. If you sleep on a quarrel it becomes less serious. *Hebrew*

13231. In a false quarrel there is no true valor. *English*

13232. In a quarrel, each side is right.
Yiddish

13233. Lovers' quarrels are love redoubled. *Portuguese*

13234. Quarrels come of laughter, and disease of coughing. *Indian (Hindi)*

13235. Quarrel is not a food which is eaten. *African (Ga)*

13236. The first quarrel is the best quarrel. *Yiddish*

13237. The noblemen's quarrels can be read on the backs of the peasants.
Russian

13238. The quarrels of married couples and the west wind stop at evening.
Japanese

13239. The quarrel that doesn't concern you is pleasant to hear about.
African (Hausa)

13240. Those who in quarrels interpose must often wipe a bloody nose.
American

13241. Without a second person a quarrel cannot start. *African (Swahili)*

QUARREL (verb)

13242. When two quarrel both are in the wrong. *Dutch*

QUESTION (noun)

13243. Ask no questions and get no lies. *American*

13244. Don't ask questions about fairy tales. *Yiddish*

13245. Every question requires not an answer. *English*

13246. Hasty questions require slow answers. *Dutch*

13247. He who asks questions hears the language, or gets interpretations. *African (Efik)*

13248. It is a blind man's question to ask why those things are loved which are beautiful. *English*

13249. Tear off the curtain of doubt by questions. *Egyptian*

QUESTION (verb)

13250. He that nothing questions, nothing learns. *English*

QUESTIONING

13251. Questioning is the door of knowledge. *Irish*

QUICK

13252. Quick and well seldom go together. *Danish*

QUIETNESS

13253. Quietness is best. *English*

QUILL

13254. One quill is better in the hand than seven geese upon the strand. *Dutch*

R

RABBI

13255. If you're at odds with your rabbi, make peace with your bartender.
Yiddish

13256. The rabbi drinks up the wine and orders his followers to be gay.
Yiddish

13257. Whether a rabbi or a bath-house keeper, all have enemies.
Yiddish

RABBIT

13258. Even the nibbling rabbit can gorge itself to death. *Tibetan*

13259. If you chase after two rabbits, you won't catch even one. *Russian*

13260. If you run after two rabbits, you won't catch either one. *Armenian*

13261. It is easier to watch a flock of rabbits than a woman. *Rumanian*

13262. When the rabbit has escaped, comes advice. *Spanish*

RABBLE

13263. Govern the rabble by opposing them. *Egyptian*

RACE

13264. The race is got by running.
English

RAG

13265. Everyone sells his rags in his own market. *Egyptian*

13266. If you must be in rags, let your rags be tidy. *Irish*

13267. Rags disgrace a handsome person. *African (Yoruba)*

13268. You may deal in rags and dress in velvet. *Yiddish*

RAGE

13269. Rage vails less than courage.
French

13270. Violent rages are soon over.
Greek

RAILLERY

13271. No raillery is worse than that which is true. *English*

RAIN (noun)

13272. A heavy rain is good for the fields and bad for the roads. *Yiddish*

13273. A little rain stills a great wind.
English

13274. After rain comes fair weather.
Dutch

13275. After rain comes sunshine.
English

13276. Don't empty your water jar until the rain falls. *Philippine*

13277. Don't put the roof on when the rain is wetting you. *African (Hausa)*

13278. Drop by drop rain fills a pot. *African (Annang)*

13279. For a morning rain leave not your journey. *English*

13280. It is better to walk in the rain than to wear a rain hat that does not fit. *Philippine*

13281. It's pleasant to look on the rain when one stands dry. *Dutch*

13282. More rain, more rest. *English*

13283. One day's rain makes up for many days' drought. *African (Yoruba)*

13284. Prepare shelter before the rain falls. *Philippine*

13285. Rain chases you into the house and a quarrelsome wife chases you out. *Yiddish*

13286. Rain has such narrow shoulders it will get in anywhere. *English*

13287. Small rain lays a great dust. *English*

13288. Though the heavy rain is over, the dropping from the trees continues. *Indian (Tamil)*

13289. Though the rain fall for forty years it does not pass into the marble. *Turkish*

13290. When rain beats on a leopard it wets him, but it does not wash out his spots. *African (Ashanti)*

13291. While the rain is still away, open up the mulch straw. *Hawaiian*

13292. While the rain is still far off, thatch your house. *Hawaiian*

13293. Who has been almost drowned fears not the rain. *Albanian*

RAIN (verb)

13294. Although it rain, throw not away your watering pot. *English*

13295. It never rains but it pours. *English*

13296. To see it rain is better than to be in it. *English*

RAINBOW

13297. Go to the end of the rainbow and you'll find a crock of gold. *English*

13298. The rainbow is not God but it prevents God sending rain. *African (Hausa)*

13299. When there's a rainbow, it's a sign that God has forgiven our sins. *Yiddish*

RAINDROP

13300. Falling raindrops will wear through a stone. *Japanese*

13301. Raindrops will hollow a stone. *Korean*

RAISIN

13302. Every raisin contains a pip. *Libyan*

RAKE

13303. What the rake gathers, the fork scatters. *English*

RANCOR

13304. Rancor sticks long by the ribs. *English*

RANK

13305. Rank does not make the man. *Greek*

RAPIER

13306. Many who wear rapiers are afraid of goose quills. *English*

RASCAL

13307. He who makes a rascal suffer obtains reward.   *Moroccan*

RASHNESS

13308. Rashness is not valor. *English*

RAT

13309. A cornered rat will bite a cat.
          Japanese

13310. A rat has never lost its hole.
          African (Fulani)

13311. A rat that gnaws pepper is desperate for food.   *African (Annang)*

13312. A rat who gnaws at a cat's tail invites destruction.   *Chinese*

13313. Although the rat may cry and lament, the cat will not relinquish its hold.   *Indian (Tamil)*

13314. An old rat easily finds a hole.
          Dutch

13315. An old rat won't go into the trap.   *Dutch*

13316. As one rat brings another, so lawyer brings lawyer.   *American*

13317. If the rat is neglectful, the cat will seize it.   *Hawaiian*

13318. One rat alone can bring trouble to many.   *African (Bemba)*

13319. One rat is outside but many rats are inside the hole.   *African (Kpelle)*

13320. Rats do not play tricks with kittens.   *Spanish*

13321. Rats fly from the falling house.
          English

13322. Rats know the way of rats.
          Chinese

13323. Rats never sleep on the mat of the cat.   *African (Jabo)*

13324. The rat does not leave the cat's house with a bellyful.   *Portuguese*

13325. The rats may safely play when the cat's away.   *English*

13326. The rat shows its teeth when crying.   *Hawaiian*

13327. The rat that has but one hole is soon caught.   *Spanish*

13328. The rat that knows but one hole is soon caught by the cat.   *Spanish*

13329. The young rat knows how to gnaw its hole.   *Chinese*

13330. Too late repents the rat when caught by the cat.   *English*

13331. When the time comes even a rat becomes a tiger.   *Japanese*

13332. You can't get rats out of mice.
          English

RAVEN

13333. A raven desires colorfulness just as an unenterprising man desires cattle.   *African (Ovambo)*

13334. Bring up a raven and he will peck out your eyes.   *French*

13335. Foster a raven and it will peck out your eyes.   *Spanish*

13336. One raven does not peck out another's eyes.   *Danish*

13337. The raven always thinks that his young ones are the whitest.
          Danish

13338. The raven thinks its own chick white.   *Irish*

13339. The young ravens are beaked like the old.   *Dutch*

RAZOR

13340. A razor may be sharper than an axe, but it cannot cut wood.
          African (Annang)

READ

13341. Read not before you learn to spell.   *English*

REAP

13342. What has been reaped green will be eaten raw. *Russian*

13343. What you reap, that you will thresh. *Russian*

REASON

13344. A woman's reason—because it is so. *English*

13345. Better die than turn your back on reason. *Chinese*

13346. He who becomes angry for no reason becomes friendly again for no reason. *Yiddish*

13347. Hearken to reason or it will be heard. *English*

13348. If it were not for fools in this world there would be no reason. *Russian*

13349. If you will not hear reason, it will surely rap your knuckles. *English*

13350. Poor men's reasons are not heard. *English*

13351. Reason does not come before years. *German*

13352. Reason governs the wise man, and cudgels the fool. *English*

13353. Reason lies between the spur and the bridle. *English*

13354. Reason rules all things. *English*

13355. Reasons are not like garments, the worse for the wearing. *English*

13356. There's reason in roasting of eggs. *English*

13357. Who gives many reasons tells many lies. *Russian*

RECEIVE

13358. Who received, should thank; who gave, should be silent. *German*

RECEIVER

13359. If there were no receiver there would be no thief. *Spanish*

13360. No receiver, no thief. *English*

13361. The receiver is as bad as the thief. *English*

RECEIVING

13362. What is worth receiving is worth returning. *French*

RECEPTION

13363. A man's reception is according to his coat; his dismissal according to his sense. *Russian*

RECKONING

13364. Even reckoning makes long friends. *English*

13365. Old reckonings breed new disputes. *French*

13366. Old reckonings make new quarrels. *English*

13367. Right reckoning makes long friends. *English*

13368. Short reckonings are soon cleared. *English*

13369. Short reckonings make long friends. *English*

13370. The reckoning does not spoil friendship. *Russian*

RECONCILEMENT

13371. Better a crooked reconcilement than a straight judgment. *Rumanian*

RECONCILIATION

13372. Nothing is preferable to reconciliation. *Irish*

RECORDER

13373. A good recorder sets all in order. *English*

RECTIFY

13374. Until you have rectified yourself, you cannot rectify others. *Chinese*

RED

13375. Today red, tomorrow dead.
German

REDEMPTION

13376. There is no redemption from hell. *English*

REED

13377. A reed need not be afraid when the winds uproot the oak. *Polish*

13378. Every reed will not make a pipe. *English*

13379. He that sits among reeds, cuts pipes as he pleases. *German*

13380. Where there are reeds, there is water. *English*

REFUSAL

13381. A refusal is better than a broken promise. *Welsh*

13382. From the front entrance, a refusal; from the back entrance, a welcome. *Russian*

REFUSE (noun)

13383. Only refuse is to be gotten free.
Yiddish

REFUSE (verb)

13384. Do not refuse to be taught.
Hawaiian

REGRET

13385. A thousand regrets do not pay one debt. *Turkish*

13386. Nobody has a monopoly on regret. *Yiddish*

13387. Regret is not first but last.
Malagasy

REGULARITY

13388. Regularity is the best medicine.
Indian (Hindustani)

REINDEER

13389. Do not examine the reindeer given you by the rich man lest you find it to be without horns. *Finnish*

REINFORCEMENT

13390. Reinforcement beats the foe.
African (Oji)

RELATION

13391. Love your relations, but live not near them. *English*

13392. Poor relations have little honor.
Danish

13393. Relations and friends should be visited but not lived with. *Swedish*

13394. When you are rich, relation exists; if you are poor, relations desist.
African (Annang)

RELATIONSHIP

13395. Blood-shared relationships are the best. *Japanese*

13396. From strong relationships often comes great grief. *Irish*

RELATIVE

13397. A relative or not, he is a fellow countryman. *Chinese*

13398. Better than strangers are relatives. *Japanese*

13399. Do not disregard a poor relative nor a slight wound. *Finnish*

13400. Eat and drink with your relatives; do business with strangers.
Greek

13401. On the day your horse dies and your gold vanishes, your relatives are like strangers met on the road.
Chinese

13402. Relatives are friends from necessity. *Russian*

RELIGION

13403. One must eat first to be able to carry out religion. *Vietnamese*

13404. Religion has two children, love and hatred. *Russian*

13405. Religion is the best armor in the world, but the worst cloak.
English

REMARK

13406. A fool's remark is like a thorn concealed in mud. *Irish*

REMEDY

13407. A remedy without pain is not to be hoped for. *Turkish*

13408. Adapt the remedy to the disease. *Chinese*

13409. Even today the remedy for dirt is water. *African (Hausa)*

13410. For compassion and for cowardice there is no remedy. *Yiddish*

13411. Galloping in water is the remedy for a vicious horse.
African (Hausa)

13412. No remedy but patience.
English

13413. Sometimes the remedy is worse than the disease. *Yiddish*

13414. The best remedy against an ill man is much ground between both.
English

13415. The remedy against bad times is to have patience with them.
Egyptian

13416. The remedy for dislike is separation. *African (Hausa)*

13417. The remedy is worse than the disease. *English*

13418. The ultimate remedy is a cautery. *Egyptian*

13419. There is a remedy for all things but death. *English*

13420. There is a remedy for everything, could men find it. *English*

13421. Tomorrow's remedy will not ward off the evil of today. *Spanish*

13422. When there's a remedy for an ailment, it's only half an ailment.
Yiddish

13423. Where remedies are needed, sighing avails not. *Italian*

REMEMBER

13424. Better twice remembered than once forgotten. *Dutch*

REMORSE

13425. Never mind the remorse; don't commit the sin. *Yiddish*

REMOVAL

13426. Three removals are as bad as a fire. *French*

RENT

13427. Rent and taxes never sleep.
German

13428. What is rent to a lord is food to a child. *Irish*

REPAIR

13429. Better to repair than to build anew. *African (Hausa)*

REPEAT

13430. If you repeat often enough that you're right, you will discover you're wrong. *Yiddish*

REPENTANCE

13431. Late repentance is seldom worth much. *Danish*

13432. Repentance always comes behind. *English*

13433. Repentance comes too late.
English

13434. Repentance costs very dear.
French

13435. Repentance for silence is better than repentance for speaking.
Moroccan

13436. Repentance is apt to follow haste.
Welsh

13437. Repentance is the heart's medicine.
German

13438. Repentance never comes beforehand.
Japanese

13439. Take nothing in hand that may bring repentance.
Dutch

13440. That may be soon done, which brings long repentance.
Danish

13441. The end of haste is repentance.
Turkish

13442. The ways of repentance are as much hidden as the ways of sin.
Yiddish

13443. There is no repentance after death.
Russian

13444. To defer repentance is dangerous.
Irish

REPETITION

13445. Repetition is beneficial.
Lebanese

13446. Repetition is the mother of learning.
Russian

13447. Repetition teaches the donkey.
Lebanese

REPLY (noun)

13448. A well-timed reply is worth its weight in gold.
Maltese

REPLY (verb)

13449. Before one replies, one must be present.
African (Wolof)

REPRIMAND

13450. A reprimand isn't a reward, it's not meted out without a reason.
Russian

REPROACH

13451. Reproach yourself ten times when you reproach others once.
Vietnamese

REPROOF

13452. A reproof is no poison.
Scottish

13453. Public reproof hardens shame.
English

REPUTATION

13454. A good reputation is a fair estate.
English

13455. A good reputation is better than a golden girdle.
Serbo-Croatian

13456. A good reputation is better than accumulated wealth.
Lebanese

13457. A good reputation sits still; a bad one runs about.
Russian

13458. A reputation is seldom cured.
English

13459. Escaping with your reputation is better than escaping with your property.
African (Hausa)

13460. Good reputation is worth more than a golden belt.
Serbo-Croatian

13461. If you are stingy, your bad reputation will spread.
African (Jabo)

13462. It is in vain for a man to rise early who has the reputation of lying in bed all the morning.
French

13463. Reputation is a jewel whose loss cannot be repaired.
American

13464. Reputation is the life of the mind, as breath is the life of the body.
English

13465. The reputation of a man is the shadow of a tree.
Indian (Hindustani)

REPUTE

13466. Good repute is better than a golden belt. *French*

REQUEST

13467. Great men's requests are commands. *Danish*

RESERVE

13468. A reserve brings no misfortune. *Russian*

13469. A reserve doesn't tear the pocket and doesn't ask to be fed. *Russian*

RESIGNATION

13470. Patient resignation is a golden word; whoever practices it will have a long life on earth. *Vietnamese*

13471. Resignation is fitting for destiny. *Turkish*

RESOLUTION

13472. No resolution without discussion. *Serbo-Croatian*

13473. Sleep over it, and you will come to a resolution. *Spanish*

13474. Too long pondering brings no resolution. *Russian*

RESOLVE

13475. A firm resolve pierces even a rock. *Japanese*

13476. Resolve lasts three days. *Korean*

RESPECT (noun)

13477. Don't have greater respect for money than for man. *Vietnamese*

13478. Respect for a stupid person is stupidity. *African (Swahili)*

13479. Respect for one's superiors, kindness for one's inferiors. *Vietnamese*

13480. Respect is given to wealth, not to men. *Lebanese*

13481. Respect is mutual. *African (Zulu)*

13482. Respect is the younger brother to love. *English*

RESPECT (verb)

13483. He that respects not is not respected. *English*

13484. Respect others if you want to be respected. *Philippine*

RESPITE

13485. There is some respite from a barking dog, but never from wagging tongues. *Rumanian*

RESPONSE

13486. There is no wise response to a foolish remark. *Slovakian*

REST

13487. A short rest is always good. *Danish*

13488. Even rest will make the lazy tired. *Hungarian*

13489. Real rest is in one's own house. *Maltese*

13490. Rest comes from unrest, and unrest from rest. *German*

13491. Rest comes only after hardship. *African (Swahili)*

13492. Rest in reason is not time lost. *Norwegian*

13493. Rest is good after the work is done. *Danish*

13494. Rest makes rusty. *Dutch*

13495. There is no rest for the poor man. *African (Hausa)*

13496. Who troubles others has no rest himself. *Italian*

RESTRAINT

13497. He who lives without restraint, will die without honor.   *Danish*

RETREAT

13498. A brave retreat is a brave exploit.   *English*

13499. A good retreat is better than a poor defense.   *Irish*

RETURN (noun)

13500. Who gives, teaches a return.   *Italian*

RETURN (verb)

13501. Better return half way than lose yourself.   *Dutch*

REVENGE (noun)

13502. He who would seek revenge must be on his own guard.   *Danish*

13503. Revenge converts a little right into a great wrong.   *German*

13504. Revenge is new wrong.   *German*

13505. Revenge is sweet.   *English*

13506. Revenge remains not unrevenged.   *German*

13507. The revenge that is postponed is not forgotten.   *Icelandic*

13508. To take revenge is not shameful.   *Lebanese*

REVENGE (verb)

13509. He who cannot revenge himself is weak, he who will not is contemptible.   *Italian*

REVERENCE

13510. Reverence ceases once blood is spilt.   *Irish*

REVOLUTION

13511. Revolutions are not made with rosewater.   *English*

REWARD

13512. Do not wait for a reward for good, the reward for ill will not miss you.   *Czech*

13513. Reward sweetens labor.   *Dutch*

13514. The reward of good and evil is like the shadow following the substance.   *Chinese*

13515. You can earn your reward from God but never from man.   *Russian*

RHINOCEROS

13516. Do not speak of a rhinoceros if there is no tree nearby.   *African (Zulu)*

RHYME

13517. It may rhyme, but it accords not.   *English*

RICE

13518. Cook only as much rice as you have.   *Philippine*

13519. Harvest the rice grains while they are ripe.   *Philippine*

13520. If rice is thrown on the roof, a thousand crows will come.   *Indian (Tamil)*

13521. If you grind damp rice, it sticks to the mortar.   *African (Jabo)*

13522. In the house where rice is pounded for sale, there is not enough to put into the mouth of a corpse.   *Indian (Tamil)*

13523. Rice and fish are as inseparable as mother and child.   *Vietnamese*

13524. Rice makes man strong, money makes him bold.   *Vietnamese*

13525. Rice obtained by crookedness will not boil up into good food.
Chinese

13526. There is no burnt rice to a hungry person. *Philippine*

13527. When the rice crop is abundant, don't look down upon potato and taro. *Vietnamese*

RICE FIELD

13528. A rice field without fertilizer is like a human body without clothes and ornaments. *Vietnamese*

13529. Don't let rice fields lay fallow; an inch of soil is an inch of gold.
Vietnamese

RICH (adjective)

13530. He is rich enough that needs neither to flatter nor borrow. *English*

13531. He is rich enough that wants nothing. *English*

13532. He is rich enough who is contented. *German*

13533. He is rich enough who owes nothing. *French*

13534. He is rich who does not know either what he has or what he has not.
Russian

13535. He that will be rich before night may be hanged before noon.
English

13536. Today rich, tomorrow a beggar.
American

13537. When one is rich, one begins to save. *German*

RICH (people)

13538. One must pluck the rich; the poor are bare. *Russian*

13539. The rich add riches to riches; the poor add years to years. *Chinese*

13540. The rich and pigs are appreciated after their death. *Russian*

13541. The rich eat the meat; the poor the bones. *Yiddish*

13542. The rich feast, the poor fast; the dogs dine, the poor pine. *English*

13543. The rich have many friends.
Dutch

13544. The rich have money; the poor children. *Estonian*

13545. The rich have no sense of justice. *Yiddish*

13546. The rich worry over their money, the poor over their bread.
Vietnamese

13547. We give to the rich, and take from the poor. *German*

RICHES

13548. He is not fit for riches who is afraid to use them. *English*

13549. He that will increase in riches must not hoe corn in silk breeches.
American

13550. No man will seek riches in a beggar's cottage. *American*

13551. One may conceal his riches but not his poverty. *Philippine*

13552. Riches abuse them who know not how to use them. *English*

13553. Riches adorn the dwelling; virtue adorns the person. *Chinese*

13554. Riches and fame are but dreams among men. *Chinese*

13555. Riches and favor go before wisdom and art. *Danish*

13556. Riches and honors unjustly gained are like floating clouds.
Japanese

13557. Riches are but the baggage of fortune. *English*

13558. Riches are gotten with pain, kept with care, and lost with grief.
English

13559. Riches are not the only wealth.
Icelandic

13560. Riches are often abused, but never refused. *Danish*

13561. Riches are the pillar of the world. *African (Kanuri)*

13562. Riches bring oft harm and ever fear. *English*

13563. Riches cause arrogance; poverty, meekness. *German*

13564. Riches have wings. *English*

13565. Riches in the shape of children make one's shank thin. *Japanese*

13566. Riches rule the roost. *English*

13567. Riches serve a wise man but command a fool. *English*

13568. The miser's riches fall into the spendthrift's hands. *Greek*

13569. The subject's riches are the king's power. *English*

13570. When riches increase, the body decreases. *English*

RIDDLE

13571. A riddle made by God is not solved. *African (Bemba)*

RIDE

13572. He rides well that never falls.
English

13573. He that never rode never fell.
Scottish

13574. Ride on, but look before you.
Dutch

13575. Who rides slowly must saddle betimes. *German*

RIDER

13576. The expert rider is the man on the horse. *African (Hausa)*

RIDING

13577. Better riding on a pad than on a horse's bare back. *English*

13578. It is good riding in a safe harbor. *English*

13579. More belongs to riding than a pair of boots. *German*

RIGHT

13580. Good right needs good help.
Dutch

13581. No right is lost which is followed up by demands. *Egyptian*

13582. Right goes with a broken head.
Rumanian

13583. Right is a piece of gold which may be cut into strips. *Russian*

13584. Right is a stubborn thing.
American

13585. Right is with the strongest.
German

13586. Right wrongs no man. *English*

13587. The greater the right, the greater the wrong. *English*

13588. What is right for the one is reasonable for the other. *German*

13589. Who is in the right fears, who is in the wrong hopes. *Italian*

RIGHTEOUSNESS

13590. He who sees righteousness and does not do it is not brave. *Japanese*

RING

13591. Better no ring than a ring of a rush. *English*

13592. Don't put too tight a ring on your finger. *Italian*

RIPE

13593. Better ripe than raw.
American

13594. Fast ripe, fast rotten. *Japanese*

13595. Soon ripe, soon rotten. *English*

13596. Soon ripe, soon rotten; soon wise, soon foolish. *Dutch*

13597. What ripens fast does not last. *German*

RISE (noun)

13598. The higher the rise the greater the fall. *French*

RISE (verb)

13599. He had need rise early who would please everybody. *French*

13600. He rises betimes that lies in a dog's lair. *English*

13601. He that rises betimes has something in his head. *English*

13602. He that rises first is first dressed. *English*

13603. He who does not rise early never does a good day's work. *English*

13604. He who rises early is rewarded doubly. *Serbo-Croatian*

13605. If you do not rise when you do not want to, you will not arrive when you want to. *African (Fulani)*

13606. In vain they rise early that used to rise late. *English*

13607. Who rises late must trot all the day. *American*

RISER

13608. An early riser gets through his business. *Irish*

13609. The early riser is healthy, cheerful, and industrious. *French*

13610. The late riser must content himself with wiping his mouth. *Slovakian*

RISING

13611. A sudden rising has a sudden fall. *English*

13612. Early rising has seven advantages. *Japanese*

13613. The rising of one man is the falling of another. *English*

RISK

13614. Better risk a little than lose the whole. *American*

13615. He who risks nothing can gain nothing. *Italian*

13616. Nothing risked, nothing gained. *American*

13617. One must risk to win. *American*

RIVER

13618. A narrow river is soon rowed. *Finnish*

13619. A river less vast than an ocean gets a bridge. *African (Annang)*

13620. A river moves a river on. *African (Ga)*

13621. A river never flows straight. *Indian (Tamil)*

13622. A river that has no bridge cannot be crossed. *Japanese*

13623. A river you would not bathe in is not drunk from. *African (Ashanti)*

13624. All rivers do what they can for the sea. *English*

13625. As far as the river flows, it carries mud. *Indian (Hindi)*

13626. Do not push the river; it will flow by itself. *Polish*

13627. Even a great river's glory ends at the sea. *Russian*

13628. Every river has its own course. *Hebrew*

13629. Follow the river and you'll get to the sea. *English*

13630. He who follows the river comes at last to the sea. *Norwegian*

13631. If the river prevents crossing it will not prevent turning back.
African (Hausa)

13632. If you saw what the river carried, you would never drink the water.
Jamaican

13633. It is easy to throw anything into the river, but difficult to take it out again.   *Indian (Kashmiri)*

13634. One can fill up a river or a well, but one cannot close a foul mouth.
Vietnamese

13635. Rivers and mountains may easily change, but human nature is changed with difficulty.   *Chinese*

13636. Rivers need a spring.   *English*

13637. Ten thousand rivers flow into the sea, but the sea is never full.
Chinese

13638. The great river refuses no streamlets.   *Korean*

13639. The river carries away him who cannot swim.   *Indian (Tamil)*

13640. The river does not swell with clear water.   *Italian*

13641. The river is never so full as to obscure the sight of the fish.
African (Yoruba)

13642. The river is no wider from this side or the other.   *Irish*

13643. The river is not crossed without a ford.   *Moroccan*

13644. The river passed and God forgotten.   *English*

13645. The way the river flows at the surface is not the way it flows underneath.   *African (Kpelle)*

13646. Till you are across the river, beware how you insult the mother alligator.   *Haitian*

13647. Trust the river but do not trust the brook.   *Russian*

13648. When the river is full the well is full.   *Chinese*

13649. When the river makes no noise, it is either dried up or much swollen.
Spanish

13650. Where the river is deepest it makes least noise.   *Italian*

RIVULET

13651. Many little rivulets make a great river.   *Danish*

ROAD

13652. A long road tests a horse; long drawn-out affairs test a friend.
Chinese

13653. A straight road has no turnings.   *African (Efik)*

13654. All roads lead to Rome.
English

13655. An old road is known.
Estonian

13656. Any road leads to the end of the world.   *English*

13657. Don't leave the high road for a short cut.   *Portuguese*

13658. Every road does not lead to Rome.   *Slovenian*

13659. Every road has two directions.
Russian

13660. Every road leads somewhere.
Philippine

13661. He keeps his road well enough who gets rid of bad company. *English*

13662. He to whom things are brought does not know the length of the road.
African (Ovambo)

13663. He who argues builds no roads.
African (Ovambo)

13664. He who knows the road can ride full trot.   *Italian*

13665. He who takes the wrong road must make his journey twice over. *Spanish*

13666. If one comes to a fork of the road in a strange country, he stops to think. *African (Jabo)*

13667. If you wish to know the road ahead, inquire of those who have traveled it. *Chinese*

13668. Keep the common road and you are safe. *Thai*

13669. Make haste before the road gets slippery. *African (Bemba)*

13670. Mock not the fallen, for slippery is the road ahead of you. *Russian*

13671. One cannot fight on two roads. *African (Jabo)*

13672. One man's road does not go far without meeting another's. *African (Ashanti)*

13673. One road for the fugitive and a hundred for the pursuer. *Russian*

13674. One road leads to heaven but many lead to hell. *Hungarian*

13675. The longest road must have an end. *American*

13676. The other side of the road always looks cleanest. *English*

13677. The road does not advise a man. *African (Ovambo)*

13678. The road from St. Petersburg to Siberia is shorter than from Siberia to Moscow. *Russian*

13679. The road is open for the mon-eyed man. *Pashto*

13680. The road that is preferred leads to destruction. *Japanese*

13681. The road to misfortune is short. *Russian*

13682. The road to ruin is paved with good intentions. *German*

13683. The road to the cemetery is paved with suffering. *Yiddish*

13684. The road to the head lies through the heart. *American*

13685. The road to the other world is the same from everywhere. *Russian*

13686. There's but one road open to a thief, but every road will do for his captors. *Latvian*

13687. There is no narrow road for the man who truly loves. *Philippine*

13688. To a friend's house the road is never long. *Danish*

13689. To go where there is no road is better than to remain without doing anything. *African (Wolof)*

13690. To spend much and gain little is the sure road to ruin. *German*

13691. Various are the roads to fame. *Italian*

13692. When you talk on the road, remember there may be men in the grass. *Chinese*

13693. Where the road is straight don't look for a short cut. *Russian*

ROADSIDE

13694. He who builds by the roadside has many surveyors. *Italian*

ROAST

13695. It is a poor roast that gives no dripping. *Danish*

13696. The roast takes a long time to a hungry man. *African (Hausa)*

ROB

13697. Rob not, repent not. *Yiddish*

ROBBER

13698. Even a robber fastens his door. *Japanese*

13699. Not even a hundred robbers can rob him who is naked. *Czech*

13700. Robbers are plundered by thieves. *Chinese*

13701. The robber does not desire a comrade to carry his knapsack for him.
Haitian

13702. The robber is expert in robbery.
Hebrew

ROBIN

13703. He that hunts robin or wren will never prosper boy nor man.
English

ROBIN HOOD

13704. Many talk of Robin Hood that never shot his bow.   *English*

ROCK

13705. Once on the down grade, even rocks have wheels.   *Mexican*

13706. One does not dive onto a rock.
African (Hausa)

ROD

13707. A rod is the cure for a boy's folly.   *African (Hausa)*

13708. An iron rod bends while it is hot.   *Greek*

13709. The rod breaks no bones.
English

ROGUE

13710. A sly rogue is often in good dress.   *Irish*

13711. Give a rogue an inch, and he will take an ell.   *Danish*

13712. He who would catch a rogue must watch behind the door.   *Dutch*

13713. Rogues hang together.
American

ROME

13714. At Rome do as Rome does.
French

13715. He who wishes to live at Rome must not quarrel with the Pope.
French

13716. It is hard to sit in Rome and strive against the Pope.   *Scottish*

13717. Rome was not built in a day.
English

13718. The farther from Rome the nearer to God.   *Dutch*

13719. When at Rome, do as the Romans do.   *English*

ROOF

13720. He who has a glass roof must not throw stones at others.   *German*

13721. He who has a glass roof should not throw stones at his neighbors.
Italian

13722. If you go up to the roof, take your provisions with you.   *Hebrew*

13723. The house roof fights with the rain, but he who is sheltered ignores it.
African (Wolof)

13724. The roof of an old hut is always full of leaks.   *Mexican*

13725. When a neighbor's roof is in flames one's own is in danger.
Indian (Tamil)

13726. When it rains, the roof always drips the same way.   *African (Jabo)*

13727. When the roof is leaky, it rains that night.   *Chinese*

ROOM

13728. Room can always be found for a delicacy.   *Hebrew*

13729. There is not enough room for two elephants to rest in the same shade.
African (Ovambo)

13730. When there is room in the heart, there is room in the house.
Danish

ROOSTER

13731. The country rooster does not crow in town.   *African (Swahili)*

ROOT

13732. The roots of learning are bitter, but the fruit is sweet.   *Polish*

13733. The roots of work are bitter, but its fruit is sweet.   *Latvian*

13734. When the root is worthless, so is the tree.   *German*

ROPE

13735. A rope that is not at hand does not bind the firewood.
  African (Swahili)

13736. A short strong rope is better than a long rotten one.   *Philippine*

13737. Even a rotten rope can be put to use.   *Japanese*

13738. Give him rope enough and he'll hang himself.   *English*

13739. He pulls with a long rope that waits for another's death.   *English*

13740. He who would hang himself is sure to find a rope.   *Danish*

13741. Never speak of a rope in the house of one who was hanged.
  German

13742. No matter how much rope is wound up, there's bound to be an end.
  Russian

13743. Pull gently at a weak rope.
  Dutch

13744. The rope has never been made that binds thoughts.   *Swedish*

13745. The rope of a lie is short.
  Lebanese

13746. The rope strong enough to bind the free man is hard to find.
  African (Hausa)

13747. You cannot pull hard with a broken rope.   *Danish*

ROSARY

13748. Beware of him that holds a long rosary.   *Maltese*

13749. Rosary in hand, the devil at heart.   *Portuguese*

ROSE

13750. A rose issues from thorns.
  Egyptian

13751. A single rose does not mean spring.   *Iranian*

13752. Among thorns grow roses.
  Italian

13753. Every rose has a thorn as its friend.   *Pashto*

13754. For the rose the thorn is often plucked.   *English*

13755. From a thorn comes a rose, and from a rose a thorn.   *Greek*

13756. He who wants a rose must respect the thorn.   *Iranian*

13757. He who would gather roses must not fear thorns.   *Dutch*

13758. No rose without a thorn.
  English

13759. Rose without thorns, love without rival, cannot be.   *Turkish*

13760. Roses and maidens soon lose their bloom.   *German*

13761. Roses fall, but the thorns remain.   *Dutch*

13762. Strew no roses before swine.
  Dutch

13763. The fairest rose at last is withered.   *English*

13764. The roses fall, and the thorns remain.   *Italian*

13765. The rose from rose is born, the thorn from thorn.   *Pashto*

13766. The rose proves a thorn.
  English

ROWING

13767. It is good rowing with set sail.
Dutch

RUB

13768. There will be rubs in the smoothest roads. *English*

RUBBISH

13769. He who sits among the rubbish must not be surprised if pigs devour him. *Serbo-Croatian*

13770. Who sieves too much keeps the rubbish. *Flemish*

RUBLE

13771. Every ruble bears a sin.
Russian

13772. He will be rich for whom the ruble prays. *Russian*

13773. When rubles fall from heaven there is no sack; when there is a sack rubles do not fall. *Russian*

13774. You don't need to have one hundred rubles if you have one hundred friends. *Russian*

RUDDER

13775. He who will not be ruled by the rudder must be ruled by the rock.
English

RULE (noun)

13776. All general rules have their exceptions. *American*

13777. It is a poor rule that will not work both ways. *American*

13778. It is no sure rule to fish with a crossbow. *English*

13779. There is no rule without an exception. *English*

RULE (verb)

13780. Better rule than be ruled by the rout. *English*

RULER

13781. A ruler cannot sleep.
African (Swahili)

13782. He that has a fellow ruler, has an overruler. *English*

13783. Only with a new ruler do you realize the value of the old. *Burmese*

RUM

13784. When the rum is in, the wit is out. *Jamaican*

RUMOR

13785. It is pleasant to spread rumors about the quarrels in other people's houses. *African (Ovambo)*

13786. Mere rumors have neither head nor foot. *Indian (Tamil)*

13787. One rumor breeds another.
Slovakian

RUN

13788. He runs far back that means to leap a great way. *English*

13789. He runs heavily who is forced to run. *Danish*

13790. He that runs fast will not run long. *English*

13791. He that runs fastest gets most ground. *English*

13792. He that runs in the dark may well stumble. *English*

13793. He that runs may rally.
English

13794. I cannot run and sit still at the same time. *English*

13795. It is not enough to run; one must start in time. *French*

13796. Who runs is followed.   *Dutch*

RUNNER

13797. Where the runner goes the walker will go with patience.

African (Hausa)

RUSH

13798. A rush for him that cares a straw for me.   *English*

RUST

13799. Nothing destroys iron like its own rust.   *Philippine*

13800. Rust consumes iron, and envy consumes itself.   *Danish*

13801. Rust eats iron.   *Russian*

13802. Rust wastes more than use.

French

S

SABRE

13803. From bad iron there cannot be a good sabre. *Turkish*

13804. The sabre cuts not its own scabbard. *Turkish*

SACK

13805. A broken sack will hold no corn. *English*

13806. A full sack pricks up its ear. *Italian*

13807. A sack full of fleas is easier to watch than a woman. *German*

13808. A sack is best tied before it is full. *French*

13809. A sack is no load for a goat. *African (Hausa)*

13810. A sack was never so full but that it would hold another grain. *French*

13811. A short sack has a wide mouth. *English*

13812. An old sack asks much patching. *English*

13813. Bad is the sack that will not bear patching. *Italian*

13814. Everyone goes with his own sack to the mill. *Italian*

13815. He who is the last to be put in the sack is the first to get out of it. *Latvian*

13816. Let every sack stand upon its own bottom. *English*

13817. Many a sack is tied up before it be full. *English*

13818. Many sacks are the death of the ass. *German*

13819. Nothing can come out of a sack but what is in it. *Italian*

13820. That which goes last into the sack comes first out. *Swedish*

13821. The best of the mill is that the sacks can't speak. *German*

13822. There comes nought out of the sack, but what was there. *English*

13823. When the sack is full it pricks up its ears. *Dutch*

13824. You can't fill a torn sack. *Yiddish*

13825. You may know by a handful the whole sack. *English*

SACRIFICE

13826. Sacrifice is bitter but its fruits are sweet. *Philippine*

SADDLE

13827. Better lose the saddle than the horse. *Italian*

13828. If there are backs, saddles will not be lacking. *Russian*

13829. One saddle is enough for one horse. *English*

13830. The saddle is a burden to the bad horse. *Serbo-Croatian*

13831. Where saddles lack, better ride on a pad than on the horse bareback. *English*

SADNESS

13832. One's own sadness is dearer than another's gladness. *Russian*

13833. Sadness and gladness succeed each other. *English*

SAFE

13834. An open safe will tempt even a bishop. *Slovenian*

SAFETY

13835. A man's safety is in holding his tongue. *Lebanese*

13836. He most values safety who experiences danger. *Iranian*

SAGE

13837. A great sage is often taken for a great fool. *Japanese*

SAID (see SAY)

13838. Least said soonest mended. *English*

13839. Little said is soon amended. *English*

13840. So said, so done. *English*

13841. Sooner said than done. *English*

13842. The less said the sooner mended. *Dutch*

13843. The more said the less done. *English*

13844. What's said can't be unsaid. *American*

13845. What is said in a drunken state has been thought out beforehand. *Flemish*

SAIL (noun)

13846. All sails do not suit every ship. *Icelandic*

13847. As sails are to a ship, so are the passions to the spirits. *English*

13848. Make not your sail too big for the ballast. *English*

13849. Set your sail according to the wind. *French*

13850. You must shift your sail with the wind. *Italian*

SAIL (verb)

13851. He that will not sail till he have a full fair wind will lose many a voyage. *English*

13852. He that will sail without danger must never come upon the main sea. *English*

SAILING

13853. It is good sailing with wind and tide. *Dutch*

13854. It is ill sailing against wind and tide. *Dutch*

13855. It is the safest sailing within reach of the shore. *Dutch*

SAILOR

13856. A sailor has a sweetheart in every port. *American*

13857. Good sailors are tried in a storm. *American*

13858. If the sailors become too numerous, the ship sinks. *Egyptian*

13859. If you are not a sailor, don't handle a boat hook. *Chinese*

13860. The better you try to serve sailors the worse they try to serve you. *American*

13861. Too many sailors drive the boat up the mountain.   *Japanese*

SAINT

13862. A saint abroad and a devil at home.   *English*

13863. A small saint is big in a small church.   *Slovenian*

13864. A young saint may prove an old devil.   *Scottish*

13865. All are not saints that go to church.   *English*

13866. All do not beg for one saint.   *Spanish*

13867. All saint without, all devil within.   *English*

13868. All saints do not work miracles.   *Italian*

13869. Among the saints there was not a single one with auburn hair.   *Russian*

13870. Don't believe in the saint unless he works miracles.   *Italian*

13871. Even a saint sins seven times a day.   *Polish*

13872. Even the saints are troubled with warts.   *Polish*

13873. Everyone praises his own saint.   *Italian*

13874. Everyone preaches for his own saint.   *French*

13875. Every saint has his festival.   *Italian*

13876. He that comes to terms with humanity must be a saint.   *Polish*

13877. Like saint, like offering.   *Italian*

13878. Little saints also perform miracles.   *Danish*

13879. Not all whose heels tread round the church are saints.   *Czech*

13880. Only saints may censure others.   *Russian*

13881. Pray to the saint until you have passed the slough.   *Portuguese*

13882. Saint cannot if God will not.   *French*

13883. Saints appear to fools.   *Portuguese*

13884. Small saints too work miracles.   *German*

13885. Such saint, such offering.   *English*

13886. The old saints are forgotten in the new.   *Portuguese*

13887. The saint has no believers unless he works miracles.   *Italian*

13888. The saint who works no cures has few pilgrims to his shrine.   *French*

13889. The village saint is a clever impostor.   *Egyptian*

13890. There is no saint who is in hell.   *Philippine*

13891. They are not all saints that use holy water.   *English*

13892. To every saint his candle.   *French*

13893. You cannot worship a saint that is unknown.   *Mexican*

13894. You must be a saint to judge and condemn others.   *Russian*

13895. Young saint, old devil. *English*

SALAD

13896. A good salad may be the prologue to a bad supper.   *English*

13897. He that sups upon salad goes not to bed fasting.   *English*

SALARY

13898. No salary without service.   *American*

SALE

13899. Better good sale than good ale.
Scottish

SALMON

13900. It is not for everyone to catch a salmon. *English*

13901. Salmon and sermon have both their season in Lent. *English*

SALOONKEEPER

13902. The saloonkeeper loves the drunkard, but he wouldn't give him his daughter in marriage. *Yiddish*

SALT

13903. Don't add salt to a boatload of salt fish. *Chinese*

13904. Even the salt on the kitchen range won't taste salty until you try it in your mouth. *Korean*

13905. If the salt is stored, the soup will not be good. *African (Fulani)*

13906. Never will salt become worm eaten. *Moroccan*

13907. Salt and bread make the cheeks red. *German*

13908. Salt enters into all food.
Turkish

13909. Salt is good to eat anywhere in the world; money is good to use anywhere in the world. *Chinese*

13910. Salt never calls itself sweet.
Jamaican

13911. Salt seasons all things. *English*

13912. Salt spilled is never all gathered. *Spanish*

13913. To know a man well one must have eaten a bushel of salt with him.
French

13914. You add salt to bread, not bread to salt. *Polish*

13915. You mustn't pour salt on a wound. *Yiddish*

SALVATION

13916. There is no salvation through excessive fasting. *Russian*

13917. Who cannot work out his salvation by heart will not do it by book.
French

SALVE

13918. Seek your salve where you got your sore. *English*

13919. There's a salve for every sore.
English

SAND

13920. The sands of a river cannot be counted. *Indian (Tamil)*

13921. What is written on sand is washed out by the tide. *Philippine*

SANDAL

13922. Walk with sandals till you can get good shoes. *Libyan*

13923. While the sandal is on your foot, tread down the thorns. *Hebrew*

SAP

13924. Sap and heart are the best of wood. *English*

13925. Sap runs best after a sharp frost. *American*

SAPLING

13926. A sapling becomes an oak.
Slovenian

SARDINE

13927. Better a sardine on the dish than a flounder in the sea. *Hebrew*

SATISFACTION

13928. Satisfaction of the heart is better than wealth. *Turkish*

13929. The satisfaction of a full man is of no use to a hungry man.
African (Fulani)

SAUCE

13930. No sauce like appetite. *French*

13931. Sauce for the goose is sauce for the gander. *English*

SAUSAGE

13932. Better a sausage in hand than a ham at the butcher's. *Polish*

13933. He who goes seeking other people's sausages often loses his own ham. *Czech*

SAVE

13934. He who does not save will live in want. *Philippine*

13935. Who nothing saves shall nothing have. *English*

13936. Who saves when he gets has when he needs. *Finnish*

SAVER

13937. A saver is better than an earner. *Yiddish*

13938. Some savers in a house do well. *English*

SAVING

13939. A little saving is no sin. *English*

13940. Of saving comes having. *English*

13941. Saving is getting. *English*

13942. Saving is greater art than gaining. *German*

13943. Saving must equal having. *English*

13944. Think of saving as well as getting. *American*

SAVOR

13945. Something has some savor, but nothing has no flavor. *English*

SAY (see SAID)

13946. Better say here it is than here it was. *Scottish*

13947. Better say nothing than not to the purpose. *English*

13948. Don't say there's a tomorrow. *Japanese*

13949. Easy to say is hard to do. *French*

13950. Everybody says it, nobody knows it. *German*

13951. He who says nothing never lies. *Italian*

13952. He who says what he likes shall hear what he does not like. *English*

13953. If you cannot say something good, don't say something bad. *Greek*

13954. Many a one says well that thinks ill. *English*

13955. No one should say that which he knows not. *African (Wolof)*

13956. Say as men say, but think to yourself. *English*

13957. Say but little, and say it well. *Irish*

13958. Say little and listen much. *Greek*

13959. Say little but think the more. *English*

13960. Say well is good but do well is better. *English*

13961. Say well or be still. *English*

13962. They say is half a lie. *English*

13963. Who says little has little to answer for. *German*

SAYING

13964. Between saying and doing there is a great distance. *Danish*

13965. Between saying and doing there is a long road. *Spanish*

13966. Saying and doing are two things.   *English*

13967. Saying is easy, but doing is difficult.   *Indian (Tamil)*

13968. Saying is one thing, doing another.   *Italian*

13969. Saying well causes a laugh, doing well produces silence.   *French*

SAYINGS

13970. An old man's sayings are seldom untrue.   *Danish*

SCALD

13971. He who has scalded himself once blows the next time.   *Italian*

SCALE

13972. Every scale has its counterpoise.   *English*

13973. Good scales bring good customers.   *Greek*

13974. Just scales and full measure injure no man.   *Chinese*

SCANDAL

13975. Scandal is like an egg; when it is hatched it has wings.   *Malagasy*

13976. Scandal will rub out like dirt when it is dry.   *English*

SCAR

13977. He who scratches a scar is wounded twice.   *Russian*

SCARCITY

13978. The best scarcity is scarcity of words.   *Welsh*

SCARECROW

13979. A garden scarecrow is not a man.   *Turkish*

SCEPTER

13980. A scepter is one thing and a ladle another.   *English*

13981. A scepter of justice is the beauty of a king.   *Indian (Tamil)*

SCHEME

13982. The myriad schemes of men do not equal one scheme of God's.
                                                                   Chinese

SCHEMING

13983. Scheming seldom has success.
                                                                   American

SCHOLAR

13984. A mere scholar, a mere ass.
                                                                   English

13985. A scholar may be gulled thrice, a soldier but once.   *English*

13986. A scholar who abandons study is like a bird that strays from the nest.
                                                                   Hebrew

13987. Every good scholar is not a good schoolmaster.   *English*

13988. Great scholars are not the shrewdest men.   *French*

13989. He that robs a scholar robs twenty men.   *English*

13990. Scholars are a country's treasure; the learned are the delicacies of the feast.   *Chinese*

13991. The scholar teaches his master.
                                                                   English

13992. When scholars vie, wisdom mounts.   *Hebrew*

SCHOLARSHIP

13993. Scholarship knows no national boundary.   *Korean*

SCHOOL

13994. All do not come from the same school.   *Hawaiian*

SCHOOLBOY

13995. Schoolboys are the most reasonable people in the world; they care not how little they have for their money.
English

SCHOOLMASTER

13996. The schoolmaster should not leave his books, nor should the poor man leave his pig.   *Chinese*

SCOLDING

13997. Scolding won't help, but the stick would.   *Yiddish*

SCORE

13998. Score twice before you cut once.
English

SCORN

13999. Scorn at first makes after-love the more.   *English*

SCORNING

14000. Scorning is catching.   *English*

SCORPION

14001. He who has been stung by the scorpion is frightened at its shadow.
Spanish

14002. The scorpion stings him who helps it out of the fire. *Indian (Tamil)*

SCRAP

14003. A scrap will not satisfy the lion.
Hebrew

SCRATCH

14004. Scratch me and I'll scratch thee.
English

SCRATCHING

14005. Scratching and borrowing do well enough, but not for long.
German

14006. Scratching and borrowing is only good for a while.   *Yiddish*

14007. Too much scratching smarts; too much talking harms.   *French*

SCRIBE

14008. Not he is a good scribe who writes well, but he who erases well.
Russian

SCYTHE

14009. Two scythes can lie together, but two spinning wheels never.
Russian

SEA

14010. Being on sea, sail; being on land, settle.   *English*

14011. Even the sea, great as it is, grows calm.   *Italian*

14012. He that is once at sea must either sail or sink.   *Danish*

14013. He who crosses the sea is wet.
African (Wolof)

14014. He who falls into the sea grasps at the eel.   *Turkish*

14015. He who is at sea does not direct the winds.   *French*

14016. In a calm sea every man is a pilot.   *English*

14017. It is hard to sail over the sea in an eggshell.   *English*

14018. It is the sea only which knows the bottom of the ship, as God only knows the time of death.
African (Efik)

14019. Praise the sea but keep on land.
English

14020. Smooth seas do not make skillful sailors.   *African (Swahili)*

14021. The sea always ebbs after high tide.   *Philippine*

14022. The sea complains for want of water. *English*

14023. The sea has fish for every man. *English*

14024. The sea is an emperor that listens to no words. *Turkish*

14025. The sea refuses no river. *English*

14026. To a drunken man the sea is only knee deep. *Russian*

14027. What the sea has swallowed it does not vomit out again. *African (Jabo)*

14028. Where the sea is deep blue, there the shark swims; when the woman is attractive, men have desire and get her. *Hawaiian*

SEAM

14029. Don't stick your seam before you've tacked it. *English*

SEAMAN

14030. A seaman is never broken till his neck be broken. *English*

14031. In bad weather, a good seaman's ability is seen on the sea. *Philippine*

14032. The good seaman is known in bad weather. *Italian*

SEARCH (noun)

14033. Desperate search doesn't cause finding. *African (Hausa)*

SEARCH (verb)

14034. Search not too curiously lest you find trouble. *English*

SEASON

14035. Everything is good in its season. *Italian*

14036. Season resembles not season. *Turkish*

14037. There is not a single season without fruit. *Turkish*

SEAT

14038. A seat in the council is honor without profit. *Portuguese*

14039. The seats in heaven which are prepared for good guardians are still vacant. *Czech*

14040. The seats in the great hall all come in rotation: the daughter-in-law will some day be the mother-in-law. *Chinese*

14041. Those who have free seats at the play hiss first. *Chinese*

SEATED

14042. Who is well seated should not budge. *German*

SECRECY

14043. In strategy secrecy is esteemed. *Japanese*

14044. What is not wished to be known is done in secrecy. *African (Yoruba)*

SECRET (adjective)

14045. There is nothing so secret but it transpires. *Dutch*

SECRET (noun)

14046. A secret between two is God's secret; a secret between three is everybody's. *Spanish*

14047. A secret imparted is no longer a secret. *Italian*

14048. A secret is a friend; an enemy if you confide it. *Russian*

14049. A secret is a weapon and a friend. *Irish*

14050. A secret known to one may spread through the world. *Indian (Tamil)*

14051. A secret stays long in darkness but it will see the light.   *Greek*

14052. A secret that should be concealed in the mind is uttered by a fool.   *Indian (Tamil)*

14053. Conceal not your secret from your friend, or you deserve to lose him.   *Portuguese*

14054. Do not tell your secrets behind a wall or a hedge.   *Spanish*

14055. Don't tell your secret even to a fence.   *Irish*

14056. He that tells a secret is another's servant.   *English*

14057. He who keeps his own secret avoids much mischief.   *Spanish*

14058. He who tells his own secret will hardly keep another's.   *Spanish*

14059. If you cast your secret into the sea, the sea will cast it out.   *Yiddish*

14060. If you tell your secret to your servant, you have made him your master.   *Scottish*

14061. If you want to know a secret ask the young children.   *Slovakian*

14062. If you want to know secrets, seek for them in trouble or in pleasure.   *Spanish*

14063. If you wish to tell a secret in your home, make sure that even your servant's shoe is out.   *Greek*

14064. If you would know secrets, look for them in grief or pleasure.   *English*

14065. It is easier to hear a secret than to keep it.   *Yiddish*

14066. Keep your secret in your own gourd.   *Jamaican*

14067. Tell your secret only to one in a thousand.   *Hebrew*

14068. The only way to keep a secret is to say nothing.   *French*

14069. The secret of a discussion is only between two.   *Moroccan*

14070. The secret of the water pot is known by the ladle.   *African (Swahili)*

14071. The secret of two is God's secret; the secret of three is everybody's secret.   *French*

14072. To a woman and a magpie tell your secrets in the marketplace.   *Spanish*

14073. To whom you tell your secret you surrender your freedom.   *Italian*

14074. Where you tell your secret you surrender your freedom.   *Portuguese*

14075. Wherever there is a secret there must be something wrong.   *English*

14076. Wine in, secret out.   *Hebrew*

SECT

14077. Every sect has its truth and every truth its sect.   *Chinese*

SECULAR

14078. The secular and the sacred are both necessary.   *Indian (Tamil)*

SECURE

14079. He that is too secure is not safe.   *English*

SECURITY

14080. Security is nowhere safe.   *German*

14081. Security is the first cause of misfortune.   *German*

SEDUCER

14082. A seducer is worse than a witch.   *African (Ovambo)*

SEE

14083. He who has seen little marvels much.   *Chinese*

14084. Only what is seen is envied.   *Russian*

14085. See all, say nothing, hold yourself content.   *English*

14086. See for your love, buy for your money. *English*

14087. See it often, it looks smaller; smell it often, it loses its scent.
Burmese

14088. Seldom seen, soon forgotten.
English

14089. The less you see him, the more you love him. *Russian*

14090. Wherever you are, do as you see done. *Spanish*

14091. Who sees you by day will not seek you by night. *English*

SEED

14092. As the seed is, so is the fruit.
Russian

14093. Even good seeds can give a poor harvest. *Russian*

14094. He that sows good seed, shall reap good corn. *English*

14095. However much you eat, leave some seed for sowing. *Latvian*

14096. If the seed is good one will have good seedlings; if the seedling is good one will have vigorous rice plants.
Vietnamese

14097. Ill seed, ill weed. *English*

14098. Some seeds will grow, others will die. *African (Zulu)*

14099. The seed that is sown is the one that sprouts. *African (Hausa)*

14100. Toasted seeds jump, but they always fall towards their companions.
African (Wolof)

14101. Unsown seeds will not sprout.
Japanese

SEEDLING

14102. A seedling is better than a cutting. *African (Hausa)*

SEEING

14103. One seeing is better than one hundred hearings. *Japanese*

14104. Seeing excels hearing.
African (Hausa)

14105. Seeing excites to knowing.
African (Wolof)

14106. Seeing is believing. *English*

14107. Seeing is believing all the world over. *Scottish*

14108. Seeing is believing, but feeling is the truth. *English*

14109. Seeing is not eating.
African (Hausa)

14110. Seeing once is better than hearing twice. *Swedish*

SEEK

14111. He that seeks finds. *English*

14112. He that seeks, finds, and sometimes what he would rather not.
Italian

14113. He that seeks to beguile is overtaken in his will. *English*

14114. He who seeks finds everywhere. *Albanian*

14115. If you seek, you will find.
Yiddish

14116. Seek till you find and you'll not lose your labor. *English*

14117. Who seeks what he should not, finds what he would not. *English*

SEEKER

14118. Pleasure seekers have no leisure. *Japanese*

SEEM

14119. Be what you seem, and seem what you are. *Scottish*

SELDOM

14120. Seldom comes the better.
English

SELF-INTEREST

14121. Self-interest is a fire which first consumes others and then self.
Russian

SELF-LOVE

14122. Self-love is a mote in every man's eye. *English*

SELF-PRAISE

14123. Self-praise is no recommendation. *English*

14124. Self-praise stinks. *German*

SELF-PRESERVATION

14125. Self-preservation is the first law of nature. *English*

SELF-RESPECT

14126. If you lose your self-respect, you also lose the respect of others. *Yiddish*

SELL

14127. Better sell than live poorly.
English

14128. Better sold than bought.
English

14129. He who sells cheap, sells quickly. *Turkish*

14130. Sell nothing on trust. *English*

14131. Sell what you have and buy what is really good. *Indian (Tamil)*

14132. Some sell and don't deliver.
French

SELLER

14133. Ale sellers should not be tale tellers. *Scottish*

14134. May both seller and buyer see the benefit. *Turkish*

14135. The seller usually asks for a high price, but the buyer should pay for a lower price. *Vietnamese*

SELVAGE

14136. The selvage shows the cloth.
English

SENSE

14137. Good sense comes only with age. *Irish*

14138. Good sense is no less important than food. *Irish*

14139. Sense doesn't come before age.
Irish

14140. Sense is required for business, music for dancing. *Finnish*

14141. Where sense is wanting, everything is wanting. *American*

14142. With another's common sense one cannot live. *Yiddish*

SENTENCE

14143. If sentence is passed on your neighbor, another time it will be passed on you. *African (Oji)*

SEPARATION

14144. Separation secures manifest friendship. *Indian (Tamil)*

SERMON

14145. Funeral sermon, lying sermon.
German

SERPENT

14146. A serpent, though it is put in a bamboo tube, won't crawl straight.
Korean

14147. He who has been stung by a serpent is afraid of a lizard. *Italian*

14148. He whom a serpent has bitten dreads a slow-worm. *African (Oji)*

14149. He whom a serpent has bitten is terrified at a rope. *Hebrew*

14150. One walks on the serpent's tracks when it is no longer there.
African (Wolof)

14151. Serpents engender in still waters. *English*

14152. The serpent brings forth nothing but a little serpent. *Egyptian*

14153. The serpent knows his own hole. *Chinese*

14154. The serpent moves deviously save when she enters her nest. *Armenian*

SERVANT

14155. A common servant is no man's servant. *English*

14156. A good servant must have good wages. *English*

14157. A servant and a cock should be kept but a year. *English*

14158. A servant is known in the absence of his master. *English*

14159. An ill servant will never be a good master. *English*

14160. Bad servants do the thing first and then seek counsel. *Hebrew*

14161. Better be a nobleman's servant than a poor man's wife. *Greek*

14162. Don't take a servant off a midden. *English*

14163. Great men's servants don't think little of themselves. *German*

14164. He can give little to his servant that licks his knife. *English*

14165. He that would be ill served should keep plenty of servants. *Italian*

14166. He that would be well served must know when to change his servants. *English*

14167. He who makes himself a servant is expected to remain a servant. *Italian*

14168. If the servant grows rich and the master poor, they are both good for nothing. *German*

14169. If you pay not a servant his wages, he will pay himself. *English*

14170. If you would have a good servant, take neither a kinsman nor a friend. *English*

14171. Many humble servants, but not one true friend. *English*

14172. One must be a servant before he can be a master. *English*

14173. One servant cannot serve two masters. *Hebrew*

14174. Servants should put on patience when they put on a livery. *English*

14175. Servants should see all and say nothing. *English*

14176. So many servants, so many foes. *English*

14177. Sometimes the servant is nobler than the master. *Yiddish*

14178. The lazy servant takes eight steps to avoid one. *Portuguese*

14179. The more servants, the worse service. *Dutch*

14180. The servant of the church eats out of the church's hand. *Mexican*

14181. Who has many servants has many thieves. *Dutch*

SERVE

14182. He that has not served knows not how to command. *English*

14183. He that's first up is not always first served. *Scottish*

14184. He that serves everybody is paid by nobody. *English*

14185. He that serves well need not be afraid to ask his wages. *English*

14186. He who has not served cannot command. *Serbo-Croatian*

14187. If you wish to be well served, serve yourself. *Spanish*

14188. If you would be well served, serve yourself.   *English*

SERVICE

14189. Good service is a great enchantment.   *English*

14190. Proffered service stinks.
English

14191. Service is no inheritance.
English

14192. Services unrequired go unrequited.   *German*

14193. Service without reward is punishment.   *English*

14194. Unwilling service earns no thanks.   *Danish*

SETTLE

14195. What can be settled amicably should not be settled violently.
Philippine

SEVEN

14196. As one is at seven, so is he at seventy.   *Yiddish*

14197. Seven don't wait for one.
Russian

14198. Seven may be company but nine are confusion.   *English*

SHADE

14199. He who is in the shade doesn't know that another is in the sun.
African (Hausa)

14200. There is no shade without a tree.   *African (Swahili)*

SHADOW

14201. A shadow is a feeble thing but no sun can drive it away.   *Swedish*

14202. A shadow reflects only the external, not the internal qualities of a person.   *Philippine*

14203. Catch not at the shadow, and lose the substance.   *English*

14204. If you are standing upright, don't worry if your shadow is crooked.
Chinese

14205. Nobody can rest in his own shadow.   *Hungarian*

SHAFT

14206. You can never make a good shaft of a pig's tail.   *English*

SHAKE

14207. All that shakes falls out.
English

SHAME

14208. He that has no shame has no conscience.   *English*

14209. He who does shame comes to shame.   *Indian (Kashmiri)*

14210. It's a shame to steal, but a worse to carry home.   *English*

14211. It is no shame to eat one's meat.
English

14212. Many a one would like to lay his own shame on another man's back.
Danish

14213. Shame in a kindred cannot be avoided.   *English*

14214. Shame induces us to fear sin.
Hebrew

14215. Shame is as it is taken.
English

14216. Shame lasts longer than poverty.   *Dutch*

14217. Shame sometimes can kill a man.   *Philippine*

14218. Shame take him that shame thinks.   *English*

14219. Some thinking to avenge their shame increase it.   *French*

14220. There is no shame in learning. *Turkish*

14221. There is nothing that hurts like shame. *African (Ashanti)*

14222. Who fears no shame comes to no honor. *Dutch*

SHAMELESS

14223. He that is shameless is graceless. *English*

SHARE

14224. Share and share alike. *English*

SHARK

14225. All kinds of fish eat man but only sharks get the blame. *Jamaican*

SHAVING

14226. After shaving there's nothing to shear. *French*

14227. Shaving is better than plucking the hair. *African (Wolof)*

SHEARER

14228. A bad shearer never had a good sickle. *English*

SHED

14229. A small shed becomes a house. *African (Ovambo)*

14230. Sleeping in a shed is better than sleeping in a two-storeyed house with no money. *African (Hausa)*

SHEEP

14231. A black sheep is a biting beast. *English*

14232. A good sheep bleats but little and gives much wool. *English*

14233. A lazy sheep thinks its wool heavy. *English*

14234. A little sheep always seems young. *French*

14235. A sheep does not give birth to a goat. *African (Ashanti)*

14236. A sheep was never known to climb a tree. *Chinese*

14237. After losing the sheep, one repairs the pen. *Korean*

14238. All the sheep are not for the wolf. *Italian*

14239. Counted sheep are eaten by the wolf. *French*

14240. Counting your sheep won't keep the wolf away. *Latvian*

14241. Coupled sheep drown one another. *Dutch*

14242. Do not kill the sheep to take its wool. *Russian*

14243. Even counted sheep are eaten by the wolf. *German*

14244. Every time the sheep bleats, it loses a mouthful. *English*

14245. He that has one sheep in the flock will like all the rest the better for it. *Scottish*

14246. He that makes himself a sheep shall be eaten by the wolf. *English*

14247. It is a bad sheep that is too lazy to carry its own fleece. *Danish*

14248. It is a foolish sheep that makes the wolf his confessor. *English*

14249. It is a silly sheep that confesses to the wolf. *Italian*

14250. It is a silly sheep that makes the wolf her confessor. *French*

14251. It is easier to take care of sheep than money. *Serbo-Croatian*

14252. It is possible for a sheep to kill a butcher. *English*

14253. Let the black sheep keep the white. *English*

14254. Many a sheep goes out woolly and comes home shorn. *Danish*

14255. No sheep runs into the mouth of a sleeping wolf. *Dutch*

14256. One bad sheep can easily lead others astray. *Philippine*

14257. One mangy sheep spoils the whole herd. *Russian*

14258. One scabbed sheep infects a whole flock. *English*

14259. One sheep follows another. *English*

14260. Outside he is clothed in a sheep's skin; inside his heart is a wolf's. *Chinese*

14261. Shear the sheep but don't flay them. *French*

14262. The dust raised by the sheep does not choke the wolf. *English*

14263. The lone sheep is in danger of the wolf. *English*

14264. The meek sheep should not try to imitate a furious bull. *Tibetan*

14265. The scabbier the sheep the harder it bleats. *Dutch*

14266. The sheep on the mountain is higher than the bull on the plain. *French*

14267. The sheep that bleats loses a mouthful. *Spanish*

14268. The sheep that bleats the most gives the least milk. *Danish*

14269. The sheep that is too tame is sucked by too many lambs. *French*

14270. There's a scabby sheep in every flock. *English*

14271. When one sheep is over the dam, the rest follow. *Dutch*

14272. When the sheep are shorn, the lambs tremble. *Yiddish*

14273. While the sheep bleats it loses its mouthful. *Flemish*

14274. You cannot shear the sheep closer than the skin. *Danish*

14275. You can't skin two hides from one sheep. *Armenian*

SHELL

14276. The rough shell may have a good kernel. *American*

14277. The shell is needed till the bird is hatched. *Russian*

SHELTER

14278. It is good to have a shelter against every storm. *English*

SHELTERING

14279. It is good sheltering under an old hedge. *English*

SHEPHERD

14280. A lazy shepherd is the wolf's friend. *Welsh*

14281. A shepherd cannot be made from a wolf. *Turkish*

14282. A shepherd strikes not his sheep. *African (Wolof)*

14283. A shepherd that is free from debt is better than a penniless prince. *Turkish*

14284. He who has daughters is always a shepherd. *French*

14285. Straying shepherd, straying sheep. *German*

14286. The good shepherd shears, not flays. *Italian*

14287. The more shepherds, the less care. *Danish*

14288. The shepherd is responsible for the shortcomings of the flock. *Lebanese*

14289. The shepherd smells of sheep even when he becomes a nobleman. *Greek*

14290. When many shepherds tend the sheep, they ever so much longer sleep. *Dutch*

14291. When shepherds quarrel, the wolf has a winning game. *German*

14292. When the shepherd is angry with his flock, he appoints a blind sheep as leader. *Hebrew*

14293. When the shepherd strays, the sheep stray. *Dutch*

SHIELD

14294. A golden shield is of great defense. *English*

SHILLING

14295. The poor man's shilling is but a penny. *English*

SHIP

14296. A dear ship stays long in the harbor. *Scottish*

14297. A great ship asks deep waters. *English*

14298. A ship and a woman are ever repairing. *English*

14299. A ship is often lost with all on board on account of one man. *Irish*

14300. A ship under sail, a man in complete armor, and a woman with a great belly are three of the handsomest sights. *English*

14301. Anchor a ship with reference to the wind. *Indian (Tamil)*

14302. Do not load everything into one ship. *German*

14303. Free ships make free goods. *American*

14304. In calm water every ship has a good captain. *Swedish*

14305. It is hard to track the path the ship follows in the ocean. *Danish*

14306. Often has a ship been lost close to the harbor. *Irish*

14307. Ships fear fire more than water. *English*

14308. The ship goes, the port remains. *Indian (Tamil)*

14309. The ship of him who confides in God founders not. *Turkish*

14310. Where the ship goes the brig can go. *Italian*

14311. You cannot damage a wrecked ship. *Italian*

SHIRT

14312. Let not your shirt know your way of thinking. *French*

14313. My shirt is nearer than my cloak. *Dutch*

14314. Near is my shirt, but nearer is my skin. *English*

14315. One doesn't spoil a shirt because of one corner. *Yiddish*

14316. One's own shirt is closer to one's body. *Russian*

14317. The shirt is nearer than the frock. *Spanish*

14318. The shirt is nearer to the body than the coat. *Danish*

SHIVE

14319. It is safe taking a shive of a cut loaf. *English*

SHOAL

14320. When the shoals are full of fish, the birds will light on the beach. *Hawaiian*

SHOE

14321. A black shoe makes a merry heart. *English*

14322. A great shoe fits not a little foot. *English*

14323. A handsome shoe often pinches the foot. *French*

14324. A mare's shoe and a horse's shoe are both alike. *English*

14325. A pair of light shoes is not all that is needed for dancing. *Danish*

14326. A sheepskin shoe lasts not long. *English*

14327. Better cut the shoe than pinch the foot. *English*

14328. Better to go barefooted than to wear shoes too narrow.
Indian (Kashmiri)

14329. Better wear out shoes than sheets. *English*

14330. Between saying and doing many a pair of shoes is worn out. *Italian*

14331. Don't throw away your old shoes till you have got new ones. *Dutch*

14332. Every shoe fits not every foot. *English*

14333. Everyone knows where his shoe pinches. *Yiddish*

14334. He knows best where the shoe pinches who wears it. *Danish*

14335. He that makes the shoe can't tan the leather. *English*

14336. He who waits for a dead man's shoes is in danger of going barefoot. *French*

14337. If the shoe fits, wear it. *English*

14338. If you stay at home, you won't wear out your shoes. *Yiddish*

14339. More belongs to dancing than a pair of dancing shoes. *Dutch*

14340. No one knows better where the shoe pinches than he who wears it. *German*

14341. No one knows where another's shoe pinches. *Dutch*

14342. Old shoes need much wax. *Swedish*

14343. One shoe will not fit all feet. *English*

14344. Only the shoe knows of the hole in the stocking. *Polish*

14345. Shoes alone know if the stockings have holes. *Jamaican*

14346. The fairest looking shoe may pinch the foot. *English*

14347. The finest shoe often hurts the foot. *English*

14348. The same shoe does not fit every foot. *Italian*

14349. The shoe should fit the foot and not the foot the shoe. *Greek*

14350. The shoe will hold with the sole. *English*

14351. The shoes of the poor man's kids grow with their feet. *Yiddish*

14352. There never was a shoe however handsome that did not become an ugly slipper. *Italian*

14353. To pass through a thicket you have to rely on shoes. *African (Shona)*

14354. When one's shoes are tight the world becomes tight on one's head. *Turkish*

14355. When you buy shoes, measure your feet. *Chinese*

14356. With shoes one can get on in the midst of thorns. *African (Yoruba)*

SHOEMAKER

14357. Shoemaker, stick to your last. *German*

14358. Shoemakers are always the worst shod. *French*

14359. The shoemaker speaks of his last and the sailor of his mast. *Yiddish*

SHOOT

14360. He shoots well that hits the mark. *English*

14361. He that shoots always aright forfeits his arrow. *English*

14362. He that shoots often shall at last hit the mark. *English*

14363. He who shoots often hits at last. *German*

SHOOTING

14364. Before shooting, one must aim. *African (Wolof)*

14365. Short shooting loses the game. *English*

SHOP

14366. A fair shop and little gain. *English*

14367. A shop is not opened for the sake of one customer. *Turkish*

14368. Keep your shop and your shop will keep you. *English*

14369. To open a shop is easy; the difficult thing is keeping it open. *Chinese*

SHORE

14370. The shore likewise belongs to the sea. *Russian*

14371. Who owns the shore owns the fish. *Russian*

SHORT

14372. Better short and sweet than long and lax. *Scottish*

SHOT

14373. Every shot does not bring down a bird. *Dutch*

14374. The first shot is worth a dozen afterward. *American*

14375. Two shots never go in the same place. *American*

SHOULDER

14376. He who rides on the giant's shoulders sees further than he who carries him. *French*

SHOUT

14377. Don't shout till you are out of the wood. *English*

14378. That what you shout out will echo back in like manner. *Russian*

SHOW (noun)

14379. The show is over. *American*

SHOW (verb)

14380. He who does not show himself is overlooked. *Spanish*

SHOWER

14381. A sunshiny shower won't last half an hour. *English*

14382. April showers bring May flowers. *English*

14383. If we stand the shower we won't flinch from the drops. *American*

SHREW

14384. A shrew gets her wish but suffers in the getting. *Irish*

14385. A shrew is better than a sheep. *English*

14386. A shrew profitable may serve a man reasonable. *English*

14387. A shrew strikes terror into a demon even. *Indian (Bihar)*

14388. One shrew is worth two sheep. *English*

14389. There is but one shrew in all the world, but every man thinks he has one. *English*

SHREWDNESS

14390. The shrewdness of the woman fails to sell the ox. *Japanese*

SHRIMP

14391. A sleeping shrimp is carried away by the current. *Philippine*

14392. Although shrimps may dance around they do not leave the river. *Japanese*

14393. Shrimps get broken backs in a whale fight. *Korean*

SHROUD

14394. Shrouds are made without pockets. *Yiddish*

SHRUB

14395. The shrub with one root is not hard to pull up. *African (Hausa)*

SICK

14396. Be long sick that you may be soon healed. *Scottish*

14397. He who was never sick dies the first fit. *English*

SICKLE

14398. One day the sickle will cut down the nettle. *Polish*

14399. Take not your sickle to another man's corn. *Danish*

SICKNESS

14400. It is all one whether you die of sickness or of love. *Italian*

14401. Sickness comes in by the bagful and goes out stitch by stitch. *Greek*

14402. Sickness comes in haste, and goes at leisure. *Danish*

14403. Sickness comes on horseback, but goes away on foot. *English*

14404. Sickness is every man's master. *Danish*

14405. Sickness is felt, but health not at all. *English*

14406. Sickness is the physician's feast. *Irish*

14407. Sickness tells us what we are. *English*

SIDE

14408. Hear the other side, and believe little. *Italian*

14409. The attractive side of the merchandise is shown. *Russian*

14410. The mother's side is the surest. *English*

SIEVE

14411. The sieve never sifts flour by itself. *African (Yoruba)*

SIGH

14412. The sighs of the happy are only featherweight. *Russian*

SIGHT

14413. Out of sight, out of heart. *Lebanese*

14414. Out of sight, out of mind. *English*

14415. Sight goes before hearsay. *Danish*

14416. The sight of a man has the force of a lion. *English*

14417. When the sight leaves the eye, love leaves the heart. *Irish*

SIGN (noun)

14418. Old signs do not deceive. *Danish*

14419. The first sign of a quarrel is gesticulation. *African (Hausa)*

14420. The sign invites you in; but your money must redeem you out. *English*

SIGN (verb)

14421. What's signed, is signed; and what's to be, will be. *American*

SILENCE

14422. A good silence is better than a bad dispute.   *Russian*

14423. Be silent, or say something better than silence.   *German*

14424. Dignified silence is better than dignified speech.   *Yiddish*

14425. He who walks in silence quarrels with nobody.   *African (Swahili)*

14426. However pleasant the sound of a drum, silence is better.
African (Hausa)

14427. However sweet talk, silence is better.   *African (Fulani)*

14428. No one betrays himself by silence.   *German*

14429. Silence and reflection cause no dejection.   *German*

14430. Silence answers much.   *Dutch*

14431. Silence catches a mouse.
Scottish

14432. Silence comes from admission.
Turkish

14433. Silence defeats the scandal monger.   *African (Hausa)*

14434. Silence does not bring harm.
African (Swahili)

14435. Silence gives consent.   *English*

14436. Silence goes better with shrewdness than with a kind heart.
Polish

14437. Silence is a fine jewel for a woman, but it's little worn.   *English*

14438. Silence is a sign of consent.
Russian

14439. Silence is an admission.   *Welsh*

14440. Silence is counsel.   *English*

14441. Silence is golden.   *English*

14442. Silence is good for the wise, how much more so for the foolish.
Hebrew

14443. Silence is profitable.
Indian (Kashmiri)

14444. Silence is talk too.
African (Hausa)

14445. Silence is the best answer to the stupid.   *Egyptian*

14446. Silence is the best ornament of a woman.   *English*

14447. Silence is the brother of acceptance.   *Lebanese*

14448. Silence is wisdom.   *English*

14449. Silence is wisdom when speaking is folly.   *English*

14450. Silence is worth a thousand pieces of silver.   *Burmese*

14451. Silence itself is eloquent.
African (Fulani)

14452. Silence profits the wise and even more the fool.   *Hebrew*

14453. Silence seldom does harm.
English

14454. Silence surpasses speech.
Japanese

14455. Speaking silence is better than senseless speech.   *Danish*

SILENT

14456. Who is silent, agrees. *German*

SILK

14457. In silk and scarlet walks many a harlot.   *English*

14458. Silk and velvet put out the kitchen fire.   *German*

14459. Silks and satins put out the kitchen fire.   *English*

14460. The fairest silk is soonest stained.   *English*

SILVER

14461. He that has not silver in his purse should have silk on his tongue.
Scottish

14462. He who does not esteem silver is not worthy to have silver. *Greek*

14463. No silver, no servant. *English*

14464. No silver, no service. *English*

14465. No silver without dross. *English*

14466. Silver and gold are all men's dears. *Danish*

14467. Silver is the father of lead; gold is the father of brass. *African (Yoruba)*

14468. When you go out to buy, don't show your silver. *Chinese*

14469. White silver draws black lines. *English*

SILVER MINE

14470. Once a silver mine, always a silver mine. *American*

SIMILARITY

14471. Similarity is not identity. *African (Hausa)*

SIMPLETON

14472. He is a great simpleton who starves himself to feed another. *Spanish*

SIMPLICITY

14473. Simplicity is the ornament of a woman. *Indian (Tamil)*

SIN

14474. A sin concealed is half forgiven. *Italian*

14475. A sin confessed is half forgiven. *Italian*

14476. A sin, even if committed by many, remains a sin. *Hungarian*

14477. A sin of gold is followed by a punishment of lead. *Russian*

14478. Citizens' sins are a city's disgrace. *Greek*

14479. Dissembled sin is double wickedness. *English*

14480. Each sin has its own excuse. *Czech*

14481. Everyone finds sin sweet and repentance bitter. *Danish*

14482. Everyone thinks himself without sin because he has not those of others. *Italian*

14483. For sins, you cry; but for debts, you pay. *Armenian*

14484. Hate the sin but do not hate the person. *Japanese*

14485. He who committed a mortal sin carries a spear. *African (Ovambo)*

14486. He who prays often has many sins. *Philippine*

14487. If there were no sin there would be no hell. *Slovakian*

14488. It is a sin to belie the devil. *English*

14489. It is a sin to have been present at a wedding without being drunk. *Russian*

14490. It is a sin to steal a pin. *English*

14491. It is no sin to cheat the devil. *English*

14492. It is no sin to see wasters want. *Scottish*

14493. It is no sin to sell dear, but a sin to give ill measure. *Scottish*

14494. It's no use hiding a sin. *Russian*

14495. Little sins have small pardons. *American*

14496. No sin, no salvation. *Russian*

14497. Old sin makes new shame. *English*

14498. Old sins breed new shame. *Scottish*

14499. One sin draws a hundred after it. *Welsh*

14500. Our sins and our debts are always greater than we take them to be. *English*

14501. Our sins and our debts are often more than we think. *Scottish*

14502. Sin cries out for retribution. *Philippine*

14503. Sin devours the one who has committed it. *African (Shona)*

14504. Sin enters laughing and comes out crying. *Rumanian*

14505. Sin has no master. *Russian*

14506. Sin is the canoe that will land you in hell. *Hawaiian*

14507. Sin is the root of the sorrow. *Chinese*

14508. Sin that is hidden is half forgiven. *English*

14509. Sins are not known till they be acted. *English*

14510. That which comes with sin goes with sorrow. *Danish*

14511. The husband's sin remains on the threshold; the wife's enters the house. *Russian*

14512. There is no sin so great as killing. *Tibetan*

14513. What is no sin is no shame. *German*

14514. When all other sins are old avarice is still young. *French*

14515. When the sin is sweet, the repentance is not bitter. *Yiddish*

14516. Where sin drives, shame sits in the back seat. *Swedish*

14517. Who avoids small sins does not fall into great ones. *German*

14518. Who swims on sin shall sink in sorrow. *English*

SING

14519. He that sings in disaster, shall weep all his lifetime thereafter. *English*

14520. He that sings worst let him begin first. *English*

14521. Many a one sings that is full sorrow. *English*

14522. Not everyone who sings is happy. *Maltese*

14523. Sing before breakfast, cry before night. *English*

14524. Who cannot sing may whistle. *German*

SINGER

14525. Singers and ringers are little home bringers. *English*

14526. Singers, lovers, and poets lie a lot. *German*

SINGING

14527. Even singing requires some effort. *Serbo-Croatian*

14528. Singing without remuneration is like a dead body without perfumes. *Egyptian*

SINGLE

14529. May the single be married and the married happy. *American*

14530. Single long, shame at last. *English*

SINNER

14531. A repentant sinner is more worthy than ten saints who never succumb to temptation. *Russian*

14532. The greater the sinner, the greater the saint. *English*

SIP

14533. A sip at a time empties the cask. *Norwegian*

14534. He who takes one sip isn't satisfied. *African (Hausa)*

14535. The first sip of broth is always the hottest. *Irish*

SIT

14536. Better sit idle than work for nothing. *English*

14537. Better sit still than rise up and fall. *English*

14538. He sits not sure that sits too high. *English*

14539. He that sits to work in the marketplace shall have many teachers. *English*

14540. He that sits well thinks ill. *English*

14541. Sit a while and go a mile. *English*

14542. Sit by the good, and by the good arise. *English*

14543. Sit in your place and none can make you rise. *English*

SITTING

14544. Sitting a lot ends by making holes in clothes. *African (Bemba)*

SIZE

14545. Dress according to your size, and associate with your equal. *Moroccan*

SKI

14546. One cannot ski so softly that the traces cannot be seen. *Finnish*

SKILL

14547. Skill and confidence are an unconquered army. *English*

14548. Skill is better than knowledge. *Vietnamese*

14549. Skill wins over noble birth. *Greek*

14550. Try your skill in gilt first, and then in gold. *English*

14551. Without skill you cannot even catch a louse. *Russian*

SKILLED

14552. You are skilled at what you are familiar with. *Burmese*

SKIN

14553. A fair skin often covers a crooked mind. *Danish*

14554. A lion's skin is never cheap. *English*

14555. A rat skin is not sufficient to cover a kettledrum. *Indian (Bihar)*

14556. Don't sell the fox skin in the wood. *Rumanian*

14557. Don't sell the skin off the bear that's still in the forest. *Yiddish*

14558. Don't sell the skin till you've caught the bear. *Dutch*

14559. He whose skin itches will scratch. *Indian (Tamil)*

14560. The skin fits closer than the shirt. *Jamaican*

14561. The skin is nearer than the shirt. *French*

14562. The skin of the young is elastic. *Finnish*

14563. The toughest skin will hold out the longest. *American*

14564. Where the lion's skin falls short, piece it out with that of the fox. *Italian*

14565. You cannot get two skins from one cow. *Chinese*

SKIPPER

14566. The good skipper proves himself during a storm. *Greek*

SKIRT

14567. Long skirts carry dust, but short skirts carry away souls. *Maltese*

14568. Who has skirts of straw needs fear the fire. *English*

SKUNK

14569. Where there was a skunk there is a smell. *African (Ovambo)*

SKY

14570. A clear sky fears not the thunder. *Rumanian*

14571. If the sky falls there will be pots broken. *Spanish*

14572. No sky without clouds. *Rumanian*

14573. There will be a way to escape even if the sky falls. *Korean*

14574. Were the sky to fall, not an earthen pot would be left whole. *Dutch*

14575. When the sky falls we shall catch larks. *English*

14576. When the sky is clear, carry an umbrella. *Chinese*

SLANDER (noun)

14577. A slander that is raised is ill to fell. *English*

14578. Slander cannot make a good man bad. *Chinese*

14579. Slander flings stones at itself. *English*

14580. Slander is a shipwreck by a dry tempest. *English*

14581. Slander leaves a scar behind it. *English*

14582. Slanders cluster thick about a widow's door. *Chinese*

SLANDER (verb)

14583. He who is slandered is great. *African (Bemba)*

SLANDERER

14584. A slanderer and a snake of deadly poison have each two tongues. *Indian (Tamil)*

14585. The most dangerous of wild beasts is a slanderer; of tame ones a flatterer. *English*

SLAP

14586. A relative's slap hurts more than a stranger's. *Rumanian*

14587. A slap heals but a harsh word is remembered. *Yiddish*

14588. A slap in hand is better than a gift to come. *Iranian*

14589. If one gets a slap in the face, one acquires an enemy as a bonus. *Yiddish*

SLAVE

14590. A slave does not choose his master. *African (Ashanti)*

14591. He's a slave that cannot command himself. *English*

14592. Never spoil a slave or deceive a small child. *Chinese*

SLAVERY

14593. One can escape from slavery but not from the grave. *Serbo-Croatian*

SLEEP (noun)

14594. Long sleep makes a bare breech. *Irish*

14595. No sleep, no dream. *African (Ga)*

14596. One hour's sleep before midnight is better than three after it. *French*

14597. One hour's sleep before midnight is better than two after it. *German*

14598. One hour's sleep before midnight is worth two after. *English*

14599. Quiet sleep feels no foul weather. *English*

14600. Seven hours' sleep will make a clown forget his design. *English*

14601. Sleep is a priceless treasure; the more one has of it, the better it is. *Chinese*

14602. Sleep is a thief. *Yiddish*

14603. Sleep is better than food. *Greek*

14604. Sleep is brother to death. *Irish*

14605. Sleep is not compared with death. *African (Ovambo)*

14606. Sleep is the best doctor. *Yiddish*

14607. Sleep is the excuse of sleep. *Turkish*

14608. Sleep is the poor man's treasure. *Latvian*

14609. Sleep is the remedy for fear. *African (Hausa)*

14610. Sleep is unconscious of enjoyment. *Indian (Tamil)*

14611. Sleep without supping, and wake without owing. *English*

14612. The sleep of a child is advantageous to the mother. *Indian (Tamil)*

14613. The sleep of kings is on an anthill. *Pashto*

SLEEP (verb)

14614. He has slept well that remembers not he has slept ill. *English*

14615. He sleeps securely who has nothing to lose. *French*

14616. He that sleeps bites nobody. *English*

14617. He who sleeps much, learns little. *Spanish*

14618. One sleeps tranquilly on the hurt of another. *Irish*

14619. The more one sleeps the less one lives. *Polish*

14620. The more you sleep, the less you sin. *Russian*

SLEEPING

14621. Early sleeping and early rising are essentials for becoming a millionaire. *Japanese*

14622. Sleeping is turning. *African (Zulu)*

14623. There will be sleeping enough in the grave. *English*

SLEIGH

14624. A sleigh demands a colt, a house needs a man. *Finnish*

SLICE

14625. Start a loaf and one slice soon follows another. *Slovakian*

SLING

14626. The sling will burst somewhere. *Greek*

SLIP

14627. A slip of the foot may be soon recovered, but that of the tongue perhaps never. *English*

14628. A slip of the tongue is worse than that of the foot. *Indian (Tamil)*

14629. Better a slip of the foot than of the tongue. *French*

14630. Every slip is not a fall. *English*

14631. It is not worth talking about a slip of the foot as if it were a fall. *African (Efik)*

14632. There's many a slip between cup and lip. *English*

SLIPPER

14633. There was never an old slipper but there was an old stocking to match it. *Irish*

14634. Though golden slippers, they must be put on the feet.

Indian (Tamil)

SLOTH

14635. Sloth breeds a scab.   *English*

14636. Sloth is the beginning of vice.

Dutch

14637. Sloth is the devil's cushion or pillow.   *English*

14638. Sloth is the key to poverty.

English

14639. Sloth, like rust, consumes faster than labor wears.   *English*

14640. Sloth makes all things difficult, but industry all things easy.   *English*

14641. Sloth turns the edge of wit.

English

SLOTHFUL

14642. The slothful is the servant of the covetous.   *English*

SLOW

14643. Slow and sure.   *English*

SLUGGARD

14644. A sluggard takes a hundred steps because he would not take one in due time.   *English*

14645. At evening the sluggard is busy.

German

14646. The sluggard makes his night till noon.   *English*

14647. The sluggard must be clad in rags.   *English*

SLUMBER (noun)

14648. One slumber invites another.

English

SLUMBER (verb)

14649. He slumbers enough who does nothing.   *French*

SLUT

14650. A slut will poison your gut.

English

SMART (verb)

14651. What smarts, teaches. *German*

SMARTEST

14652. The smartest of us gets tripped up sometimes.   *American*

SMELL (noun)

14653. Even bad smell is found in sweet places.   *Hawaiian*

14654. No bad smell can be hidden.

Philippine

14655. The smell of gain is sweet.

English

SMELL (verb)

14656. He smells best that does of nothing smell.   *English*

14657. He that smells the first savor is the fault's first father.   *English*

SMILE

14658. Better is the last smile than the first laughter.   *English*

14659. The smile on a hungry man's face is a lie.   *Polish*

SMITH

14660. By working in the smithy one becomes a smith.   *French*

14661. He is a bad smith who cannot bear smoke.   *German*

14662. The smith always follows a pattern.   *African (Yoruba)*

14663. The smith and his penny are both black.   *English*

SMOKE

14664. Much smoke, little fire.

English

14665. No smoke without fire, and no rumor without foundation.   *Lebanese*

14666. Smoke and a scolding woman drive one out of the house.   *Rumanian*

14667. Smoke does not rise where there is no fire.   *African (Shona)*

14668. Smoke follows the fairest.
English

14669. Smoke from roasting meat does not irritate the eyes.   *African (Shona)*

14670. Smoke is seen when a village burns, but hearts aflame, no one discerns.   *Malaysian*

14671. Smoke, rain, and a troublesome wife are enough to drive a man out of his house.   *French*

14672. Smoke, rain, and a very cursed wife makes a man weary of house and life.   *English*

14673. The smoke of a man's own house is better than the fire of another.
English

14674. There is no smoke without fire.
English

14675. They who shun the smoke often fall into the fire.   *Italian*

14676. When the smoke rises, there is fire below.   *Hawaiian*

14677. When there's a lot of smoke, there's little heat.   *Latvian*

14678. Where there's smoke, there's fire.   *Yiddish*

14679. You cannot cover or hide smoke.
Philippine

14680. You have to suffer smoke in order to keep warm.   *Czech*

SNAIL

14681. The snail slides up the tower at last though the swallow mounts it sooner.   *English*

14682. Tread on a snail, and he'll shoot out his horns.   *Scottish*

14683. When a snail travels, he'll get there sometime.   *Russian*

14684. When the snail crawls, its shell accompanies it.   *African (Yoruba)*

SNAKE

14685. A snake does not bite a man without cause.   *African (Ashanti)*

14686. A snake is not killed by its own poison.   *Lebanese*

14687. A snake is not taken with the hand.   *Turkish*

14688. A snake rears snakes.   *Iranian*

14689. A snake that has entered a hole should not be provoked.
African (Shona)

14690. A young snake is more poisonous and vigorous than an old one.
Indian (Tamil)

14691. Big snakes do not live in the same hole.   *African (Ovambo)*

14692. Continued beating kills the snake.   *African (Fulani)*

14693. Don't drive a snake from a bamboo thicket.   *Japanese*

14694. Do not play with a snake offspring as if it could never bite.
African (Annang)

14695. Don't trouble a quiet snake.
Greek

14696. Even though a snake enter a bamboo tube, it still inclines to wriggle.   *Chinese*

14697. Fear surrounds the place where a snake disappeared in the bush.
African (Jabo)

14698. He who has been bitten by a snake fears a decayed rope.   *Japanese*

14699. He who has been bitten by a snake fears a piece of string.   *Iranian*

14700. He who has been bitten by a snake is afraid of an eel.   *Danish*

14701. He who has been bitten by a snake is afraid of lizards.
Serbo-Croatian

14702. He who is bitten once by a snake will not walk a second time in the grass. *Chinese*

14703. If a snake bites your neighbor, you too are in danger.
African (Swahili)

14704. If you strike a snake without killing it, it will turn and bite you.
Chinese

14705. It is owing to being disturbed that a snake bites. *African (Ashanti)*

14706. Kill the snake as well as save the stick. *Indian (Bihar)*

14707. One does not fight with a spitting snake. *African (Ovambo)*

14708. One does not follow a snake into its hole. *African (Zulu)*

14709. One doesn't throw the stick after the snake has gone.
African (Jabo)

14710. One year bitten by a snake, for three years afraid of a grass rope.
Chinese

14711. Press not the tail of a sleeping snake. *Turkish*

14712. Snakes follow the way of serpents. *Japanese*

14713. The snake distills her venom and the bee her honey from the same flower. *Armenian*

14714. The snake does not bite itself.
Moroccan

14715. The snake goes crookedly, yet it arrives straight within its hole.
Indian (Kashmiri)

14716. The snake grows with every repetition of the story. *Philippine*

14717. The snake is feared because of its mouth. *African (Fulani)*

14718. The snake issues from a hole you would not have supposed.
Turkish

14719. The snake that wishes to live does not travel on the highway.
Haitian

14720. The snake, unless he be straightened out, cannot enter his hole.
Turkish

14721. Warm up a frozen snake and she will bite you first. *Armenian*

14722. When the snake is old, the frog will tease him. *Iranian*

14723. Who has been bitten by a snake dreads even earthworms. *Russian*

SNIPE

14724. Every snipe is great in his own swamp. *Russian*

14725. Every snipe praises his own swamp. *Russian*

SNORE

14726. All who snore are not asleep.
Danish

SNOW

14727. From snow whether cooked or pounded you will get nothing but water. *Italian*

14728. However much snow falls, still it does not endure the summer.
Turkish

14729. Let each sweep the snow from before his own door; let him not be concerned about the frost on his neighbor's tiles. *Chinese*

14730. No one thinks of the snow that fell last year. *Swedish*

14731. What lay hidden under the snow comes to light at last. *Dutch*

SOAP

14732. It is a loss of soap to wash the ass's head.   *Spanish*

14733. Like soap for the body, so are tears for the soul.   *Yiddish*

14734. When the soap comes to an end, the washerwoman rejoices. *Moroccan*

SOFT

14735. Soft and fair goes far.   *English*

SOIL

14736. As fallow soil gives birth to weeds, old age gives birth to disease.
Vietnamese

14737. If you take care of the soil, the soil will take care of you.   *Latvian*

14738. Soil that is fertile is unfit for the road.   *Indian (Hindi)*

SOLDIER

14739. A soldier becomes smart after eating some warm food.   *Yiddish*

14740. All are not soldiers who go to the wars.   *Spanish*

14741. Away from the battle all are soldiers.   *German*

14742. If one soldier knew what the other thinks, there would be no war.
Yiddish

14743. It is better to be a soldier than a priest.   *Greek*

14744. Soldiers in peace are like chimneys in summer.   *English*

14745. The bravest soldiers are the most civil to prisoners.   *American*

14746. The common soldiers do the fighting, and the officers claim the victory.   *Hebrew*

14747. The summer soldier and the sunshine patriot will shrink from the service of their country.   *American*

SOLE

14748. One pair of good shoes is worth two pairs of upper leathers.   *Irish*

14749. The sole of the foot is exposed to all the dirt of the road.
African (Yoruba)

SOMETHING

14750. Better something than nothing at all.   *German*

14751. Something is better than nothing.   *German*

14752. Who has something is something.   *Italian*

SOMEWHAT

14753. Somewhat is better than nothing.   *English*

SON

14754. A carpenter's son knows how to saw; a duckling, how to swim.
Chinese

14755. A runaway son is still precious; a runaway daughter loses her value.
Chinese

14756. A shoemaker's son is a prince born.   *English*

14757. A son is the bone of hard times.
African (Ovambo)

14758. A son should begin where his father left off.   *American*

14759. Better be a poor man's son than the slave of a rich.   *Rumanian*

14760. Better even a son given to gambling than a son given to drink.   *Irish*

14761. Brainless sons boast of their ancestors.   *Chinese*

14762. By renown and estimation the son of the noble is noble.   *Turkish*

14763. Happy is she who marries the son of a dead mother.   *Scottish*

14764. If your son turns out to be a thief, give him up even though he will be mad. *Moroccan*

14765. Marry your son when you will, your daughter when you can. *Danish*

14766. Send your son to the marketplace and you shall find out with whom he will associate. *Lebanese*

14767. Teach your son in the hall, your wife on the pillow. *Chinese*

14768. The magistrate's son gets out of every scrape. *Spanish*

14769. The son disgraces his father by bad conduct. *African (Efik)*

14770. The son of a wolf will be a wolf, even if he grows up with man. *Turkish*

14771. The son of an ass brays twice a day. *Spanish*

14772. The son of an old man is an orphan, and his wife is a widow. *Lebanese*

14773. To raise a son without learning is raising an ass; to raise a daughter without learning is raising a pig. *Chinese*

SONG

14774. A good song may be sung three times. *Czech*

14775. A silly song may be sung in many ways. *Danish*

14776. Every song has its end. *Slovenian*

14777. He who pitches too high, won't get through his song. *German*

14778. Let him that begins the song make an end. *English*

14779. New songs are eagerly sung. *German*

14780. New songs are liked the best. *Danish*

14781. Sweet song has betrayed many. *German*

14782. The song of the stomach is hard to hear. *African (Wolof)*

14783. To every new song one can find an old tune. *Yiddish*

14784. You will hate a beautiful song if you sing it often. *Korean*

SON-IN-LAW

14785. A son-in-law never becomes a son and a daughter-in-law never quite becomes a daughter. *Greek*

14786. With a good son-in-law you find a son, with a bad one you lose your daughter, too. *Hebrew*

SOON

14787. Better too soon, than too late. *American*

SORCERER

14788. The sorcerer mutters but knows not what he mutters. *Hebrew*

SORE

14789. A small sore wants not a great plaster. *English*

14790. An inward sore puts out the physician's eye. *English*

14791. Different sores must have different salves. *English*

14792. Old sores are hardly cured. *English*

14793. Though the sore be healed, yet a scar may remain. *English*

14794. Where there is no sore there is no need for a plaster. *French*

SORROW

14795. A child's sorrow is short lived. *Danish*

14796. A lean sorrow is hardest to bear. *English*

14797. He gains enough who loses sorrow. *French*

14798. He who loves sorrow will always find something to mourn over. *Danish*

14799. He who sings drives away sorrow. *Italian*

14800. Little sorrows are loud, great ones silent. *Danish*

14801. Make not two sorrows of one. *English*

14802. One doesn't know another's sorrow. *Yiddish*

14803. Sorrow and an evil life makes soon an old wife. *English*

14804. Sorrow and ill weather come unsent for. *Scottish*

14805. Sorrow at parting if at meeting there be laughter. *English*

14806. Sorrow comes unsent for. *English*

14807. Sorrow ends not when it seems done. *English*

14808. Sorrow follows in gaiety's footsteps. *Russian*

14809. Sorrow for a husband is like a pain in the elbow, sharp and short. *English*

14810. Sorrow is born of excessive joy. *Chinese*

14811. Sorrow is dry. *English*

14812. Sorrow is good for nothing but sin. *English*

14813. Sorrow is soon enough when it comes. *Scottish*

14814. Sorrow makes silence her best orator. *English*

14815. Sorrow makes the bones grow thinner. *Yiddish*

14816. Sorrow seldom comes alone. *Danish*

14817. Sorrow will pay no debt. *English*

14818. The sorrow of a widow can be understood only by the widowed. *Korean*

14819. When sorrow is asleep, wake it not. *English*

14820. Without sorrows none become Buddhas. *Chinese*

SORT

14821. It takes all sorts to make a world. *English*

SOUL

14822. You can't climb into someone else's soul. *Russian*

SOUND

14823. Confused sounds will not make speech. *African (Hausa)*

14824. No sound comes forth from a single hand. *Turkish*

14825. Sounds often terrify more than realities. *American*

14826. The sound of the carpenter does not remain secret. *Indian (Kashmiri)*

SOUP

14827. A soup that tastes good by licking must taste better by eating. *African (Annang)*

14828. Between the hand and the lip the soup may be spilled. *German*

14829. Between the hand and the mouth the soup is lost. *Spanish*

14830. Between the hand and the mouth the soup is spilled. *Italian*

14831. Eat bad soup with a big spoon. *Armenian*

14832. Having learned his lesson with hot soup, he blows cold fish salad. *Japanese*

14833. He who burnt himself with soup blows also in the sour milk. *Rumanian*

14834. Much soup is better than much broth. *African (Wolof)*

14835. One cannot make soup out of beauty. *Estonian*

14836. Who has been scalded with hot soup blows on cold water. *Russian*

SOUR

14837. After the sour comes the sweet. *Dutch*

SOURCE

14838. If the source of the water is bad, the dirt will reach to the low lands. *Hawaiian*

SOVEREIGNTY

14839. There is no sovereignty like bachelorhood. *Turkish*

SOW (noun)

14840. A barren sow was never good to pigs. *English*

14841. A fat sow causes her own bane. *English*

14842. A sow is always dreaming of bran. *French*

14843. A sow prefers bran to roses. *French*

14844. A still sow eats up all the draff. *Dutch*

14845. Every sow to her own trough. *English*

14846. If you raise a sow, payment is inside of her. *Hawaiian*

14847. Little knows the fat sow what the lean does mean. *English*

14848. The fat sow knows not what the hungry sow suffers. *Danish*

14849. The full sow knows not the squeak of the empty one. *Welsh*

14850. The sow, when washed, returns to the muck. *Czech*

14851. The still sow eats up all the draff. *English*

SOW (verb)

14852. As you sow so will you reap. *English*

14853. Early sow, early mow. *English*

14854. He that sows trusts in God. *English*

14855. He who sows little, reaps little. *Danish*

14856. He who sows well, reaps well. *Spanish*

14857. Nobody sows a thing that will not sell. *Spanish*

14858. One sows, another reaps. *English*

14859. Sow dry and set wet. *English*

14860. Sow early and you will reap early. *Chinese*

14861. Sow much, reap much; sow little, reap little. *Chinese*

14862. We must sow even after a bad harvest. *Danish*

14863. Who sows little mows the less. *English*

SOWER

14864. Ill sowers make ill harvest. *English*

14865. The early sower never borrows of the late. *English*

SOWING

14866. Forebear not sowing because of birds. *English*

14867. Unless there be a sowing there will be no reaping. *Turkish*

SPADE

14868. To a long illness the spade is the end. *Slovenian*

SPARE

14869. Better spare to have of thine own than ask of other men.   *English*

14870. Better spared than ill spent.
English

14871. He that spares something today will have something tomorrow. *Dutch*

14872. It is too late to spare when all is spent.   *English*

14873. It is too late to spare when the bottom is bare.   *English*

14874. Spare well and spend well.
English

14875. Spare when you are young and spend when you are old.   *English*

SPARING

14876. Always to be sparing is always to be in want.   *Danish*

14877. Sparing is a rich purse.
English

14878. Sparing is the first gaining.
English

SPARK

14879. A little spark kindles a great fire.   *Spanish*

14880. A little spark shines in the dark.   *French*

14881. A single spark can burn the whole quarter.   *Egyptian*

14882. A small spark makes a great fire.   *English*

14883. Every spark adds to the fire.
American

14884. From a spark grows a blaze.
Irish

14885. One spark burned down a forest.   *African (Ovambo)*

SPARROW

14886. A sparrow in hand is worth a pheasant that flies by.   *English*

14887. A sparrow in the hand is better than a bustard on the wing. *Spanish*

14888. A sparrow in the hand is better than a crane on the wing.   *French*

14889. A sparrow in the hand is better than a pigeon on the roof.   *German*

14890. A sparrow in the hand is better than a pigeon on the wing.   *French*

14891. A sparrow suffers as much when it breaks its leg as does a flanders horse.   *Danish*

14892. Better a sparrow in the granary than an eagle in heaven.   *Russian*

14893. Better a sparrow in the hand than a falcon in the forest.
Serbo-Croatian

14894. Better a sparrow in the hand than two flying.   *Portuguese*

14895. Better a sparrow today than a grouse on the morrow.   *Slovakian*

14896. It does not become the sparrow to mix in the dance of the cranes.
Danish

14897. Let him who dreads the sparrows sow no oats.   *Serbo-Croatian*

14898. Sparrows fight for corn which is none of their own.   *English*

14899. Sparrows who emulate peacocks are likely to break a thigh.
Burmese

14900. The sparrow has no song, but plenty of twitter.   *Turkish*

14901. The sparrow, though small, can lay eggs well.   *Korean*

14902. Two sparrows on one ear of corn make an ill agreement.   *English*

14903. Two sparrows on one ear of corn never agree.   *Spanish*

14904. Two sparrows on the same ear of corn are not long friends.   *French*

14905. You can't trick an old sparrow with chaff.   *Russian*

SPARROW HAWK

14906. You can't make a sparrow hawk of a buzzard.   *English*

SPEAK

14907. Better be ill spoken of by one before all, than by all before one.
English

14908. Better to be silent than to speak ill of another.   *African (Hausa)*

14909. Everyone speaks as he is.
Portuguese

14910. He cannot speak well that cannot hold his tongue.   *English*

14911. He that speaks lavishly shall hear as knavishly.   *English*

14912. He that speaks, sows, he that hears, reaps.   *English*

14913. He that speaks well fights well.
English

14914. He that speaks without care, shall remember with sorrow. *English*

14915. He who does not speak does not argue.   *African (Ovambo)*

14916. He who speaks ill of himself is praised by no one.   *Danish*

14917. He who speaks much, errs much.   *Turkish*

14918. Many speak much who cannot speak well.   *English*

14919. Some that speak no ill of any, do no good to any.   *English*

14920. Spare to speak and spare to speed.   *English*

14921. Speak fair and think what you will.   *English*

14922. Speak fitly or be silent wisely.
English

14923. Speak little, speak truth; spend little, pay cash.   *German*

14924. Speak no ill of another until you think of yourself.   *English*

14925. Speak of a man as you find him.
English

14926. Speak well of the dead.
English

14927. Speak what you will, an ill man will turn it ill.   *English*

14928. Speak when you are spoken to.
English

14929. That is well spoken that is well taken.   *English*

14930. What is long spoken of happens at last.   *Dutch*

14931. Who speaks much, either knows or lies much.   *Hungarian*

14932. Who speaks not, errs not.
English

14933. Who speaks of the wolf sees his tail.   *English*

14934. Who speaks, sows; who listens, reaps.   *French*

SPEAKER

14935. Though the speaker be a fool, let the hearer be wise.   *Spanish*

SPEAKING

14936. Speaking comes by nature, silence by understanding.   *German*

14937. Speaking is silver, silence is gold.   *German*

SPEAR

14938. Do not go between a spear and a bull.   *African (Ovambo)*

14939. It is easy to dodge a spear in the daylight, but it is difficult to avoid an arrow in the dark.   *Chinese*

SPECK

14940. A speck will produce a storm.
American

14941. One speck of rat's dung spoils a whole pot of rice.   *Chinese*

SPECTACLE

14942. Spectacles are death's arquebus.   *English*

SPECTATOR

14943. The spectator is a great hero.
Pashto

SPEECH

14944. A fool's speech is a bubble of air.
English

14945. Honeyed speech often conceals poison and gall.   *Danish*

14946. If speech is silver, patience is gold.   *African (Fulani)*

14947. If speech is silver, silence is gold.   *Lebanese*

14948. If speech is worth a shilling, silence is worth a pound.   *Jamaican*

14949. Speak softly, and be slow to begin your speech.   *Chinese*

14950. Speech and action make the perfect conduct.   *Moroccan*

14951. Speech is difficult, but silence is impossible.   *Yiddish*

14952. Speech is good, silence even better.   *Yiddish*

14953. Speech is often repented, silence seldom.   *Danish*

14954. Speech is pulling a straw out of thatch—once out it cannot be replaced.
African (Hausa)

14955. Speech is silver, silence golden.
English

14956. Speech is the index of the mind.
English

14957. Though speech be silver, yet silence is gold.   *Turkish*

SPEED

14958. All the speed is in the spurs.
English

14959. Hasty speed doesn't often succeed.   *Dutch*

14960. Speed and accuracy do not agree.   *Irish*

14961. Speed breeds delay.
African (Hausa)

14962. Speed is only good for catching flies.   *Yiddish*

14963. The speed of the boat depends, not upon the wood of which it is made, but upon the pilot's skill and upon favorable winds.   *Philippine*

14964. Too much speed breeds delay.
African (Shona)

SPEND

14965. Better spent than spared.
English

14966. Know when to spend and when to spare, and you need not be busy; you'll never be bare.   *English*

14967. Spend and be free, but make no waste.   *English*

14968. Spend and God will send.
English

14969. Spend not where you may save; spare not where you must spend.
English

14970. Who more than he is worth does spend, he makes a rope his life to end.   *English*

14971. Who spends before he thrives will beg before he thinks.   *English*

14972. Who spends more than he should shall not have to spend when he would.   *English*

SPENDER

14973. Great spenders are bad lenders.
English

SPENDING

14974. Through not spending enough, we spend too much.   *Spanish*

451

SPICE

14975. If you beat spice, it will smell the sweeter. *English*

14976. The best spices are in small bags. *Italian*

14977. Who has spice enough may season his meat as he pleases. *English*

SPIDER

14978. Kill the spider and you will destroy the cobweb. *Maltese*

14979. The spider does not weave his web for one fly. *Slovenian*

SPINACH

14980. Little by little the spinach is cooked. *Maltese*

SPINDLE

14981. By one and one spindles are made. *English*

SPINNING

14982. Spinning out of time never made good cloth. *English*

SPINSTER

14983. An old spinster is not worth more than an unposted letter.

Hungarian

SPIRIT (ghost)

14984. Raise no more spirits than you can conjure down. *English*

14985. The spirits hover but three feet above your head. *Chinese*

14986. You may hide a thing from men; from the spirits you cannot hide it. *Chinese*

SPIRIT (mind)

14987. A broken spirit is hard to heal. *Yiddish*

14988. A poor spirit is poorer than a poor purse. *English*

14989. It needs a light spirit to bear a heavy fate. *Danish*

14990. When the spirits are good, the step is light. *Norwegian*

14991. When the spirit is light the foot also is light. *Japanese*

SPIT

14992. Spit against the wind and you spit in your own face. *Armenian*

14993. Who spits against heaven, spit falls in his face. *English*

SPITE

14994. There is no spite like that of a proud beggar. *French*

SPLINTER

14995. He that cuts above himself will get splinters in his eye. *Danish*

SPOIL

14996. It is impossible to spoil what never was good. *American*

14997. Too little and too much spoils everything. *Danish*

SPOKE

14998. The highest spoke in fortune's wheel may soon turn lowest. *English*

14999. The worst spoke in a cart breaks first. *English*

SPONGE

15000. What is said is said, and no sponge can wipe it out. *German*

SPOON

15001. A dry spoon irritates the mouth. *Russian*

15002. A spoon is most valuable at dinnertime. *Russian*

15003. He needs a long spoon that would eat out of the same dish with the devil. *Danish*

15004. He who is not satisfied with a full spoon will never be satisfied with the scrapings.   *Serbo-Croatian*

15005. The spoon is prized when the soup is being eaten.   *Czech*

SPOOR

15006. The elephant's spoor treads out the camel's.   *African (Hausa)*

SPORT

15007. In sports and journeys men are known.   *English*

15008. Some sport is sauce to pains.   *English*

15009. Sport is sweetest when no spectators.   *English*

15010. The strong man's sport is the sickly man's death.   *German*

15011. What is sport to the cat is death to the mouse.   *German*

SPOT

15012. A spot is most seen upon the finest cloth.   *English*

15013. A spot shows most on the finest cloth.   *Spanish*

15014. All spots can be removed with a little gold.   *Yiddish*

15015. By seeing one spot you know the entire leopard.   *Japanese*

15016. Even in the sun there are spots.   *Hungarian*

15017. Every spot is not the leprosy.   *English*

15018. One spot spots the whole dress.   *Flemish*

15019. The spot will come out in the washing.   *Spanish*

SPRING (season)

15020. Every spring has an autumn and every road an ending.   *Iranian*

15021. Spring is as changeable as a stepmother's face.   *Chinese*

15022. That which does blossom in the spring will bring forth fruit in the autumn.   *English*

SPRING (water)

15023. Defile not the spring from which you may drink.   *Russian*

15024. Muddy springs will have muddy streams.   *English*

15025. Not every spring becomes a stream.   *German*

SPROUT

15026. Don't sprout up where you have not been planted.   *Greek*

SPUR (noun)

15027. A spur in the head is worth two in the heel.   *English*

15028. One's own spurs and another's horse make the miles short.   *Italian*

15029. The spur won't hurt where the hide is thick.   *American*

SPUR (verb)

15030. Spur not a willing horse.   *French*

SPY

15031. Spies are the ears and eyes of princes.   *English*

SQUINTING

15032. Better squinting than blind.   *Dutch*

STAB

15033. Better ten stabs than ten bad words.   *Greek*

STABILITY

15034. One knows not the stability of his life.   *African (Efik)*

STAFF

15035. If the staff be crooked, the shadow cannot be straight.   *English*

15036. Trust not to a broken staff.   *English*

STAIN

15037. Stains are not seen at night.   *Hebrew*

15038. The stain upon a person's character without fault will vanish.   *Hawaiian*

STAIR

15039. The stairs are mounted step by step.   *Turkish*

15040. The stairs are swept downwards, not upwards.   *Rumanian*

15041. Too many stairs and back doors make thieves and whores.   *English*

STAKE

15042. A loose stake may stand long.   *English*

15043. The low stake stands long.   *English*

STAND

15044. He stands not surely that never slips.   *English*

STANDING

15045. The higher standing, the lower fall.   *English*

STAR

15046. Even a small star shines in the darkness.   *Finnish*

15047. He who reaches for the stars must be willing to pay the cost.   *Mexican*

15048. In the absence of moonlight the star shines.   *African (Hausa)*

15049. Stars are not seen by sunshine.   *English*

15050. The stars are indeed the spies of heaven.   *Hawaiian*

15051. The stars make no noise.   *Irish*

STARLING

15052. Starlings are lean because they go in flocks.   *Italian*

START (noun)

15053. A bad start means a good end.   *Latvian*

15054. A good start wins the race.   *American*

START (verb)

15055. He who starts well ends badly.   *African (Zulu)*

STATE

15056. Talk not too much of state affairs.   *English*

STATEMENT

15057. A statement once let loose cannot be caught by four horses.   *Japanese*

STAY (noun)

15058. One day's stay does not empty a granary.   *African (Shona)*

STAY (verb)

15059. He that can stay obtains.   *English*

15060. He that stays does the business.   *English*

15061. He who stays last takes the most.   *Philippine*

STEAL

15062. He that steals can hide.   *English*

15063. He that will steal an egg will steal an ox. *English*

15064. It is not enough to know how to steal; one must know also to conceal. *Italian*

STEALING

15065. It's not for stealing that you are punished, but for getting caught. *Russian*

15066. Stealing and giving away for charity is still stealing. *Yiddish*

STEED

15067. It is too late to lock the stable door when the steed is stolen. *Dutch*

STEERING

15068. It's good steering with wind and tide. *Dutch*

STEP

15069. A step over the threshold is half the journey. *Welsh*

15070. Between the word and the deed there's a long step. *French*

15071. Every step leads to death. *Philippine*

15072. If you take one step in the wrong direction, a hundred steps in the right direction will not atone for it. *Chinese*

15073. If you tell every step, you will make a long journey of it. *English*

15074. Step by step one goes far. *Dutch*

15075. Step by step one goes to Rome. *Italian*

15076. The best step, the first step. *Welsh*

15077. The first man's steps become a bridge for the second one. *Greek*

15078. The first step binds one to the second. *French*

15079. The first step is all the difficulty. *French*

15080. The first step is the only difficulty. *English*

15081. The greatest step is that out of doors. *English*

15082. The hardest step is that over the threshold. *Italian*

15083. The steps at court are slippery. *Danish*

15084. There is but a slight step from the privateersman to the pirate. *American*

15085. Whoever falls and gets up gains a step. *Hebrew*

STEW

15086. The stew mixed by many is ill-seasoned and worse cooked. *Spanish*

15087. The stew that boils much loses flavor. *Spanish*

15088. With two cooks the stew will be salty or tasteless. *Iranian*

STICK

15089. A crooked stick will have a crooked shadow. *English*

15090. A single stick upon the hearth does not burn. *Indian (Kashmiri)*

15091. A stick can break a bone, but not a vice. *African (Swahili)*

15092. A stick has two ends. *Iranian*

15093. A stick is a peacemaker. *French*

15094. A stick is quickly found to beat a dog with. *English*

15095. A stick that goes into fire will begin to burn. *African (Ga)*

15096. A straight stick is crooked in the water. *English*

15097. It is easy to find a stick to beat a dog. *Dutch*

15098. It's not the stick that helps but the kind word.   *Yiddish*

15099. It is the raised stick that makes the dog obey.   *Danish*

15100. Little sticks kindle the fire, great ones put it out.   *English*

15101. One does not feel twenty-five strokes of a stick on a stranger's back.
                Serbo-Croatian

15102. The same stick that beats the black dog may beat the white one.
                Haitian

15103. The stick in the hand is the one that kills the snake. *African (Swahili)*

STILE

15104. He that will not go over the stile must be thrust through the gate.
                English

STING

15105. Watch for the sting after your fling.   *English*

STIR

15106. The more you stir, the worse it will stink.   *English*

STITCH

15107. A stitch in time saves nine.
                English

15108. A stitch in time saves two stitches.   *Irish*

15109. Better a stitch now than ten stitches later.   *Japanese*

STOCKING

15110. It's hard to get a stocking off a bare leg.   *English*

STOMACH

15111. A full stomach gladdens the heart.   *Mexican*

15112. A sharp stomach makes short devotion.   *English*

15113. An empty stomach cannot tolerate anything.   *Yiddish*

15114. Better a light stomach than a heavy conscience.   *Greek*

15115. Full stomach, full happiness.
                Lebanese

15116. Good stomachs make good savor.   *American*

15117. He whose stomach is full increases deeds of evil.   *Hebrew*

15118. If the stomach be not strong, do not eat cockroaches.
                African (Yoruba)

15119. If you go to sleep with an empty stomach, you will count the beams on the ceiling.   *Yiddish*

15120. If your stomach is not strong, do not swallow cactus seed. *Jamaican*

15121. It is the stomach which rules the man.   *African (Efik)*

15122. One with a full stomach will not learn anything.   *Armenian*

15123. Rather let it hurt your stomach than give it away to enemies.
                Lebanese

15124. Small stomachs, light heels.
                English

15125. The full stomach does not understand the empty one.   *Irish*

15126. The stomach has no windows.
                Albanian

15127. The stomach is the power of the legs.   *African (Ovambo)*

15128. The stomach is the workshop of the body.   *Swedish*

15129. The stomach is to be toiled for.
                African (Shona)

15130. The stomach keeps a secret better than the heart.   *Yiddish*

15131. The stomach knows no day of rest.   *African (Swahili)*

15132. The stomach never becomes full with licking.   *Estonian*

15133. Though your stomach is full, carry provisions.   *Chinese*

15134. When the stomach is concerned, wisdom withdraws. *Egyptian*

15135. When the stomach is empty, so is the brain.   *Yiddish*

15136. When the stomach is full the heart is glad.   *Dutch*

15137. You know not what man's stomach can contain.   *African (Wolof)*

STONE

15138. A large stone will never be thrown.   *Iranian*

15139. A little stone may overturn a great wagon.   *English*

15140. A little stone may upset a large cart.   *Danish*

15141. A rolling stone gathers no moss.   *English*

15142. A rolling stone, it stops not till the bottom is reached.   *Malagasy*

15143. A rugged stone grows smooth from hand to hand.   *English*

15144. A single stone is enough for a house of glass.   *Iranian*

15145. A stationary stone gathers moss.   *Russian*

15146. A stone from the hand of a friend is an apple.   *Moroccan*

15147. A stone in a well is not lost.   *English*

15148. A stone thrown at the right time is better than gold given at the wrong time.   *Iranian*

15149. A stone you would not have expected hurts your head.   *Turkish*

15150. A tumbling stone never gathers moss.   *Scottish*

15151. Boil stones in butter, and you may sip the broth.   *English*

15152. By the continual creeping of ants a stone will wear away.
Indian (Tamil)

15153. Constant dropping will wear away a stone.   *English*

15154. Don't throw stones in the well you drink from.   *Libyan*

15155. Even the stone upon which you stumble is a part of fate.   *Japanese*

15156. He who cannot carry the stone must roll it.   *Swedish*

15157. He who throws stones on another gets them back on his own bones.
Yiddish

15158. He who will throw a stone at every dog which barks has need of a great satchel or pocket.   *English*

15159. If many spit on a stone it becomes wet at last.   *Icelandic*

15160. If one throws stones into mud, his own cloth and those of others will be spattered.   *Indian (Tamil)*

15161. It is difficult to throw a stone at a lizard which is clinging to a pot.
African (Ashanti)

15162. It is easier to roll stones up a mountain than to talk to a fool.
Serbo-Croatian

15163. Many stones will bring down the walnut.   *Greek*

15164. Never take a stone to break an egg when you can do it with the back of your knife.   *Scottish*

15165. No one throws stones at a tree without fruit.   *Rumanian*

15166. Not all stones are building stones.   *Lebanese*

15167. Seldom mosses the stone.
English

15168. Stone will not become water.
African (Hausa)

15169. Stones are cheap; the problem is weight.   *African (Annang)*

15170. Stones or bread, one must have something in hand for the dogs.
Italian

15171. Stones rain upon a broken door.
Iranian

15172. The hardest stone is eroded by constant dropping of water. *Philippine*

15173. The often-moved stone gathers no moss. *Danish*

15174. The stone is hard and the drop is small, but a hole is made by the constant fall. *Spanish*

15175. The stone that everybody spits upon will be wet at last. *Danish*

15176. The stone that lies not in your gate breaks not your toes. *Scottish*

15177. The stone that lies not in your way need not offend you. *English*

15178. Though stone were changed to gold, the heart of man would not be satisfied. *Chinese*

15179. Throw no stones at a sleeping dog. *Danish*

15180. Two hard stones do not make good flour. *Finnish*

15181. When a big stone rolls it carries many with it. *Norwegian*

15182. When everyone spits on a stone it is always wet. *Norwegian*

15183. Who remove stones bruise their fingers. *English*

15184. Who throws a stone above himself may have it fall on his own head.
German

15185. You must not throw stones into your neighbor's garden. *French*

STOOL

15186. It isn't easy to sit on a borrowed stool. *Norwegian*

STOP

15187. If you know where to stop and stop there, you will never be disgraced.
Chinese

STORE (noun)

15188. A store of food is the best equipment for war: when war is proclaimed, every man takes up his wallet.
African (Yoruba)

15189. Store is no sore. *English*

STORE (verb)

15190. He who stores will take; he who does not store will not take.
African (Fulani)

STORM

15191. A storm destroys the field, bad manners destroy the country.
African (Ovambo)

15192. After a storm comes a calm.
English

15193. Let the guest go before the storm bursts. *German*

15194. The sharper the storm, the sooner it's over. *English*

15195. The storm blows over but the driftwood remains. *Yiddish*

15196. There is no storm that will not subside. *Philippine*

15197. Where there was a storm, there is calm. *African (Swahili)*

STORY

15198. A false story has seven endings.
African (Swahili)

15199. A good story badly told soon loses its effect. *Indian (Tamil)*

15200. An old story does not open the ear as a new one does.
African (Yoruba)

15201. If you don't hear the story clearly, don't carry it off with you under your arm. *Thai*

15202. The story is only half told when one side tells it. *Icelandic*

15203. The story of former wealth does not satisfy man. *African (Annang)*

STOUP

15204. The stoup that goes often to the well, comes home broken at last. *Scottish*

STRAIN

15205. He who strains himself grows old quickly. *Greek*

STRANGER

15206. A stranger does not know the back door. *Jamaican*

15207. A stranger is blind even though he have eyes. *African (Hausa)*

15208. A stranger is like a child. *African (Ashanti)*

15209. A stranger is like running water. *African (Hausa)*

15210. A stranger is not gossiped about. *African (Shona)*

15211. A stranger though he has a bed will return home. *African (Fulani)*

15212. Strangers forgive, friends forget. *Slovenian*

15213. The stranger eats with care. *African (Jabo)*

15214. The stranger who does not know where the spring is will draw water in a dirty pool. *African (Bemba)*

15215. The stranger who is not generous is not generous in his own land. *African (Bemba)*

15216. You may boast to strangers, but tell the truth to your own people. *Serbo-Croatian*

STRATAGEM

15217. All stratagems are fair in war. *American*

STRAW

15218. Even old straw may be of use sometime or other. *Indian (Tamil)*

15219. In a long journey, straw weighs. *English*

15220. On a long journey even a straw is heavy. *Italian*

15221. Straws show which way the wind blows. *English*

15222. The last straw breaks the camel's back. *English*

STREAM

15223. A little stream may quench thirst as well as a great river. *English*

15224. A little stream will drive a light mill. *English*

15225. A stream coming down won't let you swim up. *African (Efik)*

15226. A stream is pure at its rising, but, like gossip, it becomes muddy. *Indian (Hindi)*

15227. Cross the stream where it is ebbest. *English*

15228. However full the stream it won't refuse to rise higher. *African (Hausa)*

15229. It is hard to swim against the stream. *Dutch*

15230. Never strive against the stream. *Scottish*

15231. The stream can never rise above the springhead. *English*

15232. The stream may dry up, but the water course retains its name. *African (Yoruba)*

STREET

15233. When the streets are muddy, the cobblers rejoice. *Yiddish*

STRENGTH

15234. A woman's strength is in her tongue. *English*

15235. Strength avails not a coward. *Italian*

15236. Strength breaks the plough. *Moroccan*

15237. Strength is defeated by strategy. *Philippine*

15238. Strength is for man, sweetness for woman. *Vietnamese*

15239. The strength of a boat is in the helm; the strength of a woman is in her husband. *Vietnamese*

15240. The strength of a fish is in the water. *African (Shona)*

15241. The strength of one person only does not go far. *African (Bemba)*

15242. The strength of the bee is its patience. *Welsh*

15243. The strength of women is but a plentitude of talk. *African (Hausa)*

15244. When your strength is not sufficient, humble yourself. *Burmese*

STRETCH

15245. No one is so tall that he has not sometimes stretched himself. *Swedish*

STRETCHING

15246. Stretching and yawning leads to bed. *English*

STRING

15247. A little string will tie up a little bird. *English*

15248. If the string is long, the kite flies high. *Chinese*

15249. It is good to have two strings to one's bow. *Scottish*

15250. One string is good enough to a good musician. *Mexican*

STRIPPING

15251. There is no stripping a naked man. *German*

STROKE

15252. Different strokes for different folks. *American*

15253. Great strokes make not sweet music. *English*

15254. If strokes are good to give, they are good to receive. *English*

15255. Little strokes fell great oaks. *English*

15256. Many strokes will fell the oak. *German*

15257. Repeated strokes by a little axe can fell a big tree. *Philippine*

STRUGGLE

15258. The harder the struggle, the more glorious the triumph. *Philippine*

STUBBORNNESS

15259. Stubbornness gets a black eye. *Greek*

STUDENT

15260. If the student is successful, the teacher gets the praise. *Yiddish*

15261. The most disorderly students make the most pious preachers. *German*

STUDIES

15262. No studies are necessary to become a fool. *Mexican*

STUDY

15263. If you neglect study when you are young, what of your old age? *Chinese*

15264. Study well, play well. *Japanese*

STUMBLE (noun)

15265. A stumble may prevent a fall.
English

STUMBLE (verb)

15266. Better to stumble once than be always tottering. *French*

15267. He that stumbles and falls not mends his pace. *English*

15268. He who stumbles twice over the same stone deserves to break his shins.
English

STUMP

15269. A low stump upsets the sledge.
Finnish

15270. A small stump upsets a big cart.
Latvian

15271. A stump is left where the tree was felled. *African (Ovambo)*

STUPID

15272. Better a little stupid than too wise. *Finnish*

15273. The more stupid, the happier.
Chinese

STUPIDITY

15274. Stupidity does not tolerate wisdom. *African (Ovambo)*

15275. Stupidity is in the mouth.
African (Ovambo)

SUBJECT

15276. A loyal subject does not serve two lords. *Japanese*

15277. Subjects and wives, when they revolt from their lawful sovereigns, seldom choose for a better. *English*

SUBTLETY

15278. Subtlety is better than force.
English

SUCCEED

15279. He who succeeds is reputed wise. *Italian*

SUCCESS

15280. Half success, half failure.
Russian

15281. He who labors incessantly attains success easily. *Philippine*

15282. Nothing succeeds like success.
English

15283. Success intoxicates without wine. *Yiddish*

15284. Success is its own reward.
American

15285. Success is never blamed.
English

15286. Success makes a fool seem wise.
English

15287. There is no success if there is no sacrifice. *Philippine*

SUCCESSOR

15288. The successor of the leopard succeeds also the spots.
African (Bemba)

SUFFER

15289. Better suffer ill than do ill.
English

15290. He that suffers patiently overcomes. *Scottish*

15291. He who at first suffers afterwards finds ease. *Turkish*

15292. Many a one suffers for what he can't help. *French*

15293. Unless one suffers one does not learn. *Greek*

15294. We must suffer much, or die young. *Danish*

15295. Who suffers lives long.
Estonian

SUFFERANCE

15296. Of sufferance comes ease.

English

SUFFERER

15297. Only the sufferer knows how his belly aches. *Burmese*

15298. Sufferer overcomes. *English*

SUFFERING

15299. Only if one accepts suffering will one enjoy benefit. *Burmese*

15300. Suffering is bitter, but its fruits are sweet. *Estonian*

SUIT

15301. That suit is best that best suits me. *English*

SUITOR

15302. It's the last suitor that wins the maid. *Irish*

15303. The last suitor wins the maid. *English*

SULTAN

15304. A tyrannical sultan is better than constant anarchy. *Egyptian*

15305. The sultan teaches and is not to be taught. *Egyptian*

SUM

15306. A small sum will serve to pay a short reckoning. *English*

SUMMER

15307. It rains in summer as well as in winter. *English*

15308. Play in summer, starve in winter. *English*

SUN

15309. He is very blind who cannot see the sun. *Italian*

15310. He who avoids the sun will always be cold. *Russian*

15311. If the sun shone at night many thieves would be discovered. *Libyan*

15312. In every country the sun rises in the morning. *English*

15313. Make use of the sun while it shines. *Danish*

15314. No sun shines without some cloud. *English*

15315. One does not look at the moon when the sun is up. *Norwegian*

15316. The sun at home warms better than the sun abroad. *Albanian*

15317. The sun can be seen by nothing but its own light. *English*

15318. The sun cannot be hidden by a hand. *Lebanese*

15319. The sun discovers the filth under the white snow. *English*

15320. The sun does not rise for one man alone. *African (Ovambo)*

15321. The sun goes down on the hungry, and also on those who eat their rice and milk. *Indian (Tamil)*

15322. The sun is never the worse for shining on a dunghill. *English*

15323. The sun is the king of torches. *African (Wolof)*

15324. The sun is the poor man's blanket. *Mexican*

15325. The sun loves to peer into a home where love is. *Slovakian*

15326. The sun passes over filth and is not defiled. *Italian*

15327. The sun rises whether the cock crows or not. *Rumanian*

15328. The sun shines brighter after a shower. *Yiddish*

15329. The sun shines even into a little room. *Swedish*

15330. The sun shines for all the world. *French*

15331. The sun shines nowhere as it shines at home. *Slovenian*

15332. The sun shines on both sides of the hedge. *English*

15333. The sun will bring to light what lay under the snow. *German*

15334. The winter sun is like a stepmother—it shines, but does not warm. *Russian*

15335. There's nothing new under the sun. *German*

15336. They that walk in the sun will be tanned at last. *English*

15337. Though the sun shine leave not your cloak at home. *English*

15338. When the sun is highest it casts the least shadow. *English*

15339. When the sun shines, it shines on everyone. *Philippine*

15340. While the sun is still up let men work that the earth may live.
Hawaiian

15341. You cannot cover the sun with the palm of your hand.
Serbo-Croatian

SUN DIAL

15342. The sun dial counts only the bright hours. *German*

SUNLIGHT

15343. You can't cut off the sunlight with one hand. *Chinese*

SUNSHINE

15344. No sunshine but has some shadow. *English*

15345. Not all sunshine warms.
Russian

15346. Where sunshine there shade.
Indian (Kashmiri)

SUP

15347. Who sups well sleeps well.
English

SUPERIOR

15348. Do not marry your superior.
Greek

15349. Everyone finds his superior once in a lifetime. *Norwegian*

15350. Superiors have others above them. *Japanese*

15351. The superior prevails, the inferior breaks. *Japanese*

SUPPER

15352. If you eat it up at supper, you cannot have it at breakfast. *Spanish*

15353. Light suppers make clean sheets. *English*

15354. Supper is soon served up in a plentiful house. *Portuguese*

15355. The good supper is known by its odor. *Moroccan*

SURE

15356. Sure and unsure are not all one.
English

SURETY

15357. He that is surety for another must pay. *English*

15358. He who is surety is never sure.
English

SURF RIDER

15359. A good surf rider will not get wet. *Hawaiian*

15360. The inexpert surf rider breaks his board. *Hawaiian*

SURGEON

15361. A pitiful surgeon spoils a sore.
English

15362. A surgeon must have an eagle's eye, a lion's heart, and a lady's hand.
English

SUSPENSE

15363. Suspense is worse than the ordeal itself. *Yiddish*

SUSPICION

15364. A slight suspicion may destroy a good repute. *Danish*

15365. An evil suspicion has a worse condition. *English*

15366. Suspicion always haunts the guilty mind. *Philippine*

15367. Suspicion generates dark devils.
Japanese

15368. Suspicion has double eyes.
English

15369. Suspicion is the poison of friendship. *French*

SWALLOW (noun)

15370. A swallow, though small, can fly to the south across the sea. *Korean*

15371. One swallow doesn't make a spring. *Russian*

15372. One swallow does not make a summer. *English*

15373. The swallow carries spring on its wings. *Czech*

15374. The swallow starts the spring and the nightingale finishes it.
Russian

SWALLOW (verb)

15375. Do not swallow before you chew. *African (Shona)*

SWAN

15376. The swan sings before death.
English

15377. When you are among the swans you become a swan. *Thai*

SWEAR

15378. He that will swear will lie.
English

SWEARING

15379. Swearing never catches fish.
English

SWEAT

15380. Sweat makes good mortar.
German

SWEEPING

15381. Continual sweepings make a high rubbish heap. *African (Yoruba)*

SWEET

15382. All sorts of sweets are not wholesome. *English*

15383. He deserves not sweet that will not taste of sour. *English*

15384. He is worthy of sweets, who has tasted bitters. *Danish*

15385. He who eats the sweets of life should be able to bear the bitters of it.
Lebanese

15386. No sweet without sweat.
English

SWEETHEART

15387. Nobody's sweetheart is ugly.
Dutch

15388. With a sweetheart you can have paradise in a hut. *Russian*

SWEETNESS

15389. If sweetness comes first, then bitterness follows. *Philippine*

15390. You will never taste sweetness if you do not like bitterness. *Estonian*

SWIM

15391. He must needs swim that is held up by the chin. *English*

15392. In the world who knows not to swim goes to the bottom.   *English*

15393. Swim on and don't trust.
French

SWIMMER

15394. A good swimmer is not safe against drowning.   *French*

15395. Even the best swimmer can drown.   *Yiddish*

15396. Good swimmers are drowned at last.   *French*

15397. There is no good swimmer against a swift current.   *Philippine*

SWINE

15398. A swine overfat is cause of his own bane.   *English*

15399. If a swine had horns, he would wipe everyone off the earth.   *Russian*

15400. If there were fewer swine, there would be fewer bastards.   *Yiddish*

15401. Old swine have hard snouts, old oxen hard horns.   *Danish*

15402. One swine recognizes another.
Polish

15403. Sit a swine at the table and he slaps his feet on it.   *Russian*

15404. Swine, women, and bees cannot be turned.   *English*

15405. The still swine eat the mash, the wild ones run past it.   *Danish*

SWORD

15406. A keen sword is no better than a dull one if it remains sheathed.
Philippine

15407. A sword does not bend and gold does not rust.   *Russian*

15408. Against reason no sword will prevail.   *Japanese*

15409. As the sword is, so is the scabbard.   *African (Oji)*

15410. Even the sword won't hack off the head of one who confessed his crimes.   *Russian*

15411. He that strikes with the sword shall be stricken with the scabbard.
English

15412. He who has nothing else to hold on to grasps even at a drawn sword.
Greek

15413. He who is hungry embraces the sword.   *Turkish*

15414. He who plays with a sword plays with the devil.   *Spanish*

15415. It is ill putting a naked sword in a madman's hand.   *English*

15416. Many shun the sword, and come to the gallows.   *German*

15417. One sword keeps another in the sheath.   *English*

15418. The keen sword cuts not its scabbard.   *Turkish*

15419. The rusty sword and empty purse plead performance of covenants.
English

15420. There is no sword that can oppose kindness.   *Japanese*

15421. Two swords do not enter one scabbard.   *Turkish*

15422. What the sword cuts will heal; what the tongue cuts will not.
Armenian

SWORDSMAN

15423. A good swordsman is never quarrelsome.   *French*

SYMPATHY

15424. Sympathy without relief is like mustard without beef.   *English*

T

TABLE

15425. A poor man's table is soon spread. *English*

15426. He who lies under the table gets kicked. *Polish*

15427. The table robs more than a thief. *English*

TACE

15428. Tace is Latin for a candle. *English*

TADPOLE

15429. A tadpole becomes a frog. *African (Ovambo)*

15430. Tadpoles will become frogs. *Japanese*

TAEL

15431. A thousand taels won't purchase a laugh. *Chinese*

15432. Even he who has accumulated ten thousand taels of silver cannot take with him at death half a copper cash. *Chinese*

TAIL

15433. A dog's tail can never be straightened. *Indian (Bihar)*

15434. A short tail won't keep off flies. *Italian*

15435. An ass's tail will not make a sieve. *Italian*

15436. Better be the tail of a horse than the head of an ass. *English*

15437. Cut off a dog's tail and he will be a dog still. *English*

15438. Do not measure the wolf's tail till he be dead. *Serbo-Croatian*

15439. He who has a straw tail is always in fear of its catching fire. *Italian*

15440. He who recovers but the tail of his cow does not lose all. *French*

15441. If the tail is too long, it will be trampled on. *Korean*

15442. Leave a little of the tail to whisk off the flies. *Chinese*

15443. Make not your tail broader than your wings. *English*

15444. Take care you don't let your tail be caught in the door. *Italian*

15445. The pig's tail will never make a good arrow. *Spanish*

15446. The tail is always the hardest part to flay. *Italian*

15447. The tail of the sheep is proportioned to its size. *Indian (Tamil)*

15448. To a tired mare even her tail seems heavy. *Slovakian*

467

TAILOR

15449. A hundred tailors, a hundred millers, and a hundred weavers are three hundred thieves.   *Spanish*

15450. A lazy tailor finds his thread too long.   *Greek*

15451. A tailor does not choose the cloth.   *African (Swahili)*

15452. A tailor's shreds are worth the cutting.   *English*

15453. Nine tailors make a man.
English

15454. Tailors and writers must mind the fashion.   *English*

15455. The tailor cuts three sleeves for every woman's gown.   *English*

15456. The tailor makes the man.
English

15457. The tailor that makes not a knot, loses a stitch.   *English*

TAKE

15458. He who likes to take does not like to give.   *Yiddish*

15459. If you would take, first give.
Japanese

15460. Take all, pay all.   *English*

15461. Take, have, and keep are pleasant words.   *English*

15462. Take what you get, and pay what you can.   *Irish*

TAKER

15463. A taker is not a giver. *Yiddish*

TALE

15464. A good tale ill told is marred in the telling.   *English*

15465. A good tale is none the worse for being twice told.   *English*

15466. A tale never loses in the telling.
English

15467. A tale twice told is cabbage twice sold.   *English*

15468. Every man's tale is good till another's be told.   *Scottish*

15469. It ought to be a good tale that is twice told.   *English*

15470. Many a good tale is spoiled in the telling.   *Scottish*

15471. One tale is good till another is told.   *English*

15472. Tell no tales out of school.
German

15473. The tale is soon told, but the job is not soon done.   *Russian*

15474. The tale runs as it pleases the teller.   *English*

TALENT

15475. All talents are not alike.
African (Swahili)

15476. Great talent takes time to ripen.
Greek

TALK (noun)

15477. Daring talk is not strength.
African (Jabo)

15478. He whom talk killed had forgotten how to keep silent.
African (Fulani)

15479. Least talk, most work. *English*

15480. Long talk makes short days.
French

15481. Mere talk does not satisfy the stomach.   *Turkish*

15482. Much talk brings on trouble; much food brings on indigestion.
Chinese

15483. Much talk, little work.   *Dutch*

15484. Much talk makes no money.
Turkish

15485. Noisy talk does not bring about a solution.   *African (Ovambo)*

15486. Old people's talk is not scorned; they saw the sun first.
African (Ovambo)

15487. Sweet talk doesn't make you warm, but sweet meaning does.
Yiddish

15488. Sweet talk makes the girls melt.
Yiddish

15489. Talk doesn't hurt. *American*

15490. Talk gets a talkative man into trouble. *African (Fulani)*

15491. Talk is but talk. *English*

15492. Talk is cheap but it takes money to buy whiskey. *American*

15493. Talk is cheap, it doesn't cost anything but breath. *American*

15494. Talk is worth a shilling; silence is worth two. *Yiddish*

15495. Talk without authority is useless talk. *African (Hausa)*

15496. The talk of many can shake the strongest mind. *Greek*

15497. The talk of the child in the street is that of his father or his mother.
Hebrew

15498. The talk of the many can cripple a man. *Greek*

15499. There is more talk than trouble.
English

15500. Too much talk is poverty.
Greek

15501. Too much talk will include errors. *Burmese*

15502. Useless talk is not worth a match. *Moroccan*

15503. Where talk is abundant, there a lie slips in. *African (Hausa)*

TALK (verb)

15504. Always talk big and you will never be forgotten. *French*

15505. Better keep silent than talk too much. *Greek*

15506. Everyone talks of what he loves.
English

15507. He that talks to himself talks to a fool. *English*

15508. He who is ignorant talks the most. *Philippine*

15509. He who talks much errs much.
Vietnamese

15510. He who talks, sows; he who listens, reaps. *Latvian*

15511. If you talk a lot, you talk of yourself. *Yiddish*

15512. One must talk little, and listen much. *African (Wolof)*

15513. One talks of what hurts one.
Russian

15514. The less you talk, the better off you are. *Yiddish*

15515. Who talks much, errs much.
Spanish

15516. Who talks, sells; who listens, buys. *Rumanian*

TALKER

15517. A good talker does not equal a good listener. *Chinese*

15518. A great talker is a great liar.
French

15519. Great talkers are commonly liars. *German*

15520. Great talkers are great liars.
English

15521. Great talkers are like leaky pitchers, everything runs out of them.
English

15522. Great talkers are little doers.
Dutch

15523. Great talkers are not great doers. *French*

15524. The greatest talkers are always the least doers. *English*

15525. The talker sows, the listener reaps. *Italian*

TALKING

15526. If you keep on talking, you will end up saying what you didn't intend to say. *Yiddish*

15527. Much talking is unbecoming in an elder. *African (Yoruba)*

15528. Much talking, much erring. *Spanish*

15529. Talking comes by nature, silence by understanding. *English*

15530. Talking is easier than doing, and promising than performing. *German*

15531. Talking isn't barking. *Yiddish*

15532. Talking is not like doing. *Lebanese*

15533. Talking is silver, silence is gold. *German*

15534. Talking pays no toll. *English*

15535. Talking will never build a stone wall or pay our taxes. *American*

15536. There is no use in talking when the harm is done. *Irish*

TALMUD

15537. To learn the whole Talmud is a great accomplishment; to learn one good virtue is even greater. *Yiddish*

TAPSTER

15538. Tapsters and ostlers are not always the honestest men. *English*

TAR

15539. If you deal with tar, expect your hands to get dirty. *Yiddish*

TART

15540. One may tire of eating tarts. *French*

TASK

15541. Difficult tasks call for strong men. *African (Shona)*

15542. Once your task is finished, you have to enjoy yourself. *Russian*

15543. To be willing is only half the task. *Armenian*

TASTE (noun)

15544. A lordly taste makes a beggar's purse. *German*

15545. All tastes are tastes. *Italian*

15546. Everyone to his taste. *English*

15547. Tastes aren't argued about. *Russian*

15548. The tastes of ten people differ as ten colors. *Japanese*

15549. The taste of the kitchen is better than the smell. *English*

15550. There is no disputing about taste. *Spanish*

15551. To him that has a bad taste, sweet is bitter. *English*

15552. Who has eaten of the pot knows the taste of the broth. *Hebrew*

TASTE (verb)

15553. He who has not tasted the bitter does not understand the sweet. *Yiddish*

15554. What tastes sweet initially may taste bitter finally. *African (Annang)*

TAVERN

15555. A tavern is a tavern. *American*

15556. He who enters the tavern, enters not to say his prayers. *Rumanian*

15557. The tavern keeper likes the drunkard but he does not want him for a son-in-law. *Greek*

TAX

15558. Taxes are taxes. *American*

15559. There's no tax on talk. *Irish*

15560. Those who are prospering do not argue about taxes.   *Chinese*

TEA

15561. Even a cup of tea will stay hunger for a time.   *Japanese*

TEACH

15562. Better untaught than ill taught.
          English

15563. He teaches ill who teaches all.
          English

TEACHER

15564. A teacher will not criticize a teacher, nor will a doctor criticize a doctor.   *Chinese*

15565. Better than a thousand days of diligent study is one day with a great teacher.   *Japanese*

15566. Hateful is a teacher without patience.   *Welsh*

15567. He who is his own teacher has a fool for his pupil.   *German*

15568. Respect your teachers more than your parents.   *Russian*

15569. Teachers without moral rules are vain.   *Indian (Tamil)*

15570. To become a teacher one must first respect one's teacher.   *Vietnamese*

15571. Your teacher can lead you to the door; the acquiring of learning rests with each person.   *Chinese*

TEACHING

15572. Teaching of others teaches the teacher.   *English*

TEAPOT

15573. The full teapot makes no sound; the half-empty teapot is very noisy.
          Chinese

TEAR (cry)

15574. A child's tears reach the heavens.   *Yiddish*

15575. A tear in place is better than a smile out of place.   *Iranian*

15576. A woman's tears and a dog's limping are not real.   *Spanish*

15577. Are there tears—there is conscience.   *Russian*

15578. Nothing dries sooner than a tear.   *English*

15579. Tears come more often from the eyes than from the heart.   *Russian*

15580. The heir's tears are but a mask to disguise his joy.   *Mexican*

15581. The rich widow's tears soon dry.   *Danish*

15582. The tears of the adultress are ever ready.   *Egyptian*

15583. The tears of the poor are as sharp swords.   *Indian (Tamil)*

15584. The tears of the poor are the happiness of the rich.   *Philippine*

TEAR (rip)

15585. A little tear if not patched will give rise to a big one.   *Philippine*

TEASING

15586. Teasing eventually turns to a quarrel.   *Burmese*

TEETH (see TOOTH)

15587. All do not bite that show their teeth.   *Dutch*

15588. Don't show your teeth if you can't bite.   *French*

15589. Do not show your teeth until you can bite.   *Irish*

15590. He that has no teeth cannot crack nuts.   *American*

15591. He who has teeth has no bread, and he who has bread has no teeth.
          Italian

15592. Infancy teeth are not for chewing nuts.   *African (Annang)*

15593. Long teeth and short teeth eat the same food.   *African (Oji)*

15594. One must chew according to one's teeth.   *Norwegian*

15595. Show not your teeth when you are unable to bite.   *Mexican*

15596. Teeth are useful to check the tongue.   *Welsh*

15597. The teeth of a gift horse are not inspected.   *Turkish*

15598. The teeth of the puppy are growing, while the old dog is gnawing bones.   *Danish*

15599. The teeth that are going to chew for a long time should try to avoid bones.   *Burmese*

15600. Thirty-two teeth can often not bridle the tongue.   *Hungarian*

15601. Those who can't bite should not show their teeth.   *Yiddish*

15602. You don't count the teeth in someone else's mouth.   *Yiddish*

TELL

15603. One who tells you about others will tell others about you.
          African (Swahili)

15604. Tell not all you know; believe not all you hear; do not all you are able.
          German

TELLING

15605. There are two tellings to every story.   *Irish*

TEMPER

15606. A quick temper does not bring success.   *Japanese*

15607. A quick temper results in loss.
          Japanese

15608. Bad temper and anger shorten the years.   *Yiddish*

15609. He who loses his temper is in the wrong.   *French*

TEMPLE

15610. An exalted temple is known by its gate.   *Japanese*

15611. Those near the temple make fun of the gods.   *Chinese*

TEMPTATION

15612. He who avoids the temptation avoids the sin.   *Spanish*

15613. If not for pretty girls, temptation would be unheeded.   *Yiddish*

15614. Temptation arrives unannounced.   *Armenian*

15615. Temptation in a maiden is asleep; in a wife it's awake.   *Yiddish*

15616. The poor man's temptation is a loaf of bread.   *Yiddish*

TENANT

15617. Better a rich tenant than a poor landlord.   *Yiddish*

TENT

15618. A tent without a wife is like a fiddle without a string.   *Rumanian*

TERMITE

15619. Small termites collapse the roof.
          African (Ovambo)

TESTIMONY

15620. The testimony of the heart is stronger than a hundred witnesses.
          Turkish

15621. The testimony of the liar is not accepted.   *Turkish*

THANK

15622. Who does not thank for little will not thank for much.   *Estonian*

THANKS

15623. Give thanks for a little and you'll find a lot.   *African (Hausa)*

15624. He loses his thanks who promises and delays. *English*

15625. Old thanks are not for new gifts. *Italian*

15626. Old thanks pay not for a new debt. *English*

15627. Thanks cause the increase of gifts. *African (Hausa)*

15628. Thanks won't fill one's belly. *Russian*

15629. Who gives not thanks to men, gives not thanks to God. *Egyptian*

THANK YOU

15630. You can't put "thank you" in your pocket. *Yiddish*

THAW

15631. Thaw reveals what has been hidden by snow. *Danish*

THICKNESS

15632. There is not the thickness of a sixpence between good and evil. *English*

THIEF (see THIEVES)

15633. A clever thief surprises the master of the house. *Turkish*

15634. A lazy thief is better than a lazy servant. *Swedish*

15635. A thief and darkness are friends. *African (Shona)*

15636. A thief had rather steal a purse than find one. *American*

15637. A thief is a king till he's caught. *Iranian*

15638. A thief is a thief, whether he steals a diamond or a cucumber. *Indian (Bihar)*

15639. A thief is always tearful, and a swindler devout. *Russian*

15640. A thief knows a thief, as a wolf knows a wolf. *English*

15641. A thief makes a good watchman for thieves. *Japanese*

15642. A thief makes opportunity. *Dutch*

15643. A thief needs no key. *Turkish*

15644. A thief profits little where his host is a thief. *Russian*

15645. A thief seldom grows rich by thieving. *German*

15646. A thief thinks every man steals. *Danish*

15647. An old thief desires a new halter. *English*

15648. An old thief will one day be caught. *Indian (Tamil)*

15649. Call one a thief and he will steal. *English*

15650. Catch the thief before he catches you. *Rumanian*

15651. Hang the young thief, and the old one will not steal. *Danish*

15652. He is a thief indeed who robs a thief. *French*

15653. He is not a thief who has stolen, but he who has been caught. *Russian*

15654. He that trusts a thief is a fool. *English*

15655. He who holds the ladder is as bad as the thief. *German*

15656. If a thief finds nothing to steal, he thinks himself honest. *Hebrew*

15657. If a thief says he knows how to steal, let him steal a cannon. *African (Ga)*

15658. No thief steals love, but love often makes thieves. *Swedish*

15659. Once a thief always a thief. *Dutch*

15660. One thief robs another. *English*

15661. Rather with a hometown thief than a strange rabbi. *Yiddish*

15662. Save a thief from the gallows and he'll cut your throat.   *English*

15663. Set a thief to catch a thief.   *English*

15664. Take the thief before he takes you.   *Egyptian*

15665. The great thief will hang the petty thief.   *Welsh*

15666. The thief and the liar fare well the first year.   *Greek*

15667. The thief does not gossip about his accomplice.   *African (Jabo)*

15668. The thief has an easy job and bad dreams.   *Yiddish*

15669. The thief is frightened even by a mouse.   *Italian*

15670. The thief is king over others' wealth.   *Indian (Hindi)*

15671. The thief is no danger to the beggar.   *Irish*

15672. The thief is sorry he is to be hanged, but not that he is a thief.   *English*

15673. The thief is suspicious and the man who itches scratches.   *Libyan*

15674. The thief on the point of breaking into a house calls on God for help.   *Hebrew*

15675. The thief only takes something, but flames take everything.   *Polish*

15676. The thief thinks that all men are like himself.   *Spanish*

15677. The thief who understands his business does not steal from his own quarter of the town.   *Egyptian*

15678. There is no greater thief than a master tailor.   *Russian*

15679. There is no thief without a receiver.   *Spanish*

15680. When it thunders the thief becomes honest.   *English*

15681. Who steals from a thief goes unpunished.   *Hebrew*

15682. Who steals once always remains a thief.   *German*

15683. Worse than the thief himself is the keeper of the thief.   *Rumanian*

15684. You're not a thief until you're caught.   *Russian*

THIEVES (see THIEF)

15685. All are not thieves that dogs bark at.   *English*

15686. Big thieves hang little ones.   *Czech*

15687. Great thieves hang the little ones.   *French*

15688. Little thieves are hanged by the neck, great ones by the purse.   *Italian*

15689. Little thieves have iron chains, and great thieves gold ones.   *Dutch*

15690. Petty thieves are hanged; big thieves are pardoned.   *Yiddish*

15691. There are more thieves than are hanged.   *Dutch*

15692. They are not all thieves at whom the dog barks.   *Norwegian*

15693. Thieves and rogues have the best luck, if they do but scape hanging.   *English*

15694. Thieves are never rogues among themselves.   *English*

15695. Thieves increase with the making of new laws.   *Rumanian*

15696. Thieves never trust one another.   *American*

15697. Thieves nowadays are not in the forests, but in the offices.   *Rumanian*

15698. We hang little thieves and let great ones escape.   *Dutch*

15699. We hang little thieves and take off our hats to great ones.   *German*

15700. When thieves fall out, honest men come to their goods. *Dutch*

15701. When thieves fall out the peasant recovers his goods. *Danish*

15702. When thieves fall out the thefts are discovered. *French*

15703. When thieves fall out the thefts come to light. *Spanish*

15704. When two thieves quarrel the farmer gets back his cow. *Finnish*

THING

15705. A bad thing leads to good fortune. *African (Ovambo)*

15706. A bad thing never dies. *English*

15707. A borrowed thing will not fulfill your desire. *African (Fulani)*

15708. A delicate thing is not difficult to be injured. *African (Yoruba)*

15709. A good thing is known when it is lost. *Portuguese*

15710. A good thing is never too late. *Philippine*

15711. A good thing lost is valued. *Italian*

15712. A good thing sells itself. *African (Hausa)*

15713. A little thing often helps. *French*

15714. A pleasant thing never comes too soon. *Danish*

15715. A thing is sooner spared than gotten. *English*

15716. A thing learned in childhood is proven in old age. *Hebrew*

15717. A thing lost is a thing known. *French*

15718. A thing put out to dry will not stop the sun. *African (Hausa)*

15719. A thing too much seen is little prized. *French*

15720. A thing which cannot be accomplished should never be undertaken. *African (Yoruba)*

15721. All the old things seem beautiful, and the rich men wise. *Greek*

15722. All things are at a price, but conversation is gratis. *Indian (Kashmiri)*

15723. All things are difficult before they are easy. *English*

15724. All things are double—one against another. *American*

15725. All things are easy that are done willingly. *English*

15726. All things are not to be granted at all times. *English*

15727. All things are soon prepared in a well-ordered house. *English*

15728. All things fit not all men. *English*

15729. All things have a beginning. *English*

15730. All things have an end. *English*

15731. All things have an end, and a pudding has two. *English*

15732. All things have their changes. *American*

15733. All things in moderation are good. *American*

15734. All things may be suffered saving wealth. *English*

15735. All things require skill but an appetite. *English*

15736. All things thrive at thrice. *Scottish*

15737. All things which make noise at the side of the path do not come down on the path. *African (Kpelle)*

15738. All things will in the long run turn to justice. *Korean*

15739. Among good things there are no cheap ones. *Japanese*

15740. An easily heated thing is easily cooled. *Japanese*

15741. Ancient things remain in the ears. *African (Ashanti)*

15742. Better one good thing that is than two good things that were. *Irish*

15743. Borrowed things will home. *English*

15744. By labor are good things obtained. *Greek*

15745. Cheap things are of no value; valuable things are not cheap. *Chinese*

15746. Don't vouch for three things—a watch, a horse, and a wife. *Russian*

15747. Even beautiful things have disadvantages and must be used with caution. *Japanese*

15748. Every new thing has a silver tail. *English*

15749. Every thing forbidden is sweet. *Egyptian*

15750. Every thing has a beginning. *English*

15751. Every thing has an ear, and a pitcher has two. *English*

15752. Every thing has an end. *English*

15753. Every thing has his seed. *English*

15754. Every thing has its time. *English*

15755. Every thing is as it is taken. *English*

15756. Every thing is for the best. *American*

15757. Every thing is good in its season. *English*

15758. Every thing is of use to a housekeeper. *English*

15759. Every thing is the worse for the wearing. *Scottish*

15760. Every thing new is fine. *English*

15761. Every thing tells. *American*

15762. Every thing would fain live. *Scottish*

15763. Fair things are soon snatched away. *French*

15764. Four things put a man beside himself—women, tobacco, cards, and wine. *Spanish*

15765. Good things are cheap. *Japanese*

15766. Good things require time. *Dutch*

15767. Have a thing yourself, or else do without it. *Irish*

15768. He is nearest a thing who has it in his hands. *Danish*

15769. He that would have a thing done quickly and well must do it himself. *Italian*

15770. He who begins many things finishes few. *Italian*

15771. He who dispraises a thing wants to buy it. *French*

15772. He who does not wish little things does not deserve big things. *Flemish*

15773. He who finds a thing rejoices and he who owns a thing brags. *Greek*

15774. He who knows one thing does not know all things. *Indian (Tamil)*

15775. He who prizes little things is worthy of great ones. *German*

15776. He who saves in little things can be liberal in great ones. *German*

15777. He who seeks many things loses even the few.   *Greek*

15778. He who was busy with two things drowned.   *African (Bemba)*

15779. He will never have a good thing cheap that is afraid to ask the price.
English

15780. He would be wise who knew all things beforehand.   *Dutch*

15781. If things were to be done twice, all would be wise.   *English*

15782. If you are not patient in small things, you will bring great plans to naught.   *Chinese*

15783. If you look up to high things, hold on to your hat.   *Yiddish*

15784. If you see a strange thing and do not regard it as strange, its strangeness will vanish.   *Chinese*

15785. It doesn't take long to get used to good things.   *Yiddish*

15786. It is a rare thing to do good.
English

15787. It is a small thing that is taken to measure a big thing.
African (Ashanti)

15788. It is the little thing you hold that will hit the dog. *African (Bemba)*

15789. Judge not things by their names.   *American*

15790. Lay things by, they may come to use.   *English*

15791. Little things are good. *English*

15792. Little things are great to little men.   *English*

15793. Little things are pretty.
English

15794. Little things please little minds.
English

15795. Many a thing whispered into one ear is heard over the whole town.
Danish

15796. Many things are lost for want of asking.   *English*

15797. Many things grow in the garden which were never sowed.
English

15798. Many things lawful are not expedient.   *English*

15799. Most things have two handles and a wise man takes hold of the best.
English

15800. New things are fair.   *English*

15801. Of a little thing, a little displeases.   *English*

15802. Pretty things are made for money.   *English*

15803. Stolen things eaten are delicious.   *Japanese*

15804. The best things are hard to come by.   *English*

15805. The best things may be abused.
English

15806. The dainty thing would have a dainty dish.   *English*

15807. The hardest thing to do is to do nothing.   *Philippine*

15808. The simplest things are the most startling.   *American*

15809. The very thing one likes, one does well.   *Japanese*

15810. The worse things are, the better they are.   *American*

15811. There is no pointed thing that does not become blunt.   *Philippine*

15812. Things are not as quickly achieved as conceived.   *Yiddish*

15813. Things are not as they are, but as they are regarded.   *Italian*

15814. Things can't be bad all the time, nor good all the time.   *Yiddish*

15815. Things carefully kept are not gotten at by rats.   *Hawaiian*

15816. Things done cannot be undone.
English

15817. Things hardly attained are long retained. *English*

15818. Things present are judged by things past. *English*

15819. Things promised are things due. *French*

15820. Things sweet to the mouth do not necessarily nourish the belly.
Japanese

15821. Things well fitted abide.
English

15822. Three things are not to be lent: the horse, the gun, and the wife.
Rumanian

15823. Three things breed jealousy: a mighty state, a rich treasure, and a fair wife. *American*

15824. Through old things, we learn new things. *Korean*

15825. To change and to better are two different things. *German*

15826. To the jaundiced all things seem yellow. *French*

15827. Too much of one thing is good for nothing. *English*

15828. Two good things are better than one. *English*

15829. Two things a man should never be angry at: what he can help, and what he cannot help. *Scottish*

15830. Two things cannot be done at one time. *Japanese*

15831. Weak things united become strong. *English*

15832. When a thing is done, don't talk about it. *Chinese*

15833. When a thing is done, make the best of it. *German*

15834. When things are at the worst they will mend. *English*

15835. When things go right, you become rich. *Yiddish*

15836. When things go well it is easy to advise. *Dutch*

15837. Where you have lost a thing, there you look for it. *Polish*

15838. Who heeds not little things will be troubled about lesser ones.
German

15839. Who undertakes many things at once seldom does anything well.
Dutch

15840. Who wants a thing is blind to its faults. *Egyptian*

THINK

15841. Everyone thinks he knows much. *English*

15842. First think, then speak.
Turkish

15843. He that seldom thinks is at ease. *English*

15844. He that thinks amiss concludes worse. *English*

15845. He thinks not well that thinks not again. *English*

15846. He who always thinks it is too soon is sure to come too late. *German*

15847. One always thinks that others are happy. *Yiddish*

15848. One may think that dares not speak. *English*

15849. Some think they have done when they are only beginning. *French*

15850. They that think no ill are soonest beguiled. *English*

15851. Think before you speak, and look before you leap. *Irish*

15852. Think much, say little, write less. *French*

15853. Think of ease, but work on.
English

15854. Think today and speak tomorrow. *English*

15855. Think well of all men. *English*

THINKING

15856. Nobody is hanged for thinking. *Hungarian*

15857. Thinking is not knowing. *Portuguese*

15858. Thinking is very far from knowing. *English*

THIRST

15859. Thirst begets thirst. *Irish*

15860. Thirst comes from drinking. *Italian*

15861. Thousands drink themselves to death before one dies of thirst. *German*

15862. Who has no thirst has no business at the fountain. *Dutch*

THISTLE

15863. A thistle is a fat salad for an ass's mouth. *English*

15864. He that sows thistles shall reap prickles. *English*

15865. He who plants thistles does not reap grapes. *Lebanese*

15866. He who sows thistles reaps thorns. *French*

15867. He who sows thistles will not reap wheat. *Welsh*

15868. Thistle blossoms last but a moment. *Japanese*

15869. Thistle doesn't catch in smooth cloth. *Rumanian*

15870. Thistles and thorns prick sore, but evil tongues prick more. *Dutch*

THONG

15871. A thong is no shorter for having been in water. *Irish*

THORN

15872. A thorn comes into the world point foremost. *French*

15873. A thorn does not pierce a rat. *African (Annang)*

15874. A thorn pierces young skin more quickly than old. *Serbo-Croatian*

15875. He that handles thorns shall prick his fingers. *English*

15876. He who is pierced with thorns must limp off to him who has a lancet. *African (Yoruba)*

15877. He who sows thorns must walk on them barefoot. *Moroccan*

15878. He who sows thorns should not walk barefooted. *Welsh*

15879. If a thorn sticks into the flesh, a sharp thorn must be used to draw it out. *Thai*

15880. It is soon espied where the thorn pricks. *English*

15881. Kicking against thorns will cause pain. *Indian (Tamil)*

15882. The more a thorn stuck in the flesh is touched, the more it hurts. *Philippine*

15883. The point of the thorn is small, but he who has felt it does not forget it. *Italian*

15884. The thorn comes forth with the point forwards. *English*

15885. The youngest thorn is the sharpest. *Irish*

15886. Thorns make the greatest crackling. *English*

15887. While the thorn is still young it produces prickles. *Hebrew*

15888. You may sow thorns, but you won't reap jasmine. *Iranian*

THOUGHT

15889. A wise man's thoughts walk within him, but a fool's without him.
English

15890. Clean thoughts are manifested in clean deeds. *Philippine*

15891. Dark thoughts lead to dark deeds. *American*

15892. Fool's thoughts often fail.
English

15893. He who takes no thought at first will at the last repent. *Turkish*

15894. If thoughts were legal witnesses, many an honest man would be proved a rogue. *Danish*

15895. If you do not have thoughts you do not have understanding.
African (Ovambo)

15896. One sincere thought can move both Heaven and earth. *Chinese*

15897. Second thoughts are best.
English

15898. Take your thoughts to bed with you, for the morning is wiser than the evening. *Russian*

15899. The thought has good legs, and the quill a good tongue. *English*

15900. Thoughts are free. *Scottish*

15901. Thought breaks the heart.
African (Efik)

15902. Thought is free. *English*

15903. Thought is silence. *Japanese*

15904. Thoughts are toll free, but not hell free. *German*

THREAD

15905. A thread breaks where it is weakest. *English*

15906. A thread from each member of the community becomes a shirt for the naked. *Russian*

15907. A thread too fine spun will easily break. *English*

15908. Cut the thread in the middle to find an end. *Greek*

15909. Every day a thread makes a skein in the year. *Dutch*

15910. One thread from each person and the naked man will have a shirt.
Russian

15911. The thread breaks where it is thinnest. *Spanish*

15912. The thread cannot pass without a needle; the boat cannot cross without water. *Chinese*

15913. The thread follows the needle.
African (Yoruba)

15914. The thread is cut where it is thinnest. *Albanian*

15915. Thread by thread the largest robe is woven. *Hebrew*

15916. Where the thread is weakest it breaks. *French*

THREAT

15917. A threat will not kill. *Welsh*

15918. Threats are arms for the threatened. *Italian*

15919. Threats without power are like powder without ball. *English*

THREATEN

15920. He threatens many that is injurious to one. *English*

15921. He who threatens is afraid.
French

15922. There are more threatened than hurt. *Spanish*

15923. Who threatens, warns.
German

THREATENER

15924. All threateners don't fight.
Dutch

15925. The threatener sometimes gets a beating. *French*

THREE

15926. Three are too many to keep a secret, and too few to be merry. *English*

15927. Three may accord, but two never can. *American*

15928. Three may keep a secret, if two of them are dead. *English*

15929. What three know will soon be known to thirty. *German*

THREE THINGS

15930. There are three things that are not to be credited: a woman when she weeps, a merchant when he swears, nor a drunkard when he prays. *English*

15931. Three things are insatiable: priests, monks, and the sea. *English*

15932. Three things are untameable: idiots, women and the salt sea. *English*

15933. Three things cost dear: the caresses of a dog, the love of a mistress, and the invasion of a host. *English*

15934. Three things drive a man out of his house: smoke, rain, and a scolding wife. *English*

THRESHOLD

15935. The most difficult mountain to cross is the threshold. *Danish*

15936. The threshold says nothing but what it hears of the hinge. *Spanish*

THRIFT

15937. Thrift is a good revenue. *English*

15938. Thrift is better than an annuity. *French*

15939. Thrift is the philosopher's stone. *English*

THRIFTY

15940. Even if you are wealthy it still pays to be thrifty. *Philippine*

THRIVE

15941. Better late thrive, as never do well. *Scottish*

15942. He that will thrive must rise at five; he that has thriven may lie till seven. *English*

15943. Well thrives that well endures. *English*

THROAT

15944. The flatterer's throat is an open sepulchre. *Italian*

THROW

15945. Don't throw away the soiled until you have the clean. *Yiddish*

15946. He that is thrown would ever wrestle. *English*

15947. That which has been thrown away has often to be begged for again. *Danish*

THUMB

15948. No one dispenses with the thumb in tying a knot. *African (Ashanti)*

15949. One thumb cannot crush a louse. *African (Shona)*

15950. The thumb cannot point straight forwards. *African (Yoruba)*

THUNDER

15951. If thunder doesn't sound, the peasant doesn't cross himself. *Russian*

15952. The thunder has but its clap. *English*

15953. Thunder will bring to a peaceful end a quarrel between husband and wife. *Japanese*

THUNDERBOLT

15954. A thunderbolt strikes a tall house most often.   *Polish*

TICKLE

15955. He who tickles himself, laughs when he likes.   *German*

15956. If you tickle yourself you can laugh when you like.   *Russian*

TIDBIT

15957. Another man's tidbits smell sweet.   *Yiddish*

TIDE

15958. Every tide will have an ebb.
                                                               English

15959. The highest tides produce lowest ebbs.   *American*

15960. The tide keeps its course.
                                                               English

15961. The tide may turn.   *American*

15962. The tide never goes out so far but it always comes in again. *English*

15963. The tide tarries no man.
                                                               English

15964. The tide will fetch away what the ebb brings.   *English*

TIDINGS

15965. Bad tidings always come too soon.   *German*

15966. Good tidings are heard from far away.   *Yiddish*

15967. Good tidings, like bad, seldom come alone.   *American*

15968. He who brings bad tidings comes soon enough.   *German*

15969. Ill tidings come soon enough.
                                                               Dutch

15970. Tidings make either glad or sad.   *English*

TIGER

15971. A tiger dies and leaves his skin; a man dies and leaves his name.
                                                               Japanese

15972. A tiger leaves its skin when dead, but men live by their fame instead.   *Malaysian*

15973. Don't caress the tiger's whiskers when he is sleeping. *Vietnamese*

15974. He painted a tiger, but it turned out a cur.   *Chinese*

15975. He who rides the tiger finds it difficult to dismount. *Chinese*

15976. If you do not enter the tiger's den, how can you get his cub?
                                                               Chinese

15977. In the valley where there is no tiger, the hare is the master.   *Korean*

15978. The tiger crouches before he leaps upon his prey.   *American*

15979. The tiger does not eat his own cubs.   *Vietnamese*

15980. The tiger does not eat its young.
                                                               Philippine

15981. There are times when even the tiger sleeps.   *Chinese*

15982. Tiger and deer do not walk together.   *Chinese*

15983. To beat a tiger one must have a brother's help.   *Chinese*

15984. Unless you enter the tiger's den you cannot take the cubs.   *Japanese*

15985. Unless you get into a tiger's den, you won't catch a tiger's cub.   *Korean*

15986. When the tiger dies, it leaves its skin; a man, his name.   *Korean*

TILE

15987. A tile, even though it be polished, does not become a jewel.
                                                               Japanese

15988. Throw a tile over the wall and you cannot know how it lands.
Chinese

TIMBER

15989. As the timber is, so are its shavings. *Philippine*

15990. If the main timbers in the house are not straight, the smaller timbers will be unsafe; and if the smaller timbers are not straight, the house will fall. *Chinese*

15991. Stolen timber also burns.
Russian

TIME

15992. A time for adversity, and a time for prosperity. *Indian (Tamil)*

15993. Any time is no time.
American

15994. As are the times, so are the manners. *Spanish*

15995. Everything in its proper time; even fertilizer for the cabbages. *Greek*

15996. Everything in time comes to him who knows how to wait. *French*

15997. Everything is good but all in its time. *Yiddish*

15998. From tomorrow till tomorrow time goes a long journey. *French*

15999. Give time time. *Italian*

16000. Have a good time if you want, but don't overdo it. *Russian*

16001. He that gains time gains all things. *English*

16002. He that has most time has none to lose. *English*

16003. He that has time and looks for a better time, loses time. *English*

16004. He that has time has life.
English

16005. He who turns to look a second time will lose nothing. *Chinese*

16006. Hour by hour time departs.
Italian

16007. In a lucky time it's good to talk; in an unlucky time, it's better to be silent. *Yiddish*

16008. In the time of rejoicing, rejoicing; in the time of mourning, mourning. *Hebrew*

16009. It is time, not the comb, that makes men bald. *Czech*

16010. Lost time is never found again.
English

16011. Morning time, golden time.
Estonian

16012. No one can blow and swallow at the same time. *German*

16013. No time is set for death.
African (Jabo)

16014. No time like the present.
English

16015. Old times are old times, the present is present. *Japanese*

16016. One cannot drink and whistle at the same time. *Italian*

16017. One time isn't the same as another time. *Russian*

16018. One who is waiting thinks the time long. *Irish*

16019. Other times, other counsels.
Portuguese

16020. Other times, other folk.
Danish

16021. Other times, other manners.
French

16022. Our time runs on like a stream; first fall the leaves and then the tree.
Dutch

16023. Suit yourself to the times.
German

16024. Take time when time comes, for time will away. *English*

16025. That which may fall out at any time, may fall out today. *English*

16026. The good time comes but once. *Italian*

16027. The third time is never like the rest. *English*

16028. The third time pays for all. *English*

16029. The time of death is no time to take a breath. *Russian*

16030. There's a proper time for every vegetable. *Russian*

16031. There is a time for all things. *English*

16032. There is a time for work and a time for play. *Russian*

16033. There is a time to speak and a time to be silent. *English*

16034. There is always a first time. *American*

16035. There is time to wink as well as to see. *English*

16036. There needs a long time to know the world's pulse. *English*

16037. They who make the best use of their time have none to spare. *English*

16038. Those who are happy do not observe how time goes by. *Chinese*

16039. Time and chance happen to all men. *English*

16040. Time and chance reveal all secrets. *English*

16041. Time and money make everything possible. *Maltese*

16042. Time and opportunity one never has in one's hand. *Norwegian*

16043. Time and patience bring roses. *Slovakian*

16044. Time and patience will wear out stone posts. *English*

16045. Time and patience would bring the snail to Jerusalem. *Irish*

16046. Time and place make the thief. *Dutch*

16047. Time and straw make medlars ripe. *English*

16048. Time and the hour are not to be tied with a rope. *Portuguese*

16049. Time and thought tame the strongest grief. *Scottish*

16050. Time and tide wait for no man. *English*

16051. Time and tide will stay for no man. *Scottish*

16052. Time at last makes all things even. *American*

16053. Time betrays and hangs the thief. *German*

16054. Time brings everything to those who can wait for it. *German*

16055. Time brings out the truth better than the judge. *Hungarian*

16056. Time brings roses. *Dutch*

16057. Time brings wounds and heals them. *Yiddish*

16058. Time builds a castle and demolishes it. *Slovenian*

16059. Time builds and destroys everything. *Slovakian*

16060. Time can alter everything. *Yiddish*

16061. Time cannot obliterate the memory of a village case. *African (Annang)*

16062. Time causes remembrance. *African (Efik)*

16063. Time covers and discovers everything. *German*

16064. Time cures all things. *English*

16065. Time destroys all things. *Dutch*

16066. Time does not wait for man.
Japanese

16067. Time flees away without delay.
English

16068. Time flies away as fast as a shuttle on the loom. *Vietnamese*

16069. Time flies like an arrow, once gone it does not return. *Japanese*

16070. Time gained, much gained.
Dutch

16071. Time goes, death comes.
Dutch

16072. Time goes, words remain; a ship goes, the shore remains.
Indian (Tamil)

16073. Time grows longer for him that gets up early and goes to bed late.
Maltese

16074. Time heals a wound, but leaves a scar. *Estonian*

16075. Time heals and yet it kills.
Mexican

16076. Time helps even the doctor.
Estonian

16077. Time is a file that wears and makes no noise. *English*

16078. Time is always before us.
Finnish

16079. Time is anger's medicine.
German

16080. Time is better spent in austerities than in vanity. *Indian (Tamil)*

16081. Time is God's and ours. *Dutch*

16082. Time is gold. *Philippine*

16083. Time is like an arrow. *Korean*

16084. Time is money. *English*

16085. Time is not tied to a post, like a horse to the manger. *Danish*

16086. Time is the best counsellor.
German

16087. Time is the best doctor.
Russian

16088. Time is the best physician.
Yiddish

16089. Time is the best preacher.
German

16090. Time is the father of truth.
English

16091. Time is the rider that breaks youth. *English*

16092. Time is the soul of everything.
Greek

16093. Time lost we cannot win.
English

16094. Time makes hay. *German*

16095. Time must elapse before one can get a good name. *Indian (Tamil)*

16096. Time passes away, but sayings remain. *Indian (Hindi)*

16097. Time passes like the wind.
Portuguese

16098. Time past never returns.
Dutch

16099. Time reveals all things.
English

16100. Time rules all things.
American

16101. Time tries all things. *English*

16102. Time tries truth. *English*

16103. Time undermines us. *English*

16104. Time waits for no man.
Danish

16105. Time will show. *American*

16106. Time, wind, women, and fortune are changing every moment.
German

16107. Time works wonders. *Hebrew*

16108. Wasting time is robbing oneself. *Estonian*

16109. What may be done at any time will be done at no time. *English*

16110. When times are easy we do not burn incense, but when trouble comes we embrace the feet of the Buddha.
Chinese

16111. When time grows long, opinion changes. *Maltese*

16112. You won't die before your time is up. *Russian*

TIMIDITY

16113. Timidity relieves one of responsibility. *Burmese*

TINKER

16114. A tinker and a piper make bad music together. *English*

16115. The tinker stops one hole and makes two. *English*

TIPPLER

16116. The tippler discloses his true character. *Japanese*

16117. The tippler does not know the poison, the teetotaler the medicine.
Japanese

16118. There are more old wine tipplers than old doctors. *German*

TIRE

16119. He who does not tire, achieves.
Spanish

TITMOUSE

16120. A titmouse in the hands is better than a crane in the sky. *Russian*

TOAD

16121. Toads will bully frogs.
Vietnamese

TOBACCO

16122. Tobacco is different from millet flour. *African (Hausa)*

16123. Tobacco is necessary for life.
Indian (Bihar)

16124. We dine together, but each one smokes his own tobacco. *Russian*

TODAY

16125. If today will not, tomorrow may. *English*

16126. One today is better than ten tomorrows. *German*

16127. One today is worth two tomorrows. *English*

TOE

16128. Better to stumble with the toe than with the tongue.
African (Swahili)

16129. The toe that is tramped on feels most. *American*

TOGETHER

16130. Both together do best of all.
English

TOIL

16131. Toil cannot be overtaken by poverty. *Japanese*

TOLL

16132. The toll is more than the grist.
English

TOMATO

16133. Every tomato is red.
African (Hausa)

TOMORROW

16134. Never put off till tomorrow what you can do today. *English*

16135. Tomorrow is a new day.
English

16136. Tomorrow is tomorrow, today is today. *Japanese*

16137. Tomorrow is untouched.
English

16138. Tomorrow is very close.
African (Fulani)

TONE

16139. It is the tone that makes the music.   *French*

16140. The tone of the bird's song is the same everywhere.   *Japanese*

TONG

16141. The tongs are at the head of the blacksmith's shop.   *African (Yoruba)*

16142. Who has the tongs does not burn his fingers.   *Albanian*

TONGUE

16143. A double tongue will slip.
                                                       Indian (Tamil)

16144. A false tongue will hardly speak truth.   *English*

16145. A fleshy tongue cuts off the bony neck.   *Estonian*

16146. A fool's tongue is long enough to cut his own throat.   *English*

16147. A good tongue is a good weapon.   *English*

16148. A honey tongue, a heart of gall.
                                                              English

16149. A long tongue has a short hand.
                                                             Scottish

16150. A nurse's tongue is privileged to talk.   *English*

16151. A quiet tongue makes a wise head.   *English*

16152. A silent tongue is better than evil speaking.   *Manx*

16153. A smooth tongue is better than smooth locks.   *Danish*

16154. A sweet tongue deceives many folks.   *Turkish*

16155. A sweet tongue hides a bad heart.   *Jamaican*

16156. A sweet tongue is seldom without a sting to its root.   *Irish*

16157. A tongue is not necessary to declare love.   *Welsh*

16158. A tongue will get you to Kiev.
                                                              Russian

16159. A wicked tongue is worse than an evil hand.   *Yiddish*

16160. A wife's long tongue is the staircase by which misfortunes ascend to the house.   *Chinese*

16161. A woman's tongue breaks bones.   *Maltese*

16162. A woman's tongue is her sword, and she does not let it rust.   *French*

16163. A woman's tongue is the last thing about her that dies.   *English*

16164. An ill tongue may do much.
                                                             Scottish

16165. Below the tongue, there is an ax hidden.   *Korean*

16166. Better a snake's tongue to sting you than a man's.   *Greek*

16167. Between evil tongues and evil ears, there is nothing to choose.
                                                              Danish

16168. Confine your tongue lest it confine you.   *English*

16169. Even four horses cannot pull back what the tongue has let go.
                                                            Slovakian

16170. Evil tongues are silenced by the tinkle of coins in your pocket. *Yiddish*

16171. Foolish tongues talk by the dozen.   *English*

16172. For evil tongues, scissors.
                                                              Spanish

16173. He loses least in a quarrel who keeps his tongue in check.   *Danish*

16174. He must have leave to speak who cannot hold his tongue.   *Scottish*

16175. He that knows not how to hold his tongue knows not how to talk.
                                                              English

16176. He that strikes with his tongue, must ward with his head.   *English*

16177. He who has a bad tongue should have good loins.   *Italian*

16178. He whose tongue is arrested by his front teeth will never offend.
Russian

16179. If the tongue were to tell all the bosom knows, none would be friends.
Welsh

16180. It is a good tongue that says no ill, and a better heart that thinks none.
Scottish

16181. It is pleasant to wag one's tongue about other people's business.
African (Ovambo)

16182. It is proper that the tongue of a debtor be short.   *Turkish*

16183. It is the frog's own tongue that betrays him.   *Haitian*

16184. It is the human tongue which makes tremble both man and beast.
Turkish

16185. Keep guard over the tongue that is in your mouth.   *Turkish*

16186. Keep not two tongues in one mouth.   *Danish*

16187. Let not your tongue cut your throat.   *Irish*

16188. Let not your tongue run away with your brains.   *English*

16189. Little can a long tongue conceal.   *Scottish*

16190. Man's tongue is more poisonous than the bee's sting. *Vietnamese*

16191. No one ever repented of having held his tongue.   *Italian*

16192. One may hold one's tongue in an ill time.   *English*

16193. One tongue is enough for a woman.   *English*

16194. Say what you want with your tongue, but don't let your hands loose.
Russian

16195. Silken tongue and hempen heart often go together.   *Danish*

16196. That tongue does lie that speaks in haste.   *English*

16197. The lame tongue gets nothing.
English

16198. The licking tongue may make a wound.   *Russian*

16199. The tongue breaks bones, though itself has none.   *English*

16200. The tongue goes where the tooth aches.   *Spanish*

16201. The tongue has no bones in it, but it breaks bones.   *Greek*

16202. The tongue having no bone will turn any way.   *Indian (Tamil)*

16203. The tongue is a sword.
Indian (Kashmiri)

16204. The tongue is ever turning to the aching tooth.   *English*

16205. The tongue is harder than a stick.   *African (Ovambo)*

16206. The tongue is like a sharp knife: it kills without drawing blood.
Chinese

16207. The tongue is mightier than the sword.   *Japanese*

16208. The tongue is not steel, yet it cuts.   *English*

16209. The tongue is only three inches long but it can kill even a king.
Philippine

16210. The tongue is soft and remains; the teeth are hard and fall out.
Chinese

16211. The tongue is the neck's enemy.
Egyptian

16212. The tongue is the pen of the heart.   *Yiddish*

16213. The tongue is the rudder of our ship.   *English*

16214. The tongue is the rudder of the words of the mouth.   *Hawaiian*

16215. The tongue is the smallest organ in the body but can do the most important tasks.   *Slovakian*

16216. The tongue kills and the tongue saves.   *Indian (Kashmiri)*

16217. The tongue kills man and the tongue saves man.   *African (Oji)*

16218. The tongue makes no profit.
          African (Swahili)

16219. The tongue of a bad friend cuts more than a knife.   *Spanish*

16220. The tongue of a woman is sharper than a Turkish sabre.
          Serbo-Croatian

16221. The tongue of experience has most truth.   *Egyptian*

16222. The tongue of idle persons is never idle.   *English*

16223. The tongue slays quicker than the sword.   *Turkish*

16224. The tongue speaks, the conduct shows.   *Welsh*

16225. The tongue talks at the head's cost.   *English*

16226. The tongue walks where the teeth speed not.   *English*

16227. The tongue wounds more than a lance.   *French*

16228. There is nothing sharper than a woman's tongue.   *Irish*

16229. Tongue, source of honor and shame.   *Indian (Bihar)*

16230. Turn your tongue seven times before speaking.   *French*

16231. Who has not a good tongue, ought to have good hands.   *English*

16232. Without a tongue is like without a bell.   *Yiddish*

16233. Women's tongues wag like lambs' tails.   *English*

16234. You can never tie up people's tongues.   *Russian*

16235. Your tongue is your power. If you preserve it it will preserve you. If you betray it it will betray you.
          Libyan

TOOL

16236. Edged tools never wound you when you are used to them. *American*

16237. The tool to hand will be used.
          African (Fulani)

16238. The tool works, the hand boasts.   *Turkish*

TOOTH (see TEETH)

16239. Better tooth out than always ache.   *English*

16240. The tooth hurts the body, the tongue hurts the soul.   *Iranian*

16241. The tooth often bites the tongue, and yet they keep together.   *Danish*

16242. There is no ease for the mouth with an aching tooth.   *Chinese*

TOOTHACHE

16243. When a toothache comes, you forget your headache.   *Yiddish*

16244. When you have had a toothache, you can understand how another's toothache feels.   *Chinese*

TOP (lid)

16245. A crooked top on a crooked kettle.   *Japanese*

TOP (summit)

16246. It is difficult to climb but it is nice to be at the top.   *Philippine*

TORAH

16247. The Torah gives light, the Torah burns, but only the dollar gives warmth.   *Yiddish*

TORCH

16248. A great torch may be lighted at a little candle. *English*

16249. Do not light a torch from both ends. *African (Ovambo)*

16250. The more light a torch gives, the less while it lasts. *English*

TORMENT

16251. He who torments others does not sleep well. *French*

TORTOISE

16252. As long as you have not got the tortoise, you do not cut the string for him. *African (Oji)*

16253. The tortoise complains of rain whereas it has only wetted its feet. *African (Annang)*

16254. The tortoise does not bite the paw of a leopard. *African (Swahili)*

16255. The tortoise is not overburdened by its shell. *African (Shona)*

TOWER

16256. Towers are measured by their shadows, great men by those who speak evil of them. *Chinese*

TOWN

16257. A starved town is soon forced to surrender. *Italian*

16258. Be the town ever so far there is another beyond it. *African (Fulani)*

16259. Every town has its fool. *Yiddish*

16260. He who skirts a town doesn't know what is inside. *African (Hausa)*

16261. If everyone swept in front of his house, the whole town would be clean. *Polish*

16262. In a town where you know nobody, do whatever you like. *Egyptian*

16263. Other towns, other lasses. *German*

16264. The whole town is friendly to a physician. *Indian (Tamil)*

TOY

16265. There are toys for all ages. *French*

TRACE

16266. That which leaves no trace has done no harm. *Icelandic*

TRADE

16267. A good trade will carry farther than a thousand florins. *German*

16268. A handful of trade is worth a handful of gold. *English*

16269. A trade is a trade. *American*

16270. A trade is better than service. *English*

16271. A trade makes you a king but robs you of leisure. *Yiddish*

16272. A trade that is not practiced is an enemy. *Irish*

16273. A trade won't burden your shoulders. *Russian*

16274. All is fair in trade. *American*

16275. Be one's trade good or bad, it is experience that makes one an adept at it. *Irish*

16276. Each trade has its own ways. *Chinese*

16277. He that changes his trade makes soup in a basket. *English*

16278. He who cannot speak well of his trade does not understand it. *French*

16279. He who has a trade has an office of profit and honor. *English*

16280. He who has a trade may travel through the world. *Spanish*

16281. He who plies many trades remains without a house. *Greek*

16282. No trade without returns.
American

16283. No trade without tools.
Serbo-Croatian

16284. One knows a man by his trade even if it is drinking beer.
African (Hausa)

16285. The parents' trade remains an inheritance to the children. *Turkish*

16286. There are no foolish trades, there are only foolish people. *French*

16287. To have a trade is to be free of worry. *Yiddish*

16288. Trade is a lottery. *American*

16289. Trade is not mutual help.
African (Hausa)

16290. Trade is the mother of money.
English

16291. Trade must regulate itself.
American

16292. Two of a trade can never agree.
English

16293. When there is much soliciting to buy and to sell, trade is not very lively. *Chinese*

TRADITION

16294. The young cannot teach tradition to the old. *African (Yoruba)*

TRAIN

16295. The train waits for no one.
Japanese

TRAITOR

16296. A traitor will never make a patriot. *Welsh*

16297. Give a traitor good words and you make him loyal. *Spanish*

16298. He who is a traitor is a coward.
Turkish

16299. Once a traitor, always a traitor.
Mexican

TRANQUILITY

16300. He who desires tranquility must be deaf, blind, and tongueless.
Turkish

TRAP

16301. A trap without a bait catches nothing. *African (Swahili)*

16302. It is easy to fall into a trap, but hard to get out again. *English*

TRASH

16303. Trash accumulates in stagnant water. *Japanese*

16304. Trash and trumpery is the highway to beggary. *English*

TRAVEL (noun)

16305. Travel is a gloomy and trying experience. *Japanese*

16306. Travel makes a wise man better, but a fool worse. *English*

16307. Travel ripens a man. *Iranian*

TRAVEL (verb)

16308. He that travels far knows much.
English

16309. The quieter you travel, the farther you'll get. *Russian*

TRAVELER

16310. A lame traveler should get out betimes. *English*

16311. A lazy traveler makes a long journey. *American*

16312. A traveler may lie by authority.
English

16313. A traveler will not consume all his provisions. *African (Ovambo)*

16314. Choose your fellow traveler before you start on your journey.
African (Hausa)

16315. The travelers are the people who bring news about the spoors of lions. *African (Bemba)*

TRAY

16316. Different trays have different stands. *Malaysian*

TREACHERY

16317. In an office of trust there must be no treachery. *Turkish*

16318. No one can guard against treachery. *German*

16319. They who guard against treachery are few. *Turkish*

16320. Treachery and slander are long lived. *Danish*

16321. Treachery lurks in honeyed words. *Danish*

TREASON

16322. The treason approved, the traitor abhorred. *Portuguese*

TREASURE

16323. The treasures turned out to be charcoal. *Greek*

16324. There are no better treasures than children. *Japanese*

16325. Treasure is tickle. *English*

16326. Treasures laid up in the mind do not decay. *Japanese*

TREE

16327. A big tree does not fall like a little child. *African (Bemba)*

16328. A creaky tree stands a long time. *Russian*

16329. A fallen tree provides plenty of kindling. *Armenian*

16330. A fruit-bearing tree is known by its flowers. *Japanese*

16331. A good tree brings forth good fruit. *English*

16332. A good tree can lodge ten thousand birds. *Burmese*

16333. A good tree is a good shelter. *English*

16334. A good tree yields not poisonous fruit, nor a poisonous tree good fruit. *Indian (Tamil)*

16335. A great tree has a great fall. *English*

16336. A rotting tree leans long before it falls. *Finnish*

16337. A single tree does not make a forest. *Chinese*

16338. A threatened tree stands long. *Scottish*

16339. A tree bears fruit even if stones are thrown at it. *Swedish*

16340. A tree does not bear fruit before it is full grown. *African (Ovambo)*

16341. A tree often transplanted is never loaded with fruit. *Italian*

16342. A tree often transplanted neither grows nor thrives. *Spanish*

16343. A tree that affords you shade, do not order it to be cut down. *Egyptian*

16344. A tree which gives too much or too little shade should be cut down. *Russian*

16345. A tree which has no fork, its ascent is difficult. *African (Ga)*

16346. A tree with holes does not call the wind to itself. *African (Kpelle)*

16347. A tree without water gives no fruit. *Turkish*

16348. A young tree bends; an old tree breaks. *Yiddish*

16349. Aged trees cannot be bent. *Japanese*

16350. All the trees which sprout do not grow. *African (Kpelle)*

16351. As a tree falls so must it lie.
English

16352. As the tree, so the pear; as the mistress, so the maid. *German*

16353. Bend the tree only while it is young. *Russian*

16354. Bend trees to the shape you want when they are still young.
Vietnamese

16355. Dead tree does not yield dew.
African (Jabo)

16356. Don't climb a tree to look for fish. *Chinese*

16357. Don't cut down the tree to get the fruit. *Philippine*

16358. Dried trees have no buds, wicked people no children.
Vietnamese

16359. Durable trees make roots first.
American

16360. Everybody loves the tree which gives him shelter. *Russian*

16361. Good tree, good fruit. *Dutch*

16362. Great trees keep under the little ones. *English*

16363. He that loves the tree loves the branch. *English*

16364. He that plants trees, loves others besides himself. *English*

16365. He who planted the tree will water it. *Indian (Tamil)*

16366. He who tries to shake the trunk of a tree only shakes himself.
African (Yoruba)

16367. Honor the tree that gives you shelter. *Danish*

16368. If you go up a tree you know how to come down. *African (Fulani)*

16369. If you would bend the tree do it while it is young. *Japanese*

16370. In a dense forest the trees grow straight. *Latvian*

16371. It is the fruitful tree that is pelted with stones. *Indian (Hindi)*

16372. It's the tall tree that is stirred by every wind. *Latvian*

16373. Large trees give more shade than fruit. *English*

16374. Large trees grow slowly and fall suddenly. *Serbo-Croatian*

16375. Look as you fell a tree.
African (Zulu)

16376. No tree bears fruit in autumn that does not blossom in the spring.
English

16377. No tree ever bore fruit without first having flowers. *African (Ashanti)*

16378. No tree falls at the first stroke.
German

16379. Nobody climbs a coconut tree without making notches in it.
Philippine

16380. Not every tree produces fruit.
Turkish

16381. Old trees are not to be bent.
Korean

16382. One climbs up the tree from the root, not from the top. *Finnish*

16383. One doesn't climb a tree by the trunk and come down by the branches.
African (Hausa)

16384. One should spare the tree that gives one shade. *Norwegian*

16385. One tree does not make a forest.
African (Hausa)

16386. One tree does not make a grove.
Slovakian

16387. One tree receiving all the wind, breaks. *African (Oji)*

16388. Other trees, other woodcutters.
Lithuanian

16389. Prickly pear trees do not produce peaches. *Maltese*

16390. Remove an old tree and it will die. *English*

16391. Soon crooks the tree that good gambrel would be. *English*

16392. Straight trees are felled first; sweet wells are drained first. *Chinese*

16393. Straight trees have crooked roots. *English*

16394. Such tree, such fruit. *English*

16395. Tall trees catch much wind. *Dutch*

16396. Tall trees, much wind. *Japanese*

16397. The bad tree, like the crooked sugarcane, says he will not straighten; he breaks. *African (Efik)*

16398. The great tree attracts the wind. *Chinese*

16399. The highest tree has the greatest fall. *English*

16400. The nobler the tree, the more pliant the twig. *Dutch*

16401. The split tree still grows. *African (Wolof)*

16402. The tree falls not at the first blow. *English*

16403. The tree is felled in the forest and the splinters fly to the village. *Russian*

16404. The tree is known by its fruit. *English*

16405. The tree is not to be judged by its bark. *Italian*

16406. The tree is sure to be pruned before it reaches the skies. *Danish*

16407. The tree must be bent while it is young. *German*

16408. The tree that grows slowly keeps itself for another. *English*

16409. The tree which is not taller than you are cannot shade you. *African (Wolof)*

16410. The trees which are growing are tomorrow's forest. *African (Bemba)*

16411. The trees which are pointed out by the axe do not cut themselves down. *African (Bemba)*

16412. There is no tree but bears some fruit. *English*

16413. There is no tree that cannot be bored by a beetle. *Indian (Tamil)*

16414. There is no tree which has not felt the force of the wind. *Pashto*

16415. There is not a tree in heaven higher than the tree of patience. *Irish*

16416. Though a tree be a thousand feet high, the leaves fall and return to the root. *Chinese*

16417. Though a tree does not bear fruit, it is not cut down. *African (Ovambo)*

16418. To dig up a tree, you must begin with the root. *Chinese*

16419. Trees growing on windy places are sturdy. *Philippine*

16420. Trees often transplanted seldom prosper. *Dutch*

16421. Trees which are near to one another do not fall to scratch one another. *African (Bemba)*

16422. Trees which bear flowers do not always bear fruit. *African (Kpelle)*

16423. Unless the tree falls, one will never get at the branches. *African (Yoruba)*

16424. When a tree dies at its roots, its branches dry up also. *African (Swahili)*

16425. When a tree falls, it is taken off for firewood. *Philippine*

16426. When a tree is cut in the forest, the echo repeats the sound. *African (Yoruba)*

16427. When a tree is falling, everyone cries, "Down with it."   *Italian*

16428. When one would climb a tree, one begins from the bottom and not from the top.   *African (Ashanti)*

16429. When the lofty trees are felled, the remaining trees look tall.
          Indian (Tamil)

16430. When the tree falls everyone runs to cut boughs.   *Dutch*

16431. When the tree falls everyone runs to gather sticks.   *Danish*

16432. When the tree falls there is no shade.   *Chinese*

16433. When the tree is down everybody runs to the branches.   *French*

16434. When the tree is fallen, all go with their hatchet.   *English*

16435. Whichever way the tree is bending, it will fall.   *Russian*

16436. While a dead tree is expected to collapse, a live one unexpectedly snaps.
          African (Annang)

16437. While the tree is a sapling it is bent.   *Turkish*

16438. Who cuts down good trees sees no profit.   *Hebrew*

TREE-KNOT

16439. The tree-knot spoils the axe; hunger spoils love.   *African (Efik)*

TRIAL

16440. There are no trials till marriage.   *Irish*

TRIBE

16441. A tribe associates with its own tribe, and goats follow their own kind.
          Indian (Tamil)

TRICK

16442. A trick is clever only once.
          Yiddish

16443. One trick needs another trick to back it up.   *English*

16444. Trick against trick.   *German*

TRICKERY

16445. Trickery comes back to its master.   *French*

TRICKSTER

16446. Buy the trickster, and you need have no fear of the honest man.   *Irish*

TRIFLE

16447. A trifle may incur murdering.
          Korean

16448. Better own a trifle than want a great deal.   *Irish*

TROOPER

16449. A young trooper should have an old horse.   *English*

TROT

16450. An ass's trot does not last long.
          Italian

TROUBLE

16451. After trouble comes peace; after darkness comes the sun.   *Philippine*

16452. Better pour out your troubles to a stone, but don't carry them within yourself.   *Yiddish*

16453. He that seeks trouble never misses.   *English*

16454. He who bears trouble patiently receives his reward.   *Turkish*

16455. He who complains about everything brings home trouble.
          African (Ovambo)

16456. He who is wasting away with trouble must seek remedy.   *Turkish*

16457. He who looks for what cannot be obtained will endure much trouble.
          African (Hausa)

16458. It is good for a man to bear trouble rather than die. *African (Efik)*

16459. It's good to talk about troubles that are over. *Yiddish*

16460. Let your trouble tarry till its own day comes. *English*

16461. Much kindred, much trouble. *French*

16462. Never trouble trouble till trouble troubles you. *English*

16463. New troubles make us forget the old. *Hebrew*

16464. No one gets into trouble without his own help. *Danish*

16465. Nobody is willing to take away your troubles; nobody can take away your good deeds. *Yiddish*

16466. None sigh deeper than those who have no troubles. *Norwegian*

16467. Not all troubles come from heaven. *Yiddish*

16468. The biggest trouble—a shrewish wife. *Yiddish*

16469. The troubles of a stranger aren't worth an onion. *Yiddish*

16470. Trouble cuts up the heart. *Yiddish*

16471. Trouble doesn't come alone. *Yiddish*

16472. Trouble has its reward. *African (Ovambo)*

16473. Trouble is like strong medicine—too much at a time is harmful. *Yiddish*

16474. Trouble isn't hiding behind the mountains. *Russian*

16475. Trouble springs from idleness. *American*

16476. Troubles don't last forever. *African (Hausa)*

16477. When troubles are few, dreams are few. *Chinese*

16478. You never know the other fellow's troubles. *Yiddish*

TROUGH

16479. Dirty troughs will serve dirty sows. *English*

TROUSERS

16480. He who wears trousers of iron will not sit down. *African (Fulani)*

TROUT

16481. A trout in the pot is better than a salmon in the sea. *Irish*

16482. There's no catching trouts with dry breeches. *Portuguese*

16483. Trouts are not caught with dry breeches. *Spanish*

TROY

16484. Troy was not taken in a day. *English*

TRUE

16485. All be not true that speak fair. *English*

16486. It must be true that all men say. *English*

16487. What is true is not always probable. *French*

TRUST (noun)

16488. A betrayed trust is a mortal thrust. *Burmese*

16489. In trust is treason. *English*

16490. Living upon trust is the way to pay double. *English*

16491. Put not your trust in a sword, woman, mare, or water. *Pashto*

16492. Put not your trust in money, but put your money in trust. *American*

16493. Sudden trust brings sudden repentance. *English*

16494. There is no trust in horse or woman. *Turkish*

16495. This day there is no trust, but come tomorrow. *English*

16496. Too much trust breeds disappointments. *Philippine*

16497. Trust draws to heaven, honor to earth. *Yiddish*

16498. Trust is before anything, but pay in advance. *Russian*

16499. Trust is dead, ill payment killed it. *English*

16500. Trust is the mother of deceit. *English*

TRUST (verb)

16501. He is ill to trust who will trust nobody. *English*

16502. He who trusts not is not deceived. *English*

16503. If you trust before you try, you may repent before you die. *English*

16504. Trust, but not too much. *German*

16505. Trust everybody, but thyself most. *Danish*

16506. Trust none better than yourself. *English*

TRUSTING

16507. Trusting often makes fidelity. *English*

TRUTH

16508. A half truth is a whole lie. *Yiddish*

16509. All the truth should not be told. *Scottish*

16510. All truths are not good to be uttered. *French*

16511. Always tell the truth in the form of a joke. *Armenian*

16512. Better suffer for truth than prosper by falsehood. *Danish*

16513. Better to suffer for the truth than be rewarded for a lie. *Swedish*

16514. Between wrangling and disputing truth is lost. *German*

16515. Drink, eat, but speak the truth. *Russian*

16516. Even if the truth be buried for hundreds of years, it will come out in due time and will flourish. *Philippine*

16517. Even truth gets drowned when gold comes to the surface. *Russian*

16518. Even truth may be bitter. *Irish*

16519. Every truth is not good to be told. *Italian*

16520. Everything will pass away, only the truth will remain. *Russian*

16521. Face to face the truth comes out. *English*

16522. From confessors, doctors, and lawyers do not conceal the truth of your case. *French*

16523. From the truth to a lie is but a hand's breadth. *Rumanian*

16524. Half the truth is often a whole lie. *English*

16525. He must keep a sharp look out who would speak the truth. *Danish*

16526. He that follows truth too closely must take care that she does not strike out his teeth. *English*

16527. He that follows truth too near the heels shall have dust thrown in his face. *English*

16528. He who speaks the truth should have one foot in the stirrup. *Indian (Hindi)*

16529. Heaven and earth have sworn that the truth shall be disclosed. *Yiddish*

497

16530. Hide not the truth from your confessor, your doctor, or your lawyer.
Italian

16531. If everybody says so, there's some truth to it. *Yiddish*

16532. If you meet with those who quarrel, you may take one side, but at least speak the truth. *African (Wolof)*

16533. In too much dispute truth is lost. *English*

16534. It is truth that makes a man angry. *Italian*

16535. Many a truth is best concealed.
Welsh

16536. Old truths, old laws, old friends, an old book, and old wine are best. *Polish*

16537. Sooner or later the truth comes to light. *Dutch*

16538. Speak the truth, but have one foot in the stirrup. *Armenian*

16539. Tell the truth and shame the devil. *English*

16540. Tell the truth and try to escape.
Russian

16541. The truth can be told even in jest. *Turkish*

16542. The truth doesn't die but it lives like a poor man. *Yiddish*

16543. The truth has charm but it's shy. *Yiddish*

16544. The truth has many faces.
Yiddish

16545. The truth is half a quarrel.
Indian (Hindustani)

16546. The truth is in sight; the lie is behind the eyes. *Yiddish*

16547. The truth is not alive, the truth is not dead—it struggles. *Yiddish*

16548. The truth may walk around naked; the lie has to be clothed.
Yiddish

16549. The truth rises to the surface like oil on water. *Slovakian*

16550. The truth stands up, a lie does not. *Hebrew*

16551. The truth surfaces like oil on water. *Yiddish*

16552. There is in the world one truth, but it seems as if there were a hundred.
Lithuanian

16553. To know the truth is easy; but, ah, how difficult to follow it! *Chinese*

16554. To withhold truth is to bury gold. *Danish*

16555. Truth and folly dwell in the wine cask. *Danish*

16556. Truth and roses have thorns about them. *English*

16557. Truth and sweet oil always come to the top. *English*

16558. Truth at times parts the best of friends. *Indian (Bihar)*

16559. Truth fears no colors. *English*

16560. Truth filters through the stone.
American

16561. Truth finds foes where it should find none. *English*

16562. Truth finds no asylum.
German

16563. Truth gives a short answer, lies go around about. *German*

16564. Truth has a good face but bad clothes. *English*

16565. Truth has a scratched face.
English

16566. Truth has always a sure bottom. *English*

16567. Truth holds though it is bitterly taken. *Greek*

16568. Truth ill timed is as bad as a lie. *German*

16569. Truth is a jewel. *American*

16570. Truth is a lion, and lies are a hyena. *Moroccan*

16571. Truth is a slowpoke. *Yiddish*

16572. Truth is better than friendship. *Indian (Kashmiri)*

16573. Truth is bitter food. *Danish*

16574. Truth is death to the guilty. *Welsh*

16575. Truth is found only with God, and with me only a little. *Yiddish*

16576. Truth is hard to tell—if you tell it look for your sandals. *African (Hausa)*

16577. Truth is lame, but it forges ahead. *Maltese*

16578. Truth is lost with too much debating. *Dutch*

16579. Truth is steadfast. *Hawaiian*

16580. Truth is stranger than fiction. *English*

16581. Truth is stronger than the mighty. *Welsh*

16582. Truth is the club that knocks down and kills everybody. *French*

16583. Truth is the daughter of the gods. *Japanese*

16584. Truth is the daughter of time. *English*

16585. Truth is the fruit of love. *Philippine*

16586. Truth is the safest lie. *Yiddish*

16587. Truth is the walking stick to grasp. *African (Swahili)*

16588. Truth is truth to the end of the reckoning. *English*

16589. Truth lies at the bottom of a well. *English*

16590. Truth lies on the surface of things. *English*

16591. Truth, like oil, always comes to the surface. *Spanish*

16592. Truth may be blamed but cannot be shamed. *English*

16593. Truth may be harsh, but pleasing to God. *Russian*

16594. Truth may be suppressed, but not strangled. *German*

16595. Truth may suffer to death, but it never dies. *Mexican*

16596. Truth needs no colors. *English*

16597. Truth needs not many words. *English*

16598. Truth never grows old. *English*

16599. Truth often comes out of a joke. *Japanese*

16600. Truth one finds only in the prayerbook. *Yiddish*

16601. Truth ought to be spoken. *American*

16602. Truth prevails, falsehood kills. *Indian (Tamil)*

16603. Truth pricks the eyes. *Russian*

16604. Truth reigns. *Greek*

16605. Truth seeks no corners. *English*

16606. Truth seldom finds a lodging. *Flemish*

16607. Truth shames the devil. *English*

16608. Truth shines in the dark. *Welsh*

16609. Truth should not always be revealed. *English*

16610. Truth stands, falsehood does not stand. *Hebrew*

16611. Truth tries. *English*

16612. Truth will prevail. *English*

16613. Truth will sometimes break out, unlooked for. *English*

16614. Truths too fine spun are subtle fooleries. *English*

16615. When the truth is told, everyone takes it ill. *Indian (Tamil)*

16616. Who tells the truth loses his friends. *Hebrew*

16617. You can't hide the truth. *Russian*

TRY

16618. He who tries again does better. *Maltese*

16619. Try before you trust. *English*

TRYING

16620. Trying again and again is better than stopping halfway. *African (Ovambo)*

TSAR

16621. Everyone has his own Tsar in his head. *Russian*

16622. If the Tsar makes you a present of an egg he takes from you a hen. *Russian*

16623. The Tsar has pity, but not the huntsman. *Russian*

16624. The Tsar has three hands but only one ear. *Russian*

16625. The Tsar is gracious, but not so his kennel keeper. *Russian*

16626. When the Tsar has a cold all Russia coughs. *Russian*

16627. When the Tsar sins the Empire must do penance. *Russian*

TUB

16628. Every tub must stand on its own bottom. *English*

TUNE

16629. There's many a good tune played on an old fiddle. *English*

TURBAN

16630. A turban does not make a man civilized. *African (Swahili)*

TURN

16631. A bad turn brings about another. *German*

16632. A turn well done is twice done. *Scottish*

16633. An ill turn is soon done. *English*

16634. He that does his turn in time, sits half idle. *Scottish*

16635. He that does you an ill turn will never forgive you. *Scottish*

16636. One good turn deserves another. *English*

16637. One never loses good turns by doing. *English*

16638. One shrewd turn asks another. *English*

16639. What's my turn today may be yours tomorrow. *Scottish*

TWIG

16640. Between ten and thirteen, bow the twig while it is green. *Scottish*

16641. Birchen twigs break no ribs. *English*

16642. One twig will not sweep. *African (Hausa)*

16643. The twigs are rarely better than the trunk. *Icelandic*

16644. When the twig grows hard it is difficult to twist it. *Irish*

16645. Young twigs may be bent, but not old trees. *Dutch*

TWO

16646. It takes two to make a quarrel. *English*

16647. It takes two to tango.
American

16648. Two are company.   *English*

16649. Two cannot walk together unless they be agreed.   *American*

16650. Two together are luckier than one.   *Hebrew*

16651. When two are fighting, a third shouldn't interfere.   *Russian*

16652. Where two fall out, the third wins.   *German*

TWO THINGS

16653. Two things a man should never be angry at: what he can help, and what he cannot help.   *English*

16654. Two things do prolong your life: a quiet heart, and a loving wife.
English

TYRANT

16655. It is time to fear when tyrants seem to kiss.   *English*

UGLINESS

16656. Ugliness with a good character is better than beauty. *African (Hausa)*

UMBRELLA

16657. Take an umbrella before you get wet. *Japanese*

16658. We remember the umbrella only when it rains. *Philippine*

UNBORN

16659. Better unborn than untaught. *Scottish*

UNCERTAINTY

16660. Continued uncertainty leads to war. *Indian (Tamil)*

UNDERLING

16661. Underlings are worse than masters. *Yiddish*

UNDERSTAND

16662. Who understands ill, answers ill. *English*

UNDERSTANDING

16663. With great doubts comes great understanding; with small doubts comes little understanding. *Chinese*

UNDERTAKE

16664. Who undertakes too much, succeeds but little. *Dutch*

UNION

16665. In union there is strength, in discord destruction. *Philippine*

16666. Union is strength. *Dutch*

UNITY

16667. Unity is strength, separation weakness. *African (Annang)*

UNKNOWN

16668. The unknown is always great. *American*

UNLOOKED

16669. Unlooked for often comes. *English*

UNMANNERLINESS

16670. Unmannerliness is not so impolite as over-politeness. *English*

UNMANNERLY

16671. Better be unmannerly than troublesome. *English*

UPBRINGING

16672. Better than birth is upbringing. *Japanese*

USE (noun)

16673. Don't count on the free use of someone else's belongings. *Russian*

16674. He who is of no use to himself is of no use to anyone else. *German*

16675. Use is a great matter. *English*

16676. Use makes everything easy. *American*

16677. Use makes perfect. *English*

16678. Use reconciles most things. *American*

USE (verb)

16679. More than we use is more than we want. *English*

16680. Use not today what tomorrow you may want. *English*

USURER

16681. A usurer, a miller, a banker, and a publican are the four evangelists of Lucifer. *Dutch*

16682. A usurer is one that torments men for their good conditions. *English*

16683. In the next world usurers have to count red-hot coins with bare hands. *Russian*

USURY

16684. To borrow on usury brings sudden beggary. *English*

VALET

16685. The clever and active valet wants no one to set him right.
Egyptian

VALIANT

16686. Assail who will, the valiant attends.
English

VALLEY

16687. He that stays in the valley shall never get over the hill.
English

VALOR

16688. Valor can do little without discretion.
English

16689. Valor that parleys is near yielding.
English

16690. Valor would fight, but discretion would run away.
English

VALUABLE

16691. One does not go into the bush with valuables.
African (Ovambo)

VALUE

16692. If you would know the value of money, try to borrow some.
English

16693. The value of each man consists in what he does well.
Egyptian

16694. The value of father is known after his decease, that of salt when exhausted.
Indian (Tamil)

16695. The value of prosperity is known by adversity.
American

16696. The value of shoes is appreciated when the sun is hot; the value of fire is known when the weather is cold.
Indian (Tamil)

16697. There's little value in the single cow.
Irish

VANITY

16698. Vanity has no greater foe than vanity.
French

VARNISHING

16699. Varnishing hides a crack.
English

VEGETABLE

16700. Take vegetables in hunger, and medicine in illness.
Vietnamese

VEIL

16701. A veil of rope is better than breach of custom.
Moroccan

16702. The veil that covers the face seldom covers beauty.
Russian

VELVET

16703. If velvet and silk are stored in the chest, one may appear among people in rags.   *Yiddish*

VENERATION

16704. Veneration and respect must be paid to the mother as well as to the father.   *Vietnamese*

VENGEANCE

16705. A woman's vengeance knows no bounds.   *German*

16706. He who often threatens takes vengeance but rarely.   *Serbo-Croatian*

16707. The smallest vengeance poisons the soul.   *Yiddish*

16708. Vengeance, though it comes with leaden feet, strikes with iron hands.   *English*

VENISON

16709. No one will throw away venison for squirrel's flesh.

African (Yoruba)

VENTURE (noun)

16710. Many ventures make a full freight.   *English*

VENTURE (verb)

16711. Boldly ventured is half won.

German

16712. He that ventures not fails not.

French

16713. He that ventures too far, loses all.   *English*

16714. Never venture out of your depth till you can swim.   *English*

16715. Nothing venture, nothing have.

English

16716. Venture little, hazard little.

English

16717. Venture not all you have at once.

English

VESSEL (container)

16718. A full vessel must be carried carefully.   *Danish*

16719. A vessel holds only its fill.

Irish

16720. Empty vessels make the most sound.   *English*

16721. Even a vessel, when it is full, will overflow.   *Korean*

16722. He is most likely to spill who holds the vessel in his hands.   *Danish*

16723. Old vessels must leak.   *English*

16724. The greatest vessel has but its measure.   *English*

16725. Whatever is in the vessel will come out of the spout.   *Indian (Bihar)*

16726. When a vessel is full it runs over.   *Estonian*

VESSEL (ship)

16727. An unpiloted vessel will not sail.   *Indian (Tamil)*

VICE

16728. After one vice a greater follows.   *Spanish*

16729. As vice wanes, virtue waxes.

Indian (Tamil)

16730. Do not think any vice trivial, and so practice it; do not think any virtue trivial, and so neglect it.

Chinese

16731. He who spares vice wrongs virtue.   *French*

16732. No vice goes alone.   *English*

16733. No vice like avarice.   *English*

16734. The second vice is lying, the first being that of owing money.

English

16735. The second vice is lying, the first is running in debt.   *American*

16736. Vices are learned without a master.   *English*

16737. Vice is learned without a schoolmaster. *Danish*

16738. Vice is often clothed in virtue's habit. *English*

16739. Vice makes virtue shine. *English*

16740. Vice rules where gold reigns. *English*

16741. Vice should not correct sin. *English*

16742. Vice will not conquer virtue. *Indian (Tamil)*

16743. Vices willingly bear the names of virtues. *Swedish*

16744. Where vice is vengeance follows. *English*

VICTIM

16745. In the world the low are the victims of the high. *Indian (Tamil)*

VICTOR

16746. The victor feels no fatigue. *Slovenian*

VICTORY

16747. Don't divide the spoil before the victory is won. *German*

16748. He who has victory, has right. *German*

16749. It is harder to use victory than to get it. *American*

16750. The only victory over love is flight. *French*

16751. There is no victory without a struggle. *Philippine*

16752. Victory does not stand in the number of soldiers. *American*

16753. Victory is a thing that is remembered. *African (Fulani)*

16754. Victory is attained through courage. *Philippine*

16755. Victory is not gained by idleness. *German*

16756. Victory or defeat is the destiny of the moment. *Japanese*

VIGILANCE

16757. Eternal vigilance is the price of travel. *American*

16758. Vigilance and precaution are safety. *Turkish*

VILLAGE

16759. A village doomed to ruin profits not by repeated precaution. *Indian (Tamil)*

16760. Every village has its inn. *Polish*

16761. In a village do as the village does. *Japanese*

16762. It is better that a village should fall than a custom. *Albanian*

16763. So many villages, so many customs. *Serbo-Croatian*

16764. The village that is in sight needs no guide. *Turkish*

16765. The village with two headmen falls into ruin. *Iranian*

16766. The whole village is mother to the motherless. *Indian (Tamil)*

VINEGAR

16767. A dull vinegar and a lenient master are good for nothing. *Serbo-Croatian*

16768. Free vinegar tastes better than bought honey. *Albanian*

16769. Sour vinegar taints the jar. *Greek*

16770. Take heed of the vinegar of sweet wine. *English*

16771. Vinegar at a cheap rate is sweeter than honey. *Turkish*

16772. Vinegar is the son of wine. *American*

16773. Vinegar offered free is as sweet as honey. *Greek*

16774. When one always drinks vinegar, he doesn't know that anything sweeter exists.   *Yiddish*

VINEYARD

16775. A vineless vineyard and smooth-running love hold out no charm.   *Greek*

16776. Fence your own vineyard, and keep your eyes from those of others.
                                   Greek

16777. He who owns vineyards admires them and he who sees them covets them.   *Greek*

16778. The vineyard needs no prayers, but a hoe.   *Serbo-Croatian*

16779. The vineyard requires a vine grower and the house a master.

VIOLENCE

16780. If violence comes by the door, law goes out by the chimney. *Turkish*

16781. Overcome violence only by gentle means.   *Burmese*

16782. Violence in a house is like a worm on vegetables.   *Hebrew*

16783. Violence spoils the game.
                                 Turkish

VIOLET

16784. Violets and lilies do not blossom always.   *Czech*

VIOLIN

16785. It is not with an axe that the violin is played.   *Welsh*

VIPER

16786. A viper is never grateful.
                           Indian (Bihar)

16787. The viper allows no insolence.
                          African (Yoruba)

16788. Vipers breed vipers.   *Danish*

VIRGIN

16789. There is no steadfast virgin to a persevering devotee.   *Philippine*

VIRTUE

16790. Age's virtues are dearly bought.
                                 Swedish

16791. All virtues spring from honor.
                                Albanian

16792. As the virtue in the tree, such is the fruit.   *Danish*

16793. Following virtue is like climbing a hill; following evil, like slipping down a precipice.   *Chinese*

16794. He that sows virtue, shall reap fame.   *English*

16795. He that thinks too much of his virtues bids others think of his vices.
                                 English

16796. He who has nothing but virtues is not much better than he who has nothing but faults.   *Swedish*

16797. He whose virtues exceed his talents is the superior man; he whose talents exceed his virtues is the inferior man.   *Chinese*

16798. The virtue of a coward is suspicion.   *English*

16799. The virtue of silence is a great piece of knowledge.   *Italian*

16800. There is no virtue in a promise unless it be kept.   *Danish*

16801. There is often virtue where no one would think it.   *Norwegian*

16802. There's virtue in a man's face.
                                  French

16803. To fall into mud is not a virtue, but it is a disgrace to remain there.
                                  Russian

16804. To walk in the path of virtue for ten years is not enough; to do evil for a single day is too much.   *Chinese*

16805. Virtue alone leads to nobility.
German

16806. Virtue and a trade are the best portion for children. *English*

16807. Virtue and beauty are a blessed association. *Slovakian*

16808. Virtue and morality keep similar company. *Burmese*

16809. Virtue consists in action.
Dutch

16810. Virtue flourishes in misfortune.
German

16811. Virtue has all things in itself.
English

16812. Virtue is but skin deep.
American

16813. Virtue is its own reward.
English

16814. Virtue is not an orphan, it will always have neighbors. *Japanese*

16815. Virtue is not knowing but doing. *Japanese*

16816. Virtue is superior to rank.
Indian (Tamil)

16817. Virtue is the mother of all happiness. *Welsh*

16818. Virtue is the only true nobility.
English

16819. Virtue is the support of dignity.
Indian (Tamil)

16820. Virtue knocks beauty dead.
Vietnamese

16821. Virtue means sweat. *Greek*

16822. Virtue never grows old.
English

16823. Virtue praised increases.
English

16824. Virtue subdues power.
German

16825. Virtue, wealth, and pleasure are not common to all. *Indian (Tamil)*

16826. Virtue which parleys is near a surrender. *English*

VISIT

16827. A short visit is best and that not too often. *Irish*

16828. Short visits make long friends.
English

16829. When someone comes to pay you a visit, he does so for a purpose.
Maltese

VISITING

16830. It's nice visiting, but better at home. *Russian*

VISITOR

16831. In the planting season visitors come singly; in harvest time in crowds.
Australian (Maori)

16832. One can't go to bed when a visitor stays late. *Burmese*

16833. The visitor is under the rule of the visited one. *Moroccan*

VODKA

16834. Vodka is aunt to wine.
Russian

VOICE

16835. One voice, no voice. *Italian*

16836. The people's voice, God's voice.
French

16837. The voice of the ass is not heard in heaven. *Rumanian*

16838. The voice of the people is the drum of God. *Indian (Hindustani)*

16839. The voice of the people, the voice of God. *English*

16840. The voice of truth is easily known. *African (Wolof)*

16841. Two voices cannot enter one ear. *Hebrew*

VOW

16842. Break not your vows.   *Irish*

16843. Men's vows are women's traitors.   *English*

VULTURE

16844. The vulture catches not the fly.
                                     Turkish

16845. The vulture has not a good name and its body has not a good smell.
                          African (Ashanti)

16846. The vulture scents the carcass, however high in the air he may be.
                          African (Yoruba)

16847. Where there is meat, the vultures congregate.   *African (Bemba)*

W

WAGE

16848. He who takes wages for work must needs perform it.

African (Fulani)

WAGER

16849. A wager is a fool's argument.

Scottish

WAGON

16850. Empty wagons make most noise. *Danish*

16851. The empty wagon must make room for the full one. *German*

16852. The wagon must go whither the horses draw it. *Danish*

16853. When the wagon is tilting everybody gives it a shove. *Danish*

WAIT

16854. He who can wait obtains what he wishes. *Italian*

WAITING

16855. Waiting is more grievous than fire. *Turkish*

WALK

16856. Before you walk you have to creep. *Jamaican*

16857. He wisely walks that does safely go. *English*

16858. If you walk straight, you will not stumble. *Yiddish*

16859. We must walk before we run.

English

WALKER

16860. Even a slow walker will arrive.

African (Ovambo)

WALL

16861. A white wall is a fool's paper.

English

16862. Bare walls make giddy housewives. *English*

16863. Even a wall may have ears.

Indian (Tamil)

16864. Even walls have ears. *Russian*

16865. If you see a wall inclining, run from under it. *Egyptian*

16866. It is bad to lean against a falling wall. *Danish*

16867. It is evil running against a stone wall. *English*

16868. Raise a wall of mortar and stone between the holy man and the saintly woman. *Mexican*

16869. Walls have ears. *English*

16870. Walls have ears, paper sliding doors have eyes. *Japanese*

16871. Walls have ears, wine bottles have mouths. *Japanese*

16872. Walls have mice and mice have ears. *Iranian*

16873. Walls sink and dunghills rise. *Spanish*

16874. You can't build a wall with just one stone. *Greek*

WALLET

16875. A beggar's wallet is never full. *Portuguese*

16876. As the wallet grows, so do the needs. *Yiddish*

16877. The beggar's wallet has no bottom. *Italian*

WALNUT

16878. All's not a walnut that's round. *Iranian*

16879. The hardest walnut has the smallest kernel. *Slovenian*

WALNUT TREE

16880. He who plants a walnut tree, expects not to eat of the fruit. *English*

WANDERER

16881. The early wanderer found a turtle. *African (Ovambo)*

WANT (noun)

16882. For want of a nail the shoe is lost; for want of a shoe the horse is lost; for want of a horse the rider is lost. *English*

16883. Want and necessity break faith and oaths. *Danish*

16884. Want is the whetstone of wit. *English*

16885. Want makes sadness. *Irish*

16886. Want makes strife. *English*

16887. Want of care admits despair. *English*

16888. Want of care does us more damage than want of knowledge. *English*

16889. Want of money, want of comfort. *English*

WANT (verb)

16890. If you want something, you have to work for it! *Yiddish*

16891. What is not wanted is not turned back for. *African (Ashanti)*

WAR

16892. At the wars do as they do at the wars. *French*

16893. Fiercer war, sooner peace. *American*

16894. He that makes a good war makes a good peace. *English*

16895. He that preaches war is the devil's chaplain. *English*

16896. He who cannot stand the smell of gunpowder should not engage in war. *Yiddish*

16897. In the war of love who flees conquers. *Italian*

16898. In war all suffer defeat, even the victors. *Swedish*

16899. Many return from the war who cannot give an account of the battle. *Italian*

16900. May he who asks for war have it in his own home. *Serbo-Croatian*

16901. No war is more bitter than the war of friends, but it does not last long. *Irish*

16902. The fear of war is worse than war itself. *Italian*

16903. There have been few wars which did not originate through priests or women. *Czech*

16904. War among grasshoppers delights the crow. *African (Swahili)*

16905. War and physics are governed by the eye. *English*

16906. War and sympathy do not exist at the same time. *German*

16907. War at the beginning is better than peace at the end. *Iranian*

16908. War begun, hell unchained. *Italian*

16909. War brings peace. *German*

16910. War does not look at the ground. *African (Jabo)*

16911. War, hunting, and love are as full of troubles as pleasures. *English*

16912. War is blind. *African (Swahili)*

16913. War is death's feast. *English*

16914. War is pleasant to those who have not tried it. *German*

16915. War makes robbers, peace hangs them. *French*

16916. War makes thieves, and peace hangs them. *English*

16917. War must be waged by waking men. *English*

16918. What is gained in war is eaten in war. *Finnish*

16919. When war begins Hell opens. *English*

16920. When war has come, rumors have come. *African (Ashanti)*

WARE

16921. Ask the seller if his ware be bad. *English*

16922. Bad ware is never cheap. *French*

16923. Good wares make a quick market. *Scottish*

16924. Good wares praise themselves. *Russian*

16925. He that sells wares for words must live by the loss. *English*

16926. Ill ware is never cheap. *English*

16927. Pleasing ware is half sold. *English*

16928. Wares which cannot sell themselves need advertising. *Slovenian*

16929. When the wares are gone, shut up the shop windows. *English*

WARM (adjective)

16930. He that is warm thinks all so. *English*

WARM (verb)

16931. He warms too near that burns. *English*

16932. Some who mean only to warm, burn themselves. *French*

WARN

16933. Be warned by others' harms. *English*

16934. Half warned, half armed. *English*

16935. Once warned, twice armed. *English*

WARNING

16936. Happy he who can take warning from the mishaps of others. *Danish*

WARRIOR

16937. A warrior deems life a light thing when compared to honor. *Japanese*

16938. No warrior without hardships. *African (Ovambo)*

WASP

16939. The wasp makes not honey. *Turkish*

16940. Wasps haunt the honeypot.
English

WASTE (noun)
16941. Willful waste makes woeful want. *English*

WASTE (verb)
16942. Waste not, want not. *English*

WASTEFULNESS
16943. Unless there is wastefulness there is no deficiency. *Japanese*

WASTING
16944. Wasting is a bad habit, sparing a sure income. *Dutch*

WATCH (noun)
16945. Bad watch often feeds the wolf.
French

16946. Good watch prevents harm.
Scottish

16947. Good watch prevents misfortune. *English*

WATCH (verb)
16948. To him who watches, everything reveals itself. *Italian*

16949. Who watches not catches not.
Dutch

WATCHING
16950. Good watching drives away ill luck. *French*

WATCHMAN
16951. It is for the watchman to watch, but it is also for the thief to steal.
Lebanese

WATER
16952. A trickle of water is better than no water. *African (Ovambo)*

16953. A very little water is a sea to an ant. *Pashto*

16954. All the water in the sea cannot wash out this stain. *English*

16955. Although cold water be heated, it will quench fire. *Indian (Tamil)*

16956. Any water puts out fire.
French

16957. Any water suits a thirsty horse.
Serbo-Croatian

16958. As good water goes by the mill as drives it. *English*

16959. As the water level sinks the stones are exposed. *Chinese*

16960. As water lends itself to the shape of the vessel which contains it, so a man is influenced by his good or bad friends. *Japanese*

16961. As water runs towards the shore, so does money towards the rich man's hand. *Danish*

16962. Before one comes out of water one does not squeeze. *African (Hausa)*

16963. Cast not out the foul water till you bring in the clean. *Scottish*

16964. Clear water is not wanted for quenching fire. *African (Ga)*

16965. Deep waters flow slowly.
Chinese

16966. Dirty water does not wash clean. *Italian*

16967. Dirty water will quench fire.
American

16968. Distant water cannot quench a fire nearby. *Chinese*

16969. Distant water will not extinguish the neighborhood fire.
Japanese

16970. Don't cross the water unless you see the bottom. *Italian*

16971. Don't pour cold water on cooked food. *Armenian*

16972. Don't pour water on a drowned mouse. *English*

16973. Don't pour water on a drowning dog. *Philippine*

16974. Don't put water into somebody else's wine. *Greek*

16975. Don't throw away dirty water till you have got clean. *English*

16976. Don't throw out even dirty water until you have the clean water in. *Irish*

16977. Everyone draws the water to his own mill. *French*

16978. Everyone wishes to bring water to his own mill and leave his neighbor's dry. *Spanish*

16979. Foul water is thrown down the sink. *English*

16980. Foul water will quench fire as well as fair. *English*

16981. From one deep ditch comes more water than from ten shallow ones. *Yiddish*

16982. Gently flowing water will hollow even a rock. *Indian (Tamil)*

16983. He knows the water best who has waded through it. *Danish*

16984. He who fetches water breaks the pot. *African (Oji)*

16985. He who has waded knows the water. *Norwegian*

16986. He who pours water hastily into a bottle spills more than goes in. *Spanish*

16987. He who would have clear water should go to the fountainhead. *Italian*

16988. Hot water is no playground for a frog. *African (Fulani)*

16989. If plain water is satisfying enough, then the fish would not take the hook. *African (Ashanti)*

16990. If the water is too clear, no fish lives in it. *Korean*

16991. If there is no water in the stream, no need to roll up your trousers. *Armenian*

16992. If water is too clear, it will contain no fish. *Chinese*

16993. If you go first you will not drink muddy water. *African (Ovambo)*

16994. If you want clear water, draw it from the spring. *Portuguese*

16995. If you want clear water, you must go to the head of the well. *English*

16996. In fleeing from the water do not run into the fire. *American*

16997. In the deepest water is the best fishing. *English*

16998. It is difficult to gather up spilled water. *Chinese*

16999. Much water goes by the miller when he sleeps. *Scottish*

17000. Much water passes by the mill that the miller perceives not. *Italian*

17001. Much water runs by while the miller sleeps. *Danish*

17002. Muddy water won't do for a mirror. *Italian*

17003. Never pour water on a drowned mouse. *Scottish*

17004. No matter how muddy the water, it will quench the fire. *Rumanian*

17005. One should fish where the water is running. *Vietnamese*

17006. Putting the water back in the well is not waste. *African (Hausa)*

17007. Running water carries no poison. *Italian*

17008. Running water does not get stale. *Japanese*

17009. Running water takes no defilement. *Turkish*

17010. Shallow waters make a great noise. *Irish*

17011. Soft water constantly striking the hard stone wears it at last. *Portuguese*

17012. Spilled water is not picked up again. *African (Bemba)*

17013. Spilled water never returns to its tray. *Japanese*

17014. Stagnant water grows stinking. *German*

17015. Stagnant water has an evil smell. *Greek*

17016. Still water breeds vermin. *Italian*

17017. Still waters become stagnant. *Iranian*

17018. Still waters can burst dams. *Russian*

17019. Still waters run deep. *English*

17020. Still waters turn no mills. *English*

17021. Store up the water while it rains. *Burmese*

17022. Swim quietly in shallow water, lest the water will splash and blind you. *Hawaiian*

17023. Take heed of still waters, the quick pass away. *English*

17024. The first drink of cold water after intoxication is unknown to the teetotaler. *Japanese*

17025. The water of a well always drawn springs up afresh. *Indian (Tamil)*

17026. The water of all brooks must empty into the river. *Philippine*

17027. The water of even the great ocean comes from one drop at a time. *Japanese*

17028. The water runs while the miller sleeps. *Danish*

17029. The water spreads and spreads but the canoe lands at last. *African (Jabo)*

17030. The water that comes from the same spring cannot be fresh and salt both. *English*

17031. There is no water without waves. *African (Swahili)*

17032. Throwing water over yourself once won't get rid of the dirt. *African (Hausa)*

17033. To pour out water is easy, to gather it up is difficult. *Chinese*

17034. To the heavy drinker on a-wakening, water tastes like nectar. *Japanese*

17035. Trust not still water nor a silent man. *Danish*

17036. Wade not in unknown waters. *English*

17037. Water afar does not quench a fire at hand. *Italian*

17038. Water afar off quenches not fire. *English*

17039. Water at a distance is not available in an emergency. *Indian (Tamil)*

17040. Water can drown the ferryman, much more the learner. *African (Hausa)*

17041. Water can never be forced into a solid bamboo. *Burmese*

17042. Water can support a ship, and water can upset it. *Chinese*

17043. Water comes where water has been. *Swedish*

17044. Water does not boil if taken away from fire. *African (Swahili)*

17045. Water doesn't flow under a rock which is lying on the ground. *Russian*

17046. Water doesn't refuse to go down, nor smoke to go up. *Malagasy*

17047. Water does not rise above its source. *Philippine*

17048. Water, fire, and soldiers quickly make room.   *English*

17049. Water flows, the rocks remain.
Rumanian

17050. Water flows to the low ground.
Turkish

17051. Water from a salt well puts out a house on fire.   *African (Ovambo)*

17052. Water in peace is better than wine in war.   *German*

17053. Water is a good servant.
English

17054. Water is as dangerous as commodious.   *English*

17055. Water is not carried out in a sieve.   *Turkish*

17056. Water is the strongest drink; it drives mills.   *German*

17057. Water may flow in a thousand channels, but it all returns to the sea.
Chinese

17058. Water never rises above its level.
American

17059. Water past will not turn the mill.   *Spanish*

17060. Water, smoke, and a vicious woman drive men out of the house.
Italian

17061. Water, though hot, is still nothing but water.   *Chinese*

17062. Water washes everything.
Portuguese

17063. We never know the worth of water till the well is dry.   *English*

17064. What water gives, water takes away.   *Portuguese*

17065. When circumstances are favorable water will flow uphill.
Burmese

17066. When you drink the water, remember the spring.   *Chinese*

17067. Where the water is shallow no vessel will ride.   *English*

17068. Where the water recedes, there is a crocodile.   *African (Bemba)*

17069. Where water has been, there it will be; where money once went, there will it go again.   *Russian*

17070. Where water has been, water will come again.   *German*

17071. Where water once has flowed it will flow again.   *Serbo-Croatian*

17072. Wherever water flows it will find a way.   *Russian*

17073. Without someone the water can't be sanctified.   *Russian*

17074. You can never divide water in the wooden bowl.   *Philippine*

17075. You cannot do without water, even if it drowned your child.
African (Ovambo)

17076. You cannot draw water with a sieve.   *Hebrew*

17077. You must drink the water of the river you are traveling on.   *Russian*

WATERFALL

17078. What the waterfall brings the stream carries away.   *Finnish*

WATERMELON

17079. A watermelon does not break knives, nor does a cabbage bend swords.   *Lebanese*

17080. A watermelon will not ripen in your armpit.   *Armenian*

17081. Two watermelons do not go under one armpit.   *Turkish*

17082. You can't carry two watermelons in one hand.   *Armenian*

WATERWHEEL

17083. A waterwheel profits from the urine of a mouse.   *Armenian*

WAVE

17084. Don't let high waves scare you to lose the oars.   *Vietnamese*

17085. One wave thrusts out another.
American

17086. The waves do not rise but when the winds blow. *American*

WAX

17087. Soft wax will take any impression. *English*

17088. The wax hardens when it's away from the fire. *Burmese*

WAY

17089. A ready way to lose your friend is to lend him money. *English*

17090. Better ask twice than lose your way once. *Danish*

17091. Every way up has its way down. *Yiddish*

17092. He knows the way best who went there last. *Norwegian*

17093. He that goes the contrary way must go over it twice. *English*

17094. He who asks his way will never go astray. *Philippine*

17095. He who does not lose his way by night will not lose his way by day. *African (Hausa)*

17096. He who rises early finds the way short. *African (Wolof)*

17097. If shy to ask, you will lose your way. *Malaysian*

17098. It is a great way to the bottom of the sea. *English*

17099. It's a long way from words to deeds. *Latvian*

17100. It is not easy to show the way to a blind man. *Italian*

17101. Let those who know the way go before. *Norwegian*

17102. The longest way round is the nearest way home. *English*

17103. The shortest way is the best way. *American*

17104. The smoothest way is full of stones. *Yiddish*

17105. The way to be gone is not to stay here. *English*

17106. The way to be safe is never to be secure. *English*

17107. The way to bliss lies not on beds of down. *English*

17108. The way to heaven is full of obstacles and brambles. *Philippine*

17109. The way to heaven is not strewn with roses. *Philippine*

17110. The way to live much is to begin to live well betimes. *English*

17111. There are endless ways to lead to death. *Indian (Tamil)*

17112. There are more ways to the wood than one. *English*

17113. There is no short cut of a way without some ill way. *English*

17114. When a way is long you shorten it with your feet, not with a hatchet. *African (Oji)*

17115. When there is a way out, there is no need for fear. *Yiddish*

17116. Who leaves the old way for the new will find himself deceived. *English*

WEAK

17117. The weak may stand the strong in stead. *English*

WEAKER

17118. The weaker has the worse. *English*

WEAKEST

17119. The weakest goes to the wall. *Scottish*

WEAL

17120. No weal without woe. *English*

17121. Whom weal pricks, sorrow comes after and licks.   *English*

WEALTH

17122. A man's wealth is his enemy.   *English*

17123. Bear wealth; poverty will bear itself.   *English*

17124. By labor comes wealth.   *African (Yoruba)*

17125. Great wealth and content seldom live together.   *English*

17126. Great wealth, great care.   *Dutch*

17127. Great wealth will marry off even an old woman.   *Yiddish*

17128. He that marries for wealth sells his liberty.   *English*

17129. If there is wealth, there is joy.   *Philippine*

17130. Ill-gotten wealth and illicit pleasure are both bad.   *Indian (Tamil)*

17131. In wealth beware of woe.   *English*

17132. Inherited wealth has no blessing.   *African (Swahili)*

17133. It will do no good to have wealth that you won't use.   *Malagasy*

17134. Little avails wealth, where there is no health.   *English*

17135. Much wealth brings many enemies.   *African (Swahili)*

17136. The best wealth is health.   *Welsh*

17137. The greatest wealth is contentment with a little.   *English*

17138. The rich man's wealth is enjoyed by crafty tradesmen.   *Greek*

17139. The rich man's wealth swallows the morsel of the poor.   *Rumanian*

17140. The unjustly acquired wealth never reaches the third generation.   *Serbo-Croatian*

17141. The wealth which enslaves the owner is not wealth.   *African (Swahili)*

17142. There is no wealth where there are no children.   *African (Jabo)*

17143. There is no wealth without pouring out one purse into another.   *Serbo-Croatian*

17144. Wealth and content are not always bedfellows.   *American*

17145. Wealth and happiness, like smoke, vanish.   *Philippine*

17146. Wealth can be concealed, but not poverty.   *Finnish*

17147. Wealth can be sought, but reputation never.   *Philippine*

17148. Wealth counts not so much as good will nor as knowledge and pleasant speech.   *Greek*

17149. Wealth is a fine thing, but to find an heir is not easy.   *African (Ashanti)*

17150. Wealth is best known by want.   *English*

17151. Wealth is cautious.   *Greek*

17152. Wealth is enemy to health.   *English*

17153. Wealth is invited but poverty invites itself.   *African (Shona)*

17154. Wealth is like a pool: as soon as you dig a channel, it all runs out.   *Rumanian*

17155. Wealth is like rheum, it falls on the weakest parts.   *English*

17156. Wealth is like smoke.   *African (Fulani)*

17157. Wealth is not his who has it, but his who enjoys it.   *English*

17158. Wealth is not picked up like lice.   *African (Bemba)*

17159. Wealth is of no use to the dead.
Philippine

17160. Wealth is short-lived.
African (Jabo)

17161. Wealth is the poison of pleasure and the root of sorrows.
Indian (Hindi)

17162. Wealth makes wit waver.
English

17163. Wealth makes worship.
English

17164. Wealth may be bequeathed to the children but it never reaches the grandchildren.
Greek

17165. Wealth will not keep death away.
Welsh

17166. Wealth without learning is like beauty without chastity.
Indian (Tamil)

17167. When there is wealth, there is power.
Indian (Tamil)

17168. When you have wealth and fame, even strangers gather around; in time of poverty and lowliness, even relatives depart from you.
Japanese

17169. Where wealth is established it is difficult for friendship to find a place.
Russian

17170. Where wealth is, there sorrow is.
Indian (Hindi)

17171. Where wealth, there friends.
English

17172. Who seeks for wealth without previous wealth is like him who carries water in a sieve.
Egyptian

WEAPON

17173. A weapon in the workroom will not help you when you are to be mauled.
African (Ovambo)

17174. A weapon is an enemy even to its owner.
Turkish

17175. A weapon not kept polished will become rusty.
Indian (Tamil)

17176. All weapons of war cannot arm fear.
English

17177. Mere weapons are ineffective.
Indian (Tamil)

17178. The best weapon is education.
Welsh

17179. They who fight with golden weapons are pretty sure to prove their right.
Dutch

17180. Weapons bode peace.
English

WEAR

17181. Better to wear out than to rust out.
English

WEARER

17182. The wearer best knows where the shoe pinches him.
Irish

WEARY

17183. Everyone is weary—the poor in seeking, the rich in keeping, the good in learning.
English

17184. Never be weary of well doing.
English

WEATHER

17185. Clean out the drainpipes while the weather is good.
Chinese

17186. Cursing the weather is bad farming.
English

17187. Everyone can navigate in fine weather.
Italian

17188. Ill weather comes unsent for.
English

17189. Ill weather is seen soon enough when it comes.
English

17190. Look at the weather when you step out; look at men's faces when you step in.
Chinese

17191. Many can brook the weather that love not the wind.   *English*

17192. Sail when the weather is fair; you do not know what the morrow will bring.   *Greek*

17193. Weather, wind, women, and fortune change like the moon. *French*

WEATHERWISE

17194. Some are weatherwise, some are otherwise.   *American*

WEAVER

17195. Even a weaver is a master in his own home.   *Hebrew*

WEB

17196. The spider's web lets the rat escape and catches the fly.   *Spanish*

WED

17197. Early wed, early dead. *English*

17198. He that weds before he's wise shall die before he thrive.   *English*

WEDDING

17199. A poor wedding is a prologue to misery.   *English*

17200. A wedding lasts a day or two, but the misery forever.   *Czech*

17201. After the wedding it's too late to have regrets.   *Yiddish*

17202. He who dances well goes from wedding to wedding.   *Spanish*

17203. If you dance at every wedding, you'll weep at every funeral. *Yiddish*

17204. One wedding begets another.   *English*

17205. There is no wedding which ever lacked spectators.   *African (Zulu)*

17206. There is no wedding without laughter and no death without tears.   *Rumanian*

17207. Wedding and ill wintering tame both man and beast.   *English*

17208. Without cake there is no wedding.   *Polish*

17209. You can't dance at two weddings at the same time!   *Yiddish*

WEDDING RING

17210. As your wedding ring wears, your cares will wear away.   *English*

WEDGE

17211. A blunt wedge will do it, where sometimes a sharp axe will not.   *English*

17212. A wedge is dislodged by a wedge.   *Russian*

17213. Hard wedges are needed for hard tree stumps.   *Norwegian*

17214. Little by little the wedge goes into the timber.   *Welsh*

17215. One wedge drives another.   *German*

17216. The wedge must go where the axe drives.   *Estonian*

17217. There goes the wedge where the beetle drives it.   *English*

17218. To a hard knot a hard wedge.   *Spanish*

WEDLOCK

17219. Wedlock is a padlock. *English*

17220. Wedlock is like an eel basket— those who are out of it want to get in, and those who are in want to get out.   *Swedish*

17221. Wedlock rides in the saddle and repentance on the crupper.   *French*

WEED (noun)

17222. A weed loves the field, a lazy man loves eating. *African (Ovambo)*

17223. Even downtrodden weeds will bear flowers. *Japanese*

17224. Ill weeds are not hurt by frost. *Portuguese*

17225. Ill weeds grow apace. *English*

17226. Ill weeds grow the fastest and last the longest. *Danish*

17227. One ill weed mars a whole pot of pottage. *English*

17228. The evil weed produces the largest number of seeds. *Maltese*

17229. The weeds overgrow the corn. *English*

17230. To the merry man every weed is a flower; to the afflicted man every flower is a weed. *Finnish*

17231. Weeds grow best in good ground. *Swedish*

17232. Weeds never die. *German*

17233. Weeds want no sowing. *English*

WEED (verb)

17234. He that neglects to weed will surely come to need. *American*

WEENING

17235. Weening is not measure. *English*

WEIGH

17236. First weigh, then venture. *German*

17237. Weigh justly and sell dearly. *English*

17238. Weigh not what you give, but what is given you. *English*

WEIGHT

17239. Good weight and measure is heaven's treasure. *English*

17240. Great weights hang on small wires. *English*

17241. Weight and measure take away strife. *English*

WELCOME

17242. A hearty welcome is the best cheer. *English*

17243. He that is welcome fares well. *English*

17244. Such a welcome, such a farewell. *English*

WELL (adverb)

17245. All is well save that the worst piece is in the midst. *English*

17246. All is well that ends well. *English*

17247. All is well with him who is beloved of his neighbors. *English*

17248. Well is that well does. *English*

17249. Well paid is well sold. *English*

WELL (noun)

17250. A well from which you drink, throw not a stone into it. *Egyptian*

17251. A well is not dug with a needle. *Armenian*

17252. A well is not to be filled with dew. *Egyptian*

17253. Don't spit in the well, you may have to drink the water. *Russian*

17254. Do not spit into a well; you do not know when you will drink out of it yourself. *Czech*

17255. Drawn wells are seldom dry. *English*

17256. Drawn wells have sweetest water. *English*

17257. He who sits in a well to look at the sky can see but little. *Chinese*

17258. It is a bad well into which one must put water. *Dutch*

17259. It is a bad well that needs water to be carried to it. *Danish*

17260. Many wells, many buckets.
English

17261. One does not descend into a well by a rotten rope. *Turkish*

17262. The more a well is drawn, the better the spring. *Indian (Tamil)*

17263. The more the well is used, the more water it yields. *German*

17264. When the well is full it will run over. *English*

17265. You never miss the water till the well has run dry. *Irish*

WENCH

17266. Young wenches make old wenches. *English*

WHALE

17267. In a fight between whales, the backs of shrimps are burst. *Korean*

WHEAT

17268. No wheat without its chaff. *English*

17269. The way of the wheat is through the mill. *Pashto*

17270. There is no wheat without chaff. *Hebrew*

17271. Wheat has chaff on every grain. *Indian (Hindi)*

WHEEL

17272. A fifth wheel to a cart is but an encumbrance. *Spanish*

17273. A turning wheel does not get rusty. *Greek*

17274. A wheel doesn't turn if it isn't greased. *Greek*

17275. From the place where the front wheel of the carriage has passed, the hind wheel also passes. *Turkish*

17276. He who greases his wheels, helps his oxen. *English*

17277. If a water wheel exerts itself, it has no time to get frozen. *Japanese*

17278. It is the master wheel that makes the mill go round. *French*

17279. Oil the wheels if you want the cart to run lightly. *Rumanian*

17280. The wheel always comes full circle. *Hebrew*

17281. The worse the wheel, the more it creaks. *Dutch*

17282. The worst wheel always creaks most. *French*

17283. The worst wheel makes most noise. *Dutch*

17284. The worst wheel of a cart creaks most. *English*

17285. The worst wheel of a cart is the one that makes most noise. *Rumanian*

17286. When one wheel in the clock stands still, all stand still. *Swedish*

WHELP

17287. When the whelp plays, the old dog grins. *English*

WHET

17288. A whet is no let. *English*

WHETSTONE

17289. A whetstone can't itself cut, yet it makes tools cut. *English*

WHILE

17290. Stay a while, and lose a mile. *Dutch*

WHIM

17291. The whims of the living become the bequests of the dead. *Greek*

WHIP

17292. A whip for a fool and a rod for a school are always in good season. *English*

17293. It is enough to show a whip to a beaten dog. *Czech*

17294. Though the whip is long it does not reach the belly of the horse. *Japanese*

17295. Whip and whirr never made good fur. *English*

WHISPER (noun)

17296. A whisper is a spoken word. *African (Shona)*

17297. A whisper is louder than a shout. *Philippine*

WHISPER (verb)

17298. He who whispers, lies. *Danish*

WHISTLE (noun)

17299. A new whistle peels off the lip. *African (Bemba)*

17300. It isn't every kind of wood that a whistle can be made from. *Latvian*

WHISTLE (verb)

17301. You can't whistle and drink at the same time. *English*

WHOLEHEARTEDNESS

17302. Wholeheartedness will pierce a rock. *Japanese*

WHORE

17303. A whore in a fine dress is like a clean entry to a dirty house. *English*

17304. A whore in a fine dress is like a dirty house with a clean door. *Scottish*

17305. A young whore, an old saint. *English*

17306. Once a whore and ever a whore. *English*

17307. One whore calls another whore names. *Maltese*

17308. Whores affect not you but your money. *English*

17309. Whores and thieves go by the clock. *English*

WHOREDOM

17310. Whoredom and grace dwelt never in one place. *Scottish*

17311. Whoredom and thieving are never long concealed. *Spanish*

WHORING

17312. Whoring and bawdry too often end in beggary. *English*

WHY

17313. Every why has its wherefore. *English*

WICKED (people)

17314. The wicked fare well in this world; the saints in the life to come. *Yiddish*

17315. The wicked shun the light as the devil does the cross. *Dutch*

WICKEDNESS

17316. Wickedness with beauty is the devil's hook baited. *English*

WIDE

17317. Wide will wear but narrow will tear. *English*

WIDOW

17318. A good occasion for courtship is when the widow returns from the funeral. *English*

17319. A rich widow weeps with one eye and laughs with the other. *Portuguese*

17320. A widow can be wooed on her return from the funeral. *Philippine*

17321. He that marries a widow and three children marries four thieves. *English*

17322. He that marries a widow and two daughters has three back doors to his house.   *Scottish*

17323. He that marries a widow, marries a pokeful of lawsuits.   *Scottish*

17324. He that will wed a widow must come day and night.   *English*

17325. He that woos a widow must woo day and night.   *Scottish*

17326. He who marries a widow will often have a dead man's head thrown in his dish.   *English*

17327. He who marries a widow with three children marries four thieves.   *Danish*

17328. It is as easy to marry a widow as to put a halter on a dead horse.   *English*

17329. It is as easy to wed a widow as to catch a dead horse.   *English*

17330. It's dangerous marrying a widow because she has cast her rider.   *English*

17331. Long a widow weds with shame.   *English*

17332. Marry a widow before she leaves mourning.   *English*

17333. When one comes to comfort a young widow, he does not mean to perform a good deed.   *Yiddish*

17334. Widows are always rich.   *English*

17335. Widows will be widows.   *American*

17336. Woo the widow while she is in mourning.   *German*

WIFE (see WIVES)

17337. A bad wife drinks a big share of her own bad buttermilk.   *Irish*

17338. A bad wife is a poor harvest for sixty years.   *Japanese*

17339. A bad wife is like a weed that kills the crop.   *Philippine*

17340. A bad wife takes advice from everyone but her own husband.   *Irish*

17341. A bad wife will lead her family to downfall.   *Korean*

17342. A debtor's wife speaks the voice of her husband.   *African (Annang)*

17343. A fair wife and a frontier castle breed quarrels.   *English*

17344. A fair wife without a fortune is a fine house without furniture.   *English*

17345. A faithful wife does not marry again.   *Japanese*

17346. A good wife and a good cat are best at home.   *English*

17347. A good wife and health is a man's best wealth.   *English*

17348. A good wife makes a good husband.   *English*

17349. A graceful wife lends grace to her husband.   *Hebrew*

17350. A man without a wife is a man without thoughts.   *Finnish*

17351. A nice wife and a back door often make a rich man poor.   *English*

17352. A nice wife and a back door will soon make a rich man poor.   *Scottish*

17353. A pretty wife is half a livelihood.   *Yiddish*

17354. A second wife is like a wooden leg.   *Yiddish*

17355. A shrewish wife can also be right.   *Yiddish*

17356. A shrewish wife is a scourge.   *Yiddish*

17357. A wife, a razor, and a horse are things not to be lent.   *Polish*

17358. A wife and floor matting are better when new.   *Japanese*

17359. A wife brings but two good days—her wedding day and death day. *English*

17360. A wife gives beauty to a house. *Indian (Tamil)*

17361. A wife is a household treasure. *Japanese*

17362. A wife is a little dove and a little devil. *Yiddish*

17363. A wife is like a blanket; when you cover yourself with it, it irritates you, and yet if you cast it aside you feel cold. *African (Ashanti)*

17364. A wife isn't a mitten—you can't take her off your hand. *Russian*

17365. A wife is one's heart's delight. *Hebrew*

17366. A wife is sought for her virtue, a concubine for her beauty. *Chinese*

17367. A wife ought to have her will during life, because she cannot make one when she dies. *English*

17368. A wife should not hold converse with her husband's younger brother. *Chinese*

17369. A wife spoils a man's life. *Estonian*

17370. A young wife is an old man's post-horse to the grave. *German*

17371. A young wife is to an old man the horse on which he rides to hell. *Polish*

17372. A young wife, new bread, and green wood devastate a house. *Flemish*

17373. An obedient wife commands her husband. *English*

17374. Beating your wife with a paddle does not make the linen white. *Yiddish*

17375. Choose a wife from a position lower than your own, and choose friends from a higher status. *Japanese*

17376. Choose a wife to please yourself, not others. *Rumanian*

17377. Commend not your wife, wine, nor house. *English*

17378. Curse not your wife in the evening, or you will have to sleep alone. *Chinese*

17379. Do not belittle the wife, she is the home. *African (Ovambo)*

17380. Do not choose your wife at a dance, but on the field among the harvesters. *Czech*

17381. Do not govern your wife with your eyes but with your ears. *Estonian*

17382. Do not praise your wife before seven years. *Russian*

17383. Do not send your wife alone to a wedding. *Rumanian*

17384. Even a blind wife is better than no wife at all. *African (Ovambo)*

17385. He drives a good wagonful into his farm who gets a good wife. *Danish*

17386. He fasts enough whose wife scolds all dinnertime. *English*

17387. He that has a wife and children must not sit with his fingers in his mouth. *English*

17388. He that has a wife and children wants not business. *English*

17389. He that has a wife has a master. *Scottish*

17390. He that has a wife has strife. *English*

17391. He that has a wife is sure of strife. *French*

17392. He that has no wife, beats her often. *English*

17393. He that lets his wife go to every feast, and his horse drink at every water shall neither have good wife nor good horse. *English*

17394. He that loses his wife and six-pence has lost a farthing.   *English*

17395. He that marries a wife is happy for a month, but he that gets a fat benefice lives merrily all his life.
English

17396. He that speaks ill of his wife, dishonors himself.   *English*

17397. He that would an old wife wed must eat an apple before he goes to bed.
English

17398. He who does not honor his wife, dishonors himself.   *Spanish*

17399. He who has a good wife can bear any evil.   *Spanish*

17400. He who has a handsome wife, a castle on the frontier, or a vineyard on the roadside is never without war.
Spanish

17401. He who has no wife is for thrashing her daily; but he that has one takes care of her.   *Spanish*

17402. He who takes a wife takes a master.   *French*

17403. If the wife sins the husband is not innocent.   *Italian*

17404. If the wife wears the breeches, the husband must rock the cradle.
Hebrew

17405. If you're faithful to your wife, you'll have a healthy body.   *Yiddish*

17406. If you love your wife, praise her only when she is dead.   *Burmese*

17407. If you take a wife from hell, she will bring you back.   *American*

17408. If you want all the world to know, tell your wife.   *Estonian*

17409. In a beloved wife there is no evil.   *African (Jabo)*

17410. It is easy to take a wife, but hard to get rid of her.   *Serbo-Croatian*

17411. Leave her now and then if you would really love your wife.
Malaysian

17412. Love your wife like your soul, shake her like a pear tree.   *Russian*

17413. Neither reprove nor flatter your wife where any one hears or sees it.
Dutch

17414. Next to no wife a good wife is best.   *English*

17415. One's wife and one's stove stay at home.   *Latvian*

17416. Refuse a wife with one fault and take one with two.   *English*

17417. She who is the wife of one man cannot eat the rice of two.   *Chinese*

17418. Take a good wife even if you have to sell your pots and kettles.
Japanese

17419. The blind man's wife needs no painting.   *English*

17420. The cunning wife makes her husband her apron.   *English*

17421. The wife is the key of the house.
English

17422. The wife should be blind and the husband deaf.   *English*

17423. The wife that expects to have a good name is always at home as if she were lame.   *English*

17424. The wife wails and the dog whimpers and the child whines and poverty howls!   *Yiddish*

17425. There is but one good wife in the world, and every man enjoys her.
English

17426. There is but one good wife in the world and every man thinks he has her.   *Scottish*

17427. There's only one thing in the world better than a good wife—no wife.   *Irish*

17428. Though you may become the wife of a divorced man, don't become the wife of a widower.   *Japanese*

17429. What the good wife spares, the cat eats.   *English*

17430. When the wife is dumb and the husband deaf, there is peace between them.   *Rumanian*

17431. When the wife wants the husband to stay at home, she talks less and cleans more.   *Yiddish*

17432. When the wife wears the pants, the husband washes the floor.   *Yiddish*

17433. When the young wife gets into the house, the mother-in-law gets out of it.   *Vietnamese*

17434. When you have a pretty wife, you are a bad friend.   *Yiddish*

17435. When your wife is a woman of no morals, then she might as well be some one else's harlot.

African (Ashanti)

17436. Who beats his wife, beats his own head; who beats his mule, beats his purse.   *Rumanian*

17437. Who has a bad wife, his hell begins on earth.   *Dutch*

17438. Wife a mouse, quiet house; wife a cat, dreadful that.   *English*

17439. Wife and children are bills of charges.   *English*

17440. Wife and children are hostages given to fortune.   *English*

17441. Without a wife a house is the abode of a devil.   *Indian (Hindustani)*

17442. Your first wife is sent to you by God, the second by man, and the third by the devil.   *Russian*

WILD

17443. Wild and stout never wants a staff.   *English*

WILE

17444. Wiles often do what force can't.

English

WILL (noun)

17445. A dead man's will is the mirror of his life.   *Polish*

17446. A man's will is his heaven.

Danish

17447. A will is a will.   *American*

17448. Free will is worse than constraint.   *Russian*

17449. God's will is stronger than the emperor's.   *Serbo-Croatian*

17450. Good will should be taken for part payment.   *Scottish*

17451. He who would have his will let him cultivate patience.   *Welsh*

17452. Ill will never speaks well.

English

17453. One man's will is another man's wit.   *English*

17454. The will gives the work its name.   *German*

17455. The will is a good horse.

Welsh

17456. The will is taken for the deed.

French

17457. The will is the soul of the work.

German

17458. The will of man is his paradise, but it often becomes his hell.

Icelandic

17459. When it is God's will to plague a man, a mouse can bite him to death.

Dutch

17460. Where the will is ready, the feet are light.   *English*

17461. Where there's a will there are thousands of ruses; when there is none, then a thousand excuses.   *Malaysian*

17462. Where there's a will there's a way. *English*

17463. Will buys and money pays. *English*

17464. Will is power. *French*

17465. Will is the cause of woe. *English*

17466. Will will have will though will woe win. *English*

17467. With will one can do anything. *English*

WILL (verb)

17468. He that will not when he may, when he will shall have nay. *English*

WILLOW

17469. A willow will buy a horse before an oak will pay for a saddle. *English*

17470. Bend the willow while it is young. *Danish*

17471. Willows are never broken by snow. *Japanese*

17472. Willows are weak, yet serve to bind bigger wood. *Italian*

17473. Willows are weak, yet they bind other wood. *English*

WIN

17474. As won, so spent. *German*

17475. Win at first and lose at last. *English*

WIND

17476. A little wind kindles, much puts out the fire. *English*

17477. As the wind blows seek your shelter. *Scottish*

17478. As the wind, so the sail. *French*

17479. Don't love wind more than water. *Thai*

17480. Every wind blows not down the corn. *English*

17481. Every wind does not shake down the nut. *Italian*

17482. Every wind is ill to a broken ship. *English*

17483. Fast goes the wind, but faster goes the thought. *Philippine*

17484. He that weighs the wind must have a steady hand. *English*

17485. He who sows wind will reap typhoons. *Philippine*

17486. High winds blow on high hills. *English*

17487. If the wind blows, it enters at every crevice. *Egyptian*

17488. If the wind is not on your road, let it blow. *Greek*

17489. If there is no wind, the trees don't move. *Chinese*

17490. If you sow the wind, you will harvest a hurricane. *African (Swahili)*

17491. It's an ill wind that blows nobody good. *English*

17492. It's an ill wind that blows nowhere. *American*

17493. It is hard to sail without wind, and to grind without water. *Danish*

17494. It is when the wind is blowing that we see the skin of the fowl. *Haitian*

17495. Let the sail come down if the wind becomes strong. *Philippine*

17496. No wind can do him good who steers for no port. *French*

17497. One can't hinder the wind from blowing. *French*

17498. The wind blows as the sailors do not wish. *Egyptian*

17499. The wind blows not always west. *English*

17500. The wind gathers the clouds and it is also the wind that scatters them. *Rumanian*

17501. The wind in a man's face makes him wise. *English*

17502. The wind keeps not always in one quarter. *English*

17503. The wind that comes in through a crack is cold. *Japanese*

17504. The wind will fell an oak, but cannot destroy the reed. *Hungarian*

17505. There is no wall through which the wind cannot pass. *Chinese*

17506. Though the wind blows, the mountain does not move. *Japanese*

17507. To a crazy ship all winds are contrary. *English*

17508. What the wind brings it will also take away. *Armenian*

17509. When the wind blows fiercely the sea is gray. *Hawaiian*

17510. When there is no wind every man is a pilot. *French*

17511. When there's no wind, there's no quivering of the leaves. *Philippine*

17512. When there is wind in the clouds there are waves on the river. *Chinese*

17513. When there is wind outside, the garbage flies high. *Yiddish*

17514. Where there is no wind, bushes don't shake. *Pashto*

17515. Who spits against the wind, fouls his beard. *Dutch*

17516. Wind and fortune are not lasting. *Portuguese*

17517. Wind and good luck are seldom lasting. *Spanish*

17518. You can't catch the wind in a net. *English*

WINDMILL

17519. There's no turning a windmill with a pair of bellows. *Italian*

17520. Windmills are not driven by bellows. *German*

17521. You can't drive a windmill with a pair of bellows. *English*

WINDOW

17522. Better to fall from the window than the roof. *Italian*

WINE

17523. Better old wine than old strength. *Yiddish*

17524. Drink the wine, but not drunk by it. *Rumanian*

17525. Drink wine and let water go to the mill. *Italian*

17526. Each cup of wine and each bite of meat is destined from aforetime. *Chinese*

17527. Fine or not, it is my country's wine. *Chinese*

17528. Good wine and a pretty wife are two sweet poisons to a man. *Rumanian*

17529. Good wine is milk for the aged. *German*

17530. Good wine makes good blood. *Italian*

17531. Good wine makes the horse go. *French*

17532. Good wine needs no bush. *English*

17533. Good wine needs no crier. *Spanish*

17534. Good wine needs no sign. *French*

17535. Good wine praises itself. *Dutch*

17536. Good wine reddens the face of man; riches excite his heart.   *Chinese*

17537. Good wine ruins the purse, and bad wine the stomach.   *German*

17538. Good wine sells itself. *German*

17539. He that loves wine wants no woes.   *American*

17540. He who drinks wine will get drunk, he who rides a horse will sometimes fall.   *Serbo-Croatian*

17541. He who has wine says it is good.   *African (Ga)*

17542. He who likes drinking is always talking of wine.   *Italian*

17543. If you don't drink, the price of wine is of no interest.   *Chinese*

17544. In wine there is happiness.   *Hungarian*

17545. In wine there is truth. *English*

17546. One cup of wine takes away the whole of a person's bashfulness.   *Turkish*

17547. Over a glass of wine, you find many good friends.   *Yiddish*

17548. Serve wine to the man used to drinking it, and greens to the gardener.   *Hebrew*

17549. Since the wine is drawn it must be drunk.   *French*

17550. Spilled wine is worse than water.   *Scottish*

17551. Sweet is the wine but sour's the payment.   *Irish*

17552. Sweet wine makes sour vinegar.   *German*

17553. Sweetest wine makes sharpest vinegar.   *English*

17554. The wine is the master's, the goodness the drawer's.   *English*

17555. There is no wine without dregs.   *Rumanian*

17556. Thick wine is better than clear water.   *Italian*

17557. Though you drink wine, do not be drunk by wine.   *Japanese*

17558. Today's wine I drink today; tomorrow's sorrow I bear tomorrow.   *Chinese*

17559. When the wine goes in, the wit goes out.   *Dutch*

17560. When the wine is in the man, the wit is in the can.   *Dutch*

17561. When the wine is run out, you'd stop the leak.   *English*

17562. When wine comes to an end, so does conversation; when money comes to end, so do friends.   *Serbo-Croatian*

17563. When wine enters modesty departs.   *Italian*

17564. When wine sinks, words swim.   *English*

17565. Where the best wine grows, the worst is drunk.   *German*

17566. Where wine goes in, modesty goes out.   *German*

17567. Where wine is not common, commons must be sent.   *English*

17568. Who loves not wine, women, and song remains a fool his whole life long.   *German*

17569. Wine and late rising are short cuts to poverty.   *Japanese*

17570. Wine and wealth change wise men's manners.   *English*

17571. Wine and wenches empty men's purses.   *English*

17572. Wine and women make fools of everybody.   *German*

17573. Wine begins with formalities and ends in a riot.   *Japanese*

17574. Wine counsels seldom prosper.   *English*

17575. Wine does not intoxicate a man; he intoxicates himself. Men are not enticed by vice; they entice themselves.
Chinese

17576. Wine has drowned more men than the sea. *English*

17577. Wine in the bottle quenches not thirst. *English*

17578. Wine in, wit out. *English*

17579. Wine is a jewel-broom to sweep away sorrow. *Japanese*

17580. Wine is a turncoat—first a friend, then an enemy. *English*

17581. Wine is a whetstone to wit.
English

17582. Wine is lunatic water.
Japanese

17583. Wine is the best of all medicines and the worst of all poisons.
Japanese

17584. Wine is the key of all evil.
Moroccan

17585. Wine is the source of all medicines. *Japanese*

17586. Wine makes all sorts of creatures at table. *English*

17587. Wine makes old wives wenches.
English

17588. Wine neither keeps secrets nor fulfills promises. *English*

17589. Wine poured out is not wine swallowed. *French*

17590. Wine reveals a person's true heart. *Japanese*

17591. Wine should be taken in small doses, knowledge in large. *Chinese*

17592. Wine that costs nothing is digested before it be drunk. *English*

17593. Wine tops the list of all medicines. *Hebrew*

17594. Wine wears no breeches.
English

17595. Wine will not keep in a foul vessel. *French*

17596. Without wine in the bottle it is hard to have guests. *Chinese*

17597. You cannot know wine by the barrel. *English*

17598. You don't get drunk on wine which you do not drink. *Japanese*

WING

17599. Don't fly till your wings are feathered. *German*

17600. No flying without wings.
Scottish

WINNING

17601. All the winning is in the first buying. *Scottish*

17602. Too light winning makes the prize light. *English*

WINTER

17603. It is a hard winter when dogs eat dogs. *English*

17604. The winter asks you what you have done during the summer.
Latvian

17605. Winter pulls the mittens out of your pocket. *Estonian*

WINTER WEATHER

17606. Winter weather and women's thoughts change often. *English*

WISDOM

17607. A child's wisdom is also wisdom. *Yiddish*

17608. A woman's wisdom is at the end of her nose. *Japanese*

17609. A woman's wisdom is monkey wisdom. *Japanese*

17610. All wisdom is not taught in your school. *Hawaiian*

17611. Each one thinks much of his own wisdom, therefore the world is full of fools.   *Swedish*

17612. For every wagonload of wisdom there are two of stupidity.
                              Serbo-Croatian

17613. He has wisdom at will that brags not of his skill.   *English*

17614. He who rises early will gather wisdom.   *Danish*

17615. He who wants wisdom lives near a cunning person. *African (Zulu)*

17616. If there were wisdom in beards, goats would be prophets.   *Armenian*

17617. It is wisdom sometimes to seem a fool.   *English*

17618. It takes great wisdom to laugh at one's own misfortunes.
                              Indian (Hindi)

17619. Much wisdom is smothered in a poor man's head.   *Dutch*

17620. No wisdom like silence.
                                   English

17621. Not to speak is the flower of wisdom.   *Japanese*

17622. One cannot teach wisdom to a fool.   *African (Ovambo)*

17623. Poor folk's wisdom goes for little.   *Dutch*

17624. That is good wisdom which is wisdom in the end.   *Dutch*

17625. The beginning of wisdom is the fear of God.   *Irish*

17626. The best wisdom is ignorance of evil.   *Welsh*

17627. The wisdom of elders is better than the learning of youth. *Slovakian*

17628. There is no wisdom like silence.   *Welsh*

17629. Too much wisdom does not produce courage.   *Czech*

17630. Too much wisdom is akin to foolishness.   *Norwegian*

17631. Too much wisdom is folly.
                                   German

17632. Up to seventy years of age we learn wisdom and then we die fools.
                                  Yiddish

17633. What is not wisdom is danger.
                                  English

17634. When wisdom fails, luck helps.
                                   Danish

17635. Where wisdom doesn't go in it doesn't come out.   *Swedish*

17636. Wisdom adorns old age.
                                  Russian

17637. Wisdom and virtue are like the two wheels of a cart.   *Japanese*

17638. Wisdom cannot be bought for money.   *African (Ovambo)*

17639. Wisdom can't be purchased in the market.   *Yiddish*

17640. Wisdom comes with the years.
                                  Yiddish

17641. Wisdom gives wealth and honor.   *Indian (Tamil)*

17642. Wisdom goes beyond strength.
                                  English

17643. Wisdom in the man, patience in the wife, brings peace to the house and a happy life.   *Dutch*

17644. Wisdom is a good purchase, though we pay dear for it.   *English*

17645. Wisdom is a precious thing.
                                  Yiddish

17646. Wisdom is better than sanctimony.   *Yiddish*

17647. Wisdom is easy to carry but difficult to load.   *Czech*

17648. Wisdom is in age.   *American*

17649. Wisdom is in the head and not in the beard.   *Swedish*

17650. Wisdom is not in the eye, but in the head. *African (Kanuri)*

17651. Wisdom is regulated by knowledge, good conduct by love.
Indian (Tamil)

17652. Wisdom is the least burdensome traveling pack. *Danish*

17653. Wisdom is wealth to a poor man. *English*

17654. Wisdom likes not chance.
English

17655. Wisdom sometimes walks in clouted shoes. *English*

17656. Wisdom travels by oxen.
Yiddish

17657. Wisdom will not prevent sin.
Welsh

17658. Wisdom without use is fire without warmth. *Swedish*

WISE (adjective)

17659. Everyone is wise until he speaks. *Irish*

17660. He is not wise that is not wise for himself. *English*

17661. He is not wise who will not be instructed. *Irish*

17662. He is wise enough that can keep himself warm. *English*

17663. He is wise that follows the wise. *English*

17664. He is wise that is honest.
English

17665. He is wise that is ware in time.
English

17666. He is wise that knows when he is well enough. *English*

17667. He seems wise with whom all things thrive. *English*

17668. He was wise that first gave reward. *English*

17669. It is not always good to be wise.
German

17670. No one is always wise.
English

17671. None are so wise as those who know nothing. *English*

17672. None is so wise but the fool overtakes him. *English*

17673. See that you are wise, but also learn how to appear ignorant.
Armenian

17674. Some are wise and some are otherwise. *English*

17675. They are wise in other men's matters and fools in their own.
English

17676. Who is wise in the day can be no fool in the night. *English*

17677. You don't have to be wise to be lucky. *Yiddish*

WISE (people)

17678. If the wise erred not, it would go hard with fools. *English*

17679. The wise and the fool have their fellows. *English*

WISH

17680. Even the wishes of an ant reach heaven. *Japanese*

17681. If wishes were butter cakes, beggars might bite. *English*

17682. If wishes were granted, even beggars would grow rich. *Greek*

17683. If wishes were horses beggars would ride. *English*

17684. If wishes were thrushes beggars would eat birds. *English*

17685. If wishes were true, shepherds would be kings. *French*

17686. If wishes would bide, beggars would ride. *English*

17687. Mere wishes are silly fishes.
English

17688. The wish is father to the thought. *English*

17689. When a thing is done wishes are too late. *English*

17690. Wishes never can fill a sack. *English*

17691. Wishes never filled the bag. *French*

WISHER

17692. Wishers and would-ers are never good householders. *English*

17693. Wishers want will. *English*

WISHING

17694. After the act, wishing is in vain. *French*

17695. With wishing comes grieving. *Italian*

WIT

17696. A knavish wit, a knavish will. *English*

17697. A little wit will serve a fortunate man. *English*

17698. All the wit of the world is not in one head. *Swedish*

17699. An ounce of mother wit is worth a pound of clergy. *Scottish*

17700. An ounce of wit that's bought is worth a pound that's taught. *English*

17701. Better wit than wealth. *English*

17702. Bought wit is dear. *English*

17703. Great wits have short memories. *English*

17704. Great wits meet. *French*

17705. It is good to buy wit with other men's money. *English*

17706. It is wit to pick a lock and steal a horse, but it is wisdom to let them alone. *English*

17707. Little wit in the head makes much work for the feet. *English*

17708. Many by wit purchase wealth, but none by wealth purchase wit. *English*

17709. The less wit a man has, the less he knows that he wants it. *English*

17710. The more wit, the less courage. *English*

17711. The wit of a woman is a great matter. *English*

17712. Two wits are better than one. *Scottish*

17713. Use your wit as a buckler, not a sword. *English*

17714. Where there is no wit within, no wit will come out. *Danish*

17715. Wit and will strive for the victory. *English*

17716. Wit and wisdom are good warison. *English*

17717. Wit and beauty seldom come together. *German*

17718. Wit bought is better than taught. *English*

17719. Wit is better than cunning. *German*

17720. Wit is folly unless a wise man has the keeping of it. *English*

17721. Wit is never good till it be bought. *English*

17722. Wit will walk where will is bent. *English*

17723. Wit without learning is like a tree without fruit. *English*

17724. Wit without wisdom cuts other men's meat and its own fingers. *English*

17725. Wit without wisdom is but little worth. *English*

WITHIN

17726. If better were within, better would come out. *English*

WITNESS

17727. A false witness is worthy of being cast to the dogs.   *Hebrew*

17728. Better one eyewitness than ten hearsay witnesses.   *Dutch*

17729. No witness can become the judge.   *Hebrew*

17730. There is no such witness as a good measure of wine.   *Spanish*

WITTICISM

17731. Witticisms spare no one.
French

WIVE (verb)

17732. It's hard to wive and thrive both in a year.   *English*

WIVES (see WIFE)

17733. Ugly wives and stupid servant girls are treasures above price.
Chinese

17734. When you have five wives, you have five tongues.   *African (Ashanti)*

17735. Wives and pots and kettles are better when old.   *Japanese*

17736. Wives and shoes are better when old.   *Japanese*

17737. Wives and wind are necessary evils.   *English*

17738. Wives must be had, be they good or bad.   *English*

17739. Wives must have their will.
English

17740. Wives, razors, and horses should never be lent.   *Russian*

WIVING

17741. In wiving and thriving a man should take counsel of all the world.
English

WOE

17742. By telling our woes we often assuage them.   *French*

17743. There is no woe to want.
English

WOLF (see WOLVES)

17744. A hungry wolf is not at rest.
Portuguese

17745. A wolf and a sheep never agree.
Greek

17746. A wolf changes his coat but never his nature.   *Serbo-Croatian*

17747. A wolf hankers after sheep even at his last gasp.   *Dutch*

17748. A wolf is happy during a storm.
Greek

17749. A wolf may grow old and his hair turn gray, but his mind doesn't change to his dying day.   *Greek*

17750. A wolf selects its prey from what has been accounted for.   *Greek*

17751. An old wolf does not lose his way.   *Turkish*

17752. An old wolf is not scared by loud cries.   *Danish*

17753. An old wolf is used to being shouted at.   *Dutch*

17754. By little and little the wolf eats the sheep.   *English*

17755. By little and little the wolf eats up the goose.   *English*

17756. Cover yourself not with the skin of a wolf if you would not be considered a wolf.   *Basque*

17757. Feed a wolf in the winter and he will devour you in the summer.
Greek

17758. For love of the ox the wolf licks the yoke.   *Spanish*

17759. For love the wolf eats the sheep.
German

17760. For the least choice the wolf took the sheep.   *English*

17761. He who feeds a wolf, strengthens his enemy.   *Danish*

17762. He who swaddles the wolf will be barked at by the dog.
African (Wolof)

17763. If the wolf feared rain, he would wear a cloak. *Greek*

17764. If the wolf would cease his running, the people would cease their shouting. *German*

17765. It is a hard winter when one wolf eats another. *English*

17766. It needs but slight provocation to make the wolf devour the lamb.
Danish

17767. Live with a wolf, howl like a wolf. *Estonian*

17768. Make yourself a sheep, and the wolf is ready. *Russian*

17769. Make yourself a sheep and the wolf will eat you. *French*

17770. No matter how much you feed a wolf, he keeps on looking into the forest. *Russian*

17771. On very small pretext the wolf seizes the sheep. *Italian*

17772. One wolf does not bite another.
Spanish

17773. One wolf does not kill another.
Portuguese

17774. Talk about the wolf, and the wolf is here. *Russian*

17775. Talk of the wolf and his tail appears. *Dutch*

17776. Talk of the wolf and you see his tail. *French*

17777. The hungry wolf goes for food even into the village. *Lithuanian*

17778. The wolf and the fox are both in one story. *Spanish*

17779. The wolf and the sheep cannot be of one mind. *Turkish*

17780. The wolf bemoans the sheep, and then eats it. *Italian*

17781. The wolf catches not the sheep that are counted. *Turkish*

17782. The wolf catches the sheep that separates from the flock. *Turkish*

17783. The wolf changes his fur, but never his habits. *Rumanian*

17784. The wolf changes his hair, but not his skin. *Albanian*

17785. The wolf changes his teeth, but not his disposition. *Spanish*

17786. The wolf commits no mischief at home. *Spanish*

17787. The wolf doesn't concern himself with the price of a sheep.
African (Hausa)

17788. The wolf doesn't devour his prey near his den. *Greek*

17789. The wolf does not fear the sheepdog, but his collar or nails.
Russian

17790. The wolf eats counted sheep.
English

17791. The wolf eats of what is counted. *Spanish*

17792. The wolf eats often of the sheep that have been warned. *English*

17793. The wolf enters a flock that is without a dog. *Turkish*

17794. The wolf is always left out of the reckoning. *Italian*

17795. The wolf is always said to be bigger than he is. *Italian*

17796. The wolf is not afraid of the dog, but he hates his bark. *Yiddish*

17797. The wolf is not always a wolf.
Italian

17798. The wolf is not so big as people make him. *French*

17799. The wolf is well pleased with the kick of a sheep. *Portuguese*

17800. The wolf knows what the ill beast thinks. *English*

17801. The wolf laments what he left behind, the shepherd what he took away. *Armenian*

17802. The wolf loses his teeth, but not his inclinations. *Spanish*

17803. The wolf must die in his own skin. *English*

17804. There's no showing the wolf to a bad dog. *French*

17805. Though the wolf be lean, he can contend with a goat. *African (Wolof)*

17806. Train a wolf cub as much as you want, he still won't become a lamb. *Armenian*

17807. Upon a slight pretext the wolf takes the sheep. *French*

17808. What the she-wolf does pleases the he-wolf. *French*

17809. When one wolf eats another, there is nothing to eat in the wood. *Spanish*

17810. Where the wolf gets one lamb it looks for another. *Spanish*

17811. Who does not wish to be like the wolf, let him not wear its skin. *Italian*

17812. Who keeps company with the wolf will learn to howl. *English*

17813. Who makes the wolf his companion should carry a dog under his cloak. *Italian*

17814. Wolf doesn't eat wolf. *Rumanian*

17815. Wolf should not eat wolf. *American*

17816. You may preach ever so long to the wolf, he will nevertheless call for lamb before night. *Danish*

WOLVES (see WOLF)

17817. He that lives with wolves must howl with them. *Dutch*

17818. He who herds with wolves, learns to howl. *Danish*

17819. He who kennels with wolves must howl. *French*

17820. He who wants to wrestle with wolves must have a bear's claws. *Swedish*

17821. If you're afraid of wolves, don't go into the forest. *Russian*

17822. Those are very hard times in the wood when the wolves eat each other. *French*

17823. When you live with the wolves, howl like a wolf. *Russian*

17824. Where wolves are full, sheep are few. *Serbo-Croatian*

17825. Who herds with wolves must howl with wolves. *German*

17826. Wolves are often hidden under sheep's clothing. *Danish*

17827. Wolves discuss the back of the leader. *African (Ovambo)*

17828. Wolves don't eat wolves. *Italian*

17829. Wolves lose their teeth but not their memory. *English*

17830. Wolves never prey upon wolves. *English*

17831. You must howl with the wolves when you are among them. *Danish*

WOMAN (see WOMEN)

17832. A bad woman is as hard as a harsh winter's day. *Hebrew*

17833. A beautiful woman is a beautiful trouble. *Jamaican*

17834. A beautiful woman is paradise for the eye, the soul's hell, and purgatory for the purse. *Estonian*

17835. A covetous woman deserves a swindling gallant. *French*

17836. A drunken woman is lost to shame. *Irish*

17837. A fair woman without virtue is like palled wine. *English*

17838. A foolish woman is known by her finery. *French*

17839. A good woman is worth, if she were sold, the fairest crown that's made of purest gold. *English*

17840. A good woman is worth more than rubies. *Philippine*

17841. A gossiping woman is the root of trouble. *African (Jabo)*

17842. A gossiping woman talks of everybody, and everybody of her. *Portuguese*

17843. A handsome woman is either silly or vain. *Spanish*

17844. A house without a woman is a meadow without dew. *Czech*

17845. A mirror and chastity are two things a woman must have. *Japanese*

17846. A plain woman with moral beauty is better than a beautiful woman. *Vietnamese*

17847. A pregnant woman wants toasted snow. *Hebrew*

17848. A reformed woman of the streets is the best of women. *Mexican*

17849. A silent woman is better than a double-tongued man. *English*

17850. A small woman can also have a big mouth. *Yiddish*

17851. A thrifty woman is the wealth of her house. *Maltese*

17852. A vain woman thinks of adorning herself only. *Indian (Bihar)*

17853. A whistling woman and a crowing hen are two of the unluckiest things under the sun. *English*

17854. A whistling woman and a crowing hen will call the old gentleman out of his den. *English*

17855. A wicked woman and an evil is three halfpence worse than the devil. *English*

17856. A wise woman is twice a fool. *English*

17857. A wise woman will marry the man who loves her rather than the one she loves. *Slovenian*

17858. A woman, a spaniel, and a walnut tree—the more you beat them the better they be. *English*

17859. A woman and a glass are ever in danger. *English*

17860. A woman and a hen are soon lost through gadding. *Portuguese*

17861. A woman and a melon are hard to choose. *French*

17862. A woman can beat the devil. *Irish*

17863. A woman can do more than the devil. *English*

17864. A woman comes out not only to see but also to be seen. *Hebrew*

17865. A woman conceals only what she does not know. *French*

17866. A woman cuts her wisdom teeth when she is dead. *Rumanian*

17867. A woman does not perish in marriage. *African (Jabo)*

17868. A woman goes mad twice—when she loves and when she begins to go gray. *Polish*

17869. A woman has long hair and short sense. *Yiddish*

17870. A woman has long hair but short brain. *Estonian*

17871. A woman has nine lives like a cat. *English*

17872. A woman has only half a brain.
Lebanese

17873. A woman is a weathercock.
English

17874. A woman is an angel at ten, a saint at fifteen, a devil at forty, and a witch at fourscore. *English*

17875. A woman is attractive when she is somebody else's wife.
African (Shona)

17876. A woman is never satisfied.
African (Swahili)

17877. A woman is not a lemon whose quality you can judge at once. *Hebrew*

17878. A woman is well either in the house or in the grave. *Pashto*

17879. A woman is young till she bears a child, and cloth is new till it is washed. *Indian (Tamil)*

17880. A woman keeps secret only what she does not know. *German*

17881. A woman laughs when she can, and weeps when she pleases. *French*

17882. A woman need but look upon her apron-string to find an excuse.
English

17883. A woman never brings a man into the right way. *African (Kanuri)*

17884. A woman that loves to be at the window is like a bunch of grapes on the highway. *English*

17885. A woman that paints puts up a bill that she is to be let. *English*

17886. A woman who accepts, sells herself; a woman who gives, surrenders. *French*

17887. A woman who has lost her rival has no sorrow. *African (Wolof)*

17888. A woman who is dignified in her ways is respected even by the irreverent. *Philippine*

17889. A woman who looks much in the mirror spins but little. *French*

17890. A woman without a husband is like a boat without a helmsman.
Vietnamese

17891. A woman without a husband is like a distaff without the spindle.
Rumanian

17892. A woman without a mate is like a garden without an enclosure.
Slovakian

17893. A woman without a veil is like food without salt. *Pashto*

17894. A woman without jealousy is like a ball without bounce. *English*

17895. A young woman, like new wine, bubbles. *Rumanian*

17896. An honest woman dwells at the sign of an honest countenance.
English

17897. An uneducated woman is like a flower without fragrance. *Philippine*

17898. An unmarried woman who is quarrelsome loses half her worth.
Philippine

17899. Beat a woman with a hammer and you'll have gold. *Irish*

17900. Beware of a bad woman and put no trust in a good one. *Spanish*

17901. Beware of the fore part of a woman, the hind part of a mule, and all sides of a priest. *English*

17902. Choose not a woman nor linen by candlelight. *English*

17903. Do not insult a woman before she has undressed. *African (Bemba)*

17904. Don't marry an old woman, even though you will eat with her young pigeons and lamb's meat.
Moroccan

17905. Even a beautiful woman is not without blemish. *African (Swahili)*

17906. Even the handsome woman experiences the misfortune of divorce.
Egyptian

17907. Every woman would rather be handsome than good. *German*

17908. Everything goes to loose ends where there is no woman. *American*

17909. He who marries a woman for her money is good for nothing.
Lebanese

17910. He who marries a young woman gets welfare and a treasure.
Moroccan

17911. He who trusts a woman and leads an ass will never be free from plague. *French*

17912. If a woman be chaste she may live in the street of the harlots.
Indian (Tamil)

17913. If a woman doesn't want to dance she says her frock is too short.
Jamaican

17914. If a woman is cold, it is her husband's fault. *Russian*

17915. If a woman speaks two words, take one and leave the other.
African (Kanuri)

17916. If a woman were as little as she is good, a peascod would make her a gown and a hood. *English*

17917. If you marry a beautiful woman, you marry trouble.
African (Jabo)

17918. In the freshness of youth a woman is like a gilded statue, but when youth has faded she looks like a beehive on a rainy day. *Vietnamese*

17919. It is as great a pity to see a woman weep as to see a goose go barefoot. *English*

17920. It's easier for the mare when the woman gets off the cart. *Russian*

17921. It is much easier to take care of a sackful of fleas than a woman.
Hungarian

17922. It is no child's play when an old woman dances. *Danish*

17923. It is not the most beautiful woman who has the most sense. *Irish*

17924. It is the woman who knows her husband. *African (Ashanti)*

17925. Mistrust the woman who speaks only of her virtue. *Russian*

17926. Never was bad woman fair.
English

17927. No woman is so old that she is not pleased when she is kissed.
Slovakian

17928. No woman is ugly if she is well dressed. *Portuguese*

17929. No woman is ugly in the dark of night. *Philippine*

17930. No woman is ugly when she is dressed. *Spanish*

17931. No woman likes another.
Maltese

17932. No woman marries an old man for God's sake. *German*

17933. She is a woman and therefore may be wooed; she is a woman and therefore may be won. *English*

17934. Tell a woman she's a beauty, and the devil will tell her so ten times.
English

17935. The handsomest woman can only give what she has. *French*

17936. The homely woman is precious in the home, but at a feast the beautiful one is preferred. *Chinese*

17937. The more a woman admires her face, the more she ruins her house.
Spanish

17938. The pretty woman in the house is the enemy of all the ugly ones.
Chinese

17939. The righteous woman has only one husband. *Vietnamese*

17940. The well-dressed woman draws her husband away from another woman's door. *Spanish*

17941. The woman cries before the wedding and the man after. *Polish*

17942. The woman who giggles much wants to be caressed. *Philippine*

17943. The woman who gives is seldom good; the woman who accepts is in the power of the giver. *Italian*

17944. The woman who is always out in the streets is likely to encounter evil. *Philippine*

17945. There was never a conflict without a woman. *Albanian*

17946. Though a beautiful woman does not say anything, she cannot be hidden. *Japanese*

17947. Though a thousand times admonished, a faithless woman will not become a faithful wife. *Indian (Tamil)*

17948. Though you speak of a beautiful woman, it is only one layer of skin. *Japanese*

17949. To educate a woman is like placing a knife in the hands of a monkey. *Indian (Hindi)*

17950. Trust not a woman: she will tell you what she has just told her companion. *African (Wolof)*

17951. What a woman wills, God wills. *French*

17952. When the beautiful woman blooms, the law bites. *Hawaiian*

17953. When the old woman is hard pressed she must needs run. *Irish*

17954. When woman reigns the devil governs. *Italian*

17955. Where a woman rules the house, the devil is serving-man. *German*

17956. Without a bright mirror a woman cannot know if the powder is smooth on her face. *Chinese*

17957. Woman and land are the causes which destroy man. *Australian (Maori)*

17958. Woman is a torment, but she is worth buying with your life. *Iranian*

17959. Woman is as double faced as a star-apple leaf. *Jamaican*

17960. Woman is like a ripe banana leaf—when poked it tears. *Hawaiian*

17961. Woman is the chief gate to hell. *Indian (Hindi)*

17962. Woman, wind, and luck soon change. *Portuguese*

WOMANKIND

17963. Womankind is long haired, short witted. *Turkish*

WOMEN (see WOMAN)

17964. All women are alike. *African (Ashanti)*

17965. All women are good: either good for something, or good for nothing. *English*

17966. All women are good Lutherans—they would rather preach than hear mass. *Dutch*

17967. Among beautiful women there are many fools. *Japanese*

17968. Beautiful women are short lived. *Korean*

17969. Beware of women with beards and men without beards. *Basque*

17970. Discreet women have neither eyes nor ears. *English*

17971. Even the best of women has still a devil's rib in her. *Rumanian*

17972. Few women turn gray because their husband dies. *Danish*

17973. Handsome women generally fall to the lot of ugly men. *Italian*

17974. If women manage a village, it will become a desert.   *Indian (Hindi)*

17975. In books there are women who appear as jewels.   *Chinese*

17976. It is difficult to trust women.   *Irish*

17977. It is easier to make a hundred watches agree than ten women. *Polish*

17978. Lazy and silly women marry well.   *Greek*

17979. Many women appear ideal in public but are not so in their homes.   *Philippine*

17980. Many women, many words.   *English*

17981. Married women take pity on single women who lie alone in their beds.   *Vietnamese*

17982. Put the light out, and all women are alike.   *German*

17983. The fewer women, the less trouble.   *Polish*

17984. The more women look in their glass, the less they look to their house.   *English*

17985. There are only two good women in the world—one is lost and the other cannot be found.   *Polish*

17986. There are only two good women in the world; the one is dead, the other not to be found.   *German*

17987. Three women and a goose make a market.   *English*

17988. Three women are a market, and seven a whole fair.   *Russian*

17989. Three women, three geese, and three frogs make a market.   *Polish*

17990. Two old women and a goose make a market.   *Slovakian*

17991. Two women, a market; three, a fair.   *Russian*

17992. Two women and a goose make a market.   *Italian*

17993. Two women are a party, three a crowd.   *Hungarian*

17994. Two women in one house will not agree long.   *English*

17995. What women say is nonsense; but he who does not listen in is a fool.   *African (Bemba)*

17996. When evening falls all women become equal.   *Lebanese*

17997. When three women meet it is worse than a hundred ducks quacking.   *Rumanian*

17998. When women are on board there is no want of wind.   *American*

17999. Where there are women and geese, there wants no noise.   *English*

18000. Women always speak the truth, but not the whole truth.   *Italian*

18001. Women and cats are both animals ungrateful.   *Mexican*

18002. Women and glass are always in danger.   *Portuguese*

18003. Women and hens by too much gadding are lost.   *English*

18004. Women and linen look best by candlelight.   *English*

18005. Women and maidens must be praised, whether truly or falsely.   *German*

18006. Women and music should never be dated.   *English*

18007. Women and their wills are dangerous ills.   *English*

18008. Women and weal can never agree.   *English*

18009. Women and wine, game and deceit, make the wealth small and the wants great.   *English*

18010. Women are as fickle as April weather. *German*

18011. Women are defective in understanding and religion. *Moroccan*

18012. Women are devilish things. *Japanese*

18013. Women are fragile things. *Japanese*

18014. Women are like shadows—follow them and they fly from you, fly from them and they follow you. *Swedish*

18015. Women are necessary evils. *English*

18016. Women are never at a loss for words. *German*

18017. Women are saints in church. *English*

18018. Women are ships and must be manned. *English*

18019. Women are wise impromptu, fools on reflection. *Italian*

18020. Women, asses, and nuts require strong hands. *Italian*

18021. Women can keep only those secrets of which they know nothing. *Serbo-Croatian*

18022. Women commend a modest man, but like him not. *English*

18023. Women conceal all that they know not. *English*

18024. Women grow more beautiful with silk; rice plants grow better with fertilizer. *Vietnamese*

18025. Women have long hair and short wisdom. *Greek*

18026. Women have long hair, but short brains and faith. *Slovenian*

18027. Women have no souls. *English*

18028. Women have their fears. *American*

18029. Women have two faults—they can neither do nor say well. *English*

18030. Women in mischief are wiser than men. *English*

18031. Women in state affairs are like monkeys in glass shops. *English*

18032. Women laugh when they can and weep when they will. *English*

18033. Women learn how to weep in order to lie. *Rumanian*

18034. Women look for talent, men for beauty. *Vietnamese*

18035. Women, money, and wine have their balm and their harm. *French*

18036. Women, money and wine, have their good and their pine. *English*

18037. Women must have the last word. *English*

18038. Women must have their wills. *English*

18039. Women, priests, and poultry never have enough. *English*

18040. Women rouge that they may not blush. *Italian*

18041. Women should associate with women. *Japanese*

18042. Women want the best first, and the best always. *English*

18043. Women, wealth and wine have each two qualities—a good and a bad. *English*

18044. Women, wind, and fortune are given to change. *English*

WONDER

18045. A wonder lasts but nine days in a town. *Scottish*

18046. No wonder lasts more than three days. *Italian*

18047. The wonders of the world are more numerous than its misfortunes. *Moroccan*

18048. Wonder is the daughter of ignorance.   *English*

18049. Wonders will never cease.
                          English

WOOD

18050. A little wood will heat a little
oven.   *English*

18051. By the side of dry wood the
green will also burn.   *Slovenian*

18052. Crooked wood burns just as
well as straight.   *German*

18053. Dry wood makes a quick fire.
                          Danish

18054. Even soaked wood when put
near the flame long enough will surely
burn.   *Philippine*

18055. Good wood is better than a
good layer of painting.   *Vietnamese*

18056. Green wood makes a hot fire.
                          English

18057. He that picks up all sorts of
wood soon gets an armful. *German*

18058. Like wood, like arrows.
                          English

18059. Little wood, much fruit. *Dutch*

18060. Not every sort of wood is fit to
make an arrow.   *French*

18061. Not every wood will make
wooden shoes.   *Danish*

18062. The wood for a temple does not
come from one tree.   *Chinese*

18063. The wood has ears, the field
has eyes.   *German*

18064. Wood half burnt is easily kindled.   *English*

18065. Wood near the fire will catch.
                          African (Fulani)

18066. Wood warms a man twice.
                          American

18067. Woods have ears and fields
have eyes.   *Dutch*

WOODCOCK

18068. One woodcock does not make a
winter.   *English*

WOODCUTTER

18069. He who stands near the woodcutter is likely to be hit by a splinter.
                          Danish

WOOER

18070. A wooer should open his ears
more than his eyes.   *Norwegian*

WOOING

18071. Happy is the wooing that is not
long a-doing.   *English*

WOOL

18072. Better give the wool than the
sheep.   *Italian*

18073. Better lose the wool than the
lamb.   *Greek*

18074. He who goes to collect wool
may come back shorn.   *French*

18075. It's ill shaving against the wool.
                          English

18076. Many go out for wool and come
home shorn.   *German*

18077. Rather lose the wool than the
sheep.   *Portuguese*

18078. There is no wool so white but a
dyer can make it black.   *English*

WOOL SELLER

18079. A wool seller knows a wool
buyer.   *English*

WORD

18080. A gentle word can break a
bone.   *Yiddish*

18081. A good word always falls on a
friendly spot.   *Estonian*

18082. A good word at court is better
than a coin in one's purse. *Irish*

18083. A good word extinguishes more than a pailful of water.   *Spanish*

18084. A good word in court is better than a pound in the purse.   *Irish*

18085. A good word is as soon said as a bad one.   *English*

18086. A good word removes anger.
          African (Ga)

18087. A harsh word is more painful than a blow.   *Indian (Tamil)*

18088. A kind word is better than a harsh one.   *Indian (Tamil)*

18089. A kind word is better than alms.   *Yiddish*

18090. A kind word is like a spring day.   *Russian*

18091. A kind word is never lost.
          American

18092. A kind word never broke anyone's mouth.   *Irish*

18093. A man's word is his honor.
          Danish

18094. A silent man's words are not brought into court.   *Danish*

18095. A single kind word keeps one warm for three winters.   *Chinese*

18096. A spoken word isn't a sparrow; if it flies out, you won't catch it.
          Russian

18097. A spoken word is silver, silence is gold.   *Russian*

18098. A straightforward word is bitter.   *Turkish*

18099. A superfluous word has no place.   *Yiddish*

18100. A true word needs no oath.
          Turkish

18101. A woman's word is a bundle of water.   *Indian (Hindi)*

18102. A word and a stone once let go cannot be recalled.   *Portuguese*

18103. A word before is worth two behind.   *English*

18104. A word helps a good person, but even a stick can't help the bad.
          Yiddish

18105. A word is enough to the wise.
          Dutch

18106. A word is like an arrow—both are in a hurry to strike.   *Yiddish*

18107. A word is more to him that has wisdom than a sermon to a fool.
          English

18108. A word is not a knife but it wounds just as deeply.   *Philippine*

18109. A word of peace redeems a crime.   *African (Ovambo)*

18110. A word once out flies everywhere.   *French*

18111. A word shoots up like the blade of grass.   *African (Annang)*

18112. A word spoken is an arrow let fly.   *English*

18113. A word stirs up anger or love.
          Indian (Kashmiri)

18114. A word that when spoken you would wish back, let it remain in your head.   *African (Ashanti)*

18115. A word to the wise is enough.
          English

18116. A word which flew out of the mouth like a sparrow cannot be drawn back, even by four horses.   *Czech*

18117. Among men of honor a word is a bond.   *Italian*

18118. An honest man's word is as good as his bond.   *English*

18119. An honest man's word is as good as the king's.   *Portuguese*

18120. An honest man's word is his bond.   *Dutch*

18121. Bad words are like bruises.
          Philippine

18122. Bad words find bad acceptance.   *English*

18123. Bad words make a woman
worse.   *English*

18124. Bare words are no good bargain.   *English*

18125. Bare words buy no barley.
                          English

18126. Bare words make no bargain.
                          Scottish

18127. Better be convinced by words
than by blows.   *Danish*

18128. Better one word in time than
two afterwards.   *English*

18129. Better one word less than one
word too many.   *Maltese*

18130. Big words seldom go with good
deeds.   *Danish*

18131. Bitter words are medicine;
sweet words bring illness.   *Chinese*

18132. Cool words scald not the
tongue.   *English*

18133. Deliver your words not by
number but by weight.   *English*

18134. Evil words corrupt good manners.   *English*

18135. Fair words and foul deeds cheat
wise men as well as fools.   *English*

18136. Fair words and foul play cheat
both young and old.   *English*

18137. Fair words break no bones.
                          English

18138. Fair words butter no parsnips.
                          English

18139. Fair words cost nothing.
                          English

18140. Fair words don't fatten the cabbage.   *German*

18141. Fair words don't fill the pocket.
                          German

18142. Fair words fill not the belly.
                          English

18143. Fair words, foul deeds.
                          English

18144. Fair words hurt not the tongue.
                          English

18145. Fair words make fools fain.
                          English

18146. Fair words please the fool, and
sometimes the wise.   *Danish*

18147. Fair words will not make the
pot boil.   *English*

18148. Fair words will not sow the
land.   *Welsh*

18149. Fair words won't feed a cat.
                          Italian

18150. Few words and many deeds.
                          English

18151. Few words are best.   *English*

18152. Few words to the wise suffice.
                          English

18153. Fine words don't fill the belly.
                          Dutch

18154. Fine words without deeds go
not far.   *Danish*

18155. Footless words may travel out a
thousand miles.   *Korean*

18156. For an intelligent man, one
word and he understands.   *Chinese*

18157. For mad words deaf ears.
                          English

18158. From the lips starts the word
and reaches thousands.   *Greek*

18159. From words to deeds is a great
space.   *English*

18160. Gentle words ease sorrow.
                          Philippine

18161. Good words and bad acts deceive both wise and simple.
                          Portuguese

18162. Good words and ill deeds deceive the wise and fools.   *English*

18163. Good words anoint us, and ill
do unjoint us.   *English*

18164. Good words are worth much and cost little. *English*

18165. Good words cost no more than bad. *English*

18166. Good words cost nothing. *English*

18167. Good words make amends for misdeeds. *English*

18168. Good words quench more than a bucket of water. *English*

18169. Good words without deeds are rushes and reeds. *English*

18170. Half a word to the wise is enough. *Dutch*

18171. He who gives fair words feeds you with an empty spoon. *English*

18172. He who is scared by words has no heart for deeds. *Danish*

18173. He who listens to the words of a woman will be accounted worthless. *Indian (Tamil)*

18174. He who pays no heed to the words of his elders mounts a wild horse. *Turkish*

18175. Heed not all the words of the doctor nor yet of the confessor. *Greek*

18176. High words break no bones. *English*

18177. If one word does not succeed, ten thousand are of no avail. *Chinese*

18178. If you haven't given your word, restrain yourself; if you have, keep it. *Russian*

18179. Ill words are bellows to a slackening fire. *English*

18180. It is a good thing to listen to the words of one woman in forty. *Turkish*

18181. It is better to keep back one word than to speak two. *Icelandic*

18182. It is bitter fare to eat one's own words. *Danish*

18183. It is difficult to get a good word; it is easy to give a bad one. *Chinese*

18184. It is good to find modest words to express immodest things. *English*

18185. Kind words don't wear out the tongue. *Danish*

18186. Like word, like deed. *English*

18187. Many a true word is spoken in jest. *English*

18188. Many words hurt. *English*

18189. Many words will not fill a bucket. *English*

18190. Mere words will not feed the friars. *Irish*

18191. More is done with words than with hands. *German*

18192. More words than one go to a bargain. *English*

18193. Nice words do not cost anything; so one should choose words which can please others' ears. *Vietnamese*

18194. Nice words penetrate into the bones. *Vietnamese*

18195. Not every word requires an answer. *Italian*

18196. Numerous words show scanty wares. *Japanese*

18197. Of big words and feathers, many go to the pound. *German*

18198. Old people's words are weighed with scales. *Greek*

18199. One cross word brings on a quarrel. *Yiddish*

18200. One good word quenches more heat than a bucket of water. *Italian*

18201. One ill word asks another. *English*

18202. One word beforehand is better than ten afterwards. *Danish*

18203. One word in its place is worth a camel. *Lebanese*

18204. Pleasant words will draw a snake from its hole. *African (Swahili)*

18205. Polite words open iron gates. *Serbo-Croatian*

18206. Poor people's words go many to a sackful. *German*

18207. Smooth words do not flay the tongue. *Italian*

18208. Soft words are hard arguments. *English*

18209. Soft words don't scotch the tongue. *French*

18210. Soft words hurt not the mouth. *Swedish*

18211. Soft words will get the snake out of its hole. *Iranian*

18212. Sugared words generally prove bitter. *Spanish*

18213. Sweet words please fools. *Japanese*

18214. The best words give no food. *African (Wolof)*

18215. The fewer the words, the better the prayer. *German*

18216. The king's word is more than another man's oath. *English*

18217. The king's word must stand. *English*

18218. The poor man's word is considered last. *African (Zulu)*

18219. The two words, "peace" and "tranquillity," are worth a thousand pieces of gold. *Chinese*

18220. The word of a man, like the tusk of an elephant, can never be withdrawn. *Indian (Bihar)*

18221. The word of slander rings like a bell. *Rumanian*

18222. The word of the destitute does not reach the assembly. *Indian (Tamil)*

18223. The word of the Tsar is a proverb. *Russian*

18224. The word that has departed grows on the way. *Norwegian*

18225. The word that lies nearest the heart comes first in the mouth. *Norwegian*

18226. There is many a true word spoken in jest. *Scottish*

18227. To shun an elder's word is to refuse advice. *African (Shona)*

18228. Wait is a hard word to the hungry. *German*

18229. Weigh your words, do not count them. *Serbo-Croatian*

18230. What words won't do, gold will. *English*

18231. When a word has once left the lips, the swiftest horse cannot overtake it. *Chinese*

18232. When the word is out, it belongs to another. *German*

18233. Where words fail beating succeeds. *Greek*

18234. While the word is in your mouth it is your own; when it is once spoken, it is another's. *English*

18235. While the word is still in your mouth, you are a lord; once you utter it, you are a fool. *Yiddish*

18236. Wise words and great seldom agree. *English*

18237. Words and feathers are tossed by the wind. *English*

18238. Words are but sands, it's money that buys lands. *English*

18239. Words are but words. *English*

18240. Words are empty, but the writing brush leaves traces. *Chinese*

18241. Words are female, deeds are male. *Italian*

18242. Words are good, but fowls lay eggs. *German*

18243. Words are good, when works follow. *German*

18244. Words are mere bubbles of water, but deeds are drops of gold. *Tibetan*

18245. Words are silver, but answers are gold. *African (Swahili)*

18246. Words are the voice of the heart. *Chinese*

18247. Words are wind. *English*

18248. Words are women. *English*

18249. Words are worthless unless backed up by deeds. *Philippine*

18250. Words can turn the course of a river. *Greek*

18251. Words cut more than swords. *English*

18252. Words have long tails. *English*

18253. Words may pass, but blows fall heavy. *English*

18254. Words must be weighed and not counted. *Yiddish*

18255. Words often do more than blows. *German*

18256. Words once spoken cannot be wiped out with a sponge. *Danish*

18257. Words once uttered cannot be overtaken even by a four-horse coach. *Korean*

18258. Words that come from the heart enter the heart. *Hebrew*

18259. Words unspoken are not known. *Chinese*

18260. Words won't feed cats. *Italian*

18261. You may gain by fair words what may fail you by angry ones. *Danish*

WORK (noun)

18262. A woman's work is never done. *English*

18263. A work ill done must be done twice. *English*

18264. All work and no play makes Jack a dull boy. *English*

18265. All work asks for diligence. *African (Ovambo)*

18266. By continually urging, the work undertaken may be completed. *Indian (Tamil)*

18267. Careless work with the hands brings unclean food to the mouth. *Hawaiian*

18268. Diligent work makes a skillful workman. *Danish*

18269. Do not put off today's work till tomorrow. *African (Ovambo)*

18270. Every work stands in awe of the master. *Estonian*

18271. Fine work is its own flattery. *Slovakian*

18272. First work, then wages. *African (Swahili)*

18273. God's work is soon done. *French*

18274. Hard work never killed anyone. *Hebrew*

18275. He does a good day's work who rids himself of a fool. *French*

18276. He who is busy with work cares little for news. *Czech*

18277. He who is without work in summer is without boots in winter. *Polish*

18278. He who likes his work, to him work comes easy. *Yiddish*

18279. He who looks for light work goes very tired to bed. *Yiddish*

18280. Hurry men at their work, not at their meals. *Chinese*

18281. If you would have your work ill done, pay beforehand. *Italian*

18282. It is harder work getting to hell than to heaven. *German*

18283. Lack of work brings a thousand diseases.   *Indian (Hindi)*

18284. Look at the work before you pay the hire.   *Indian (Tamil)*

18285. Neglect not a work in which you are skillful.   *Indian (Tamil)*

18286. No work can be finished if one does not have patience.   *Philippine*

18287. No work, no honey.   *American*

18288. The hard work of a hundred years may be destroyed in an hour.
Chinese

18289. The hardest work is to do nothing.   *American*

18290. The work meant to be performed by two cannot be done by one alone.   *African (Bemba)*

18291. The work of two is not meant to be done by one alone.
African (Bemba)

18292. The work praises the master.
Estonian

18293. The work praises the workman.
German

18294. There is no work in the grave.
American

18295. To the spectator no work is too hard.   *German*

18296. Weighty work must be done with few words.   *Danish*

18297. When everyone minds his own business the work is done.   *Danish*

18298. Who loves his work and knows to spare may live and flourish anywhere.   *German*

18299. Women's work is never done.
Scottish

18300. Work and overtime are the father and mother of wealth.   *Maltese*

18301. Work depends on tools.
Japanese

18302. Work done at the proper time is like a king's throne.
Indian (Kashmiri)

18303. Work done expects money.
Portuguese

18304. Work done quickly gives pleasure.   *Greek*

18305. Work for the sake of the children is better than pilgrimage and the holy war.   *Moroccan*

18306. Work half done is no work at all.   *Slovakian*

18307. Work has bitter roots, but sweet fruits.   *Rumanian*

18308. Work is a golden bracelet.
Rumanian

18309. Work is afraid of a resolute man.   *Chinese*

18310. Work is for men and thrift for women.   *Serbo-Croatian*

18311. Work is not a hare, it won't run away.   *Latvian*

18312. Work isn't a wolf, it won't run off into the forest.   *Russian*

18313. Work is the mother of life.
Slovakian

18314. Work loves fools.   *Russian*

WORK (verb)

18315. He that will not work will want.   *English*

18316. He that works after his own manner, his head aches not at the matter.   *English*

18317. He who will not work of his own accord will find himself forced to work by another.   *African (Hausa)*

18318. Work as if you were to live forever; pray as if you were to die tonight.   *Russian*

WORKER

18319. The hard worker and good health are always friends.   *Estonian*

18320. The hard worker toiled and the lazy man rejoiced.   *Greek*

WORKING

18321. It is working that makes a workman.   *English*

WORKMAN

18322. A bad workman blames his tools.   *African (Swahili)*

18323. A bad workman never finds a good tool.   *French*

18324. A good workman is known by his chips.   *English*

18325. An ill workman quarrels with his tools.   *English*

18326. As is the workman so is the work.   *English*

18327. He is a bad workman who cannot talk of work.   *German*

18328. Not to oversee workmen is to leave them your purse open.   *English*

18329. The better workman, the worse husband.   *English*

18330. The workman is known by his work.   *Italian*

18331. The workman is worthy of his hire.   *Dutch*

18332. What is a workman without his tools.   *English*

18333. Where there are too many workmen, there is little work.
                                                German

18334. Workmen are easier found than masters.   *German*

WORLD

18335. All the world goes by fair speech.   *English*

18336. Better be out of the world than out of the fashion.   *English*

18337. Better the world should know you as a sinner than God know you as a hypocrite.   *Danish*

18338. Better to see the world than not to see it.   *African (Fulani)*

18339. Eat and drink, and let the world go to ruin.   *Egyptian*

18340. Half the world knows not how the other half lives.   *English*

18341. Half the world laughs at the other half.   *German*

18342. He that has the world at will, seems wise.   *English*

18343. He that will not strive in this world should not have come into it.
                                                Italian

18344. He who is angry with the world must be tired of it.   *African (Hausa)*

18345. If the world will ever be redeemed, it will be only through the merit of children.   *Yiddish*

18346. It is a wicked world, and we make part of it.   *English*

18347. Let every man have his own world.   *Irish*

18348. Let the world pass.   *English*

18349. One half of the world laughs at the other.   *French*

18350. Take the world as it is, not as it ought to be.   *German*

18351. The whole wide world isn't dear.   *Russian*

18352. The whole world isn't crazy.
                                                Yiddish

18353. The whole world is one thief.
                                                Yiddish

18354. The world befriends the elephant and tramples on the ant.
                                        Indian (Hindustani)

18355. The world belongs to the scoundrel.   *Maltese*

18356. The world consists of cogs—one depends on the other.   *Yiddish*

18357. The world does not belong to the staring buck, but to the fox that is not eaten tomorrow. *African (Ovambo)*

18358. The world has been based on injustice since time immemorial. *Russian*

18359. The world has no secrets. *African (Swahili)*

18360. The world hates the informer and the moralist. *Yiddish*

18361. The world holds more for the healthy than the wealthy. *Slovakian*

18362. The world is a cage of madmen. *Maltese*

18363. The world is a cattle post where the herdsman serves one today, another tomorrow. *African (Ovambo)*

18364. The world is a chain, one link in another. *Maltese*

18365. The world is a cheat. *American*

18366. The world is a ladder for some to go up and some down. *English*

18367. The world is a sure teacher, but it takes a big payment. *Finnish*

18368. The world is a theatre of love. *Indian (Kashmiri)*

18369. The world is a wheel. *Greek*

18370. The world is big, its troubles still bigger. *Yiddish*

18371. The world is but a day's walk, for the sun goes about it in twenty-four hours. *English*

18372. The world is for him who has patience. *Italian*

18373. The world is full of falsehood; it cheats and deludes. *English*

18374. The world is full of fools. *English*

18375. The world is full of troubles, but each man feels his own. *Yiddish*

18376. The world is good, only bad luck casts a pall over it. *Yiddish*

18377. The world is governed with little brains. *Italian*

18378. The world is his who enjoys it. *English*

18379. The world is his who knows how to wait for it. *English*

18380. The world is like a staircase; some go up, others go down. *Italian*

18381. The world is not without good people. *Russian*

18382. The world is ruined by tyranny, it is not ruined by pickaxe and spade. *Turkish*

18383. The world is the world for the world. *Japanese*

18384. The world is too narrow for two fools a-quarrelling. *English*

18385. The world is wide, yet there is little room in it. *Polish*

18386. The world likes to be cheated. *Dutch*

18387. The world runs on wheels. *English*

18388. The world stands on money. *Yiddish*

18389. The world stands on three things: money, money, and money. *Yiddish*

18390. The world wags on with three things: doing, undoing, and pretending. *Italian*

18391. The world was never so dull, but if one will not, another will. *English*

18392. The world was not made in a day. *American*

18393. The world will do its own business. *American*

18394. There's more to the world than you can see through your window; get outside and you'll see more. *Russian*

18395. This world is the unbeliever's paradise. *Turkish*

18396. This world is the world of everyone in turn. *Irish*

WORM

18397. A little worm will lie under a great stone. *English*

18398. Nourish no worms that eat timber. *Thai*

18399. Silent worms dig holes in the walls. *Japanese*

18400. Tread on a worm, and he'll turn his head. *Scottish*

18401. Tread on a worm and it will turn. *English*

18402. Worms eat you up when dead and worries eat you up alive. *Yiddish*

18403. Worms that live on mahogany do not know that dates are sweet. *African (Fulani)*

WORRY

18404. Put off your worries for the morrow. *Yiddish*

18405. Worries about children continue until death. *Lebanese*

18406. Worries are easier to bear with soup than without it. *Yiddish*

18407. Worry, not work, kills man. *Maltese*

WORSHIP

18408. Much worship, much cost. *French*

WORTH

18409. No worth is attached to turbans, but to professions. *Indian (Kashmiri)*

18410. The worth of a thing is known by its want. *English*

18411. The worth of a thing is what it will bring. *English*

WOUND

18412. A bad wound may be cured, bad repute kills. *Spanish*

18413. A wound heals but bad words never fade. *Philippine*

18414. A wound in the hand is well, but to be wounded by unkind words is not well. *Indian (Kashmiri)*

18415. A wound never heals so well that the scar cannot be seen. *Danish*

18416. An ill wound is cured, not an ill name. *English*

18417. He that's afraid of wounds must keep from a battle. *Scottish*

18418. If you cannot heal the wound, do not tear it open. *Danish*

18419. Old wounds easily become painful. *Japanese*

18420. Old wounds easily bleed. *German*

18421. The evil wound is cured, but not the evil name. *English*

18422. The wound caused by words is worse than the wound of bodies. *Moroccan*

18423. The wound heals, the scar remains. *Serbo-Croatian*

18424. The wound of a knife is easily healed, but the wound in the heart, never. *Rumanian*

18425. The wound of the hand heals; the wound of the tongue heals not. *Turkish*

18426. The wound that a friend gives you hurts. *Greek*

18427. When the wound is healed the pain is forgotten. *Danish*

18428. Wounds by a sharp knife are easily cured. *American*

18429. Wounds from the knife are healed, but not those from the tongue. *Spanish*

18430. Wounds heal, but not ill words. *Spanish*

WRANGLER

18431. Wranglers are never in the wrong.   *English*

WRATH

18432. When wrath and vengeance marry, cruelty is born.   *Russian*

WRECK

18433. A wreck on shore is a beacon at sea.   *Dutch*

WREN

18434. A wren in the hand is better than a crane to be caught.   *Irish*

18435. Wrens may prey where eagles dare not perch.   *English*

WRETCH

18436. That which the wretch does spare the waster spends.   *English*

WRETCHED

18437. It is hard to be wretched, but worse to be known so.   *English*

WRINKLE

18438. An old wrinkle never wears out.   *English*

WRITING BRUSH

18439. He who can handle a writing brush will never have to beg. *Chinese*

WRONG

18440. All wrong comes to wrack.
                                                            English

18441. He who does the wrong forgets it, but not he who receives it.   *Italian*

18442. Revenge a wrong by forgiving it.   *English*

18443. To forget a wrong is the best revenge.   *English*

18444. Truly it is much better to suffer wrong than to do wrong! *American*

18445. Two wrongs will not make one right.   *English*

18446. What is wrong today won't be right tomorrow.   *Dutch*

WRONG-DOER

18447. The wrong-doer never lacks excuses.   *Italian*

Y

YARDSTICK

18448. We measure others with our own yardstick. *Greek*

YARN

18449. It is good spinning from another's yarn. *Dutch*

YAWNING

18450. Yawning goes from man to man. *Scottish*

YEAR

18451. A bad year has thirteen months. *Greek*

18452. A hundred years cannot repair a moment's loss of honor. *Italian*

18453. A hundred years is not much, but never is a long while. *French*

18454. A hundred years of regret pay not a farthing of debt. *German*

18455. A hundred years of wrong do not make an hour of right. *German*

18456. A year is a day if life continues. *African (Hausa)*

18457. Another year will bring another Christmas. *Danish*

18458. As the years go by, the teeth and the memory grow weaker. *Yiddish*

18459. Better die ten years earlier than live those years in poverty. *Chinese*

18460. He who remembers last year finds not this year good. *African (Hausa)*

18461. It's not the years that age, but sorrow. *Russian*

18462. It will be all the same a hundred years hence. *American*

18463. Lost years are worse than lost dollars. *Yiddish*

18464. Men's years and their faults are always more than they are willing to own. *English*

18465. Say no ill of the year till it be past. *English*

18466. The fewer his years, the fewer his tears. *English*

18467. The more your years, the nearer your grave. *English*

18468. The year does nothing else but open and shut. *English*

18469. The years are gravediggers of our joys and sorrows. *Finnish*

18470. To complete a thing, a hundred years is not sufficient; to destroy it, one day is more than enough. *Chinese*

18471. What does not happen in a year may happen in a moment. *Spanish*

18472. Years and months are like a flowing stream. *Japanese*

18473. Years and months wait for no man. *Korean*

18474. Years know more than books. *English*

YEAST

18475. Too much yeast spoils all the dough. *Maltese*

YESTERDAY

18476. Yesterday and the day before yesterday are not like today. *African (Swahili)*

YIELDING

18477. Yielding stops all war. *German*

YOKE

18478. Once you're taken on the yoke, don't say that you're not strong enough. *Russian*

YOUNG

18479. The young may die, the old must. *Dutch*

18480. The young rely on their fathers, the old on their children. *Vietnamese*

18481. Young, one wears flowers; old, one bears disease. *Vietnamese*

YOUTH

18482. A good youth, a good old man. *Greek*

18483. A growing youth has a wolf in his belly. *English*

18484. A lazy youth, a lousy age. *English*

18485. A prudent youth is superior to a stupid old man. *Indian (Tamil)*

18486. An idle youth, a needy age. *English*

18487. An unsubmissive youth is useless. *Indian (Tamil)*

18488. He that corrects not youth controls not age. *French*

18489. He who in youth is idle will experience hardships in old age. *Philippine*

18490. If youth knew what age would crave, it would both get and save. *English*

18491. Inferior in youth, not much use in old age. *Chinese*

18492. Rule youth well, for age will rule itself. *English*

18493. That which is practiced in youth will be pursued in old age. *Yiddish*

18494. What you learn in youth you do not unlearn in old age. *Greek*

18495. What youth learns, age does not forget. *Danish*

18496. Youth and age will not agree. *English*

18497. Youth and white paper take any impression. *English*

18498. Youth and wine are like a whip to a galloping horse. *Japanese*

18499. Youth comes never again. *Korean*

18500. Youth easily grows old yet becomes learned with difficulty. *Japanese*

18501. Youth—folly; old age—illness. *Russian*

18502. Youth goes in a flock, manhood in pairs, and old age alone. *Swedish*

18503. Youth has a beautiful face and old age a beautiful soul. *Swedish*

18504. Youth is a crown of roses; old age a crown of willows. *Hebrew*

18505. Youth is green, age is sturdy. *Russian*

18506. Youth is no virtue.   *Slovakian*

18507. Youth likes to flit away.   *Irish*

18508. Youth likes to wander.   *Irish*

18509. Youth may stray afar yet return at last.   *French*

18510. Youth often sheds its skin.
    Irish

18511. Youth riotously led breeds a loathsome old age.   *English*

18512. Youth will be served.   *English*

18513. Youth will have his swing.
    English

YOUTHS

18514. Untraveled youths have ever homely wits.   *English*

ZEAL

18515. An intense zeal prevails upon heaven. *Japanese*

18516. Blind zeal only does harm. *German*

18517. Too much zeal spoils all. *French*

18518. Zeal without knowledge is fire without light. *English*

18519. Zeal without knowledge is the sister of folly. *English*

18520. Zeal without prudence is frenzy. *English*

SELECTED BIBLIOGRAPHY

This bibliography includes only collections and secondary literature in English. It is by no means an inclusive list of the hundreds of proverb collections that exist for the many languages and cultures of the world. Also only the most significant bibliographies and scholarly books on the proverb can be mentioned here. The following sources are intended to give the reader at least a survey of the most important books on the proverb.

I. BIBLIOGRAPHIES:

BARTLETT, JOHN. *Catalogue of a Choice and Valuable Collection of Rare Books of Proverbs and Emblems, Dance of Death, etc., Including Many Books Printed in the Sixteenth and Seventeenth Centuries and Curiously Illustrated Works.* Boston: Little, Brown & Co., 1888.

BONSER, WILFRID. *Proverb Literature: A Bibliography of Works Relating to Proverbs.* London: William Glaisher, 1930. Reprint. Nendeln, Liechtenstein: Kraus Reprint, 1967.

DE CARO, FRANCIS A. AND WILLIAM K. MCNEIL. *American Proverb Literature: A Bibliography.* Bloomington, Indiana: Folklore Forum, Indiana University, 1971 (Folklore Forum, Bibliographic and Special Series, No. 6).

MIEDER, WOLFGANG. *International Bibliography of Explanatory Essays on Individual Proverbs and Proverbial Expressions.* Bern: Peter Lang, 1977.

————. *International Proverb Scholarship: An Annotated Bibliography.* New York: Garland Publishing, 1982.

————. *Investigations of Proverbs, Proverbial Expressions, Quotations and Clichés. A Bibliography of Explanatory Essays Which Appeared in "Notes and Queries" (1849-1983).* Bern: Peter Lang, 1984.

————. *Proverbs in Literature: An International Bibliography.* Bern: Peter Lang, 1978.

STIRLING-MAXWELL, SIR WILLIAM. *An Essay Towards a Collection of Books Relating to Proverbs, Emblems, Apophthegms, Epitaphs and Ana, Being a Catalogue of Those at Keir.* London: Privately Printed, 1860.

II. STUDIES

ALSTER, BENDT. *Studies in Sumerian Proverbs.* Copenhagen: Akademisk Forlag, 1975.

BARAKAT, ROBERT A. *A Contextual Study of Arabic Proverbs.* Helsinki: Suomalainen Tiedeakatemia, 1980.

BLACKWOOD, ANDREW J. *In All Your Ways: A Study of Proverbs.* Grand Rapids, Michigan: Baker Book House, 1979.

BOAS, GEORGE. *Vox Populi: Essays in the History of an Idea.* Baltimore, Maryland: Johns Hopkins University Press, 1969.

BRIDGES, CHARLES. *An Exposition of the Book of Proverbs.* London: Seeley, Jackson, and Halliday, 1859. Reprint with the title *Proverbs: A Commentary on Proverbs.* Edinburgh: The Banner of Truth Trust, 1977.

BRYANT, MARGARET M. *Proverbs and How to Collect Them.* Greensboro, North Carolina: American Dialect Society, 1945.

CHEALES, ALLAN BENJAMIN. *Proverbial Folklore.* London: Simpkin, Marshall & Co., 1874. Reprint. Darnby, Pennsylvania: Folcroft Library Editions, 1976.

DUNDES, ALAN. *Life is Like a Chicken Coop Ladder. A Portrait of German Culture Through Folklore.* New York: Columbia University Press, 1984.

DUNDES, ALAN AND CLAUDIA A. STIBBE. *The Art of Mixing Metaphors: A Folkloristic Interpretation of the "Netherlandish Proverbs" by Pieter Bruegel the Elder.* Helsinki: Suomalainen Tiedeakatemia, 1981.

ELMSLIE, WILLIAM ALEXANDER. *Studies in Life from Jewish Proverbs.* London: James Clarke, 1917.

FONTAINE, CAROLE R. *Traditional Sayings in the Old Testament: A Contextual Study.* Sheffield: The Almond Press, 1982.

FRANK, GRACE AND DOROTHY MINER. *Proverbes en Rimes: Text and Illustrations of the Fifteenth Century from a French Manuscript in the Walters Art Gallery, Baltimore.* Baltimore, Maryland: Johns Hopkins University Press, 1937.

GORDON, EDMUND I. *Sumerian Proverbs: Glimpses of Everyday Life in Ancient Mesopotamia.* Philadelphia: University of Pennsylvania Press, 1959.

GRAULS, JAN. *The Proverbs of Pieter Bruegel the Elder (1527–1569).* Antwerp: Gevaert, 1938.

GRIFFIS, WILLIAM. *Proverbs of Japan: A Little Picture of the Japanese Philosophy of Life as Mirrored in Their Proverbs.* New York: Japan Society, 1924.

GUERSHOON, ANDREW. *Certain Aspects of Russian Proverbs.* London: Frederick Muller, 1941.

HABENICHT, RUDOLPH E. ed. *John Heywood's "A Dialogue of Proverbs".* Berkeley, California: University of California Press, 1963.

HASAN-ROKEM, GALIT. *Proverbs in Israeli Folk Narratives: A Structural Semantic Analysis.* Helsinki: Suomalainen Tiedeakatemia, 1982.

HOUGHTON, HERBERT. *Moral Significance of Animals as Indicated in Greek Proverbs.* Amherst, Massachusetts: Carpenter & Morehouse, 1915.

HULME, F. EDWARD. *Proverb Lore: Being a Historical Study of the Similarities, Contrasts, Topics, Meanings, and other Facets of Proverbs, Truisms, and Pithy Sayings, as Expressed by the Peoples of Many Lands and Times.* London: Elliot Stock, 1902. Reprint. Detroit: Gale Research Co., 1968.

HUZII, OTOO. *Japanese Proverbs.* Tokyo: Japanese Government Railways, 1940.

KIDNER, FRANK DEREK. *The Proverbs. An Introduction and Commentary.* London: Tyndale Press, 1964.

KRIKMANN, ARVO. *On Denotative Indefiniteness of Proverbs.* Tallinn: Academy of Sciences of the Estonian SSR, Institute of Language and Literature, 1974.

———. *Some Additional Aspects of Semantic Indefiniteness of Proverbs.* Tallinn: Academy of Sciences of the Estonian SSR, Institute of Language and Literature, 1974.

KUUSI, MATTI. *Towards an International Type-System of Proverbs.* Helsinki: Suomalainen Tiedeakatemia, 1972.

LEVY, ISAAC JACK. *Prolegomena to the Study of the Refranero Sefardi.* New York: Las Americas Publications, 1968.

MAHGOUB, FATMA MOHAMMED. *A Linguistic Study of Cairene Proverbs.* Bloomington, Indiana: Indiana University Press, 1968.

MARVIN, DWIGHT EDWARDS. *The Antiquity of Proverbs: Fifty Familiar Proverbs and Folk Sayings with Annotations and Lists of Connected Forms, Found in All Parts of the World.* New York: G.P. Putnam's Sons, 1922.

MARZAL, ANGEL. *Gleanings from the Wisdom of Mari.* Rome: Biblical Institute Press, 1976.

MATISOFF, JAMES A. *Blessings, Curses, Hopes, and Fears. Psycho-Ostensive Expressions in Yiddish.* Philadelphia: Institute for the Study of Human Issues, 1979.

McKANE, WILLIAM. *Proverbs. A New Approach.* London: SCM press, 1970.

MIEDER, WOLFGANG, ed. *Selected Writings on Proverbs by Archer Taylor.* Helsinki: Suomalainen Tiedeakatemia, 1975.

MIEDER, WOLFGANG AND ALAN DUNDES, eds. *The Wisdom of Many: Essays on the Proverb.* New York: Garland Publishing, 1981.

PARKER, A. A. *The Humour of Spanish Proverbs.* London: The Hispanic & Luso-Brazilian Councils, 1963.

PENFIELD, JOYCE. *Communicating with Quotes: The Igbo Case.* Westport, Connecticut: Greenwood Press, 1983.

PERMYAKOV, G. L. *From Proverb to Folk-Tale: Notes on the General Theory of Cliché.* Moscow: "Nauka" Publishing House, 1979.

PFEFFER, J. ALAN. *The Proverb in Goethe.* New York: Columbia University Press, 1948.

PLOPPER, CLIFFORD H. *Chinese Proverbs: 1. The Relationship of Friends as Brought out by the Proverbs; 2. Economics as Seen through the Proverbs.* Peking: North China Union Language School, 1932.

———. *The Religious Life of the Chinese as Disclosed in Their Proverbs.* Shanghai: China Press, 1926. Reprint. New York: Paragon Book Reprint Corp., 1969.

ROBINSON, BENJAMIN WILLARD. *The Sayings of Jesus, Their Background and Interpretation.* New York: Harper, 1930.

SCOTT, R. B. Y. *The Anchor Bible: Proverbs, Ecclesiastes. Introduction, Translation, and Notes.* Garden City, New York: Doubleday, 1965.

SMITH, ARTHUR HENDERSON. *Proverbs and Common Sayings from the Chinese.* Shanghai: American Presbyterian Mission Press, 1914. Reprint. New York: Paragon Book Reprint Corp. and Dover Publications, 1965.

SMITH, CHARLES G. *Shakespeare's Proverb Lore: His Use of the Sententiae of Leonard Culman and Publilius Syrus.* Cambridge, Massachusetts: Harvard University Press, 1963.

TAYLOR, ARCHER. *Comparative Studies in Folklore: Asia–Europe–America.* Taipei: The Orient Cultural Service, 1972.

———. *The Proverb.* Cambridge, Massachusetts: Harvard University Press, 1931. Reprint. Hatboro, Pennsylvania: Folklore Associates, 1962.

THISELTON-DYER, T. F. *Folklore of Women: As Illustrated by Legendary and Traditionary Tales, Folk-Rhymes, Proverbial Sayings, Superstitions, etc.* London: Elliot Stock, 1905. Reprint. Williamstown, Massachusetts: Corner House Publishers, 1975.

THOMPSON, JOHN MARK. *The Form and Function of Proverbs in Ancient Israel.* The Hague: Mouton, 1974.

TRENCH, RICHARD CHENEVIX. *On the Lessons in Proverbs: Being the Substance of Lectures Delivered to Young Men's Societies at Portsmouth and Elsewhere.* New York: Redfield, 1853. Reprint with the title *Proverbs and Their Lessons.* London: Macmillan, 1869, and London: George Routledge, 1905.

TURNER, CHARLES W. *Studies in Proverbs. Wise Words in a Wicked World.* Grand Rapids, Michigan: Baker Book House, 1976.

WHITING, BARTLETT JERE. *Chaucer's Use of Proverbs.* Cambridge, Massachusetts: Harvard University Press, 1934. Reprint. New York: AMS Press, 1973.

———. *Proverbs in the Earlier English Drama with Illustrations from Contemporary French Plays.* Cambridge, Massachusetts: Harvard University Press, 1938. Reprint. New York: Octagon Book, 1969.

WILSON, F. P. *The Proverbial Wisdom of Shakespeare.* New York: Modern Humanities Research Association, 1961. Reprint. Norwood, Pennsylvania: Norwood Editions, 1978.

YOUNG, BLAMIRE. *The Proverbs of Goya: Being an Account of "Los Proverbios", Examined and Now for the First Time Explained.* New York: Houghton Mifflin, 1923.

III. COLLECTIONS

1. *International:*

BECHTEL, JOHN H. *Proverbs: Maxims and Phrases Drawn from All Lands and Times.* London: Gay & Bird, 1906.

BLAND, ROBERT. *Proverbs, Chiefly Taken from the Adagia of Erasmus, with Explanations and Examples from the Spanish, Italian, French and English Languages.* 2 vols. London: T. Egerton, 1814.

BOHN, HENRY G. *A Polyglot of Foreign Proverbs, Comprising French, Italian, German, Dutch, Spanish, Portuguese, and Danish, with English Translations & a General Index.* London: Henry G. Bohn, 1857. Reprint. Detroit: Gale Research Co., 1968.

BUSH, WILLIAM. *1800 Selected Proverbs of the World, Ancient, Medieval and Modern.* Boston: Meador, 1838.

CHAMPION, SELWYN GURNEY. *Racial Proverbs: A Selection of the World's Proverbs Arranged Linguistically with Authoritative Introductions to the Proverbs of 27 Countries and Races.* London: George Routledge & Sons, 1938. Reprint. London: Routledge & Kegan, 1963.

———. *The Eleven Religions and Their Proverbial Lore.* New York: E. P. Dutton, 1945.

———. *War Proverbs and Maxims from East and West.* London: Probsthain, 1945.

CHRISTY, ROBERT. *Proverbs, Maxims and Phrases of All Ages.* New York: G. P. Putnam's Sons, 1887. Reprint. Norwood, Pennsylvania: Norwood Editions, 1977.

CODRINGTON, ROBERT. *A Collection of Many Select and Excellent Proverbs out of Several Languages.* London: W. Lee, 1664.

COHEN, ISRAEL. *Dictionary of Parallel Proverbs in English, German and Hebrew.* Tel Aviv: Machbarot Lesifrut Publishers, 1961.

CONKLIN, GEORGE W. *The World's Best Proverbs.* Philadelphia: Mackay, 1906.

DAVIDOFF, HENRY. *A World Treasury of Proverbs from Twenty-Five Languages.* New York: Random House, 1946; also published with the title *Speakers' and Writers' Treasury of Proverbs.* New York: Grosset & Dunlap, 1946.

DENNYS, E. M. *Proverbs and Quotations of Many Nations.* London: Simpkin, Marshall & Co., 1890.

FERGUSSON, ROSALIND. *The Facts on File Dictionary of Proverbs.* New York: Facts on File, 1983; also published with the title *The Penguin Dictionary of Proverbs.* New York: Penguin Books, 1983.

FULLER, THOMAS. *Gnomologia; Adagies and Proverbs; Wise Sentences and Witty Sayings, Ancient and Modern, Foreign and British.* London: B. Barker, 1732.

GENT, N. R. *Proverbs English, French, Dutch, Italian and Spanish.* London: no publisher given, 1659.

GLUSKI, JERZY. *Proverbs. A Comparative Book of English, French, German, Italian, Spanish and Russian Proverbs with a Latin Appendix.* New York: Elsevier Publishing Co., 1971.

GUINZBOURG, LT. COLONEL VICTOR S. M. DE. *Wit and Wisdom of the United Nations: Proverbs and Apothegms on Diplomacy.* New York: privately printed, 1961.

———. *Supplement: Wit and Wisdom of the United Nations or The Modern Machiavelli.* New York: privately printed, 1965.

GUZZETTA-JONES, ANGELINE, JOSEPH ANTINORO-POLIZZI AND CARL ZOLLO. *We Remember ... A Collection of 200 Years of Golden Sayings of Some of the Ethnic Groups that Made America Great.* Rochester, New York: Flower City Printing Co., 1975.

HOUGHTON, PATRICIA. *A World of Proverbs.* Poole: Blandford Press, 1981.

HOWELL, JAMES. *Lexicon Tetraglotton. An English–French–Italian–Spanish Dictionary with the Choicest Proverbs.* London: Bee, 1660.

HUNT, CECIL. *Hand-Picked Proverbs, Selected from the Storehouse of the World's Wisdom.* London: Methuen, 1940.

JONES, H. P. *Dictionary of Foreign Phrases and Classical Quotations Comprising 14,000 Idioms, Proverbs, Maxims and Mottoes.* Edinburgh: Deacon, 1929.

KELEN, EMERY. *Proverbs of Many Nations.* New York: Lothrop, Lee & Shepard, 1966.

KELLY, WALTER K. *A Collection of the Proverbs of All Nations. Compared, Explained, and Illustrated.* Andover, Massachusetts: Warren F. Draper, 1879. Reprint. Darby, Pennsylvania: Folcroft Library Editions, 1972. Reprint. Philadelphia: R. West, 1978.

KING, WILLIAM FRANCIS HENRY. *Classical and Foreign Quotations, Law Terms and Maxims, Proverbs, Mottoes, Phrases, and Expressions in French, German, Greek, Italian, Spanish and Portuguese.* New York: T. Whitaker, 1888. Reprint. Detroit: Gale Research Co., 1968.

KONSTANDT, OSCAR. *One Hundred Proverbs with Their Equivalents in German, French, Italian and Spanish.* Great Malvern, Worcester: Edelweiss House, 1958.

LAWSON, JAMES GILCHRIST. *The World's Best Proverbs and Maxims.* New York: Grosset & Dunlap, 1926.

LONG, JAMES. *Eastern Proverbs and Emblems Illustrating Old Truths.* London: Trübner, 1881.

MAIR, JAMES ALLAN. *A Handbook of Proverbs: English, Scottish, Irish, American, Shakespearean and Scriptural.* London: Routledge, 1873.

MAPLETOFT, JOHN. *Select Proverbs. Italian, Spanish, French, English, Scottish, British, etc. Chiefly Moral. The Foreign Languages Done into English.* London: Monckton, 1707.

MARVIN, DWIGHT EDWARDS. *Curiosities in Proverbs: A Collection of Unusual Adages, Maxims, Aphorisms, Phrases and Other Popular Dicta from Many Lands.* New York: G. P. Putnam's Sons, 1916. Reprint. Darby, Pennsylvania: Folcroft Library Editions, 1980.

MAWR, E. B. *Analogous Proverbs in Ten Languages.* London: Elliot Stock, 1885.

MIDDLEMORE, JAMES. *Proverbs, Sayings and Comparisons in Various Languages.* London: Isbister, 1889.

O'LEARY, C. F. *The World's Best Proverbs and Proverbial Phrases.* St. Louis, Missouri: Herder, 1907.

OPDYKE, GEORGE HOWARD. *The World's Best Proverbs and Short Quotations.* Chicago: Laird, 1920.

ORTON, JAMES. *Proverbs Illustrated by Parallel, or Relative Passages, to which are Added Latin, French, Spanish and Italian Proverbs with Translations.* Philadelphia: E. H. Butler, 1852.

PROCHNOW, HERBERT V. AND HERBERT V. PROCHNOW, JR. *The Toastmaster's Treasure Chest.* New York: Harper & Row, 1979 (chapter XI: "The Proverbs of Many Nations", pp. 430–444).

RAY, JOHN. *Proverbial Sayings, or a Collection of the Best English Proverbs by John Ray, Scots Proverbs by Allan Ramsay, Italian Proverbs by Orlando Pescetti, Spanish Proverbs by Ferdinand Nuñez. With the Wise Sayings and Maxims of the Ancients.* London: no publisher given, 1800.

ROBACK, ABRAHAM AARON. *A Dictionary of International Slurs.* Cambridge, Massachusetts: Sci-Art Publishers, 1944. Reprint. Waukesha, Wisconsin: Maledicta Press, 1979.

ROSENZWEIG, PAUL. *The Book of Proverbs: Maxims from East and West.* New York: Philosophical Library, 1965.

SADÁSHEW, WISHWANÁTH. *Select Proverbs of All Nations: Four Thousand and Upward Alphabetically Arranged and Translated into Maráthi Couplets.* Bombay: Crishnajee, 1858.

SHEARER, WILLIAM JOHN. *Wisdom of the World in Proverbs of All Nations.* New York: MacMillan, 1904.

STEVENSON, BURTON. *The Macmillan (Home) Book of Proverbs, Maxims, and Famous Phrases.* New York: Macmillan, 1948.

WADE, JOHN (Pseud. THOMAS FIELDING). *Select Proverbs of All Nations with an Analysis of the Wisdom of the Ancients.* London: Berger, 1824.

WALKER, J. *Handy Book of Proverbs.* New York: Crowell, 1910.

WARD, CAROLINE. *National Proverbs in the Principal Languages of Europe.* London: Parker, 1842.

2. Anglo-American

ABEL, ALISON M. *Make Hay While the Sun Shines: A Book of Proverbs.* London: Faber, 1977.

ANGLUND, JOAN WALSH. *A Pocketful of Proverbs.* New York: Harcourt, Brace & World, 1964.

ANONYMOUS. *Book of Proverbs and Epigrams.* New York: Ottenheimer, 1954.

———. *National Proverbs: England.* London: Palmer, 1912.

———. *Proverbs for Daily Living.* Mount Vernon, New York: The Peter Pauper Press, 1949.

———. *Treasury of Proverbs and Epigrams.* New York: Avenel Books, 1954.

APPERSON, G. L. *English Proverbs and Proverbial Phrases. A Historical Dictionary.* London: J. M. Dent, 1929. Reprint. Detroit: Gale Research Co., 1969.

BAILEY, NATHAN. *Divers Proverbs with Their Explication & Illustration.* No place: no publisher given, 1721. Reprint. New Haven, Connecticut: Yale University Press, 1917.

BARBER, JOHN WARNER. *The Book of 1000 Proverbs.* New York: American Heritage Press, 1971.

BARBOUR, FRANCES M. *A Concordance to the Sayings in Franklin's "Poor Richard".* Detroit: Gale Research Co., 1974.

————. *Proverbs and Proverbial Phrases of Illinois.* Carbondale, Illinois: Southern Illinois University Press, 1965.

BARTLETT, JOHN. *Familiar Quotations: A Collection of Passages, Phrases and Proverbs Traced to Their Sources in Ancient and Modern Literature.* Boston: Little, Brown & Co., 1855 (14th ed., 1968).

BARTLETT, JOHN RUSSELL. *Dictionary of Americanisms.* Boston: Little, Brown & Co., 1877.

BAZ, PETROS D. *A Dictionary of Proverbs.* New York: Philosophical Library, 1963.

BEAR, JOHN. *The World's Worst Proverbs.* Los Angeles: Price, Stern, Sloan Publishers, 1976.

BENHAM, WILLIAM GURNEY. *Putnam's Complete Book of Quotations, Proverbs and Household Words.* New York: G. P. Putnam's Sons, 1926.

BLUE, JOHN S. *Hoosier Tales and Proverbs.* Rensselaer, Indiana: J. S. Blue, 1982.

BOATNER, MAXINE, JOHN GATES AND ADAM MAKKAI. *A Dictionary of American Idioms.* Woodbury, New York: Barron's Educational Series, 1975.

BOHN, HENRY G. *A Hand-Book of Proverbs Comprising an Entire Republication of Ray's Collection of English Proverbs, with His Additions from Foreign Languages.* London: H. G. Bohn, 1855.

BOURDILLON, FRANCIS. *The Voice of the People: Some Proverbs and Common Sayings Examined and Applied.* London: The Religious Tract Society, 1896.

BREWER, EBENEZER C. *Dictionary of Phrase and Fable.* New York: Harper & Row, 1870 (Centenary Edition revised by Ivor H. Evans, 1970).

BROWN, RAYMOND LAMONT. *A Book of Proverbs.* Newton Abbot: David & Charles, 1970.

BROWNING, DAVID C. *Everyman's Dictionary of Quotations and Proverbs.* London: Dent, 1951. Reprinted as *Dictionary of Quotations and Proverbs.* London: Octopus Books, 1982.

BRUNVAND, JAN HAROLD. *A Dictionary of Proverbs and Proverbial Phrases from Books Published by Indiana Authors before 1890.* Bloomington, Indiana: University of Indiana Press, 1961.

CHIU, KWONG KI. *A Dictionary of English Phrases with Illustrative Sentences.* New York: A. S. Barnes, 1881. Reprint. Detroit: Gale Research Co., 1971.

COLLINS, VERE HENRY. *A Book of English Proverbs, with Origins and Explanations.* London: Longmans, 1959.

COLOMBO, JOHN ROBERT. *Colombo's Little Book of Canadian Proverbs, Graffiti, Limericks & Other Vital Matters.* Edmonton, Alberta: Hurtig, 1975.

CURRAN, PETER. *Proverbs in Action.* Hove: Editype, 1972.

DENT, R. W. *Shakespeare's Proverbial Language: An Index.* Berkeley, California: University of California Press, 1981.

DOWNEY, WILLIAM SCOTT. *Proverbs.* New York: Edward Walker, 1858.

DRAKEFORD, JOHN W. *A Proverb a Day Keeps the Troubles Away.* Nashville, Tennessee: Broadman Press, 1976.

EWART, NEIL. *Everyday Phrases. Their Origins and Meanings.* Poole, Dorset: Blandford Press, 1983.

FEIBLEMAN, JAMES KERN. *New Proverbs for Our Day.* New York: Horizon Press, 1978.

FUNK, CHARLES EARLE. *"A Hog on Ice" and Other Curious Expressions.* New York: Harper & Brothers, 1948. Reprint. New York: Warner Paperback, 1972.

GRAY, MARVIN L. *I Heard Somewhere: A Book of Contemporary American Proverbs.* New York: Pageant Press, 1961.

HALL, JOSEPH S. *Sayings from Old Smokey: Some Traditional Phrases, Expressions, and Sentences Heard in the Great Smokey Mountains and Nearby Areas.* Asheville, North Carolina: The Cataloochee Press, 1972.

HARGRAVE, BASIL. *Origins and Meanings of Popular Phrases and Names.* London: T. Werner Laurie, 1925. Reprint. Detroit: Gale Research Co., 1968.

HAZLITT, W. CAREW. *English Proverbs and Proverbial Phrases.* London: Reever and Turner, 1869. Reprint. Detroit: Gale Research Co., 1969.

HENDERSON, GEORGE SURGEON. *The Popular Rhymes, Sayings, and Proverbs of the County of Berwick.* Newcastle-on-Tyne: For the Author, 1856. Reprint. Darby, Pennsylvania: Folcroft Library Editions, 1977.

HINES, DONALD M. *Frontier Folksay: Proverbial Lore of the Inland Pacific Northwest Frontier.* Norwood, Pennsylvania: Norwood Editions, 1977.

HOLT, ALFRED H. *Phrase and Word Origins: A Study of Familiar Expressions.* New York: Dover, 1961.

HYAMSON, ALBERT M. *A Dictionary of English Phrases.* New York: E. P. Dutton, 1922. Reprint. Detroit: Gale Research Co., 1970.

INWARDS, RICHARD. *Weather Lore: A Collection of Proverbs, Sayings, and Rules Concerning the Weather.* London: Elliot Stock, 1898.

JAUSS, ANNE MARIE. *Wise and Otherwise, the Do's and Don'ts of Sundry Proverbs.* New York: McKay, 1953.

JENSEN, IRVING LESTER. *Proverbs.* Chicago: Moody Press, 1982.

JOHNSON, ALBERT. *Common English Proverbs.* London: Longmans, Green & Co., 1954.

KANDEL, HOWARD. *The Power of Positive Pessimism: Proverbs for Our Times.* Los Angeles: Price, Stern, Sloan Publishers, 1964.

KIN, DAVID. *Dictionary of American Maxims.* New York: Philosophical Library, 1955.

———. *Dictionary of American Proverbs.* New York: Philosophical Library, 1955.

KING, VICTOR LOUIS. *Yes You Can Say That: The Wisdom of the People.* Brand Brook, New Jersey: no publisher given, 1956.

LEAN, VINCENT STUCKEY. *Lean's Collectanea. Collections of Proverbs (English and Foreign), Folklore, and Superstitions, also Compilations Towards Dictionaries of Proverbial Phrases and Words, Old and Disused.* Ed. by T. W. Williams. 4 vols. Bristol: J. W. Arrowsmith, 1902–1904. Reprint. Detroit: Gale Research Co., 1969.

LURIE, CHARLES N. *Everyday Sayings: Their Meanings Explained, Their Origins Given.* London: G. P. Putnam's Sons, 1928. Reprint. Detroit: Gale Research Co., 1968.

MAKKAI, ADAM. *Handbook of Commonly Used American Idioms.* Woodbury, New York: Barron's Educational Series, 1984.

MARCHA, E. F. *Handy Book of English Proverbs.* Toledo, Ohio: E. F. Marcha, 1905.

MATHEWS, MITFORD M. *A Dictionary of Americanisms on Historical Principles.* Chicago: University of Chicago Press, 1951.

NARES, ROBERT. *A Glossary of Words, Phrases, Names, and Allusions in the Works of English Authors, Particularly of Shakespeare and His Contemporaries.* London: George Routledge, 1905. Reprint. Detroit: Gale Research Co., 1966.

NELSON, THOMAS H. *Modern Proverbs.* Grand Rapids, Michigan: Zondervan, 1937.

PARTRIDGE, ERIC. *A Dictionary of Catch Phrases.* New York: Stein and Day, 1977.

———. *A Dictionary of Clichés.* London: George Routledge, 1940.

———. *A Dictionary of Slang and Unconventional English.* New York: Macmillan, 1937.

PENDELL, ELMER. *Wisdom to Guide You.* Jacksonville, Alabama: The Author, 1960.

PETERSON, GAIL. *Proverbs to Live by.* Kansas City, Kansas: Hallmark Cards, 1968.

PULLAR-STRECKER, HERBERT. *Proverbs for Pleasure: Uncommon Sayings Collected, Arranged and Annotated.* New York: Philosophical Library, 1955.

RANDOLPH, VANCE AND GEORGE P. WILSON. *Down in the Holler: A Gallery of Ozark Folk Speech.* Normen, Oklahoma: University of Oklahoma Press, 1953.

RAYNER, JOHN L. *Proverbs and Maxims.* London: Cassell, 1910.

READ, ALLEN WALKER. *Classic American Graffiti.* Paris: Privately printed, 1935. Reprint. Waukesha, Wisconsin: Maledicta Press, 1977.

REID, JOHN CALVIN. *Proverbs to Live by.* Glendale, California: Regal Books, 1977.

RHYS, ERNEST. *The Dictionary of Best Known Quotations and Proverbs.* New York: Garden City Publishing Co., 1939.

RIDOUT, RONALD AND CLIFFORD WHITING. *English Proverbs Explained.* London: Pan Books, 1969.

SEWELL, HELEN. *Words to the Wise: A Book of Proverbs for Boys and Girls.* New York: Dodd, 1932.

SIMPSON, J. A. *The Concise Oxford Dictionary of Proverbs.* Oxford: Oxford University Press, 1982.

SKEAT, WALTER. *Early English Proverbs: Chiefly of the Thirteenth and Fourteenth Centuries.* Oxford: Clarendon, 1910. Reprint. Darby, Pennsylvania: Folcroft Library Editions, 1974.

SMITH, WILLIAM GEORGE. *The Oxford Dictionary of English Proverbs.* Oxford: Clarendon, 1935 (3rd ed. by F. P. Wilson, 1970).

SPURGEON, CHARLES HADDON. *The Salt-Cellars, Being a Collection of Proverbs.* New York: A. C. Armstrong, 1889. Reprinted with the title *Spurgeon's Proverbs and Sayings with Notes.* Grand Rapids, Michigan: Baker Book House, 1975.

STARK, JUDITH. *Priceless Proverbs from the Tongue of the Young.* Los Angeles: Price, Stern, Sloan Publishers, 1982.

STEVENSON, BURTON. *The Macmillan (Home) Book of Proverbs, Maxims and Familiar Phrases.* New York: Macmillan, 1948.

SWAINSON, C. *A Handbook of Weather Folk-Lore, Being a Collection of Proverbial Sayings Relating to the Weather, with Explanatory and Illustrative Notes.* London: William Blackwood, 1873. Reprint. Detroit: Gale Research Co., 1974.

TAYLOR, ARCHER AND BARTLETT JERE WHITING. *A Dictionary of American Proverbs and Proverbial Phrases, 1820–1880.* Cambridge, Massachusetts: Harvard University Press, 1958.

TAYLOR, JOSEPH. *Antiquitates Curiosae: The Etymology of Many Remarkable Old Sayings, Proverbs, and Singular Customs.* London: T. and J. Allman, 1818.

TILLEY, MORRIS PALMER. *A Dictionary of the Proverbs in England in the Sixteenth and Seventeenth Centuries.* Ann Arbor, Michigan: University of Michigan Press, 1950.

TONN, MARYJANE HOOPER. *Proverbs to Live by.* Milwaukee, Wisconsin: Ideals Publishing Corp., 1977.

TRUSLER, JOHN. *Proverbs Exemplified, and Illustrated by Pictures from Real Life.* London: Literary Press, 1790. Reprint. New York: Johnson Reprint Corp., 1970.

URDANG, LAURENCE AND FRANK R. ABATE. *Idioms and Phrases Index.* 3 vols. Detroit: Gale Research Company, 1983.

URDANG, LAURENCE AND NANCY LAROCHE. *Picturesque Expressions: A Thematic Dictionary.* Detroit: Gale Research Co., 1980.

WHITING, BARTLETT JERE. *Early American Proverbs and Proverbial Phrases.* Cambridge, Massachusetts: Harvard University Press, 1977.

————. *Proverbs, Sentences, and Proverbial Phrases from English Writings Mainly Before 1500.* Cambridge, Massachusetts: Harvard University Press, 1968.

WIESNER, WILLIAM. *Too Many Cooks.* Philadelphia: Lippincott, 1961.

WILDER, ROY. *You all Spoken Here.* New York: Viking, 1984.

WILKERSON, DAVID. *Pocket Proverbs: Wisdom to Live by.* Ventura, California: Regal Books, 1983.

3. Western European

ALBERTI, LEONORA DE. *Proverbs in Italian and English.* London: Hill, 1920.

————. *Proverbs in Portuguese and English.* London: Hill, 1920.

————. *Proverbs in Spanish and English.* London: Hill, 1920.

ANDERSON, M. L., ED. *The James Carmichaell Collection of Proverbs in Scots.* Edinburgh: Edinburgh University Press, 1957.

ANONYMOUS. *National Proverbs: France.* London: Palmer, 1913.

————. *National Proverbs: Holland.* London: Palmer, 1915.

————. *National Proverbs: Ireland.* London: Palmer, 1913.

————. *National Proverbs: Italy.* London: Palmer, 1913.

————. *National Proverbs: Portugal.* London: Palmer, ca. 1915.

————. *National Proverbs: Scotland.* London: Palmer, 1913.

————. *National Proverbs: Spain.* London: Palmer, ca. 1915.

————. *National Proverbs: Wales.* London: Palmer, 1920.

ARANDA, CHARLES. *Dichos: Proverbs and Sayings from the Spanish.* Santa Fe, New Mexico: Sunstone Press, 1977.

BARTON, JOHN. *A Select Collection of English and German Proverbs, Proverbial Expressions, and Familiar Quotations, with Translations.* Hamburg: Conrad Kloss, 1896.

BAUER-CZARNOMSKI, FRANCIS. *Proverbs in German and English.* London: Hill, 1920.

BELCOUR, G. *A Selection of the Most Used French Proverbs with English Equivalents.* London: E. Stanford, 1882.

BEVERIDGE, ERSKINE, ed. *Fergusson's Scottish Proverbs from the Original Print of 1641, Together with a Larger Manuscript Collection of about the Same Period Hitherto Unpublished.* Edinburgh: Scottish Text Society, 1924.

BOGGS, RALPH S. AND I. JOSEPH DIXSON. *Everyday Spanish Idioms.* New York: Regents Publishing, 1978.

BUCUVALAS, ELAINE, CATHERINE LAVRAKAS AND POPPY STAMATOS. *Treasured Greek Proverbs: The Greeks Have a Saying for It.* New York: D. C. Divry, 1980.

BURKE, ULRICH RALPH. *Spanish Salt: A Collection of All the Proverbs which are to be Found in Don Quixote.* London: no publisher given, 1872. Reprint. Philadelphia: R. West, 1977.

CARBAJO, ANTONIO. *Spanish Proverbs: A Compendium of the Philosophy and Wisdom of the Spanish Race.* Miami Springs, Florida: Language Research Press, 1964.

CELORIO, MARTA AND ANNETTE C. BARLOW. *Handbook of Spanish Idioms.* New York: Regents Publishing, 1973.

CHEVIOT, ANDREW. *Proverbs, Proverbial Expressions, and Popular Rhymes of Scotland.* London: Alexander Gardner, 1896. Reprint. Detroit: Gale Research Co., 1969.

COBOS, RUBÉN. *Southwestern Spanish Proverbs / Refranes españoles del sudveste.* Cerrillos, New Mexico: San Marcos Press, 1973.

COLLINS, JOHN. *A Dictionary of Spanish Proverbs. Compiled from the Best Authorities in the Spanish Language, Translated into English with Explanatory Illustrations from the Latin, Spanish, and English Authors.* London: S. Brooke, 1823. Reprint. Darby, Pennsylvania: Folcroft Library Editions, 1977.

FOGEL, EDWIN MILLER. *Proverbs of the Pennsylvania Germans.* Lancaster, Pennsylvania: The Pennsylvania-German Society, 1929.

GAFFNEY, SEAN AND SEAMUS CASHMAN. *Proverbs & Sayings of Ireland.* Dublin: Wolfhound Press, 1974.

GALLOWAY, CLIFFORD H. *Spanish Proverbs, Sayings, Idioms and Random Selections, with Their English Translations.* New York: Spanish-American Printing Co., 1944.

GLICK, DAVID I. *Proverbs of the Pennsylvania Dutch.* Smoketown, Pennsylvania: Brookshire, 1972.

GUZZETTA-JONES, ANGELINE, JOSEPH ANTINORO-POLIZZI AND CARL ZOLLO. *Diceva la Mia Honna ... / My Grandmother Used to Say ...* Rochester, New York: Flower City Printing, 1972.

HASSELL, JAMES WOODROW. *Middle French Proverbs, Sentences and Proverbial Phrases.* Toronto: Pontifical Institute of Mediaeval Studies, 1982.

HENDERSON, ALFRED. *Latin Proverbs and Quotations, with Translations and Parallel Passages.* London: Sampson Low, 1869.

HENDERSON, ANDREW. *Scottish Proverbs.* Glasgow: Thomas D. Morison, 1881. Reprint. Detroit: Gale Research Co., 1969.

HISLOP, ALEXANDER. *The Proverbs of Scotland with Explanatory and Illustrative Notes and a Glossary.* Edinburgh: Alexander Hislop & Co., 1868. Reprint. Detroit: Gale Research Co., 1968.

KELLY, JAMES. *A Complete Collection of Scottish Proverbs. Explained and Made Intelligible to the English Reader.* London: William and John Innys, 1721. Reprint. Darby, Pennsylvania: Folcroft Library Editions, 1976.

KREMER, EDMUND PHILIPP. *German Proverbs and Proverbial Phrases with Their English Counterparts.* Stanford, California: Stanford University Press, 1955.

LUCIANI, VINCENT. *Italian Idioms with Proverbs.* New York: S. F. Vanni, 1964.

MACDONALD, T. D. *Gaelic Proverbs and Proverbial Sayings with English Translations.* Stirling: Mackay, 1926.

MACGREGOR, FORBES. *Scots Proverbs and Rhymes.* Edinburgh: Pinetree Press, 1976.

MACINTOSH, DONALD. *A Collection of Gaelic Proverbs and Familiar Phrases.* Edinburgh: D. Macintosh, 1785. Reprint. Glasgow: Caledonian Press, 1951.

MARCHAND, CHARLES M. *Five Thousand French Idioms, Gallicisms and Proverbs.* Paris: J. Terquem, 1905.

MARIETTE, A. *French and English Idioms and Proverbs.* 3 vols. London: Hachette, 1896–1897.

MARKETOS, B. J. *Proverb for It: 1510 Greek Sayings.* New York: New World Publishers, 1945.

MASSA, GAETANO. *Italian Idioms and Proverbs.* New York: Las Américas, 1940.

McCORMICK, MALACHI. *A Collection of Irish Proverbs.* Staten Island, New York: Stone Street Press, 1981.

MEEK, DONALD E., ed. *The Campbell Collection of Gaelic Proverbs and Proverbial Sayings.* Inverness: Gaelic Society, 1978.

MURISON, DAVID. *Scots Saws: From the Folk-Wisdom of Scotland.* Edinburgh: Mercat Press, 1981.

NEGRIS, ALEXANDER. *A Dictionary of Modern Greek Proverbs with an English Translation.* Edinburgh: Thomas Clark, 1831.

NICOLSON, ALEXANDER. *A Collection of Gaelic Proverbs and Familiar Phrases Based on Macintosh's Collection.* Edinburgh: Maclachlan and Stewart, 1881.

O'FARRELL, PADRAIC. *Gems of Irish Wisdom.* Dublin: Mercier Press, 1980.

O'RAHILLY, THOMAS F. *A Miscellany of Irish Proverbs.* Dublin: Talbot Press, 1922. Reprint. Darby, Pennsylvania: Folcroft Library Editions, 1976.

PAYEN-PAYNE, JAMES BERTRAND DE VINCHE. *French Idioms and Proverbs.* London: Nutt, 1893. Reprint. Oxford: Oxford University Press, 1924.

RAMSAY, ALLAN. *A Collection of Scots Proverbs.* Edinburgh: Ramsay, 1737. Reprint. Edinburgh: Harris, 1979.

ROBERTS, T. R. *The Proverbs of Wales: A Selection of Welsh Proverbs with English Translations.* Penmaenmawr: Jones, 1885. Reprint. London: Griffiths, 1909.

ROVIRA, LUIS ISCLA. *Spanish Proverbs. A Survey of Spanish Culture and Civilization.* Lanham, Maryland: University Press of America, 1984.

SHOEMAKER, HENRY. *Scotch-Irish and English Proverbs and Sayings of the West Branch Valley of Central Pennsylvania.* Reading, Pennsylvania: Reading Eagle Press, 1927.

SPALDING, KEITH AND KENNETH BROOKE. *An Historical Dictionary of German Figurative Usage.* Oxford: B. Blackwell, 1952ff.

STRÖMBERG, REINHOLD. *Greek Proverbs: A Collection of Proverbs and Proverbial Phrases Which Are Not Listed by the Ancient and Byzantine Paremiographers.* Göteborg: Wettergren, 1954.

TRATSAERT, JAN. *National Proverbs: Belgium.* London: Palmer, 1915.

TRICOMI, G. *A Handbook of English Proverbs with Their Equivalents in Italian.* Catania: N. Giannotta, 1900.

UTHE-SPENCKER, ANGELA. *English Proverbs / Englische Sprichwörter.* München: Deutscher Taschenbuch Verlag, 1977.

VAUGHAN, HENRY HALFORD. *Welsh Proverbs with English Translations.* London: Kegan Paul, Trench, and Co., 1889. Reprint. Detroit: Gale Research Co., 1969.

4. *Eastern European*

ALLER, SIMEON. *The Russians Said It First: A Heritage of Proverbs.* Los Angeles: Ward, 1963.

ANONYMOUS. *National Proverbs: Rumania.* London: Palmer, ca. 1915.

———. *National Proverbs: Russia.* London: Palmer, ca. 1915.

AYALTI, HANAN J. *Yiddish Proverbs.* New York: Schocken Books, 1963.

BAERLEIN, HENRY. *The Shade of the Balkans, Being a Collection of Bulgarian Folk-Songs and Proverbs.* London: Nutt, 1904. Reprint. New York: R. West, 1977.

BAUER-CZARNOMSKI, FRANCIS. *Proverbs in Polish and English.* London: Hill, 1920.

———. *Proverbs in Russian and English.* London: Hill, 1920.

BERNSTEIN, IGNAZ. *Yiddish Sayings Mama Never Taught Us.* Ed. by Gershon Weltman and Marin Zuckerman. Van Nuys, California: Perivale Press, 1975.

BEZA, MARCU. *Rumanian Proverbs.* London: A. M. Philpot, 1921.

CHIMCZUK, JOSEPH. *Ukrainian-Canadian Folk Wisdom. Texts in English Translation.* Windsor: Summer, 1959.

DAVIS, E. J. *Osmanli Proverbs and Quaint Sayings: 4300 Sentences in Turkish, Printed in Roman Characters, with English Translations, Explanations, and a Guide to the Pronunciation.* London: Sampson, Low, Marston and Co., 1897.

GURVITCH, DOLLY AND A. HERENROTH. *Russians Say It this Way: Ninety-Nine Russian Idiomatic Expressions and Their American Equivalents.* New York: International University Press, 1945.

KOGOS, FRED. *1001 Yiddish Proverbs.* Secaucus, New Jersey: Castle Books, 1970.

KRYLOV, C. A. *Russian Proverbs and Sayings in Russian and English.* New York: United States Army Russian Institute, 1973.

LANGNAS, ISAAC A. *1200 Russian Proverbs.* New York: The Wisdom Library, 1960.

MANYASIG, MÜBIN. *A Brief Selection of Turkish Proverbs.* Ankara: Turkish Press, 1961.

SEGAL, LOUIS. *Russian Proverbs and Their English Equivalents.* London: Kegan Paul, 1917.

TURNER, K. AMY. *National Proverbs, Serbia.* London: Palmer, 1915.

VELIMIROVIC, NIKOLAJ. *Serbia in Light and Darkness.* London: Langmans, 1916.

WEINGARTEN, JOSEPH A. *Yiddish Proverbs.* New York: no publisher given, 1941.

————. *Yiddish Proverbs and Proverbial Expressions.* New York: no publisher given, 1944.

———— AND NAOMI VINOGRADOFF. *Russian Proverbs.* New York: no publisher given, 1945.

YURCHAK, PETER. *Slovak Proverbs and Sayings.* Scranton, Pennsylvania: Obrana Press, 1947.

5. *African*

AJIBOLA, J. O. *Owe Yoruba.* Ibadan: Oxford University Press, 1971.

BENDER, CARL JACOB. *Proverbs of West Africa.* Girard, Kansas: Haldeman Hulius, 1924.

BURTON, RICHARD E. *Wit and Wisdom from West Africa; or, A Book of Proverbial Philosophy, Idioms, Enigmas, and Laconisms.* London: Tinsley Brothers, 1865. Reprint. New York: Negro Universities Press, 1969.

DELANO, ISAAC O. *Owe L'esin Oro: Yoruba Proverbs—Their Meaning and Usage.* Ibadan: Oxford University Press, 1966.

EKWULO, S. A. *Elulu Ikwerre: Ikwerre Proverbs.* Port Harcourt, Nigeria: Rivers State Council for Arts and Culture, 1975.

ESSIEN, PATRICK PAUL. *The Use of Annang Proverbs as Tools of Education in Nigeria.* Ph.D. dissertation Saint Louis University, 1978 (includes a collection of Annang proverbs).

FARSI, S. S. *Swahili Sayings from Zansibar.* Nairobi: East African Literature Bureau, 1958.

GIRARD, FERNAND JOSEPH. *Ideology Local and National: Continuation and Accommodation (Comparisons and Relationships Between Bemba Proverbs and Zambian Humanism).* Ph.D. dissertation Michigan State University, 1981 (includes a collection of Bemba proverbs).

HAMUTYINEI, MORDIKAI A. AND ALBERT PLANGGER. *Tsumo-Shumo: Shona Proverbial Lore and Wisdom.* Gwelo, Rhodesia: Mambo, 1974.

HERZOG, GEORGE. *Jabo Proverbs from Liberia: Maxims in the Life of A Native Tribe.* London: Oxford University Press, 1936.

JOHNSON, WILLIAM PERCYVAL. *Chinyanja Proverbs.* Cardiff: Smith, 1922.

JUNOD, H. P. AND A. A. JACQUES. *The Wisdom of the Tonga-Shangaan People.* Pretoria: Central African Press, 1936.

KALUGILA, L. *Swahili Proverbs from East Africa / Methali za kiswahili toka Afrika Mashiriki.* Uppsula: Scandinavian Institute of African Studies, 1977.

KUUSI, MATTI. *Ovambo Proverbs with African Parallels.* Helsinki: Suomalainen Tiedeakatemia, 1970.

LAMBIE, N. *Where Continents Meet: African Proverbs.* New York: John Day, 1972.

LESLAU, CHARLOTTE. *African Proverbs.* Mount Vernon, New York: Peter Pauper Press, 1962.

LINDFORS, BERNTH AND OYEKAN OWOMOYELA. *Yoruba Proverbs: Translation and Annotation.* Athens, Ohio: Ohio University Center for International Studies, 1973.

MALCOLM, D. *Zulu Proverbs and Popular Sayings.* Durban: Griggs, 1949.

MERRICK, CAPTAIN G. *Hausa Proverbs.* London: Kegan, Paul, Trench, Trübner & Co., 1905. Reprint. New York: Negro Universities Press, 1969.

MURPHY, WILLIAM PETER. *A Semantic and Logical Analysis of Kpelle Proverb Metaphors of Secrecy.* Ph.D. dissertation Stanford University, 1976 (includes a collection of Kpelle proverbs).

NJOKU, JOHN E. *A Dictionary of Igbo Names, Culture, and Proverbs.* Washington, D.C.: University Press of America, 1978.

NYEMBEZI, CYRIL L. SIBUSISO. *Zulu Proverbs.* Johannesburg: Witwatersrand University Press, 1963.

OPOKU, KOFI ASARE. *Speak to the Winds: Proverbs from Africa.* New York: Lothrop, Lee & Shepard, 1975.

PLAATJE, SOLOMON TSHEKISKO. *Sechuana Proverbs, with Literal Translations and Their European Equivalents.* London: Kegan, Paul, Trench, Trübner & Co., 1916.

RATTRAY, R. SUTHERLAND. *Ashanti Proverbs. The Primitive Ethics of a Savage People.* Oxford: Clarendon Press, 1916. Reprint. Oxford: Clarendon Press, 1981.

SABBAGHA, N. G. AND M. S. B. KRITZINGER. *English Proverbs and Expressions with Afrikaans Equivalents.* Pretoria: J. L. van Schaik, 1968.

SCHEUB, HAROLD. *African Oral Narratives, Proverbs, Riddles, Poetry, and Songs.* Boston: G. K. Hall, 1977.

SCHEVEN, ALBERT. *Swahili Proverbs: Nia zikiwa moja, kilicho mbali huja.* Washington, D.C.: University Press of America, 1981.

TAYLOR, WILLIAM ERNEST. *African Aphorisms; or Saws from Swahili-Land Translated and Annotated.* London: Sheldon, 1924.

WHITTING, C. E. J. *Hausa and Fulani Proverbs.* Lagos: Printed by the Government Printer, 1940.

6. *Near Eastern*

ABDELKAFI, MOHAMED. *One Hundred Arabic Proverbs from Libya.* London: Vernon & Yates, 1968.

ALCALAY, REUVEN. *Words of the Wise: An Anthology of Proverbs & Practical Axioms Drawn from Hebrew Literature Throughout the Ages.* Jerusalem: Massada Press, 1970.

ANONYMOUS. *National Proverbs: Arabia.* London: Palmer, 1913.

AQUILINA, JOSEPH. *A Comparative Dictionary of Maltese Proverbs.* Malta: The Royal University of Malta, 1972.

BAYYAN, KEWORK. *Armenian Proverbs and Sayings.* Venice: Academy of S. Lazarus, 1889.

BURCKHARDT, JOHN LEWIS. *Arabic Proverbs, or the Manners and Customs of the Modern Egyptians, Illustrated from Their Proverbial Sayings Current in Cairo.* London: John Murray, 1830. Reprint. London: Curson, 1875.

COHEN, A. *Wisdom of the East: Ancient Jewish Proverbs.* London: John Murray, 1911. Reprint. Darby, Pennsylvania: Folcroft Library Editions, 1980.

ELWELL-SUTTON, L. P. *Persian Proverbs.* London: John Murray, 1954.

FREYHA, ANIS. *A Dictionary of Modern Lebanese Proverbs.* Beirut: Librairie de Liban, 1974.

GOLDMAN, M. *Proverbs of the Sages: Collection of Proverbs, Ethical Precepts, from the Talmud and Midrashim.* New York: Goldman & Steinberg, 1911.

HANKI, JOSEPH. *A Collection of Modern Egyptian Proverbs.* Cairo: Al-Baian Printing Office, 1897.

KHERDIAN, DAVID. *Pigs Never See the Stars: Proverbs from the Armenian.* Aurora, Oregon: Two Rivers Press, 1982.

LINDENBERGER, JAMES M. *The Aramaic Proverbs of Ahiqar.* Baltimore, Maryland: Johns Hopkins University Press, 1983.

LUNDE, PAUL AND JUSTIN WINTLE. *A Dictionary of Arabic and Islamic Proverbs.* London: Routledge & Kegan Paul, 1984.

MANUELIAN, P. M. *Seven Bites from a Raisin: Proverbs from the Armenian.* New York: Ararat Press, 1980.

McCOY, RAYMOND. *Ancient Egyptian Proverbs.* Menomonie, Wisconsin: Enchiridion Publications, 1971.

MOUSER, WILLIAM E. *Walking in Wisdom: Studying the Proverbs of Solomon.* Downers Grove, Illinois: Intervarsity Press, 1983.

NAIMAN, ARTHUR. *Every Goy's Guide to Common Jewish Expressions.* Boston: Houghton Mifflin, 1981.

SAFADI, DALAL KHALIL AND VICTORIA SAFADI BASHA. *A Thousand and One Arabic Proverbs.* Beirut: American Press, 1956.

SINGER, A. P. *Arabic Proverbs.* Cairo: Diemer, 1913.

WESTERMARCK, EDWARD. *Wit and Wisdom in Morocco: A Study of Native Proverbs.* London: George Routledge, 1930. Reprint. New York: AMS Press, 1980.

WORTABET, JOHN. *Arabian Wisdom.* London: John Murray, 1910.

7. Far Eastern

AKIYAMA, AISABURO. *Japanese Proverbs and Proverbial Phrases.* Yokohama: Yoshikawa Book Store, 1940.

ANONYMOUS. *National Proverbs: China.* London: Palmer, 1913.

————. *National Proverbs: India.* London: Palmer, ca. 1914.

————. *National Proverbs: Japan.* London: Palmer, 1913.

BEILENSON, PETER. *Chinese Proverbs from Olden Times.* Mount Vernon, New York: Peter Pauper, 1956.

BROWN, BRIAN. *The Wisdom of the Chinese: Their Philosophy in Sayings and Proverbs.* New York: Brentano, 1921.

BROWN, CHARLES CUTHBERT. *Malay Sayings.* London: George Routledge, 1951.

BUCHANAN, DANIEL CRUMP. *Japanese Proverbs and Sayings.* Norman, Oklahoma: University of Oklahoma Press, 1965.

CARR, MARK WILLIAM. *A Selection of Telugu Proverbs.* Madras: Christian Knowledge Press, 1868.

CHRISTIAN, JOHN. *Behar Proverbs. Classified and Arranged According to Their Subject Matter, and Translated into English with Notes.* London: Kegan, Paul, Trench, Trübner & Co., 1891.

DUNCAN, MARION H. *Love Songs and Proverbs of Tibet.* London: The Translator, 1961.

EUGENIO, DAMIANA L. *Philippine Proverb Lore.* Quezon City: University of the Philippines, 1967.

FALLON, S. W. *A Dictionary of Hindustani Proverbs.* Benares: Medical Hall Press, 1886.

GRANT, BRUCE K. *Korean Proverbs: Dragon Head, Snake Tail, and A Frog in a Well.* Salt Lake City, Utah: Moth House, 1982.

GRAY, JAMES. *Ancient Proverbs and Maxims from Burmese Sources.* London: Trübner, 1886.

GRIFFIS, WILLIAM ELLIOT. *Proverbs of Japan: A Little Picture of the Japanese Philosophy of Life as Mirrored in Their Proverbs.* New York: Japan Society, 1924.

GUITERMAN, ARTHUR. *Chips of Jade: Being Chinese Proverbs with More Folk-Sayings from Hindustan and other Oriental Countries.* New York: E. P. Dutton, 1920.

GURDON, PHILIP RICHARD. *Some Assamese Proverbs.* Shillong: Assam Secretariat Printing Office, 1896.

HAMILTON, A. W. *Malay Proverbs-Bidal Melayu.* Singapore: Printers, 1937. Reprint. Singapore: Eastern Universities Press, 1961.

HART, HENRY H. *Seven Hundred Chinese Proverbs.* Stanford, California: Stanford University Press, 1937.

HOSE, E. S. *Malay Proverbs.* Singapore: Singapore Government Printing Office, 1934.

HSIEH, TEHYI. *Chinese Epigrams Inside Out and Proverbs.* New York: Exposition Press, 1948.

HUA, ELLEN KEI. *Kung Fu Meditations and Chinese Proverbial Wisdom.* Ventura, California: Farout Press, 1973.

HUA, ELLEN KEI. *Wisdom from the East: Meditations, Reflections, Proverbs & Chants.* Ventura, California: Farout Press, 1974.

JAMSHEDGI, NASARVANJI PITIT. *Gujarati Proverbs.* Bombay: no publisher given, 1903.

JENSEN, HERMAN. *A Classified Collection of Tamil Proverbs.* London: Trübner, 1897.

JOHNSON, WILLIAM F. *Hindi Arrows for the Preacher's Bow.* Ludhiana: Ludhiana Mission Steam Press, 1909.

————. *Hindi Proverbs with English Translations.* Allahabad: Christian Literature Society, 1898.

KNOWLES, JAMES. *A Dictionary of Kashmiri Proverbs and Sayings.* Bombay: Education Society's Press, 1885.

LAI, TIEN CHANG. *Chinese Proverbs.* Hongkong: Swindon Book, 1979.

————. *Selected Chinese Sayings.* Hongkong: University Book Store, 1960.

LAI, TIEN CHANG AND Y. T. KWONG. *Chinese Proverbs.* Hongkong: Kelly & Walsh, 1970.

LAZARUS, JOHN. *A Dictionary of Tamil Proverbs with an Introduction and Hints in English on Their Meaning and Application.* Madras: Albinion Press, 1894.

LIN, SUN-PO. *Words of Wisdom from Chinese Sages.* New York: Walters & Mahon, 1933.

LONG, JAMES. *Bengali Proverbs.* Calcutta: no publisher given, 1851.

MANWARING, ALFRED. *Marathi Proverbs.* Oxford: Clarendon Press, 1899.

NARASIMHA ACHARYULU, A. *Vakyamanjari: A Collection of Telugu Idioms, Colloquial Expressions, and Proverbs.* Madras: Kalaratnakaram Press, 1882.

OKADA, ROKUO. *Japanese Proverbs and Proverbial Phrases.* Tokyo: Japan Travel Bureau, 1960.

PAHK, INDUK. *The Wisdom of the Dragon: Asian Proverbs.* New York: Harper & Row, 1970.

PE, HLA. *Burmese Proverbs.* London: John Murray, 1962.

PERCIVAL, PETER. *Tamil Proverbs with Their English Translations.* Madras: Dinavartamani Press, 1842.

PLOPPER, CLIFFORD H. *Chinese Religion Seen Through the Proverb.* Shanghai: China Press, 1926. Reprint. New York: Paragon Book Reprint Corp., 1969.

ROCHIRAM, GAJUMAL. *A Handbook of Sindhi Proverbs with English Renderings and Equivalent Sayings.* Karachi: Commissioner Press, 1895.

ROEBUCK, T. *A Collection of Proverbs and Proverbial Phrases in the Persian and Hindustanee Languages.* Calcutta: Hindoostanee Press, 1824.

SCARBOROUGH, WILLIAM. *A Collection of Chinese Proverbs.* Shanghai: Presbyterian Mission Press, 1875.

SMITH, ARTHUR H. *Proverbs and Common Sayings from the Chinese.* Shanghai: Presbyterian Mission Press, 1914. Reprint. New York: Paragon and Dover, 1965.

TÊ, HUYNH DINH. *Vietnamese Cultural Patterns and Values as Expressed in Proverbs.* Ph.D. dissertation Columbia University, 1963 (includes a collection of Vietnamese proverbs).

WILKINSON, RICHARD JAMES. *Malay Proverbs on Malay Character.* Kuala Lampur: F. M. S. Government Press, 1907.

WINSTEDT, RICHARD OLOF. *Malay Proverbs.* London: John Murray, 1950.

YOO, YOUNG H. *Wisdom of the Far East. A Dictionary of Proverbs, Maxims, and Famous Classical Phrases of the Chinese, Japanese and Korean.* Washington, D.C.: Far Eastern Research and Publications Center, 1972.

8. *Mexican*

BALLESTEROS, OCTAVIO. *Mexican Proverbs: The Philosophy, Wisdom and Humor of a People.* Burret, Texas: Eakin Press, 1979.

GOMEZ DE ESTAVILLO, G. *Mexican Proverbs.* Delicias, Mexico: José Ismael Velázquez, 1948.

9. *West Indian*

ANDERSON, IZETT AND FRANK CUNDALL. *Jamaican Negro Proverbs and Sayings.* London: Institute of Jamaica, 1910. Reprint. Shannon: Irish University Press, 1972.

BECKWITH, MARTHA WARREN. *Jamaica Proverbs.* Poughkeepsie, New York: Vassar Cooperative Book Shop, 1925. Reprint. New York: Negro Universities Press, 1970.

BIGELOW, JOHN. *The Wit and Wisdom of the Haytians.* New York: Scribner & Armstrong, 1877.

HOARD, WALTER B. *Anthology: Quotations and Sayings of People of Color.* San Francisco: R. & E. Research Associates, 1973.

10. *Oceanian*

COLLOCOTT, E. E. V. AND JOHN HAVEA. *Proverbial Sayings of the Tongans.* Honolulu: Bishop Museum Press, 1922.

GREEN, L. S. *Hawaiian Stories and Wise Sayings.* Poughkeepsie, New York: Vassar College, 1923.

JUDD, HENRY P. *Hawaiian Proverbs and Riddles.* Honolulu: Bishop Museum Press, 1930. Reprint. Millwood, New York: Kraus Reprint, 1978.

McDONNELL, A. F. *Maori Songs and Proverbs. Ancient and Modern.* Auckland: privately printed, 1923.

SCHULTZ, ERICH BERNHARD. *Proverbial Expressions of the Samoans.* Wellington, New Zealand: Polynesian Society, 1953.